Georg Benedikt Winer

A comparative view of the doctrines and confessions of the various communities of Christendom

With illustrations from their original standards

Georg Benedikt Winer

A comparative view of the doctrines and confessions of the various communities of Christendom
With illustrations from their original standards

ISBN/EAN: 9783337260835

Printed in Europe, USA, Canada, Australia, Japan

Cover: Foto ©Lupo / pixelio.de

More available books at **www.hansebooks.com**

CLARK'S

FOREIGN

THEOLOGICAL LIBRARY.

FOURTH SERIES.

VOL. XXXV.

Winer on the Doctrines and Confessions of Christendom.

EDINBURGH:
T. & T. CLARK, 38, GEORGE STREET.
MDCCCLXXIII.

PRINTED BY MURRAY AND GIBB,

FOR

T. & T. CLARK, EDINBURGH.

LONDON,	. HAMILTON, ADAMS, AND CO.
DUBLIN,	. JOHN ROBERTSON AND CO.
NEW YORK,	. . SCRIBNER, WELFORD, AND CO.

OF

THE DOCTRINES AND CONFESSIONS OF THE VARIOUS COMMUNITIES OF CHRISTENDOM.

WITH ILLUSTRATIONS FROM THEIR ORIGINAL STANDARDS.

BY

DR. GEORGE BENEDICT WINER,
FORMERLY PROFESSOR OF THEOLOGY IN THE UNIVERSITY OF LEIPSIG.

EDITED FROM THE LAST EDITION, WITH AN INTRODUCTION, BY

REV. WILLIAM B. POPE,
PROFESSOR OF THEOLOGY, DIDSBURY COLLEGE, MANCHESTER.

EDINBURGH:
T. AND T. CLARK, 38, GEORGE STREET.
MDCCCLXIII.

CONTENTS.

	PAGE
INTRODUCTION BY THE EDITOR,	xi

INTRODUCTION, ... 1
   I. ON THE DOCTRINE OF THE SEVERAL COMMUNIONS, AS EXHI-
      BITED IN THEIR STANDARDS, ... 1
   II. THE SYMBOLICAL DOCUMENTS, ... 8
      1. Romish Church, 8; 2. Greek Church, 12; 3. Evangelical (Lutheran) Church, 15; 4. Reformed Church, 20; Arminians, 28; 5. Baptists (Anabaptists, Mennonites), 29; 6. Socinians, 31; 7. Quakers, 34.

I. THE SOURCE OF CHRISTIAN KNOWLEDGE, AND FOUNDATION OF CHRISTIAN DOCTRINE, ... 37
   I. First Point of Divergence: Symbolical Testimonies: 1. Greek, 37; 2. Roman, 38; 3. Protestant, 41; 4. Socinian, 45; 5. Quaker, 46.
   II. Second Point of Divergence, 49. 1. Roman, 50; 2. Greek, 51; 3. Protestant, 53; 4. Socinian, 55; 5. Quaker, 55.
   III. Divergences of less import in relation to Scripture, . 57

II. THE TRINITY, ... 63
   Symbolical Testimonies: 1. Romish and Protestant, 63; 2. Socinian, 64; 3. Arminian, 66. Differences of less moment, 67.

III. CULTUS OF THE VIRGIN; INVOCATION OF SAINTS; VENERATION OF PICTURES AND RELICS, ... 68
   I. Invocation of Saints.—1. Roman, 69; 2. Greek, 70; 3. Protestant, 73.
   II. Veneration of Pictures and Relics.—1. Roman, 75; 2. Greek, 76; 3. Protestant, 77.

IV. ORIGINAL STATE OF MAN; THE IMAGE OF GOD, . . 78
   1. Roman, 79; 2. Greek, 80; 3. Lutheran, 81; 4. Reformed, 81; 5. Mennonites, 82; 6. Arminian, 83; 7. Socinian, 84; 8. Quaker, 85.

V. RESULTS OF THE FALL; PRESENT STATE OF MAN, . . 86
   I. First Point of Divergence: 1. Roman, 87; 2. Greek, 89; 3. Lutheran, 89; 4. Reformed, 92; 5. Arminian, 94; 6. Socinian, 95; 7. Quaker, 96; 8. Mennonites, 97.

II. Second Point of Divergence, 98. 1. Socinian, 100 ; 2. Arminian, 100 ; 3. Roman, 102 ; 4. Greek, 104 ; 5. Lutheran, 104 ; 6. Reformed, 105.
Original Sin and Baptism : 1. Roman, 108 ; 2. Greek, 108 ; 3. Protestant, 109 ; 4. Arminian, 109 ; 5. Quaker and Mennonite, 110.
III. Third Point of Divergence, 110. 1. Roman, Greek, etc., 111 ; 2. Lutheran, 112 ; 3. Reformed, 113 ; 4. Quaker, 114.

VI. PERSON OF CHRIST, AND HIS DIVINITY, . . . 116
Socinian Symbols : the Human Nature of Christ, . . . 116
Relation of the two Natures : 1. Lutheran, 118 ; 2. Reformed, 121 ; 3. Quaker, 124 ; 4. Anabaptist, 125.

VII. REDEMPTION : THE MERITS OF CHRIST, ... 127
First Point of Divergence, 127. Symbolical Testimonies : 1. Roman, 128 ; 2. Greek, 129 ; 3. Protestant, 129.—Sinlessness and Obedience of Christ, 130. Symbols, 131 : 1. Protestant, 132 ; 2. Socinian, 132 ; 3. Quaker, 136.
Second Point of Divergence, 138. Symbolical Testimonies : 1. Roman Catholic Decrees, 139 ; 2. Protestant Antitheses from the Symbols, 140 ; 3. Arminian Doctrine, 142. Indulgences, 143.

VIII. CONVERSION AND GRACE, ... 145
I. That the Divine Grace is indispensable to Conversion : 1. Roman, 146 ; 2. Greek, 146 ; 3. Lutheran and Reformed, 146 ; 4. Arminian, etc., 147.
II. Relation of Divine Grace to Human Ability : 1. Protestant Symbols, 148 ; 2. Roman, 152 ; 3. Greek, 153 ; 4. Socinian, 154 ; 5. Arminian, 155 ; 6. Mennonites, 157 ; 7. Quaker, 158.

IX. UNIVERSALITY OF GRACE : PREDESTINATION, . . 161
I. Reformed Symbols, ... 162
II. Anti-Predestinarian Symbols : 1. Arminian, 169 ; 2. Lutheran, 172 ; 3. Socinian and Mennonite, 173 ; 4. Roman and Greek, 174 ; 5. Quaker, 175.

X. JUSTIFICATION : FAITH, WORKS, ... 178
First Point of Divergence, 178. Symbolical Testimonies : 1. Roman, Mennonite, and Quaker, 179 ; 2. Protestant, 180.
Second Point of Divergence, 183. 1. Roman, 183, 189 ; 2. Protestant, 185, 191 ; 3. Socinian, 191 ; 4. Arminian and Mennonite, 192 ; 5. Greek, 195 ; 6. Quaker, 195.
Third Point of Divergence, 196. 1. Roman, 196 ; 2. Greek, 198 ; 3. Protestant, 199 ; 4. Reformed, 200 ; 5. Arminian, 201 ; 6. Socinian, 202 ; 7. Quaker, 202.

XI. THE HOLINESS OF THE REGENERATE, AND WORKS OF SUPEREROGA-
TION, ... 205
Point of Divergence, 205. Symbolical Testimonies: *a.* As to
whether the Justified may perfectly fulfil the Law of God—1.
Roman and Quaker, 205 ; 2. Protestant, 206. *b.* Whether the
Justified can do more than keep the Commandments—1. Roman
and Greek, 207 ; 2. Protestant, 209. *c.* Monasticism and Vows,
210 ; Protestant Symbols, 211.

XII. LOSS OF GRACE : MORTAL AND VENIAL SINS, . . . 214
Point of Divergence, 214. Symbolical Testimonies : *a.* The Defectibility of Justification—1. Roman, Lutheran, and Arminian,
214 ; 2. Reformed, 215 ; 3. Quaker, 217. *b.* Relation of Mortal
Sins to Faith—1. Roman Catholic, 218 ; 2. Protestant, 218.
c. Venial Sins, and their proper Nature—1. Roman and Greek,
219 ; 2. Protestant, 220 ; 3. Arminian, 220.

XIII. THE MEANS OF GRACE : THE WORD OF GOD, . . . 222
1. Roman, 222 ; 2. Protestant, 223 ; 3. Socinian, 225 ; 4. Arminian, 226.
Law and Gospel : 1. Protestant, 227 ; 2. Socinian, 231.

XIV. SACRAMENTS GENERALLY, ... 232
First Point of Divergence : 1. Quaker, 232 ; 2. Roman, Greek,
and Lutheran, 234 ; 3. Reformed, 234 ; 4. Socinian, 237 ; 5.
Arminian, 238.
Second Point of Divergence, 239. 1. Roman and Greek, 240 ; 2.
Protestant, 241 ; 3. Arminian, 242.
Third Point of Divergence, 243. 1. Roman, 244 ; 2. Protestant,
246.

XV. BAPTISM, ... 249
First Point of Divergence : Socinian Symbols, 249.
Second Point of Divergence : 1. Socinian Symbols, 251 ; 2. Arminian and Mennonite, 252 ; 3. Roman, Greek, and Protestant,
253.
Third Point of Divergence, 255. 1. Roman, 256, 258 ; 2. Protestant, 256, 259 ; 3. Socinian, 260 ; 4. Arminian, 261 ; 5. Anabaptist, 261 ; 6. Quaker, 262.

XVI. THE LORD'S SUPPER, ... 264
First Point of Divergence : 1. Socinian, 264 ; 2. Arminian, 265 ;
3. Greek and Roman, 266 ; 4. Protestant, 267.
Second Point of Divergence : 1. The Eucharistic Doctrine of
Zwingli and Calvin, 269 ; 2. Symbolical Testimonies, 271.
Third Point of Divergence : 1. Roman, 280, 285 ; 2. Greek,
281 ; 3. Lutheran and Reformed, 283, 286.
Fourth Point of Divergence, 287. 1. Roman, 288, 291 ; 2. Greek
and Protestant, 289, 290.

Fifth Point of Divergence, 292. 1. Roman and Greek, 293; 2. Protestant, 296.

XVII. PENANCE, ... 297
Divergence, 297. *a.* Repentance, and the Sacrament of Penance generally, and Satisfactions in particular—1. Roman and Greek, 298; 2. Protestant, 301. *b.* Confession and Absolution—1. Roman and Greek, 303; 2. Protestant, 304.
Penances, 307. 1. Roman and Greek, 308; 2. Protestant, 309.
Purgatory, 310. 1. Roman, 311; 2. Greek, 312; 3. Protestant, 313.
Indulgence: Romish Symbols, 314.
Prayers for the Dead, 316. Evangelical Protests, 317.

XVIII. CONFIRMATION; MARRIAGE; SUPREME UNCTION; ORDERS, . 318
a. Confirmation—1. Greek and Latin, 318; 2. Protestant, 320.
b. Marriage, Divorce—1. Roman, 321, 323; 2. Greek, 322; 3. Protestant, 324. *c.* Extreme Unction—Roman and Greek, 325.
d. Orders—1. Roman and Greek, 327; 2. Protestant, 329.

XIX. THE CHURCH: ITS IDEA AND AUTHORITY, . . . 330
First Point of Divergence: 1. Roman, 331; 2. Greek, 332; 3. Protestant, 332; 4. Arminian, 335; 5. Quaker, 335; 6. Socinian, 336.
Second Point of Divergence: 1. Roman, 336, 338; 2. Protestant, 337, 338.
Third Point of Divergence: 1. Roman, 339; 2. Greek and Protestant, 340.

XX. THE MINISTRY, ... 344
First Point of Divergence: 1. Quaker, 344; 2. Roman and Protestant, 346.
Second Point of Divergence, 347. 1. Roman and Greek, 348; 2. Protestant, 349.
Third Point of Divergence: 1. Roman, 351; 2. Protestant, 352; 3. Socinian, 353.
Fourth Point of Divergence, 353.
Fifth Point of Divergence: 1. Roman, 354; 2. Protestant, 355; 3. Greek, 356.
Sixth Point of Divergence: 1. Roman and Greek, 357; 2. Protestant, 359.
The Power of the Keys: 1. Protestant, 361; 2. Roman, 362.

XXI. DIVINE WORSHIP: LITURGY, ... 363
1. Quaker, 364; 2. Roman and Greek, 365; 3. Protestant, 367.
The Vernacular: 1. Roman, 369; 2. Protestant, 370.
Images and Pictures: 1. Reformed, 371; 2. Lutheran, 371.

COMPARATIVE TABLES, ... 374

INDEX, ... 391

INTRODUCTION BY THE EDITOR.

ON many accounts it is necessary that this work of Winer's should not go before the English public without some kind of formal Introduction. The grounds of that necessity may be stated in very few words. Comparative dogmatics, or symbolism, as a branch of historical theology, has not had much attention paid to it by English theologians: a few remarks, therefore, on this subject will be expedient. Winer's treatment of the Confessions is distinguished from that of most other authors by being absolutely free from polemics; the statements of the standard being simply placed in juxtaposition, and without much, if any, doctrinal decision of his own: the reproduction of such a neutral exhibition of rival beliefs will demand a certain amount of justification or apology. Finally, the book was written by a German, and dated, as it were, from an earlier period in the century; whence it results that certain Continental systems have a disproportionate place, and certain other systems more familiar to us are either left in obscurity or omitted altogether: it will therefore be necessary at least to indicate how this obliquity may be corrected by the student. Whilst disposing of these preliminaries, opportunity will be afforded to point out the value of the work and the importance of the kind of theological study of which it is one of the best auxiliaries.

I. Symbolism, in the conventional theological meaning of the word, embraces the science of the various Confessions into which the Church has from the beginning condensed the substance of Christian doctrine. In its widest comprehension, therefore, it includes every formula of faith from the Apostles' Creed downwards; and constructs what may be called a confessional theology, based on the historical development of these documents. In its more restricted application, it deals only with the characteristic differences of these Confessions; and, inasmuch as the era of Confessions began, strictly speaking, with the Reformation, symbolism, or comparative symbolism, resolves itself into an exhibition of the doctrinal points that have divided, since the sixteenth century, the various communities that bear the Christian name. In fact, at that time the ancient œcumenical *Creeds* gave place to the modern *Confessions*, as the universal badges or standards of professing Christendom. Hence the present volume, like all others of its kind, begins its statistical survey with the modern estate of the Christian Church. It has little or nothing to do with the ancient developments of truth and error, of which the earlier symbols are the record. It virtually makes symbolism a comparative view, not of the creeds, but of the confessions of Christianity. Conventions rule the terminology of all the sciences, the theological science included; and this term is now fixed to signify the science of the modern differences of Christian doctrine.

It ought to be remembered, however, by the student that there is another and much older convention which vindicates for three, and for three only, of the Confessions of Christian faith, the name of symbols. The term carries us back to the earliest ages of theological phraseology, when ecclesiastical Greeks adopted the word from classical usage to signify generally every outward sign or token of an inward mystery, and, more particularly, those compendiums of the faith which were held as pledges of fidelity by the soldiers of Christ, and signs or marks distinguishing the orthodox from all others. The former use, that made the sacraments and other rites symbols, pointed to the Tessera or pledge divided as the remembrancer of a covenant: so baptism was a symbol between God and man in the Christian covenant. The latter use, that made the Confessions of Faith symbols, pointed to the watchword, or sign, by which the soldiers might distinguish friends from enemies. The first of these symbols was the Apostles' Creed, gradually compacted to its present form, as note after note was added for the contradiction of heresy. The second was the Nicene Creed, which, with its subsequent appendages, established the divinity of the second and the third persons in the Trinity. The third was the Athanasian Creed, of later date and unknown origin, which was accepted, however, by the entire Christian world, as its symbol of belief as touching the Trinity and the Person of Christ in particular, and the cardinal truths of Christianity in general.

These three œcumenical or universal Creeds occupy the same place in the ancient and comparatively uncorrupt church which the confessions occupy in the modern church as in the process of reform from its corruptions. The long interval produced all the corruptions of Christian doctrine, but no creeds or confessions to formulate and sustain them. In arming itself against the perversions of the faith, the Reformation fell back upon the ancient creeds in their integrity. For the most part, those symbols were laid as the foundation of the new superstructure, and were assumed into its formularies; thus establishing at the very outset a broad basis of connection and unity with the faith as delivered by the apostles to the church, and by the learning, zeal, and fidelity of the church expressed in these primitive standards. Apart from controversy, and viewed only as an historical fact, this is of great importance, and must always be remembered in the study of Winer's impartial exhibition, which takes this fact indeed for granted, but does not of necessity make it prominent. Its bearing upon the fair estimate of the relative Confessions of

Christendom is manifold. Some few aspects of it may be stated here with advantage.

First, as it respects the Greek Church. This vast community, which, almost as literally now as at the beginning, occupies the eastern portion of the old-world Christendom, makes its boast that it is the Orthodox Church, never having had any complicity with either heresy or schism. It knows nothing of any doctrinal development in its faith since the time when the three creeds were sent forth from its own bosom to control the belief of the world. Whatever it holds in common with Romanism or Protestantism, it holds as the heritage of the earliest ages. It disavows any œcumenical council of Christendom, from the sixth downwards. It protests, not loudly indeed, but with a stern and most obdurate tenacity, against the later additions that Rome has introduced; and does not side with Protestantism simply because it holds Romanism and Protestantism to be alike systems that are contending on the basis of private judgment against the fixed faith of the true and only Catholic Church. The addition of *Filioque*, "proceeding from the Father *and the Son*," was an offence against the one Christian creed that has never been forgiven. In the high and serene theology of the Eastern Church, most of the destructive doctrines of Romanism are denounced with a vigour that Protestantism cannot surpass. The supremacy of the Pope is a gigantic absurdity. Romanism itself is the archetypal Protestantism; and has begotten the sects of the Protestant world in its own image and likeness. Hence the Oriental Church disdains to enter the arena of controversy. It would not consent to have a table in the comparative survey of the present volume. Indeed, it could not have a place here were it not for the accident that a few —a very few—Confessions have been sanctioned by isolated synods, and have come to be regarded as authorized exponents of Eastern doctrine.

The student must carry this suggestion with him in his

estimate of the relative place of the Greek Church among these standards. It will help to clear his ideas on many points. It will explain, for instance, the scanty place which that old community—for, with all its diversities, it is but one—holds in the volume. The Orientals decline the entire theory of "development," and reject it with all its consequences. It declares every theory new: its cry is "the old is better." It holds that the whole faith, in its integrity, was once delivered to the saints; and that the earliest creeds were simply the scriptural doctrine set in a frame of new words—only new *words*—according to the necessities of controversy. Its never-failing watchword, which it has always had in readiness to meet every advance and every protest from Western Christendom, is that "the faith was given to the charge of Christian love, and only by love can be defended." It regards the Church from age to age as the living interpreter as well as guardian of the mysteries of faith. It denies that the Church has ever spoken in a collective and universal character, or with an œcumenical voice, since the earliest times. Hence it has no confessions with which to meet the counter-confessions of modern times. Those which are collated in this volume, for instance, bear the signature after all only of individual men, "profitable for doctrine, reproof, correction, and instruction in righteousness:" nothing more. This will explain, further, the attitude of the East towards the Pontifical system: it is that of the "Catholic, Orthodox Church," or rather "the Church," towards "Romanism," the mother of Protestantism and of error. Eastern Christendom knows no date later than Pentecost: it has a date for the beginning of the carnal and human system of Rome; and, *à fortiori*, for every system of Protestantism. Its proud boast is that it has never changed; that it is unchangeable; and that both Romanism and Protestantism are seas the waves of which are spent when they reach its territory, and can never overflow its borders.

It is obvious that Rome stands in a different relation to

these ancient œcumenical symbols, and to the general scope of our modern tabulation of the standards. A few remarks, purely historical and by no means controversial, may be useful in reference to two points: first, as to the fact of the faithful transmission of the ancient faith to modern times; and, secondly, as to the equally certain fact that modern Romanism is only one of the many parties in the general controversy of Christendom. What is involved in these affirmations will appear in the sequel.

The three ancient symbols were preserved faithfully during the ages of corruption. Not one of their positive statements was formally contradicted. However near the errors of the middle ages might approach to some of their positions, and affect them indirectly and by implication, the old communities never formally violated the articles of their creeds. These always occupied their central or fundamental place, monuments of a purer age, and silent protests against innumerable heresies that were clustering around their statements, though not actually contradicting them. One word alone separated East and West in relation to those symbols. But that one word does not separate between Romanism and Protestantism; and it is with the Roman doctrine that we have now to do. Those ancient Confessions of Faith were common property at the Reformation, and have always continued to be such. This is a fact of great significance, of much more significance than is conceded to it by many superficial controversialists. It is of great moment in relation to the continuity of the kingdom of Christ upon earth: the heavenly treasure of truth has existed always, though in earthen vessels; or, to make a large application of St. Paul's words, in vessels not of "gold and of silver," but "of wood and of earth," and some of them entirely to "dishonour." This is a plain historical fact. It cannot be denied, either by the sceptical critic of Christianity on the one hand, or by the severest Christian polemic on the other. It explains the vigorous life of the older systems: a phenomenon not otherwise to be accounted for. But it is not referred to now in anything like an apologetic interest. The fact does not soften down or palliate the enormous differences between the Roman system and that modern theology which is a return to the ancient. It does not suggest a basis of union: the fabric and constitution of Papal doctrine renders that of all impossible compromises the most impossible. The additions to the simple faith—ranging from the supreme doctrine of mediation, through the whole economy of the work of Christ, objective and subjective, down to the authority of the Church and the last things, or at least the penultimate things, of Eschatology—can never be tolerated by the Protestant mind. But still the fact remains; and it suggests the abstract possibility at least that interior fires, more searching even than those of the Reformation, may burn up the wood and the hay and the stubble, leaving the pure and unadulterated gold of truth. A merely historical consideration of the question can, of course, go no further in this direction.

The other point in reference to the relation of Rome to the subject of this Treatise is this, that, whatever may be said of the Oriental community, Roman Christendom has since the Council of Trent descended to the arena of a common competition, and its faith is to be numbered among the rival confessions. This, of course, is flatly contradicted by those whom it concerns. They acknowledge but one organized Church, which has been the kingdom of Christ from the beginning, and in the sixteenth century broke a long silence to contradict heresy and declare its faith to the world. As to the theory of the Church involved in this, nothing need now be said. In controversy between Rome and the Reform, that, of course, would be the all-deciding question. But, apart from controversy, the broad historical facts give their evidence; and, in relation to our present work, they must be allowed their full significance. Comparative dogmatics, or symbolism, must take the standards of the Council of Trent, not as the doctrine of the catholic and universal Church, but as the fixed expression of the Roman dogma, as distinguished from the Oriental and from the formularies of the Protestant communions. Those standards are framed in accordance with that idea. They keep rival standards always in view: offensive or defensive, they contend step by step for their theory and interpretation as against others. The fathers of Trent were just like other fathers; their sessions were marked by just the same characteristics which marked those from which proceeded the confessions of the Lutherans and the Reformed. It is an open conflict. There is not on the one hand a catholic, universal, and divine Church, laying down its tranquil and everlasting doctrines; and on the other a combination of heresies formulating their deviations from ancient truth. While we hold fast this, that the modern Roman decrees and canons and catechisms have only one column among many in the tabulation of rivalry, we can also give them the benefit of the fact. In theology, historical theology, Roman doctrine must be regarded as a systematized confession of faith. This is not a question of charity, or of toleration. The authorities quoted in the following work, public and private, are documents put in the court theological, to be examined and tested like all others. The canons of the Council, setting aside their anathemas, are theological determinations which demand to be carefully weighed on their merits; and the apologies and defences of Bellarmine and others, though admitted only on sufferance in such a court as this, must be allowed the same fair hearing that is accorded to Luther, Calvin, and Melanchthon. In short, and to sum up: the original symbols are in this branch of historical theology somewhat like standards of appeal; and nothing is lost, but everything is gained, by frankly admitting the elaborate system of Romanist dogmatics into the court, to give account of its additions to the œcumenical creeds which all accept, the final appeal being the Word of God.

As to the relations of the Protestant Confessions themselves to the original formulas of Christianity, the same principle of historical justice demands that fair account should be taken of the absolute fidelity of the bulk of Protestant Christendom to the ancient faith, and of the difference which this establishes among the several parties in this work placed on the same level. The propriety of a juxtaposition so impartial will be considered hereafter. Meanwhile, the fact of this distinction ought to be made prominent.

The great bodies into which the fermenting elements of the Reformation resolved themselves, were one in the maintenance of the ancient creeds. Many differences separated the Evangelical or Lutheran Churches from the Reformed or Calvinistic; and the Anglican Confession differed from both, by combining the leading characteristics in its composite system of articles and ritual. But all were as one in the acceptance of the doctrinal formulas with which the early Church had been content to declare its faith. Luther and Calvin widely separated as to the sacraments and the doctrines of grace; and their two theologies diverged widely as to many of the subordinate questions affecting the Person of Christ, the nature of the Atonement, and the means of grace. These differences are reflected in the Anglican system, and have always been evident enough in English divinity. Arminianism also, as a subsequent development, brought into Reformation theology what it regarded as the doctrine of grace taught in the Scripture and in the Church before the days of Augustine; and it has, partly as a separate Remonstrant community, but chiefly as an element pervading some other systems, exerted a deep and always increasing influence. But these great communities, forming together the Protestant Christian world of the Reformation and post-Reformation age, held firmly to the three creeds, and to the fundamentals of the doctrine concerning the person and mediation of Christ, the reality and perfection of His atonement for human sin, the work of the Holy Spirit, the constitution of the Christian Church, the office of the ministry, and the means of grace, of which those creeds are the foundation. All this is undeniable truth. It is not denied by any reasonable theologian. It is once plainly stated by Winer, and everywhere assumed. But it should be constantly kept in mind by those who study his survey of the innumerable variations of the Protestant Confessions.

Polemics apart, it must also be remembered in the estimate formed of these bodies which, on the one hand, have introduced opposing Confessions, or, on the other, have been content to decline altogether the formation or avowal of any specific creed. As it respects the former, the Socinians, who have no inconsiderable place in these tables, avowedly introduced a new formula, taught as new, and supported as such by a copious literature of catechisms and apologies. Whatever they might plead as to the teaching of Scripture, and the latent, misunderstood faith of antiquity, and the deep-rooted corruptions of the Trinitarian Christendom, they never pretended to join in any ancient Confessions of Christian Faith. In a symbolical and confessional point of view—and that alone is ours here—they came into the court with a new testimony. Their creed was written afresh. Doctrine after doctrine—Trinity, Person of Christ, Sin, Atonement, Grace, Righteousness, Sacraments—was remodelled. Their Confessions and Catechisms are admitted, simply because all communities professedly Christian are admitted. They claim to be heard, and they are heard. As it respects the latter, those who decline altogether to come into this court, and deny its jurisdiction, they also must take the consequences of their silence or contempt. Their faith, however vague and unformulated, has a substance, and cannot be hid; its documents must be found somewhere, whether authoritative or not. The further question must not be discussed, whether a Christian Church or a Christian community ought to exist without its specific and definite testimony to the Christian truth. All that need now be asserted is, that so it was not from the beginning, and that the representatives of comparative dogmatics, collating the formularies of Christendom, have some show of reason in their complaint of this deviation from the usage of Christendom as a whole. There are indeed some chaotic combinations of Christian men from whose confessions it is a great comfort to be relieved. No skill in the synoptist could locate or adjust them. But there are some orthodox bodies, and many isolated orthodox churches, the absence of whose standards is much to be deplored.

The current of these remarks has been determined by the relation of the ancient symbols to the present work. A few additional observations must be made upon the nature of the modern Confessions themselves; obviously only a few, because Winer's work will here speak for itself. It gives a clear, historical account of the standards, their origination, their growth, their secret history, their literature, and, in fact, all that pertains to them as a distinct theological literature. This is done so completely as to render any addition superfluous, and so systematically as to make a closer analysis of them impossible. But it may not be inexpedient to point out some of the prominent notes that mark the distinction between the modern Confessions and the ancient Creeds; especially as the tendency of the preceding observations has been to regard them as co-ordinate and on the same footing as declarations of Christian Faith.

The first and most obvious distinction is to be found in the fact, that the early symbols were the personal profession of faith, representing the characteristic of the man as he was a Christian man. This was the case especially with the Apostles' Creed, the parent and fountain of all innumerable subsequent Confessions,—unless, indeed, we carry their parentage higher and up to the baptismal formula in St. Matthew. Be that as it may, the earliest use of the earliest creed, in its simplest form as the expansion of the baptismal formula, was the individual avowal of faith in the leading verities of Christian faith. As such it was expounded to the catechumen, and as such it was engraven on the mind of the baptized child. As time rolled on, article after article was added for the contradiction of heresy; but its original use was not lost. It was the genuine "milk" for the babes of the Church, which was not withdrawn, even after the "strong meat" of the two later creeds was prepared for a more adult Christendom. As a personal confession it has never entirely lost its place, at least in the West. The Nicene symbol may have superseded it in the East; but has been only combined with it throughout a large portion of the West. A mass of superstitious legends has been connected with its origin, especially by the Romanists; and various opinions have been entertained as to its authority and value; but it cannot be denied that it lingers still among the majority of modern Christian communities as an individual testimony of Christian belief. The same may be said of its ampler representative and successor: that also has been from age to age in some of its forms, over the greater part of Christendom, both a private and public avowal of faith. In a much more limited degree, the stern Athanasian has served the same purpose: rightly or wrongly, a great multitude of Christian people on the most solemn occasions use it as the formula of their general belief. This does not hold good of any modern Confessions. They represent the convictions, not of Christian men as Christian men, but of Churches as Churches. What the symbols were to the individual, the Confessions are to the community. The former were binding on the members of the Church, the latter only on its ministers as the expounders of its doctrine. There is no modern formulary that has ever been imposed upon the individual as necessary to his communion with his brethren; but there are few which have not been more or less obligatory on those who have been entrusted with ministerial functions and responsibilities.

The ancient symbols were, broadly speaking, notes of the unity of the Church; the modern Confessions are, broadly speaking again, notes of its necessary diversity. The question need not be discussed, where the responsibility of Christian differences lies. That must be referred to a higher tribunal. Suffice that the internal unfaithfulness of the witnessing Church has been the cause of them; and that the great and all-important separation on which modern Confessions mainly rest, was an absolute necessity to the life and health of Christianity. As to the lesser divisions among the evangelical communities themselves, all that need be said is, that they have been overruled for good. It would be presumptuous to add that they have been ordained of God; or that, in the Holy Ghost's catholic administration of the many Churches by means of which His one Kingdom is maintained, these divisions have been provided for and subordinated to His purpose. But it is the very wisdom of charity to maintain that they have never been disowned by Him. His spiritual kingdom ruleth over all the several manifestations of its earthly and transitory form. Unless this is believed, there can be no satisfaction in the study of a book like that which now lies before us. He who entertains the rigid conviction that the variations in evangelical Confessions are no other than the record of heresies that never should have existed, or of differences that are fatal to the unity of the Church, or of perversions of the simplicity of the faith that obstruct its diffusion, is without the first requisite for an intelligent study of symbolical theology. He may enter thoroughly into comparative dogmatics, as a controversialist; but the true and profound secret of historical theology is closed against him. Indeed, to such a student the history of the Christian Church must be from the beginning downwards a bewildering chaos. But, studying on other and better principles, he will see that manifold corruptions of doctrine have never suppressed the glorious unity or the fundamental truth as it is in Jesus. He will see that the general history of the three centuries past has been on the whole a mighty vindication of original, catholic Christianity.

He will learn to be tolerant of the differences among the evangelical Confessions; recognising their essential oneness amidst their accidental divergences, and deeply convinced, that whatever clothing wrought by human hands may be thrown around the Protestant doctrine, its "body is of Christ." Nor will he value his own Confession less, or hold to it less tenaciously, because he is constrained to admit, that communities adopting other standards are carrying on the cause of the universal kingdom in a different style, as it respects subordinate matters, but with equal zeal, and an equal blessing.

Another important difference is suggested by the fact, that the ancient symbols were mainly designed to be incorporated in the worship of the Church, while the modern Confessions are exclusively theological documents, deposited in the ark of every community as its standard of truth and protest against error. The profession of Christian faith in the public congregation, as part of the liturgical service of the worshipping assembly, may be traced to times beyond which the memory of the Church cannot go, and is continued to the present day throughout a large portion of Christendom, both reformed and unreformed. Indeed, there are very few Christian communities which do not, in some form or other, if not by creeds, yet by hymns which embody their substance, lift up to the Supreme their devout profession of faith. As to the ancient symbols, it cannot be denied that this service was bound up with their original design, and has been from the beginning their characteristic function. The modern Church has not constructed its formulas on the same principle; no new creed has been constructed to supersede in public worship the old ones; none have been devised to accompany them. The formularies, articles, and Confessions of the later evangelical communities are theological documents, belonging rather to the teaching than to the worshipping service of the Church. They are not symbols of belief, which give pledges to God of fidelity to His truth, so much as symbols that give pledges of fidelity to that truth in the presence of the world. It is necessary to remember this clear line of distinction. It explains the marked difference in tone and phraseology between the older and the more modern formularies. The former, as uttered to God, make mention of His name and His truth only, keeping human names and human errors out of view; the latter, as uttered to man, deal largely in the enumeration of heresies, and in their elaborate confutation, and in their earnest rebuke and rejection.

Lastly, it must not be omitted that the modern Confessions stand in relation to the early Creeds as their necessary supplements, filling up their deficiencies, and so rounding them into the perfect fulness of Christian doctrine. It is not meant that this was their design; only that this makes the difference which the comparison suggests. Where the older documents are scanty, the later are full; and what the earlier omit, the latter amply supply. Some such difference, indeed, may be observed to exist between those original Creeds themselves: the exterior relations of the Trinity are not hinted at in the Apostles'; they are sharply defined in the Nicene; they are exhibited with all the exquisite refinement possible to human language in the Athanasian. But with the doctrines of the Trinity and the Person of Christ, or the Incarnation, the process of expansion ends. The mediatorial office and ministry of Christ, and the work of the Holy Spirit, in the application of redemption to the individual, are scarcely indicated in any of them. There lies their deep deficiency, the effect of which on the history of theology and the Christian Church can hardly be estimated. Now where the ancient creeds are silent, the modern Confessions are most copious and explicit. The nature, and penalty, and universality of sin, the expiatory sacrifice of Christ, and all that its operation and its defence demand, the righteousness of faith, with all its definitions and safeguards, the inspiration and authority of the

Holy Scriptures, the true characteristics and notes of the Church,—the relation of the sacraments to the means, are *loci communes* of theology, which the ancient creeds touch lightly where they touch them at all. It might seem as if the assaults of heresy had never been directed against these vital doctrines when they were constructed. A mere censorious criticism would go further, and say that the " doctrine of the cross," and the connected truths with which man's acceptance and final salvation are essentially bound up, are not made as prominent as they should be. Upon these the modern Confessions throw a flood of light. That is, they exhaustively bring out the scriptural doctrine, and reproduce its harmonies: under various aspects, indeed, according to their several theories, but all uniting in certain most important elements, and, by their differences on subordinate points, only furnishing a more thorough view of the one subject. It may fairly be said of the leading formularies of the Lutheran and Reformed types of doctrine, which in some sort have regulated the rest, that they none of them fail to instruct sinful men aright in the nature of the common ground of hope, and in the methods and conditions of the attainment of the common salvation. Thus they collectively and individually may lay claim to the earliest honour put upon the creeds: they are emphatically each the *Rule of Faith* to its own communion ; always understanding by that expression, a common directory of faith and practice subordinate to the supreme standard of Holy Scripture. This is true, notwithstanding that in many points they offend all. By the very fact of their differences on many comparatively subordinate topics, their imperfection and incompleteness is proved. They cannot all be in all things right. But they conspire to indicate the way in which the perfect faith is to be sought ; and predict a time when they will, if it seem good to the Holy Ghost, be merged in one general Confession, as true to the Scriptures as the Scriptures are to the truth of God.

II. It was mentioned at the outset, and the reader will soon discover for himself, that this work is simply an historical exhibition of the differences of the Confessions, without any infusion of the controversial element. It adheres stedfastly to its one and ruling principle, that of letting the standards speak for themselves. There is no polemic on the one hand, no harmonizing irenicum on the other. This is a characteristic of Winer's book, which makes it almost unique in this branch of theological literature. But a glance at that literature will better locate the work than any general description.

When the several Confessions of the Lutheran and Reformed Churches were produced, they speedily gave birth to a vigorous series of works devoted to their explanation. First came the polemical writers, of whom Chemnitz on the Lutheran and Bellarmine on the Romanist side were the most eminent as between Rome and the Reformation, while the contest between the Lutheran and the Reformed themselves was conducted by Hospinian in his *Concordia discors*, and Hutter in his *Concordia concors*. After nearly a century had passed, the symbolical books, as they had by this time been termed, required historical introductions. This service was rendered by Carpzov, and Walch, and Semler: the two latter especially have left little to be desired as to the literature of the question. The comparative treatment of the Confessions was begun by Planck, who, however, made Protestantism his starting point; and in a theological interest, as the titles of his works show, including as they do, " the fundamental ideas, the specific differences and the practical consequences." Then followed, in the early part of the present century, Marheincke's work, which, though the title hardly betrays it, is coloured by a Lutheran dogmatic influence, and in a masterly manner exhibits the internal development and harmony of each system apart. Winer then followed, in 1824, with a comparative view of the several doctrinal systems arranged in a tabular form, and supported by copious quotations from the standards in the original. This work was a novelty in its strictly historical character. It was the first and the last that appeared on this purely undogmatic principle; and as such it has held its ground, having appeared in successive editions, the last of which, now translated, appeared as lately as 1866, substantially unchanged. After the publication of Winer's treatise, the tide of symbolical literature set in with great strength. Möhler, one of the ablest and most conscientious of modern Romanist divines, led the way in his *Symbolism*, which brought all the doctrinal standards of Protestantism to the bar of Roman Catholic orthodoxy. His work is a subtle though clear apology for Tridentine doctrine; and is exceedingly valuable to the theologian, even in the English translation of Robertson, as giving all that can be said on that side of the question. What Bossuet attempts in an oratorical and unsatisfactory, because unreal manner, in his *Variations of Protestantism*, Möhler essays to establish in a calm and scientific manner: the deviation of Protestantism from the consensus of Catholic doctrine in regard to every cardinal article of the Christian faith. His work was held in unbounded esteem by his own community; and it was highly regarded even by his opponents. The challenge he threw down was immediately taken up by some of the foremost divines of the Evangelical Church; and, indeed, by some who would scarcely be acknowledged as evangelical. The leader of the Tübingen School, Baur, was the first who replied; and the final form of his answer, *The Antithesis of Catholicism and Protestantism*, remains a very valuable work, as it were an atonement for much that is destructive in his writings. Marheineke, attacked in his own province, roused himself to expose many of Möhler's fallacies. Nitzsch also, the most consistent Protestant of all these advocates, came forward with an exhaustive reply, which is full of symbolical learning, and exhibits a fine appreciation of the points in which a profound study will find elements of agreement where a superficial glance will find only variance. Sack, Tafel, and others joined in the theological tournament; it may, indeed, be said that each of the systems of Continental Protestantism, from Luther to Swedenborg, which Möhler had attacked, furnished its own champion. Since Möhler's time a great variety of treatises have appeared, most of which need no allusion here, as they are referred to in the notes of the following work. Suffice that through the whole range of them there is not found one which occupies the position that Winer's took. Either they present the several Confessions of each particular communion; or they survey the several standards from their own individual point of view, and for controversial purposes; or, if they furnish a general sketch, it is in their own words, and in the way of synopsis. Winer still stands alone, in his three characteristics: first, that of exhibiting all the standards of the Christian world (with the exceptions hereafter to be mentioned); secondly, that of giving the very words of the standards themselves in apt juxtaposition; and, thirdly, that of abstinence from polemical dissertation or harmonizing. It must be observed, however, that this last observation holds good only of Winer's original. The edition presented to the English reader was edited by Dr. Preuss, a Protestant controversialist, who will be found to have here and there added some incisive notes, retained in this edition for the sake of completeness, and indeed for their own value. Their value is not a whit lessened by the fact that Dr. Preuss has yielded in America to influence that need not be here further referred to, and become reconciled to Rome, his former deadly enemy. It is only right to mention this. For the rest, these notes are so few that they by no means affect the purely historical and uncontroversial character of Winer's work, as here given to the English reader.

But before another word is said on this subject, it must be admitted that this is a great achievement. To set forth in order, and with absolute impartiality, the endless variations of Christian thought, through the entire process of the *loci communes* of theology, in all their dogmatic comprehensiveness and subtlety, is a task for which very few men could be found competent. Many have taken it in hand; but, before proceeding far, have been overpowered by their honest prepossessions, and surrendered themselves to the *genius loci* of their own Confession. But Winer has held the scales with an even and untremulous hand. He has done justice to every side of every question: the copious extracts from the standards are left to speak for themselves; while innumerable points of less importance, both in dogma and its history, are thrown into the notes and observations. Now, there is no question here as to the character of a theology that is capable of dealing thus impartially with all sides. Opinions will differ widely on this subject. Some would regard it as a brand upon the theologian, that he should be capable of sustaining his neutrality equally and everywhere in the sacred domain of truth; others would count that his highest recommendation, and regard him as the type of what all teachers of theology should be. This question need not be touched here. Suffice, that a man was found competent to the task, and who has accomplished it in such a manner that his work might be taken as a textbook in almost all the schools of modern theology. Suspicion might be aroused here and there; but no more than suspicion.

This leads at once to the question of the practical benefit of such an impartial survey. Assuming that the present work is what it professes to be, a clear and undistorted reflection of the forms into which the Christian formularies have been shaped, to what use can the student apply it? This question is best answered by considering briefly the relation such a comparative view bears to the several branches of theological study.

To begin with the most important, there is a pure Biblical theology which is the standard and test of every other; that is, the exhibition of truth as it is found in the Scriptures, in its variety of definition and statement, in its gradual development from dispensation to dispensation, in its different types as presented by the several schools of inspired teachers, and in its organic unity as the result of the superintending inspiration of the Divine Spirit. This must needs be the norm and criterion of all that is called theology in the Christian Church. That it is so, is the theory, it may boldly be said, of every community under heaven known by the name of Christ. What may seem to be exceptions are not really exceptions. The old and corrupt Churches, that live and move and have their being in tradition, profess, these standards being judges, the same allegiance to Scripture which the purer Churches that protest against them profess. What in act they may deny, in word they maintain. The Romanist apology, for instance, for the existence of the Roman Catholic system of church doctrine and discipline is, in the last resort, an appeal to Scripture. It is true that there is an enormous qualification of this fact. The Tridentine dogma of inspiration, in other respects as true as that of the Protestants, is, as it were, nullified by a series of figments: it extends that inspiration to more than the Bible contains; it tacitly transfers its virtue to an "authentic" Vulgate; and, above all, it establishes a co-ordinate inspiration directing the ecclesiastical traditions which interpret, by development or otherwise, the unwritten Scripture handed down by the apostles, and the truths that the Bible contains only in germ. This concurrent endowment of the visible Church with inspiration, as having its organ and living voice in the infallible Pontiff, is the fundamental error that vitiates all. But there stands the original theory still. Tradition and development, with their living interpreter, alike are driven by an absolute necessity into the supreme court for a last decision. In every controversy with Rome this is a tacit, if not expressed, assumption of both parties: the one cannot, the other dares not, deny that there is a law, and a testimony concerning that law, surrounding and higher than all the decisions of men. To that supreme court all evangelical communities, without reserve, carry their appeal. Here, again, the seeming exceptions are not real exceptions. Some of them may betray mystical tendencies which would bring the soul of men into more immediate relations with God, and make the Church a recipient of revelation *without the Word*. The Quakers, for instance, who hold a large place in this volume, may seem to waver between two theories—for mysticism, like every other tendency, must have its theories —as to the supremacy of Scripture. One side may hold that the internal light in every redeemed man is to be the test of Scripture, another that Scripture is to be the test of the internal light; but both practically agree to solve these difficulties by a more or less consistent or inconsistent appeal to the words of the written oracles. It is needless to dilate further upon this fact. Its application to the theological use of this comparative survey is obvious. Here we have no Biblical theology; that is entirely excluded. The tables are constructed without any reference to Scripture; the sayings of God's Word being, as it were, the only thing omitted. But he who uses the volume must not fail to do for himself what the book does not do. He has the sum of all the creeds before him, his own included; and must conscientiously examine all in the light of the infallible Word. Doing this, he will understand better both the systems he has to study and the standard to which they are all brought. There is no more effectual method of studying the variations of rival systems than that of hearing their pleas before this bar; and certainly, on the other hand, one of the best commentaries upon the New Testament is to be found in the comparison of the interpretations put upon it by the rival theologies. No one who has studied the controversies concerning the Person of Christ, or Justification by Faith, as registered in this volume, will hesitate to acknowledge that they have shed a clear light upon the terminology of the New Testament epistles. In fact, however paradoxical the assertion may seem, it is one that all thorough students of these controversies will verify: that the subtle discussions of the polemics on the one person and two natures of the Redeemer, the bearings of active and passive righteousness, the nature of imputation in all its aspects, shed much more light upon the Scriptures to which they appeal than they shed upon the subject they deal with. A yet bolder word may be spoken. There are many topics in Biblical theology which cannot be thoroughly understood but by those who study them in the light of the polemics of the sixteenth century. It would be an offence against the fundamental hermeneutical canon of the self-interpreting sufficiency and perspicuity of Scripture to say generally that its interpretation as Scripture is in any sense dependent on controversy. But it may safely be affirmed, that few subordinate helps can be mentioned which are more effectual than the careful comparison of the various constructions that have been put upon the same words and sentences by the framers of the several Confessions of Christendom. The Bible that settles all differences often has a reflex light thrown upon it by the differences that it settles.

Again, the catholic exhibition of the Confessions of Christendom, without polemics or harmony, is of great value in the study of historical theology, or the development of Christian doctrine. Perhaps it would be better to correct the usual phrase, and say Christian *dogma*. The doctrine of Christianity was not left for development; its development ran through the ages of gradual revelation, but was ended with the faith once for all delivered through the apostles to the saints. As Moses began, so St. John ended, the slow process by which the truth as it is in Jesus was unfolded to the Church. Development in the history of theology, as such, has been only the more and perfect definition and systematization of the doctrines already given in their full sufficiency: a development governed mainly by the operation of two laws. On the one hand, the necessity of formal instruction in a

Church which gradually pervaded all ranks of society, incorporated all grades of culture, and adapted itself to all ranges of human civilisation, would lead to a scientific arrangement of truth, and deduction of consequences from each truth in particular, and application of the whole to the unvarying problems of human life. Hence a sure development of dogma, throwing the Divine doctrine into moulds fashioned by men. On the other hand, the necessity of encountering false doctrine and condemning it, whether the errors of unbelief without or the errors of heresy within, would lead to the same result. The history of the development of Christian theology in its Creeds and Confessions, is mainly occupied with the decisions of contested questions; in fact, had there been no such contests, there would have been but a scanty development of dogma. It is needless to say that the student of theology must needs study it historically; unless he does so, his views will be narrow and superficial. This being assumed, he cannot do better than make Winer's one of his text-books. Not by any means the only one; for its service in this department, though extremely important, is limited. For instance, it touches only in an indirect manner the grand development of dogma which formed its final expression in the three Creeds. It is true that most of the early questions of contention were brought again into the arena after the Reformation, and have the record of their settlement in the modern Confessions. But that is not the case with all of them; and our present volume, a good adjunct of other books, will not supersede the elaborate works that make the universal development of Christian doctrine their subject.

Finally, it follows as matter of course, that this work is a useful aid to the student of dogmatic theology as such; that is to say, of every minister of the gospel, whatever may be the Confession to which he owes allegiance. Of course, it is not here that he will learn his theology, or find the system that represents his creed. The book is too general and scanty for that. Sketches and outlines of theological doctrine ought not to satisfy the teacher of divinity, whose business is to make his own dogmatic system as familiar to his mind in all its details as it is precious to his heart in its fundamental principles. But it is of inestimable service to mark the doctrinal definitions of systems other than our own; to use them as interpreters, as correctives, and as supplements. No sound theologian inherits a dogmatic system so complete as to defy improvement in his own hands, and no theologian is bound by any dictate of humility or modesty to abstain from amending the best definitions of his predecessors and masters. Let the student, even the young student, make the experiment upon any doctrine: say the doctrine of the Eucharist, which, beyond every doctrine, has taxed and exhausted the energies of the confessional divines. Let him attempt an analytical reconstruction of the dogma, noting some points among the erroneous theories of Confessions other than his own which are perhaps by his own too much neglected, and observing refinements of phraseology to which his line of thought may not have accustomed his mind, and especially paying attention to aspects of the question which in the heat of controversy have by his own confession had slight justice done them. The result will be useful to him, while the process will have been stimulating. In general, and to dismiss this subject, it may be averred that he will have the best dogmatic system at his command who, faithful to his particular Confession, has carefully collated every other with it.

The transition is easy to the polemical theology which has occupied so large a space in theological literature during the last three hundred years,—indeed, more or less, from the beginning. The impartial survey of the entire field of results which this volume contains, is of essential service in this branch of study: perhaps its service is more marked here than anywhere else. Controversies there must be among the churches visible on earth; in this sense also the estate of

Christendom is that of a militant Church contending for the faith against the infidel, and about the faith within itself. It would be wrong to say that the Redeemer decreed that it should be so; but it is right to say that He foresaw it, predicted it, and has by His Spirit overruled it for good, and taken it up into the administration of the government of His kingdom. Of polemics there are many kinds. There is the controversy that pursues the antichrist, who goes out from the community of Christ because his doctrine never was *of it;* there is the controversy that is waged in defence of the purity and the integrity of the faith against those who seem to hold its fundamentals and grievously disfigure the superstructure; there is the controversy which brethren maintain with brethren, building on the same foundation the same superstructure, but differing about the arrangement of the material, and certain very important laws that regulate the process of the construction itself; and, finally, there are controversies among the same brethren, often raging with an intensity in the inverse proportion of their importance, concerning what may be called the ornamentation and finishing touches of the edifice of systematic doctrine. But these are figures, and must be reduced to plain terms. Then the first are represented by the unfailing polemics of Christendom against the Socinians, and others like-minded, who deny the doctrines of the Trinity, the Incarnation and Person of Christ, Original Sin, the Atonement, and other truths which necessarily hang upon these; the second are represented by the permanent controversy of Protestantism with the old communities which retain those doctrines, but encumber them with additions that mar their simplicity and defeat their power; the third are represented by the Eucharistic controversies between Lutheranism and the Reformed, by what may generally be called the Calvinistic controversy, and by the unsettled question as to the relation of baptism to the Christian covenant; the last are represented by such discussions as concern some non-essential points of church government, some inscrutable questions touching the nature and limits of Christ's exinanition, the precise relation of the active and the passive obedience of the Redeemer. Of course, this very classification of the controversies may itself be controverted. Some would place the second class at the head of the list, and make mediæval Christendom no other than a Satanic caricature of Christianity; some would place the questions noted last under the third head, and regard them as gravely affecting the very essentials of a systematic doctrine; some would dismiss the fourth altogether, and count everything, down or up to the minutest finial of every pinnacle in the edifice, matter of deep importance; while there are not wanting those who in their latitudinarian charity or indifference smile compassionately at all alike, and think they justify themselves by quoting the apostle's words, though not his meaning in the words, *I am of Christ!* But there would be no propriety in argument on this subject here; suffice, that the value of this book is established for those who hold all truth precious, however won, and therefore love the very dust of Christian controversy.

It is a considerable advantage to the student of the controversies that he should have lying before him the very terms in which the contending parties have formulated their beliefs. Very much of the confusion, and of the acrimony, and of the barrenness, of religious dissensions has been the result of misstatement of opponents' views and misquotation of their language. Many polemic divines, faithful to the truth in "that which is much," loyal to the great principle for which they contend, have not been also faithful in "that which is least," have not been careful of minute accuracy in the presentation of the error they would refute. And what holds good of the principals in the controversy, holds good also of those who only assist at it, or study it in its results. They never see the bearings of the question, or get a clear conception of its issues, simply because they have never defined its starting-point, or mastered its exact terminology. The student who would avoid this evil must not be content with current and traditional notions of the dogmas of rival communities. He must examine for himself, and make his own the *ipsissima verba* of the canon, decree, article, or catechetical definition. They are given fairly and fully in this volume; and the selection is not the less valuable because it is confined always to the question in hand. The passages are in every case the proof passages of the Creed or Confession; and given in the original, even to the retention of the modern Greek phraseology. Moreover, as a handbook or guide in Christian Polemics proper, Winer's book has the additional recommendation of including excerpts from some of the leading controversialists all round, from Bellarmine to Barclay. Fortified by this compendium of fixed and sure authorities, the student may safely explore his way. He will see what men have said and what they have not said. He will see some errors to be worse than he has been in the habit of thinking them to be; others will be robbed of some of their conventional evil characteristics. He will often perceive, what otherwise would not be perceived, the reason why one opinion has been held as the necessary result of another, and why a certain truth has been renounced because a previous error had made it inconvenient. He will learn that there is an analogy of untruth as well as of truth, an analogy of infidelity as well as an analogy of faith. Above all, he will not fail, if working on sound principles, to see more and more clearly the longer he studies, that the innumerable variety of contradictory opinions only tends to bring out into more luminous distinctness the glorious outline of the one system of truth on which Christianity rests.

A word must be said, before passing, on the Comparative Tables at the end of the volume. They deserve attention as the product of no little thought and skill: in fact, no part of the work made a heavier demand upon the ability of the author, certainly no part has occasioned the editor more trouble in the reproduction; and, in this case, what required much care in the preparation will require equal care in the use. The student—and by the student is meant especially the young student, for whom this work is mainly designed—will do well to make himself master of the technical principle on which the Table—it is only one in reality—is constructed; and reward his author by noting the tact with which a multitude of harmonious and discordant elements are articulated into one homogeneous structure. He should then, and will if he is thoroughly in earnest, commit to memory the entire table, first as a whole, and then in its divergent lines. If memory is made only the minister of the judgment, he will have acquired a good general view of the entire body of Christian theology in its leading outlines, and have lodged safely in his mind a sort of nucleus around which may crystallize a miscellaneous mass of knowledge otherwise acquired.

But here lies a danger, to the consideration of which a separate paragraph may be allotted, as it concerns not these tables only, but the subject and treatment of this work generally. It would be a fatal mistake to think that an intimate familiarity with tables like these makes a theologian. It is the very principle and theory of the volume to preclude that supposition. It gives only the materials, which the intelligent reader must use according to his own discretion and the exercise of his own rightly directed and rightly guarded private judgment. The present section of this Introduction has been occupied with the fact that Winer gives only a comparative view of the doctrinal systems as they are, and as they are supported by authorized documents and standard expositors. This law of the work must be again made prominent. The function and glory of theology is, after all, not the knowledge of these confessional statements, but the fine perception of their broader or more refined distinctions, and the thoughtful, not to say philosophical, appreciation of the underlying spirit of these distinctions, and the education of the theological eye to perceive the process by which they shade into each other. What kind of labour this involves, and how richly that labour is rewarded, this is not the place to say. But it is the place to say that it is indispensable: unless the student will undertake it, he must be content to remain a sciolist in a science which, equally with all others, if not more than all others, demands profoundness and exactitude. He will be "ever learning, never coming to a knowledge of the truth,"—to quote the apostle's words in a sense somewhat different from their first intention. He will acquire, perhaps, a certain expertness in words, but the things that are the soul of these words will remain hidden from him. He will be in great danger of sinking into the number, only too large, of conventional theologians, confident enough until their neighbour comes and searches them. He is exposed, moreover, to a worse peril than even this: to the peril of joining the herd of those babblers who in the present day seem to have made Christian dogma, as they delight to call it, the arena or rather the victim of their superficial exercitations, and use the scanty knowledge which they have acquired in pastime to point their ridicule at mysteries as far beyond their capacity as are the interior secrets of the familiar sun. Unless that spirit, in all its forms and manifestations and works, is as abhorrent to him as anything that he can possibly abhor, he may call himself indeed a theologian, but theology has no part in him.

Therefore the student should make these tables only the basis of other tables of his own. In constructing them he is not cramped as the printer has been cramped in the endeavour to present them. He has an unlimited scope, and an unlimited margin. Then he must go to work on certain principles of his own. As to the more formal and mechanical part of his work, he may fill in the vacant places of the table— of which more hereafter—and give their location and general character to some systems of faith that ought to be included: this will enlarge his classification to some extent, though not so much as might be expected. Then, as to what is rather material than formal, he should give a separate table to each of the *loci* of theology, from the Scriptures downwards: taking, that is, the order of them as given in this volume, which is not necessarily the best.

Supposing him to begin with the sources or documents of theology, he must dedicate to this subject a table in which the relative place of every Confession is assigned, studying his definitions well, and showing the influence of every divergency upon the community that represents it, and upon the system of doctrine held by that community. If he has a quick eye and sure hand, this sketch will itself expand into a very complete digest of Christian theology: for, which of the religious communions does not bear in almost every article of its creed the stamp and influence of its peculiar view of the inspiration and authority of the Word of God? It is patent enough that this differentiates Romish doctrine from every other. It is not so patent that here lies a marked distinction between Rome and the East, to the advantage of the latter; and that the difference between the Lutheran and the Reformed theologies is not slightly affected by their relative view of the Word of God; and that each of the subordinate systems shows to a quick perception the effect of aberrations, sometimes almost imperceptible, on this subject.

Having thus practised his hand, the student may easily and surely go on. The doctrine of the Holy Trinity will be the superscription of one of his most important tables: one of his most important; in some respects one of the easiest, but in others one of the most difficult. Here he will have, though it is a bold word to say, more unanimity than on any other subject. But there are shades of difference between East and West—between Lutheran, Reformed, and Arminian—which will task his subtlety; especially when he goes beyond his guide in this volume, and traces the influence of the Subordination and Arian theories on those Confessions which hold fast their integrity in general, but show the particular effect of theory on their doctrine of mediation and atonement, and the Person of Christ. Moreover, he must learn to trace the delicate influence of Sabellianism on modern Confessions, venial in some forms of mysticism, but fatal in the grotesque theology of Swedenborg. And he will not have thoroughly accomplished this part of his task, unless he indicates, or tries to indicate—his very failure here will be profitable—the effect on modern theology of a careful distinction between the absolute or immanent, and the relative or economical, Trinity. But this will require that he should descend from the general doctrine to the intricacies of the minor presentations of it, as represented by the federal theology of a past age, which, however eternally true in some of its broad principles, has never been formulated in any Confession. A more obvious effect of the distinction may be traced in the variations of statement, if not of doctrine, as to the final subjection of the Son, and the nature of the kingdom that has "no end." And, lastly, it may be observed to have its effect upon the entire system of mediatorial worship, which in some Confessions is more anxious to emphasize the coequal dignity and interchangeable homage of the Three Persons, and in others lays great stress on the unity of the object of worship through the mediation of the Son, and under the influence of the Holy Spirit, while a third class, in harmony with ancient catholic usage, thinks to follow the Scripture precedent by uniting the two.

It may be said, generally, of most of the other great topics made prominent in this work, that each might with advantage be made the basis of a separate classification. Every system and every Confession has its estimate, for instance, of Sin : it would be more than a mere paradox to say that the dogma of original sin stamps a character for good or evil upon every type of Christian doctrine. The same may be said, with equal but not with more propriety, of the redeeming work of Christ, objective between heaven and earth, and subjective in the human soul. So also Righteousness or justification, the doctrine that presides in the Mediatorial Court of Christ, brings into its own court every individual standard of faith that has ever been set up. In this case, however, the table must needs be a long and elaborate one. For, whatever may be the variety of opinion entertained as to the propriety of Luther's *articulus stantis vel cadentis ecclesiæ*, none will deny that it is a topic literally all-pervading in theology. Every exhibition of the truth of the gospel must have its clear deliverance on this subject. But those deliverances, however clear in the general, are sufficiently vague and indeterminate when the interior distinctions of the communities are introduced. Imputation, faith, works, faith and works, active and passive obedience imputed, formal and efficient cause, condition and instrument, are terms that have a volume of meaning linked with each, and all of them in turn cry from their respective Confessions for adjustment. The task of arranging them is one that it is far easier to recommend than to accomplish. But even here nothing is impossible to the energy that loves its work. The dogma of the Church also presents a fine nucleus for classification: in the nature of things the dogma, like that which it defines, is catholic, and all the tribes of theology must flow into it. None is exempt; for, though there are some systems that glory in their emancipation from the word and the very idea, with all its appendages, and profess to wish that it were exterminated from the theological vocabulary, it will be found on close scrutiny, if indeed any scrutiny is needed, that the great reality is their very life. No communities are more churchly than those which think they have unchurched themselves: witness the close, compact, and orderly Body that calls Christian brethren "Friends."

There is one topic that may be singled out for special remark. It is that of the Person of Christ: a dogma, or doctrine, that does not generally stand at the head of a theological department. Winer makes it one of his *loci*, and gives it ample prominence; but then he is careful to connect with it the term "Divinity," as if the Person of Christ and His Godhead were convertible terms. To do him justice, however, the observations which he appends to the exhibition of the authorities, shows that he included the true doctrine of Christ's Person, as a subordinate branch of a subject over which it should have presided as supreme. The Godhead of Christ is a doctrine that belongs to the Trinity; it belongs to His Person only as pertaining to one of His two natures, which in their indissoluble unity constitute His Person. In making this doctrine the superscription of a distinct branch, the student will have before him one of the finest subjects in theology. He must not make haste; but contemplate it long, reverently, and loyally, before he begins. When he begins, he may take Winer's comparative view to a certain extent; but he will soon have to desert his guide, or rather his guide will desert him. He must go to the ancient symbols, and even higher than that. They will show him what was the Catholic doctrine, as formulated by the first four Councils, against sundry heresies that denied the verity of the human nature of Christ, the absoluteness of His divine nature, the unity of His one Person, and the distinction of His two natures. And, as his table is not exactly a classification of heresies, but rather of the doctrine of the Confessions on all sides, his task will be a simple one down to the Reformation. He will have to show the unity of Christendom on this great subject,—no solitary, surviving symbol or Confession of Faith, bearing witness to any doctrine on Christ's Person but one. He may tabulate if he will, and as much as he pleases, the sporadic and speedily obsolete opinions of men and of schools, from the Docetics downwards; but that is at his own discretion. After the Reformation, the Socini and the Polonian Brethren will demand to be heard. Their places must be found for them, and a place also for their descendants, of every degree, who have greatly varied their doctrine—but never in the ascending scale, always rather in the line of a sure descent. So far, however, all has been general, and comparatively easy. The plain answer to the plain question, "What think ye of Christ? whose son is He?" or that other, "Whom say ye that I am?" is frankly given by the several Confessions, and cannot easily be mistaken. But the subject does not end there. Now comes its difficulties, which are, if such a term may be admitted, its fascinations. They search into all the nooks and corners of this confessional temple, and try sharply the spirits of theological science. It will be sufficient here to indicate in what direction those crucial tests and minor amenities of the doctrine lie: as these remarks are not intended to do the work, but to indicate how it is to be done. And, first, it must be shown what specific dogmas of the old communions have tended to mar or obscure a doctrine otherwise correctly held. It is not doing justice to the subject to say that Christendom was united upon the confession of the Person of Christ at the time of the Reformation. Protestant theologians would demur to this statement as such, and unqualified: Romanist delinquencies, running over so wide a range of vital topics, would scarcely leave this, the most vital of all, untouched. It will be necessary, then, to show how what may be called the application of the doctrine has suffered in the hand of Greek and Romish theology: the latter especially, but noting the difference in this respect between the two. What effect upon the humanity of our Lord in His one Person has the dogma of the Immaculate Conception of the Virgin, which makes Him in His human nature no longer the solitary sinless representative of mankind? What influence is exerted upon it by the dogma of the Mediatorship confined to the Manhood, always supposing that, in the indivisible as well as undivided Person, there could be no merely human agent? What cross-lights, or rather shadows, are thrown upon it by the dogma of Transubstantiation: not only as impairing its dignity, but as seeming to transfer the office of the Holy

Spirit, the mediator between the Person of Christ and our persons, to a Sacrament which gives the whole Christ to man, directly, and in another form, and through a priestly mediator? These are questions to be profoundly studied, and their answer will greatly enrich the tabular view.

But the doctrine carries its inquisition into the Protestant as well as the Romanist standards, and becomes the watchword of some strange varieties of discussion. It will be necessary to show how Lutheran theology stands in relation to it. That relation is in some respects peculiar; unshared by any other Confession in Christendom. Consubstantiation, however widely different from Transubstantiation in some most fundamental respects, is akin in its influence upon the doctrine of the Person in relation to the Holy Ghost. But the specialty of this theory of the Eucharist is that it limits the impartation of Christ in the Sacrament to His human nature, or His glorified corporeity, which is communicated to the recipient in and with and under the elements. This is, in a certain sense, a division of the one Person of the Redeemer. But the doctrine is perhaps saved from such an imputation by another kindred dogma, that of the *communicatio idiomatum*, or the communication of the properties of the Divine nature to the human. Thus the manhood of the Saviour has all the virtue of His divinity, and can be imparted from a thousand altars. To show the bearing of this upon the Lutheran sacramental theology, and indeed upon the entire economy of union with Christ in its system, will be a necessary task, as well as to indicate the marked difference between it and the Reformed theology in general, with the mediation scheme of Calvin. The doctrine must also be traced in another and widely different range: that, namely, which opens to our view the theories of our Lord's exinanition, or the measure and laws of His humiliation in the assumption of human nature. Though the questions arising out of this subject are not precisely confessional questions, belonging rather to the minor controversies, they are more and more active in their influence on Lutheran theology, and must have a place in its department of the tabular view. Nor must it be omitted that the doctrine of Christ's Person is closely connected with the nature of that obedience which He wrought out as one agent, not man only, though representing man, not God only, though the manifestation of God, but the Incarnate Son, the unity of whose Person raises Him absolutely above the law to which He voluntarily submitted. But there lies the question in discussion; and fairly to discuss it requires a careful study of the doctrine now before us. In fact, it is scarcely possible to limit the application of this subject. No topics in theology more aptly represent the central truth. For, from the absolute and the economical Trinity down to the judgment and the final consummation, the true idea of Christ's Person has in all things the pre-eminence. The student who shall achieve well, or fairly well, this individual table, will have learnt more by the process than many a goodly volume on the divinity of Christ could teach him.

Once more, the Holy Spirit, as the centre of a dogmatic system, might advantageously command another line in such tables as these. The place assigned to the Third Person in the economical Trinity in the several Confessions, defines their character with almost as much precision as that of Christ's Person. Here would recur, of course, the question of the *Filioque*, which divides East from West, and has already been viewed under the doctrine of the immanent Trinity. But now it would introduce the bearing of the double procession upon the theology of redemption. For, if Father and Son are names belonging to the God of the mediatorial economy, and the Holy Ghost proceeds from both, then we gain an important basis for a double doctrine of the Spirit's relation to the Mediator. In the one He is sent from the Father through the Son's intercession to discharge a distinct function, to be the administrator of redemption generally, to fill up as it were the measure of Christ's Work, and act upon earth in the place of Him whom the heavens have received. In the other, He is the Spirit proceeding from Christ Himself, whose presence is the presence of our very Lord. "The Lord is that Spirit," whose indwelling fulfils all that the Scripture says in its profoundest passages concerning the mystical union of Christ's Person with believers. The former view, unqualified by the latter, lays the foundation of a superstructure in which the Saviour and the Holy Ghost are often too much separated: the actual miraculous presence of Christ being the result of a perpetual miracle, the continuation of His work in the Church; and the office of the Comforter being limited to the particular functions of enlightenment and sanctification. The latter view allows of no Christ in the mediatorial economy who is to be regarded as apart from the Spirit, who proceedeth from the Son as well as from the Father, and is therefore what the Lord has termed Him, His other Self within the Christian Church. It is the union of these two counterpart ideas that gives the perfect doctrine of the Holy Ghost as a centre in theology. But the doctrine does not end there. That is only its beginning. The Spirit's work in the world is as all-pervasive as that of the Son. Every theological system has its distinct relation to it; and no two assign precisely the same function to Him whose ministration the gospel is. It will be a difficult but valuable exercise to determine the posture of all the Confessions to the Holy Ghost as inspirer and witness of the Scriptures, as bearing testimony to believers and working within them. It is under this head that some of the distinguishing characteristics both of Romanism and of Arminianism would best be exhibited. In the former system the Holy Ghost was in the original constitution of man a kind of mediator before the Mediator: being the bond of perfection in man's first estate, the superadded gift of original righteousness, whose departure was the fatal fall, and His restoration in baptism the free gift that restores mankind.

Arminianism has no more imposing doctrine than that which it teaches concerning the Spirit's universal influence as the representative of Christ's redemption, pervading the outer court with that preliminary grace which leads to the Holy and the Holiest. These are but specimens, serving to show in what way the Third Person might occupy a place as central as Christ Himself in the exhibition of Christian doctrine. Before leaving the topic, the observation may be allowed, in the way of marginal note only, that there is no one subject in Christian theology more neglected than this. Let our imaginary student take care not to neglect it.

Yet one more subject shall detain us for a while. It is at first sight somewhat remarkable that Winer has not included Eschatology, or the Doctrines of the Last Things, in his tabulation. But, when we consider attentively, we find that the symbolical interest of these subjects is exhausted by the section on the doctrine or sacrament of Penance. This is one of many instances in which the place occupied by a subject in the old Confessions is far from being the measure of its absolute importance. The Comparative Tables now recommended must have a department for the Last Things, and give it plenty of space. For it is a vast as well as an awful branch of theology, and, though scarcely mentioned at any length in our volume, occupies in some form or other the anxious thought of every Church in Christendom. In filling up the table, our student will have to introduce a great number of theories, more or less fanciful and speculative, which glimmer in some of the Confessions,—for instance, on the subject of the Resurrection, and the circumstantials of the consummation of all things. There is one branch—the Intermediate State—in which the Romanist and Greek, the Lutheran and the Reformed, will all be found in their Confessions more or less to differ. The differences are easily stated, but they are enormous in their bearing upon theology. The Advent of Christ is another subject which enters little into the Creeds and Confessions, save in connection with the Judgment; but there is a world of unwritten Creeds on the subject of the Millennium which must be epitomized, if justice is to be done to the table. And finally the Judgment, with its eternal issues, must enter. Here again it is remarkable that the Creeds and Confessions of Christendom, whether ancient or modern, have little to say, simply because they were generally constructed more or less with reference to the suppression of error, and there has been a most solemn unanimity among the Christian communities on this subject from the beginning.

It will strike the reader's mind, and possibly take the form of an objection, that this enlarged series of comparative tables must needs involve a constant repetition of the leading topics of theology. That, indeed, is the characteristic difference between such a synoptical view as is here proposed and that which is given in this volume. But the very repetition, that might on a first glance seem wearisome or distracting, will on deeper consideration approve itself to be a peculiar and great advantage. It would be hard to exaggerate the importance of that kind of theological study which makes every cardinal topic in its turn a centre, and brings all other themes to revolve around it. Thus, and thus only, we see the various bearings and relations of every subject, and come to understand it thoroughly. Indeed, it is not possible in any other way to do justice to some of the leading doctrines. The Person of Christ cannot be studied under the dogma of the Trinity, though it must necessarily enter there so far as concerns the Divine nature. On the other hand, the doctrine of the Trinity, both as immanent and as economical, must recur under the dogma of the Person of Christ, but in such a way as to avoid the semblance of repetition. It is impossible to do justice to the doctrine of the Holy Ghost as an isolated subject; it must run more or less through all theology. So is it with the Atonement, which, however clear it may be made in itself, is made much more clear when it returns in the doctrine of justification. In fact there is nothing that the student of a book like this should have more diligently impressed upon his mind, than the necessity of not studying the several subjects of theological science in an isolated manner. This is the manifest evil connected with most of the systems that are commonly adopted. Topic after topic—from Revelation to Judgment—is introduced, discussed, and despatched, often with a special care that it shall return no more. It was not after this manner that the Christian Church was taught the rudiments of its theology in the New Testament; and on such a principle the truth can never be adequately unfolded in the scientific theology of the Christian Church. What is to be desired and recommended as the perfection of divinity, is that in which the freedom of Biblical theology is preserved and harmonized with the results of systematizing art. The bearings of every doctrine on every other doctrine should be indicated at least: that being briefly and subordinately touched upon under one head, which takes the leading place under another. Now the same observation will apply to the task now recommended. Our Table is not an exhibition of systematic theology, but of the relation of every Creed to its leading doctrines. But the result, if it is skilfully done, will be as good as any system of theology. It remains only that the student make the experiment: commencing on a small scale, enlarging it as he goes on. Let him insert at first the judgments of every Confession on the fundamental subjects, much after the manner of Winer, but in his own words. If his tables are in a worthy volume, well articulated, and with ample room for fuller detail of minor differences, for dates and names and all the other accessories of his subject, the accumulation of a few years will be more valuable to him than any book in his library.

III. Hitherto these introductory observations have gone on the supposition that Winer's work is a calm, impartial, comprehensive, and universal view of the Confessions of Christendom; and that as such it may be made a text-book by the theologian of every doctrinal type. It is time now to specify certain necessary qualifications of this tribute: qualifications, however, which point only to the kind of supplement which his work requires for the English reader, and for the English reader of the present day. This has no reference to the mere literature of the question. The last German editor of the work has supplied all that could be desired in this department; and the student who desires to possess the amplest materials for the prosecution of his researches in Symbolical Theology, will find the latest and best collections of the several Creeds of the Churches indicated for his benefit. A judicious selection of these would be a valuable addition to his library, and give him a firm foundation on which to build. In fact, so complete and well digested are these summaries and collections, that no man need quote at second hand the statements of either the ancient or the modern Confessions of Christian Faith; and, as truth should reign in every department of theology, so accuracy in literary quotation should be its faithful minister. But neither truth in the thing expressed, nor accuracy in the expression of it, can long be maintained in this branch of study unless the habit is formed of examining, wherever that is possible, the original standards as they speak for themselves.

Whatever supplement the work may require has reference rather to its presentation for English readers. And this in two directions. First, the Continental systems of theology are by the necessity of the case looked at from a German point of view, and, when the point of view is transferred to this side of the Channel, though the geographical change is not great, the theological parallax is considerable, bearing no precise proportion to the distance in space. Secondly, to the English eye of the present day there are many and most important varieties of Confession which, whether formulated or not, ought to be admitted into the survey, but have no place in Winer's tabulation. It may be suggested that this was a fair reason for an editorial reconstruction of the work itself; or for running dissertations adapting the foreign element to the English standard of comparison, and such insertions of our more modern representatives of belief as would have made the book complete. As to the first suggestion, he who would offer it has never made the experiment of recasting the work of a great man, and yet preserving its identity; and he must have failed to notice how miserably such processes have generally issued. There is no extant illustration of its success; at least of such complete or even partial success as would encourage any sound-minded editor to the attempt. As to the third suggestion, that of adding the later Confessions, the question must first be answered, Where are they to be found? Most of our modern communities have declined to formulate their peculiarities by express articles, at any rate by any such precise form of sound words as might be appealed to as declaring their common sentiment. It is far easier to understand the general type of Congregationalist or Baptist or Methodist doctrine than to quote the terms in which they have agreed to define it. So also it is much easier to summarize in the mind than to exhibit on paper the congeries of beliefs, positive and negative, that make up the religion of Millenarians, Unitarians, Friends, Swedenborgians, Irvingites, and others, too many to be enumerated. Some of these bodies fall back upon old standards, such as the Thirty-nine Articles and the Westminster Confession. So far as that holds good, their case is met. The definitions of the Anglican Church have been given by Winer himself, and he has done more than justice to the question; the testimonies of the Westminster Confession have been carefully given in this English edition, in justice to that very large portion of the Christian world which owes it allegiance more or less absolute. The third suggestion remains, the running dissertations;˙ and that is provided for in what remains of this Introduction, so far as such fleeting notices as the following may deserve the name of dissertation.

First, as to the two great types of Protestant doctrine, the Lutheran and the Reformed, it may not be a superfluous task to make a few remarks that shall round them off to the English student in their united and several significance. It would be a work of supererogation to indicate their doctrinal distinction, from Rome on the one hand, and, on the other hand, as sharply defined between themselves. That is done effectually in the volume, and need not be twice done. But a German author would take some things for granted which an English reader would need to have explained to him.

These two systems of Christian doctrine in the German theory rule the Protestant world. As such they are not Lutheranism and Calvinism, but, dropping the names of men, they are the Evangelical and the Reformed Confessions. Lutheranism is the Evangelical Church : having adopted that term for its theology, not as against its Swiss coadjutor in the Reformation, but as against Rome, and as the symbol of its protest for the pure gospel. The Swiss or Calvinistic movement, as nearly as possible simultaneous, produced the Reformed Confession : having adopted that term Reformed for its theology, not as against its German coadjutor, of course, but still as against Rome, and as the symbol of its protest against the Papal Church. It would perhaps be hypercriticism to say that the two terms obscurely indicate a certain difference between the two systems, as the former was more concerned with Christian doctrine, the latter more concerned with the Christian State, while they in some sense alike contended for both. There is a truth in this which might be pleaded for, were it worth while. But let it pass : the distinction is one that has not so much significance among us as it has in German theology, but it is one that requires to be understood : we must be familiar with many things in our neighbours' nomenclature which we do not ourselves adopt. Returning to the starting-point, the German survey of the Christian world makes the Evangelical and Reformed types govern all Protestant theology. To change the figure, the river that went out of the new Eden to water the garden was parted and became two streams to fertilize the entire theological earth. To drop figures altogether, Lutheranism as a form of Christianity is held by the German heart of Europe, by the Scandinavian nations, by part of Britain and America, reckoning itself the standard and director of an immense body of science theological that bears not its name; whilst the Reformed form of Christianity is held by Switzerland and France, its ancient seats, by the Netherlands, by much of Great Britain—Scotland particularly, but not exclusively,—and by the greater part of North America. Whatever Christian symbols bear not the signature of the Augsburg Confession have that of the Helvetic; in other words, those have written broadly upon them the name of Luther, these the name of Calvin. Hence the arrangement of the Confessions in the present volume. The English Articles and the Westminster Confession drop quietly into the ranks of the Reformed. Evangelical and Reformed are the two central superscriptions made one in the unity of Protestant doctrine. To the left lie the corrupt Confessions of East and West; and to the right, in a confraternity forced upon them rather by science than truth, the Arminian, Anabaptist, and Socinian forms of faith. This style of German unification has not been interfered with in our edition.

It has at the first glance some measure of justification in the facts of the case, especially as regards the Reformed type of Confession. This has been stamped, with some modifications, on a larger number of Christian formularies. The die was new cut, and its edges keenly sharpened at the Synod of Dort; it took a completer form and was engraved afresh in good English letters in the Westminster Confession, and that Confession is an elect symbol of Calvinistic Presbyterianism all over the world, as well as of most congregational communities in England and America. Moreover, the Anglican formularies were constructed very much under the influence of the Augsburg and the Swiss Confessions: being in many respects a composite of the two, deriving, when the articles, canons, and rites of the English Church are viewed as a whole, a peculiar and unshared character from the combination. He who reads the doctrinal standards is constantly reminded of Calvin; he who follows its liturgical service feels that he is much more under the influence of a sacramental religion than Calvin ever was. But, on the other hand, there is much to be set against all this. It is not true that Luther and Calvin moulded the Reformation so absolutely. In our own land, Christian theology had been before their time undergoing its silent but sure transformation. There lived brave men before Agamemnon: there were true interpreters of God's Word in England and Scotland who did more for subsequent Christian truth than any of the Confessions of Germany and Switzerland. Moreover, the doctrinal system of the English Churches varies in many things from the Continental type; and varies in a way which absolutely proves it independent of both the forms of that type. The dogma of Transubstantiation has never had a formula that expresses it in the English language; the Anglican Real Presence is more nearly allied to Calvin's doctrine, though essentially diverging from that. The theology of the Puritans, however much like that of Calvin, held very different theories as to the relation of Christianity to the State, and the authority of man in things divine. And, if we come down to our own times, it cannot be said that the great bulk of English theology is under the influence of either Luther or Calvin. In all its branches it is independent of Continental Confessions, however much in all its branches indebted to Continental learning and criticism.

Passing from that subject—which, however, will presently be resumed—the internal relations of Lutheranism and the Reformed demand a moment's attention. A careful study of their documents will show how widely they diverge on many fundamental points: so widely, that the experiment of their union in Germany, now nearly half a century made, can never hope to be a complete success. It may be wrong to say fundamental points, for the two Confessions are perfectly at one as to the deepest basis of human hope. But as to the universality of the grace of the gospel, and the means of grace by which it is applied, and the sacramental participation of Christ, they are very widely separated. The absolute sovereignty of God over man's will and destiny, declared in the doctrine of Election, sways with a dread supremacy the Reformed Confessions; the Lutheran allow free play for human responsibility and a predestination based upon the foresight of faith and obedience. In the Reformed Confessions the means of grace are reduced finally to the Word of God; in the Lutheran they really become the sacraments alone: for, in the former, the emphasis is laid upon the living word, which makes all other means what they are; while, in the latter, grace is in its strictest meaning the justification, quickening, and sanctification of the soul, which are imparted in the order of the gospel only through the two sacraments. It is, however, in the nature of eucharistical communion with Christ that the two Confessions betray the widest difference. In the Reformed the Lord's Supper is the sign and pledge of a union with Christ which is produced independently by the Spirit through faith. In the Lutheran, the glorified corporeity of Christ, His real body and blood, are in verity and deed received by all who partake : to their salvation by the worthy, to their condemnation by the unworthy. It is only right to add on this subject, that, while the Lutheran doctrine has remained almost unvaried from the beginning—taking its stand with desperate tenacity on the words, *This is my Body!*—the Reformed has known many varieties of statement. Calvin, for instance, who denied the ubiquity of the Saviour's body, and therefore rejected the idea of its impartation in and under and with the elements to all who received them, nevertheless held firmly that the very body of Christ is the spiritual sustenance of the soul, which ascends to touch it as it were in heaven by faith. Zwingli fixed his eye solely on the symbol and sign in the sacrament: at least that is the prevalent tendency of his teaching, the language of which varies considerably. The representatives of the Reformed Confessions in England have, as has been already affirmed, maintained their independence. The Presbyterian type of doctrine in the Westminster Confession gives much prominence to the sealing efficacy of the Lord's Supper, as an instrument that not only pledges but conveys over the blessings of which it is the sign, the benefits, that is, of the Christian covenant. From this the Congregationalist standards recede, and go beyond Zwingli in the opposite direction. But we are trespassing into a region where our volume itself is the best guide.

Before leaving these venerable Confessions, or rather families of Confessions, a word may be said as to their influence upon the theologies which they severally regulated. At the outset they each gave birth to as noble a series of dogmatic writers as Christian literature has ever known: as subtle as the schoolmen, whose methods they inherited, but baptized richly with the spirit of the new evangelical doctrine. The enumeration of their names in both communions would literally fill more than one of these pages: of divines, that is, who wrote on Systematic Theology, whose works were not practical or controversial treatises so much as bodies of divinity, constructed on the most comprehensive system, arranged with consummate analytical art, and still held in repute as the standard of Orthodoxy. These are the treasures of Lutheran and Reformed Theology, bequeathed to it by the first century after the Reformation. But here we are encountered by the objection, that this immense phalanx of divines failed to defend Germany and Switzerland and Holland from the irruption of Rationalism, and Transcendental Philosophy, and Confessional indifference and lawlessness. It is hard to meet that objection. The fact must be left among those mysteries of Divine Providence which are the common burden, and which happily we are not required to solve. But we may demur to the inference drawn from the fact in disparagement of these Confessions themselves, and of Confessions generally. Granted that neither of the two great Reformation Standards has preserved its community from error—that Germany and Holland, their headquarters in the present day, have a large number of destructionist critics in their midst—that is no argument against the value of the formularies against which these critics have revolted. The vital essential truth that is common to them all has preserved them to this day: the errors they contain—for, being in some things contradictory, errors they must hold, each or both—may be to a great extent chargeable with the recoil into Rationalism.

An intelligent, not to say charitable, estimate of the present influence of the two great families of Confessions on Continental Theology will discover much to plead in their favour. First, it cannot be denied that they have never failed from the beginning to keep their place as the two centres of a Christian literature generally sound. This holds good of both. A stream of rich, fresh, edifying German theology may be traced flowing steadily within its more or less definite banks from Melanchthon to the present day. A censorious observer may point to periods when those banks were effaced, and the healthy and impure waters flowed indistinguishably through one turbid mass: the more catholic-minded observer will see it far otherwise. The same may be said of the Reformed Theology, especially if its tributaries in Holland and England and America are taken into account. Again, it is no slight evidence of the inherent vigour of these Confessions that they are rallying around them many of the ablest thinkers and writers of the age. These are so earnest in their allegiance that they are beginning to receive a common name from their confessional ardour. Some of them are rigorous and almost bigoted in their adherence to their respective formularies, emulating the old dogmatic divines in the systematic presentation of Lutheran and Reformed Theology, as reconstructed in the presence of Rationalism and with a constant reference to its attacks. Some of them base their labours on the theory of a union of the Confessions. These Union theologians are rapidly increasing. They labour, of course, under great disadvantages. It cannot be denied that the original framers of the Confessions finished their work in such a manner that the types can never coalesce,—the two theologies can never run into the same mould. This does not, however, preclude the possibility that the resulting system may be one better on the whole than any which either Confession could produce alone: a question, however, which this is not the place to enter upon. The union of the two Churches, begun at the Tercentenary of the Reformation, and gradually spreading through Germany down to the present time, is, after half a century, only an experiment.

In our own day Protestant Europe is witnessing a new and strange kind of controversy, waged furiously on the Continent, but more or less involving Great Britain. There is, to use a bold word, a contest between the modern Confessions and the ancient symbols, or rather the one ancient symbol from which the others sprang—the Apostles' Creed. The German Protestant Alliance—for by such a term we must translate its paradoxical name in the original—is waging a steady and relentless war against the Reformation symbols, and uses for convenience the earliest Christian rule of faith as its standard and battery. As the campaign goes on, and its tactics and evolutions become more evident, it begins to appear that the old symbol has been, after all, deceitfully used. The contest is really the old one between a human and a divine Christianity under another form. The question soon arose, What is the *symbolum apostolicum?* One by one it lost its articles, until it was disintegrated into a meaningless symbol of an original legendary faith. But the gradual accumulation of the articles of that Creed was step by step a series of victories over the heresies of early times; and now it remains that, article by article, it must be defended in these later ages. Lutheranism has to fight resolutely now for the veriest foundation facts of the Christian faith; and it is no small evidence of the value of its old Confessions that the ablest defenders of the early faith are also the most strenuous adherents of their own modern form of it.

But Protestant Christendom was not long divided between the two Confessions in their integrity. Other systems of faith have arisen, and exerted vast influence. A few words will be necessary in explanation of the place assigned in this work to Arminian doctrine, as the first and most important of these. The idea suggested to the English mind by the term Arminianism is not precisely the same as that which it suggests to the German divine. To us it is simply the antithesis of Calvinism, and stands rather for a tendency of thought than for a definite Confession. To the German, and to the Continental student of historical theology generally, it stands for a Dutch religious community with a dogmatic standard and a developed history not yet ended.

The Arminian or Remonstrant divinity has always had a sore ordeal to pass through. To the Lutherans it has been a degenerate branch of the Reformed, and to the Reformed an unworthy offshoot which it would fain disavow. It is not necessary here to trace its history, nor to characterize its leading theologians, for both these have justice done them in the volume. Suffice that the names of Arminius, Episcopius, Curcellæus, Hugo Grotius, Limborch, Le Clerc, and Wetstein are a septemvirate not easily to be paralleled. But the taint of latitudinarianism is upon the later Remonstrant theology,— to the susceptibilities at least of the more orthodox Lutherans and Reformed. It is almost universally thought that the older quinquarticular Arminianism betrayed a tendency towards laxity in doctrine almost as soon as the Remonstrant stage of its history was entered upon. Episcopius had to defend his party against the charge of Socinianism: an easier task than to defend it against the imputation of carrying too far the subordination in the Trinity. It has been an offence to the Confessional divines that the Arminians have been lax as it regards symbols. The Calvinistic controversialists, in particular, have never forgiven them their consistently-held dogma concerning the human will, and have freely given them the name of semi-Pelagians. Thus, on all hands, the Arminian theology has been, and still is, where it lingers in the Netherlands, condemned: where it escapes one enemy, it falls under the censure of another. To the strict adherent of the symbols, it is Rationalism; to the hyper-orthodox, it is semi-Socinianism; to the rest, it is semi-popish Pelagianism. All this is here stated as matter of fact. It is a necessary explanation of the circumstance that the Arminian and the Socinian standards are in such suspicious juxtaposition. The student must bear in mind that Winer only falls in with the conventional manner of speaking and principle of classification. A careful examination of the authorities cited will suffice to exhibit the truth as it respects an important body of theological teachers and doctrines which have exerted no slight influence on the Christianity of the world.

But there is an Arminianism in this country which is a very different matter, and must be regarded under other lights. It is its peculiarity that it has one history on the Continent and another in England or among the English-speaking races. Whereas in most Continental reviews of historical theology Arminianism is regarded as a suspicious transitional stage between Orthodoxy and Rationalism, and its evil communications with Socinianism are supposed to have corrupted its good morals, in the English estimate Arminianism is mainly regarded as the diffused corrective of Calvinism. It represents a doctrine of the Atonement, whether objective in the finished work of Christ or subjective in the personal application of that work, which opposes the doctrine held by the Calvinistic Reformed communities everywhere. The satisfaction of Christ is viewed rather as offered to the righteous Governor of the universe, and counted by Him sufficient for the relief of the world from the sentence of the law, than as a strict equivalent for the guilt of the elect, and imputed to them as such. And the application of Christ's merit is regarded as an appropriation on the part of man through the Spirit's grace, leaving it as the issue of his probation to hold it fast for ever or lose it, rather than as the absolute and irreversible interest in salvation secured by Christ for His own. This is English Arminianism, as it reigns in a very large section of the Anglican divinity, more ancient and more modern, and as it has been accepted throughout the wide-spread Methodist denominations. It may be said, indeed, that Arminianism in England further represents a doctrine of the Trinity and the Person of Christ which has its peculiarities. But an accurate theological criticism will not allow this. The subordination in the interior relations of the triune nature, which, as a subordination that does not impair the essential equality and consubstantiality of the Divine Persons, was taught by Pearson, for instance, the representative of a large body of divines, was not derived from Arminianism. It descended to these writers from the earliest theology of the Church, and is supported by them by Scripture and the fathers. It is true that the doctrine luminously reigns in the writings of the second generation of Dutch Arminianism, but Anglican divinity was no borrower from the Continent in this department. Nor was it, strictly speaking, in the other; that is, in the doctrines of Grace. Neither the older divines of the English Church, nor the modern Methodists, thought themselves to have received what they taught on these questions, either "from man or by man." But undoubtedly the reflex and indirect influence of the Synod of

Dort was very great in this country. For a long time Arminianism was a watchword as against Calvinism. This, however, gradually ceased to be an acknowledged watchword; it was suppressed in the Methodist literature, and is not used save by the Calvinistic opponents of the doctrines referred to. For the rest, and to sum up these merely historical remarks, it must be remembered by the English student of this work, that while Arminians, or rather Remonstrants, have never ceased to be a corporate body in the Reformed Netherlands, Arminianism in England has never been more than a tendency and an influence, a theory and norm of doctrine, and consequently without a Confession of its own.

Strictly speaking, Arminianism has not, either on the Continent or in England, had a Confession. One of the characteristic principles of the party was a comparative indifference to formal symbols and creeds. But this fact must be rightly understood; the Remonstrant divines were never lax either in the systematization or the definition of their faith. Their dogmatic writers were quite worthy to take rank with their rivals in these respects, and that is no small praise. Nothing can be more luminous than the exposition of doctrine by Episcopius and Limborch. And it cannot be denied that their entire theory of Christianity from end to end is articulated, uniform and consistent; it would not otherwise have lodged so firmly in the Anglo-Saxon mind. But the leaders of this movement were not ambitious to form a distinct community; they were content to protest against what they thought exaggerations in the Confessions which they in the main agreed with and adopted. Arminians they never called themselves; and their name Remonstrants was derived from their honourable but firm remonstrance presented to the States-General of Holland in 1611. Arminius was originally a disciple of Beza, and through him of Calvin. He never ceased to respect the Reformed Confessions; and never, any more than his successors, set up a rival formulary. He was content, so far as concerned that, with establishing negations of some of what he thought the too severe statements of the doctrines of Grace. It must be added to this, that the community carried to an excess their estimate of the greater importance of a sound life in comparison with a sound Creed; forgetting, in later times especially, that, if doctrine is according to godliness, godliness is also according to doctrine. Hence, on the whole, it may be said that the Remonstrant community abjured the thought of any such separation from the Reformed communion as would have been involved in the construction of a distinct Creed.

On the other hand, there are certain Arminian documents which have all the force and authority of a Confession. For the character and history of these the reader is referred to Winer. They have reference to the five points in particular that defined the differences between the old and the new types of doctrine. The other standards are appealed to as containing the more general exposition of doctrine. And the whole may be said to be the most remarkable instance Christianity has known of an eclectic faith. This term is a branded one; and as such will be very welcome to those who are the overzealous enemies of Arminianism. But it is used here in an historical and conventional sense of our own, to meet the facts of the case. It absorbs the greater part of the doctrines of the Lutheran and Reformed standards, using honestly the terms satisfaction, original sin, effectual grace, but throwing over them the influence of a doctrine concerning the universal effect of the redeeming work of Christ which gives each of them a distinct and qualified character: to reconcile them with vain reasoning, their enemies say; to reconcile them with Scripture and the facts of human consciousness, they say themselves. In this they are eclectic enough to borrow from later Lutheranism, the early Greek Churches, and in some sense the later doctrine of Rome. Semi-Pelagianism, both Roman and Greek, might seem to have lent them some of its few unexceptionable principles as to the freedom of the human will. But they contracted no further debt to that system, as the Remonstrants have never denied that the first as well as all subsequent movements of the soul towards God are of the operation of the Holy Ghost. To go a step further back: there may appear to be a strain of the Romanist doctrine in the Arminian view of the effects of the fall. But in the latter, the restoration of the Spirit to man through Christ's mediation is made a general gift to the race; in the former, the Sacrament of Baptism removes every trace of original sin as such. This line of observation might easily be pursued; but enough has been said for our merely historical object. Justice would not have been done to the Arminian section of our comparative view without so much: more would carry us beyond our present design. Let it suffice, that the eclecticism of the Remonstrant divinity must indicate its character in the following work, which will show that the importation of the older theology into the new, for which it is responsible, will hardly justify Möhler's patronizing terms concerning it, and still less the calm verdict of Dr. Hodge, in an essay on the "History of Creeds": "The theology taught in all these Papal standards is Arminianism."

From a German point of view the Anabaptists and Mennonites are necessary factors in a comparison of the Confessions. But to an English eye they seem like fossils even in a German work, and in every sense are obsolete in a symbolical survey. They pertain to one family, the badge of which was the rejection of infant baptism, a badge less honourable in its history on the Continent than in its history in England and America. The Anabaptists proper belong rather to ecclesiastical than to dogmatic history. By their frightful excesses they disturbed the progress of the Reformation more than any other among the elements of Luther's difficulty. Melanchthon did them too much honour in 'his elaborate refutation of their Montanistic and other extravagances. Their name, if not their memory, has perished: one of their principles, however, having survived in a purer form. Towards the middle of the seventeenth century Menno Simonis formed a Baptist community in Holland, which mingled with its own creed many of the fanatical notions of the Anabaptists, and some of those which Quakerism has made familiar to us, adding to the whole a rite peculiar to itself, the feet-washing. They have since multiplied into smaller sects with which our subject is not concerned. As to the original body, nothing need be added to the information of our work, save that the limitation of the Sacrament of Baptism to adult believers is the only point in common between them and the Baptists known to ourselves.

Finally, on this branch of the subject, it must be remembered that the elaborate Socinian Confessions and catechisms which figure so largely in our volume are, strictly speaking, as much extinct as those of the Anabaptists. This is a plain fact, but it is one the significance of which is sometimes lost sight of. What the Socinian doctrine was, and what its links were with the primitive heresies of the second century—lineal descent it had none,—Winer's work will show. What it does not indicate, the affinity with Arianism on the one hand and the doctrine of Praxeas and the rest on the other, must be gathered from the history of Christian doctrine. What is here necessary is to indicate that our English Socinianism, so called, is a very different thing from that which figures in these columns. It is as far removed from its prototype in Poland as the Baptist doctrine in England is from its Anabaptist representative in the Reformation age. But in an opposite direction; for, whereas among our Baptists the stream has run clear of its defecations, Unitarianism in England and America has thrown off much, if not all, of the dogmatic precision and doctrinal consistency and supernatural dignity of its Continental ancestry. The term supernatural will point the way to what we mean. The old Socinianism adopted Rationalist principles at the outset, rejected the traditional Christianity of past ages, and constructed its theory of Christ's Person and work by the light of its own rational interpretation of the Scriptures. But it held fast the doctrine of the inspiration of Scripture, or of its quasi-inspiration; though it had no inspiring Person, it had an inspiring influence, to elevate the Bible above other literature. It also perceived clearly the supernatural element that pervades the Bible, and its Christ therefore was not in the world under the ordinary conditions of mankind. Hence the modern historians of theology in Germany, generalizing after their fashion, represent Socinianism as the beginning of Rationalism with the supernatural added. The effect of this is apparent in the Socinian formularies, especially as they refer to the Person of Christ. Not divine, He is nevertheless preternaturally conceived and endowed; He is capable of receiving communications from God denied to all others, and of imparting those communications as no others could impart them; and the honour put upon Him is such as no mere mortal could bear and live. At three points in the Saviour's history, Socinianism set upon Him a remarkable seal of dignity. In His birth, when God created Him not after the manner of men; at His rapture into heaven, where, lifted nearer to God than Paul was, He received such knowledge of divine things as neither man nor angels had ever received; and at His ascension, when He was raised to a supreme dignity over the universe. This strain of comment might be pursued, but here also we must forbear from going out of our prescribed sphere. Enough is said to indicate why the Socinian is placed among the Christians, and his Creed as carefully examined and collated as any other. Now that old Socinianism is extinct saving in annals, it marks a stage in a great development no more. It did not rise high enough to admit of recovery to the truth; it did not sink low enough to satisfy the proclivities of rationalistic error. Its Confessions remain simply to show that in that sifting age it had its probation.

The consideration of modern Unitarianism leads to the second branch of this topic, and the last of our general observations: the supplement that the English reader must bring to Winer's Collection of Creeds. It may be as well to say at once that there are no Confessions which have to be added. The old Confessions are still used, though with certain modifications, by those communities which hang upon Creeds and Articles. The majority, however, dispense with them, and content themselves with a more or less defined tradition of faith. In fact, the ancient symbols which at the Reformation became Confessions, have in these last days become Platforms, to use the American word, Standards, as the English call them. A few general observations on these will close our preparatory labours.

The modern Unitarians are not included in Winer's symbolical survey. In fact they were not known to him. The representatives in Germany of their type of doctrine were not reckoned among Christian communities; not indeed that they existed in numbers too small to form congregations,—they formed many congregations that did not bear their name, or betray outwardly their departure from the old faith,—but the far greater part of them were content with a practical indifference and literary infidelity; they were the Illuminati who retired from the communion of the Church, and calmly sat over against the cross, pondering and criticising. Among the churches of Germany and Switzerland there have been many ruled by Socinian opinions, but there have been none that avowed any obligation to the Socini. They have reserved their allegiance for a mightier potentate, the human reason. In other words, they do not give themselves the name of any man; because no one man in any one age can represent the flux of opinions that change with the progression of the race. Nor do they set up any Confession of Faith; and for the same reason: the next generation ought not to be bound by the opinions or prejudices of its predecessor. Nor do they condescend to adopt an appellation that might simply negative some current opinion,—such, for instance, as Unitarianism; for their opinions negative not one current opinion only, but the entire code of Christian beliefs. On the Continent, Socinianism is as extinct as it is with us; but there it has not our substitute. Unitarianism is an English and American system of doctrine, comprising an infinite variety of opinions on all religious subjects, which are kept in a sort of cohesion by the central affirmation that Christ was and is only man. That is their Creed, Confession, and Standard reduced to unity. If that be maintained, every dogma of the old Creed may be held, or renounced, or modified, according to the measure of the illumination of every man or every church. Confessions, or Articles of Faith, or terms of concord, are out of the question. They are at once needless and impossible : needless, because the simplicity of the one article needs no formula; and impossible, because there are and always have been among them as many opinions as there are teachers, in regard to the variety of topics that enter into the construction of a Confession of Faith. When, therefore, in an adaptation of Winer to the English point of view, we substitute Unitarianism for ancient Socinianism, or rather make the former an appendage of the latter, it must be with a considerable reservation. In fact, all that is necessary is to insert among the observations the note, that the modern representatives of Socinus have no Confession or Standard from which an authoritative statement may be extracted on any one point in Christian theology. In leaving the subject thus, we abstain from entering upon any historical review of the variety of phases through which the Unitarian theory has passed in reaching its present stage of creedless development. That would be an interesting, however painful, task; there is abundance of materials for it at hand, but it does not belong to our province. A comparative survey of the Confessions cannot include a community whose Confession is limited to one negation, and beyond that has no standard of appeal and no force of general obligation.

Before leaving the Unitarians, we may observe that there seems to be a tendency among the writers of some communities to put such an interpretation upon the doctrine of the Trinity as would issue in a dogma never yet found in any Confession or heresy. Many a theologian in Germany, loyal in general to the Augsburg Confession, nevertheless indulges in speculations, and shapes them into definitions, which are neither Trinitarian, nor Tritheistic, nor Arian, nor Sabellian, but simply their own. The fashion set abroad has been copied at home. How many writers are there owning a professed allegiance to the Thirty-nine Articles, whose teaching on this subject bears the same character! Stripped of their refinements, their definitions would be reduced to naked Unitarianism. Were such Trinitarians in profession, but Unitarians in heart, to define honestly their Creed to themselves, they must needs join this community. There are not wanting indications that this method of refining upon the doctrine of the Trinity finds favour in some other communities not so rigidly bound to their articles as the Church of England. Of course, the Unitarian Creed—using that term in a conventional sense—may claim these teachers; and, taking them into account, its influence may be said to be extending in England. Apart from that, however, and viewed as a distinct type of Christian belief, it holds but a slight and waning position in English Christendom.

The doctrinal Confession of the Presbyterians and Congregationalists of Great Britain and America may be said to be shaped generally by the Westminster Confession, with its accompanying Catechism. The history of this celebrated formulary is given in our work: any one who desires to enlarge its scanty notices has abundant materials for doing so. Not excepting the Canons of Dort, no Confession so fully expresses the doctrine of the Reformed branch of the Reformation, and none has exerted so much influence in Christendom. It is the common formulary of the Presbyterian Churches in the old and new world. The Congregational Convention, which met at the Savoy in 1658, declared their acceptance of the doctrinal part of the Confession and Catechisms of the Westminster Assembly; and, in fact, formed their Savoy Confession on its basis. For a long time the Assembly's Catechisms were generally used by all these communities; and to some extent even now that is the case. They were adopted in America by the Puritan founders of American Christendom. Since the seventeenth century, platform after platform has reconstructed or modified the original form to harmonize it with American institutions, but the essential body of the old Confession has remained intact. It remains to this day the avowed or unavowed directory of the religious faith of all who, throughout the English-speaking world, hold to the traditions of Puritan theology. Broadly speaking, then, the citations from the Westminster Confession in this volume may be taken as representing the faith of Presbyterians and Congregationalists, whether Independent or Baptist. This, however, is speaking very broadly. Both the latter branches have again and again published documents which have the character of Confessions.

A large number of Baptist congregations adopted, in 1677, a modification of the Westminster Confession, which contains the following articles:—"Baptism is an ordinance of the New Testament. . . . Those who do actually profess repentance towards God, faith in and obedience to our Lord Jesus Christ, are the only proper objects of this ordinance. . . . Immersion, or dipping of the body in water, is necessary to the due administration of that ordinance. . . . All ignorant and ungodly persons, as they are unfit to enjoy communion with Christ, so are they unworthy of the Lord's table." An earlier Confession, in 1646, dilates more fully upon one point: "The way and manner of dispensing this ordinance is dipping or plunging the body under water. It, being a sign, must answer the things signified; which is, that interest the saints have in the death, burial, and resurrection of Christ; and that, as certainly as the body is buried under water, and risen again, so certainly shall the bodies of the saints be raised by the power of Christ in the day of the resurrection, to reign with Christ." In our own day, the formulary from which this last extract is taken has been republished with general acceptance. It may be said that the Baptist Confession of Faith, though not binding as such, and free in lesser details, is consistently and firmly held as a general tradition in England. With its Westminster type of the doctrines of Grace, its congregational principles of church government, its own peculiar theory of one of the Sacraments, and in some respects of both, it is a clear and definite system. Placed, however, among the Confessions of Christendom, whether of ancient or modern times, it is an isolated, exceptional, and very fragmentary representation of Christian doctrine.

The modern Independents have found it necessary to add some kind of standards to their original Confession, though in the adoption of these standards they do not forget the idea that lurks in their general designation. A few extracts from a "Declaration of Faith, Church Order, and Discipline" will explain very clearly their position. Among the preliminary notes are these:—" 1. It is not designed in the following summary to do more than to state the leading doctrines of faith and order maintained by Congregational Churches in general. 4. It is not intended that the following statement should be put forth with any authority, or as a standard to which assent should be required. 5. Disallowing the utility of creeds and articles of religion as a bond of union, and protesting against subscription to any human formularies as a term of communion, Congregationalists are yet willing to declare, for general information, what is commonly believed among them, reserving to every one the most perfect liberty of conscience. 7. They wish it to be observed that, notwithstanding their jealousy of subscription to creeds and articles, and their disapproval of the imposition of any human standard, whether of faith or discipline, they are far more agreed in their doctrines and practices than any Church which enjoins subscription and enforces a human standard of orthodoxy; and they believe that there is no minister and no Church among them that would deny the substance of any one of the following doctrines of religion, though each might prefer to state his sentiments in his own way." These assertions might seem sufficient to vindicate the propriety of passing on, since a place among the Confessions must needs be denied to those who protest against symbols in every form. But a few more extracts may be useful as showing where the Congregationalists would be found were they to accept a place:—" 9. They believe that, in the fulness of the time, the Son of God was manifested in the flesh, being born of the Virgin Mary, but conceived by the power of the Holy Spirit; and that our Lord Jesus Christ was both the Son of man and the Son of God, partaking fully and truly of human nature, though without sin; equal with the Father, and 'the express image of His Person.' 14. They believe that all who will be saved were the objects of God's eternal and electing love, and were given by act of divine sovereignty to the Son of God; which in no way interferes with the system of means, nor with the ground of human responsibility, being wholly unrevealed as to its objects, and not a rule of human duty. 15. They believe in the perpetual obligation of Baptism and the Lord's Supper: the former to be administered to all converts to Christ and their children, by the application of water to the subject 'in the name of the Father, and of the Son, and of the Holy Ghost;' and the latter to be celebrated by Christian Churches as a token of faith on the Saviour, and of brotherly love." If carefully examined, these declarations will be found to allow a wide latitude as to the Calvinistic peculiarities of the Westminster Confession, as also upon the Sacraments, while strictly

faithful, in articles not quoted, to the doctrines of the Trinity and the Person of Christ, and the authority of the Scriptures. As to the specific principles of the church government of the Congregationalists, the following is the final statement:—
" 7. The power of admission into any Christian Church, and rejection from it, they believe to be vested in the Church itself, and to be exercised only through the medium of its own officers. 9. They believe that the power of a Christian Church is purely spiritual, and should in no way be corrupted by union with temporal or civil power. 12. They believe that it is the duty of Christian Churches to hold communion with each other . . . but that no Church, nor union of Churches, has any right or power to interfere with the faith or discipline of any other Church, further than to separate from such as, in faith and practice, depart from the gospel of Christ. 13. They believe that church officers, whether bishops or deacons, should be chosen by the free voice of the Church; but that their dedication to the duties of their office should take place with special prayer and by solemn designation, to which most of the Churches add the imposition of hands by those already in office." If such clauses as these are added to the several Reformed testimonies in Winer's list, English Congregationalism, and American also, would be fairly represented. But it is only historical justice to add that Independent Churches claim their prerogative of independence. Their trust-deeds may be orthodox in most cases, and there may reign throughout their denomination a noble tradition of evangelical orthodoxy: but there is no universal safeguard by the very terms of their Declaration. There is no Confession, Standard, or Declaration that would in any sense represent the teaching of many of its ministers, both in America and in England. But we are interdicted from pursuing this topic any further. Suffice that the Congregationalist Confession of Faith is one that cannot be made a supplement to our volume, inasmuch as it does not exist in any available form. The

doctrine of these Churches is represented, so far as it is represented, by the testimonies of the Westminster Confession.

Among the communities of English origin to which Winer gives no place, must be reckoned those which fall under the general denomination of Methodist. Methodism in its original form, as it first assumed the character of a Society within the Church of England, and afterwards by force of circumstances took rank among the Connexional Churches of Presbyterian Christendom, was not forgotten by Möhler, who has traced its doctrinal characteristics with a fair degree of precision. But it escaped the notice of Winer, partly because to his view it was an adherent of the Thirty-nine Articles, so far as the Christian Faith was concerned; and partly because whatever doctrinal peculiarities it held were never formulated in any Confession. Hence a few general observations are necessary to show the relation of the Methodist community to the general question of the Symbols.

It may be said that English Methodism has no distinct Articles of faith. At the same time it is undoubtedly true that no community in Christendom is more effectually hedged about by confessional obligations and restraints. Reference has been made to the distinction of Creeds, Confessions, and Standards. Methodism combines the three in its doctrinal constitution after a manner on the whole peculiar to itself. Materially if not formally, virtually if not actually, implicitly if not avowedly, its theology is bound by the ancient Œcumenical Creeds, by the Articles of the English Church, and by comprehensive standards of its own the peculiarity of its maintenance of these respectively having been determined by the specific circumstances of its origin and consolidation, circumstances into which it is not our business here to enter. In common with most Christian Churches it holds fast the Catholic Symbols: the Apostolical and Nicene are extensively used in its Liturgy, and the Athanasian, not so used, is accepted so far as concerns its doctrinal type. The doctrine of the Articles of the Church of England is the doctrine of Methodism. This assertion must be, of course, taken broadly, as subject to many qualifications. For instance : the Connexion has never avowed the Articles as its Confession of Faith ; some of those Articles have no meaning for it in its present constitution ; others of them are tolerated in their vague and doubtful bearing rather than accepted as definitions; and, finally, many Methodists would prefer to disown any relation to them of any kind. Still, the verdict of the historical theologian, who takes a comprehensive view of the estate of Christendom in regard to the history and development of Christian truth, would locate the Methodist community under the Thirty-nine Articles. He would draw his inference from the posture towards them of the early founders of the system ; and he would not fail to mark that the American branch of the family, which has spread simultaneously with its European branch, has retained the Articles of the English Church, with some necessary modifications, as the basis of its Confession of Faith. Setting aside the articles that have to do with discipline rather than doctrine, the Methodists universally hold the remainder as tenaciously as any of those who sign them, and with as much consistency as the great mass of English divines who have given them an Arminian interpretation. That is to say, where they diverge in doctrine from the Westminster Confession, Methodism holds to them ; while this Confession rather expresses their views on Presbyterian Church government. It may suffice to say generally on this subject, that so far as concerns the present volume, every quotation from the English Articles may stand, if justly interpreted, as a representative of the Methodist Confession. Finally, we have the Methodist Standards, belonging to it as a society within a church, which entirely regulate the faith of the community, but are binding only upon its ministers. Those Standards are to be found in certain rather extensive theological writings which have none of the features of a Confession of Faith, and are never subscribed or accepted as such. More particularly, they are some Sermons and Expository Notes of John Wesley; more generally, these and other writings, catechisms, and early precedents of doctrinal definition; taken as a whole, they indicate a standard of experimental and practical theology to which the teaching and preaching of its ministers are universally conformed. What that standard prescribes in detail it would be impossible to define here. It is not our task to furnish the supplement to our volume, but to point out what it includes, and how it may be made. Suffice that the Methodist doctrine is what is generally termed Arminian as it regards the relation of the human race to redemption; that it lays great stress upon the personal assurance which seals the personal religion of the believer; and that it includes a strong testimony to the office of the Holy Spirit in the entire renewal of the soul in holiness as one of the provisions of the covenant of grace upon earth. It may be added, though only as an historical fact, that a rigorous maintenance of this common standard of evangelical doctrine has been attended by the preservation of a remarkable unity of doctrine throughout this large communion.

Omitting Swedenborgianism, a system not indigenous in England, which we are not bound to regard as one of the Confessions of Christendom, the "Catholic and Apostolic Church" represents a certain aggregate of tendencies, doctrines, and ritual that is in process of forming a confession, though it has none as yet to furnish. This community sprang, in the person of its founder, from what would be called, in the language of historical theology, a modern Montanistic spirit. Its tenets include the renewal of the apostolate, the restoration of the miraculous signs of the early Church, and a consequent reconstruction of the estate of Christ's Body upon earth. Its early doctrine as to the identity between the Lord's human nature and that of man as fallen, has fallen into the category of unformulated beliefs. Its importations from Catholic antiquity, as interpreted by Rome, are not clearly defined: for, though transubstantiation is denied, and the repetition on human altars of the one oblation, what its sacramental doctrine is can be determined by no adequate authority. Its high millenarian theories are left in the same indefinite state. And, as a whole, this modern phenomenon cannot as yet be classed among the Confessions of Christendom. It is a composite of all the Confessions, as its ritual is a composite of all the Rites of Christendom. The reader who would add this community to his supplement must take the pains to read many a treatise, and to explore a very miscellaneous service-book. He will find much to reward his curiosity as a student of the developments of the Christian Church; but he will find it difficult to construct the appropriate confessional column.

After all that has been said, there remains another supplementary question which the student of Symbolism must add in his own way. It does not refer to any particular class of doctrinal judgment that might be added to the tabulation, nor is it confined to English Christianity. It is more or less common to all forms of the Christian religion, and includes many very important elements of belief and teaching which defy systematization, but nevertheless enter largely into many systems and exert a mighty influence in the Church's development. These tendencies represent the body of unformulated opinions which belong to all Confessions: undertones of Christian doctrine which characterize men rather than communities, and act upon them rather as modes of thinking than as definite beliefs. Tendencies to Millenarianism, which Judaizes the second coming of Christ as St. Paul's enemies Judaized the first coming; tendencies to a ritualistic Christianity which would restore to it a symbolical character from which the New Testament declares it free; tendencies to modify the traditional faith of Christendom as to the justice of God, the atonement for human sin, and the everlasting issues of the judgment; tendencies generally to make the reason of man the standard instead of the Scripture:—these, and many others which are subordinate expressions of these, are obvious enough to the intelligent survey of the Christian theologian. But, generally speaking, they make no sign: they take no form, they construct no creed, and they have only to be watched and guarded against as passing phenomena. One tendency there is which steadily aims to dissipate the Dogma of Christianity altogether, and to set free the mind of man from any restraint whatever upon its religious sentiments. Against this tendency, which would issue, if unchecked—but that is a thing impossible— in the subversion of the Christian Faith, the study of the present work is one the most effectual safeguards.

CONFESSIONS OF CHRISTENDOM.

INTRODUCTION.

I.

ON THE DOCTRINE OF THE SEVERAL COMMUNIONS, AS EXHIBITED IN THEIR STANDARDS.

1. [THE scientific exhibition of the doctrinal systems of the several Christian communions has occupied the earnest attention of evangelical theologians from the times of the Reformation. As these theologians, however, mostly wrote under the conviction that they had to maintain a pure confession of the truth of God's word, their treatment of the opposite doctrine naturally assumed the form of a warfare conducted in God's name against error. From this spirit sprang the *Examen Concilii Tridentini* of Martin Chemnitz, itself not the least significant production of the sixteenth century. The devastation which Rationalism wrought in the Church set a limit to this kind of work. What interest had the question concerning a sinner's justification before God through the blood of Christ, for men who believed neither in the divinity of the Son nor in the existence of God the Father? Planck, indeed, recalled attention to the half-forgotten doctrinal antitheses, but only as an historical writer; and it was reserved for this last age to summon back the science of Polemics, even to its very name.

Among the older polemic works of our Church may be mentioned, as the most important:
Schlüsselburg, *Hæreticorum Catalogus.* Frankfurt, 1597–1599.

Calovius, *Synopsis Controversiarum.* Wittemberg, 1653.
Fr. Bechmann, *Theologia Polemica.* Jena, 1710.
Olearius, *Synopsis Controversiarum Selectiorum.* Leipzig, 1710.
Schubert, *Institutiones Theologiæ Polemicæ.* Jena, 1756.]
To which may be added the works of Planck, *Abriss der dogmat. Systeme;* Marheinecke, *Christ. Symbolik,* and *Institutiones Symbolicæ;* and the English Bishop Marsh.

[Of late years, the controversy with Rome has stimulated this literature. In 1832 appeared Möhler's *Symbolik,* a book from which we can learn neither the Evangelical nor the Romish doctrine. The author created for himself a fantastic system, and seeks to set forth its advantages in the most favourable light. F. C. Baur answered him by the *Gegensatz des Katholicismus und Protestantismus,* Nitzsch by the *Protestantische Beantwortung der Symbolik Möhlers,* and E. Sartorius by the *Soli Deo Gloria.* After Möhler arose on the Romish side Perrone, an Italian Jesuit, superior to his German predecessor in keenness and in power of systematization: he wrote the *Prælectiones Theologicæ,* and, in its German form, *Der Protestantismus und die Glaubensregel.* Hase replied in his *Handbuch der protestantischen Polemik.* Works of more general interest are: Guerike, *Allgemeine christl. Symbolik;* Köllner, *Symbolik;* Karsten, *Populäre Symbolik;* and Graul, *Die Unterscheidungslehren.*]

2. It is obvious that Symbolical Theology must regard as the exclusive source of its scientific material the written exhibitions of doctrine which every ecclesiastical communion has put forth as the authentic confession of its faith. It is true that those individual divines who bear an orthodox character in their own party, may be supposed to have this advantage in their favour, that even their private writings will be in conformity with their standards. But then this report of orthodoxy, which proceeds not from the Church itself, but from the theologians of a particular age, does not exclude the possibility of deviations from the strict confession; and it is the object of Symbolic Theology to exhibit the dogmatic convictions of any community down to the finer details. Moreover, in the learned treatises of systematic divinity, there

is always more or less concomitant of scientific apparatus; and this makes it difficult to distinguish between what is symbolical and what is merely the deduction of the author, or his particular manner of clothing the truth, that is, between the confession of faith and dogmatic theology. Consequently, it is equally safe and becoming to fall back upon the confessions, and to make them the sole basis of Symbolics as a science. Now every Christian communion has such confessions, since each was once under the obligation of proclaiming publicly its distinctive faith. These documents are sometimes in the form of specific articles of faith, sometimes in the form of catechisms.[1] Generally, however, every community has both kinds of authentic symbolic writings at once. In this case the confessions have the precedence; yet the catechisms must not be overlooked, since in them there often reigns more perspicuity than in the confessions, which are sometimes drawn up in ambiguous phraseology.

Against Symbolic Theology, as limiting itself to the authentic symbolical documents, two objections may be urged. First, it may be said that it presents, at least in regard to such communities as have anything like a continuous growth of doctrine, an obsolete system, in a certain sense long ago petrified; hence, indeed, Planck thought it needful to append to his sketch a glance at the more recent dogmatic teachings (of Rationalism). But since Symbolics must, in order not to lose its independent character, proceed from the idea of what has been ecclesiastically sanctioned, and since a symbolical system must needs be valid as such until the Church itself has remodelled, improved, or retracted it, that fixed standard must always be kept in view. The exhibition of the deviations in dogmatical teaching, even when they have become predominant among the doctors of the community in question, must be handed over to the history of Christian Doctrine.[2]

---

[1] The liturgical books of a Christian community have inferior value in Symbolics, although they also are really public (indirect) confessions of doctrine. They are seldom needed in this branch of theology.

[2] It is well known that the Reformed theologians do not acknowledge to the same extent as the Lutherans the obligatory character of their (in themselves almost only provincial) symbols, and that in the lapse of time even catechetical instruction has receded from its ancient symbolical rigour. But even in this

The second objection has been urged against Symbolical Theology mainly by Romish theologians. They maintain that he who holds fast to the symbols exhibits only a school theology, to which their Church attaches little value; moreover, that he deals only with the forms, which are only symbols of higher religious ideas, and should serve only as *involucra* to them. But inasmuch as the Church has never openly declared that it was willing to let one part of its teaching fall away as mere school theology, and be struck out of the series of its articles of faith, and has never even distantly hinted that its dogmatic sanctions were to be regarded as only the symbols of a spiritual religion, the Protestant must, following the older and orthodox dogmatic divines, who apprehended them all literally, disapprove of every endeavour on the part of Romish theologians to idealize the doctrines of their Church, even as they resist the unregulated essays of Protestant divines to adapt the symbolical standards to a new philosophy, and exhibit them as the wisdom of reason. Symbolics must needs go on in the historical way, avoiding all references to more recent Romanist dogmatists, and all idealizing remonstrances; taking extracts from the Romish symbols with the same literal fidelity as those of the *Formula Concordiæ*; convinced that the original framers of both gave a genuine account of their belief, and did not aim to delude the world by secret symbolism. And, in fact, the most recent Romish symbolical divines and polemics have renounced those idealizing tactics.

3. Another question may arise, as to the compass of what may be called Symbolics, and as to the principles which should be laid down for this science and its internal organization. Planck embraced only the three leading Christian Confessions and the Socinians within the circle of his plan; Marheinecke does not in his greater work go beyond this, though in his *Institutes* he has devoted some attention to the

case Symbolics must go back to the confessions, since the Church, at the time when they appeared, recognised the doctrinal system they contain as its own, and never publicly sanctioned any transformation of it. The same holds good of the Arminians, who are less favourable to all symbolical forms of doctrine.

Mennonites, the Moravians, and the Quakers. Now it can scarcely be doubted that the doctrine of the Greek Orthodox Church,[1] which contains much that deviates from the Romish, and is exhibited in symbols expressed in clear though not always scientifically rigorous terms, as much merits a specific presentation as the Reformed doctrine does by the side of the Lutheran. The Arminians might perhaps urge a fainter plea for such a distinction, since they sprang from the bosom of the Reformed Church, and agree with it still in all but a few leading points, which are themselves not always of a dogmatic character. Yet, inasmuch as the differences do involve leading points, and the community is externally a firmly consolidated one, it is impossible to deny to the Arminian system of doctrine a place in our Symbolics. The Quakers and the Mennonites have little that is peculiar in the detail of doctrine; and where a precise definition of faith according to the fundamental ideas of theology is in question, they might be omitted, because they do little more than repeat the words of Scripture, and keep clear of the theology of the schools: therefore we do not devote a special column to them in our tables, but refer to them only in the explanatory notes.

All these various religious communities, however, may fitly be ranked by Symbolical Theology under two heads, according to their several principles. The one class acknowledge as the source of Christian revelation the Holy Scriptures alone, limiting the acting of direct inspiration to these, though distinguished among themselves by different explanations of that inspiration. Here we have the principle of Protestantism The other class place by the side of Scripture, or above it, a second source of knowledge, believing in a continuous inspiration within the Christian Church. They either (1) assign to the Church, led by the Spirit, the right of constructing Christian saving truth out of a supposed oral tradition of the apostles,—which is Catholicism; or (2) they assume an immediate illumination of every individual through the Holy Ghost,—which is Quakerism. These two principles, for the

[1] The schismatical sects of the East cannot well be introduced into Comparative Symbolics, inasmuch as their dogmatic testimony is not expressed in authorized writings, or their present faith is only imperfectly known.

designation of which the historically known names are not definitive enough, are precise antitheses. [The Mennonites are, as a rule, and not without reason, classed with the Protestants. So are the Socinians, but only by abuse of terms.]

4. If we take a comparative view of the dogmatic deviations of the individual communities, we find at once the following results:—First, the greatest number and the most important revolve around three centres: the relation of human power to the work of sanctification proposed to it; the extent and the influence of the merit of Christ; the manner in which, and the means by which, man appropriates the merit of Christ, and attains to justification before God. All start from the universal principle of Christianity, that man is in a religious and ethical point of view fallen from God, but that in Christ there is a possibility of a return, and that he must accomplish that return in the use of the means provided for him in the economy of the Christian salvation. Secondly, those individual deviations of the individual communions do indeed always stand in evident and clear connection, and are formed into a system; but yet they do not flow from *one* material principle (*principium constitutivum*) by an internal necessity,—a fact which gave the older polemical divines occasion to distinguish between *errores systematici* and *errores extra systematici*. Accordingly we have thought fit here and there to make a difference between main dogmas and subordinate dogmas.

5. The business of the symbolical theologian, to extract from the documentary Confessions of the various communities their doctrinal systems, is not without difficulty. On the one hand, these Confessions do not always embrace the entire dogmatic beliefs of the Communion; and, on the other, they are not all drawn up with the precision which science loves and demands. To illustrate both these points: 1. In the Council of Trent, the dogmas of the Image of God, and of Justification, and of Works of Supererogation, and of Indulgences, are only imperfectly exhibited. In the Reformed Confessions nothing is said about Infant Communion; in the Lutheran, the intention of the priest at the administration of

the sacraments is not expressly contested. 2. As it respects dogmatic precision, the Tridentine Council and the Lutheran formularies (especially the *Formula Concordiæ*) are far above the Reformed Confessions, which (particularly in the Eucharist doctrine) use many figurative expressions; while they still more surpass the Greek, which indeed sometimes contradict each other. Symbolics, therefore, cannot accomplish its task by drawing simply from the symbols, but must sometimes apply critical combinations in order to arrive at a full and clear understanding of the doctrine of any community. If a dogma is merely indicated, our science does not err when it exhibits it in that form which, when the Confession was drawn up, was the current one. (For instance: the Romish doctrine *de merito congrui et condigni*, that of Indulgences, and that of the effect of the sacraments *ex opere operato*.)

If a doctrinal point has been entirely passed over, because it was held unimportant or already sufficiently treated, or because at the time when the Confession appeared it was not contested, in that case the historically demonstrated doctrine or observance of the Church must represent the symbol: for instance, as to the communion of children in the Reformed Church. If a dogma is indistinctly expressed, the symbolist must seek to define it, either by comparison with such dogmas as are in close connection with the one in question, and must be regarded as the grounds of it, or deductions from it; or, where such combination is impossible, he must faithfully preserve the indistinct expressions of the symbol itself, and adduce, apart from the doctrinal standard, explanations from the writings of theologians counted orthodox by the community. When, finally, a difference occurs between the several Confessions of one Communion, it is to be expressly stated if this was founded in a gradual change in the doctrinal standard; or only indicated, if a merely wavering point.

II.

THE SYMBOLICAL DOCUMENTS; OR, LITERARY ANALYSIS OF THE PUBLIC CONFESSIONS AND STANDARDS OF THE SEVERAL COMMUNIONS.

I. THE ROMISH CHURCH.

1. *Primary Sources of the Roman Catholic Doctrine.*

Canones et Decreta Concilii Tridentini.—The Canons and Decrees of the Council of Trent, which was opened at Trent, in the Tyrol, on the 13th Dec. 1545; removed, after eight sessions, to Bologna on 28th April 1552; re-opened May 1551 in Trent, and closed there on 28th April 1552; once more renewed on the 18th Jan. 1562; and finally closed, with the twenty-fifth session, on the 3d and 4th Dec. 1563.[1] This was reckoned, till lately, the eighteenth and last Œcumenical Council, acknowledged as such throughout the Roman Catholic Church, and even in France, so far as dogma is concerned. Its Decrees were, after Pope Pius IV. had confirmed them by a Bull (*Benedictus Deus*), 26th Jan. 1564, published authoritatively through the press of Paulus Manutius at Rome in 1564.[2] Other editions followed in the same year at Rome, Venice, Antwerp, Lyons, Cologne; in 1580 an edition was sent out at Lyons, with observations, and the *Index libror. prohibit.* The most trustworthy, for correctness and completeness, of the later editions are those of Gallemart, Chiflet, and Le Plat. These Decrees have been translated into several living tongues:

---

[1] The history of this Council, which of itself explains much in the Decrees, must be sought in two older works, written in a very different spirit: 1. That of Fra Paolo (Paul Sarpi), originally in Italian; 2. That of Sforza Pallavicini, also originally in Italian. A. Saliq wrote a complete history of the Council, Halle 1741. Bungener's is less trustworthy. A general view is given by Preuss, *das Concil von Trident.* (Berlin, 1862.) But he who would gain a thoroughly complete insight into the history of the Council, must go to Le Plat's collection of its Acts in *Monumentorum ad hist. Conc. Trid. illustrandam spectantium amplissima Collectio* (Lovanii, 1781). G. J. Planck's *Anecdota ad hist. Conc. Trid.* (Göttingen, 1791) may be added with advantage.

[2] Certain errors that crept in (De Euchar. Sess. 13, where the words *Spiritus sancti* were omitted after *non absque peculiari ductu et gubernatione*) were cancelled in the octavo edition, Rome 1564.

see Walch, *Bibl. Theol.* i. 407. For the purpose of Symbolics only Sess. 4–7, 13, 14, 21–25 are to be taken into account. The *Decreta*, moreover, are distributed, where they are more diffuse, into chapters, which must be carefully distinguished from the appended *Canones*, that is, brief propositions, which always end with 'anathema sit.'

2. *Symbolical Writings of the Second Rank.*

1. *Professio Fidei Tridentinæ.*—After the Synod at Trent had declared a confession of faith to be obligatory (Sess. 24, reform. capp. 1–12 ; Sess. 25, reform. cap. 2), this was drawn up at the command of Pope Pius IV., 1564, and established as a formulary binding on all who assumed any spiritual office or any academical function or dignity, in a Bull dated 13th Nov. 1564. It is found in the *Magn. Bullarium Rom.* t. 11, p. 127, under the title *Forma professionis fidei cath.*, and has been often reproduced in modern languages. This Formula expresses itself on some points more precisely than the Tridentine Council.

2. *Catechismus Romanus.*—This Catechism was, after a decree of the Council of Trent (Sess. 25, p. 627), drawn up by Archbishop Leon Marino, Bishop Egid. Foscarari, and the Portuguese Fr. Fureiro, under the supervision of three Cardinals. It was fairly latinized by P. Manutius and some others ; published, under the authority of Pius V., 1566, in Latin and Italian by Manutius ; and approved by many Provincial Synods, including even French. It was reproduced often in Latin, with observations by Fabricius in 1602, and translated into several modern languages. The older editions give the text without break or division ; in that of Cologne, 1572, books and chapters appeared ; and in that of Antwerp, 1574, questions and answers. This Catechism is divided into four parts : *de Symbolo apostolico, de Sacramentis, de Decalogo, de Oratione dominica.* The form of a catechetical book of instruction, adapted to the use of beginners, is not enough distinguished from that of a directory for ministerial catechization : in fact, through the constant recurrence of exhortations to the

pastors, it rather assumes the character of a pastoral guide. Reference is made to the Council of Trent on many points; but the Catechism further developes many doctrines, and touches some which had been passed over by the Tridentine Fathers: *e.g.*, on the *Limbus patrum*, and on the dignity of the Pontiff. On the other hand, other ecclesiastical institutes are omitted: *e.g.*, Indulgences, the Rosary, etc. The estimation of this Catechism was much lowered by the Jesuits at the end of the sixteenth century, on occasion of the controversies about the *auxilia gratiæ* and Predestination; and the Roman Curia did nothing to counteract this. Meanwhile, in Symbolics, the Catechism is safe. For, since it coincides with the Decrees of the Tridentine Council, and has been accepted by Popes and Bishops, it cannot possibly contain any doctrine essentially opposed to Catholicism: hence even Bossuet adduces it as one of the witnesses of genuine Catholicism (*Monit. in expos. doct. cath.*).

Other Catechisms have attained a high consideration in the Romish Church, but no proper pontifical approbation. The most celebrated among these are the two Catechisms of the Jesuit P. Canisius: the Larger was published first in 1554, the Smaller in 1559; and both have often appeared in modern languages. As to other Romish Catechisms, see the works of Walch, Steudlin, and Köcher.

[3. The *Bullarium Romanum.*—For we are not here dealing with an imaginary Catholic Church, which believes nothing but what has been taught by the Tridentine Synod: we deal with a palpable Romish Church, the Church which regards the Pontiff at Rome as its head; with a Church which believes and confesses the immaculate conception of the Virgin on no other authority than that of a single Papal Bull. And has the Bull *Ineffabilis* any pre-eminence over the other Bulls in the Romish Bullarium?—The chief editions are: *Bullarium magnum Romanum*, Romæ 1739–1849, 32 tom. fol.; *Bullarium magnum Romanum a Leone magno usque ad Benedictum* XIV., Luxemburg 1727–1753, 19 tom. fol., with three continuations.]

4. The *Confutatio Aug. Confess.*—prepared by a college of

Romish theologians, to whom the Emperor Charles V. gave his confidence—may be included here; for it undoubtedly exhibits the then current faith of the Church, though wanting in ecclesiastical authorization. (See below, iii. 1.)

Two collective editions of the Symbolical sources of Romanism have lately been published: *Libri Symbolici eccl. Romano-cathol.*, ed. cur. J. T. L. Danz, Weimar 1835; *Libri Symb. ecc. cathol. conjuncti atque notis prolegomenis indic. instructi, op. et stud.* F. G. Streitwolf et R. E. Klener, Göttingen, 1846. [Still more available is Denziger, *Enchiridion Symbolorum et definitionum quæ de rebus fidei et morum a conciliis œcumenicis et summis pontificibus emanarunt*, Wirceburgi 1856–1865. It contains over 130 documents: among them the *Symbolum apostolicum* in thirteen forms, the *Symbolum Nicænum*, the *Constantinopolitanum*, the *Ephesium*, the *Epist. Flav.* of Leo, the *Chalcedonense;* the Dogmatic Decrees of the so-called 5th, 6th, 7th, and 8th General Councils; some of the most important ordinances of Popes Innocent III., Gregory IX., Clement V., and John XXII.; the most important decrees of the Councils of Constance and Florence; Bulls of Pius II. and Leo X.; the Tridentine Decrees in full; the Constitutions of Alexander VII., Innocent XI., Alexander VIII., Innocent XII., Clement XI., Benedict XIV., Pius VI., Pius VII. and VIII., Gregory XVI., and Pius IX.]

As witnesses of the Romish authoritative doctrine, may be cited also:—

1. The Liturgical Books, which have been sanctioned by the Roman Curia, and have obtained in all countries and provinces public ecclesiastical approval, especially the Missals. Among these last, none is more celebrated and generally used than the *Missale Romanum*, first printed under Sixtus IV. in 1475, and improved in 1570 under Pius V., in 1604 under Clement VIII., and in 1634 under Urban VIII. [The most recent change in it is due to Pius IX., who removed the old liturgy of the Feast of the Conception of the Virgin, and substituted a new one.]

2. The Confessions of Faith which were imposed upon those who joined the Romish Church. Originally the *Prof. fidei Trident.* was used for this purpose. There are, indeed, private writings of unknown authors, and on the Roman side all dogmatic authority has been denied them of late. But in a Church the doctrine of which is fixed and unchangeable, the bishops must be supposed to know what that doctrine is; and they must be assumed conscientiously to deliver, when they speak in the name of the Church, only acknowledged and accepted dogmatic statements. See, for many such convert-professions, Wald, *De hæresi abjuranda quid statuat ecclesia rom. cathol.*, Regiom. 1821.

The most important Roman Catholic apologies for their doctrine are: Rob. Bellarmini (Jesuit and Cardinal, † 1621), *Disputationes de Controversiis christ. fidei adv. huj. temp. hæreticos.* Of this work the edition of Lyons, 1610, is used, which was the last *aucta et recognita* by the author. Mart. Becani (Jesuit and Confessor of the Emperor Ferdinand II., † 1624), *Manuale controvers. huj. temporis*, Heidelberg 1759 [best edition, Cologne 1696]. F. Coster (Jesuit, † 1619), *Enchiridion controvers. præcip. nostri temporis de relig.*, Colon. 1585. J. B. Bossuet (Bishop of Meaux, † 1704), *Exposition de la doctrine de l'église catholique sur les matières de controverse:* the edition here used is that of Paris, 1761. Seb. a S. Christophoro, *Theologia histor. polem.*, Bamb. 1751. [Melchior Canus, *De locis theologicis* (Salamanca, 1563), departs from the Romish doctrine now accepted. On the other hand, Bossuet, Costerus, and Becanus are far surpassed by Perrone, *Prælectiones theologicæ quas in collegio Romano societatis Jesu habebat* (best edition, Rome, 1840–1842, but often reprinted).][1]

II. The Greek Church.[2]

1. *Confessions.*

The Confession presented to the Sultan Mahmoud II., after the fall of Constantinople, 1453—that of the Patriarch Gennadius or Georg. Scholarius—extends only over the common Christian dogmas, and does not touch the points of difference between the Greek and the Roman doctrine. It is printed in Greek and Turkish, in M. Crusii *Turcogræcia* (Basil. 1584), and in Chytræi *Orat. de eccl. gr. statu* (Fref. 1583). [Recently Greek and Latin, in Kimmel, *Libri symbolici ecclesiæ orientalis* (Jenæ 1843).]

The Calvinistic tendencies and efforts of Cyril Lucar gave

---

[1] Eck's dry *Loci Communes*, to which Klee thinks every unprejudiced reader must give the palm over Melanchthon's for learning, method, and dialectical tact, I have not thought it necessary to quote. Klee's judgment must have been written in the hope that no reader would compare the two books.

[2] Augusti, 2 *Progrr. de nonnullis eccles. gr., quæ nuper jactatæ sunt, virtut.*, Bonn 1821, with reference to Stourdza, *Considérations sur la doctrine et l'esprit de l'église orthodoxe*, Stutt. 1816. The system of Greek doctrine is fully exhibited in Heineccius, *Abbild. der alten und neuern gr. K.* As to the too highly estimated coincidence between the East and West, see Leo Allatius, *De ecc. occ. atq. orient. perp. consens.*, Cöln 1648. The harmony of Greek and Lutheran dogmas is seen in Kohl, *Ecclesia gr. lutheranizans*, Lubec. 1723.

occasion for a public Confession of the proper orthodox Greek faith (a Confession ἣν ἐδέξατο καὶ δέχεται ἀπαξαπλῶς πᾶσα ἡ ἀνατολικὴ ἐκκλησία, as the Synod of Jerusalem, 1672, expressed it). This man, who became Patriarch first in Alexandria and then in Constantinople, but in 1638 lost his life by ecclesiastical visitation, acquired, through a residence in Geneva, a strong preference for Calvinism, and drew up, in conformity with the Reformed doctrine, a confession of faith, which was first published in Latin, 1629–1630, and then at Geneva in Greek and Latin, 1633. In 1613, M. Caryophilus, Bishop of Iconium, published a reply. In 1638, a Synod was held in Constantinople against Cyril Lucar, the decrees of which were, together with the synodal document of the Patriarch Parthenius, 1642 (Synod of Jassy), appended to the edition of that Confession, Geneva 1645. It is found, Greek and Latin, in Hottinger, *Append. ad analect. hist. theol.*; Greek and French, in Aymon, *Monumens authentiques de la religion des Grecs* (La Haye, 1708); and Latin, in *Corp. et Syntagma conf. fidei*, 1654.

The genuine faith of the orthodox Greek Church was now laid down in the Ὀρθόδοξος ὁμολογία τῆς καθολικῆς καὶ ἀποστολικῆς ἐκκλησίας τῆς ἀνατολικῆς, drawn up by Petr. Mogilas, Metropolitan of Kiew, primarily for the Russian Church. This was, in consequence of a conference between Russian and Constantinopolitan clergy, and after the revision of Meletius Syrigus, accepted as an orthodox confession of faith. It was issued in 1643 by the four Patriarchs, Parthenius of Constantinople, Joannicius of Alexandria, Macarius of Antioch, and Parisius of Jerusalem, and others; and it was finally once more sanctioned by a Synod at Jerusalem, 1672. It was originally printed only in the Russian language; the first modern Greek edition appeared under the auspices of Minsius, with a Latin translation and preface by the Jerusalem Patriarch Nectarius. This Confession divides into three sections, which treat περὶ πίστεως, περὶ ἐλπίδος, and περὶ τῆς εἰς Θεὸν καὶ τὸν πλησίον ἀγαπῆς, and in the form of question and answer. [Kimmel's work, already referred to, gives it in Greek and Latin.]

At the Synod in Jerusalem, which was held under the

Patriarch Dositheus, a combination was formed for a new vindication of the orthodox faith (ἀσπὶς ὀρθοδοξίας) against Calvinism. The decrees are found in Harduin, *Acta Conc.* xi., and embrace a Confession drawn up by Dositheus in eighteen sections, which Harduin gives in Greek and Latin, but Aymon in Greek and French. Its undeniable approximation in many points to the Roman doctrine has brought the Synod under the suspicion of Latinizing, a suspicion which Tzschirner has not succeeded in altogether removing (Schröckh, *Kirchengesch. n. d. Ref.* ix. 91).[1]

The following are private writings, but very useful :—
1. The Confession (ὁμολογία τῆς ἀνατολικῆς ἐκκλησίας τῆς καθολικῆς καὶ ἀποστολικῆς ἐν ἐπιτομῇ) of Metrophanes Critopulus, a Greek ecclesiastic, born in Berœa, afterwards Patriarch in Alexandria, drawn up in ancient Greek during a journey to Helmstädt in 1625. It falls into twenty-three chapters. [Weissenborn has edited in his *Appendix librorum symbolicorum ecclesiœ orientalis*, Jenœ 1850.] To the same category belong, 2. The *Acta et scripta theol. Wirtemberg. et patriarch. Const. D. Hieremiœ, quœ utrique ab anno* 1576 *usque ad* 1581 *de August. Conf. inter se miserunt.* They contain the Augsburg Confession in Greek; then three documents of the Patriarch Jeremias, wherein he criticises the doctrines of the Augsburg Confession, with the answers of the Tübingen theologians; and finally some letters of the same Patriarch. 3. The Confession of the Moscow Metropolitan Philarete (in Pinkerton's *Russia*).

2. *Catechisms.*

There are many of these, but not universally accepted. The best known are Archbishop Plato's *Orthodox Doctrine, or Brief Summary of Christian Theology*, drawn up primarily for Prince Paul Petrowitzsch (1764 ?). Plato leans, in the doctrine of justification, and in many other dogmas, to a more decidedly scriptural theory; and many of the specific teachings of his own Church he throws into the background. Peter the Great

[1] The chief ground of suspicion was not its passing over the points of difference with the Romish Church, but the presentation of the dogmas themselves, which, with their proofs, contain evident tendencies to Latinizing. I refer only to the fact that the Apocrypha of the Old Testament are placed on a level with the canonical books. In any case, the decrees of this Synod bear witness to a further development and fuller definition of Greek orthodox dogmas.

also commanded a catechism to be drawn up for the Russian youth, which was translated into German.

[The Confessions of the Greek Church are collected in *Libri Symbolici eccl. orientalis*, E. J. Kimmel, Jenæ 1843; with *Appendix* by Weissenborn, 1850.] The most complete dogmatic handbook is Th. Procopowicz, *Christ. orthod. theologiæ*, Regiom. 1773-1775. See, for others, Walch, *Bibl. theol.* ii. 570. To these may be added Hyac. Karpinski, *Compend. orthod. theolog. doct.*, L. 1786.

III. EVANGELICAL (LUTHERAN) CHURCH.[1]

1. *Confessions.*

Confessio Augustana.—The Confession of Augsburg—on the basis of the seventeen articles of Torgau, 1529, which seem to have been indistinguishable from the articles settled in the Convent of Schwabach, 1529—was composed by Melanchthon, and, in the name of the evangelical states of Germany, presented in German and Latin to the Emperor Charles V. at the Diet of Augsburg on 25th June 1530. It consists of twenty-one articles, which discuss the principal doctrines of theology with reference to Roman Catholic doctrine, briefly but succinctly; and seven more which treat of the *abusus mutatos*.[2]

The first authorized and original edition was printed in 1530 at Wittenberg by G. Rhaw. It has, however, ordinarily a common title, including the *Apologia*, and at the end of the book stands, *Impressum per G. Rhaw*, 1531. The text is on the title-page announced as 'deudsch und latinisch;' but in many copies only the Latin text appears. I edited an impression of the latter at Erlangen, 1825; and Tittmann one of both texts at Dresden, 1830. It is not to be disguised that the extant copies of this primary edition do not agree in all places; the difference is more marked in the German text than in the Latin; and the whole state of things justifies the

---

[1] [See Walch, *Introductio in Libros ecclesiæ Lutheranæ symbolicos*, Jena 1732.] Feuerlein, *Biblioth. symb. ev. Luth.*, Würn 1768.
[2] Cf. Chytræus, *Hist. der A. C.*, Rostock 1576; Salig, *Vollständ. Hist. der A. C.*, Halle 1730; Planck, *Gesch. d. protest. Lehrbegr.* iii. 1.

supposition that single sheets and pages were corrected before the issue of the copies, and that Melanchthon took occasion to amend certain places. This original edition must of course in Symbolics be regarded as the authentic one, since the originals of the Confession as presented to the Emperor are not to be recovered; while the copies which are found in the libraries and archives of the evangelical states, and have partly been printed, do not agree among themselves and with that *editio princeps*, and may really be copies of the first sketch of the Confession which Melanchthon copiously revised before it was delivered. It was not his text of 1530 that was received into the German *Concordienbuch*, but that of the copy preserved in the imperial archives at Mayence, although it has been since proved that this copy was not taken from the original Confession. On the other hand, the second edition of the Latin *Concordia* of 1584 has the text of the *editio princeps*. Among the editions edited by Melanchthon himself, the Latin one of 1540 is named the *Variata*, because the author made alterations in the tenth article concerning the Supper.

A confutation of the Confession of Augsburg (*Confutatio Aug. Confess.*) was drawn up in Latin by a commission of Roman Catholic divines (among whom were Eck and Faber), and read aloud in German in the Diet, August 3, 1530. But no copy was given to the Protestant Estates. It appeared first in Latin in A. Fabricii *Harmonia Conf. A.*, Colon. 1573. The German text was first edited by C. G. Müller, from the Mayence archives (Lips. 1808), with a Latin text from a manuscript. Pfaff, Weber, and Hase printed this Confutation in their editions of the symbolical books. This document was met, on the part of the Protestants, by the *Apologia Confessionis Augustanæ*, which also was drawn up by Melanchthon. The first sketch of it, written on the basis of what was remembered of the Confutation as publicly read, was delivered to the Emperor on 22d September 1530, but given back by him. Melanchthon then finished the Apology on the basis of a written copy of the Confutation; and it appeared in Latin and German (this latter translated by J. Jonas), just as we now have it, in connection with the Confession itself. The octavo edition of 1531 contains a Latin text with variations, which the learned have regarded as a counterpart of the *Confessio Variata*, and termed *Apologia Variata*. Melanchthon follows in the Apology the order of the Confession, but sometimes groups several articles together when they deal with one main topic; and thus the opponents are refuted in sixteen sections.

The *Articles of Smalkald, Articuli Smalcaldici*, were drawn up in German by Luther, to be presented at the General Council summoned by Paul III. in July 1536, and signed at Smalkald by an assembly of very many evangelical theologians in February 1537. The first German edition appeared at Wittenberg in 1538, revised in 1543: the Latin, translated by P. Generanus, was published in 1541 at the same place; but it was a later translation that was received into the Latin *Concordienbuch*, that of N. Selneccer (1579 and 1582). The work consists of three parts: De summis articulis divinæ majestatis (4); De articulis qui officium et opus J. C. seu redemtionem nostram concernunt (4); Articuli de quibus agere potuerimus cum doctis et prudentibus viris vel etiam inter nos ipsos (15). To these articles there is appended now a treatise of Melanchthon, De potestate et primatu Papæ. It appeared at first in Latin, without the author's name. Dietrich in 1541 published it in German with the name of Melanchthon. It was taken into the *Concordienbuch* with the signatures of many theologians. (Compare Bertram, *Geschichte des symbol. Anhangs der schmalk. AA.* 1770.)

The *Formula Concordiæ* was based upon a formula of union drawn up at Torgau in 1576.[1] It was composed in the monastery of Bergen, near Magdeburg, in 1577, by six theologians,—Jac. Andreæ, Mt. Chemnicius, Nic. Selneccer, Dav. Chytræus, And. Musculus, and Christ. Körner,—and acquired symbolical authority in Saxony, Weimar, Coburg, Würtemberg, Baden, Mecklenburg, Lübeck, Hamburg. On the other hand, it was not accepted in Hesse, Anhalt, Pomerania, and the free cities Frankfurt, Nuremberg, Magdeburg, Bremen, Danzig. In the Palatinate and Brandenburg it was first

[1] This formula was printed by Semler from a contemporary MS. under the name of the *Torgauisches Buch*—the Torgau Book. Halle, 1760.

B

adopted, but afterwards rejected in consequence of a change of confession. [Hutterus, *Concordia concors.* Francf. 1690; Chemnicii *Examen conc. Trid.* ed. E. Preuss, Berolini 1861.] The language originally was German; it was translated into Latin by Luc. Osiander, and in this form was taken into the Latin *Liber Concordiæ.* The *editio princeps* of the German Formula is that of the German *Concordienbuch*, Dresd. 1580. The whole falls into two parts, an *epitome* and a *solida declaratio*: the former, the Epitome, treats more briefly, the latter more fully, all contested dogmas. First the point of dispute is exhibited, then the doctrine of the evangelical Church is laid down (*affirmativa*), and finally the false positions of opponents are refuted by arguments (*negativa*).

2. *Catechisms.*[1]

The *Catechismus Major* and *Catechismus Minor* (*Enchiridion*) were both issued by Luther, 1529; the larger first in quarto, the smaller afterwards in octavo. Their matter is distributed into five sections: Decalogue, Apostles' Creed, the Lord's Prayer, Baptism, and the Eucharist. The larger Catechism contained in the second edition of 1529 an instruction and exhortation to confession (whether Luther's is doubtful). The smaller was, in the oldest German edition, 1529—probably the second—provided with forms of prayer, daily watchwords, marriage and baptismal chapters, short instructions as to the manner of confession, etc. These additions were taken up into the first authentic edition of the German *Concordienbuch.* The section on confession appears in a Latin edition of 1532 to be enlarged into a catechization on confession, and takes its place immediately after the chapter on baptism. A special section on the power of the keys was not added by Luther to either of the editions published by himself. But as early as the third decennium of the sixteenth century this is found in various editions of the smaller Catechism; and from 1531 it was made in Nuremberg matter of preaching. Whence came this article, reproducing as it does Luther's

[1] Cf. Augusti *Versuch einer histor.-krit. Einleitung in die beiden Hauptkatechismen der ev. K.*, Elberfeld 1824.

ideas, and in part his words, can only be conjectured; but, as this subject has no symbolic importance, it does not lie within our plan to investigate it further. The larger Catechism was in 1529 put into Latin by Lonicer; this was revised by Selneccer, and in this form entered the *Concordienbuch*. The smaller Catechism appeared in Latin, 1529, at Wittenberg. The translator is not known, though some think him Justus Jonas. (See Illgen, *Memoria utriusque catech. Luth.*, Lips. 1829.)

The collective symbolical documents of the Lutheran Church were called the *Concordienbuch* (*Concordia, Liber Concordiæ*, Book of Concord). It was issued in German at the command of the Elector Augustus in Dresden 1580, and often afterwards: the Latin was by N. Selneccer, Lips. 1580. The most important Latin editions are those of Rechenberg, Leipz. 1678; Pfaff, Tüb. 1730; Tittmann, Meissen 1827; Hase, Leipz. 1827, Berlin 1857. The German *Concordienbuch* was edited by S. J. Baumgarten, Halle 1747. [Reineccius published it in German and Latin at Leipsig 1708, Walch at Jena in 1750, and Müller at Stuttgart in 1860.[1]]

[The same doctrine as that contained in the *Concordienbuch* may be found in sundry other *corpora doctrinæ*, of which the three most important are: 1. The *Corpus Doctrinæ Prutenicum*, or *Repetitio Doctrinæ ecclesiasticæ*, Königsb. 1567; 2. The *Corpus Doctrinæ Thuringicum*, or *Corpus Doctrinæ Christianæ*, Jena 1570; 3. The *Corpus Doctrinæ Julium*, Heinrichstadt 1576.]

Among particular Provincial Confessions may be mentioned: 1. The *Confessio Ecclesiarum Saxonicarum*, prepared for the Council of Trent, under the direction of the Elector Maurice, by Melanchthon, 1551. From the original in the library of the Thomaskirche at Leipzig. J. Quodvultdeus Bürger edited this in 1722; it is found also in Melanch. *Opera*, i. 121; in Chytræi *Hist. Conf. Aug.* 2. The *Confessio Wirtembergica* (Suevica) was drawn up with the same design by J. Brenz, at the request of Duke Christopher, and on 24th Jan. 1552 given in to the Council of Trent. It treats in its thirty-five articles of many points passed over or lightly indicated in the

[1] Under the title *Libri Ecclesiæ Dan. symbolici* a book has appeared, containing the three Œcumenical Councils, the Conf. August., and Luther's Smaller Catechism, edited by J. C. Lindberg. (The *Confess. Havn.*, drawn up in forty-three articles, 1530, and presented to King Frederic I., is to be regarded as superseded by the A. C. It was published in Danish and Latin by Wöldiche, Kopen. 1736.)

other Confessions: *e.g.* the Sacrament of Confirmation, and Extreme Unction, Fasting, Benedictions, the Authority of Councils. It was published in German in 1552, as also in Latin. 3. The *Confessio Bohemica*, or the confession of faith of the Lutherans and Moravian Brethren in Bohemia, drawn up in 1575, and published at Amberg in German, 1609. To be distinguished from this is the Conf. Bohemica received into the second part of the Corpus et Syntagma, which the Moravian Brethren alone presented to the Emperor Charles v., 1535, and has often appeared in German. (See Walch, *Bibl. Theol.* i. 401, and Baumgarten, *Erläut. der symb. Schr.* S. 247.)[1] 4. The *Articles of Visitation*, which were drawn up under the Saxon Administrator Fr. William in 1592, in order to extirpate Crypto-Calvinism; even the Professors in Saxony having been bound by it. [Printed first in 1593. They appear in the beginning of the older Saxon editions of the *Concordienbuch.*] Cf. Walch, *Bibl. Theol.* i. 398.

[The most important works of Lutheran theologians in defence of their doctrine are: Martini Chemnicii *Examen concilii Tridentini* (ed. pr. Frankf. 1566; last edited by E. Preuss, 1862, with a triple Appendix and Indexes); the *Loci Theologici* of the same author, Frankf. 1591; and Gerhard, *Loci Theologici*, Jena 1610 (by E. Preuss, Berlin 1863). For the illustration of points only indicated in the Symbolical Books, it is well to consult Hutter, *Compendium locorum theologicorum*, Vitembergæ 1610 (by Twesten, Berlin 1863).]

IV. THE REFORMED CHURCH.

1. *Confessions.*

A collection of Reformed Confessions (with some Lutheran included) appeared at Geneva under the title, *Corpus et Syntagma Confessionum fidei quæ in diversis regnis et nationibus ecclesiarum nomine fuerunt authenticæ editæ* (Aurel. Allobrog. 1612; second and enlarged edition, 1654).[2] The *Confessio Marchica* was not included in the last edition. Before this there had been issued a combination of symbolical dogmas drawn from the Reformed Confessions, and the Confessions of

[1] The little work which appeared under the title *Confessio fidei Suecanæ in conc. Upsal.* 1593, contains only three Œcumenical Symbols and the Aug. Conf.

[2] The Latin Conf. of Cyril Lucar, and the Canons of Dort, are included in the last edition. We have printed the passages of the Reformed Symbols from this edition.

Augsburg, Würtemberg, and Bohemia, as *Harmonia Confessionum fidei orthodoxarum et reform. eccles.*, in nineteen sections (Geneva, 1581).[1] Recently, however, the following collections and translations of the Reformed Symbols have appeared: *Corpus librorum symbol. qui in eccles. reform. autoritatem publ. obtinuerunt*, curâ J. C. A. Augusti, Elberfeld 1827 (this contains also the Dort Canons, the Heidelberg and Geneva Catechism, and the March. Confessions, but is uncritical, and in a high degree incorrect); *Confessions de foi des églises réformées de France et de Suisse*, Montpellier 1826 (containing only the Conf. Gall., Helv. II., and the Thirty-nine Articles of the English Church); *Sammlung symb. Bücher der Ref. K.*, edited by Mess, Neuwied 1830; the *Symbolical Books translated from the Latin*, Neustadt. [*Collectio confessionum in ecclesiis reformatis publicatarum*, ed. H. A. Niemeyer, Lips. 1840, contains thirty-one Confessions on 1050 pages. Finally: Böckel, *Bekenntnissschriften der ev. ref. K.*, Leipzig 1847.] The individual Confessions will now be arranged in periods:—

a. Before Calvin, or apart from his influence.

The *Confessio Tetrapolitana* (also *Argentinensis* or *Suevica*), the Confession of the four cities Strassburg, Constance, Memmingen, and Landau,—all disposed towards the Zwinglian sacramental doctrine. It was drawn up by M. Bucer, and presented in Latin and German to the Emperor Charles V. at Augsburg, 1530. It appeared in print at Strassburg, both in German and in Latin; and consists of twenty-three articles, of which eighteen present a view of the Supper somewhat deviating from that of the Augsburg Confession (cf. Planck, *Prot. Lehrb.* iii. 1. 83). With the title *Conf. Argentinensis* it appears in the Latin of the *Corp. et Syntagma* [and as *Confessio Tetrapolitana* in Niemeyer]; the *Confutatio* which the Emperor procured in opposition to it was first printed in Müller's edition of the *Conf. A. C.*, Lips. 1808. See Wernsdorf, *Hist. Conf. Tetrap.*, Viteb. 1721; Fels, *de Variâ Conf. Tetrap. fortunâ*, Göttingen 1755.

---

[1] The editors of the two collections have suppressed their names. The *Harm. Conf.* is thought to have been drawn up by Beza, and the *Corp.* and *Syntagma* by Caspar and Aurentius.

Ulr. Zwingli *ad Carol. Imp. fidei ratio*, 30th July 1530, has remained a private document: it was presented to the Emperor at the Diet in Augsburg, and consisted of twelve articles. Eck prepared in three days an answer to this. Zwingle's *Christianæ fidei brevis et clara expositio* was held by the Swiss in higher estimation than the former Confession, but still without symbolical authority: it was drawn up in eleven sections; from the original Latin it passed into the German of Leo Judæ 1535, and is found in Zwingle's *Opp.* ii. 550. [The Latin is in Niemeyer.]

The *Confessio Basileensis* (Mülhusana), 1534, the Confession of Bâsle, was published there under the title, *Bekantnus unsers heylig. christl. Glaubens, wie es die Kylch zu Basel haldt.* It is thought to have been drawn up by Oswald Myconius after a project of Œcolampadius, and contains twelve articles. Mühlhausen adopted this Confession, and it was printed there in 1537. The Latin appears in the *Corp. et Syntagma* [and both Latin and German in Niemeyer].

The *Confessio Helvetica* I., drawn up at Basel by appointed theologians of the towns of Zürich, Bern, Basel, Schaffhausen, St. Gallen, Mühlhausen, Biel, that is, by Bullinger, Myconius, Grynæus, Leo Judæ, and Grossmann, was accepted and signed by those cantons and towns, and sent also to the Lutheran divines assembled at Smalkald in 1537. It consists of twenty-seven articles; appeared first in Latin, and afterwards in a German translation of Leo Judæ, 1536, 1587. It is in the first part of the *Corp. et Syntagma* [and in Niemeyer, Latin and German].

The *Wahrhaft Bekenntniss der Diener der Kirche zu Zürch, was sie aus Gottes Wort mit der heil. christl. Kirche glauben und lehren, insonderlich von dem Nachtmahl unsers Herrn*, etc., contains the genuine Zwinglian doctrine of the Eucharist.

β. After Calvin; under his influence or supervision.

The *Consensio mutua in re sacramentariá ministror. Tigur. et J. Calvini*, drawn up in 1549, and consisting of twenty-six articles, was intended to effect a mediation between the Zürich-Zwinglian and the Genevese-Calvinian doctrine of the Supper. It is printed in Calvin's *Opp.* viii. 648, and in his *Tractatus Theologici* (Gen. 1611), and separately in 1564 by Robert Stephens.

There was another Consensus: *De æternâ Dei prædestinatione, qua in salutem alios ex hominibus elegit, alios suo exitio reliquit, item de providentiâ quâ res humanas gubernat, consensus pastorum Genevensis ecclesiæ* a J. Calvino expositus, Genev. 1552. According to Planck, *Lehrbeg.* vii. 805, whom Marheinecke follows, this Consensus was accepted by Zürichers, 1544, and under the title *Consensus Tigurinorum* is found in Calvini *Opusc.* p. 754. By this title only the seventh volume of Calvin's works, which contains the *Tract. Theolog.*, is known to me, and I find there the *Consensio mutua in re sacramentariâ*. That statement, therefore, might rest on an error. Esscher also knew nothing of any *Consensus de prædestinatione* on the part of the Zürichers.

The *Confessio Gallicana* was drawn up (by Calvin?) in forty articles, accepted by a Synod in Paris, 1559, in 1560 presented to Francis II. of France, and once more to King Charles IX. in 1561. At a Synod in Rochelle, 1571, it was confirmed anew, and found approval and acceptance also beyond France. In its Latin form (1566) it was printed in the *Comment. de statu rel. et reipubl. in regno Galliæ* (1571), as also in the *Corp. et Syntagma;* in its French form it was printed in Beza's *Histoire ecclés. des églises réform. au royaume de France,* ii. 173. An original of the French is in the State archives of Geneva.

Separate from this, and by no means a translation of it, is the *Confession und Kurze Bekanntnuss des Glaubens die reform. Kirchen in Frankreich,* Heidelb. 1566. It was intended to be presented to Maximilian II., 1564, and the Estates of the German Empire at the Diet in Frankfurt; but the war prevented the accomplishment of this purpose. It is specially full on the doctrine of the Eucharist. The Latin (from the French original) is in Calv. *Opp.* viii., and in the *Tractatus Theol. Omnes,* p. 107.

The *Articuli* xxxix. *Eccles. Anglicanæ*—the Thirty-nine Articles of the Church of England—on the basis of the forty articles drawn up in Edward the Sixth's reign (by Cranmer and Ridley, 1551), were fixed under Queen Elizabeth, 1562, and formally accepted by the Episcopal Church at a Synod in London. Comp. Burnet, *On the Articles.*

The *Scoticana Confessio fidei*, in twenty-five articles, had for its chief author John Knox. It tends in a marked manner towards Calvin's doctrine, yet more in the sacramental dogma than in that of predestination. In the *Corp. et Syntagma* [and in Niemeyer also] the so-called negative Confession of 1581 is included.¹

The *Westminster Confession* is perfectly distinct from the old Scottish. It was drawn up by a convention of theologians, under the authority of Parliament, termed the Westminster Assembly, 1643–1648, and has in Scotland symbolical authority.

The *Confessio Hungarica* or *Czengerina*, drawn up by a Synod of Hungarian Reformers in 1557 or 1558, consists of eleven articles. It is found in the *Corp. et Syntagma*, i. 148 [and in Niemeyer, 539–550].

The *Confessio Belgica*, in thirty-seven articles, was originally a private document of Guido v. Bres, and printed in French, 1562. It presently appeared in Dutch, and attained during the sixteenth century general acceptance on the part of the Netherlands congregations, and the signatures even of many princes. At the Synod of Dort it was, after a revision of the text, publicly confirmed.² The most complete edition, with polemical remarks, is that of Festus Homm, Leiden 1618. It is found also in *Corpus et Syntagma*, in the *Actis Synodi Dordr.*, under the 146th session. Since the Dort Synod the text has been firmly fixed. It was edited in Greek (by Revius), with Latin text, Leiden 1623, and Amsterdam 1638.

The *Confessio Helvetica* II. was drawn up by Bullinger, at

---

[1] This was mainly directed against Roman Catholicism, and couched in the most vehement terms, being in this respect very similar to the Smalkald Articles. The decrees of the Council of Trent are termed *erronea et sanguinolenta*, and rejected *cum omnibus subscriptoribus et approbatoribus crudelis et sanguinei illius fœderis conjurati contra dei ecclesiam.*

[2] The judgment of the Remonstrants on this point, *Apol. Confess. Rem.*, was very vigorous. They who attentively read it will find strong reason for thinking that it was written by some individual hastily, without much judgment, or the serious scrutiny of others, and therefore for doubting whether such a document ought to be regarded as expressing the mind of a whole community. Adr. Saravia says that it was first written by Guido von Bres, communicated to a few here and there, and, without any very solemn examination or approbation of any synod, gradually passed into use as a formula of the churches.

the request of Frederick III., Elector of the Palatinate, in 1564. It was issued in the Latin original, 1566, and in a German translation by the author himself, having been often reprinted, alone and in collections. It contains thirty chapters, and was held in the very highest esteem among the Confessions of the Reformed Church, not only in Switzerland, but in the Palatinate and in Scotland, as well as in the Polish, Hungarian, and even the French, Reformed Churches. A French translation by Beza appeared at Geneva in 1566.

The *Confessio fidei Friderici* III. *Elector. Palat.* was published at the request of his successor, the Elector John Casimir, 1577, and is found under the Latin title, *Confessio Palatini*, in the *Corpus et Syntagma*. Other Palatinate Confessions (of theologians) see in Walch, *Biblioth. Theol.* i. 421.

The *Repetitio brevis, simplex et perspicua orthodoxæ Confessionis, quam amplectuntur ecclesiæ principatus Anhalt.*, Neap. Casimir, 1581, was drawn up, according to the advertisement of the publisher, in a theological assembly at Cassel in March 1859. It consists of eleven articles. The latest separate edition is, *Das Bekennt. der Anhalt landesk.*, or *Repetitio Anhaltina*, by Valentiner, Bernburg 1859.

The *Confessio Brandenburgica*, drawn up under the direction of the Prince John Sigismund (mainly by Mt. Füssel), appeared in 1614 by the title, *Des hochgeborn. Fürst. Joh. Sig. Bekänndniss von jetzigen unter den Evangelischen sevebenden u. in Streitgezogenen Punkten*. It contains sixteen articles, and must be distinguished from the Confession of the Reformed Churches in Germany, which the same Prince caused to be published at Frankfurt-on-the-Oder in 1614, already printed, it is thought, before the end of the sixteenth century in South Germany. Combined with the *Colloq. lips.* of 1631, the *Declaratio Thorun.* of 1645, it appeared with the title, *The Three Confessions*. The three documents appear as an appendix in Hering's *Hist. Nachricht*, Halle 1778. [Niemeyer has the three.] The *Declaration of Thorn* is cited below as it is printed in Hering.

The *Decrees of the Synod of Dort* — during 154 sessions, from 13th November 1618 to 9th May 1619 — are printed in Latin in the *Acta Synodi national. in nomine J. C. autor.*

ordinum general. fœderat. Belgii prov. Dordrechti habitæ, 1620. They were published also apart by the title, *Judicium synodi nation. Dord.* 1619. The Calvinistic dogma of election is laid down in all its strictness as the orthodox faith. The Netherlands, most of the Swiss cantons, the Rhenish Palatinate, the French churches, and the Puritans in England, accepted these canons. The English Episcopal Church, however, in fact renounced them; and the Brandenburg Church took no part in the Synod.

The *Formula Consensus eccles. Helveticarum reform. circa doct. de gratia univ. et connexa aliaq. nonnulla capita* was drawn up, 1674, against the specific doctrine of Particularism which appeared in the Reformed Church, by J. H. Heidegger, Professor in Zürich, and printed in German and Latin, Zürich 1675. It consists of twenty-six articles, and was accepted by Zurich, Berne, Basel, Schaffhausen, Glarus, Appenzell, S. Gallen, Mühlhausen, Biel, Neufchatel; later also by Geneva and, with certain limitations, by Lausanne. But dissensions were soon excited by it throughout the Swiss churches, as the consequence of which, and about the beginning of the eighteenth century, this Consensus gradually lost its symbolical importance. Compare Hottinger, *Succincta ac genuina formulæ consensus Helv. historia;* and Pfaff, *Schediasma de form. consens. Helv.,* Tübing. 1723, where the Formula itself is printed, which has also been often printed alone, and as appendix to the *Conf. Helv.* II.

2. *Catechisms.*[1]

The *Heidelberg Catechism*—*Catechismus Heidelbergensis s. Palatinus*—was composed by Olevianus and Ursinus, at the command of the Elector Frederick III., in 1562, translated by Lagus and Pithopœus into Latin, and then published both in Latin and German (*Christliche Underricht wie der in Kirchen und Schulen der churf. Pfalz getrieben wirdt*), Heidelb. 1563. The German text is reckoned the authentic one, and has often been republished. It has been translated into many languages, even into Spanish, 1628, and in every kind of way

[1] Cf. J. C. Köcher, *Catech. Hist. der ref. Kirche,* Jen. 1756.

has been commented on. It consists of three main divisions: 1. The miserable estate of man; 2. Redemption from that state; 3. Gratitude for that redemption. It is divided into 129 questions, distributed over 52 Sundays: of these questions, the 80th and the most celebrated was omitted in many editions through unevangelical respect for man. The Synod of Dort approved it, sess. 148.[1] See Von Alpen's *Gesch. u. liter. des Heid. Cat.*, Frankf. 1810; [Hasse, *Nachrichten ueber die Verf., die Entsteh., u. Verbr. des Heid. Cat.*, Mörs 1863.]

The *Catechismus Ecclesiæ Genevensis*, 1545, by Calvin; in French earlier, 1541. (Calvin had in 1536 published a book of instruction for youth in French, and 1538 in Latin.) It contains four divisions (of Faith, Law of God, Prayer, Sacraments), is distributed over fifty-five Sundays, and was esteemed especially in France. It appeared in German, Heidelberg 1563. The Latin text is in the Calv. *Opp.* viii.

The *Catechismus Tigurinus* was collected from the Catechisms of Leo Judæ (1554) and Bullinger (1559), and in 1609 brought to its present settled form. It consists of four divisions and one hundred and ten questions, distributed over forty-eight Sundays.

The *Church Catechism*, prepared under Edward VI., and first printed in English and Latin 1553, was revised by Nowell, 1572, and accepted by the English Episcopal Church. It falls into four sections. The Puritan Westminster Confession has also a twofold Catechism appended to it. [See *Appendix collectionis Confessionum in ecclesiis reformatis publicatarum*, ed. Niemeyer, Lipsiæ 1840.]

The *Catechesis Belgica*, connected with the *Confessio Belgica*, is by many regarded as a specific Belgian Catechism. But it is, as Köcher has shown, no other than the Heidelberg Catechism. It was first translated into Dutch in 1568.

---

[1] Declaratum fuit, consentientibus omnium tam exterorum quam Belgic. theologorum suffragiis, doctrinam in catechesi Palat. comprehensam verbo Dei in omnibus esse consentientem neque ea quidquam contineri, quod ut minus eidem consentaneum mutari aut corrigi debere videretur cet.

The Arminians.[1]

1. *Confessions.*

Remonstrantia, libellus supplex exhibitus Hollandiæ et West-frisiæ Ordinibus, 1610. They are five articles, in which the Dutch advocates of universal redemption just briefly expressed their faith. In the *Scriptis advers. collation. Hag.* they stand at the head. They have also been often reprinted. Walch, *Religion streitigk. ausser der Luther. K.* iii. 540.

Confessio seu Declaratio sententiæ Pastorum, qui in fœderato Belgio Remonstrantes vocantur, super præcip. articulis rel. Christ., Harderov. 1622 (Simon. Episcop. *Opp.* ii. 69). It consists of twenty-six chapters, and its author was Simon Episcopius († 1643). The first edition is said to have appeared in Latin and Dutch as early as 1621 (cf. Limborch, *Vita Episcop.* 279), the Dutch having preceded (Brandt, *Hist. der Reformatie,* iv. 648). Uytenbogard is, however, stated to be the Dutch translator; consequently the Latin was the original text. Against four professors in Leyden, Polyander, Rivetus, Walæus, and Thysius, who had issued a *Censura in confess. Remonst.,* Episcopius wrote his *Apologia pro confessione seu declaratione sententiæ,* 1630. Many polemical treatises followed on both sides, especially Sim. Episcopii *Verus theologus remonstrans* (*Opp.* ii. 508).

Scripta adversaria collationis Hagiensis habitæ anno 1611 *de Divinâ prædestinatione et capitibus ei annexis,* L. B. 1616. The translation was by Bertius; for these records of the Hague Conference had been published before in Dutch. The most important thing in them is the defence of the five articles. *Epistola ecclesiastarum, quos in Belgio Remonstrantes vocant, ad exterarum eccles. reform. doctores cet. qua sententiam suam de prædestinatione cet. exponunt,* L. B. 1617. This epistle, indicating the opinions of the Remonstrants, was drawn up by Barlæus. *Acta et Scripta synodalia Dordracena ministror. remonstrant.,* Herderwici 1620.

[1] Cf. Franke, *De Historia dogmatum Arminianorum,* Kil. 1814.

2. Catechisms.

Onderwysinge in de christ. Religie—Instructions in the Christian Religion, given in question and answer, according to the Confessions of the Remonstrant Reformed Christians, Rotterd. 1644. The author is supposed to have been Uytenbogard. A shorter text-book is: *Onderwys in de christ. Rel.*, by Barth. Prævostius. This appeared, in a revised form, at Amsterdam in 1733.

The most important dogmatic writings of the theologians of this community are: Sim. Episcopii *Institutt. theol.* libb. 4 (this was only half finished, including in Christology only the chapter on Redemption); Steph. Curcellæi († 1659) *Institutio rel. Christ.* libb. 7 (this also is incomplete); Ph. a Limborch († 1712), *Theologia Christiana*, Amst. 1686, 1730; Adr. a Cattenburg, *Spicilegium theol. christ. Phil. a Limborch*, Amst. 1726. Especially Jac. Arminii († 1609) *Opera theol.*, L. B. 1609 (Frankf. 1635), contain dogmatic treatises on the chief dogmas on which the Arminian differs from the Calvinistic faith.

V. Baptists (Anabaptists, Mennonites).

1. *The Older Anabaptists at the Time of the Reformation.*

Their doctrinal positions are briefly, and of course with a polemical bearing, exhibited by Melanchthon, *Vorlegung etlicher unchr. Artik. welche die Wiedertäufer vorgeben*, in Luther's German works; and in Menius, *Der Wiedertäufer Lehre widerlegt.* Compare *Form. conc.* p. 622.

2. *Mennonites.*

(Herm. Schyn, *Hist. Christ. qui in Belgi fœderato Mennonitæ appellantur*, Amstel. 1723, and *Hist. Menn. plenior deductio*, 1729. Hunzinger, *Das rel. Kirch. u. Schulwesen der M.*, Speier 1831.)

a. Confessions (Schyn, *Plen. Deduct.* c. iv.).

Their number is tolerably large, but they have not reached any general importance; and there are many differences among them, as this party have never been consistent in their doctrinal opinions.

Korte Belydenisse des Geloofs, or *Præcipuorum Christianæ fidei articulorum brevis Confessio*, was prepared in 1580 by J. Ris (Hans de Ris) and L. Gerardi. It was turned into Latin in Schyn, *Histor. Menn.* It consists of forty articles, and exhibits the common faith of the Waterlandian congregations: cf. Schyn, *Pl. Ded.* 280. Besides this, Schyn gives prominence to five Confessions, which the United Flemings, Frisians, and Germans in 1665 issued: *De algemeene Belydenissen der vereenighde Vl., Vr., en Hooghd. Doopgesinde Gemeynte.* First, the articles of faith which had been formulated on 1st May 1591; secondly, the *Bekänntniss vom einigen Gott.*, etc., 1628, whose author was Ontermann; thirdly, the *Chr. Geloofsbelyd. des Olyf-Tacx* (*ramus olivæ*), 1629; fourthly, the *Brevis Confessio* of the united Frisian and German Baptists, 1630 (drawn up, it is said, by J. Centzen); and, fifthly, *Voorstell. van de princ. artic.*, consisting of a Confession, in fifteen articles, drawn up by A. Cornelis. There was, sixthly, a Confession accepted at Leyden, 1664, by Flemish, Frisian, and German divines, which appeared in the same year at Amsterdam; seventhly, an evangelical Confession of the Baptists as preached and taught at Altona, by Roose; and, eighthly, Ris' *Glaubenslehre der wahren Mennoniten*, which was drawn up in 1765, and in 1766 was published in Dutch at Hoorn. It obtained in 1773 the approval of many churches, and appeared with their sanction expressed, Hamburg 1776.

As to some protocols, the result of religious conversations and discussions between the Mennonites and the Reformed theologians, at Frankenthal in 1571, and Linden in 1578, and Leuwarden in 1597, see Schyn, who gives extracts, and Köcher, p. 461. A private document, but one very useful, is the so-called *Hornische Bekenntniss*, a Confession written at Hoorn, 1618, in thirty-three articles, which Schyn, *Plen. Deduct.* 295, ascribes to P. J. Twisk, a very prolific Mennonite author, who died in 1636.

β. Catechisms.

Kort Onderwys, or Instruction drawn up by the appointment of a Synod in Amsterdam, in 1697, by A. A. Dooregest, P. Beets, and H. Schyn, and, when approved by the Synod, printed at Amsterdam in 1697, and again in 1723. It consists of twenty-eight chapters. H. Schyn arranged an extract: see his *Plen. Ded.* 361. Other Mennonite Catechisms are mentioned by Köcher, *Bibl. symb.* i. 647; Walch, *Bibl. Theol.* i. 547. Most complete is reckoned that of P. Baudouin, Haarlem, published in Dutch in that town, 1743. I have never seen this. Hunzinger alludes to *Christl. Gemüthsgespräch von dem geistl. u. seligm. Glaube*, 1783, in twenty-four articles, and one hundred and forty-eight questions and answers, with a smaller Catechism appended, as the most extensively used handbook of Christian instruction.

3. *The Baptists in England and America.*

These are represented by two Confessions: the one, that of the Particular Baptists, was drawn up in 1689, and consists of thirty-two chapters; the other, that of the General Baptists, dates from the year 1691, and embraces twenty-seven chapters. Other older Confessions of this community may be seen in Crosby's *History of the English Baptists*, Lond. 1738.

VI. THE SOCINIANS.[1]

1. *Confessions.*

Confessio fid. Christ. edita nomine ecclesiarum quæ in Polonia unum Deum et Filium ejus unigenitum J. C. et Sp. S. corde sancto profitentur per divinæ veritatis confessionem, 1642. This Socinian Confession was composed by J. Schlichting in the form

---

[1] Cf., for the Socinian literature generally, C. Sand, *Biblioth. Antitrin.*, Freystadt (Amst.) 1684. Bock, *Historia Antitrin. maxime Socianianismi et Socinianorum*, Regiom. 1714–1784. As to the substance and matter of it, Flatt's *Beiträge zur christ. Dogma*, Tüb. 1792; Bengel, in *Süskind's Mag. für Dogma;* Kaiser, *Pr. de Ethice eccl. Socin. symb. ad symbol. protestant. ethicen comparata*, Erlangen 1830. [O. Fock, *Der Socinianismus nach seiner stellung in der Gesammtwickelung des christl. Gentes, nach s. hist. Verlauf u. nach s. Lehrbegriff dargestellt*, Kiel 1847.]

of an exposition of the Apostles' Creed, with plentiful scriptural demonstrations. It appeared in French, 1646, and in Polish the same year. The latter translation was, under the direction of the Diet, burnt by the common executioner. An enlarged and improved edition of the Latin appeared in 1651, and a defence of it against N. Cichovius in 1652, both from the same Schlichting. Besides these there is a French translation of 1642, a Dutch of 1652, and a German of 1653 by J. Felbinger. In this Confession the deviations of the Socinians from the universal Christian faith are exhibited with far less completeness and decisiveness than in the Catechism presently to be named. The Confession of the Prussian Socinians, which they presented in 1666 to their sovereign, is only an extract from the former. See Bock, *Historia Socinianismi Prussici* (Regiom. 1754).

2. *Catechisms.*

(*Catechesis et Confessio fidei coetus per Polon. congregati in nomine Domini J. C. Domini nostri crucifixi et resuscitati*, Cracov. 1574. The author of this Catechism was G. Schomann, Socinian preacher in Cracow, † 1591. The answers are usually given in scriptural language.)

Fausti Socini († 1604) *Christianæ rel. brevissima Institutio per interrogationes et responsiones, quam catechismum vulgo vocant*, Racov. 1618. This is *Bibl. fratrum Polonorum*, i. 651, a fragment which includes only the doctrines concerning God and Christ.

The Smaller Catechism, for the discipline of children in divine service, written in Polish and German, Rakau 1605, was also published in Latin with the title, *Brevis Institutio relig. Christianæ*, 1629.

The latter Socinian Catechism, constructed by V. Schmalz, a Socinian preacher who died in 1622, and Hieron. Moscorovius, a Polish nobleman who died in 1625, on the basis of the Fragment of Faustus Socinus, appeared first in Polish at Rakau in 1605. In German it was issued in 1608, with a dedication to the University of Wittenberg. In Latin it was edited by Moscorovius, but with some alterations, under the title, *Catechesis ecclesiarum, quæ in regno Polon. et magno ducatu Lithuaniæ et aliis ad istud regnum pertinentibus provinciis adfirmant, neminem alium præter patrem Domini nostri J. C. esse illum unum Deum Israelis, hominem autem illum, Jesum Nazarenum, qui ex virgine natus est, nec alium præter aut ante ipsum, Dei filium unigenitum et agnoscunt et confitentur*, Racov. 1609. ("Catechetical Instruction of those Churches in the kingdom of Poland and the grand duchy of Lithuania, and other provinces pertaining to that kingdom, which acknowledge and confess that no other besides the Father of our Lord Jesus Christ is the one God of Israel, and that He, the man Jesus Christ, who was born of the Virgin, nor any other besides or before Him, is the only-begotten Son of God.") Moscorovius dedicated the edition to James I., King of Great Britain, in a special address; but, by the decree of the Parliament, it was publicly burnt in 1614 (or 1653). An impression, with copious refutation, was published by G. L. Oeder at Frankfort and Leipzig in 1739. A new German edition was issued at Rakau, 1612; and a new Latin and enlarged one, with remarks of M. Ruar, a zealous Socinian († 1657), and Jonas Schlichting († 1661), Irenop. 1659 or 1665. The last known edition, with annotations of many hands, was published at Stauropoli, 1684. A German translation appeared in 1666, written by Knoll, who indulged in many alterations of which the Socinians highly disapproved. This Catechism is in ten sections, and the sections are partially subdivided into chapters. Oeder was the first to number the questions.

The following are the most important dogmatic writings of the theologians of the Socinian school:—Fausti Socini *De Auctoritate Scripturæ sacræ libellus; Lectiones sacræ* (imperfect); *Prælectiones theol.; De statu primi hominis ante lapsum Disp.; De Justificatione; De J. Ch. servatore Disp.; De baptismo aquæ Disp.; De cœnâ Domini tract. brevis*,—all which, with many others, are collected together in the *Bibliotheca fratrum Polonorum, quos Unitarios vocant* (Irenop. 1656, 6 vols. fol.), 1 and 2 vol.—J. Völkel, preacher in Smigla († 1618), *De verâ relig. libb. quinque*, Racov. 1630 (edited by Crell, Amst. 1640). This edition was publicly burnt in Amsterdam, 1642. A Dutch translation appeared in 1649. The Latin is incorporated in Maresii *Hydra Socinianismi expugnata*, Groen. 1651–1663. It is a comprehensive and systematically arranged handbook of instruction in Socinian dogmatics,

c

and highly prized by the Socinians themselves.—J. Crell, pastor and professor in Rakau, who died in 1633, *De uno Deo patre*, libb. 2, Racov. 1631; contained, at least so far as concerns God and His attributes, in the *Biblioth. frat. Polon.* vi. His exegetical writings are printed in the third, fourth, and fifth volumes of the *Bibl. f. Polon.*—Ch. Ostorodt, Socinian preacher at Buskow, near Danzig, who died in 1611, *Unterrichtung von der wichtigsten Hauptpunkten der Chr. Religion*. The full title is, 'Instruction in the leading Doctrines of the Christian Religion, containing nearly the entire Confession of the Churches in the kingdom of Poland, etc., which, because they confess that only the Father of our Lord Jesus Christ is the only God, etc., are contemptuously branded as Arians (!) and Ebionites,' Rakau 1604. It is in forty-two chapters, and almost verbally taken from the writings of Socinus.—Val. Smalz, pastor in Rakau, who died 1624, *Wahrhaft. Erklärung*, or True Explanation out of Scripture concerning the Deity of the Lord Jesus, Rakau 1598. In a Latin form, *De divinitate J. C.* 1608.—J. Ludw. Wolzogen (Lord of Tarenfelt, who died in 1658), *Erklär. der beiden unterscheidl. Meinungen von der Natur und dem Wesen des einen allerhöchsten Gottes*, 1646.— And. Wissowatius von Szumski († 1678), *Religio naturalis seu de rationis judicio in controversiis etiam theologicis ac relig. adhibendo*, 1685.—Joach. Stegmann the elder, a Unitarian preacher at Clausenburg in Siebenbürgen, who died in 1632, *De judice et normâ Controv. fidei*, libb. 11, Eleutherop. 1644; and *Prob. der einfält. Warnung für der neu Photinian. oder Arian. Lehr von J. Botsacco*, Rakau 1638.—Sam. Crell († 1747), *Cogitationes novæ de primo et secundo Adamo, seu de ratione salutis per illum amissæ, per hunc recuperatæ*, Amsterd. 1700.— The *Summa univ. theol. christ. secund. Unitarios* (Clausenb. 1787) contains the doctrinal scheme of the Siebenbürg Unitarians, which in some not unimportant points deviates from the older Socinianism. See J. G. Rosenmüller, in Staüdlin u. Tzschirner, *Archiv. für Kirchengesch.* i. 1. 83. The author is generally reputed to have been G. Markos, but this is far from certain. (A short sketch of the doctrine of the English Unitarians, by an anonymous hand, appears in the *Theol. Nachr.* 1822, i. 20.)

VII. THE QUAKERS.

Catechism and Confession.

The *Catechism and Confession of Faith* of which Robert Barclay was the author, appeared originally in English: it was translated into Dutch in 1674, into German in 1679.

It appeared also in Latin under the title: *Catechismus et fidei confessio approbata et confirmata communi consensu et consilio patriarcharum, prophetarum et apostolorum, Christo ipso inter eos præsidente et prosequente*, cet., Roterod. 1676. The answers in the Catechism, and the entire Confession, consist of sentences of Scripture. Another Catechism for Children appeared in London, by G. F. (Fox), 1660.

An Apology for the True Christian Divinity, being an Explanation and Vindication of the Principles and Doctrines of the People called Quakers; written in Latin and English by Robert Barclay, and since translated into High Dutch, Low Dutch, French, and Spanish; Baskerville, Birmingham 1765. The doctrinal scheme is reduced to fifteen theses, which Barclay had in 1675 laid down, and here defends at large. J. W. Baier published certain anti-Quaker dissertations, which were collected under the title, *Synopsis et examen theol. enthusiast.* (Jena, 1701); and these were replied to by G. Keith, in a defence of Barclay's Apology, *Amica responsio ad Baieri dissertationes*, Amst. 1683, which specially seeks to justify the principle of the Quaker faith, the doctrine of the *lumen internum*, or Inner Light.

(Clarkson's *Portraiture of Quakerism, as taken from a view of the moral, educational, and religious principles, etc.*, London 1806.)

I.

THE SOURCE OF CHRISTIAN KNOWLEDGE, AND FOUNDATION OF CHRISTIAN DOCTRINE.

I. FIRST POINT OF DIVERGENCE.

ALL communities of Christendom, with the exception of the Socinians, agree that the divine revelation of truth is contained simply and purely in the Holy Scriptures. But they differ from each other in this: the Protestant Confessions alone regard the written volume of revelation as complete in itself; while all others either (1) place in juxtaposition with Scripture certain co-ordinate sources of Christian knowledge and instruction, the Greeks a so-called tradition, and the Romanists tradition and its living teaching authority, that is, the Pope, or, (2) holding the proper source of the knowledge of divine things to be a direct illumination of every individual by the Holy Ghost, subordinate the Scripture to this personal enlightenment, as merely its testimony (or *regula secundaria*) and witness. These are represented by the Quakers.

> [The Socinians arbitrarily cut off the half of God's word, that is, the Old Testament, and correct the New Testament also after their own manner.]

SYMBOLICAL TESTIMONIES.

I. GREEK.

Conf. orthod. p. 18 : Φανερὸν πῶς τὰ ἄρθρα τῆς πίστεως ἔχουσι τὸ κῦρος καὶ τὴν δοκιμασίαν, μέρος ἀπὸ τὴν ἁγίαν γραφήν, μέρος ἀπὸ τὴν ἐκκλησιαστικὴν παράδοσιν. ... Ἥγουν δύο λογίων εἶναι τὰ δόγματα. Ἄλλα (δόγματα) παραδίδει ἡ γραφή, τὰ ὁποῖα περιέχονται εἰς τὰ θεολογικὰ βιβλία τῆς ἁγίας γραφῆς· καὶ ἄλλα εἶναι δόγματα παραδεδομένα ἐκ στόματος ἀπὸ τοὺς ἀποστόλους, καὶ τοῦτα ἑρμηνεύθησαν ἀπὸ τὰς συνόδους καὶ τοὺς ἁγίους πατέρας· καὶ εἰς τὰ δύο τοῦτα ἡ πίστις εἶναι τεθεμελιωμένη.

Metroph. Critop. Conf. c. 7, p. 82: Διαιρεῖται τὸ θεῖον ῥῆμα εἴς τε τὸ γραπτὸν καὶ ἄγραφον. καὶ ἄγραφον μὲν εἶεν ἂν αἱ ἐκκλησιαστικαὶ παραδόσεις. P. 85: Θεωροῦνται δὲ αἱ παραδόσεις περί τε τὰς τελετὰς τῶν ἁγίων μυστηρίων καὶ περὶ ἄλλα τινὰ χρήσιμα καὶ τὴν ἐκκλησίαν κοσμοῦντα, cct. (P. 123, the most important traditions of the Church are enumerated, as the veneration of saints and relics, the forty days' fast, the institution of monachism, prayers for the dead, etc.) Comp. Theodos. Zygomalas, in Crusii *Turcogræc.* p. 97, and Plato's *Katech.* S. 112, 115, 135 f.

II. ROMAN CATHOLIC.

Conc. Trid. sess. 4, *Decr. de canonic. scripturis:* Synodus ... hoc sibi perpetuo ante oculos proponens, ut sublatis erroribus puritas ipsa evangelii in ecclesiâ conservetur, ... perspiciensque hanc veritatem et disciplinam contineri in libris scriptis et sine scripto traditionibus, quæ ex ipsius Christi ore ab apostolis acceptæ, aut ab ipsis apostolis, Spiritu sancto dictante, quasi per manus traditæ, ad nos usque pervenerunt: orthodoxorum patrum exempla secuta, omnes libros tam V. quam N. T., cum utriusque unus deus sit auctor, nec non traditiones ipsas, tum ad fidem tum ad mores pertinentes, tanquam vel ore tenus a Christo, vel a Spiritu sancto dictatas et continuâ successione in ecclesiâ catholicâ conservatas, pari pietatis effectu ac reverentiâ suscipit et veneratur. ... Si quis autem ... traditiones prædictas sciens et prudens contemserit, anathema sit. Omnes itaque intelligant, quo ordine et viâ ipsa synodus post iactum fidei confessionis fundamentum sit progressura et quibus potissimum testimoniis ac præsidiis in confirmandis dogmatibus et instaurandis in ecclesia moribus sit usura.

Cat. Rom. præf. 12: Omnis doctrinæ ratio, quæ fidelibus

tradenda sit, verbo dei continetur, quod in scripturam traditionesque distributum est.—The *Cat. Rom.* contains no more on this subject.

For appeals to apostolical tradition concerning individual dogmas, and religious ceremonials connected with them, see *e.g.* Trid. sess. 14, Extreme Unction, cap. 1; sess. 22, cap. 4 and 9; *Cat. Rom.* i. 6. 3, ii. 7, 29.

[The Council of Trent begins to indicate a third source of knowledge by the side of Scripture and tradition, when it says, in the introduction to the decrees of the fifth session : S. S. Tridentina synodus sacrarum scripturarum et sanctorum patrum ac probatissimorum conciliorum testimonia *et ipsius ecclesiæ judicium et consensum secuta* hæc de ipso peccato originali statuit fatetur et declarat. Le Plat, *Canones* 24. But that this judgment of the Church is no other than the judgment of the Pope, is shown by the Bull *Ineffabilis* of 8th December 1854. For, after Gregory XV. had declared that Eternal Wisdom had *not yet revealed* to their Church the inmost secret of the mystery of the immaculate conception of Mary, and that therefore he could not define it (Wadding, *Legatio*, Lovaniæ 1624, S. 452), Pius IX., on December 8, 1854, declared that the doctrine of the Immaculate Conception *was revealed of God*, and therefore to be firmly and stedfastly believed, *esse a Deo revelatam atque idcirco ab omnibus fidelibus firmiter constanterque credendam.* And in Lect. vi. of the Officium of 25th September 1863, the Pope commands as follows: Deiparæ virginis in suâ conceptione victoriam Pius nonus pontifex maximus totius ecclesiæ votis annuens statuit *supremo suo atque infallibili oraculo* solemniter proclamare. Accordingly there must be, for all who are subject to the Roman bishop, three sources of knowledge,—Holy Scripture, Tradition, and the Pope.]

For the elucidation of what in the symbol is merely hinted, we extract a few passages from Bellarmine and others:[1]—

---

[1] Comp. Cani *Loc. Theol.* iii. ; Becani *Manuale Controv.* i. 2 ; Bossii *Institt. Theol.* i. 66 ; B. Galura, *Diss. de Tradit., altera revel. fonte*, Friburg 1790 ; Klee, *kath. Dog.* i. 232 ; Schlier, *Die göttl. Trad. n. Gesch. u. Idee*, in Pletz, *Th. Zeitsch.* 1833, iii. On the Protestant side, Chemnicius, *Exam.* i. loc. 2 ; Weinmann, *Darst. u. Kritik der Streitf. üb. die Tradition*, Hildburgh 1825.

Bellarmini *De Verbo Dei,* iv. 3 : Nos asserimus, in scripturis non contineri expresse totam doctrinam necessariam sive de fide sive de moribus, et proinde præter verbum Dei scriptum requiri etiam verbum Dei non scriptum, i.e. divinas et apostolicas traditiones.

iv. 2 : Vocatur doctrina non scripta non ea, quæ nusquam scripta est, sed quæ non est scripta a primo auctore. E. c. parvulos baptizandos vocatur traditio apostolica non scripta, quia non invenitur hoc scriptum in ullo apostolico libro, tametsi scriptum est in libris fere omnium veterum patrum. . . . Est partitio traditionum in traditiones divinas, apostolicas, ecclesiasticas. Divinæ dicuntur, quæ acceptæ sunt ab ipso Christo apostolos docente, et nusquam in divinis literis inveniuntur. . . . Apostolicæ traditiones proprie dicuntur illæ, quæ ab apostolis institutæ sunt, non tamen sine assistentiâ Spiritus sancti et nihilominus non exstant in eorum epistolis. . . . Ecclesiasticæ traditiones proprie dicuntur consuetudines quædam antiquæ vel a prælatis vel a populis inchoatæ, quæ paulatim tacito consensu populorum vim legis obtinuerunt. Et quidem traditiones divinæ eandem vim habent, quam divina præcepta sive divina doctrina scripta in Evangeliis. Et similiter apostolicæ traditiones non scriptæ eandem vim habent, quam apostolicæ traditiones scriptæ. . . . Ecclesiasticæ autem traditiones eandem vim habent, quam decreta et constitutiones ecclesiæ scriptæ.

[On the third source of knowledge, co-ordinate with Scripture and tradition, compare the fourth commission of the seven Consultores of Pius IX. : Caterini, Audisio, Perrone, Passaglia, Schrader, Spada, and Trullet, for the year 1853 : " It is not necessary, in order to establish tradition, that we produce an uninterrupted series of testimonies of the Fathers,—a series which should go up to the apostles, in order to come down to ourselves. It must be confessed that Catholic tradition is proved, when we can establish the general consent of the Church at any particular epoch, or produce a certain number of testimonies that presuppose it." Malou, *L'immaculée conception de la b. v. M. considérée comme dogme de foi,* Bruxelles 1857. And Malou himself in this work, which was undertaken in the cause of the episcopate assembled in Rome, dedicated to Pius ix., says: "The promises of infallibility which our Lord Jesus Christ made to His Church are of such a kind, that neither the body of the pastors in proposing a doctrine of faith, nor the faithful in adhering to it, can be deceived. It is impossible that the entire body of the Church should adopt and believe a doctrine contrary to divine revelation. From the moment that the pastors and the flock profess with unanimous accord a doctrine dogmatic in its nature, or are certain that this doctrine is true, and that it has been revealed, from that time it bears the seal by which the Divine Master has willed that His teaching should be recognised. . . . If this accord should appear only in our days, it is no less decisive than it would have been in the era of the martyrs, because it has the same guarantee as it would have had at that epoch. *The Catholic Church enjoys to-day the same authority and the same divine assistance as in the days of the apostles; it therefore possesses the same infallibility.*" The infallible organ of this infallible Church is, however, the Pope. So the Romish synod of 1854; so Pope Pius ix. *Syllabus errorum d. d.* 8th December 1864, No. xxiii.]

III. PROTESTANT.

The older Lutheran symbols reject, it is true, the *humanas traditiones*, valid in the Roman Catholic Church (*Confess. Aug.* pp. 13, 28 seq.; *Apol.* p. 205 seq.; *Art. Smal.* p. 337); they do not, however, mean thereby the apostolical doctrinal tradition generally, as a source of Christian truth and knowledge, but those meritorious works of justification which obscured the doctrine of (justifying) faith (trad. ad placandum Deum, ad promerendam gratiam et satisfaciendum pro peccatis, *Conf. Aug.* p. 28; *Apol.* 151).[1] Compare, however, *Aug. Conf.* præfat.

---
[1] Since these symbols understand by *traditiones* observances and usages, and of that kind much was retained from the old Church, they might rightly maintain (*Aug. Conf.* p. 31): servantur apud nos pleræque traditiones, quæ conducunt ad hoc, ut res ordine geratur in ecclesiâ, ut ordo lectionum in missâ et præcipuæ feriæ. *Apol.* pp. 209, 212. But every notion of meritoriousness was to be excluded from them. Calvin also, in conformity with the position polemics then assumed, contended against these traditions primarily (traditiones humanas): v. *Instit.* iv. 10.

p. 6 : offerimus . . . nostram confessionem, ejusmodi doctrinam ex S. S. et puro verbo Dei hactenus illi (concionatores) . . . tractaverint. It is the *Form. Conc.* p. 570, which first speaks out more definitely : Credimus . . . unicam regulam et normam, secundum quam omnia dogmata omnesque doctores æstimari et judicari oporteat, nullam omnino aliam esse, quam prophetica et apostolica scripta cum V. tum N. T. . . . Reliqua vero sive patrum sive neotericorum scripta, quocunque veniant nomine, sacris literis nequaquam sunt æquiparanda. [Cf. *Sol. Dec.* p. 632. In explanation, L. Hutter, *Comp. loc. Th.* No. 1 seq. : Scriptura sacra est verbum Dei, impulsu Spiritus s. a prophetis et apostolis literarum monumentis consignatum, de essentiâ et voluntate Dei nos instruens. *Est* (autem) *plena et sufficiens quoad informationem tum fidei tum morum.*]

Conf. Helv. ii. 1 : In Scripturâ sanctâ habet universalis Ch. ecclesia plenissime exposita, quæcunque pertinent cum ad salvificam fidem tum ad vitam deo placentem recte informandam. . . . Sentimus ergo ex hisce scripturis petendam esse veram sapientiam et pietatem, ecclesiarum quoque reformationem et gubernationem, omniumque officiorum pietatis institutionem, probationem denique dogmatum reprobationemque aut errorum confutationem omnium, sed admonitiones omnes. — Cap. 2 : Non alium sustinemus in causâ fidei judicem, quam ipsum deum per script. s. pronunciantem, quid verum sit, quid falsum, quid sequendum sit quidve fugiendum. . . . Repudiamus traditiones humanas, quæ tametsi insigniantur speciosis titulis, quasi divinæ apostolicæque sint, vivâ voce apostolorum et ceu per manus virorum apostolicorum, succedentibus episcopis ecclesiæ traditæ, compositæ tamen cum scripturis ab his discrepant, discrepantiaque illa sua ostendunt, se minime esse apostolicas. Sicut enim apostoli inter se diversa non docuerunt, ita et apostolici non contraria apostolis ediderunt. Quin imo impium esset asseverare, apostolos viva voce contraria scriptis suis tradidisse.

Conf. Gall. art. 5 : Quum hæc (s. s.) sit omnis veritatis summa, complectens quidquid ad cultum dei et salutem nostram requiritur, neque hominibus neque ipsis etiam angelis fas esse dicimus, quidquam ei verbo adjicere vel detrahere vel quidquam prorsus in eo immutare.

Conf. Belg. 7 : Credimus sacram scripturam dei voluntatem perfecte complecti, et quodcunque ab hominibus, ut salutem consequantur, credi necesse est, in illa sufficienter edoceri. Nam quum illic omnis divini cultus ratio, quem deus a nobis exigit, fusissime descripta sit, nulli hominum . . . fas est, aliter docere. . . . Quum enim vetitum sit, ne quis dei verbo quidquam addat aut detrahat, satis eo ipso demonstratur, doctrinam illius perfectissimam omnibusque modis consummatam esse. Sed nec cum divinis iisdem scripturis ulla hominum, quantavis sanctitate præditorum scripta, neque ulla consuetudo cum divinâ veritate (veritas enim rebus omnibus antecellit), neque multitudo, neque antiquitas, neque temporum personarumque successio, neque concilia, decreta aut statuta comparari possunt.

Thirty-nine Articles.—Art. vi. : Holy Scripture containeth all things necessary to salvation ; so that whatsoever is not read therein, nor may be proved thereby, is not to be required of any man that it should be believed as an article of the Faith, or to be thought requisite or necessary to salvation. Comp. Art. xix. and xxi. : Wherefore things ordained by them as necessary to salvation have neither strength nor authority, unless it may be declared that they are taken out of Holy Scripture.

Confess. Scot. 18 : Doctrina, quæ ab ecclesiis nostris docetur, verbo dei scripto continetur, videl. in libris V. et N. T. canonicis, in quibus omnia credenda ad hominum salutem sufficienter expressa affirmamus.—19 : Sicut confitemur scripturas dei sufficienter instruere et hominem dei perfectum reddere, ita ejus auctoritatem a deo esse . . . affirmamus. Asserimus itaque, quod qui dicunt scripturas non aliam habere auctoritatem sed eam, quam ab ecclesia accipit, sunt in deum blasphemi cet. Compare the Negative, p. 159.

[*West. Conf.* ch. i. sec. 6 : The whole counsel of God, concerning all things necessary for His own glory, man's salvation, faith, and life, is either expressly set down in Scripture, or by good and necessary consequence may be deduced from Scripture ; unto which nothing at any time is to be added, whether by new revelations of the Spirit or traditions of men. Nevertheless we acknowledge the inward illumination of the Spirit of God to be necessary for the saving understanding of such things as are revealed in the word; and that there are some circumstances concerning the worship of God, and government of the Church, common to human actions and societies, which are to be ordered by the light of nature and Christian prudence, according to the general rules of the word, which are always to be observed.

Declar. Thorun. p. 47: Nullum hodie verbum dei exstat aut certo ostendi potest de dogmatibus fidei aut præceptis vitæ ad Salutem necessariis, quod non sit scriptum aut in scripturis fundatum, sed solâ traditione non scriptâ ecclesiæ commissum.

Conf. Remonstr. i. 13: Libris sacris perfecte continetur plena et plus quam sufficiens revelatio omnium fidei mysteriorum inprimis eorum, quæ universis et singulis hominibus simpliciter ad æternam salutem consequendam scitu, creditu, speratu, factu necessaria sunt.

Ib. i. 10 sqq.: Quia solis libris sacris divina auctoritas competit, necessarium etiam est, ut ad eos solos tanquam ad Lydios lapides controversiæ et lites omnes ad religionem pertinentes exigantur et ex iis solis disceptentur; . . . dirimi enim eas jure judiciali aut potestativo per judicem aliquem visibilem ac ordinarie loquentem in ecclesia deum minime voluisse censendum est, cum normam tantum dirigentem sive directive duntaxat, non etiam coactive judicantem nobis in verbo suo relinquere voluerit, judicem vero infallibilem semper in ecclesiâ loquentem esse debere nusquam significaverit. — *Ib.* i. 10: Etsi vero primitiva ecclesia certissime rescire potuit et indubie etiam rescivit, libros istos ab apost. scriptos esse vel saltem approbatos nobisque istius rei scientiam quasi per manus tradidit, non tamen idcirco sacri hi libri a nobis pro veris ac divinis habentur, quod eos veros esse sive divinos continere sensus ecclesia prim. judicio suo irrefragabili censuerit cet.

Observations.

It is easily inferred that the Protestant symbols did not so much reject apostolical tradition in itself (in the ideal sense), as rather those traditions which by the Romanists were counted apostolical, but could not be reconciled with Scripture, or sustain by demonstration their apostolical origin (Chemnitz, *Exam.* i. 2). The utterances of the Councils and of the Fathers have obviously, on these principles, no co-ordinate consideration, nor, as against Scripture, decisive authority;

but, found true in accordance with Scripture, they are venerable testimonies of the Christian truth never altogether extinguished in the Church. *Art. Sm.* 308; *Form. Conc.* 570; *Conf. Helv.* i. 3, ii. 2; *Gall.* 5; *Scot.* 20; *Belg.* 7; *Conf. Remonst.* i. 12, 18. The same may be said of the three Œcumenical Creeds, by adopting which the Protestant Church gave documentary evidence of its union in sentiment with the ancient Church. *Form. Conc.* 571. Comp. *Helv.* ii. 17; *Conf. Gall.* 5; *Eng. Artt.* 8; *Belg.* 9; *Bohem.* 2; *March.* 2; *Dec. Thorun.* p. 45. Comp. also Chemnitz, *Examen* 1, *Præf.* 10; Calvin, *Institt.* iv. 9. 1.

It needs only to be lightly indicated, that the construction or adoption of the symbolical books furnishes no analogy with Roman Catholic tradition. Comp. *Form. Conc.* p. 572. Among the Reformed Confessions, that of Basel thus concludes: Finally, we would submit this our Confession to the judgment of the divine written Scriptures; . . . and we in this and all will be thankfully obedient to the direction of God and His holy word. Similarly, *Conf. Helv.* ii., and *Conf. Scot.*, at the end of the preface. However, in the *Conclusio* of the Canons of Dort, and in the *Form. Cons. Helv.* 26, the symbols are named in conjunction with the Scripture. In the latter passage the term *Libri Symbolici* is used of the public confessions.

IV. SOCINIAN.

The Socinians regard the New Testament books as the only source of the knowledge of the Christian Church, so far as this is doctrine, that is, a new divine legislation. They attach to the Old Testament, which is supposed to have been rendered obsolete by the New, only an historical, and not a dogmatic value.

Cat. Rac. p. 1 (final Revision): Unde discere possumus religionem christ.? Ex sacris literis præsertim N. T. Exstant igitur aliæ sacræ literæ præter literas N. T.? Exstant, nempe scripta V. T.—*Ib.* p. 6: Quæ (religionis christianæ veritas) cum iis (scriptis Novi Testamenti) tantum, nec ullis aliis libris comprehensa sit, apparet, iis libris necessario propterea habendam esse fidem.

Socin. de auctorit. S. S. cap. 1, p. 271 b: Considerandum est, si recipiatur Novum Testamentum, non posse ad ipsam religionis summam quidquam fere momenti habere quamcumque Veteris Testamenti depravationem, cum nihil non levis momenti potuerit esse in Vetere Testamento, quod Novo non contineatur, nec quidquam illius recipiendum sit, quod non conveniat cum iis, quæ in hoc sunt scripta. Adeo ut utilis quidem plures ob causas sit lectio Veteris Testamenti iis, qui Novum recipiunt, id est hominibus christianæ religionis, sed non tamen necessaria.

Cat. Rac. qu. 31 : (Scripta divinarum literarum) prorsus sufficientia sunt ad eam rem (ut in rebus ad salutem necessariis iis solis acquiescendum sit) : eo quod fides in Jesum Christum et obedientia mandatorum ejus sit in iis scriptis N. Fœderis sufficientissime tradita et explicata, quam ex dei promissione vita æterna consequitur.

Ib. qu. 33 : (De traditionibus rom. eccles. sentiendum est) eas non solum sine causâ et justâ necessitate confictas et inventas esse, verum etiam summo cum discrimine fidei christianæ.

The Protestant symbols designate the Old and New Testaments in common, and without distinction, as *Scriptura sacra.* Comp. *Conf. Helv.* ii. 1 ; *Conf. Gall.* 3 ; *Thirty-nine Artt.* vi. ; *Conf. Belg.* 4. How far the Old Testament still retains its authority as *Law*, see below, under XIII.

V. Quaker.

Barclay, *Apol.* Prop. ii. : Seeing no man knoweth the Father but the Son, and he to whom the Son revealeth Him ; and seeing the revelation of the Son is in and by the Spirit ; therefore the testimony of the Spirit is that alone by which the true knowledge of God hath been, is, and can be only revealed. . . . By the revelation of the same Spirit He hath manifested Himself all along unto the sons of men, both patriarchs, prophets, and apostles : which revelations of God by the Spirit, whether by outward voices and appearances, dreams, or inward objective manifestations in the heart, were of old the formal object of their faith, and remain yet so to be. Moreover, these divine inward revelations, which we make absolutely necessary for the building up of true faith, neither do, nor can ever, contradict the outward testimony of the Scriptures, or right and sound reason ; yet from hence it will not follow that these divine revelations are to be subjected to the test either of the outward testimony of the Scriptures or of the natural reason of man, as to a more noble or certain rule and touchstone: for this divine revelation and inward illumination is that which is evident and clear of itself, forcing, by its own evidence and clearness, the well-disposed understanding to assent irresistibly the same thereunto, even as the common principles of natural truths do move and incline the mind to a natural assent: as, that the whole is greater than its part; that two contradictories can neither be both true nor both false. . . . *Comment.* on Prop. ii. § 15: He, then, that acknowledges himself ignorant, and a stranger to the inward inbeing of the Spirit of Christ in his heart, doth thereby acknowledge himself to be yet in the carnal mind, which is enmity to God, whatever he may otherwise know or believe of Christ, or however much skilled or acquainted with the letter of the Holy Scripture; not yet to be, notwithstanding all that, attained to the least degree of a Christian; yea, not once to have embraced the Christian religion. For take but away the Spirit, and Christianity remains no more Christianity than the dead carcase of a man, when the soul and spirit is departed, remains a man, which the living can no more abide, but do bury out of the sight, as a noisome and useless thing, however acceptable it hath been when actuated and moved by the soul. § 15: Yet those that have their spiritual senses, and can savour the things of the Spirit, as it were *in primâ instantiâ*, *i.e.* at the first blush, can discern them without, or before they apply them either to Scripture or reason. But to make an end, I shall add one argument to prove that this inward, immediate objective revelation, which we have pleaded for all along, is the only sure, certain, and unmoveable foundation of all Christian faith; which argument, when well considered, I hope will have weight with all sorts of Christians; and it is this: That which all professors of Christianity, of what kind soever, are forced ultimately to recur unto, when pressed to the last, that for and because of which all other foundations are recommended, and accounted worthy to be believed, and without which they are granted to be of no weight at all, must needs be the only most true, certain, and unmoveable foundation of all Christian faith. § 11: But there are some that will confess that the Spirit doth now lead and influence the saints, but that He doth it only subjectively, or in a blind manner, by enlightening their understandings to understand and believe the truth delivered in the Scriptures, but not at all by presenting those truths to the mind by way of object; and this they call *medium incognitum assentiendi*, as that of whose working a man is not sensible. This opinion, though somewhat more tolerable than the former, is nevertheless not altogether according to truth, neither doth it reach the fulness of it. Because there be many truths which, as they are applicable to particulars and individuals, and most needful to be known by them, are in nowise to be found in the Scripture, as in the following proposition shall be shown. Besides, the arguments already adduced do prove that the Spirit doth not only subjectively help us to discern truths elsewhere delivered, but also objectively present those truths to our minds. For that which teacheth me all things, and is given me for that end, without doubt presents those things to my mind which it teacheth me. It is not said, *It shall teach you to understand those things that are written;* but, *It shall teach you all things.* Again, that which brings all things to my remembrance, must needs present them by way of object; else it were improper to say it brought them to my remembrance, but only that it helpeth to remember the objects brought from elsewhere.

Prop. iii.: From these revelations of the Spirit of God to the saints have proceeded the Scriptures of truth, which, because they are only a declaration of the fountain, and not the fountain itself, therefore they are not to be esteemed the principal ground of all truth and knowledge, nor yet the adequate primary rule of faith and manners; yet, because they give a true and faithful testimony of the first foundation, they are and may be esteemed a secondary rule, subordinate to the Spirit, from which they have all their excellency and certainty. For as by the inward testimony of the Spirit we do alone truly know them, so they testify that the Spirit is that guide by which the saints are led into all truth; therefore, according to the Scriptures, the Spirit is the first and principal leader. . . . *Commentary* on Prop. iii. § 2: Though, then, we do acknowledge the Scriptures to be very heavenly and divine writings, the use of them to be very comfortable and necessary to the Church of Christ, and that we also admire and give praise to the Lord for His wonderful providence in preserving these writings so pure and uncorrupted as we have them, through so long a night of apostasy, to be a testimony of His truth against the wickedness and abominations even of those whom He made instruments in preserving them, so that they have kept them to be a witness against themselves; yet we may not call them the principal fountain of all truth and knowledge, nor yet the first adequate rule of faith and manners: because the principal fountain of truth must be the truth itself, that is, that whose certainty and authority depends not upon another. . . . That which is given to Christians for a rule and guide must needs be so full, that it may clearly and distinctly guide and order them in all things and occurrences that may fall out. But in that there are numberless things, with regard to their circumstances, which particular Christians may be concerned in, for which there can be no particular rule had in the Scriptures, therefore the Scriptures cannot be a rule to them. —§ 6: Moreover, because they are commonly acknowledged by all to have been written by the dictates of the Holy Spirit, and that the errors which may be supposed by the injuries of times to have slipt in, are not such but that there is a sufficient clear testimony left to all the essentials of the Christian faith, we do look upon them as the only fit outward judge of controversies among Christians, and that whatsoever doctrine is contrary unto their testimony may therefore justly be rejected as false; and for our parts, we are very willing that all our doctrines and practices be tried by them.

II. SECOND POINT OF DIVERGENCE.

[The decision as to the true meaning and interpretation of Holy Scripture rests, according to the Roman Catholic doctrine, with the Church, that is, in the last appeal, with the Pope. Every one must submit to it, or rather to him. The Council of Trent limited this absolute right of determination by a clause which referred to the clear and consentient voice of the Fathers; but in later times this limitation has been allowed by the Papal Church to drop out. Protestants, on the other hand, maintain that the true meaning of Holy Writ, so far as its contents are the sum of what constitutes the faith necessary for salvation, may be plainly extracted from Holy Writ itself. The Quakers separate the Holy Spirit from the written word, and teach that the internal light suffices for the understanding of the nature and of the will of God. The question as to the interpretation of the written word is for them a very subordinate one. They deal with it, however, thus: He whom the Holy Spirit has previously inwardly enlightened, will also understand and be able to expound the Bible.]

SYMBOLICAL TESTIMONIES.

I. ROMAN.

Conc. Trid. sess. 4, *Decr. de edit. et usu S. S.*: Ad coërcenda petulantia ingenia decernit (synodus), ut nemo suæ prudentiæ innixus, in rebus fidei et morum ad ædificationem doctrinæ christianæ pertinentium, sacram scripturam ad suos sensus contorquens contra eum sensum, quem tenuit et tenet sancta mater ecclesia, *cujus est judicare de vero sensu et interpretatione scripturarum sanctarum*, aut etiam contra unanimem consensum patrum ipsam scripturam sacram interpretari audeat, etiamsi hujusmodi interpretationes nullo unquam tempore in lucem edendæ forent. Qui contravenerint, per ordinarios declarentur et pœnis a jure statutis puniantur.

[The Pope has recently explained Holy Scripture in a manner *contra unanimem consensum patrum;* for in his Bull *Ineffabilis* he has, contrary to that *consensus,* interpreted many passages (Gen. iii. 15, Jer. i. 28, Luke i. 42, etc.) of the Immaculate Conception. And nevertheless he condemns in his Bull, delivered from the chair, every one who shall think in his heart otherwise than the Pope thinks.]

(Bellarmini *de verbo dei,* iii. 3: Convenit inter nos et adversarios, scripturas intelligi debere eo spiritu, quo factæ sunt i. e. spir. sancto. . . . Tota igitur quæstio in eo posita est, ubi sit iste spiritus. Nos enim existimamus, hunc spiritum, etsi multis privatis hominibus saepe conceditur, tamen certo inveniri in ecclesiâ i. e. in concilio episcoporum confirmato a summo ecclesiae totius pastore sive in summo pastore cum concilio aliorum pastorum.—*Ib.* cap. 9 : Non ignorabat deus multas in ecclesiâ exorituras disputationes circa fidem, debuit igitur judicem aliquem ecclesiae providere. At iste judex non potest esse scriptura, neque spiritus revelans privatus, neque princeps secularis, igitur princeps ecclesiasticus vel solus vel certe cum consilio et consensu coöpiscoporum. Ac primum non esse judicem scripturam, planum est, quia varios sensus recipit nec potest ipsa dicere, quis sit verus. Praeterea in omni republ. bene instituta et ordinata lex et judex distinctae res sunt. Lex enim docet quid agendum, et judex legem interpretatur et secundum eam homines dirigit. Denique de scripturae interpretatione quaestio est, non autem se ipsa interpretari potest.— *Ib.* cap. 10 : Verbum ecclesiae i. e. concilii vel pontificis docentis ex cathedrâ non est verbum hominis i. e. verbum errori obnoxium, sed aliquo modo verbum dei i. e. prolatum assistente et gubernante Sp. sancto. Cf. Cani *Loci*, lib. iv.; Becani *manuale*, i. 5; Klee, *kathol. Dogmat.* i. 243 ff.)

II. GREEK.

The *Conf. orthod.* plainly lays down the position, that the Church *alone* has the power to expound Scripture; for what occurs on p. 140, ἡ ἐκκλησία ἔχει τὴν ἐξουσίαν ταύτην, ὥστε . . . δοκιμάζῃ τὰς γραφάς, must be understood of human writings. To the œcumenical synods, which were no other than the Church itself deciding on this authoritative dogma, this confession expressly ascribes a judicial power in regard to the orthodox faith. Other Confessions laid down the principle, that none must deviate from the traditional interpretations of the holy Fathers which have been approved by the synods (Jerem. *in actis Wirtemb.* p. 260). Moreover, that principle follows from the dogma as to the inspiration of the Church, which the Greeks hold in common with the Romanists. Cf. *Conf. orthod.* p. 152. The Confession of Dositheus speaks on this subject plainly.

Conf. orthod. p. 17 : Πρέπει νὰ κρατῇ διὰ βέβαιον καὶ ἀναμφίβολον ὁ ὀρθόδοξος χριστιανός, πῶς ὅλα τὰ ἄρθρα τῆς πίστεως τῆς καθολικῆς καὶ ὀρθοδόξου ἐκκλησίας εἶναι παραδεδομένα ἀπὸ τὸν κύριον ἡμῶν Ἰησοῦν Χριστόν· . . . καὶ αἱ οἰκουμενικαὶ σύνοδοι τὰ ἑρμηνεύουσαν καὶ τὰ ἐδοκίμασαν καὶ νὰ πιστεύῃ εἰς αὐτά. —P. 18 : Φανερὸν πῶς τὰ ἄρθρα τῆς πίστεως ἔχουσι τὸ κῦρος καὶ τὴν δοκιμασίαν . . . μέρος ἀπὸ τὴν ἐκκλ. παράδοσιν, καὶ ἀπὸ τὴν διδασκαλίαν τῶν συνόδων καὶ τῶν ἁγίων πατέρων.— P. 19 : καὶ τοῦτα (the dogmas of apostolical tradition) ἑρμηνεύθησαν ἀπὸ τὰς συνόδους καὶ τοὺς ἁγίους πατέρας.

Metroph. Critopul. *Conf.* c. 7, p. 84 : ἡ ἁγία γραφὴ ἐνεπιστεύθη τῇ ἐκκλησίᾳ ὑπὸ θεοῦ, ὡς δοκεῖν τὴν ἐκκλησίαν φύλακα καὶ ὁδηγὸν εἶναι τῆς θεοπνεύστου γραφῆς . . . ὁδηγόν, ὅτι πρὸς ταύτην ἡμᾶς ὁδηγεῖ, τὰ ἀσαφῆ δοκοῦντα σαφηνίζουσα καὶ ἀνακαλύπτουσα τὰ κεκαλυμμένα πάνυ ὀρθοδόξως καὶ θεαρέστως.

Jerem. in act. *Wirtemb.* p. 142 : Οὐχ ἡμῖν ἔξεστι, τῇ ἰδίᾳ καταθαρροῦσιν ἐξηγήσει, τι τῶν τῆς θεοπνεύστου γραφῆς ῥητῶν συνιέναι καὶ κατανοεῖν ἢ διερμηνεύειν εἰ μὴ κατὰ τῶν παρὰ τῶν ἁγίων συνόδων ἐν ἁγίῳ πνεύματι, πρὸς τὸν εὐσεβῆ σκόπον δοκιμασθέντας θεολόγους.

Id. p. 260 : Διὸ καὶ αὖθις ἀξιοῦμεν ὑμᾶς, οὕτω νοεῖν τὰ ῥητὰ ὡς οἱ οἰκουμενικοὶ διδάσκαλοι τῆς ἐκκλησίας ἐξηγήσαντο, ὧν τὰς ἐξηγήσεις αἵτε οἰκουμενικαὶ ζ΄ σύνοδοι καὶ αἱ λοιπαὶ τοπικαὶ ἐκεκύρωσαν. Ὡς γὰρ προείπομεν, οὐ χρὴ μεταίρειν ὅρια αἰώνια ἃ ἔθεντο οἱ πατέρες, ἵνα μὴ τὸν ὅρον ἐν ἀρχῇ ῥηθέντα τῆς ς΄ παραβαίνοντες, τοῖς ἐκιτιμίοις ὑποκεισώμεθα.

Cf. pp. 114, 116, 139, 250, and in Crusii *Turco-Graecia*, p. 440.

Dosithei *Conf.* c. 2 : Πιστεύομεν τὴν θείαν γραφὴν εἶναι θεοδίδακτον, καὶ διὰ τοῦτο ταύτῃ ἀδιαστάκτως πιστεύειν ὀφείλομεν, οὐκ ἄλλως μέντοι ἀλλ᾽ ἢ ὡς ἡ καθολ. ἐκκλησία ταύτην ἡρμήνευσε καὶ παρέδωκεν. . . . τὴν τῆς καθολ. ἐκκλησίας μαρτυρίαν οὐχ ἧττον τῆς ἣν κέκτηται ἡ θεία γραφή, εἶναι πιστεύομεν· ἑνὸς γὰρ καὶ τοῦ αὐτοῦ ἁγίου πνεύματος ὄντος ἀμφοτέρων δημιουργοῦ, ἴσον ἐστι πάντως ὑπὸ τῆς γραφῆς καὶ ὑπὸ τῆς καθολ. ἐκκλησ. διδάσκεσθαι. . . . τὴν καθολ. ἐκκλησ. ὡς λαλοῦσαν ἐκ τοῦ πνεύματος τοῦ θεοῦ ἀδύνατον πάντῃ ἁμαρτῆσαι, ἢ ὅλως ἀπατῆσαι καὶ ἀπατηθῆναι. Cf. c. 12.

III. PROTESTANT.

The Lutheran symbols, as a whole, do not speak expressly on interpretation of Scripture independent of ecclesiastical authority. But their meaning is plain from their fundamental principles, as to the nullity of all tradition, and of any infallibility in the visible Church ; as also from the fact that the Reformation sprang from that very freedom, and that the symbolical books argue exegetically against the Roman Catholic Church. Only the *Conf. Wirt.* p. 130, expressly rejects the *jus interpretandæ s. scripturæ in potestate summorum pontificum situm.* The Lutheran theologians, following the symbols, lay down, like the Reformed, this antithesis to the Catholic position : *S. S. est sui ipsius legitimus interpres* (comp. under *Helv. Conf.* i.), and avow the *perspicuitas S. S.*, which makes an exegetic-dogmatic tribunal superfluous.

Conf. Helv. i. art. 2 : Scripturæ sacræ interpretatio ex ipsâ solâ petenda est, ut ipsa interpres sit sui, caritatis fideique regulâ moderante.

Conf. Helv. ii. c. 2 : Scripturas sanctas dixit apost. Petrus (2 Pet. i. 20) non esse interpretationis privatæ. Proinde non probamus interpretationes quaslibet : unde nec pro verâ aut genuinâ scripturarum interpretatione agnoscimus eum, quem vocant sensum Romanæ ecclesiæ, quem scilicet simpliciter Romanæ ecclesiæ defensores omnibus obtrudere contendunt recipiendum. Sed illam duntaxat scripturarum interpretationem pro orthodoxâ et genuinâ agnoscimus, quæ ex ipsis est petita scripturis (ex ingenio utique ejus linguæ, in quâ sunt scriptæ, secundum circumstantias, item expensæ et pro ratione locorum vel similium vel dissimilium, plurium quoque et clariorum, expositæ), cum regulâ fidei et caritatis congruit et ad gloriam dei hominumque salutem eximie facit.

Conf. Scot. 18 : Scripturæ sacræ interpretationem neque ad privatam aliquam aut publicam personam pertinere confitemur, neque ad ecclesiam aliquam, . . . sed jus et auctoritas hæc est solius spiritus dei, per quem sacræ scripturæ literis sunt mandatæ. Cum ergo contingit, quod contravertitur pro recto sensu alicujus loci vel sententiæ scripturæ, . . . non tam videndum nobis est, quid homines ante nos vel dixerint vel fecerint, quam quid Spiritus sanctus uniformiter in corpore sacræ scripturæ dicat. . . . Si itaque interpretatio, determinatio vel sententia cujusvis doctoris ecclesiæ vel concilii expresso dei verbo in quovis alio scripturæ loco repugnet, certum est, illam interpretationem non esse mentem et sensum sancti Spiritus. Nullum enim interpretationem admittere audemus, quæ alicui principali articulo fidei aut alicui plano textui scripturæ aut caritatis regulæ repugnat.

Conf. Remonstr. i. 14 : Librorum sacrorum, licet alicubi præsertim indoctis et minus exercitatis satis obscuri sint, tanta est claritas ac perspicuitas in sensibus inprimis ad æternam salutem intellectu necessariis, ut omnes lectores non docti tantum sed et idiotæ, quantum satis est, mentem eorum assequi possint ; modo præjudicio, vanâ confidentiâ aliisque pravis affectibus sese occæcari non sinant, etc.

[Baier, *Compendium theologiæ positivæ*, ed. E. Preuss, Berolini 1864, viii. S. 95, 96 : Inter affectiones Scripturæ locum habet perspicuitas, seu quod ea quæ creditu et factu homini ad salutem tendenti sunt necessaria, verbis et phrasibus ita claris et usu loquendi receptis in Scriptura proponuntur, ut quilibet homo, linguæ gnarus et vel mediocri judicio pollens, verbisque attendens, verum verborum sensum, quoad ea, quæ sibi sunt scitu necessaria, assequi, et capita ipsa doctrinæ simplici mentis apprehensione amplecti possit : prout ad assensum fidei verbo apprehenso et rebus significatis præbendum intellectus hominis per scripturam ipsam ejusque lumen supernaturale seu virtutem divinam illi conjunctam perducitur.—The analogy of faith was regarded by the older theologians as the guiding principle of exposition (*Apol. A. C.* 290 ; Luther's *Werke*, Walch, iii. 2042). They never, indeed, denied that false interpretations of Scripture might be found, and have been found, by the side of the true and only right one. But the notion was to them unknown, that every passage may be expounded in three-and-twenty various ways, and that it was the business of every man to select from this fortuitous mass his own opinion.] Cf. Twesten, *Vorlesung*, i. 450.

IV. Socinian.

Cat. racov. p. 15 (qu. 36): Etsi difficultates quædam in S. S. occurrunt, tamen multa alia tum ea, quæ sunt ad salutem necessaria ita perspicue aliis in locis S. S. sunt tradita, ut ab unoquoque maxime vero pietatis ac veritatis studioso et divinam opem implorante possint intelligi (qu. 37). Quâ ratione id demonstrabis? Primum, cum deus eo fine atque consilio S. Scripturam hominibus tradi voluerit, ut ex ea voluntatem ipsius cognoscerent, incredibile prorsus est, ejusmodi scripta tradi voluisse, e quibus voluntas ipsius perfici et cognosci ab omnibus non posset. Deinde, quod in ipsis religionis chr. principiis apostoli epistolas suas, in quibus præcipua religionis chr. mysteria continentur, ad homines simplices scripserint. In qu. 39 it is then shown whence have sprung the many *dissidia in eruendo scripturæ sensu;* and among other reasons this is assigned, that men do not as much as they ought, and with as much desire, seek the divine help of the Holy Spirit, promised by God to those who daily and nightly invoke Him. Comp. also Socinus, *Opp.* i. 344; Ostorodt, *Unterricht.* S. 2, 426; and the references in Bengel, xv. 115.

V. Quaker.

Barclay, *Apol.* x. 19 : For all that which man, by his own industry, learning, and knowledge in the languages, can interpret of the Scriptures, or find out, is nothing without the Spirit; we cannot be certain, but may still miss of the sense of it : whereas a poor man, that knoweth not a letter, when he heareth the Scriptures read, by the same Spirit he can say, *This is true;* and by the same Spirit he can understand, open, and interpret it, if need be. . . . iii. 4 : And therefore He [Christ] gave them His Spirit as their principal guide, which neither moths nor time can wear out, nor transcribers nor translators corrupt ; while none are so young, none so illiterate, none in so remote a place, but that they may come to be reached and rightly informed by it. Through and by the clearness which that Spirit gives us, it is that we are only best rid of those difficulties that occur to us concerning the Scriptures.

General Remarks.

According to the early theologians, the Church uttered her infallible declarations through the collective episcopate, legitimately assembled in one œcumenical council (*ecclesia repræsentans*). Bellarmin. *Eccl. Mil.* c. xiv., says: Our opinion is that the Church cannot possibly err, neither in things absolutely necessary, nor in others which she proposes to our faith and duty, whether they are expressly declared in Scripture or not; and when we say that the Church cannot err, we understand that as well of the whole body of the faithful as of the whole body of the episcopate. But the latter are, as we say, the *ecclesia repræsentiva*. Cf. Cani *Loci*, 5; Möhler, *Symbolik*, § 37; Klee, *kath. Dogm.* i. 246. According to Bellarmine, *Conc.* i. 4, an œcumenical council is that " cui interesse possunt et debent episcopi totius orbis, nisi legitime impediantur, et cui nemo recte præsidet, nisi Summus pontifex aut alius ejus nomine."[1] In such a council the bishops decide as judges (*judices*), for they alone have ordinarily the *jus suffragii;* while others are in the council only *ex privilegio et consuetudine*, or as learned co-assessors giving their aid. Bellarmine, *l.c.* i. 15. [Of late the Roman Catholic Church has receded from these principles of Bellarmine. Comp. the Encyclical of 8th December 1864, § *Atque silentio præterire non possumus.*] Compare with this the fundamental principles of the Greek Church, *Conf. orthod.* pp. 18, 122, 153; Dosithei *Conf.* c. xii.; Jerem. *in Act. Wirt.* p. 139; Plato, *Catech.* S. 118. The orthodox Greek Church reckons such œcumenical councils *seven:* the Council of Nicæa, 325; Constantinople, 381; Ephesus, 431; Chalcedon, 451; Constantinople, 553, and again 680 (Trullanum); Nicæa again, 787. The Roman Catholic, on the other hand, acknowledges eighteen general synods accepted by Popes, among which that of Trent was [till lately] the last; Bellarm. *Concil.* i. 5. About some of these, however, the Romanists themselves are not agreed. The Protestant Church has given no symbolical decision as to the number of the œcumenical councils; but comp. *Decl. Thor.* p. 45, and Baumgarten, *Polem.* iii. 395. The idea of universal synods, in which an utterance is made by good and learned men from Holy Scripture on points of difference that may have arisen as to faith and truth, is one that is not alien to the Protestant Church: it is well known that the Evangelicals long and earnestly appealed to a free universal council (*Aug. Conf.* p. 7; *Artt. Sm.* p. 300). The symbols which touch upon this point distinguish, however, between the ideal

---

[1] See, however, for the relation, contested even among the Romanists, between the Pope and the Œcumenical Council, Marheineeke, *Katholicismus*, ii. 206. Walter, *Kirchenrecht*, S. 306; Klee, *kath. Dogm.* i. 248, have recently ascribed to the Pope as Primus the convoking, the precedence, and the approval of the decrees of the council.

and the reality (*Conf. Wirt.* p. 134; *Thirty-nine Artt.* xxi.; *Conf. Scot.* xx.; Calvin, *Institt.* iv. 9. 13; *Conf. Remonst.* 25), and reject every authority co-ordinate with that of Holy Scripture. It is certain that in practice the idea has never been carried out, and that it could not be carried out without many inconveniences.

III. DIVERGENCES OF LESS IMPORT IN RELATION TO SCRIPTURE.

1. If the Holy Scripture, and especially the New Testament, be a written revelation, it follows that all which it contains as dogma, interpreted by a correct exposition, is an element of the Christian revelation. Reason, therefore, has no prerogative of distinguishing in the material which, as constituting the Bible, lies before it; of so dividing, namely, that what reason could not of itself discover, would therefore not be part of the Christian dogma. And in this matter all the Christian symbols agree; the Socinians forming, in the estimate of many, the one exception (Baumgarten, *Polemik*, iii. 196; Mosheim, *Institt. hist. ecc.* 820; Schröckh, *KG. n. d. R.* v. 560). But that even they do not *in thesi* make reason the absolute judge in matters of the Christian faith, is evident from the distinction they draw between those mysteries in revelation which are against and those which are above reason. It also follows from their ancient view of the inability of the reason to discern God and His will.[1] They admit only a *negative* right in reason to test a revelation presented as divine, and teach that nothing in Christendom or Christian truth may *contradict* reason. In exegetical practice, however, they apply this fundamental principle to all passages of Scripture which contain the *supra-rational*, or the so-called

[1] Socinus, *Opp.* ii. 454. Man himself, of himself, cannot know either himself, or God or His will: it is necessary, on the other hand, that God should reveal these things to him by some reason. Ostorodt, *Unterr.* S. 10. That man knows anything of God or divinity is not from nature, nor from observation of the creation, but from the tradition of what God has from the beginning revealed to man. But those have not heard this voice who have entertained an indifferent thought about any divinity at all. Cf. especially Socinus, *Prælect. Theol.* cap. 2. How the Socinians have fallen away from this higher view, see in Zerrenner.

mysteries of the symbolical Christian faith. For, according to their notions, mysteries of faith, once revealed, must be *comprehensible* by reason ;[1] and thus, in fact, the Socinian exegesis of Scripture is governed by reason, and is constantly subject to violent distortions in interpretation.[2] Compare, generally, J. J. C. Zerrenner, *Neuer Versuch*, Jena 1820.

2. The precise relation of the Latin version known as the Vulgate to the original, as established by the Tridentine Synod, has been matter of controversy. The words of the decree (sess. iv. *decr. de edit. et usu S. S.*) run thus : Synodus, considerans non parum utilitatis accedere posse ecclesiæ dei, si ex omnibus latinis editionibus, quæ circumferuntur, sacrorum librorum, quænam pro authenticâ habenda sit, innotescat, statuit et declarat, ut hæc ipsa vetus et vulgata editio, quæ longo tot sæculorum usu in ipsâ ecclesiâ probata est, in publicis lectionibus, disputationibus, prædicationibus et expositionibus pro authenticâ habeatur et ut nemo eam rejicere quovis prætextu audeat vel præsumat.—At the first glance, it might appear as if the Council would merely say that, if a Latin version was to be used (as in the divine service), the Vulgate alone among all those extant was to be regarded as having sanction for the Church : at least in these words no definite antithesis is established between it and the original. There is, however, undoubtedly in the permission to use the Latin translation in all theological controversies (*disputationibus*), a certain undervaluation of the original text which was not to be expected from the representatives of the Church. And, in fact, the transactions of the Council which preceded the decrees show that the Tridentine Fathers aimed to establish the authenticity of the Vulgate, the original being left in the background, in order to obtain an advantage in disputes with the Protestants, who appealed always to that original ; or, as it follows in the immediate sequel of the decree, to restrain *petulantia ingenia*, and to obviate such interpretations of Scripture as de-

---

[1] Schlichting, *Diss. de Trinitate*, p. 70 : *Mysteria divina*, divine mysteries, are so called, not because as revealed they transcend our intelligence and apprehension, but because they cannot be known otherwise than by revelation.

[2] Cf. *e.g. Cat. Rac.* qu. 89, 97, 111, 392. As to Socinus' exegetical maxims in reference to many biblical sentences, see *De Christo servatore*, iii. 7. Cf. Bengel in *Süskind's Mag.* xv. 132.

parted from the mind of the Church.¹ Finally, many even of the most orthodox Romish theologians have so understood the decree as to make the Vulgate dogmatically as trustworthy as the original ; and even the Church (in general councils²) might establish its decisions by appeal to the Vulgate.³ Recently it has been attempted to explain away every allusion in the decree to the original; or, since the plain words of it cannot be forced, to interpret the whole as a merely provisional disciplinary enactment for a good purpose.⁴ An antithesis of the Tridentine sanction of the Vulgate is found in the *Declar. Thorun.* ii. 1. 4.

3. On the reading of Scripture by the laity the Roman symbols have nothing definitive. The Popes, however, have repeatedly interdicted it, especially Innocent III. (Concil. Tolos. 1229), and Clement XI. in the Bull *Unigenitus* (1713). Pius VII. disapproved of the use of Bible translations which had not the sanction of the Roman chair ; and the *Index lib. prohib.*

---

¹ [Jud. le Plat, *Monumentorum ad historiam concilii Tridentini*, Lovanii 1783.] Cf. Schröckh, *KG.* iv. 132 ; Marheineckc, *System der Kathol.* i. 231.

² The decree does not mention the acts of councils in which the Church herself sits in judgment. But Bellarmine, *de verbo dei*, ii. 10, says with great simplicity: In the general councils of the Church there are but few, sometimes no, men skilled in Hebrew ; it would be a bad thing for the Church if on grave questions she could not confide in the Latin version, etc.; and from what Canus says, ii. 15, *de linguarum hebr. et grœcœ utilitate*, it may be gathered how orthodox Catholic theologians regard the use of the original as compared with that of the Vulgate.

³ According to this, the Vulgate was on a level of itself with the original, and only in and by the use made of it had the pre-eminence. The decree is not that the truths of faith may be more surely known from the Vulgate than from the original (the Church never asserted that), but that they may be known with equal assurance, and therefore that the Church adhered to the Vulgate because it was in more general use and better understood. Accordingly the old Protestant polemics addressed themselves to the task of showing that the Vulgate, as compared with the original, was corrupt. Chemnitz, *Exam.* 1, i. 7, 13 ; Sixt. Amama, *Censura Vulgatœ et a Tridentinis canonizatœ* (!) *versionis Pentat.*, Francq. 1628. See also the same author's *Antibarbarus Bibl.*, Amst. 1628, in answer to which Bellarmine, *de verbo dei*, ii. 12, sought to make out that the Vulgate is free from errors. Still more successfully the old polemics pointed to the discrepancy between the Clement. and Sixtine authentic editions. Cf. James, *Bellum papale*, London 1600.

⁴ Cf. L. van Ess. *Pragm. doctor. cath. Trid. circa Vulgatam decreti sensum nec non licitum textus origin. usum testantium historia*, Sulzbach 1816 ; Herber, *de Vers. Lat. Vulg. ex conc. Trid. decreto authenticâ,* Vratis. 1815.

which Pius IV. issued makes the reading of (Catholic) translations of Scripture dependent on the permission of the pastors and heads of monasteries. However, there have never been wanting prelates and theologians of the Romish Church who have desired to make the reading of the Bible as common as possible, proceeding from the principle, *Lectio S. S. est pro omnibus.* But in consequence of the other principle predominant in that Church, of the essential obscurity of Scripture, it is perfectly consistent that but little stress is laid upon the individual and private reading of the Bible on the part of the laity, and that the common people are referred mainly to the oral instruction of the clergy: Bellarmine, *de verbo dei,* ii. 15. The Greek Church never made Scripture accessible to the laity. In their divine service it is still read in a language not understood by the people, and translations have till lately not been widely diffused. The Synod of Jerusalem, in 1672, was made to utter a condemnation of the reading of Scripture by the laity: Harduin, *Concil.* xi. 255. Even the Quakers attach little importance to the private reading of the Bible, since the people are always dependent upon the correctness of the translation, which they themselves are not able to decide upon: see Barclay, Prop. iii. The learned themselves derive, according to them, no real advantage from reading the word of God, if they are destitute of the true internal light. If the Protestant Church is zealous in putting the Scriptures into the hands of the laity, it is under the full conviction that the proper clearness of the original is unimpaired in those passages which make up the constituent elements of necessary faith.

4. The Roman Catholics reckon as part of Holy Scripture, besides the canonical books, the so-called Apocrypha (that is, Tobit, Judith, Ecclesiasticus, Wisdom of Solomon, 1 and 2 Maccabees, Baruch, parts of Esther, the Hymn of the Three, Susannah, Bel and the Dragon), and ascribe to them divine authority, appointing portions of them to be read at certain festivals; cf. Conc. Trid. sess. iv. dec. 1. It is true that many Romish theologians make an historical distinction between the canonical and apocryphal books, terming the former proto-canonical, and the latter deutero-canonical (see Jahn, *Einleitung,* i. 140). But the Church takes no notice of any

such distinction, which indeed is of itself without any significance for dogmatics. How it came to pass that the Tridentine Synod denied the distinction already existing in the Jewish Church between the canonical and the apocryphal books, is matter of fruitless conjecture. It was the long prevalent custom in the Latin Church to use the canonical books and the non-canonical promiscuously; and there was a desire (not without the influence of doctrinal bias) to be faithful to the old habit. In the Lutheran symbols there is found no decided negative, though they do in fact declare the canonical books alone to be dogmatically binding: Bretschneider, *Dogmatik*, cap. 1; *Conf. Gall.* iii. 4; *Conf. Belg.* 6: libri apocryphi, quos quidem ecclesia legere et ex iis documenta de rebus cum libris canonicis consentientibus desumere potest: at nequaquam ea ipsorum vis et auctoritas est, ut ex ullo testimonio ipsorum aliquod dogma . . . certo constitui possit. *Dec. Thorun.* p. 46, *Conf. Remon.* i. 6, and the *Conf. Gall.*, the English Article vi., the *Conf. Remonst.* i. 3, give express lists of the canonical books of the Old Testament. The Socinians also (Ostorodt, *Unterr.*), and the Mennonites (Ris, *Conf.* c. 29), agree in this with the Protestant Churches. Barclay mentions the exclusion of the Apocrypha from the collection of the divinely-inspired books, but only in passing, and as an historical fact.

Metrophanes Critop. *Conf.* c. 7, attests, for the Greek Church, that it assigned no canonical authority to the Old Testament Apocrypha. "As to the other books, which some would combine together with the Holy Scriptures, such as Tobit and the like, we do not hold that they are to be rejected, for they hold much that is moral and worthy of all praise. But as canonical and authentic they were not formerly received by the Church of Christ. . . . Wherefore we do not seek to establish our dogmas by them, but from the three-and-thirty canonical and authentic books, which we call the inspired and holy Scripture." On the other hand, the Apocrypha are placed in co-ordination with the canonical books by the Synod at Jerusalem, 1672, [at least according to] Harduin, *Concil.* xi. 258.

5. As to the inspiration of Holy Writ, the Racovian Cate-

chism does not speak expressly; it aims merely to demonstrate the *certitudo S. S.* Socinus, however, not only admits that the apostles, in the announcement of doctrines necessary to salvation, enjoyed a special guidance of the Divine Spirit [1] (which therefore would not fail them in writing), but says of them that they wrote certain things "vel ab ipso div. spiritu impulsi *eoque dictante* vel spiritu sancto pleni;" and even in the Racovian Catechism there occur traces here and there of a faith in inspiration. See Zerrenner, *Neuer Versuch*, etc., S. 132-198. In the *Conf. Remonst.* i. 3, the authors of the canonical books are said to be *spiritu dei sancto afflati, instructi et directi.* In the *Form. Cons. Helv.* ii. 1, moreover, we have an assertion of the inspired character of the Hebrew vowels.

[1] Socini *Opp.* i. 3746: Apostolos in iis, quæ ad æternam salutem omnino pertinent, errare non potuisse et ratio manifesta et Christi apertissima verba atque promissa plane demonstrant.

II.

THE TRINITY.

ALL Christian communities agree that God is in His nature one; but the great majority acknowledge, according to the definitions of the ancient Church, in this one divine essence three persons or hypostases, inseparably united, co-equal in eternity and perfection. They separate to some extent from the Arminians, who, because the Son is generated, and the Spirit proceeds eternally from the Father, teach a subordination among the three Persons; and they differ wholly from the anti-Trinitarians or Socinians, who, denying the Trinity in the divine essence, hold the supreme and only God, who is one in essence, to be one in person also, and regard Christ as only a man exalted to divine majesty (a God who became such in time: Osterodt, S. 65), and that which the Scripture calls the Holy Ghost as merely the power of God efficient in the sanctification of men. In the symbols of the Quakers, the doctrine of the Trinity is not exhibited as such; nor are the biblical passages which touch on the Trinity in the divine essence ever collected. All is reduced to the one declaration in Proposition ii. of Barclay: No man knoweth the Father but the Son, and he to whom the Son revealeth Him; the revelation of the Son is in and by the Spirit.

SYMBOLICAL TESTIMONIES.

I. ROMISH AND PROTESTANT.

As the declarations of the Roman Catholic and Protestant symbols alike and almost literally coincide with, or as comments arise out of, the statements of the ancient œcumenical symbols,—which symbols themselves, moreover, have been accepted generally by the Protestants,—it is unnecessary to set those statements in order here. Comp. however, Gennadius, *Conf.* art. 3; *Metrop. Critop.* 1; *Conf. orth.* i. qu. 8–10; *Aug. Conf.* 1; *Apol.* p. 50; *Artt. Sm.* p. 303; *Conf. Helv.* ii. cap. 3; *Conf. Gall.* art. 6; *Eng. Artt.* 1–3; *Conf. Belg.* art. 8. As to the Mennonites, comp. Ris, *Conf.* artt. 2 and 3.

II. SOCINIAN.

1. *The Trinity generally.*

Cat. Rac. p. 31: Qui fit, ut Christiani non solum patrem, verum etiam filium et spiritum sanctum personas esse in unâ deitate vulgo statuant? Graviter in eo errant, argumenta ejus rei afferentes e scripturis male intellectis.

2. *Deity of Christ.*

Ib. p. 32: Vox *deus* duobus potissimum modis in scripturis usurpatur: prior est, cum designat illum, qui in cœlis et in terrâ omnibus ita dominatur et præest, ut neminem superiorem agnoscat . . . atque in hac significatione scriptura unum esse deum asserit. Posterior modus est, cum eum denotat, qui potestatem aliquam sublimem ab uno illo deo habet aut deitatis unius illius dei aliquâ ratione particeps est. Etenim in scripturis propterea deus ille unus deus deorum vocatur. Psalm. l. 1. Et hac quidem posteriore ratione filius dei vocatur deus in quibusdam scripturæ locis.

Ib. p. 48: An præter humanam Ch. naturam s. substantiam non agnoscis etiam in eo divinam? Siquidem hoc loco naturæ divinæ nomine ipsam dei essentiam intelligimus, non agnoscimus hoc sensu divinam in Ch. naturam, cum id non solum rationi sacræ verum etiam divinis literis repugnet.

Ib. p. 58: Si Chr. ex essentiâ patris genitus fuisset, aut partem essentiæ sumsisset aut totam. Essentiæ partem sumere non potuit eo quod sit impartibilis essentia divina, neque totam, nam hac ratione pater desiisset esse pater . . . adde quod cum ess. div. sit una numero ac proinde incommunicabilis, fieri istud nullo pacto potuit (after the latest revision).

Ib. p. 47 : Non solum est Ch. filius dei unigenitus . . . sed etiam propter divin. tum potentiam ac virtutem tum auctoritatem ac potestatem, quæ in eo adhuc mortali eluxit, jam tum deus fuit, multo magis nunc, postquam omnem in cœlo et in terrâ potestatem accepit et omnia deo solo excepto ejus pedibus sunt subjecta (wanting in first edition).

Ib. p. 50 : Quidquid divinum Chr. habet, scriptura eum patris dono habere aperte docet.

Ib. p. 164 : Primo præcepto Jes. addidit id, quod ipsum Jesum pro eo, qui in nos potestatem habeat divinam istoque sensu pro deo agnoscere . . . ac divinum ei honorem exhibere tenemur.

Ib. qu. 237 : (Honor divinus Christo debitus consistit) in eo, quod, quemadmodum adoratione divinâ eum prosequi tenemur, ita in omnibus necessitatibus nostris ejus opem implorare possumus. Adoramus vero eum propter ipsius sublimem et divinam ejus potestatem.

Ib. qu. 245 : (Is honor et cultus Christo tribuitur, ut inter Christum et deum discrimen) permagnum sit. Nam adoramus et colimus deum tanquam causam primam salutis nostræ, Christum tanquam secundam : aut, ut cum Paulo (1 Cor. viii. 6) loquamur, deum tanquam cum ex quo omnia, Christum ut cum per quem omnia.

Thus the Socinian doctrine as to the deity of Christ is in its connection this : The man Jesus, who, born as the Son of God, accomplished the purposes of God on earth for the salvation of men, was by God exalted in the ascension to almighty dominion over His Church (the people of God), and therefore over the whole world. Consequently He was exalted to a participation in the divine glory, and in this state Christ may receive, as God, adoration or worship. Christ is not *naturâ Deus;* did not from eternity pre-exist with God ; never became participant ipsius *essentiæ* divinæ (which is absolutely indivisible and incommunicable); and all the divine that He possesses He received as the gift of God. (A contention arose between Socinus and others, especially the Siebenburg Unitarians, as to the divine honour to be paid to Christ. On this, consult the tractates of Socinus in the *Bibl. Frat. Polon.* ii. 709 sqq. The *Summa theol. Unit.* agrees generally with the

E

views of Socinus. But on what ground does Hase assert, *K. G. S.* 593, that the English Unitarians have renounced the worship of Christ?)

3. *Divine Personality of the Holy Ghost.*

Cat. Racov. qu. 80 : Sp. s. nusquam in s. s. vocatur expresse deus. Quia vero quibusdam locis ea attribuit ipsi scriptura, quæ dei sunt, non eo facit ac si ipse vel deus sit vel persona divinitatis.

Ib. qu. 371 : Sp. s. non esse in deitate personam, hinc dicere potes, primum, quod ea, quæ Spiritui s. in scripturis attribuuntur, nulla prorsus ratione personæ conveniant, ut sunt: quod detur, quod ex eo detur idque aut secundum mensuram aut absque omni mensurâ, quod effundatur ipse et ex ipso effundatur et quod eo potentur homines, quod augeatur, in duplo detur, in partes distribuatur, tollatur ipse et ex ipso tollatur, quod interdum sit, interdum non sit, denique quod exstinguatur, et similia in scripturis exstant (Act. v. 32, cet.). Deinde idem ex eo patet, quod non sit extra deum natura, sed in ipso deo. . . . Quoniam vero Sp. s. in deo est, nec tamen in Spiritu s. reciproce dici potest esse deum, hinc apparet, Sp. s. non esse personam.

F. Soc. breviss. inst. p. 652 b : Quid de Spiritu sancto dicis ? Nempe illum non esse personam aliquam a deo, cujus est spiritus, distinctam, sed tantummodo (ut nomen ipsum spiritus, quod flatum et afflationem, ut sic loquar, significat, docere potest) ipsius dei vim et efficaciam quandam, i. e. eam, quæ secum sanctitatem aliquam afferat cet.[1]

III. Arminian.

The *Conf. Remonst.* c. 3 says nothing of a subordination, expresses itself on this subject with very great prudence; and expressly ascribes to the Holy Spirit also a *communicatio deitatis ab æterno.*

Episcopius, *Inst. Theol.* iv. 2. 32, p. 333 : Sed addo, certum esse ex scripturis, personis. his tribus divinitatem divinasque

---

[1] Cf. Soc. *Bibl. Fr. Pol.* ii. 455 ; *Tr. de Deo, Christo et Sp.* ; Ostorodt, *Unterricht,* c. iv. 6 ; Crell, *de uno Deo patre.*

perfectiones tribui non collateraliter aut co-ordinate, sed subordinate, ita ut pater solus naturam istam divinam et perfectiones istas divinas a se habeat sive a nullo alio, filius autem et Spiritus sanctus a patre : ac proinde pater divinitatis omnis, quæ in filio et Spiritu sancto est, fons ac principium sit. . . . Dignius autem est, esse a nullo, quam esse ab alio, et generare, quam generari, spirare quam spirari cet.

Limborch, *Theol. Christ.* ii. 17, sec. 25 : Colligimus, essentiam divinam et filio et Spiritui sancto esse communem. Sed et non minus constat, inter tres hasce personas subordinationem esse quandam, quatenus pater naturam divinam a se habet, filius et Spiritus sanctus a patre, qui proinde divinitatis in filio et Spiritu sancto fons est et principium. Communis christianorum consensus ordinis ratione prærogativam hanc agnoscit, patri semper tribuens primum locum, secundum filio, tertium Spiritui sancto. Sed est et quædam supereminentia patris respectu filii, et patris ac filii respectu Spiritus sancti, ratione dignitatis ac potestatis. Dignius siquidem est generare quam generari, spirare quam spirari cet.

DIFFERENCES OF LESS MOMENT.

The Greek Church teaches, following John xv. 26, that the Holy Ghost proceeds only from the Father. But the Roman Catholic and Protestant Churches, including the Mennonites and Arminians, teach, with the Nicene and Athanasian symbols, in harmony with the orthodox view of the essential relation of the Father and the Son in the holy Trinity, that He proceeds from the Father and the Son together. See *Cat. Rom.* i. 9. 6 (cf. Klee, *Dogm.* ii. 182); *Form. Conc.* p. 781; *Conf. Helv.* ii. 3 ; *Conf. Gall.* art. 6 ; *Eng. Artt.* ii. ; *Conf. Belg.* art. xi. ; *Conf. Rem.* iii. 2 ; Ris, *Conf. Menn.* art. 3. The passage in the Greek formulary is as follows : διδάσκει [ἐκκλησία] πᾶς τὸ πνεῦμα τὸ ἅγιον ἐκπορεύεται ἐκ μόνου τοῦ πατρός, ὡς πηγῆς καὶ ἀρχῆς τῆς θεότητος. More explicit statements are found in Metrop. Critop. c. i. 11 ; Jerem. *in Actis Wirt.* pp. 57, 200. Cf. Zernicav. *Tract. de Process. Sp. s. a solo patre*, Regiom. 1774 ; Th. Procopowitz, *de Process. Sp.*, Goth. 1772.

III.

CULTUS OF THE VIRGIN; INVOCATION OF SAINTS; VENERATION OF PICTURES AND RELICS.

POINT OF DIVERGENCE.

ALL Christian Churches agree that to God alone belongs adoration. But the Papists and Greeks connect with this an invocation and reverence of angels and saints—that is, of the dead who for their sanctity have already attained to their felicity in God [1]—as intercessors with God; and they believe that even the pictures and the relics of these saints should be reverenced. The more this part of the Roman dogmatics has been contested,[2] the more necessary does it become to let the symbols themselves speak which declare the Church's doctrine; so that we may separate what is merely the superstition of the crowd from the dogma which the Church itself holds and decrees.

---

[1] Bellarmini *de Beatitud. sanct.* cap. 1 : The spirits of pious men, who are released from the body and need no purgation, but are already admitted to the fruition of blessedness which consists in the clear vision of God. The Tridentine expression says the same thing : *una cum Christo regnantes.*

[2] The Romanists are themselves partly responsible for this : for, to *intercedere precibus* is added by the *canon missæ* and Bellarmin (i. 17) the word *meritis*, which, however easily explicable on the principles of the Romish doctrine, must needs suggest to Protestants the idea that independent merits are meant which are co-ordinate with the merits of Christ. See *Apol. Aug. Conf.* p. 227 ; Chemnitz, *Exam. Conc. Trid.* iii. 4. 2. The remarks of Bellarmine, *de Imag. Sanct.* ii. 21, are very objectionable to the Protestant mind.

I. INVOCATION OF SAINTS.

SYMBOLICAL TESTIMONIES.

I. ROMAN.

Conc. Trid. sess. 25, *Decr. d. invocat. sanctor:* (Doceant episcopi), sanctos una cum Christo regnantes orationes suas pro hominibus deo offerre (cf. Trid. sess. 22, cap. 3), bonum atque utile esse, suppliciter eos invocare et ob beneficia impetranda a deo per filium ejus Jesum Christum, qui solus noster redemtor et salvator est, ad eorum orationes, opem, auxiliumque confugere; illos vero, qui negant, sanctos æternâ felicitate in cœlo fruentes invocandos esse, aut qui asserunt, vel illos pro hominibus non orare, vel eorum, ut pro nobis etiam singulis orent, invocationem esse idololatriam, vel pugnare cum verbo dei adversarique honori unius mediatoris dei et hominum Jesu Christi, vel stultum esse, in cœlo regnantibus voce vel mente supplicare, impie sentire.

Cat. Rom. iii. 2. 10 : Invocandi sunt (angeli), quod et perpetuo deum intuentur et patrocinium salutis nostræ sibi delatum libentissime suscipiunt. Exstant divinæ scripturæ testimonia hujus invocationis.

Ib. iv. 5. 8 : Jure ecclesia gratiarum actioni preces etiam et implorationem sanctissimæ dei matris adjunxit; qua pie atque suppliciter ad eam confugeremus, ut nobis peccatoribus suâ intercessione conciliaret deum, bonaque tum ad hanc tum ad æternam vitam necessaria impetraret. Ergo nos . . . assidue misericordiæ matrem ac fidelis populi advocatam invocare debemus, ut oret pro nobis peccatoribus, ab eâque hac prece opem et auxilium implorare, cujus et præstantissima merita apud deum esse et summam voluntatem juvandi humanum genus, nemo nisi impie et nefarie dubitare potest.

Ib. iii. 2. 8 : Docendum est, venerationem et invocationem sanctorum angelorum ac beatarum animarum, quæ cœlesti gloriâ perfruuntur, . . . huic legi (de uno deo colendo) non repugnare. Quis enim adeo demens est, qui edicente rege, ne se pro rege quisquam gerat aut regio cultu atque honore affici patiatur, continuo putet nolle regem, suis ut magistratibus

honos deferatur? Etsi enim angelos christiani adorare dicuntur exemplo sanctorum veteris testamenti, non eam tamen illis venerationem adhibent, quam deo tribuunt. Quodsi legimus interdum angelos recusasse, ne se homines venerarentur, eo fecisse intelligendum est, quod sibi eum honorem haberi nolebant, qui soli deo deberetur.
Cf. *Conf. A. C.* p. 89 seq.; Eck, *Loci,* cap. 14; Bellarm. *de Ecc. triumph.* lib. i.; Becan. *Man. controv.* i. 7; Bossuet, *Ex. Doct. Cath.* c. 4; Sailer, *Ecc. Cath. de cult. sanct.*

[Pius IX., in his Encyclical of 2d February 1849: Optime enim nostis, venerabiles fratres, *omnem fiduciæ nostræ rationem in sanctissima virgine esse collocatam;* quandoquidem Deus totius boni plenitudinem posuit in Maria, ut proinde, si quid spei in nobis est, si quid gratiæ, si quid salutis, ab eâ noverimus redundare, quia sic est voluntas ejus, qui totum nos habere voluit per Mariam.]

II. GREEK.

Conf. orthod. p. 77 : Ἔχουσι χρέος ὅλοι οἱ ὀρθόδοξοι, νὰ τὴν (Μαρίαν) δοξάζουσι πρεπούμενα καὶ νὰ τὴν εὐλαβοῦνται, ὡς μητέρα τοῦ κυρίου ἡμῶν Ἰησοῦ Χριστοῦ ἢ μᾶλλον εἰπεῖν, ὡς θεοτόκον.

Ib. p. 317: Ἐπικαλούμεθα τὴν μεσιτείαν τῶν ἁγίων πρὸς τὸν θεόν, διὰ νὰ παρακαλοῦσι δι' ἡμᾶς· καὶ ἐπικαλούμεθα αὐτούς, ὄχι ὡς θεοὺς τινας, ἀλλ' ὡς φίλους αὐτοῦ· τοῦ ὁποίου δουλεύουσι καὶ τὸν ὁποῖον δοξολογοῦσι καὶ λατρεύουσι· καὶ χρειαζόμεθα τὴν βοήθειάν τους, ὄχι ὡς ἂν νά μας ἐβοηθοῦσαν ἐκεῖνοι ἀπὸ τὴν ἐδικήν τους δύναμιν· μὰ διατὶ ζητοῦσιν εἰς ἡμᾶς τὴν χάριν τοῦ θεοῦ μὲ ταῖς πρεσβείαις τους.

Ib. p. 321: Ἀκόμι τοὺς ἀγγέλους ἐπικαλούμεθα νὰ μεσιτεύουσι μὲ ταῖς προστασίαις τοὺς ὑπὲρ ἡμῶν πρὸς τὸν θεόν· διατὶ ἐκεῖνοι προσφέρουσιν εἰς τὴν τοῦ θεοῦ μεγαλειότητα τὰς προσευχὰς καὶ ἐλεημοσύνας καὶ πάντα τὰ καλὰ ἔργα τῶν ἀνθρώπων· οἱ δὲ ἅγιοι μετὰ θάνατον εἶναι ὥσπερ ἄγγελοι, καὶ ἠμποροῦσι τότε νὰ ἠξεύρουσι ταῖς χρείαις μας, καὶ νὰ ὑπακούουσι ταῖς προσευχαῖς μας· καὶ νὰ μεσιτεύουσιν ὑπὲρ ἡμῶν. ἀπὸ τὸ ὁποῖον γίνεται φανερόν, πῶς ἡμεῖς δὲν ἐναντιούμεθα εἰς τὴν ἐντολὴν τοῦ θεοῦ, μὲ τὸ νὰ παρακαλοῦμεν τοὺς ἁγίους· οἱ ὁποῖοι ἅγιοι ὡς πιστοὶ δούλοι παρεστώτες εις την του θεού μεγαλοπρέπειαν, μεσιτεύουσι δι' ημάς προς τον μόνον αληθινον θεόν· μάλιστα αν καταφρονήσωμεν την μεσιτείαν των αγίων παροξύνομεν τα μέγιστα την θείαν μεγαλειότητα, δεν τιμώντες τους ειλικρινώς δουλεύσαντας αυτή.

Metroph. Critop. *Conf.* cap. 17, p. 132: *Δεῖ καὶ τοῖς ἁγίοις τρόπον τινὰ εἶναι τῆς τῶν πόρρω γνώσεως*. . . . "Εστιν οὖν αὐτοῖς τρόπος οὔθ' ἱστορίαι, οὔτ' ἐπιστολαί, ἀλλ' ἡ ἀποκάλυψις τοῦ παναγίου πνεύματος τοῦ . . . πάντα εἰδότος καὶ τούτων ὅσα βούλεται τοῖς πιστοῖς τῶν δούλων ἀποκαλύπτοντος, κἀκείνους εἰς ἔντευξιν ὑπὲρ τῶν δεομένων ἐγείροντος, καὶ τὰς τοιαύτας ἐντεύξεις καὶ ἀποδεχομένου καὶ πληροῦντος. Τοῦτο οὖν εἰδοῦσα ἡ τοῦ Χριστοῦ ἐκκλησία καὶ πάλαι τούτους (ἁγίους) ἐπεκαλεῖτο καὶ μέχρι σήμερον τοῦτο ποιεῖ. Οὐδὲν ἕτερον παρὰ τούτων αἰτοῦσα, ἢ τὸ πρεσβεύειν τὸν πάντα δυνάμενον θεὸν ὑπὲρ ἡμῶν, πολλαῖς θλίψεσι καὶ ἀνωμαλίαις τοῦ βίου περικυκλουμένων ὁσημέραι, ἵν' ὑπομονὴν ἐν ταῖς θλίψεσι δῷ ὁ οἰκτίρμων θεὸς καὶ τὴν ἀπὸ τούτων ἀπαλλαγὴν ἐν τάχει. Οὐ γὰρ λέγομεν πρός τινα τῶν ἁγίων, ἅγιε σῶσον, ἢ λύτρωσαι, ἢ προνοοῦ μοι ἀγαθά, ή τι τοιοῦτον, οὐδαμῶς. (ταῦτα γὰρ μόνῳ τῷ θεῷ δυνατὰ, καὶ οὐδενὶ ἄλλῳ.) ἀλλὰ λέγομεν ἅγιε Ο. Δ. πρέσβευε ὑπὲρ ἡμῶν. Ἔτι οὐ λέγομεν τοὺς ἁγίους μεσίτας· εἷς γάρ ἐστι μεσίτης θεοῦ καὶ ἀνθρώπων, ἄνθρωπος Ἰησοῦς Χριστὸς, ὃς μόνος ἀμέσως δύναται τῷτε πατρὶ καὶ ἡμῖν μεσιτεύειν*. — P. 133: *Οὐ μεσίτας τοίνυν τοὺς ἤδη μεταστάντας ἁγίους καλοῦμεν, ἀλλὰ πρέσβεις καὶ ἱκέτας πρὸς τὸν θεὸν ὑπὲρ ἡμῶν ἀδελφῶν ἐκείνων ὄντων. Οἱ πρεσβεύοντες οὐ τοῖς αὐτοῖς ῥήμασιν οἷς καὶ ὁ υἱὸς μεσιτεύων κέχρηνται, ἀλλ' ἄλλοις πολὺ διαφέρουσι τοῖς ἐκείνου, καὶ μεγίστην τὴν αὐτῶν πρὸς τὸν θεὸν ταπεινότητα καὶ δουλείαν ἐμφαίνουσιν*. Cf. Dosithei *Confess*. c. 8.

Ibid. p. 135: *ἡ καθολικὴ ἐκκλησία πλὴν τοῦ πρεσβεύειν τὸν θεὸν ὑπὲρ ἡμῶν καὶ πάντα τἀναγκαῖα ἡμῖν παρ' ἐκείνου αἰτεῖν, οὐδενὸς ἄλλου δεῖται παρά του τῶν ἁγίων, οὐδὲ παρ' αὐτῆς τῆς ἁγίας θεοτόκου· ἣν ὡς μὲν πάντων τῶν ἁγίων ὑπερέχουσαν καὶ πολλῷ πλείονα ἐκείνων παρρησίαν πρὸς τὸν υἱὸν ἔχουσαν, πρώτην τῶν ἄλλων ἐπικαλούμεθα εἰς πρεσβείαν, ὡς δὲ τῇ ἑαυτῆς δυνάμει μηδὲν δυναμένην ποιῆσαι πλὴν τοῦ πρεσβεύειν, καὶ ἡμεῖς οὐδενὸς ἄλλου παρὰ ταύτης δεόμεθα πλὴν τοῦ πρεσβεύειν καὶ ἱκετεύειν τὸν αὐτῆς υἱὸν καὶ θεὸν ὑπὲρ ἡμῶν*.

However, the character of μεσίται is assigned to the saints, *Acta Wirt.* p. 128. Plato, in his *Catech.* S. 159, warns against the abuse of the veneration offered to saints.

Observations.

The foregoing testimonies establish the following propositions: 1. The Roman and Greek Churches make a clear distinction between the worship of God (and Christ) and that of the saints. God is prayed to as the independent Author and Giver of all good; the saints are invoked as the mediators of the divine benevolences, that is, by means of their prayer, addressed to God in the name of Christ:[1] cf. the passage cited above, *Cat. Rom.* iv. 6. 3. The merit of Christ is declared not to be hereby invaded,[2] inasmuch as the impartation of benefits is not connected with any specific merit of the saints, which before and independently of Christ availed with God, but merely with their intercession, which itself is based on Christ's merit, and is offered in His name. It is not, indeed, of much moment here that the word *invocare* is used, and not *adorare*; for in the Romish ecclesiastical language the *adorare* is, like *preces*, just as seldom used as concerning God: cf. *Cat. Rom.* iii. 2. 4, Sancti viri . . . reges adorabant; and Bellarm. *de Ecc. triumph.* ii. 21. 2. The Tridentine Council commands the *invocatio sanctorum*, not as a religious duty, but as good and wholesome. The Protestant, however, cannot anywhere find the biblical ground of such *invocatio*; and, when any intercession with God is in question, will be content with that of Christ, lamenting meanwhile that the Roman Catholic Church, or the Roman Catholic clergy, have not more earnestly sought to obviate the easily possible and actual superstition and abuse of this doctrine.

The *canonized* saints receive from the Romish Church *public* veneration: festivals are held in their honour, masses are read, churches are built. The non-canonized it is permitted only in secret to honour: cf. Bellarm. *l.c.* cap. 10. Canonization is, according to Bellarmine, cap. 7, " nothing more than the public testimony of the Church concerning the true sanctity and glory of any man now dead; at the same time it is the judgment and opinion by which are decreed the honours due to those who reign in blessedness with God, which are generally held to be seven." The right of canonization the Pope alone now holds. As to this canonization in the Eastern Church, see Heineccius, iii. S. 50.

[1] The distinction is well known between λατρεία and δουλεία. Eck. *Loc.* c. 14: licet sancti non sint adorandi latriâ, quia soli deo debetur, tamen venerandi sunt duliâ. Cf. Bellarmin. *l.c.* cap. 12.

[2] According to Möhler, the invocation of saints is itself an honour to Christ.

III. PROTESTANT (INCLUDING ARMINIAN AND SOCINIAN).

C. A. art. 21 : De cultu sanctorum docent, quod memoria sanctorum proponi potest, ut imitemur fidem eorum et bona opera juxta vocationem.—Sed scriptura non docet invocare sanctos, seu petere auxilium a sanctis, quia unum Christum nobis proponit mediatorem, propitiatorium, pontificem et intercessorem. Hic invocandus est et promisit se exauditurum esse preces nostras, et hunc cultum maxime probat.

Apol. C. A. p. 223 : Confessio nostra probat honores sanctorum. . . . Præterea et hoc largimur, quod angeli orent pro nobis. Exstat enim testimonium Zachariæ (i. 12), ubi angelus orat : Domine exercituum, usque quo tu non miserebaris Jerusalem cet. De sanctis etsi concedimus, quod sicut vivi orant pro ecclesiâ universâ in genere, ita in cœlis orent pro ecclesiâ in genere, tametsi testimonium nullum de mortuis orantibus exstat in scripturis, præter illud somnium sumtum ex libro Machabeorum posteriore. Porro ut maxime pro ecclesiâ orent sancti, tamen non sequitur, *quod sint invocandi*. Quanquam confessio nostra hoc tantum affirmat, quod scriptura non doceat sanctorum invocationem, seu petere a sanctis auxilium. Cum autem neque præceptum, neque promissio, neque exemplum ex scripturis de invocandis sanctis afferri possit, sequitur, conscientiam nihil posse certi de illa invocatione habere. Cf. *Conf. Wirtemberg*, p. 122 sq. ; and *Conf. Bohem.* art. 17.

A. Sm. p. 310 : Invocatio sanctorum est etiam pars abusuum et errorum antichristi, pugnans cum primo principali articulo et delens agnitionem Christi. Non etiam est mandata, nec consilio, nec exemplo, nec testimonio scripturæ nititur. Omnia in Christo melius et certius nobis sunt proposita, ut non egeamus invocatione sanctorum, etiamsi res pretiosa esset, cum tamen sit res maxime perniciosa.

Cat. Racov. p. 173 : An quisquam præter Chr. colendus sit, doce. Nullo prorsus modo. Nec enim ullum exstat divinum testimonium, ex quo cuiquam . . . hunc honorem a deo datum esse appareat. Quod vero hodie in rom. ecclesiâ virgini Mariæ et sanctis defertur, id totum in ipsorum opinione fundatum est. Cf. Ostorodt, *Unterricht*. c. 42, S. 424.

Conf. Helv. ii. cap. 5 : Divos nec contemnimus, nec vulgariter de eis sentimus. Agnoscimus enim eos esse viva Christi membra, amicos dei, qui carnem et mundum gloriose vicerunt. Diligimus ergo illos ut fratres, et honoramus etiam, non tamen cultu aliquo, sed honorabili de eis existimatione, denique laudibus justis. Imitamur item eos. Nam imitatores fidei virtutumque ipsorum, consortes item æternæ salutis esse, illis æternum apud deum cohabitare, et cum eis in Christo exsultare desideriis votisque ardentissimis exoptamus. . . . Honorandi ergo sunt propter imitationem, non adorandi propter religionem cet.

Conf. Gall. art. 24 : (Credimus) quidquid homines de mortuorum sanctorum intercessione commenti sunt, nihil aliud esse, quam fraudem et fallacias satanæ.

Conf. Belg. art. 26 : Hic mediator, quem pater inter se et nos constituit, suâ majestate haudquaquam nos terrere debet, ut ad alium, arbitrio nostro quærendum, ideo impellat. Nemo enim neque in cœlo, neque in terrâ inter creaturas est, qui nos impensius amet, quam Christus. . . . Sola igitur diffidentia morem hunc induxit, ut sanctos ignominia honoris loco afficiant, dum id agunt, quod illi nunquam fecerunt, nec sibi deferri postularunt, sed constanter et pro officio suo rejecerunt, sicut ex scriptis eorum patet. Neque hic nostra indignitas prætexenda est. . . . Sciebat enim probe deus, cum hunc nobis daret, peccatores nos esse.

Against the cultus of Mary is specially decisive *Declar. Thorun.* ii. 2, 3.

Conf. Remonstr. xvi. 3 : Præter hunc unicum mediatorem (Christum) alios ullos vel angelos vel homines sive vivos sive mortuos religiose colere i. e. plus quam civiliter adorare vel invocare, tanquam scilicet patronos et advocatos nostros ap. deum, aut templa, altaria, festa iis consecrare . . . prorsus illicitum deoque ingratum esse statuimus. . . . Memoriam tamen (sanctorum) sancte colendam et virtutes cum præconio digne celebrandas et ad imitationem . . . proponendas esse jure censemus. (Cf. Limborch, *Theol. christ.* v. 19 ; Sim. Episcop. *disput.* 15, in s. *Opp.* ii. ii. 207 sqq.)

II. VENERATION OF PICTURES AND RELICS.

SYMBOLICAL TESTIMONIES.

I. ROMAN.

Conc. Trid. sess. 25, *Decr. de invoc. sanctor.*: (Doceant episcopi) sanctorum quoque martyrum et aliorum cum Christo viventium sancta corpora, quæ viva membra fuerunt Christi et templum Spiritus sancti, ab ipso ad æternam vitam suscitanda et glorificanda, a fidelibus veneranda esse, per quæ multa beneficia a deo hominibus præstantur; ita ut affirmantes, sanctorum reliquiis venerationem atque honorem non deberi vel eas aliaque sacra monumenta a fidelibus inutiliter honorari atque eorum opus impetrandæ causa sanctorum memorias frustra frequentari, omninq damnandos esse, prout jam pridem eos damnavit et nunc etiam damnat ecclesia. Imagines porro Christi, deiparæ virginis et aliorum sanctorum in templis præsertim habendas et retinendas eisque debitum honorem et venerationem impertiendam, non quod credatur inesse aliqua in iis divinitas vel virtus, propter quam sint colendæ, vel quod ab eis sit aliquid petendum, vel quod fiducia in imaginibus sit figenda, veluti olim fiebat a gentibus, quæ in idolis spem suam collocabant: sed quoniam honos, qui eis exhibetur, refertur ad prototypa, quæ illæ repræsentant: ita ut per imagines, quas osculamur et coram quibus caput aperimus et procumbimus, Christum adoremus et sanctos, quorum illæ similitudinem gerunt, veneremur. Id quod conciliorum, præsertim vero secundæ Nicænæ synodi decretis contra imaginum oppugnatores est sancitum.

Cat. Rom. iii. 2. 23: Cum Christus ejusque sanctissima et purissima mater ceterique omnes sancti humanâ præditi naturâ humanam speciem gesserint, eorum imagines pingi atque honorari non modo interdictum non fuit, sed etiam sanctum, et grati animi certissimum argumentum semper habitum est.— 24: Non solum in ecclesiâ imagines habere et illis honorem et cultum adhibere ostendet parochus, cum honos, qui illis exhibetur, referatur ad prototypa, verum etiam maximo fidelium bono factum declarabit cet.

Ib. iii. 2. 8 : Docendum est (venerationem sanctorum angelorum ac beatarum animarum, quæ cœlesti gloria perfruuntur) aut etiam corporum ipsorum sanctorumque cinerum cultum, quem semper cath. ecclesia adhibuit, huic legi (de colendo uno deo) non repugnare. . . . iii. 2. 15 : Cui fidem non faciant et honoris, qui sanctis debetur, et patrocinii, quod nostri causâ suscipiunt, mirabiles effectæ res ad eorum sepulcra, et oculis et manibus membrisque omnibus captis in pristinum statum restitutis, mortuis ad vitam revocatis, ex corporibus hominum ejectis dæmoniis? . . . Quid plura? si vestes, sudaria, si umbra sanctorum, priusquam e vitâ migrarent, depulit morbos viresque restituit, quis tandem negare audeat, deum per sacros cineres, ossa ceterasque sanctorum reliquias eadem mirabiliter efficere?

Cf. Eck, *loci*, c. 15 ; Bossuet, *expos.* c. 5 ; Bellarmin. *de eccles. triumph.* lib. ii. ; Klee, *Dogmat.* iii. 407 ff.

II. Greek.

Conf. orthod. p. 328 : Ἡμεῖς ὅταν τιμῶμεν τὰς εἰκόνας καὶ τὰς προσκυνοῦμεν, δὲν προσκυνοῦμεν τὰ χρώματα ἢ τὰ ξύλα· μὰ τοὺς ἁγίους ἐκείνους, τῶν ὁποίων εἶναι αἱ εἰκόνες, δοξάζομεν μὲ προσκύνησιν δουλείας, βάλλοντας μὲ τὸν νοῦν μας τὴν ἐκείνων παρουσίαν εἰς τὰ ὀμμάτιά μας.

Metroph. Critopul. Conf. p. 125 : Ταῖς ἁγίαις εἰκόσι καὶ τιμὴν τὴν προσήκουσαν ἀπένειμεν, οὐ λατρευτικὴν ἢ δουλικήν, ἄπαγε· αὗται γὰρ θεῷ μόνῳ προσήκουσιν· ἀλλὰ σχετικὴν καὶ φιλικήν· ἀναφέρουσα μέν τοι καὶ ταύτην ἐπὶ τὰ ἐκείνων πρωτότυπα· ὥς φησιν ὁ ἐν ἁγίοις Βασίλειος ὁ μέγας. Ἡ τιμὴ τῆς εἰκόνος ἐπὶ τὸ πρωτότυπον διαβαίνει.

Ibid. p. 128 : Τὴν αὐτὴν διὰ τιμὴν ἀπονέμει ἡ ἐκκλησία καὶ τοῖς ἁγίοις λειψάνοις, εἰ μόνον ἀληθῆ καὶ ἀνόθευτα εἴη, πολλαὶ γὰρ πανουργίαι καὶ καπηλίαι ἐπενοήθησαν περὶ ταῦτα. ὡς συμβαίνειν τὸν αὐτὸν ἅγιον, οὗ τὰ λείψανα ὀνομάζουσι, τρικέφαλον καὶ τετρακέφαλον εἶναι, τοσαυτόχειρά τε καὶ τοσαυτόποδα. πολλαχοῦ γὰρ δεικνύουσι τὰ αὐτὰ μέλη τοῦ αὐτοῦ ἁγίου. ὅπερ ὡς ἄτοπον καὶ καπηλευτικὸν ἡ ἐκκλησία μισεῖ καὶ ἀποτρέπεται.

Cf. *Synod. Hierosol.* in Harduin, *Concil.* xi. p. 257 sqq.;

Jerem. in *Act. Wirtcmb.* p. 369; Plato, *Catech.* S. 164 f.; Heinecc. *Abbild.* ii. 82 ff.

Observations.

In respect to the pictures of the saints, the Eastern Church differs from the Western in this, that it tolerates no sculptured or hewn images, only painted ones. *Metroph. Critop.* cap. xv. p. 125: τούτων [τῶν ἁγίων] εἰκόνας ἡ ἐκκλησία ἔχει οὐ γλυπτὰς οὐδὲ λαξευτὰς ἀλλὰ γραπτὰς μόνον.

III. PROTESTANT.

Apol. C. A. p. 229 : Ab invocatione (sanctorum) ad imagines ventum est, hæ quoque colebantur et putabatur eis inesse quædam vis, sicut magi vim inesse fingunt imaginibus signorum cœlestium certo tempore sculptis. . . .

Art. Sm. p. 310 : Reliquiæ sanctorum refertæ multis mendaciis, ineptiis et fatuitatibus. Canum et equorum ossa ibi sæpe reperta sunt. Et licet aliquid forte laudandum fuisset, tamen propter imposturas istas, quæ diabolo risum excitarunt, jam dudum damnari debuissent, cum præsertim careant verbo dei et non necessariæ et inutiles sint. Estque hoc omnium teterrimum, quod . . . loco cultus dei et boni operis, sicut missam reliquias venerati sunt.

Conf. Helv. ii. cap. 4 : Quando beati spiritus ac divi cœlites, dum hic viverent, omnem cultum sui averterunt et statuas oppugnarunt, cui verisimile videatur divis cœlitibus et angelis suas placere imagines, ad quas genua flectunt homines, detegunt capita, aliisque prosequuntur honoribus ?

Ibid. c. 5 : Multo minus credimus reliquias divorum adorandas esse aut colendas. Veteres isti sancti satis honorasse videbantur mortuos suos, si honeste mandassent terræ reliquias, postquam astra petiisset spiritus : ac omnium nobilissimas reliquias majorum æstimabant esse virtutes, doctrinam et fidem, quas ut commendabant cum laude mortuorum, ita eas exprimere annitebantur, dum vivebant in terris.

Cf. against veneration of pictures generally, *Cat. Rac.* qu. 252; and against the Romish cultus of pictures and relics, Curcellæi *Institt.* vii. 9. 14.

IV.

ORIGINAL STATE OF MAN: THE IMAGE OF GOD.

POINT OF DIVERGENCE.

It is admitted on all sides that primitive mankind, or the first pair, before the Fall and in a state of innocence, were both in body and soul more perfect than all men have been since the Fall.[1] Only in the definition of the compass of this primitive perfection, and its relation to human nature, the Christian standards differ; although these differences are rather indicated than expanded in the symbols. Some attribute to the original man only unimpaired faculties of knowledge and will, sinlessness but not virtue, as also freedom from bodily death. Among these are Socinians and Arminians. Others ascribe to him an habitual wisdom and holiness, with immortality of the body: these are the Romanists, Greeks, and Protestants. The latter section are divided: the Protestants regard these advantages as natural and increated in man; the Romanists regard them divine gifts of grace, which were superadded to the natural endowments of men, reason and free-will. The Socinians once more unite with the Arminians in regarding immunity from bodily death as something imputed by God to our first parents as their destiny, consequently not as resulting from the nature of man.

---

[1] The Protoplasts had, that is, those qualities, not for themselves alone, but as heads and representatives of the race; consequently that they might transmit them by generation to all men, which would indeed have been the case if the Fall had not intervened. Comp. among others, the *Conf. Gall.* 10.

SYMBOLICAL TESTIMONIES.

I. ROMAN.

Conc. Trid. sess. 5 : Si quis non confitetur, primum hominem . . . sanctitatem et justitiam, in qua constitutus fuerat,[1] amisisse incurrisseque . . . mortem, quam antea illi comminatus fuerat deus, . . . anath. sit.

Cat. Rom. i. 2. 19 : Postremo deus ex limo terræ hominem sic corpore effectum et constitutum effinxit, ut non quidem naturæ ipsius vi, sed divino beneficio immortalis esset et impassibilis. Quod autem ad animan pertinet, eum ad imaginem et similitudinem suam formavit liberumque ei arbitrium tribuit, omnes præterea motus animi atque appetitiones ita in eo temperavit, ut rationis imperio nunquam non parerent. Tum originalis justitiæ admirabile donum addidit, ac deinde cæteris animantibus præesse voluit.

(Bellarmini *Gratia primi hom.* 2 : Integritas illa, cum qua primus homo conditus fuit et sine qua post ejus lapsum homines omnes nascuntur, non fuit naturalis ejus conditio, sed supernaturalis evectio.—*Ib.* 5 : Sciendum est primo, hominem naturaliter constare ex carne et spiritu, et ideo partim cum bestiis partim cum angelis communicare naturam ; et quidem ratione carnis et communionis cum bestiis habere propensionem quandam ad bonum corporale et sensibile, in quod fertur per sensum et appetitum ; ratione spiritus et communionis cum angelis habere propensionem ad bonum spirituale et intelligibile, in quod fertur per intelligentiam et voluntatem. Ex his autem diversis vel contrariis propensionibus existere in uno eodemque homine pugnam quandam, et ex eâ pugnâ ingentem bene agendi difficultatem, dum una propensio alteram impedit. — Sciendum secundo, divinam providentiam initio creationis, ut remedium adhiberet huic morbo seu languori naturæ humanæ, qui ex conditione materiæ oriebatur, addidisse

---

[1] As to the choice of this word, see Nitzsch in the *Stud.* 1834, S. 31. Even rigorous theologians of the Roman Church say positively : Primos homines *creatos* esse *cum* or *in* justitiâ orig. (Bellarmini *Grat. hom. primi*, c. 5). The distinguishing point lies rather in the *supernaturale ;* for, as Bellarmine says, "gratiam gratum facientem (justit. orig.) *in creatione* accepit homo."

homini donum quoddam insigne, justitiam videlicet originalem, qua veluti aureo quodam fræno pars inferior parti superiori et pars superior deo facile subjecta contineretur; sic autem subjectam fuisse carnem spiritui, ut non posset ipso invito moveri, neque ei rebellis fieri, nisi ipse fieret rebellis deo, in potestate tamen spiritus fuisse, rebellem deo fieri, et non fieri.—Nos existimamus, rectitudinem illam etiam partis inferioris fuisse donum supernaturale, et quidem per se, non per accidens, ita ut neque ex naturæ principiis fluxerit, neque potuerit fluere. Et quia donum illud supernaturale erat, ut statim probaturi sumus, eo remoto, natura humana sibi relicta pugnam illam experiri coepit partis inferioris cum superiore, quæ naturalis futura erat, id est ex conditione materiæ secutura, nisi deus justitiæ donum homini addidisset.)

Cf. Möhler, *Symbol.* § 1, and *Neue Untersuch.* S. 60 ff.; Klee, *kathol. Dogmat.* ii. 318 f.

II. GREEK.

Conf. orthod. p. 50 : Ἡ κατάστασις τῆς ἀκακίας καὶ ἀθωότητος εἶναι ἡ ἄγνοια καὶ ἡ ἀπειρία τοῦ κακοῦ, ἤγουν ὅταν δὲν γνωρίζῃ οὔτε ἐδοκίμασε καθόλου τὸ κακόν, ἢ διὰ τὴν ἡλικίαν τοῦ ἢ δι' ἄλλαις αἰτίαις. Καὶ κατὰ τοῦτον τὸν τρόπον ἦτον εἰς τὸν Ἀδὰμ ἡ ἀθωότης καὶ ἡ ἀκακία, πρὶν ἁμάρτῃ, κατὰ πᾶσαν τελειότητα καὶ δικαιοσύνην ἔμφυτον, τόσον ἀπὸ τὸ μέρος τῆς διανοίας, ὅσον καὶ ἀπὸ τὸ μέρος τῆς θελήσεως, εἰς τὴν διάνοιαν περικλείεται πᾶσα ἐπιστήμη· καὶ εἰς τὴν θέλησιν πᾶσα χρηστότης καὶ καλοσύνη. Διατὶ γνωρίζωντας ὁ Ἀδὰμ τὸν θεὸν καλώτατα (καθ' ὅσον εἰς τὸν καιρὸν ἐκεῖνον τοῦ ἦτον συγκεχωρημένον, καὶ καθ' ὅσον ἔπρεπε) μὲ τοῦτο ὁποῦ ἐγνώριζε τὸν θεόν, ἐγνώριζεν ὅλα τὰ πράγματα μετ' ἐκεῖνον. . . . P. 51 : Περὶ δὲ τῆς θελήσεως, αὕτη πάντοτε ὑποτάσσετο εἰς τὸν λόγον. καλὰ καὶ πάντοτε νὰ ἦτον ἐλεύθερα, καὶ ἦτον ἐξουσία εἰς τὸν ἄνθρωπον νὰ ἁμάρτῃ ἢ νὰ μὴν ἁμάρτῃ.

Metroph. Critop. indicates a distinction between natural and supernatural elements in the first man. *Conf.* c. 3, p. 51 : The Protoplasts, having lost all their divine and spiritual gifts, remained devoid of these, only the natural light being left. Cf. cap. 8, p. 88, and Dositheus, c. 14.

III. LUTHERAN.

Apol. C. A. p. 53 sq.: Justitia originalis habitura erat non solum aequale temperamentum qualitatum corporis, sed etiam haec dona, notitiam dei certiorem, timorem dei, fiduciam dei, aut certe rectitudinem et vim ista efficiendi.[1] Idque testatur scriptura, cum inquit, hominem ad imaginem et similitudinem dei conditum esse (Gen. i. 27). Quod quid est aliud, nisi in homine hanc sapientiam et justitiam effigiatam esse, quae deum apprehenderet et in quâ reluceret deus, hoc est, homini dona esse data notitiam dei, timorem dei, fiduciam erga deum et similia? (Cf. p. 52: Propriis viribus posse diligere deum super omnia, facere praecepta dei, quid aliud est quam habere justitiam originis?)

(*Conf. Sax.* ii. p. 53, more precise as to the inborn character: Justitia originalis non tantum fuit acceptatio generis. hum. coram deo, sed etiam in ipsâ naturâ hominum lux in mente, quia firmiter assentiri verbo dei poterat, et conversio voluntatis ad deum et obedientia cordis congruens cum judicio legis dei, quae menti insita erat.)

F. C. p. 640: (Peccatum orig.) est privatio concreatae in paradiso justitiae originalis s. imaginis dei, ad quam homo initio in veritate, sanctitate atque justitiâ creatus fuerat.

IV. REFORMED.

Conf. Helv. ii. 8: Fuit homo ab initio a deo conditus ad imaginem dei, in justitiâ et sanctitate veritatis, bonus et rectus. Sed instinctu serpentis et suâ culpâ a bonitate et rectitudine deficiens, peccato, morti variisque calamitatibus factus est obnoxius.

Conf. Belg. art. 14: Credimus, deum ex terrae pulvere hominem creasse et ad suam imaginem et similitudinem fecisse atque efformasse, bonum nempe, justum et sanctum, qui suo sese arbitrio ad divinam voluntatem per omnia componere posset.

---

[1] That Melanchthon meant, not a mere capacity or ability, but a power which confers that to which it is directed, an active *habitus*, is clear from his definitions elsewhere. The bias of the first man to goodness, well-pleasing to God, was so strong and decisive, that he in fact did only what was good. Cf. *Apol.* p. 51. This was the perfection of human nature, as it proceeded from the hands of the Creator: Nitzsch in *Stud.* 1834, 37. On *rectitudo*, see Nitzsch, *id.*

Conf. Scot. art. 2 : Confitemur, deum creasse hominem, videlicet ... Adamum, in imaginem et similitudinem suam, cui sapientiam, dominium, justitiam, liberum arbitrium et claram sui ipsius notitiam dedit, adeo ut in totâ hominis naturâ nulla potuerit notari imperfectio.

Canon. Dordrac. iii. 1 : Homo ab initio ad imaginem dei conditus verâ et salutari sui creatoris et rerum spiritualium notitiâ in mente, et justitiâ in voluntate et corde, puritate in omnibus affectibus, exornatus adeoque totus sanctus fuit.

Cf. *Cat. Heidelb.* 6 ; *Form. Cons. Helv.* 7. [*West. Conf.* ch. iv. sect. 2.]

V. MENNONITES.

The Mennonites also, at least in the *Conf.* which is now to be quoted, appear to distinguish between natural and non-natural endowments in the first man, terming the latter *imago Dei.* The *Conf.* of Ris does not go beyond general expressions.

Conf. Fris. et Germ.: Hominem fecit deus, quem prorsus condecoravit sapientiâ, ingenio et intellectu super creaturas omnes cumque dominum omnium illarum constituit et praeterea secundum imaginem suam divinam in justitiâ et sanctimoniâ verâ ad immortalitatem creatum in paradiso posuit cet.

Observations.

1. The distinction between the natural and the supernatural in the original man is not expressed with as much clearness by the symbols as it is by the theologians, especially Bellarmine, in the passages quoted. The *Cat. Rom.*, however, leaves not much difficulty about the question. On the other hand, the Protestant symbols do not expressly declare that the *justitia originalis* was an integral and necessary element of man's primitive nature itself. Luther is very clear, on Gen. iii., that righteousness was not a certain gift which came from without, separate from the nature of man, but was natural, so that it was the nature of Adam to love God. Cf. Melanc. *Loc.* i. 85. Thus we are to interpret the *concreata* of *Form. Conc.* p. 640 ; and in the clause p. 645 : originale peccatum, quod *in hominis naturâ et essentiâ* habitat. Now, as the *peccatum originis*, total corruption, came into the place of the original righteousness (see below, v.); since, once more, the *liberum arbitrium* in spiritual things is denied to fallen human nature, that is, the right direction of the natural will, it follows that

the *justitia originalis* must be thought of as natural to man. *Immortality*, a *posse non mori*, the Protestant symbols do not reckon an element in the image of God; but this follows *per consequens* from what had been said about the punishment of Adam (*Conf. Aug.* 2; *Conf. Helv.* ii. 2; and *Conf. Belg.* 14), and that *æquale temperamentum qualitatis corporis* could hardly have any other result than immunity from physical death (Baier, *Theol. Pos.* p. 258).

VI. ARMINIAN.

Conf. Remonstr. v. 5 : (Primos homines) intellectu etiam puro animoque recto et liberâ voluntate aliisque affectibus integris ornavit deus, quin et necessariâ in isto statu sapientiâ, integritate gratiâque variâ sufficienter instruxit, non solum ut glorioso in cæteras creaturas imperio ac dominio recte uti scirent, sed ut dei etiam . . . erga se voluntatem imprimis recte intelligerent suamque propriam voluntatem deo . . . ultro subjicerent cet.

Apol. Conf. Rem. p. 60 b : Qualemcunque justitiam originalem Adamo et Evæ attribueris . . . eam volentibus ac lubentibus Remonstrantibus Adamo et Evæ attribueris, dummodo justitiam orig. ejusmodi qualitatem aut formam esse non dicas, quâ positâ impossibile fuerit peccare Adamum et quâ non positâ impossibile fuerit Adamum non peccare.—P. 42 a : Falsum est, corpus Adami immortale h.e. incorruptibile fuisse; corpus omne animale . . . corruptibile esse, ratio recta docet.

Limborch, *Theol. christ.* ii. 24. 5 : Justitiam originalem solent collocare in mentis lumine ac rectitudine, in voluntatis sanctitate et justitiâ, in sensuum et affectuum harmoniâ atque ad bonum promptitudine. Sane homines primos in primævo suo statu longe perfectioris fuisse conditionis, quam nos, cum in lucem edimur, evidentissimum est. Non enim mens ipsorum fuit tabulæ instar rasæ, omnique cognitione destitutæ, sed ipsi scientiâ actuali fuere præditi et necessariâ sapientiâ in statu illo a deo instructi ; aderat et capacitas ad scientiam ulteriorem acquirendum per ratiocinationem, experientiam et revelationem. Non tamen erant omniscii, aderat et ignorantia quorundam, nesciebant se nudos esse, vel potius, nuditatem esse indecoram ; ignorasse videntur, serpentem animal esse mutum, alias fraudem metuissent, aliaque similia. Quin et tanta non erat sapientia, quin in errorem seduci possent, quod in Evâ patuit. Voluntas eorum non fuit neutra, in bonum ac malum æque indifferens, sed antequam ei lex a deo posita erat, rectitudinem habuit naturalem, ut inordinate nec concupisceret nec posset. Ubi enim lex non est, ibi liberrimus voluntatis usus absque culpâ.—ii. 24. 10: Primum hominem, nisi peccasset, non fuisse moriturum, dubitandum non est, mors enim pœna peccati fuit. Inde vero non recte hominis immortalitas infertur. . . . Attamen mortalitatem istam, nisi homo peccasset, in perpetuum a moriendi actu immunem conservasset deus.

VII. SOCINIAN.

Cat. Racov. p. 18: Ab initio homo mortalis creatus fuit i. e. talis, qui non solum naturâ suâ mori potuerit sed etiam, si naturæ suæ relinqueretur, non potuerit non mori, licet divino beneficio semper in vitâ conservari posset. Cf. Socin. *Prælect.* c. 1, with the *Responsio ad defens;* F. Puccii in *Opp.* ii. 272 sqq.

Socin. *Prælect.* c. 3: Si justitiæ originalis nomine eam conditionem intelligunt, ut non posset (primus homo) peccare, eam certe non habuit Adamus, cum eum peccasse constet. Neque enim peccasset, nisi prius peccare potuisset. . . . Concludamus igitur, Adamum etiam antequam mandatum illud dei transgrederetur, revera justum non fuisse, cum nec impeccabilis esset nec ullam peccandi occasionem habuisset; vel certe justum eum fuisse affirmari non posse, cum nullo modo constet, eum ullâ ratione a peccato abstinuisse. Sed sunt, qui dicant, originalem primi hom. justitiam in eo fuisse, quod rationem appetitui ac sensibus dominantem haberet eosque regentem, nec ullum inter ipsam et illos dissidium esset. Verum nullâ ratione adducti hoc dicunt, cum potius ex eo, quod Adam deliquit, appareat appetitum ac sensus rationi dominatos fuisse nec bene inter hanc et illos antea convenisse.

Cat. Racov. q. 22 (final Revis.): Certum est, primum hominem ita a deo conditum fuisse, ut libero arbitrio præditus esset, nec vero ulla causa subest, cur deus post ejus lapsum illum eo privarit, ac neque æquitas ac justitia seu rectitudo dei permittit, ut hominem recta agendi voluntate ac facultate privet, præsertim cum post illud tempus nihilominus ut recta velit atque agat, ab eo sub comminatione pœnæ exigat; nec etiam inter pœnas, quibus Adæ peccatum punivit deus, ejusmodi pœnæ mentio exstat.

VIII. QUAKER.

The Quakers do not commit themselves to a definition of *justitia originalis*. Barclay, *Apol.* prop. ii. 4: Not to dive into the many curious notions which many have concerning the condition of Adam before the Fall, all agree in this, that thereby he came to a very great loss, not only in the things which relate to the outward man, but in regard to that true fellowship and communion he had with God.—We shall not attempt to fill up the blank in the doctrine of the Quakers by inferences drawn from their teaching as to the state of man *after* the Fall.

Observations.

2. The original perfections of the first man are classed together in the Protestant symbols as the *Imago Dei: Apol. C. A.* p. 54; *Conf. Helv.* xi. c. 8; *Gall.* 9; *Belg.* 14; *Scot.* 2; *Canon Dordr.* iii. 1. The *Cat. Rom.* refers this expression only to the freedom of the will.[1] The Arminians (*Conf. Rem.* v. 4; *Apol.* 60; Curcellæi *Instit.* iii. 8) and the Socinians (*Cat. Racov.* qu. 42, F. Socin. *passim*) apply it (following Gen. i. 26, Ps. viii. 7) to the dominion over the creatures. The Mennonites seem to include in it the holiness imparted to man, and his destination to immortal life (Schyn, *Plen. Ded.* p. 89). With the Greeks this expression has never gained any symbolical significance; it does not occur in the *Conf. orthod.* Metroph. Critop. gives a very strange explanation of the image of God; and in a form of prayer (Goar, *Euchol og.* p. 684) that image is, it would seem, referred to the external beauty of the body. The patriarch Jeremias, however (*Act. Wirt.* 366), distinguishes between εἰκών and ὁμοίωσις θεοῦ; he regards the former as something belonging to man naturally, the latter as the result of his moral endeavours. On the contrary, the *Conf. orthod.* declares that man in his state of innocence was ὅμοιος τοῖς ἀγγέλοις, like the angels (p. 52). As an idea disputed in theology, the image of God is treated by Karpinski, *Comp. theol.* p. 59 seq.

[1] The distinction between the *Imago Dei* and the *similitudo cum Deo* may be passed over, having no relation to Symbolism.

V.
RESULTS OF THE FALL: PRESENT STATE OF MAN.

I. FIRST POINT OF DIVERGENCE.

IT is agreed upon by all, that in the sin of Adam (Gen. iii.; cf. Rom. v. 12 seq.), *qui non sibi tantum, sed et nobis nocuit,*— who hurt not himself only, but also us,—the ultimate reason is to be found why all men naturally descended from him (*since the Fall*) are born without those prerogatives and advantages which the first human pair had before the Fall. But in the definition of the manner how, and of the degree in which, the sin of Adam wrought ruinously upon all men, the communions of Christendom differ. For the Roman and Greek Churches, in harmony with the positions laid down by them on the preceding subject (IV.), regard as the true and proper result of the first sin, as the divine punishment of Adam's transgression, only the loss of those gifts of the divine favour in the possession of which the first man stood, that is to say, of original holiness and immortality: both Churches, however, connecting strictly with this a certain enfeebling of the natural powers for good in consequence of this loss.[1] Protestants, on the other hand, deem that with the loss of *justitia originalis* there entered an entire depravation of human nature in spiritual

---

[1] The theologians call this *vulnera naturæ*, which must be regarded as the results, not the constituents, of the original sin: Bellarm. *Amiss. Grat.* v. 4. c. 9. He also says (*Grat. prim. hom.* c. 2): homo nunc *nascitur* pronus ad malum, infirmus, ignorans. But that this weakness does not belong to the corruptio *naturæ*, Bellarmine expressly declares, *De grat. prim. hom.* c. 5.

respects, so that the natural man is turned away from God, and inclined only to evil (*prava concupiscentia*); and this they regard as the immediate and proper consequence of the sin of Adam. Man after the Fall has, according to the Roman Catholic doctrine, the very same nature, that is, as to all its faculties, which Adam had, but now without those *dona supernaturalia*; he has the *pura naturalia*, yet as to their strength greatly weakened. According to the Protestant standards, the nature of man is deprived of essential and increated advantages and powers: therefore robbed of its integrity.[1] The Socinians reckon as the consequence of Adam's sin, as resting upon all men, only the resulting necessity of dying; although they do not deny that, as the effect of the entrance of sin through that first sin into mankind, a moral weakness has by degrees entered, with which every one is now born. The Quakers speak more decisively of a *semen peccati*, which has penetrated from Adam to mankind: the capacity for the divine grace, for the internal light, being however left to man. But withal, the Quakers do not carry back their doctrine to the original perfections of the first man.

SYMBOLICAL TESTIMONIES.

I. ROMAN.

The Roman Catholic doctrine is not expanded either in the *Conc. Trid.* or in the *Cat. Rom.*: the latter appeals simply to the former (i. 3. 2). But from the definition of the original state of man (see the previous article), compared with the decrees concerning sin, what we have said above follows of itself. Bellarmine with great precision states the doctrine (*De Grat.* iv. 15, vi. 10).

Concil. Trid. sess. v. 1: Si quis non confitetur, primum hominem Adam, cum mandatum dei in paradiso fuisset trans-

---

[1] To the Romanists original sin is something negative; to the Protestants inherited sin is something positive (Möhler). When Melanchthon accepts the Romish definition of inherited sin as *carentia justitiæ originalis (inesse debitæ)*, *Apol.* p. 53 (cf. *Sax. Conf.* p. 53), he does so under the supposition of the Protestant idea of *justitia originalis* being essentially *concreata* (*naturalis*).

gressus, statim sanctitatem et justitiam . . . amisisse incurrisseque per offensam prævaricationis hujusmodi iram et indignationem dei atque ideo mortem . . . totumq. Adam per illam prævaricationis offensam secundum corpus et animam in deterius commutatum fuisse, anath. sit.—2 : Si quis Adæ prævaricationem sibi soli et non ejus propagini asserit nocuisse et acceptam a deo sanctitatem et justitiam, quam perdidit, sibi soli et non nobis etiam eum perdidisse, aut inquinatum illum per inobedientiæ peccatum mortem et pœnas corporis tantum in omne genus hum. transfudisse, non autem et peccatum, quod mors est animæ, anath. sit.

Ib. sess. 6, cap. 1 : Declarat synodus—oportere, ut unusquisque agnoscat et fateatur, quod cum omnes homines in prævaricatione Adæ innocentiam perdidissent, facti immundi . . . usque adeo servi erant peccati, . . . tametsi in eis liberum arbitrium minime exstinctum esset, viribus licet attenuatum et inclinatum.—Can. 5 : Si quis liberum hominis arbitrium post Adæ peccatum amissum et exstinctum esse dixerit cet. anathema sit.

(Bellarmin. *Amiss. grat.* iii. 1 : Pœna, quæ proprie primo peccato quasi e regione respondet, jactura fuit originalis justitiæ et supernaturalium donorum, quibus deus naturam nostram instruxerat.—*De gratia primi hom.* 1 : Docent, per Adæ peccatum totum hominem vere deteriorem esse factum et tamen nec liberum arbitrium neque alia naturalia dona, sed solum supernaturalia perdidisse.—*Ibid.* c. 5 : Quare non magis differt status hominis post lapsum Adæ a statu ejusdem in puris naturalibus, quam differat spoliatus a nudo, neque deterior est humana natura (si culpam originalem detrahas), neque magis ignorantiâ et infirmitate laborat, quam esset et laboraret in puris naturalibus condita. Proinde corruptio naturæ non ex alicujus doni carentiâ, neque ex alicujus malæ qualitatis accessu, sed ex solâ doni supernaturalis ob Adæ peccatum amissione profluxit.)

Cat. Rom. iii. 10. 6 : Recta quidem concupiscendi vis deo auctore a naturâ nobis insita est, sed primorum parentum nostrorum peccato factum est, ut illa naturæ fines transsiliens usque adeo depravata sit, ut ad ea concupiscenda sæpe excitetur, quæ spiritui ac rationi repugnant.

(Bellarmini *Amiss. grat.* v. 5 : Non est quæstio inter nos et adversarios, sitne humana natura graviter depravata per Adæ peccatum. Id enim libentur fatemur. Neque etiam quæstio est, an hæc depravatio aliquo modo ad peccatum originale pertineat, ita ut materiale ejus peccati dici possit. Id enim S. Thomas concedit cet. Sed tota controversia est, utrum corruptio naturæ ac præsertim concupiscentia per se et ex naturâ suâ, qualis invenitur etiam in baptizatis et justificatis, sit proprie peccatum originale. Id catholici negant cet.)

II. Greek.

Conf. orth. p. 52 : Ὡς ἂν ἔσφαλε μὲ τὴν παράβασιν, παρευθὺς εἰς τὸν ἴδιον τόπον τοῦ παραδείσου, πέρνωντας τὴν κατάστασιν τῆς ἁμαρτίας ἐγίνηκε θνητός.—Καὶ τότε παρευθὺς ἔχασε τὴν τελειότητα τοῦ λόγου καὶ τῆς γνώσεως· καὶ ἡ θέλησις ἔκλινε περισσότερον εἰς τὸ κακόν, παρὰ εἰς τὸ καλόν· καὶ οὕτως ἡ κατάστασις τῆς ἀθωότητος καὶ ἀκακίας, ἔστωντας καὶ νὰ δοκιμάσῃ τὸ κακόν, ἄλλαξεν εἰς κατάστασιν ἁμαρτίας. P. 58 : Ὁ λόγος, ὅταν ὁ ἄνθρωπος ἦτον εἰς τὴν κατάστασιν τῆς ἀθωότητος, ἤγουν πρὶν ἁμάρτῃ, ἦτον ἀδιάφθορος εἰς τὴν τελειότητά τοῦ, καὶ διὰ τὴν ἁμαρτίαν ἐφθάρη· μὰ ἡ θέλησις, καλᾶ καὶ νὰ ἔμεινεν ἄβλαβη, εἰς τὸ νὰ ἐπιθυμᾷ τὸ καλὸν ἢ τὸ κακόν, ἔγινεν μ' ὅλον τοῦτο εἰς κάποιους, πλέον ἐπιρρεπὴς καὶ κλίνει πρὸς τὸ κακόν· καὶ εἰς ἄλλους πρὸς τὸ καλόν. P. 59 : Δείχνει ὁ ἅγιος διδάσκαλος (Basilius), πῶς καλᾶ καὶ ἡ ἀνθρωπίνη θέλησις, ἐβλάβη μὲ τὸ προπατορικὸν ἁμάρτημα, μ' ὅλον τοῦτο καὶ τῶρα κατὰ τὸν παρόντα καιρὸν εἰς τὴν προαίρεσιν τοῦ καθ' ἑνός, στέκεται τὸ νὰ εἶναι καλὸς καὶ τέκνον θεοῦ, ἢ κακὸς καὶ υἱὸς διαβόλου. Comp., on the freedom of the will in the natural man, Jerem. *in Art. Wirtemb.* p. 367 ; Metroph. Critop. *Conf.* c. 4, p. 66 ; Dosithei *Confess.* cc. iii. and xiv.

III. Lutheran.

C. A. p. 9 : Docent, quod post lapsum Adæ omnes homines, secundum naturam propagati, nascantur cum peccato h. e. sine metu dei, sine fiduciâ erga deum et cum concupiscentiâ.

Apol. A. C. p. 51 : Hic locus testatur, nos non solum

actus, sed potentiam seu dona efficiendi, timorem et fiduciam erga deum, adimere propagatis secundum carnalem naturam. Dicimus enim, ita natos habere concupiscentiam nec posse efficere verum timorem et fiduciam erga deum.

Ib. p. 53: . . . Voluimus significare, quod peccatum originis hos quoque morbos contineat, ignorationem dei, contemtum dei, vacare metu dei et fiduciâ erga deum, non posse diligere deum. Hæc sunt præcipua vitia naturæ humanæ, pugnantia proprie cum primâ tabulâ decalogi.

Ib. p. 55: Nos recte expressimus utrumque in descriptione peccati originalis, videlicet defectus illos, non posse deo credere, non posse deum timere ac diligere, item habere concupiscentiam, quæ carnalia quærit contra verbum dei, hoc est, quærit non solum voluptates corporis, sed etiam sapientiam et justitiam carnalem, et confidit his bonis contemnens deum.

Art. Sm. p. 317: Peccatum hæreditarium tam profunda et tetra est corruptio naturæ, ut nullius hominis ratione intelligi possit, sed ex scripturæ patefactione agnoscenda et credenda sit.

F. C. p. 573: Credimus, quod sit aliquod discrimen inter ipsam hominis naturam, non tantum quemadmodum initio a deo purus et sanctus et absque peccato homo conditus est, verum etiam qualem jam post lapsum naturam illam habemus.

Ib. p. 574: Credimus, peccatum originis non esse leve, sed tam profundam humanæ naturæ corruptionem, quæ nihil sanum, nihil incorruptum in corpore et animâ hominis, atque adeo in interioribus et exterioribus viribus ejus, reliquit. . . .

Ib. p. 640: (Credimus est), quod sit per omnia totalis carentia, defectus seu privatio concreatæ in paradiso justitiæ originalis seu imaginis dei, ad quam homo initio in veritate, sanctitate atque justitia creatus fuerat, et quod simul etiam sit impotentia et inaptitudo, ἀδυναμία et stupiditas, quâ homo ad omnia divina seu spiritualia sit prorsus ineptus.—Præterea, quod peccatum originale in humanâ naturâ non tantummodo sit ejusmodi totalis carentia seu defectus omnium bonorum in rebus spiritualibus ad deum pertinentibus, sed quod sit etiam loco imaginis dei amissæ in homine intima, pessima, profundissima, (instar cujusdam abyssi) inscrutabilis et ineffabilis corruptio totius naturæ et omnium virium, imprimis vero superiorum et principalium animæ facultatum, in mente, intellectu, corde et voluntate. Itaque jam post lapsum homo hæreditario a parentibus accipit congenitam pravam vim, internam immunditiem cordis, pravas concupiscentias et pravas inclinationes : ita, ut omnes naturâ talia corda, tales sensus et cogitationes ab Adamo hæreditariâ et naturali propagatione consequamur, quæ secundum summas suas vires et juxta lumen rationis naturaliter e diametro cum deo et summis ipsius mandatis pugnent atque inimicitiâ sint adversus deum, præsertim quantum ad res divinas et spirituales attinet. In aliis enim externis et hujus mundi rebus, quæ rationi subjectæ sunt, relictum est homini adhuc aliquid intellectus, virium et facultatum : etsi hæ etiam miseræ reliquiæ valde sunt debiles : et quidem hæc ipsa quantulacunque per morbum illum hæreditarium veneno infecta sunt atque contaminata, ut coram deo nullius momenti sint.

Against Flacius, who maintained that inherited sin, as a *totalis corruptio naturæ humanæ*, is and exists in the very substance of man himself, the *Formula Conc.* thus protests : Etsi peccatum originale totam hominis naturam, ut spirituale quoddam venenum et horribilis lepra (quemadmodum D. Lutherus loquitur) infecit et corrupit, ita quidem, ut jam in nostrâ naturâ corruptâ ad oculum non monstrari possint distincte hæc duo, ipsa natura sola et originale peccatum solum : tamen non unum et idem est corrupta natura seu substantia corrupti hominis, corpus et anima, aut homo ipse a deo creatus in quo originale peccatum habitat, (cujus ratione natura, substantia, totus denique homo corruptus est) et ipsum originale peccatum, quod in hominis naturâ aut essentiâ habitat eamque corrumpit; quemadmodum etiam in leprâ corporali ipsum corpus leprosum et lepra ipsa in corpore non sunt unum et idem, si proprie et distincte eâ de re disserere velimus. Discrimen igitur retinendum est inter naturam nostram, qualis a deo creata est hodieque conservatur, in quâ peccatum originale habitat, et inter ipsum peccatum originis, quod in naturâ habitat. Hæc enim duo secundum sacræ scripturæ regulam distincte considerari, doceri et credi debent et possunt.

IV. Reformed.

Conf. Basil. 2 : Through Adam's fall the entire human race is corrupted and subject to condemnation; our nature has been weakened, and affected with such a bias to sin that, unless the Spirit of God restores it, man of himself can do nothing good.

Conf. Helv. ii. cap. 8 : Qualis (homo, Adam) factus est a lapsu, tales sunt omnes, qui ex ipso prognati sunt, peccato inquam, morti variisque obnoxii calamitatibus. Peccatum autem intelligimus esse nativam illam hominis corruptionem ex primis illis nostris parentibus in nos omnes derivatam vel propagatam, quâ concupiscentiis pravis immersi et a bono aversi, ad omne vero malum propensi, pleni omni nequitiâ, diffidentiâ, contemtu et odio dei, nihil boni ex nobis ipsis facere, imo ne cogitare quidem possumus.

Ib. cap. 9 : Considerandum est, qualis fuerit homo post lapsum. Non sublatus est quidem homini intellectus, non erepta ei voluntas, et prorsus in lapidem vel truncum est commutatus. Ceterum illa ita sunt immutata et imminuta in homine, ut non possint amplius quod potuerunt ante lapsum. Intellectus enim obscuratus est, voluntas vero ex liberâ facta est voluntas serva. Nam servit peccato, non nolens sed volens. Etenim voluntas, non noluntas dicitur. Ergo quoad malum sive peccatum homo non coactus vel a deo vel a diabolo, sed suâ sponte malum facit et hac parte liberrimi est arbitrii. . . . Quantum vero ad bonum et ad virtutes, intellectus hominis non recte judicat de divinis ex semet ipso.

Confess. Gall. art. 9 : Credimus, hominem . . . suâ ipsius culpâ excidisse a gratiâ, quam acceperat ac proinde seipsum a deo omnis justitiæ et bonarum omnium fonte abalienasse, adeo ut ipsius naturâ sit prorsus corrupta et spiritus excœcatus ac corde depravatus, omnem illam integritatem sine ullâ prorsus exceptione amiserit. Etsi enim nonnullam habet boni et mali discretionem, affirmamus tamen, quidquid habet lucis, mox fieri tenebras, cum de quærendo deo agitur, adeo ut suâ intelligentiâ et ratione nullo modo possit ad eum accedere. Item, quamvis voluntate sit præditus, qua ad hoc vel illud movetur, tamen, cum ea sit penitus sub peccato captiva, nullam prorsus habet ad bonum appetendum libertatem, nisi quam ex gratia et dei dono acceperit.

Thirty-nine Articles, art. 9 : Original sin standeth not in the following of Adam (as the Pelagians do vainly talk), but it is the fault or corruption of the nature of every man that naturally is engendered of the offspring of Adam, whereby man is very far gone from original righteousness—*ab originali justitiâ quam longissime distet*—and is of his own nature inclined to evil, so that the flesh lusteth always contrary to the Spirit, and therefore, in every person born into the world, it deserveth God's wrath and damnation; and this infection of nature doth remain, yea, in them that are regenerated, whereby the lust of the flesh, called in Greek φρόνημα σαρκὸς, which some do expound the wisdom, some sensuality, some the affection, some the desire of the flesh, is not subject to the law of God; and though there is no condemnation for them that believe and are baptized, yet the apostle doth confess that concupiscence and lust hath of itself the nature of sin.

Conf. Scot. 3 : (Adami) transgressione, quæ vulgo dicitur originale peccatum, prorsus deformata est illa dei in homine imago ipseque et ejus posteri naturâ facti sunt inimici dei, mancipia satanæ et servi peccati, adeo ut mors æterna habuerit et habitura sit potentiam et dominium in omnes etc.

[*Westm. Conf.* vi. 23 : By this sin they fell from their original righteousness and communion with God, and so became dead in sin, and wholly defiled in all the faculties and parts of soul and body. They being the root of all mankind, the guilt of this sin was imputed, and the same death in sin and corrupted nature conveyed to all their posterity, descending from them by ordinary generation. From this original corruption, whereby we are utterly indisposed, disabled, and made opposite to all good, and wholly inclined to all evil, do proceed all actual transgressions.]

Conf. Belg. art. 15 : (Peccatum originis) est totius naturæ corruptio et vitium hæreditarium, quo et ipsi infantes in matris suæ utero polluti sunt, quodque veluti radix omne peccatorum genus in homine producit ideoque ita fœdum et exsecrabile est coram deo, ut ad generis hum. condemnationem sufficiat.

Canon. Dordr. cap. iii. art. 1 : Liberâ suâ voluntate a deo desciscens (homo) eximiis istis donis (justitiæ cet.) se ipsum orbavit, atque e contrario eorum loco cœcitatem, horribiles tenebras, vanitatem ac perversitatem judicii in mente, malitiam, rebellionem ac duritiem in voluntate et corde, impuritatem denique in omnibus affectibus contraxit.

Catech. Heidelb. 7 : Through the fall and disobedience of our first parents . . . our nature has been so poisoned that we are all conceived and born in sin. 8 : Are we then so corrupted that we are altogether unable for anything good and inclined only to evil? Yes, unless we are regenerate through God's Spirit.

V. Arminian.

Conf. Rem. vii. 3 sq. : Per transgressionem factus est homo (Adam) ex vi comminationis divinæ reus æternæ mortis ac multiplicis miseriæ, exutus est primævâ illâ felicitate, quam in creatione acceperat cet. Quia vero Ad. stirps ac radix erat totius generis humani, ideo non se ipsum tantum sed omnes etiam posteros suos, qui quasi in lumbis ipsius conclusi erant et ex ipso per naturalem generationem prodituri, eidem morti ac miseriæ involvit et una secum implicuit, adeo ut omnes hom. sine ullo discrimine, excepto solo J. Ch., per hoc unicum Ad. peccatum privati sint primævâ illâ felicitate et destituti verâ justitiâ ad æt. salutem consequendam necessariâ, adeoque morti illi et multiplici miseriæ etiam nunc obnoxii nascantur.

Limborch, *Theol. Christ.* iii. 3. 4 : Fatemur, etiam infantes nasci minus puros, quam Adamus fuit creatus, et cum quadam propensione ad peccandum : illam autem habent non tam ab Adamo, quam a proximis parentibus, cum, si ab Adamo esset, in omnibus hominibus debeat esse æqualis. Jam autem admodum est inæqualis, et ordinarie inclinant liberi in peccata parentum.

Id. v. 15. 15 : Haud illubentes fatemur, nos temperamento minus puro nasci ac proinde inclinationem nostram in res carni gratas esse vehementiorem, quam in primis nostris parentibus fuit, unde fit, ut facilius incitemur ad motus inordinatos. Quoniam enim nascimur ex parentibus peccato assuetis atque istâ assuetudine ratione temperamenti non parum immutatis, fieri non potest, quin et temperamentum minus purum in nos propagent. Atqui illa physica est impuritas, non moralis, et tantum abest ut sit vere ac proprie dictum peccatum, ut motus primi inde orti materia sint virtutis exercendæ.—Thus is vindicated for man the natural ability to know God by the light of nature. *Vid.* Limb. *Theol. Ch.* iii. 4. 2, iv. 11. 7.

VI. SOCINIAN.

Cat. Racov. p. 21 : Homo morti est obnoxius, quod primus homo apertum dei mandatum, cui adjuncta fuit mortis comminatio, transgressus fuit. Unde porro factum est, ut universam suam posteritatem secum in eâdem mortis jura traxerit, accedente tamen cujusvis in adultioribus proprio delicto, cujus deinde vis per apertam dei legem, quam homines transgressi fuerant, aucta est. Cf. F. Socin. *Opp.* i. p. 122 b.

Ib. p. 294 : Peccatum originis quid sit, nondum inter auctores ipsos convenit. Hoc certum est, per Ad. lapsum haudquaquam hominis naturam ita vitiatam esse, ut in iis, quæ deus ab ipso idque sub pœnæ comminatione aut præmii pollicitatione requirat, obediendi vel non obediendi deo libertate et arbitrio privatus sit. . . . Et lapsus Adæ, cum unus actus fuerit, vim eam, quæ depravare ipsam naturam Adami, multo minus vero posterorum ipsius posset, habere non potuit. Non negamus tamen, assiduitate peccandi naturam hominum labe quadam et ad peccandum nimiâ proclivitate infectam esse. Sed eam vel peccatum per se esse vel talem esse negamus, ut homo vim sibi facere non possit, divino spir. hausto, et hactenus deo obedire quatenus id ab ipso pro suâ summâ bonitate et æquitate exigit. Cf. Socin. *prælect.* c. iv. p. 541 ; c. 5, *de libero arbitrio.*

F. Socini *de Christo servat.* iv. 6 : Falluntur egregie, qui peccatum originis imputatione aliquâ pro eâ parte, quæ ad reatum spectat, contineri autumant, cum omnis reatus ex solâ generis propagatione fluat. Gravius autem multo labuntur, qui pro eâ parte, quæ ad corruptionem pertinet, ex pœnâ ipsius delicti Adami illud fluxisse affirmant. Quâ enim vel auctoritate vel ratione unquam, non dicam probabunt, sed leviter alicui persuadebunt, Adamum ut sui delicti pœnam mentis ac voluntatis corruptionem incurrisse, quæ deinde in nobis propagatione ingenita fuerit? Imo quid absurdius et deo indignius excogitari potuit, quam Adamo ejusmodi pœnam ob delictum inflictam fuisse, propter quam a peccando in futurum abstinere non posset? . . . Corruptio nostra et ad peccandum proclivitas non ex uno illo delicto in nos propagata est, sed continuatis actibus habitus modo hujus modo illius vitii est comparatus, quo naturam nostram corrumpente ea corruptio deinde per generis propagationem in nos est derivata. Neque vero si Ad. non deliquisset, propterea vel nos a peccatis immunes fuissemus vel in hanc naturæ corruptionem incurrere non potuissemus, dummodo ut ille habuit, sic nos quoque voluntatem ad malum liberam habuissemus.

VII. QUAKER.

Barclay, *Apol.* Prop. iv. 5: That Adam is a public person is not denied, and that through him there is a seed of sin propagated to all men, which in its own nature is sinful, and inclines men to iniquity; yet it will not follow from thence that infants, who join not with this seed, are guilty. As for these words in the Romans, the reason of the guilt there alleged is, *For that all have sinned.* Now no man is said to sin unless he actually sin in his own person; for the Greek words ἐφ' ᾧ may very well relate to θανάτῳ, which is the nearest antecedent, so that they hold forth how that Adam, by his sin, gave an entrance to sin in the world; *and so death entered by sin.* That we confess, then, that a seed of sin— *semen peccati*—is transmitted to all men from Adam, although imputed to none, until by sinning they actually join with it, in which seed he gave occasion to all to sin; and it is the origin of all evil actions and thoughts in men's hearts, ἐφ' ᾧ, to wit, θανάτῳ, as it is in Rom. v., *i.e. in which death all have sinned.* For this seed of sin is frequently called death in the

Scripture, and the *body of death*, seeing, indeed, it is a death to the life of righteousness and holiness; therefore its seed and its product is called the old man, the old Adam, in which all sin is, for which we use this name to express this sin, and not that of *original sin*, of which phrase the Scripture makes no mention, and under which invented and unscriptural barbarism this notion of *imputed sin to infants* took place among Christians.—Prop. v. 17: Human nature, which, though of itself wholly corrupted and defiled, and prone to evil, yet is capable to be wrought upon by the grace of God; even as iron, though an hard and cold metal of itself, may be warmed and softened by the heat of the fire, and wax melted by the sun.

VIII. MENNONITES.

According to the Mennonites, Adam and his descendants lost through the first sin the divine image, holiness, and immortality. Schyn, *Plen. deduct.* p. 240 : An evil concupiscence is inherited by all; but with this there is a permanent facultas occurrens et adeo oblatum bonum audiendi, admittendi aut rejiciendi—the faculty of hearing, and receiving or rejecting good (Ris, *Conf.* art. 5).

Observations.

1. How it was possible to Adam to transgress the divine commandment, the symbols nowhere attempt to investigate. They allude to seduction through the serpent, and teach that Adam fell *suâ culpâ* (*Conf. Helv.* p. 54 ; *Helv.* ii. 8; *Gall.* 9 ; *Belg.* 14 ; *Syn. Dord.* iii. 1), or through *abuse of his freedom* (*Conf. Sax.* p. 54; *Helv.* ii. 9). As to the relation of this sin to the *sanctitas concreata*, or increated holiness, the Protestant symbols maintain silence. So also they say nothing as to the relation which God may be supposed to bear to this sin, save that the *Form. Cons. Helv.* 4 speaks of a *permittere lapsum*, while the other symbols are content to specify that God was not the *causa* and *auctor mali* (*A. C.* p. 15 ; *F. C.* 799 ; *Dec. Thor.* ii. 3. 1). But the Arminian *Conf. Rem.* is more full on this subject.

2. As original sin is propagated by natural generation (*A. C.* p. 9 ; *F. C.* 644 ; *Eng. Art.* ix. ; *Conf. Belg.* 15), it follows that Christ, as conceived supernaturally in the womb of the Virgin, was free from original sin (*Cat. maj.* 495 ; *F. C.* 574, 648 ; *Eng. Art.* xv. ; *Conf. Belg.* 18 ; *Dec. Thor.* 23). Withal, the Virgin herself in the Pro-

G

testant symbols is not excepted from the general law of the race in relation to original sin (*Dec. Thor.*).

3. [The Roman Catholic Church, on the other hand, teaches that the Virgin Mary was protected from original sin at the first moment of her being conceived, by a special privilege. Pius IX. in his Bull *Ineffabilis* (Dec. 8, 1854): Declaramus, pronuntiamus et definimus, doctrinam, quæ tenet, beatissimam virginem Mariam in primo instanti suæ conceptionis fuisse singulari omnipotentis Dei gratiâ et privilegio, intuitu meritorum Christi Jesu salvatoris humani generis, ab omni originalis culpæ labe præservatam immunem, esse a Deo revelatam, atque idcirco ab omnibus fidelibus firmiter constanterque credendam. Quâpropter si qui secus ac a nobis definitum est, quod Deus avertat, præsumpserint corde sentire, ii noverint ac porro sciant, se proprio judicio condemnatos, naufragium circa fidem passos esse, et ab unitate ecclesiæ defecisse. This Bull is printed fully in Chemnicii *Exam. Conc. Trid.* (ed. Preuss), Berlin 1862. Its explanation, however, is to be sought in the *Constit. Sollicitudo* of Pope Alexander VII., to which it expressly refers; and this is found in the same edition of Chemnitz. The originator of this new Romish doctrine was Duns Scotus; its promoters have been the University of Paris and the Franciscans. The salient points in its development have been the Council of Basle, and the Popes Sixtus IV., Alexander VII., and Clement XI. The history of the dogma has been given in a work on the subject by Preuss, Berlin 1865.]

II. SECOND POINT OF DIVERGENCE.

All the communities which assume a corruption of mankind as it now is, inherited or transmitted from Adam, with the solitary exception of the Quakers, regard that corruption under the aspect of *sin* properly so called, or of an inherited condemnation, on account of which men are regarded as sinners in the sight of God. The Roman Catholic standards, in harmony with their views of the evil resulting from the Fall, make original sin consist only in the *habitualis aversio a deo* resulting from the *carentia just. orig.*; while they regard the *prava concupiscentia*, being something belonging to man's nature itself, that is, the *vulnera* or wound of that nature, not as sin properly so called. The Protestants, on the other hand, call original sin the total depravation of human nature (in spiritual things); consequently they regard it as the *prava concupiscentia* itself, and before it issues in actual sin. The Quakers would have the universal depravation of the natural man, the wicked *semen* in him, to be called sin only when it is developed into actual sin. Similarly the Mennonites. The Socinians and later Arminians reject the idea of original condemnation altogether, and regard even the death which has been transmitted from Adam to all his posterity as not being, touching the latter, the punishment of sin, but as something brought upon man by generation, and consequently natural evil alone. The inborn tendency to sin they cannot, according to their views of the Fall, reckon as something inherited from Adam..

Since the Romanists deem the *concupiscentia carnis*, concupiscence, not to be an evil quality introduced into human nature, but something natural[1] springing from the sense-element in man, or his sensuousness, they therefore cannot regard this as having in it anything imputable, and consequently do not hold it to be sin properly so called: the mere *pronitas ad malum* is not sin of itself (Bellarmine, *Amiss. Grat.* v. 7). It is sin only metonymically, inasmuch as actual sin springs out of this concupiscence (*Confut. A. C.* 2); not so much *peccatum* as *materiale peccati*.[2] The *reatus*, or guilt, of original sin extends therefore only to the *carentia justitiæ originalis*, which is an habitual departure from God. As to the *vulnera naturæ*, which are not the very original sin itself, see Bellarmine, *Amiss. Grat.* v. 4.

[1] That is to say, if we suppose the supernatural gift of original righteousness withdrawn from man, the contest between the flesh and the spirit would arise naturally of itself (Möhler). The lusts of the flesh, if they overpower the spirit, engender sin; but they are not of themselves, and as such, sin (Baur, *Gegensatz*, S. 33). Thus is explained the origination of actual sin in human nature, without the necessity of assuming any evil quality or bias additionally infused into that nature. Hence Bellarmine, *De gratiâ prim. hom.* c. 5 : non deterior est humana natura, si culpam naturalem detrahat, neque magis ignorantiâ et infirmitate laborat, *quam esset et laboraret* in puris naturalibus condita.

[2] Duns Scotus says : Peccatum originale formaliter est carentia justitia orig. debitæ, concupiscentia est materiale peccati originalis, quia per privationem justitiæ originalis ipsa non positive, sed per privationem fit prona ad concupiscendum delectabilis.

SYMBOLICAL TESTIMONIES.

I. SOCINIAN.

Cat. Rac. qu. 423 : Peccatum originis nullum prorsus est. Nec enim e scriptura id peccatum originis doceri potest, et lapsus Adæ cum unus actus fuerit, vim eam, quæ depravare ipsam naturam Adami, multo minus vero posterorum ejus posset, habere non potuit. Ipsi vero id (depravationem naturæ) in pœnam irrogatum fuisse, nec scriptura docet, uti superius exposuimus, et deum illum, qui æquitatis fons est, incredibile prorsus est id facere voluisse.

F. Socin. *Prælect.* c. 4 : Concludimus . . . ex peccato illo primi parentis nullam labem aut pravitatem universo generi hum. necessario ingenitam esse, nec aliud malum ex primo illo delicto ad posteros omnes necessario manasse, quam moriendi omnimodam necessitatem, non quidem ex ipsius delicti vi, sed quia, cum jam homo natura mortalis esset, ob delictum illud suæ naturali mortalitati a deo relictus est. . . . Quare, qui ex ipso nascuntur, eadem conditione nasci omnes oportet.

Only in one passage (*de Christo Servo*, iv. 6) does Socinus call the necessity of dying a *reatus* delictorum nostrorum. But this does not indicate that the sin of Adam had been actually *imputed* to his descendants ; for this would be in direct opposition to the whole Socinian system. *Reatus* signifies to him only *damnum, noxa, malum ex alterius culpâ proficiscens.*

II. ARMINIAN.

Apol. Conf. Remonstr. p. 84 b : Peccatum originale nec habent (Remonstrantes) pro peccato proprie dicto, quod posteros Adami odio dei dignos faciat, nec pro malo, quod per modum proprie dictæ pœnæ ab Adamo in posteros dimanet, sed pro malo, infirmitate, vitio aut quocunque tandem alio nomine vocetur, quod ab Adamo justitia originali privato in posteros ejus propagatur : unde fit, ut posteri omnes Adami eadem justitia destituti, prorsus inepti et inidonei sint ad vitam æternam consequendum, aut in gratiam cum deo redeant, nisi deus nova gratia sua eos præveniat, et vires novas iis restituat ac sufficiat, quibus ad eam possint pervenire. Atque hoc significatum a deo credunt ejectione Adami ex paradiso, typo cœli, et obsidione viæ, qua ad illum patebat aditus: Hæc enim calamitas non tantum evenit Adamo, sed posteris omnibus Adami fuit cum eo communis. Peccatum autem originis non esse malum culpæ proprie dictæ, quod vocant, ratio manifesta arguit: malum culpæ non est, quia nasci plane involuntarium est, ergo et nasci cum hac aut illâ labe, infirmitate, vitio vel malo. Si malum culpæ non est, nec potest esse malum pœnæ, quia culpa et pœna sunt relata. Culpa autem in posteris Adami alia esse non poterat, quam hæc; alia enim prior concipi non potest, quia alioquin non esset culpa seu peccatum originis. Multo minus itaque fieri potest, ut sit culpa simul et pœna. Præterquam enim quod nihil indignius deo tribui possit, quam quod peccatorum peccato, quo de novo reus sit pœnæ, puniat; adeo diversa sunt culpa et pœna, ut prorsus sint incompatibilia. Pœna enim est actus dei et actus justitiæ; culpa actus hominis et ἀδικία. Pœna est involuntaria: culpa, nisi sit voluntaria, culpa esse non potest. Et cum deus puniendo hominem in ordinem cogere intendat, ista punitione novam inordinationem voluntati hominis injiceret, et suâ punitione sibi ipsi novæ pœnæ occasionem daret, atque ita rationem justitiæ et ordinem omnem pœnæ turbaret in infinitum usque. Malum itaque cum sit, necesse est, ut sit illud malum, quod Remonstrantes statuunt.

Limborch, *Theol. christ.* iii. 4. 4: Nullam scriptura in infantibus corruptionem esse docet, quæ vere ac proprie sit peccatum.—4. 5: Absurdum est statuere, deum homines punivisse corruptione tali, quæ vere ac proprie dictum est peccatum, et ex quâ omnia actualia peccata tanquam ex fonte necessario scaturiunt, et deinde propter illam corruptionem homines denuo punire pœnâ inferni.—4. 6: Concipi non potest, quomodo peccatum hoc propagetur. Non enim inhæret animæ, quæ immediate, etiam juxta communem horum doctorum opinionem, a deo creatur, ac proinde, si peccato esset infecta, peccatum illud a deo esset.—4. 7: Nullum peccatum pœnâ dignum est involuntarium, quia nihil magis debet esse voluntarium, quam quod hominem pœnæ et quidem gravissimæ, æternæ nempe et summorum cruciatuum, reum facit. Atqui corruptio originaria est involuntaria.

Ib. iii. 4. 1 : Inclinatio illa (ad peccandum) proprie dictum peccatum non est aut peccati habitus ab Adamo in ipsos propagatus, sed naturalis tantum inclinatio habendi id, quod carni gratum est, quæ proprie oritur a temperamento corporis, quod a proximis parentibus propagari scimus. Pro diversâ enim temperamenti ratione animus hominis diversimode a variis objectis afficitur, quodque uni gratum alteri ingratum est ; inde diversæ adeo in hominibus cupiditates, dum unusquisque appetit, quod pro temperamenti sui ratione ipsi gratum est, ac aversatur ingratum. Quia vero carni nostræ grata plerumque voluntati divinæ adversantur, quoniam deus in hisce abnegandis promtam animi nostri obedientiam explorare vult, inde est, quod illa inclinatio in objecta carni nostræ grata sit etiam inclinatio in peccatum (cf. iii. 3. 4).—iii. 4. 24 : Ad ejusmodi generis mala, quæ neutra sunt, corruptio illa, quæcunque nobis a natura inest, referri debet ; nempe non est peccatum neque pœna, nostri respectu : est tamen malum aliquod naturale, quod ex occasione pœnæ Adamo inflictæ ad nos promanavit, seu carentia boni cujusdam, quo alias gavisi fuissemus, quoniam Adamus bonum, quo ipse propter peccatum spoliatus est, ad nos propagare non potuit.

Ib. iii. 3. 19 : Dicimus, deum innoxios posteros non punire ob peccatum Adami ; pœna enim delictum non excedit, sed malis hujus vitæ ac tandem morti subjicere, quia ex Adamo peccatore geniti sunt, non ut in ipsis Adami peccatum puniat cet.—iii. 3. 1 : Mors non habet rationem pœnæ proprie dictæ in posteris, fieri enim nequit, ut insontes propter alterius peccatum puniantur, sed est naturalis tantum moriendi necessitas ab Adamo mortis pœna punito in ipsos derivata.

III. ROMAN.

Whether the relation of man, naturally engendered of the offspring of Adam, to God is that of *a sinner*, cannot be determined with any certainty from the *Cat. Rom.* i. 3. 2 : *peccatum* et peccati pœnam in uno Adamo non constitisse, sed ex eo tanquam ex semine et caussâ ad omnem posteritatem jure permanasse. For *peccatum* here may be the sin which springs from the inborn concupiscence. So also Conc. Trid.

sess. v. 2 is ambiguous. But a proper *inherited sin* (or moral condemnation in the sight of God) is enforced on us by No. 3 of that session : hoc Adæ peccatum, quod origine unum est et propagatione, non imitatione transfusum, omnibus inest unicuique proprium (cf. Trid. sess. vi. 3). The declaration that even the children of Christians, before they themselves can sin, originalis peccati nihil non traxisse ex Adam, and therefore need an *expiatio* through baptism, confirms the same argument. So also No. 5, where we read of a *reatus* ex Adami semine. Bellarmine, *Amiss. gr.* iv. 2 : " We confess that in man, born of seed propagated from Adam, there is *reatus quidam*, a certain guilt and spot, which makes the man himself truly and properly a sinner, and marks him for eternal banishment from God." Cf. v. 17 : " Original sin is not less properly and truly sin than personal."

But what is it that in the natural man has the character of (inherited) *sin?* The symbols give this no direct answer. The Romish theology, however, has always explained the carentia justitiæ originalis inesse debitæ as being *original sin*, although with a variety of defining clauses ; or, as Bellarmine expresses it, the habitualis aversio et obliquitas voluntatis, quæ et macula mentem deo invisam reddens appellari potest. Cf. *De Amiss. gr.* v. 19 : " Therefore the privation of the gift of original righteousness is called original sin, so far as this is connected with habitual aversion from God." Klee, *Dogm.* ii. 346. On this point some extended extracts from Bellarmine may be given :—

Bellarmini *Amiss. grat.* v. 17 : Sciendum est, peccati nomen bifariam accipi solere. Uno modo pro transgressione præcepti, alio modo pro eo, quod remanet in animâ peccatoris post actionem illam transgressionis præcepti. . . . Quod autem post actionem peccati aliquid maneat, quod sit et dicatur proprie peccatum, ex eo potest intelligi, quod, qui peccatum commiserunt, dicuntur ab omnibus post actionem peccati proprie et formaliter peccatores ; item dicuntur esse in peccato, habere peccatum, mundati a peccato cet. . . . Quamvis autem id, quod remanet post actionem, sit aliquo modo effectus ejusdem actionis, tamen est etiam aliquo modo idem cum ipsâ actione, et ideo non per figuram metonymiæ, sed proprie dicitur peccatum ;

et duplex illa significatio peccati non est significatio duarum rerum sive duorum peccatorum, sed unius et ejusdem alio atque alio modo se habentis. . . . l'eccati perversio sive obliquitas, ut est in motu, dicitur peccatum in priore significatione, ut autem permanet in animâ peccantis, dic. peccatum in significatione posteriore. Nam sicut, qui a sole avertitur, manet aversus in tenebris, donec ad solem iterum revertatur, et qui ab aliquo recedit, manet in eâ distantiâ, donec iterum accedat: sic etiam qui per peccatum a deo avertitur et recedit, non solum dum peccat, sed etiam postquam peccavit, manet a deo aversus et longe dissitus, donec per pœnitentiam convertatur et revertatur ad deum.—Itaque peccatum in priore significatione unum est duntaxat omnium hominum, sed in Adamo actuale et-personale, in nobis originale dicitur. Solus enim ipse actuali voluntate illud commisit: nobis vero communicatur per generationem eo modo, quo communicari potest id quod transiit, nimirum per imputationem. Omnibus enim imputatur, qui ex Adamo nascuntur, quoniam omnes in lumbis Adami existentes in eo et per eum peccavimus, cum ipse peccavit.

IV. GREEK.

The Greek symbols only assert firmly the reality of original sin, without more distinctly indicating wherein that sin consists. *Conf. orthod.* p. 53 : Καθὼς ὅλοι οἱ ἄνθρωποι ἦσαν εἰς τὴν κατάστασιν τῆς ἀθωότητος εἰς τὸν 'Αδάμ, τέτοιας λογῆς καὶ ἀφ' οὗ ἔσφαλεν, ὅλοι ἔσφαλαν εἰς αὐτὸν καὶ ἔμειναν εἰς τὴν κατάστασιν τῆς ἁμαρτίας· διὰ τοῦτο ὄχι μόνον εἰς τὴν ἁμαρτίαν ὑπόκεινται, μὰ καὶ εἰς τὴν τιμωρίαν διὰ τὴν ἁμαρτίαν.

From the Greeks' doctrine (see below) on the extinction of original sin by baptism, it may be seen that they cannot have held evil concupiscence as the properly sinful thing in the natural man.

V. LUTHERAN.

C. A. p. 10 : Docent, quod hic morbus seu vitium originis vere sit peccatum, damnans et afferens nunc quoque æternam mortem his, qui non renascuntur per baptismum et Spiritum sanctum.

A. Sm. p. 315 : Per Adami inobedientiam omnes homines facti sunt peccatores, morti et diabolo obnoxii.

F. C. p. 639: (Lutherus significavit) etiamsi homo prorsus nihil mali cogitaret, loqueretur aut ageret, tamen nihilominus hominis naturam et personam esse peccatricem, h. e. peccato originali prorsus et totaliter . . . coram deo infectam, venenatam. . . . Et propter hanc corruptionem atque primorum nostrorum parentum lapsum natura aut persona hominis lege dei accusatur et condemnatur cet.—Ibid. quod hoc hæreditarium malum sit culpa seu reatus, quo fit, ut omnes propter inobedientiam Adæ et Hevæ in odio apud deum et naturâ filii iræ simus. Cf. p. 642.

Apol. A. C. p. 57 : Disputant (adversarii), concupiscentiam pœnam esse, non peccatum, Lutherus defendit peccatum esse. Supra dictum est (p. 54), Augustinum definire peccatum originis, quod sit concupiscentia. Expostulent cum Augustino, si quid habet incommodi hæc sententia. Præterea Paulus ait (Rom. vii. 7): concupiscentiam nesciebam esse peccatum, nisi lex diceret: Non concupisces. Item (Rom. vii. 23): Video aliam legem in membris meis repugnantem legi mentis meæ et captivantem me legi peccati, quæ est in membris meis. Hæc testimonia nulla cavillatione everti possunt. Clare enim appellant concupiscentiam peccatum cet.

F. C. p. 575 : Rejicimus et damnamus dogma illud, quo asseritur, concupiscentias pravas non esse peccatum sed concreatas naturæ conditiones et proprietates quasdam essentiales.

VI. REFORMED.

Conf. Gall. art. 11 : Credimus hoc vitium (originis, as defined in Art. ix.) esse vere peccatum, quod omnes et singulos homines, ne parvulis quidem exceptis adhuc in utero matrum delitescentibus, æternæ mortis reos coram deo peragat.

Conf. Belg. art. 15 : Est peccatum originis . . . vitium hæreditarium, quo et ipsi infantes in matris suæ utero polluti sunt . . . estque ita fœdum et exsecrabile coram deo, ut ad generis humani condemnationem sufficiat.

Declar. Thorun. ii. 3. 7 : . . . pravitatis reliquiæ (in renatis) videl. praviæ inclinationes et motus concupiscentiæ, quæ proinde vere et proprie peccatum dicitur, non tantum, quatenus est pœna et causa peccati, sed etiam quatenus ipsa cum legi dei tum spiritui gratiæ repugnat.

Thirty-nine Articles, art. ix. *ut supra*.

Calvin, *Institt. christ*. i. 1. 8 : Hæc duo distincte observanda : nempe, quod sic omnibus naturæ nostræ partibus vitiati perversique, jam ob talem duntaxat corruptionem damnati merito convictique coram deo tenemur, cui nihil est acceptum nisi justitia, innocentia. Neque ista est alieni delicti obligatio ; quod enim dicitur, nos per Adami peccatum obnoxios esse factos dei judicio, non ita est accipiendum, ac si insontes ipsi et immerentes culpam delicti ejus sustineremus, sed quia per ejus transgressionem maledictione induti sumus omnes, dicitur ille nos obstrinxisse. Ab illo tamen non sola in nos pœna grassata est, sed instillata ab ipso lues in nobis residet, cui jure pœna debetur. Quare Augustinus, utcunque alienum peccatum sæpe vocet (quo clarius ostendat propagine in nos derivari), simul tamen et proprium unicuique asserit. Et apostolus ipse disertissime testatur, ideo mortem in omnes pervagatam, quod omnes peccarint, i.e. involuti sint originali peccato et ejus maculis inquinati. Atque ideo infantes quoque ipsi, dum suam secum damnationem a matris utero afferunt, non alieno, sed suo ipsorum vitio sunt obstricti. Nam tametsi suæ iniquitatis fructus nondum protulerint, habent tamen in se inclusum semen : ideo non odiosa et abominabilis deo esse non potest.

Observations.

If original sin is supposed to be only a defect, or an evil that has come upon mankind, the inheriting of such an evil is sufficiently explained by pointing to the fact that Adam was the original progenitor of the race. But if an original *guilt* is imported into the doctrine,—a guilt that, since the transgression of Adam, has clung to all human individuals,—there arises a more important question, that is, how far anything inherited may involve guilt. The Romish symbols say nothing on this subject ; but the theologians (including in the notion of sin the free consent of the individual; cf. Bellarm. *De amiss. gr.* i. 1) adopt the idea of an imputation, the foundation of which is laid by the derivation of all from Adam. Bellarm. *Amiss. Gr.* v. 17; Möhler, *Symb.* 5 (cf. *Conf. orthod.* 53). This thought is not absent from the Protestant symbols, at least they do not exclude an *imputatio peccati Adamitici* (*Apol.* p. 51 ; *F. C.* 642), though rejecting this as the *sole* foundation for original sin. The *Form. Conc.* says: Propter nostram corruptionem et primorum parentum lapsum natura aut persona hominis lege dei accusatur et condemnatur. And again: Hæreditarium malum est culpa seu reatus, quo fit, ut omnes propter inobedientiam Adæ et Hevæ in odio apud deum et naturâ filii iræ simus, though this latter *propter* may be viewed as an immediate cause. But this view is found in the private writings of Luther and Melancthon. An imputation is plainly taught by the *Form. Cons. Helv.* 10: Censemus, peccatum Adami omnibus ejus posteris judicio dei arcano et justo imputari. . . . Duplici nomine post peccatum homo naturâ indeque ab ortu suo, antequam illum actuale peccatum in se admittat, iræ et maledictioni divinæ obnoxius est, primum quidem ob παράπτωμα et inobedientiam, quam in Adami lumbis commisit, deinde ob consequentem in ipso conceptu hæreditariam corruptionem insitam cet. In this passage, it is at the same time indicated that by the *in quo* peccarunt the theory of imputation receives its welcome support. But, in fact, the Reformers did not reduce the original guilt of the natural man to mere imputation: they saw in the inborn corruption itself something offensive to the all-holy God, and therefore condemnable in His sight; whence it appears that they held a definition of sin which does not necessarily require the free consent of the individual (cf. *Apol. A. C.* 581 ; Parei *Corp. Doct. Chr.* 38, 41) as lying at the foundation of their doctrine. See Melanc. *Loci*, i. 86; Calvin, *Institt.* ii. 1. 8. And this explains the *propter alienam culpam* of *Apol.* 51 ; cf. Heidegger, *Corp.* x. 48. The Socinians must naturally, as denying all original sin, reject the imputation of Adam's transgression. Cf. on Rom. v. 12 : Socin. *Prælect.* c. 4; *De Chr. Serv.* iv. 6; *Cat. Rac.* qu. 426.

ARMINIAN SYMBOLS.

Apol. Conf. Rem. p. 84 a : Fatentur Rem., peccatum Adami a deo imputatum dici posse posteris ejus, quatenus deus posteros Ad. eidem malo, cui Adamus per peccatum obnoxium se reddidit, obnoxios nasci voluit, sive quatenus deus malum, quod in pœnam Adamo inflictum fuerat, in posteros ejus dimanare et transire permisit. At nihil cogit eos dicere, peccatum Ad. posteris ejus sic fuisse a deo imputatum, quasi deus posteros

Ad. revera censuisset ejusdem cum Adamo peccati et culpæ, quam Ad. commiserat, reos. . . .

Limborch, *Theol. christ.* iii. 3. 8 : Quod itaque imputationem peccati Adami attinet, quâ statuitur, deum primum Adami et Evæ peccatum omnibus ipsorum posteris ita imputasse, ut omnium peccatum sit omnesque in Adamo peccaverint et propterea mortis ac condemnationis æternæ rei facti sint, eam impugnamus.

Original Sin and Baptism.

Original sin, as defined by the Protestants, is not effaced by baptism; the imputation of it is removed. Its total abolition must, as it has seized human nature in its inmost recesses, be awaited in the resurrection alone. The Romish Church, on the other hand, hold original sin to be removed by baptism, which restores the righteousness acceptable to God; for the *prava concupiscentia*, which remains even in the baptized as the *fomes peccati*, or fuel of sin, is not in itself of the nature of sin.

I. Roman.

Concil. Trid. sess. v. 5 : Si quis per J. Ch. gratiam, quæ in bapt. confertur, reatum originalis peccati remitti negat, aut etiam asserit non tolli totum id, quod veram et propriam peccati rationem habet, sed illud dicit tantum radi aut non imputari, anathema sit, in renatis enim nihil odit deus cet. Manere autem in baptizatis concupiscentiam vel fomitem, sancta syn. fatetur et sentit, quæ cum ad agonem relicta sit, nocere non consentientibus, sed utiliter per Ch. gratiam repugnantibus non valet. Hanc concupiscentiam, quam aliquando Apost. peccatum appellat, sancta syn. declarat, ecclesiam cath. nunquam intellexisse peccatum appellari, quod vere et proprie in renatis peccatum sit, sed quia ex peccato est et ad peccatum inclinat.

Cf. Bellarmini *Amiss. grat.* v. 5. 7.

II. Greek.

Confess. orthod. p. 282 : Τὸ προπατορικὸν ἁμάρτημα μὲ οὐδεμίαν μετάνοιαν εἶναι δυνατὸν νὰ ἐξαλειφθῇ, μόνον μὲ τὴν χάριν τοῦ θεοῦ ἀφανίζεται διὰ τῆς ἐν σαρκὶ οἰκονομίας τοῦ κυρ. Ἰ. Χ. καὶ τῆς ἐκχύσεως τοῦ τιμίου αἵματος αὐτοῦ, καὶ τοῦτο γίνεται μὲ τὸ μυστήριον τοῦ ἁγ. βαπτίσματος. Cf. p. 157.

III. Protestant.

Apol. A. C. p. 56: Semper ita scripsit (Luth.), quod baptismus tollat reatum peccati orig., tametsi materiale, ut isti vocant, peccati maneat, videl. concupiscentia. Cf. p. 57.

F. C. p. 575: Affirmamus, quod hanc naturæ corruptionem ab ipsâ naturâ nemo nisi solus deus separare queat, id quod per mortem in beatâ illâ resurrectione plene fiet. Ibi enim ipsa natura nostra absque peccato orig. et ab eodem omnino separata et remota resurget et æternâ felicitate fruetur.

Conf. Gall. art. 11: Affirmamus, hoc vitium (orig.) etiam post bapt. esse vere peccatum, quod ad culpam attinet, quamvis qui filii dei sunt, minime idcirco condemnentur, quoniam videl. deus illud ipsis non imputat.

Conf. Belg. art. 15: Nec per bapt. (peccatum orig.) penitus exstinguitur aut radicitus evellitur, . . . quamvis dei filiis in condemnationem id non imputetur, verum gratiâ et misericordiâ ejus condonetur.

Thirty-nine Artt. art. ix.: And this infection of nature doth remain, yea in them that are regenerated; whereby the lust of the flesh is not subject to the law of God. And though there is no condemnation for them that believe and are baptized, yet the apostle doth confess that concupiscence and lust hath of itself the nature of sin.

Cf. *Dec. Thorun.* ii. 3. 7.

IV. Arminian.

The Arminians do not discern sin in the *inclinatio ad peccandum;* not only so, they also deny that this inclination remains necessarily in the regenerate all through life, or that there must of necessity be in consequence a conflict between the flesh and the spirit: vid. *Apol. Conf. Rem.* p. 128; Limborch, *Theol. christ.* v. 12. 2 seqq.

V. Quaker and Mennonite.

Barclay, *Apol.* Prop. iv.: This evil and corrupt seed is not imputed to infants, until they actually join with it. . . . Those who are under a physical impossibility of either hearing, knowing, or understanding any law, where the impossibility is not brought upon them by any act of their own, but is according to the very order of nature appointed by God, to such there is no law. Moreover, the Quakers reject the expression *original sin* as unbiblical.

Ris, *Confess.* art. 4: Primus homo in peccata lapsus . . . et a deo per consolatoria promissa iterum erectus et ad vitam æt. admissus est simul cum omnibus illis, qui lapsi erant, eousque ut *nemo posterorum* ipsius respectu hujus restitutionis *aut peccati aut culpæ reus nascatur.*

Schyn, *Plen. deduct.* p. 229: Quoted from the Frankenthal Protocol: fatetur, omne id, quod in peccato Adami ad æt. condemnationem facit, in Christo ademtum esse, quare infantes quoad reatum æt. damnationis per Christi obedientiam absolvantur, et absolute negat, peccatum originale in infantib. esse ad mortem æt. vel ipsos adhuc esse filios iræ naturâ reosque æt. mortis. (Condemnation rests upon man only through the peccata actualia which spring from the concupiscentia carnis.)

III. THIRD POINT OF DIVERGENCE.

Man, being born with moral inability, does also, during his life which lies under the imputation of sin, go on increasing the evil of his nature by actual transgression. No man doeth what is well-pleasing to God, so that he may be justified before God. In this all communions agree, and therefore hold in common that the divine help of grace through Christ is indispensable. But the Romanists, Greeks, Socinians, and Arminians believe that not everything the natural man does is simply sin in the sight of God; while the Lutherans and Calvinists teach that nothing but sin can proceed from the total corruption of the natural man in spiritual things, and that the natural man has free-will only *in rebus civilibus*. [The *Form. Conc.* (p. 675), however, makes the express reservation that this holds good only of the unbaptized, not of baptized Christians.]

I. Roman, Greek, etc.

Conc. Trid. sess. 6, can. 7 : Si quis dixerit, opera omnia, quæ ante justificationem fiunt, quacunque ratione facta sint, vere esse peccata vel odium dei mereri, aut, quanto vehementius quis nititur se disponere gratiam, tanto eum gravius peccare, anath. sit.

Cf. Möhler, *Symbol.* § 7 ; espec. Bellarmini *De gratia*, lib. 5. Dosithei *Confess.* c. 14 : ὅτι δύναται ὁ ἄνθρωπος φύσει ἐργάζεσθαι τὸ ἀγαθὸν ὑπαινίττεται μὲν καὶ ὁ κύριος, λέγων καὶ τοὺς ἐθνικοὺς ἀγαπᾶν τοὺς ἀγαπῶντας αὐτούς, διδάσκεται δὲ καὶ ὑπὸ τοῦ Παύλου (Rom. ii. 14), ἐξ ὧν φανερὸν καὶ τοῦτο, ὅτι δηλαδὴ ἀδύνατον, ὅτι ὃ ποίησει ὁ ἄνθρωπος ἀγαθὸν ἁμαρτίαν εἶναι· τὸ γὰρ καλὸν ἀδύνατον κακὸν εἶναι γινόμενον μέντοι φύσει μόνῃ καὶ ψυχικόν, οὐχὶ δὲ καὶ πνευματικὸν ποιεῖν τὸν μετερχόμενον, οὐ συμβάλλεται πρὸς σωτηρίαν ἁπλῶς ἄνευ πίστεως ἀλλ' οὐδὲ μὴν πρὸς κατάκρισιν.

F. Socin. *Opp.* ii. p. 463 b : Quilibet homo, ubi ad eam ætatem pervenerit, ut rationis usum habeat, si nullâ malâ institutione aut usu corruptus fuerit, posset si plane id vellet, nullum ex iis peccatis committere, quæ cum ipsâ ratione pugnant, eique per se omnino adversantur ; sed ut ea peccata vitare possit, quæ ipsi rationi per se non omnino adversantur, necesse est præterea, ut sibi persuadeat ac speret, si illa vitaverit, se ingens aliquod inde bonum consecuturum. Propterea deus præceptis suis, quæ per Chr. dedit, . . . addidit vitæ æternæ promissum cet.

Limborch, *Theol. christ.* iv. 11. 11 : Quodsi quidem gratiâ communi (d. i. ea, quam deus per opera creationis ac providentiæ omnibus hominibus communicat) recte utantur et pro virium sibi per illam concessarum modulo honestati naturali operam dent, illos etiam pro ratione status, in quo degunt, deo gratos esse credimus neque a salute prorsus exclusos, saltem igni infernali non adjudicandos.

II. Lutheran.

A. C. p. 15 : Humana voluntas habet aliquam libertatem ad efficiendam civilem justitiam et deligendas res rationi subjectas. Sed non habet vim sine Spiritu sancto efficiendæ justitiæ dei seu justitiæ spiritualis, quia animalis homo non percipit ea, quæ sunt Spiritus dei (1 Cor. ii. 14) ; sed hæc fit in cordibus, cum per verbum Spiritus sanctus concipitur. Hæc totidem verbis dicit Augustinus lib. 3. *Hypognosticon:* esse fatemur liberum arbitrium omnibus hominibus, habens quidem judicium rationis, non per quod sit idoneum in iis, quæ ad deum pertinent, sine deo aut inchoare aut certe peragere : sed tantum in operibus vitæ præsentis tam bonis, quam etiam malis. Bonis dico, quæ de bono naturæ oriuntur, i. e. velle laborare in agro, velle manducare et bibere, velle habere amicum, velle habere indumenta, velle fabricare domum, uxorem velle ducere, pecora nutrire, artem discere diversarum rerum bonarum, vel quicquid bonum ad præsentem pertinet vitam. Quæ omnia non sine divino gubernaculo subsistunt, imo ex ipso et per ipsum sunt et esse cœperunt. Malis vero dico, ut est velle idolum colere, velle homicidium cet.

F. C. p. 640 : Post lapsum homo hæreditario a parentibus accipit congenitam pravam vim, internam immunditiem cordis, pravas concupiscentias et pravas inclinationes, ita ut omnes naturâ talia corda, tales sensus et cogitationes ab Adamo hæreditaria et naturali propagatione consequamur, quæ secundum summas suas vires et juxta lumen rationis naturaliter e diametro cum deo et summis ipsius mandatis pugnent, atque inimicitiâ sint adversus deum, præsertim quantum ad res divinas et spirituales attinet. In aliis enim externis et hujus mundi rebus, quæ rationi subjectæ sunt, relictum est homini adhuc aliquid intellectus, virium et facultatum.

Ib. p. 657 : Etsi humana ratio seu naturalis intellectus hominis obscuram aliquam notitiæ illius scintillulam reliquam habet, quod sit deus, et particulam aliquam legis tenet : tamen adeo ignorans, cœca et perversa est ratio illa ut etiamsi ingeniosissimi et doctissimi homines in hoc mundo evangelion de filio dei et promissiones divinas de æternâ salute legant vel audiant, tamen ea propriis viribus percipere, intelligere, credere et vera esse statuere nequeant. Quin potius, quanto diligentius in eâ re elaborant, ut spirituales res istas suæ rationis acumine indagent et comprehendant, tanto minus intelligunt et credunt, et ea omnia pro stultitiâ et meris nugis et fabulis habent, priusquam a Spiritu sancto illuminentur et doceantur.

Ib. p. 661: Sacræ literæ hominis non renati cor duro lapidi, qui ad tactum non cedat, sed resistat, idem rudi trunco, interdum etiam feræ indomitæ comparant, non quod homo post lapsum non amplius sit rationalis creatura, aut quod absque auditu et meditatione verbi divini ad deum convertatur, aut quod in rebus externis et civilibus nihil boni aut mali intelligere possit, aut libere aliquid agere vel omittere queat.

Apol. A. C. p. 64: Quanquam justitiæ rationis lubentur tribuimus suas laudes, nullum enim majus bonum habet hæc natura corrupta... tamen non debet cum contumeliâ Christi laudari.... Falsum est et contumeliosum in Chr., quod non peccent homines facientes præcepta dei sine gratiâ.—P. 218: Illud falsum est, non peccare hominem, qui facit opera præceptorum extra gratiam.

F. C. p. 700 : Etsi opera illa, quæ ad conservandam externam disciplinam faciunt (qualia etiam ab infidelibus fiunt . . .) suam coram mundo dignitatem et laudem habent et temporalibus quibusdam præmiis in hoc mundo a deo ornantur, attamen, cum non ex verâ fide proficiscantur, revera coram deo sunt peccata, h. e. peccatis contaminata et a deo pro peccatis et immunditiâ reputantur propter naturæ hum. corruptionem et quia persona cum deo non est reconciliata. Cf. p. 667.

[*Form. Conc.* p. 675: Quapropter ingens discrimen est inter homines baptizatos et non baptizatos. Cum enim juxta Pauli doctrinam omnes qui baptizati sunt, Christum induerint, et revera sint renati: habent illi jam liberatum arbitrium, hoc est, rursus liberati sunt, ut Christus testatur. Unde etiam non modo verbum Dei audiunt, verum etiam, licet non sine multâ infirmitate, eidem assentiri illudque fide amplecti possunt.— It is under this aspect that we must view all that the Confessions, especially the *F. C.*, say of the " unregenerate."]

III. REFORMED.

Conf. Helv. ii. 9 : Nullum est ad bonum homini arbitrium

liberum nondum renato, vires nullæ ad perficiendum bonum.—
Terrenarum rerum intelligentia in lapso homine non est nulla.
Reliquit enim deus ex misericordiâ ingenium, multum tamen
distans ab eo, quod inerat ante lapsum. Nemo negat, in
externis et regenitos et non regenitos habere liberum arbitrium;
habet enim homo hanc constitutionem cum animantibus aliis
communem, ut alia velit, alia nolit. Ita loqui potest aut
tacere, domo egredi vel domi manere cet.

Conf. Gall. 9 : Etsi enim nonnullam habet boni et mali discretionem, affirmamus tamen, quidquid habet lucis, mox fieri tenebras, quum de quærendo deo agitur, adeo ut suâ intelligentiâ et ratione nullo modo possit ad eum accedere; item, quamvis voluntate sit præditus, quâ ad hoc vel illud movetur, tamen quum ea sit penitus sub peccato captiva, nullam prorsus habet ad bonum appetendum libertatem, nisi quam ex gratiâ et dei dono acceperit.

Thirty-nine Artt. art. xiii. : Works done before the grace of Christ and the inspiration of His Spirit are not pleasant to God; forasmuch as they spring not of faith in Jesus Christ, neither do they make men meet to receive grace; yea, rather, for that they are not done as God hath commanded and willed them to be done, we doubt not but that they have the nature of sin.

Canon. Dordrac. iii. 4. : Residuum quidem est post lapsum in homine lumen aliquod naturæ, cujus beneficio ille notitias quasdam de deo, de rebus naturalibus, de discrimine honestorum et turpium retinet et aliquod virtutis ac disciplinæ externæ studium ostendit. Sed tantum abest, ut hoc naturæ lumine ad salutarem dei cognitionem pervenire et ad eum se convertere possit, ut ne quidem eo in naturalibus ac civilibus recte utatur, quin imo qualecunque id demum sit, id totum variis modis contaminet atque in injustitiâ detineat. Quod dum facit, coram deo inexcusabilis redditur.·

Declar. Thorun. ii. 3. 6.

IV. QUAKER.

Barclay, *Apol.* Prop. v. : For we affirm that, as all men partake of the fruit of Adam's fall, in that, by reason of that evil seed which through him is communicated unto them, they are prone and inclined only to evil, though thousands of thousands be ignorant of Adam's fall, neither ever knew of the eating of the forbidden fruit. . . . This light, seed, etc., appears to be no power or natural faculty of man's mind. This light and seed of God in man he cannot move and stir up when he pleaseth.

As to the works of the natural man, and their value, see Prop. vii. 10; and as to the religious and moral powers of the natural man, see Prop. v. vi.: This most certain doctrine being then received, that there is an evangelical and saving light and grace in all, the universality of the love and mercy of God towards mankind, both on the death of His beloved Son, the Lord Jesus Christ, and in the manifestation of the light in the heart, is established and confirmed against all the objections of such as deny it. . . . By whose inward and secret touches they feel themselves turned from the evil to the good, and learn to do to others as they would be done by, in which Christ Himself affirms all to be included.

VI.

PERSON OF CHRIST, AND HIS DIVINITY.

DIVERGENCE.

To save mankind from ruin, and to bring men back to Himself, God sent forth His Son. It is agreed on all sides that Christ is true man; but, at the same time, in some sense *God*. The Socinians maintain that Christ, by His nature man, became only in time partaker of divine power and glory, and therefore is not essentially equal with God. The other Christian communions, however, ascribe to Christ eternal Deity, and therefore perfect equality of nature with God the Father. These speak of an incarnation of the Son of God; the former of an exaltation of the *man Jesus*, conceived of the Holy Ghost, and consequently begotten as the Son of God, to divine majesty. The latter acknowledge in Christ two distinct but internally united natures; but the former only one nature, and that the human.

THE SOCINIAN SYMBOLS.

THE HUMAN NATURE OF CHRIST.

Catech. Racov. p. 45 : Quænam ea sunt, quæ ad Christi personam referuntur ? Id solum, quod naturâ sit homo verus, olim quidem, cum in terris viveret, mortalis, nunc vero immortalis.—P. 46 : (Final Revision) Jesus nullo pacto est purus et vulgaris homo. Quia licet naturâ sit homo, nihilominus tamen simul est unigenitus dei filius idque etiam a primo ortu. Etenim conceptus e Spiritus s. et e virgine, sine ullo viri congressu natus, nullum alium patrem hactenus præter deum habuit.

F. Socin. *Breviss. Inst.* p. 654 a: De Christi essentiâ ita statuo, illum esse hominem in virginis utero et sic sine viri ope divini spiritus vi conceptum ac formatum indeque genitum, primum quidem patibilem et mortalem, donec scilicet munus sibi a deo demandatum in terris obivit, deinde vero, postquam in cœlum ascendit, impatibilem et immortalem factum.

Ostorodt, *Unterr.* c. 6, p. 48 : We therefore hold that the essence or the nature of the Son of God is no other than man's essence : He was true man, and we know no other nature in Him. But we acknowledge this also, that He had a beginning different from that of other men ; that is, that He received His origin and existence not from a man, but from God Himself ; since the Virgin Mary conceived Him of the Holy Ghost, that is, by the power of God, for which reason He was to be called the Son of God. He is therefore God's Son, yea, His only-begotten Son, from the beginning of His existence. God never had another son like Him, who by His own power alone was conceived in His mother's womb and born : yea, he was the natural Son of God for the same reason, since he was not adopted, and had never been the son of another before, but always and only and from the beginning the Son of God.

On the Deity of Christ, see the Socinian propositions above (No. ii.) ; and, against the incarnation, comp. *Cat. Racov.* qu. 144–156.

Since the Socinians deny the eternal Godhead of the Redeemer, they cannot admit that He had naturally the knowledge of the counsels of God for human salvation. Hence they assume that Christ was caught up into heaven before His appearance in His mission ; and that thus He received immediately from God the doctrines of the new economy which He was to unfold to the world.

Cat. Rac. p. 146 : Quâ ratione ipse Jesus ad ipsius divinæ voluntatis notitiam pervenit ? Eâ ratione, quod in cœlum ascenderit ibique patrem suum et eam, quam nobis annunciavit, vitam et beatitatem viderit, et ea omnia, quæ docere deberet, ab eodem patre audierit : a quo deinde e cœlo in terram demissus, Spir. s. immensâ copiâ perfusus fuit, cujus afflatu cuncta, quæ a patre didicit, prolocutus est. (John iii. 13, vi. 46, viii. 26, cet.)

Observations.

It is not necessary to adduce testimonies from the several symbols of the communions on a subject which is perfectly clear. Romanists, Greeks, and Protestants agree in accepting on this matter the Three Creeds. Cf. *Cat. Rom.* i. 3, viii. 4, 5 ; Gen. *Conf.* 23 ; *Conf. orth.* 66 ; *Metr. Critop.* c. 1 ; *Conf. Helv.* ii. 11 ; *Gall.* 14 ; *Thirty-nine Artt.* ii. ; *Belg.* 19 ; *Conf. Aug.* p. 10 ; *Apol.* p. 50 ; *A. Sm.* p. 303 ; *Cat. maj.* 493 ; *F. C.* art. viii. ; *Conf. Rem.* viii. 3 ; Ris, *Conf.* 8.

THE RELATION OF THE TWO NATURES.

A subordinate controversy has been raised as to the mutual relation of the two natures in Christ. It had its origin in the sacramental contention between Luther and Zwingli. Luther and the Lutheran Church affirmed that the *communio naturarum* in the *unio personalis*, which is matter of Christian faith involves a real mutual *communicatio idiomatum*, or interchange of properties, so that the divine nature imparts to the human its attributes, that is, omnipotence, omnipresence, and omniscience : whence, of course, it follows that the body of Christ may be everywhere present in the Eucharist.[1] But Zwingli, and with him the Reformed Church, maintained that such a real communication was a thing impossible, and therefore denied it : the scriptural phrases on which the doctrine is supposed to depend he treated as merely figures of speech. The Roman Catholic Church, as such, took no part in the controversy : only a few of her polemical divines have expressly declared against the *communicatio idiomatum.* Bellarm. *de Christo*, iii. 10 seq. ; Becan. *Man. Cont.* ii. 1 ; Klee, *Kath. Dog.* i. 435.

I. LUTHERAN.

F. C. p. 767 : Postquam Ch. non communi ratione, ut alius

---

[1] The main points in this controversy revolve around the first of the three kinds of *communicatio* laid down by theologians, the *genus majestaticum* (cf. *Conf. Helv.* ii. 11). How far the other two were affected, see Schubert, *Theol. Pol.* iii. 157.

quispiam sanctus in cœlos ascendit, sed, ut apostolus (Eph. iv. 10) testatur, super omnes cœlos ascendit, et revera omnia implet et ubique non tantum ut deus, verum etiam ut homo, præsens dominatur et regnat a mari ad mare, et usque ad terminos terræ, quemadmodum olim prophetæ de ipso sunt vaticinati, et apostoli (Mrc. xvi. 20) testantur, quod Christus ipsis ubique co-operatus sit, et sermonem ipsorum sequentibus signis confirmaverit. Hæc autem non terreno modo, sed, ut D. Lutherus loqui solet, pro modo et ratione dexteræ dei facta sunt, quæ non est certus aliquis et circumscriptus in cœlo locus (ut Sacramentarii sine testimonio sacræ scripturæ fingunt), sed nihil aliud est, nisi omnipotens dei virtus, quæ cœlum et terram implet, in cujus possessionem Christus, juxta humanitatem suam, sine confusione tamen et exæquatione naturarum, et in essentiâ, et in essentialibus proprietatibus, realiter seu revera venit. Ex hac communicatâ sibi divinâ virtute homo Christus, juxta verba Testamenti sui, corpore et sanguine suo in sacrâ cœnâ, ad quam nos verbo suo ablegat, præsens esse potest et revera est.

Ib. p. 768 : Ex hoc fundamento, cujus jam facta est mentio, et quod unio personalis docet, quomodo videlicet divina et humana natura in personâ Christi sint unitæ, ut non modo nomina communia, sed realiter etiam et re ipsâ inter se, sine omni confusione et exæquatione essentiarum, communicent, promanat etiam doctrina illa de communicatione idiomatum duarum in Christo naturarum.

Ib. p. 773 : Quantum ad divinam in Christo naturam attinet, cum in ipso nulla sit transmutatio, divinæ Christi naturæ per incarnationem nihil (quoad essentiam et proprietates ejus) vel accessit vel decessit, et per eam in se vel per se neque diminuta neque aucta est. . . . Quod ad humanam naturam in personâ Christi attinet, non defuerunt quidam, qui contenderent, eam in personali etiam cum divinitate unione nihil amplius habere, quam duntaxat suas naturales essentiales proprietates, quarum ratione fratribus suis per omnia similis est. Unde affirmarunt, humanæ in Christo naturæ nihil eorum tribui vel debere vel posse, quod sit supra vel contra naturales ipsius proprietates, etiamsi scripturæ testimonia humanæ Christi naturæ talia tribuant. Hanc vero ipsorum opinionem falsam esse, verbo dei adeo perspicue demonstrari potest, ut etiam ipsorum consortes cum ipsum errorem reprehendere et rejicere tandem cœperint. Sacræ enim literæ et orthodoxi patres scripturæ verbis edocti præclare testantur, quod humana natura in Christo eam ob causam et inde adeo, quod cum divinâ naturâ personaliter unita est, (deposito servili statu et humiliatione, jam glorificata et ad dexteram majestatis et virtutis divinæ exaltata) præter et supra naturales, essentiales atque in ipsa permanentes humanas proprietates, etiam singulares, excellentissimas, maximas, supernaturales, impervestigabiles, ineffabiles atque cœlestes prærogativas majestatis, gloriæ, virtutis ac potentiæ super omne, quod nominatur, non solum in hoc seculo, sed etiam in futuro, acceperit, ut ita humana in Christo natura (suo modo et ratione) in exsequendo officio Christi simul adhibeatur, co-operetur et suam efficaciam, id est virtutem et operationem habeat, non tantum ex suis naturalibus proprietatibus aut secundum essentiales proprietates aut quousque earum virtus et efficacia progreditur, sed præcipue secundum majestatem, gloriam, virtutem atque potentiam, quam per unionem hypostaticam, glorificationem et exaltationem accepit.

Ib. p. 778 : His vocabulis (realis communicatio, realiter communicari) nunquam ullam physicam communicationem vel essentialem transfusionem (quâ naturæ in suis essentiis aut essentialibus proprietatibus confunderentur) docere voluimus, ut quidam vocabula et phrases illas astute et malitiose falsâ interpretatione, contra conscientiam suam, pervertere non dubitarunt, tantum ut piam doctrinam suspicionibus iniquissimis gravarent : sed vocabula et phrases illas verbali communicationi opposuimus, cum quidam fingerent, communicationem idiomatum nihil aliud, nisi phrasin et modum quendam loquendi, hoc est mera tantum verba, nomina et titulos inanes esse ; et hanc verbalem communicationem adeo urserunt, ut de nullâ aliâ communicatione audire quidquam vellent. Quapropter ad recte declarandam majestatem Christi vocabula (de reali communicatione) usurpavimus, ut significaremus, communicationem illam vere et reipsâ (sine omni tamen naturarum et proprietatum essentialium confusione) factam esse.

Ib. 779 : Quare testimonia illa sacræ scripturæ, quæ de eâ majestate loquuntur, ad quam humana in Christo natura exaltata est, non in eam sententiam accipimus, quod divina illa majestas (quæ divinæ naturæ filii dei propria est) in personâ filii hominis tantum secundum divinam naturam Christo sit adscribenda aut quod majestas illa tantum eâ ratione sit in humanâ Christi naturâ nudum tantum titulum et nomen solum divinæ illius majestatis, per phrasin et modum loquendi, revera autem nullam prorsus cum ea communicationem habeat.

Ib. p. 780 : Credimus, docemus et confitemur, non fieri talem majestatis dei et omnium proprietatum ejus effusionem in humanam naturam Christi, quâ divinæ naturæ aliquid decedat, aut ut de suo alii ita largiatur aliquid, quod hac ratione sibi ipsa non in se retineat aut quod humana natura in substantiâ atque essentiâ suâ parem majestatem acceperit, quæ a naturâ et essentiâ divinæ naturæ sit separata et divisa, quasi cum vinum, aqua aut oleum de uno vase in aliud transfunditur. Neque enim vel humana in Christo natura vel ulla alia creatura in cœlo aut in terrâ eo modo omnipotentiæ divinæ capax est, ut per se omnipotens essentia et natura fiat aut omnipotentes proprietates in se et per se habeat. Hac enim ratione humana natura in Christo abnegaretur et in divinitatem prorsus transmutaretur.

II. Reformed.

Wahr. Bek. der Diener der Kirche zu Zürch. 1545 : The true human body of Christ has not been, since the ascension, with His rational human soul deified, that is, changed into God, but has only been glorified. By that glorification, however, the nature of the human body has not been abolished; its infirmities have been removed, and that body has been made glorious, illustrious, and immortal. Since the ascension Christ has been no longer corporeally upon earth ; for, according to the attributes of His real human body, He can be only in one place, and not everywhere present.

Conf. Helv. ii. 11 : Non docemus, veritatem corporis Christi a clarificatione desiisse aut deificatam adeoque sic deificatam esse, ut suas proprietates, quoad corpus et animam, deposuerit ac prorsus in naturam divinam abierit unaque duntaxat substantia esse cœperit.

Conf. Gall. 15 : Credimus, in unâ eademque personâ, quæ est Jesus Christus, vere et inseparabiliter duas illas naturas sic esse conjunctas, ut etiam sint unitæ, manente tamen unaquaque illarum naturarum in suâ distinctâ proprietate, ita ut, quemadmodum in istâ conjunctione, divina verbi natura proprietates suas retinens mansit increata, infinita et omnia replens, sic etiam natura humana manserit mansuraque sit in æternum finita, suam illam naturalem formam, dimensionem atque adeo proprietatem habens, cui nimirum veritatem humanæ naturæ non ademerit resurrectio et glorificatio sive assumtio ad dexteram patris.

Conf. Angl. p. 89 sq. . . . (Credimus) quamvis majestas et divinitas Christi ubique diffusa sit, tamen corpus ejus . . . in uno loco esse oportere : Christum corpori suo majestatem dedisse, naturam tamen corporis non ademisse : neque ita asserendum esse Christum deum, ut cum negemus esse hominem.

Conf. Belg. art. 19 : Sed duæ naturæ in unam personam unitæ, quarum utraque proprietates suas distinctas retineat, adeo ut sicut natura divina semper increata permansit absque initio dierum et vitæ fine, cœlum et terram implens, sic humana natura proprietates suas non amiserit, sed creatura remanserit, initium dierum et naturam finitam habens, omniaque illa, quæ vero corpori conveniunt, retinens. Et quamvis eidem naturæ immortalitatem resurrectione suâ dederit, nihilominus veritatem ejus non commutavit, si quidem . . . resurrectio nostra etiam a veritate ejus corporis dependet.

The *Admonitio de lib. Concordiæ*, which was issued, 1581, from Neustadt, states the point of controversy thus : Naturis singulis in personâ Ch. realiter communicari proprietates essentiales alterius naturæ, negamus et pernegamus cum scripturâ et universâ orthodoxâ ecclesiâ. Personæ autem Ch. utriusque naturæ nomina, proprietates et operationes omnes communicari realissime, cum iisdem asserimus . . . contra nostros adversarios, qui aliqua deo humana et homini aliqua divina tribuentes confundunt naturas, et aliqua adimentes personam Ch. dissolvunt. Etenim personæ, quia realiter utramque naturam in suâ substantiâ complectitur, realiter et verissime competit, quidquid sive utriusque sive alterutrius est naturæ, propter naturarum unionem. At naturæ uni nequaquam est commune, quod alterius est proprium propter naturarum essentiale et æternum discrimen. Hoc est illud, quod dicitur . . . permutari prædicata s. attributa Ch. de subjectis concretis tantum, non autem de abstractis. . . . Non est igitur quæstio, an deo, sed an deitati realiter humana competant, neque an homini, sed an humanitati realiter divina competant. Illud enim confitemur, hoc negamus.

Conf. Brand. 4 : They confess that they, in the article of the Person of Christ, heartily believe that in Christ there are two inseparable natures, the divine and the human, so personally united and conjoined, that they cannot be and never will be separated. Each nature we hold to retain its natural properties even after this personal union, while at the same time there is a true communion and fellowship. We believe that Christ is with us, and abides with us to the end of the world, according to His infinite nature, that is, according to His divine majesty, but not according to that nature in which He ascended to heaven, and in which He will come again from heaven, which cannot, even in its highest glory, be everywhere present without the abolition of its own attributes. We believe also that the Lord Christ has been in His assumed humanity enriched and crowned with high and supernatural gifts, as in Ps. viii.; yet that the human nature has not been transformed into deity, nor made like unto God, which is the Eutychian error.

(Zwinglii *Exegesis eucharisticæ negotii* (*Opp.* iii. p. 525): Est ἀλλοίωσις, quantum huc attinet, desultus vel transitus ille aut si mavis permutatio, qua de alterâ in Chr. naturâ loquentes alterius vocibus utimur. Ut cum Ch. ait : caro mea vere est cibus, caro proprie est humanæ in illo naturæ, attamen per commutationem h. l. pro divinâ ponitur naturâ. Quâ ratione enim filius dei est, eâ ratione est animæ cibus. . . . Rursus cum perhibet filium familias a colonis trucidandum, cum filius familias divinitatis ejus nomen sit, pro humanâ tamen naturâ accipit, secundum enim istam mori potuit, secundum divinam minime. Cum, inquam, de alterâ naturâ prædicatur, quoad alterius, id tandem est alloeosis aut idiomatum communicatio aut commutatio.)

Cf. *Conf. Czengeri.* art. 8 ; *Colloq. Lips.* p. 33 ; *Conf.*

Anhalt. art. 8; and the appended *Ass. Cath. de mysterio incarnationis cct.*; also Calvin, *Institut.* iv. 17. 30; Heidegger, *Corp. theol.* xvii. 46 sqq.; Wyttenbach, *Theol. dogm.* ii. p. 708 sqq.

[The passages by which the fathers of the Lutheran Church thought themselves bound to defend and teach the real impartation of the properties of the divine nature to the human in the personal union, are especially Col. ii. 9, John vi. 53 seq., John v. 27, Matt. xxviii. 18, Phil. ii. 9, 10, John i. 14.]

III. QUAKER.

With respect to the Somatic or corporeity in Christ, there are two singular opinions of the Quakers and the Anabaptist Mennonites which must be adduced. The former ascribe to Christ a double body; that is, besides the earthly and visible body with which He was clothed in the womb of the Virgin, He had a heavenly and spiritual body, by means of which He has from the beginning communicated Himself to men, and effects continuously the union of the enlightened with God. The Anabaptists and older Mennonites did not regard the human body of Christ as having been begotten in the womb of the Virgin, but as created by the Holy Ghost, thus removing every possibility of original sin in Christ.

Barclay, *Apol.* Prop. xiii. 2: The body, then, of Christ which believers partake of is spiritual, and not carnal; and His blood which they drink of is pure and heavenly, and not human or elementary. . . . If it be asked, What that body, what that flesh and blood is? I answer, It is that heavenly seed, that divine, spiritual, celestial substance, that spiritual body of Christ, whereby and through which He communicateth life to men, and salvation to as many as believe in Him and receive Him, and whereby also man comes to have fellowship and communion with God. This is proved from the sixth chapter of John, from ver. 32 to the end, where Christ speaks more at large of this matter than in any other place. . . . From this large description of the origin, nature, and effects of this body, flesh and blood of Christ, it is apparent that it is spiritual, and to be understood of a spiritual body or temple of Jesus Christ, which was born of the Virgin Mary, and in which He walked, lived, and suffered in the land of Judæa, because it is said that it came down from heaven, yea, that it is He that came down from heaven. Now all Christians at present generally acknowledge that the outward body of Christ came not down from heaven; neither was it that part of Christ which came down from heaven; and, to put the matter out of doubt, when the carnal Jews would have been so understanding it, He tells them plainly, ver. 63, *It is the spirit that quickeneth, the flesh profiteth nothing.* . . . So, then, as there was the outward visible body and temple of Jesus Christ, which took its origin from the Virgin Mary, there is also the spiritual body of Christ, by and through which He that was *the Word in the beginning with God*, and was and is God, did reveal Himself to the sons of men in all ages, and whereby men in all ages come to be made partakers of eternal life, and to have communion and fellowship with God and Christ. Now, as the outward body and temple was called Christ, so was also His spiritual body no less properly, and that long before that outward body was in being. Hence the apostle saith, 1 Cor. x. 3, 4, that *the fathers did eat the same spiritual meat, and did all drink the same spiritual drink: for they drank of that spiritual rock that followed them, and that rock was Christ.* This cannot be understood otherwise than of the spiritual body of Christ; which spiritual body of Christ, though it was the saving food of the righteous both before the law and under the law, yet under the law it was veiled and shadowed, and covered under divers types, ceremonies, and observations; yea, and not only so, but it was veiled and hid in some respect under the outward temple and body of Christ, or during the continuance of it; so that the Jews could not understand Christ's preaching about it while on earth.

IV. ANABAPTIST.

For the Anabaptist dogma above referred to (to which the *Conf. Belg.* art. 18 refers), see *F. C.* p. 828. Menno Sim. had adopted it; it was accepted in the Emden *Colloquium*, and in the *Hoorns. Conff.* But the other Mennonite Confessions contain nothing on the subject; and a Synod at Strasburg, 1555, decreed: Christum suam carnem et sanguinem a Mariâ accepisse. Cf. *Pr. Mennon. de origine hum. Ch. nat. vera sententia,* Jena 1753.

VII.
REDEMPTION: THE MERITS OF CHRIST.

FIRST POINT OF DIVERGENCE.

ALL Christians are agreed that Christ is the supreme Benefactor of the world in a religious point of view, and that we all, in particular, owe to Him the possibility of return to God, and of obtaining the forgiveness of sins, with that eternal life which is dependent on forgiveness. But difference arises as to the medium through which Christ effected the reconciliation between men and God. The greater number of Christian communities acknowledge this medium to be the substitutionary death of Christ, the passion and cross, and regard the reconciliation as a divine act of grace, based immediately upon this meritorious act of Christ. The Socinians deny altogether the procurement of forgiveness through the death of Christ, rejecting the satisfaction of the Redeemer. They hold the death of Christ to have been merely the powerful seal and confirmation, as of the doctrine of Jesus, so also of the forgiving grace of God, and at the same time as a mighty incitement to departure from sin.[1] Christ, on their principles, only mediately redeemed from sin; His merit consisted mainly in His perfect and efficient announcement of the will and the promises of God. Thus He showed mankind the infallible way of blessedness; and every man who chooses this way, that is, fulfils the commandments of Christ, attains through Him to salvation.

[1] In the *Cat. Rac.* the death of Christ is significantly included in the *munus propheticum*, the prophetic office.

While, therefore, among all other Christian confessions, the death of Christ is the centre or consummation of all that Christ accomplished and provided for man, the Socinians repute that death only as a co-operant element in the meritorious service of Christ. The former hold that the resurrection was the seal and consummation of the death of Christ as an expiatory death; but the Socinians regard the death of Jesus mainly as the basis of His resurrection, because without the death there could have been no rising again, without the rising again there could have been no confirmation of the hope of eternal life, and no elevation of Christ to that place of heavenly dignity where He could act efficiently for the salvation of His people. The former Christian communions maintain that the doctrine, and also the example of Christ, were only part of His work, standing in the closest and most necessary connection with His atoning death; but the Socinians unite the two in one, and make this the essential matter in Christ's work, His death being subordinate and ministrant to it. Christianity is to them, in fact, essentially a revelation of the divine will, and Christ a new and more perfect divine lawgiver.[1]

SYMBOLICAL TESTIMONIES.

I. Romish.

Conc. Trid. sess. vi. cap. 7 : Christus, qui, cum essemus inimici, propter nimiam caritatem, quâ dilexit nos, nobis suâ sanctissimâ passione ligno crucis justificationem meruit et pro nobis deo patri satisfecit. Cf. sess. v. 3.

Cat. Rom. i. 5. 11 : Hoc in passione et morte filius dei spectavit, ut omnium ætatum peccata redimeret ac deleret et pro eis patri abunde cumulateque satisfaceret. — ii. 5. 63 : Prima satisfactio et præstantissima illa est, quâ pro scelerum

---

[1] Hence the definition of the Christian religion in Socinus : Religio Christiana est doctrina cœlestis docens veram viam perveniendi ad vitam æternam. Hæc autem via nihil est aliud quam obedire Deo juxta ea quæ ille nobis præcepit per Dom. nostr. J. C. A celestial doctrine, that is, teaching the way of life, which way is obedience to the commandments given through Christ.

nostrorum ratione, etiamsi deus summo jure nobiscum velit agere, quidquid a nobis debeatur, cumulate persolutum est: hæc vero ejusmodi esse dicitur, quæ nobis deum propitium et placatum reddidit, eamque uni Christo acceptam ferimus, qui in cruce pretio pro peccatis nostris soluto plenissime deo satisfecit.

II. GREEK.

Conf. orthod. p. 85 sq.: Ὁ θάνατος τοῦ Χριστοῦ, νὰ ἦτον μὲ διαφορώτερον τρόπον, παρὰ ὅπου ἦτον τῶν ἄλλων ὅλων ἀνθρώπων, διὰ ταῖς ἀφορμαῖς τούταις· πρῶτον διὰ τὸ βάρος τῶν ἁμαρτιῶν μας, δεύτερον διατὶ εἰς τὸν σταυρὸν ἀπάνω ἐπλήρου τὴν ἱερωσύνην· ἑαυτὸν προσενέγκας τῷ θεῷ καὶ πατρὶ εἰς ἀπολύτρωσιν τοῦ γένους τῶν ἀνθρώπων. Ἐκεῖ ἀκόμι εἰς τὸν σταυρὸν ἐτελείωνε τὴν μεσιτείαν ἀνάμεσον θεοῦ καὶ ἀνθρώπων. (Col. i. 20, ii. 14.)
Cf. Plato, *Catech.* S. 95 f.

III. PROTESTANT.

C. A. p. 10: (Docent, quod filius dei sit) vere passus, crucifixus, mortuus et sepultus, ut reconciliaret nobis patrem et hostia esset non tantum pro culpâ originis, sed etiam pro omnibus actualibus hominum peccatis. *Ibid.* art. 4: Peccata remitti propter Christum, qui suâ morte pro nostris peccatis satisfecit.

Apol. A. C. p. 93: Christus, quia sine peccato subiit pœnam peccati et victima pro nobis factus est, sustulit illud jus legis, ne accuset, ne damnet hoc, qui credunt in ipsum, quia ipse est propitiatio pro eis, propter quam nunc justi reputantur.

Catech. maj. p. 495: Dominus ad hæc passus, mortuus et sepultus, ut pro me satisfaceret meamque culpam, quæ mihi luenda fuerat, persolveret, non auro neque argento, sed proprio et pretioso suo sanguine.

Conf. Helv. ii. cap. 15: Christus peccata mundi in se recepit et sustulit divinæque justitiæ satisfecit. Deus ergo propter solum Christum passum et resuscitatum propitius est peccatis nostris nec illa nobis imputat.

Conf. Gall. art. 17 : Credimus, eo unico sacrificio, quod J. C. in cruce obtulit, nos esse deo reconciliatos. . . . Testamur, Christum esse integram et perfectam nostram ablutionem, in cujus morte plenam satisfactionem nanciscimur cet.

Conf. Belg. art. 21 : Credimus, J. C. summum illum sacerdotem esse, . . . qui se nostro nomine coram patre stitit ad iram ipsius plenâ satisfactione suâ placandum, offerens se ipsum in ligno crucis pretiosumque sanguinem suum ad purgationem peccatorum nostrorum effundens. *Cat. Heidelb.* 37–40 ; Calvin, *Instit.* ii. 14. 5 ; comp. *Conf. Remonstr.* viii. 7, 9.

West. Conf. ch. viii. sec. 5 : The Lord Jesus, by His perfect obedience and sacrifice of Himself, which He through the Eternal Spirit once offered up unto God, hath fully satisfied the justice of His Father, and purchased not only reconciliation, but an everlasting inheritance in the kingdom of heaven, for all those whom the Father hath given unto Him. Sec. 6 : Although the work of redemption was not actually wrought by Christ till after His incarnation, yet the virtue, efficacy, and benefits thereof were communicated unto the elect in all ages successively from the beginning of the world, in and by those promises, types, and sacrifices wherein He was revealed and signified to be the Seed of the woman which should bruise the serpent's head, and the Lamb slain from the beginning of the world, being yesterday and to-day the same, and for ever.

The Sinlessness and Obedience of Christ.

The life of Jesus, as preceding His death, is introduced by the older Protestant symbols, only so far as it involves the perfect sinlessness of Christ: *Apol.* p. 93 ; *Eng. Artt.* 15 ; *Conf. Gall.* 14. The perfect goodness of Christ fitted Him, as man, to be the effectual atonement for all, since for Himself He had not to suffer death. The sinless obedience was the necessary antecedent of the atonement. On the other hand, the *Form. Conc.* describes the sinless life of Jesus, referred to the divine law, as the perfect fulfilment of that law by Christ in the stead of men; consequently as itself an act of satisfaction—the *obedientia activa.* On the Reformed side this is given in the form of a hint, *Helv.* ii. 11, *Cat. Heid.* 36 ; and as an express and plain affirmation in *Form. Cons. Helv.* c. xv. (against Piscator).

SYMBOLS.

F. C. p. 684: Justitia illa, quæ coram deo fidei aut credentibus ex merâ gratiâ imputatur, est obedientia, passio et resurrectio Ch., quibus ille legi nostrâ causâ satisfecit et peccata nostra expiavit. Cum enim Ch. non tantum homo, verum deus et homo sit, in unâ personâ indivisâ, tam non fuit legi subjectus, quam non fuit passioni et morti (ratione suæ personæ) obnoxius, quia dominus legis fuit. Eam ob causam ipsius obedientia non ea tantum, quâ patri paruit in tota suâ passione et morte, verum etiam, quâ nostrâ causâ sponte sese legi subjecit eamque obedientiâ illâ suâ implevit, nobis ad justitiam imputatur, ita ut deus propter totam obedientiam, quam Christus agendo et patiendo in vitâ et morte suâ nostrâ causâ patri suo cœlesti præstitit, peccata nobis remittat, pro bonis et justis nos reputet et salute æternâ donet. . .

P. 697: Fides nostra respicit in personam Christi, quatenus illa pro nobis legi sese subjecit, peccata nostra pertulit et cum ad patrem suum iret, solidam, absolutam et perfectissimam obedientiam jam inde a nativitate suâ sanctissimâ usque ad mortem patri suo cœlesti pro nobis miserrimis peccatoribus præstitit.

Form. Consens. Helv. c. 15: Ita Chr. vice electorum obedientia mortis suæ deo patri satisfecit, ut in censum tamen vicariæ justitiæ et obedientiæ illius universa ejus, quam per totius vitæ suæ curriculum legi . . . sive agendo sive patiendo præstitit, obedientia vocari debeat. Rotundo asserit ore spiritus dei, Christum sanctissima vita legi et justitiæ div. pro nobis satisfecisse et pretium illud, quo emti sumus deo, non in passionibus duntaxat sed totâ ejus vitâ legi conformatâ collocat. . . . 16. Hæc cum ita se omnino habeant, haud sane probare possumus oppositam doctrinam illorum, qui . . . justitiam Ch. activam et passivam ita partiuntur, ut asserant, activam cum sibi pro suâ vindicare, passivam vero demum electis donare et imputare. (Cf. Wyttenbach, *Theol. dogm.* ii. p. 789 sqq.)

Against the *obedientia activa Christi* protested Soc. *Prælect.* c. 18; Limborch, *Th. ch.* iii. 21; and many Romanists. Barclay, *Apol.* vii. 8, mentions, in passing, the complete obedience of Christ as, together with His passion and death, belonging to the atonement. Episcopius abolishes the *obed. act. satisfactoria*, by asserting that Christ must needs fulfil the divine law for Himself.

I. Protestant.

The older symbols did not touch the question whether Christ was Mediator in one or in both natures; but the controversy between Osiander and Stancarus gave occasion for the decision of the Lutheran Church in the *F. C.* art. 3, in harmony with the œcumenical doctrine of the inseparable union of the two natures in Christ.

Form. Conc. art. 3 : Quod Ch. vere sit nostra justitia sed tamen neque secundum solam div. naturam neque sec. solam hum. naturam, sed totus Chr. sec. utramque naturam in solâ videlicet obedientiâ suâ, quam patri ad mortem usque absolutissimam deus et homo præstitit eaque nobis peccatorum omnium remissionem et vitam æt. promeruit. Cf. *Conf. Belg.* art. 19.—Against the scholastic assertion that Christ was Mediator only in the human nature (si sermo sit de principio formali, non de ipso supposito), which Bellarmine defended, the symbols do not enter any special protest.

II. Socinian.

The prophetic office of Christ consists, according to the *Cat. Rac.* p. 145, in this, that Christ perfectly manifested, confirmed, and surrounded by sanctions, the will of God otherwise hidden from us. But this will embraces, p. 148, the perfect precepts and promises of God; and among the latter life eternal is reputed the greatest, the remission of sins promised freely of the divine grace being included in this. The confirmation of the divine will was given through Christ, in harmony with the divine counsels, among other means by His death. But Christ suffered death for our sins : how and wherefore is declared as follows :—*Cat. Rac.* p. 261 seq. : Ch. pro pecc. n. passus est, primo, ut omnibus peccatoribus hac ratione jus certissimum fieret peccatorum remissionis ipsiusque adeo vitæ æt., proinde etiam non dubia fides. Secundo, ut omnes peccatores ad Ch. incitarentur et traherentur, in hoc et per hunc solum peccatorum remissionem quærentes, qui pro iis esset mortuus. Tertio, ut suam hac ratione deus humano generi immensam testaretur caritatem illudque sibi penitus reconciliaret. — P. 262 : At quæ ratio erat, quia iisdem afflictionibus et morti ejusmodi credentes sint obnoxii, easdem afflictiones et mortem Christo perferendi ? Duæ ejus rei extitere causæ, quemadmodum etiam duplici ratione Christus nos servat: primum enim, et certam nobis salutis spem facit, et, ut salutis viam tum ingrediamur, tum in eâ persistamus, nos movet. Deinde nobis in omni tentationum, laborum, et periculorum certamine adest, opitulatur et tandem ab ipsâ æternâ morte liberat.—P. 265 : (Mors Ch. nobis voluntatem dei confirmavit) duplici ratione, primum quod ab asserendâ suâ doctrinâ ne acerbissimâ quidem morte deterreri se passus est, nominatim vero, quod novum fœdus sanguine suo sanxerit; . . . deinde quod per mortem pervenerit ad resurrectionem, ex quâ maxima oritur divinæ voluntatis confirmatio deque nostrâ resurrectione et vitæ æternæ adeptione certissima persuasio. — P. 266 : Expone eam rem fusius, quâ ratione resurrectione Christi, atque ad eum modum ipsius morte de resurrectione nostrâ et vitâ æternâ confirmati simus ? Primum morte et resurrectione Christi certi sumus facti de nostrâ resurrectione ad eum modum, quod in exemplo Christi propositum esse nobis spectemus, quod in Christi doctrinâ promissum est: eos, qui deo obtemperent, e quovis mortis quantumvis atrocis genere liberari. Deinde, cum Christus ita resurrexit, ut supremam in omnia potestatem fuerit adeptus, omnis de salute nostrâ dubitandi causa sublata est.[1] — P. 267 : Hinc igitur perspicio, plus in resurrectione quam in Christi morte situm esse in nostræ salutis negotio ? Hactenus sane, quatenus mors Christi inutilis et inefficax futura fuisset, nisi eam consecuta fuisset Christi resurrectio (quod tamen decreti divini respectu haud fuit possibile), quæ mortem quoque illius mirum in modum animavit et efficacissimam in salutis nostræ negotio effecit.—P. 268 sqq. : Nonne etiam ideo Christus est mortuus,

[1] This exaltation of Christ was a reward for obedience shown unto death (Soc. *Pr. th.* c. 23) ; that is, God had decreed thus to impart His sin-destroying grace.

ut salutem nostram proprie loquendo mereretur et peccatorum nostrorum debita proprie itidem loquendo dissolveret ? Etsi nunc vulgo ita Christiani sentiant, tamen ea sententia tum fallax est et erronea tum admodum perniciosa, siquidem id sibi volunt, Christum æquivalentes pro peccatis nostris pœnas persolvisse et obedientiæ suæ pretio inobedientiam nostram exacte compensasse. . . . Id scripturis repugnat ad cum modum, quod scripturæ passim deum peccata hominibus gratuito remittere testentur. . . . Rationi repugnat, quod sequeretur, Ch. æternam mortem subiisse, . . . ut taceamus unam per se mortem, etiamsi tandem æterna fuisset, nedum adeo brevem, innumeris æternis mortibus æqualem non esse. —P. 277 : Quo sensu Ch. pro peccatis nostris seu propter peccata dicitur esse mortuus? Eodem sensu, quanquam longe pleniore ac perfectiore, quo victimæ pro peccatis cædi dicebantur. Nempe . . . Ch., omnis peccati insonti, peccata nostra causa mortis fuerunt, quam ille subiit, ut nos ab eorum omnium reatu solveret et quæ mortis illius vis est ; ut ea simul in nobis tolleret et aboleret. Ideo enim Christo pro peccatis nostris in mortem se tradidit, us nos sibi assereret ac manciparet, . . . suo livore nos sanavit; nam tantâ suâ caritate errantes ad se convertit.—P. 284 : Quid de reconciliatione sentis ? Christum J. nobis, qui propter peccata nostra dei inimici eramus et ab eo abalienati, viam ostendisse, quemadmodum nos ad deum converti atque ad eum modum ei reconciliari oporteat; et ad id faciendum morte etiam suâ, in quâ tanta erga nos caritas dei apparuit, nos vehementer impulisse.

The priestly office of Christ is referred by Socinianism only to His state of exaltation. *Cat. Rac.* p. 476 : In eo situm est, quod quemadmodum pro regio munere potest nobis in omnibus nostris necessitatibus subvenire, ita pro mun. sacerdotali subvenire vult ac porro subvenit atque hæc illius subveniendi s. opis afferendæ ratio *sacrificium* ejus appellatur. qu. 477 quod, quemadmodum in V. T. summus pontifex . . . ea, quæ ad expianda peccata populi spectarent, perficiebat, ita Ch. nunc penetravit cœlos, ut illic deo appareat pro nobis et omnia ad expiationem peccatorum nostr. spectantia peragat. [Qu. 479 indicates How.] Qui expiationem peccatorum nostrorum Jesus in cœlis peragit ? Primum a peccatorum pœnis nos liberat, dum virtute et potestate, quem a patre plenam et absolutam consecutus est, perpetuo nos tuetur et iram dei interventu suo quodammodo a nobis arcet; deinde ab ipsorum peccatorum servitute nos liberat, dum eadem potestate ab omni flagitiorum genere nos retrahit et avocat, id vero in suâ ipsius personâ nobis ostendendo, quid consequatur is, qui a peccando desistit.—P. 280 sq.: A peccatorum poenâ nos liberavit, cum se ipsum pro nobis, deo sic volente, in mortem tradidit et per sanguinem proprium in coelesti sacrario obtulit, quam filii sui ad mortem, eamque crucis, obedientiam deus pro omnium gratissimâ sibi victimâ accepit. Neque tamen hoc eam vim habet, quasi deus debita nostra sibi proprie persoluta acceperit, cum Christus illius proprius victimaque ab ipsomet data fuerit, quod et in anniversario illo sacrificio (sacrificii Christi figura) fiebat, et omnia ipse per se suoque nomine deo debuerit, et quamvis omnium maxima ac perfectissima ejus fuerit obedientia, nihilominus incomparabiliter majora pro illâ praemia acceperit; proinde hoc immensæ dei gratiæ et liberalitati adscribendum est, quod non solum nihil eorum, quæ sibi a nobis debebantur, receperit, non solum omnia debita nobis condonaverit, sed etiam victimam de suo eamque filium suum proprium et unigenitum uniceque dilectum, agnum illum immaculatum pro nobis peccatisque nostris impenderit, non ut sibi quidquam pro nobis persolveret, (ficta enim solutio hæc foret, non vera solutio) sed ut nobis tanto majus certiusque jus veniæ et æternæ vitæ faceret, seseque ad eam dandam tanto pignore obstringeret nosque ad se converteret, aliisque ingentibus bonis, de quibus egimus, per mortem filii sui bearet.

Still more plainly is it declared by Socinus, *Præl. theol.* c. 24, that with this oblation of Christ in heaven the idea of satisfaction may easily be connected, and that this idea, and all belonging to it, has been taken up out of predilection for the Epistle to the Hebrews. For the explanation of some of the remarks on the Catechism, see c. 28 : A Chr. in coelis manens non ideo expiat peccata nostra, quod vis atque efficacia expiationis ab ipso in cruce peractæ perpetuo duret, sed quia is, ad dei dextram in coelis collocatus, divinæ liberalitatis nos perpetuo admonet ad eamque amplectendam jugiter movet, et summâ potestate sibi a deo in coelo et in terrâ concessâ a divina ira, quæ de cœlo identidem adversus impios et peccatores exseritur et in die illâ extremâ adversus omnes simul cumulatissime exseretur, nos et servat et servaturus est.

Socin. *Prælect. theol.* c. 16–29 ; *de J. Ch. servatore in der biblioth. fratr. Polon.* i. ; Ostorodt, *Unterricht.* c. 37, 40 ; *Summa theol. Unitar.* ii. 4.

III. QUAKER.

The Quakers, like the Romanists and Protestants, speak of the atoning death of Christ, and in scriptural expressions. But they make a double atonement, distinguishing the actual and external, which was accomplished on the cross, and has brought to the sinner the possibility of obtaining salvation, from the internal atonement, through the communication of the inner power of the light of life flowing from Christ into the soul. Both and together effect the deliverance of man from sin ; the one being as necessary as the other.

Barclay, *Apol.* vii. 2 : Forasmuch as all men who have come to man's estate (the man Jesus only excepted) have sinned, therefore all have need of this Saviour to remove the wrath of God from them due to their offences. In this respect He is truly said to have borne the iniquities of us all in His body on the tree, and therefore is the only Mediator, having qualified the wrath of God towards us, so that our former sins stand not in our way, being by virtue of His most satisfactory sacrifice removed and pardoned. Neither do we think that remission of sins is to be expected, sought, or obtained any other way, or by any works or sacrifice whatsoever ; though, as has been said formerly, they may come to partake that are ignorant of the history. So, then, Christ by His death and sufferings hath reconciled us to God, even while we are enemies ; that is, He offers reconciliation unto us, we are put into a capacity of being reconciled. . . . We consider then our redemption in a twofold respect or state, both which in their own nature are perfect, though in their application to us the one is not, nor cannot be, without respect to the other. . . . The first is the redemption performed and accomplished by Christ for us in His crucified body without us ; the other is the redemption wrought by Christ in us, which no less properly is called and accounted a redemption than the former. The first, then, is that whereby a man, as he stands in the Fall, is put into a capacity of salvation, and hath conveyed unto him a measure of that power, virtue, spirit, life, and grace that was in Christ Jesus, which, as the free gift of God, is able to counterbalance, overcome, and root out the evil seed wherewith we are naturally, as in the Fall, leavened. The second is that whereby we witness and know this pure and perfect redemption in ourselves, purifying, cleansing, and redeeming us from the power of corruption, and bringing us into unity, favour, and friendship with God. By the first of these two, we that were lost in Adam, plunged into the bitter and corrupt seed, unable of ourselves to do any good thing, but naturally joined and united to evil, forward and propense to all iniquity, servants and slaves to the power and spirit of darkness, are, notwithstanding all this, so far reconciled to God by the death of His Son, while enemies, that we are put into a capacity of salvation, having the glad tidings of the gospel peace offered unto us; and God is reconciled unto us in Christ, calls and invites us to Himself. . . . By the second, we witness this capacity brought into act, whereby, receiving and not resisting the purchase of His death, to wit, the light, spirit, and grace of Christ revealed in us, we witness and possess a real, true, and inward redemption from the power and prevalency of sin, and so come to be truly and really redeemed, justified, and made righteous, and to a sensible union and friendship with God. Thus He died for us, that He might redeem us from all iniquity; and thus we know Him, and the power of His resurrection, and the fellowship of His sufferings, being made conformable to His death. This last follows the first in order, and is a consequence of it, proceeding from it as an effect from its cause, so as none could have enjoyed the last without the first had been, such being the will of God; so also can none now partake of the first, but as he witnesseth the last. Wherefore, as to us, they are both causes of our justification; the first the procuring efficient, the other the formal cause. . . . 4. That the obedience, sufferings, and death of Christ is that by which the soul obtains remission of sins, and is the procuring cause of that grace, by whose inward workings Christ comes to be formed inwardly, and the soul to be made conformable unto Him, and so just and justified. And that, therefore, in respect of this capacity and offer of grace, God is said to be reconciled ; not as if He were actually reconciled, or did actually justify, or account any just, so long as they remain in their sins really impure and unjust.

SECOND POINT OF DIVERGENCE.

The Confessions which acknowledge a reconciliation of the world through the vicarious death of Christ differ again in this : some hold the atoning death of Christ as perfectly sufficient; others as sufficient in part; and others, again, as more than sufficient. The Lutherans take the first view, that of a perfectly sufficient value: the death of Christ was a ransom-price perfectly proportioned to the guilt and punishment of all those whom He should redeem—a *plenaria satisfactio*. The second view, that of a partly sufficient value, is held by various classes : 1. As to its value (*intensive*), the Arminians so regard it, inasmuch as they assert that the vicarious death of Christ, as His alone, had not in itself the power of expiating the sins of all ; but that the compassion of God reckoned it as perfectly sufficient—a disproportionate ransom-price, instead of one exactly proportioned to the demerit of the sin.[1] 2. As to its application, there is again a difference in the second class : *a.* The Roman Catholics belong to it in a certain sense, as they think that Christ's death has provided a full satisfaction only for the guilt contracted before baptism, while for mortal sins committed after baptism only the guilt and eternal penalty are abolished, the temporal or limited punishments requiring the expiation of Christians themselves ; β. The Calvinists, according to whom God applies the merit of Christ only to the elect. In another sense, how-

[1] Our theologians call this *Acceptilatio*. *Acceptatio*, on the other hand, is the acceptance of or satisfaction with the sufficient ransom-price offered to God on the death of Jesus.

ever, the Romanists make the third class: they esteem the death of Christ to have a superfluity of merit; as the sufferings of the God-man necessarily bear an infinite value, while the applications of His satisfaction to man must ever be finite. On the application of this superabundant merit, see xvii. 2.

SYMBOLICAL TESTIMONIES.

I. ROMAN CATHOLIC DECREES.

As to the satisfaction of Christ which is applied in baptism, see below, xv. 2. Compare Bellarmine, *Pœnit.* iv. 14 : " We acknowledge this difference : In baptism the blood of Christ operates so fully, so perfectly, so abundantly, as to destroy all sins, not only as to their guilt, but also as to all the penalty of another life, whether eternal or temporal. But in the sacrament of penance, the same blood of Christ destroys indeed the guilt and the eternal pains, but does not expiate the whole temporal penalty, unless the sinner's own satisfaction co-operates." The necessity of our own expiation springs from the principle, that " it is false and contrary to the word of God to affirm that guilt is never remitted by our Lord without the forgiveness of its universal penalty." Conc. Trid. sess. 14. It is thus admitted, that the Christian who has committed mortal sins receives for Christ's sake forgiveness of his guilt, and remission of the eternal penalty, but that he must himself temporally make expiation for his sins here or in purgatory; that is, he must either suffer certain temporal punishments inflicted on him by God, or make satisfaction by personal penal visitations on himself. Conc. Trid. sess. 14, can. 13. The satisfying operation, however, of these penances, it must be remembered, rests upon the merit of Christ, and is therefore, according to Roman Catholic argument, far from dishonouring or obscuring those supreme merits. Trid. sess. 14 ; *Pœnit.* c. 8 ; *Cat. Rom.* ii. 5. 72 ; Bellar. *Pœn.* iv. 7.

Conc. Trid. sess. 14, *de Pœn.* cap. 8 : Sane et divinæ justitiæ ratio exigere videtur, ut aliter ab eo in gratiam recipiantur, qui ante baptismum per ignorantiam deliquerint, aliter vero, qui semel a peccati et dæmonis servitute liberati et accepto

Spiritus sancti dono scienter templum dei violare non formidaverint; et divinam clementiam decet, ne ita nobis absque ullâ satisfactione peccata dimittantur, ut occasione accepta peccata leviora putantes in graviora labamur. . . . Accedit, quod dum satisfaciendo patimur pro peccatis, Christo, qui pro peccatis nostris satisfecit, conformes efficimur. . . . Neque vero ita nostra est satisfactio hæc, quam pro peccatis nostris exsolvimus, ut non sit per Christum; nam qui ex nobis tanquam ex nobis nihil possumus, eo co-operante omnia possumus. Ita non habet homo unde glorietur, sed omnis gloriatio nostra in Christo est cet.

Cat. Rom. ii. 5. 65: Docendi sunt, duo esse, quæ peccatum consequuntur, maculam et pœnam. Ac quamvis semper culpâ dimissâ simul etiam æternæ mortis supplicium ap. inferos constitutum condonetur, tamen non semper contingit, ut dom. peccatorum reliquias et pœnam certo tempore definitam, quæ peccatis debetur, remittat. — As to penances imposed by the priest, or self-inflicted, see qu. 63, 73; as to temporal pains as satisfying, qu. 75.

Conc. Trid. sess. 14, *de pœn.* can. 13: Si quis dixerit, pro peccatis quoad pœnam temporalem minime deo per Christi merita satisfieri pœnis ab eo inflictis et patienter toleratis vel a sacerdote injunctis, sed neque sponte susceptis . . . , anathema sit.—Can. 15: Si quis dixerit, . . . fictionem esse, quod, virtute clavium sublata pœna æterna, pœna temporalis plerumque exsolvenda remaneat, anath. sit.

Cf. *Confut. A. C.* p. 84 sq.

II. Protestant Antitheses from the Symbols.

Apol. A. C. p. 184: Fatentur adversarii, quod satisfactiones non prosint ad remissionem culpæ. Verum fingunt, satisfactiones prodesse ad redimendas pœnas seu purgatorii seu alias. Sic enim docent, in remissione peccati deum remittere culpam, et tamen, quia convenit justitiæ divinæ punire peccatum, mutare pœnam æternam in pœnam temporalem. Addunt amplius, partem illius temporalis pœnæ remitti potestate clavium, reliquum autem redimi per satisfationes. P. 185: Et has satisfactiones dicunt valere, etiamsi fiant ab his, qui relapsi sunt in peccatum mortale, quasi vero divina offensa placari queat ab his, qui sunt in peccato mortali. Hæc tota res est commentitia, recens conficta, sine auctoritate scripturæ et veterum scriptorum ecclesiasticorum. Ac ne Longobardus quidem de satisfactionibus hoc modo loquitur. *Ib.* p. 189 : Cum scripturæ citatæ non dicant, quod operibus non debitis pœnæ æternæ compensandæ sint, temere affirmant adversarii, quod per satisfactiones canonicas pœnæ illæ compensentur. *Ib.* p. 192 : Cum mors Christi sit satisfactio pro morte æternâ, et cum ipsi adversarii fateantur, illa opera satisfactionum esse opera non debita, sed opera traditionum humanarum, de quibus Christus inquit, quod sint inutiles cultus : tuto possumus affirmare, quod satisfactiones canonicæ non sint necessariæ jure divino ad remissionem culpæ aut pœnæ æternæ aut pœnæ purgatorii. Sed objiciunt adversarii, vindictam seu pœnam necessariam esse ad pœnitentiam, quia Augustinus ait, pœnitentiam esse vindictam punientem cet. Concedimus vindictam seu pœnam in pœnitentiâ necessariam esse, non tanquam meritum, seu pretium, sicut adversarii fingunt satisfactiones, sed vindicta formaliter est in pœnitentiâ, hoc est quia ipsa regeneratio fit perpetua mortificatione vetustatis. *Ib.* p. 193 : At, inquiunt, convenit justitiæ dei, punire peccatum. Certe punit in contritione, cum in illis terroribus iram suam ostendit, sicut significat David, cum orat : (Ps. vi. 2) domine, ne in furore tuo arguas me. Et Jeremias cap. x. (24) : corripe me, domine ; veruntamen in judicio, non in furore, ne ad nihilum redigas me. Hic sane de acerbissimis pœnis loquitur. Et fatentur adversarii contritionem posse tantam esse, ut non requiratur satisfactio. *Ib.* p. 194 : Objiciunt de Adam, de Davide, qui propter adulterium punitus est. Ex his exemplis faciunt universalem regulam, quod singulis peccatis respondeant propriæ pœnæ temporales in remissione peccatorum. Prius dictum est, sanctos sustinere pœnas, quæ sunt opera dei, sustinent contritionem seu terrores, sustinent et alias communes afflictiones, ita sustinent aliqui proprias pœnas a deo impositas, exempli causâ. *Ib.* p. 195 : Ubi docet hoc scriptura, non posse nos a morte æternâ liberari, nisi per illam compensationem certarum pœnarum præter communes afflictiones ? At contra sæpissime docet, remissionem peccatorum gratis contingere propter Christum, Christum esse victorem peccati et mortis: quare non est assuendum meritum satisfactionis. Et quamvis afflictiones reliquæ sint, tamen has interpretatur præsentis peccati mortificationes esse, non compensationes æternæ mortis seu pretia pro æternâ morte.

Conf. Helv. ii. cap. 14: Improbamus illos, qui suis satisfactionibus existimant se pro commissis satisfacere peccatis. Nam docemus, Christum unum morte vel passione suâ esse omnium peccatorum satisfactionem, propitiationem vel expiationem. Cf. *Conf. Gall.* art. 17 u. 24; *Conf. Eng. Artt.; Conf. Belg.* art. 23; *Declar. Thorun.* ii. 6, *pœnit.* 3; Calvin, *Institut.* iii. 4. 25 sqq. (and Limborch, *Theol. christ.* v. 77. 16). Especially, however, as to the mass in its limitation of the power of the Redeemer's cross, s. *A. C.* p. 25; *Apol.* p. 265; *Art. Angl.* 31; *Conf. Angl.* p. 97.

III. Arminian Doctrine.

The *Conf. Rem.* contains no adequate statement as to the value of the satisfaction of Christ. The specific doctrine of the Arminians was formed after the Synod of Dort, and is found in the writings of the leading Arminians.

Limborch, *Apol. thes.* iii. 22. 5: Quæri hic posset, quomodo *unius* hominis victima sufficere possit et revera suffecerit ad tot hominum myriades eorumque peccata innumera expiandum. Resp. Sufficit illa duplici respectu. Primo, respectu *voluntatis divinæ*, quæ ad generis humani liberationem nihil ultra requisivit, sed *in unicâ hac victimâ acquievit.* . . . Secundo, respectu dignitatis personæ Jesu Christi. Quamvis enim Jesus non sit passus nisi in humanâ suâ naturâ, tamen quia illa in personæ unitatem assumta est a naturâ divinâ, recte ipse dei filius æternus tulisse dicitur, quidquid homo Jesus Christus in carne pro peccatoribus sustinuit. Quin et, licet Christus solummodo consideretur ut homo, excellentia personæ ipsius tanta est, ut omnium hominum longissime superet. 21. 6: Satisfactio Christi dicitur, quâ pro nobis pœnas omnes luit peccatis nostris debitas, easque perferendo et exhauriendo divinæ justitiæ satisfecit. Verum illa sententia nullum habet in scriptura fundamentum. Mors Christi vocatur sacrificium pro peccato; atqui sacrificia non sunt solutiones debitorum, neque *plenariæ pro peccatis satisfactiones;* sed illis peractis conceditur *gratuita peccati remissio. Ib.* 21. 8 : In eo errant quam maxime, quod velint redemtionis pretium per omnia *æquivalens* esse debere miseriæ illi, e quâ redemtio fit. Redemtionis pretium enim constitui solet pro liberâ æstimatione illius, qui captivum detinet, non autem solvi pro captivi merito.

Curcellæi *Rel. christ. instit.* v. 19. 15 sq. : Non ergo, ut vulgo putant, satisfecit Ch. patiendo omnes pœnas, quas peccatis nostris merueramus; nam primo istud ad sacrificii rationem non pertinet, sacrificia enim non sunt solutiones debitorum; secundo Ch. non est passus mortem æternam, quæ erat pœna peccato debita, nam paucis tantum horis in cruce pependit et tertiâ die resurrexit. Imo etiamsi mortem æternam pertulisset, non videtur satisfacere potuisse pro omnibus totius mundi peccatis; hæc enim fuisset tantum una mors, quæ omnibus moribus, quas singuli pro suis peccatis meruerant, non æquivaluisset. . . . Quarto ista sententia non potest consistere cum illâ remissione gratuitâ omnium peccatorum, quam deum nobis in Ch. ex immensâ suâ misericordiâ concedere, sacræ literæ passim docent.

Indulgences.

As to the superabundant satisfaction of Christ, on which the institute of indulgences rests, the Romish symbols contain no specific teaching. The *Cat. Rom.* only hints at it, but Bellarmine gives it a full exposition.

Cat. Rom. i. 5 : Pretium, quod Ch. pro nobis persolvit, debitis nostris non par solum et æquale fuit, verum *ea longe superavit.*

Bell. *De ind.* i. 2 : Exstat in ecclesiâ thesaurus satisfactionum ex Christi passionibus infinitus, qui nunquam exhauriri poterit. Nam Christi passio pretii fuit infiniti, cum esset passio personæ infinitæ. Deus est, qui sanguinem fudit pro ecclesiâ. Dignitas autem satisfactionis mensuram accipit a dignitate personæ satisfacientis. Deinde Christus pro hominibus omnibus mortuus est. Certum est autem, non omnibus hominibus, qui hactenus vixerunt, pretium mortis Christi reipsa applicatum fuisse ad eorum expianda peccata, imo majorem partem hominum morti æternæ addictam esse. Superest igitur multum illius pretii, quod semper applicari possit, præsertim cum tota Christi satisfactio nobis applicari possit, cum ipse per se nullâ satisfactione indiguerit, qui peccatum non fecit, nec facere potuit. — C. 4: Verissime scripsit Clemens VI. in constitut. Unigenitus, unam sanguinis Ch. guttam propter unionem ad verbum toti mundo reconciliando satis esse potuisse. Et cum Ch. non unam sang. guttam, sed totum sanguinem pro nobis fuderit, . . . dubium esse non potest, quin semper supersit pretium, idque justissimum, quo debita nostra solvi possint. Cf. Klee, *Dogmat.* ii. S. 475, iii. S. 285.

The Protestant symbols do not enter upon the question, save as they condemn the indulgences based upon the superabundant satisfaction.

VIII.
CONVERSION AND GRACE.

ALL Christians agree that the regeneration of man, wherein he is restored to righteousness in Christ and acceptableness to God, takes place under the influence of divine grace and of the Holy Spirit. But, in conformity with their several doctrines as to the depravity of the natural man, they differ as to the degrees and steps of this influence, and as to the relation it bears to human ability. Some deny to man, as in a state of nature, all ability to begin the work of regeneration: the Roman Church, the Lutheran and Reformed Churches, the Arminians, Mennonites, and Quakers. Others maintain—the Socinians—that man, by means of his natural ability, animated by the promises of God, may begin his own amendment; but that when he has begun it, and become a believer, he receives the seal and special power of the Holy Spirit. The former are divided into two classes, with reference to the development of the renewal, which can be commenced only by the Holy Ghost. The Romanists, like the Arminians and Mennonites, teach that the Holy Ghost awakens and strengthens the ability slumbering in the natural man, but that man must in free self-decision give himself up to this influence, which indeed he can never acquire by merit, in order that the work of regeneration may be effected through his own power united with the divine. Protestants generally, on the contrary, refer regeneration back entirely to the influence of the Holy Ghost, who restores in the natural man the power of willing. After that restoration, and in the subsequent process of renewal, the regenerate uses this newly-bestowed power only in co-operation. The Quakers, deriving all renewal from the divine light kindled in the spirit, are far from speaking of any co-operation of human power with the divine grace. They ascribe to human nature, as spirit, only a capacity for the internal light, and regard it as the foundation for the gracious energy and influence of the Divine Spirit.

SYMBOLICAL TESTIMONIES.

I. *That the Divine Grace is Indispensable to Conversion.*

I. ROMAN.

Conc. Trid. sessio 6, can. 1 : Si quis dixerit, hominem suis operibus, quæ vel per legis doctrinam fiant, absque divinâ per Christum gratiâ, posse justificari coram deo, anathema sit.— *Ib.* can. 2 : Si quis dixerit, ad hoc solum divinam gratiam per Christum dari, ut facilius homo juste vivere ac vitam æternam promereri possit, quasi per liberum arbitrium sine gratiâ utrumque, sed ægre tamen et difficulter, possit, anathema sit. —*Ib.* can. 3 : Si quis dixerit, sine præveniente Spiritus sancti inspiratione atque ejus adjutorio hominem credere, sperare, diligere aut pœnitere posse, sicut oportet, ut ei justificationis gratia conferatur, anathema sit. Cf. also cap. 3.

(Bellarmini *De amiss. grat.* vi. 16 : Nos libenter admittimus, non posse homines solis viribus naturæ corruptæ quidquam boni præstare, quod ad pietatem et vitam æternam pertineat.)

II. GREEK.

Jerem. *in Actis Wirtemb.* p. 367 sq. : Δείκνυται, ὡς τὸ μὲν ἀναστῆναι καὶ ἀκολουθῆναι ἐφ᾽ ἡμῖν καὶ δύναμιν ἔχομεν ὥστε ἑλέσθαι τὸ ἀγαθὸν οὐχ ἧττον ἢ τὸ κακόν. Ἑνὸς δὲ καὶ μόνου χρῄζομεν, τῆς παρὰ θεοῦ δηλαδὴ βοηθείας, ἵνα τὸ ἀγαθὸν κατορθώσωμεν καὶ σωθῶμεν, ἧς χωρὶς οὐδὲν ἀνύσαι ἰσχύομεν.

III. LUTHERAN AND REFORMED.

A. C. p. 14 : De libero arbitrio docent, quod humana voluntas . . . non habeat vim sine Spiritu sancto efficiendæ justitiæ dei seu justitiæ spiritualis, . . . sed hæc fit in cordi-

bus, cum per verbum Spiritus sanctus concipitur. Cf. *Apol.*
A. C. p. 84 sq.

Conf. Helv. i. art. 9 : Sic homini liberum arbitrium tribuimus, ut qui scientes et volentes agere nos bona et mala experimur, mala quidem agere sponte nostrâ queamus, bona vero amplecti et persequi, nisi gratiâ Chr. illustrati, excitati atque impulsi non queamus cet.

West. Conf. ch. ix. sec. 3 : Man, by his fall into a state of sin, hath wholly lost all ability of will to any spiritual good accompanying salvation ; so as a natural man, being altogether averse from that good, and dead in sin, is not able by his own strength to convert himself, or to prepare himself thereunto. Sec. 4 : When God converts a sinner, and translates him into the state of grace, He freeth him from his natural bondage under sin, and by His grace alone enables him freely to will and to do that which is spiritually good ; yet so as that, by reason of his remaining corruption, he doth not perfectly nor only will that which is good, but doth also will that which is evil.

Conf. Gall. art. 9 : Etsi (homo naturâ) nonnullam habet boni et mali discretionem, affirmamus tamen, quidquid habet lucis, mox fieri tenebras, cum de quærendo deo agitur ; adeo ut suâ intelligentiâ et ratione nullo modo posit ad eum accedere. Item, quamvis voluntate sit præditus, quâ ad hoc vel illud movetur, tamen cum ea sit penitus sub peccato captiva, nullam prorsus habet ad bonum appetendum libertatem, nisi quam ex gratiâ et dei dono acceperit.

Cf. *Declar. Thorun.* ii. 4. 1.

IV. ARMINIAN, ETC.

Conf. Remonstr. vii. 10 : Summa gratiæ divinæ in Christo nobis reparatæ necessitas et utilitas evidenter apparet, quippe sine quâ nec miserabile peccati jugum excutere, nec quidquam in totâ religione vere bonum operari, nec denique mortem æternam effugere unquam possumus. Comp. 3 and 4 of the Five Artt. *Conf. Rem.* xvii. 6.

F. Socin. *Opp.* ii. p. 464 : Homo in hac vitâ non quidem viribus naturalibus, sed viribus sibi a deo per spem vitæ æternæ sibi ab eo factam subministratis potest dei voluntatem perficere. Cf. *Cat. Racov.* qu. 427.

Ris, *Conf.* art. 22 : Regeneratio est divina quædam qualitas in animâ hominis vere resipiscentis, erectio imaginis dei in homine, renovatio mentis seu animi, vera cum veritatis cognitione animi illuminatio secum afferens mutationem voluntatis. . . . Ortum habet ex deo per Christum. Medium sive instrumentum, per quod in nobis generatur, est Spiritus sanctus . . . absque ullâ ullius creaturæ co-operatione. Cf. Schyn, *Plen. deduct.* p. 240.

Barclay, *Apol.* Prop. v. ; s. above.

II. *Relation of Divine Grace to Human Ability.*

I. PROTESTANT SYMBOLS.

The passages which most decisively exclude human co-operation are found in the symbols which deal with Synergism [1] and Arminianism.

A. C. p. 15 : Esse fatemur liberum arbitrium omnibus hominibus, . . . non per quod sit idoneum in iis, quæ ad deum pertinent, sine deo aut inchoare aut certe peragere cet. Cf. *Conf. Wirtemb.* p. 104.

F. C. p. 579 : Credimus, quantum abest, ut corpus mortuum se ipsum vivificare atque sibi ipsi corporalem vitam restituere possit, tantum abesse, ut homo, qui ratione peccati spiritualiter mortuus est, se ipsum in vitam spirit. revocandi ullam facultatem habeat.

Ib. p. 662 : Antequam homo per Sp. s. illuminatur, convertitur, regeneratur et trahitur, ex sese et propriis naturalibus

---

[1] Synergism is described in *F. C.* 677. Melancthon, *Loci* (1535) : Videmus (in conversione) conjungi has causas, verbum, Spiritum sanctum et voluntatem non sane otiosam sed repugnantem infirmitati suæ. . . . Si de totâ vitâ piorum loquamur, etsi est ingens imbecillitas, tamen est aliqua libertas voluntatis, quum quidem jam adjuvetur a Sp. sancto cet. And in the Definit. of *liberum arbitrium:* esse in homine facultatem *applicandi se ad gratiam.* Cf. *Conf. Anhalt.* p. 15. Semper ecclesiæ nostræ docuerunt, in conversione hominis concurrere hæc tria, verbum dei, Spiritum sanctum, quem pater et filius mittunt, ut accendat nostra corda et trahat per verbum, voluntatis denique per verbi meditationem divinitus motæ assensum.

suis viribus in rebus spiritualibus et ad conversionem aut regenerationem suam nihil inchoare, operari aut co-operari potest, nec plus quam lapis, truncus aut limus (cf. Luther *ad Gen.* cap. 19).

Ib. p. 666: Quamvis renati etiam in hac vitâ eo usque progrediantur, ut bonum velint eoque delectentur, et bene agere atque in pietate proficere studeant: tamen hoc ipsum non a nostrâ voluntate aut a viribus nostris proficiscitur, sed Spiritus sanctus operatur in nobis *illud velle et perficere.*

Ib. p. 674: Consequitur, quam primum Spiritus sanctus per verbum et sacramenta opus suum regenerationis et renovationis in nobis inchoavit, quod revera tunc per virtutem Spiritus sancti co-operari possimus ac debeamus, quamvis multa adhuc infirmitas concurrat. Hoc vero ipsum, quod co-operamur, non ex nostris carnalibus et naturalibus viribus est, sed ex novis illis viribus et donis, quæ Spiritus sanctus in conversione in nobis inchoavit.

Ib. p. 582: Quod D. Lutherus scripsit, hominis voluntatem in conversione pure passive se habere, id recte et dextre est accipiendum, videl. respectu divinæ gratiæ in accendendis novis motibus, h. e. de eo intelligi oportet, quando Sp. dei per verbum auditum aut per usum sacramentorum hominis voluntatem aggreditur et conversionem atque regenerationem in homine operatur. Postquam enim Sp. s. hoc ipsum jam operatus est atque effecit, hominisque voluntatem solâ suâ divinâ virtute et operatione immutavit atque renovavit, tunc revera hominis nova illa voluntas instrumentum est dei Spiritus sancti, ut ea non modo gratiam apprehendat, verum etiam in operibus sequentibus Spiritui sancto co-operetur.

Ib. p. 677: Rejicitur Papistarum et Scholasticorum error, qui docuerunt, quod homo naturalibus suis viribus initium ad agendum bonum et ad conversionem suam facere possit, sed quia infirmior sit, quam ut bene cœpta perficere queat, quod Spiritus sanctus illa, quæ naturalibus propriis viribus inchoata erant, adjuvet et absolvat.

Ib. p. 677: Item (rejicitur) Synergistarum dogma, qui fingunt, hominem in rebus spiritualibus non prorsus ad bonum esse emortuum, sed tantum graviter vulneratum et semimortuum esse. Et quamvis liberum arbitrium infirmius sit, quam ut initium facere et se ipsum propriis viribus ad deum convertere et legi toto corde obedire possit, tamen si Spiritus sanctus initium faciat et nos per evangelium vocet, gratiam suam, remissionem peccatorum et æternam salutem nobis offerat, tunc liberum arbitrium propriis suis naturalibus viribus deo occurrere, aliquo modo (aliquid saltem, etsi parum et languide) ad conversionem suam conferre, eam adjuvare, co-operari, sese ad gratiam præparare et applicare, eam apprehendere, amplecti, evangelio credere, et quidem in continuatione et conservatione hujus operis propriis suis viribus una cum Spiritu sancto *co-operari posse.* Contra hunc errorem supra demonstratum est, quod facultas applicandi se ad gratiam non ex nostris naturalibus propriis viribus, sed ex solâ Spiritus sancti operatione promanet.

The conversion here spoken of is not to be understood of the so-called conversion of a baptized Christian, still less of his daily renewal; it is the conversion of one not yet baptized. *This* conversion is identical with regeneration. *Form. Conc.* p. 675.

Conf. Helv. ii. cap. 9: Quantum ad bonum et virtutes, intellectus hominis non recte judicat de divinis ex semetipso. . . . Constat vero, mentem vel intellectum ducem esse voluntatis, cum autem cœcus sit dux, claret, quousque et voluntas pertingat. Proinde nullum est ad bonum homini arbitrium liberum nondum renato, vires nullæ ad perficiendum bonum.—In regeneratione . . . voluntas non tantum mutatur per Spiritum, sed etiam instruitur facultatibus, ut sponte velit et possit bonum. Nisi hoc dederimus, negabimus christianam libertatem et inducemus legalem servitutem.—Observandum est . . . regeneratos in boni electione et operatione non tantum agere passive, sed active. Aguntur enim a deo, ut agant ipsi, quod agunt.

Thirty-nine Artt. art. x.: The condition of man, after the fall of Adam, is such that he cannot turn and prepare himself by his own natural strength and good works to faith, and calling upon God; wherefore we have no power to do good works, pleasant and acceptable to God, without the grace of God by Christ preventing us, that we may have a good will, and working with us, when we have that good will.

Conf. Scot. art. 12 : Naturâ ita sumus mortui, cœci et perversi, ut nec sentiamus cum pungimur, . . . nec dei voluntati, cum nobis revelatur, queamus assentiri, nisi Spiritus domini nostri, quod mortuum est, vivificet, auferat tenebras mentium nostrarum et rebellionem cordium in obsequium benedictæ voluntatis ipsius flectat. Itaque confitemur . . . Spiritum s. sine omni meriti nostri respectu, sive sit ante sive post regenerationem, nos sanctificasse et regenerasse cet.

Cf. *Conf. Gall.* art. 12 ; *Conf. Tetrap.* 3 ; *Conf. Belg.* art. 14.

Can. Dordr. cap. 3, art. 3 : Omnes homines in peccato concipiuntur . . . inepti ad omne bonum salutare . . . et *absque Spiritus sancti regenerantis gratiâ* ad deum redire, naturam depravatam corrigere, vel ad ejus correctionem se disponere nec volunt, nec possunt.

Ibid. art. 14 : Fides dei donum est non eo, quod a deo hominis arbitrio offeratur, sed quod homini re ipsâ conferatur, inspiretur et infundatur. Non etiam, quod deus potentiam credendi tantum conferat, consensum vero seu actum credendi ab hominis deinde arbitrio exspectet, sed quod et velle credere et ipsum credere in homine efficiat.

Ibid. cap. 3, reject. error. 4 : (Rejiciuntur) qui docent, hominem irregenitum non esse proprie nec totaliter in peccatis mortuum aut omnibus ad bonum spirituale viribus destitutum, sed posse justitiam vel vitam esurire ac sitire, sacrificiumque spiritus contriti, . . . quod deo acceptum est, offerre.

Ibid. art. 11 : Quando deus . . . veram in electis conversionem operatur, non tantum evangelium illis externe prædicari curat et mentem eorum per Sp. s. potenter illuminat, . . . sed ejusdem etiam Sp. regenerantis efficacia cor clausum aperit, durum emollit, voluntati novas qualitates infundit facitque eam ex mortuâ vivam, ex nolente volentem cet. Art. 12 : Tum voluntas jam renovata non tantum agitur et movetur a deo, sed a deo acta agit et ipsa. Cf. art. 16. S. *Form. Consens. Helv.* 21 (Heidegger, *Corp. theol. christ.* x. 85 sq.).

Thus the natural man has only the power of resisting grace. [All else is wrought by the Holy Spirit. He opens the heart, enlightens the understanding, and softens the will. Thus a co-operation of the human will in conversion on the part of unbaptized persons is not taught. It is otherwise with the baptized. Of them it must, however, be maintained that they co-operate with the Spirit. And that is no Synergism.]

II. ROMAN.

Conc. Trid. sess. 6, cap. 5 : Vocantur (adulti), ut, qui per peccata a deo aversi erant, per ejus excitantem atque adjuvantem gratiam ad convertendum se ad suam ipsorum justificationem, eidem gratiæ libere assentiendo et co-operando, disponantur, ita, ut tangente deo cor hominis per Spiritus sancti illuminationem, neque homo ipse nihil omnino agat, inspirationem illam recipiens, (quippe qui illam et abjicere potest), neque tamen sine gratiâ dei movere se ad justitiam coram illo liberâ suâ voluntate possit.

Ib. cap. 6 : Disponuntur ad ipsam justitiam, dum excitati divinâ gratiâ et adjuti, fidem ex auditu concipientes, libere moventur in deum, credentes vera esse, quæ divinitus revelata et promissa sunt atque illud imprimis : a deo justificari impium per gratiam ejus, per redemtionem, quæ est in Christo Jesu ; et dum peccatores se esse intelligentes, a divinæ justitiæ timore, quo utiliter concutiuntur, ad considerandam dei misericordiam se convertendo in spem eriguntur (fidentes Deum sibi propter Christum propitium fere ; illumque tanquam omnis justitiæ fontem diligere incipiunt).

Ib. cap. 7 : . . . justitiam in nobis recipientes unusquisque . . . secundum propriam dispositionem et co-operationem.

Ib. can. 3 : Si quis dix., sine præveniente Sp. s. inspiratione atque ejus adjutorio hominem credere, sperare, diligere aut pœnitere posse, sicut oportet, ut ei justificationis gratia conferatur, anathema sit.

Ib. can. 4 : Si quis dix., liberum hominis arbitrium a deo motum et excitatum nihil co-operari assentiendo de excitanti atque vocanti, quo ad obtinendam justificationis gratiam se disponat ac præparet, neque posse dissentire, si velit, sed veluti inanime quoddam nihil omnino agere mereque passive se habere, anath. sit.

In a very luminous sketch, Bellarmin, *De grat.* vi. 15, gives the Roman doctrine of the relation of lib. arbitr. to gratia

div. dar. Cf. Möhler, *Symbol.* § 11; Klee, *Dogmat.* iii. S. 25 ff.
[Perrone, *Prælectiones theologicæ Romæ*, 1837, v. 135, 136: Inst. Peccatores in Scripturis passim mortui ac sepulti dicuntur; nihil igitur operantur cum per Christi gratiam in vitam revocantur. R. N. Cons. Licet enim peccatores reipsâ mortui sint in ordine ad vitam spiritualem, fruuntur tamen vitâ naturali, dum propterea per gratiam prævenientem excitantur, capaces fiunt ad assensum præstandum, si eidem gratiæ velint obtemperare.]

III. GREEK.

Conf. orthod. p. 59 : Δείχνει ὁ ἅγιος διδάσκαλος (Basilius), πῶς καλᾶ καὶ ἡ ἀνθρωπίνη θέλησις, ἐβλάβη μὲ τὸ προπατορικὸν ἁμάρτημα, μ' ὅλον τοῦτο καὶ τῶρα κατὰ τὸν παρόντα καιρὸν εἰς τὴν προαίρεσιν τοῦ καθ' ἑνὸς στέκεται τὸ νὰ εἶναι καλὸς καὶ τέκνον θεοῦ, ἢ κακὸς καὶ υἱὸς διαβόλου. ὅλον τοῦτο εἶναι εἰς τὸ χέρι καὶ ἐξουσίαν τοῦ ἀνθρώπου· καὶ εἰς μὲν τὸ καλὸν ἡ θεία χάρις συμβοηθᾷ· ἀλλὰ καὶ ἀπὸ τὸ κακὸν ἡ ἰδία γυρίζει τὸν ἄνθρωπον, χωρὶς νὰ ἀναγκάσῃ τὸ αὐτεξούσιον τοῦ ἀνθρώπου.

Jerem. *in Act. Wirtemb.* p. 367: Οὐδὲν κωλύει καὶ μετὰ τὴν ἐκ παραβάσεως πτῶσιν ἐκκλίναι μὲν ἀπὸ τοῦ κακοῦ τὸν ἄνθρωπον, ἐπεισάκτου ὄντος ποιῆσαι δὲ τὸ ἀγαθὸν καὶ τὸ καλὸν αἱρεῖσθαι, ὡς ἔχοντα τὸ αὐτεξούσιον. . . . Ἐκ δὴ τούτων πάντων δείκνυται, ὡς τὸ μὲν ἀναστῆναι καὶ ἀκολουθῆσαι ἐφ' ἡμῖν καὶ δύναμιν ἔχομεν ὥστε ἐλέσθαι τὸ ἀγαθὸν οὐχ ἧττον ἢ τὸ κακόν. Ἑνὸς δὲ καὶ μόνου χρήζομεν, τῆς παρὰ θεοῦ δηλαδὴ βοηθείας, ἵνα τὸ ἀγαθὸν κατορθώσωμεν καὶ σωθῶμεν, ἧς χωρὶς οὐδὲν ἀνύσαι ἰσχύομεν.

The former passage from the *Conf. orth.* speaks merely in general of a divine assistance in man's renewal; the second, that of Jeremias, appears to declare that man can voluntarily turn to good, or begin his change, but that for the full accomplishment of his renewal the divine aid is needful. On the other hand, Plato (*Cat.* 107) refers all to grace, defined as preventing, awakening, justifying, and co-operating in the justified. Dositheus, *Conf.* 3, expresses himself in a Roman manner, laying down a χάρις προκαθαρτική (*gratia prævcnicns*) and a συνεργεῖν of grace, and the human αὐτεξουσία.

IV. Socinian.

Cat. Racov. qu. 422: Estne liberum arbitrium situm in nostrâ potestate, ut deo obtemperemus? Prorsus. Etenim certum est, primum hom. ita a deo conditum fuisse, ut libero arbitrio præditus esset. Nec vero ulla caussa subest, cur deus post ejus lapsum illum eo privaret cet.

Ib. qu. 427: Expone, quam longe vis ipsa liberi arbitrii pateat. Communiter in hominibus naturâ exiguæ admodum sunt vires ad ea quæ deus ab illis requirit perficiendum, at voluntas ad ea perficiendum omnibus adest natura. Nihilominus tamen eæ vires non ita prorsus exiguæ sunt, ut homo si vim sibi facere velit divino auxilio accedente, non possit voluntati divinæ obsecundare. Cf. qu. 447.

Ib. qu. 428-30: Auxilium divinum duplex est, interius et exterius. — (Exterius auxilium divinum) sunt promissa et minæ, quorum tamen promissa vim habent longe majorem. Unde etiam, quod sint sub novo fœdere longe præstantiora promissa, quam sub vetere fuerint, facilius est sub novo quam sub vetere fœdere voluntatem dei facere.[1]—(Interius auxilium divinum est) id, cum deus in cordibus eorum, qui ipsi obediunt, quod promisit (vitam æternam), obsignat. Later revision: Quod Sp. sancti donum est? Est ejusmodi dei afflatus, quo animi nostri vel uberiore rerum div. notitiâ vel spe vitæ æt. certiore atque adeo gaudio ac gustu quodam futuræ felicitatis aut singulari ardore complentur.

(F. Socin. *Prælect. theol.* cap. 5: Interius auxilium duplex est, unum, cum deus id, quod sibi obedientibus promisit, eorum etiam cordibus quodammodo inscribit; alterum, cum ad ipsius voluntatem recte percipiendam, quæ in externo verbo propter res infinitas, de quibus in humanâ vitâ agere et deliberare

---

[1] F. Socin. *Opp.* ii. p. 463: Quilibet homo, ubi ad eam ætatem pervenerit, ut rationis usum habeat, si nullâ malâ institutione aut usu corruptus fuerit, posset, si plane id vellet, nullum ex iis peccatis committere, quæ cum ipsâ ratione pugnant eique per se omnino adversantur. Sed, ut ea peccata vitare possit, quæ ipsi rationi per se non omnino adversantur, necesse est præterea, ut sibi persuadeat ac speret, si illa vitaverit, se ingens aliquod inde bonum consecuturum. Propterea deus præceptis suis, quæ per Christum dedit, . . . addidit vitæ æternæ promissum, cui ut fidem adhibere possint, iis omnibus generatim concedit, quibus ipse Christus ejusque evangelium annunciatur.

contingit, expresse omnino contineri nequit, mentem erudit, eamque illustrat. — Ex his duobus interioribus auxiliis prius magis proprium est N. T., posterius vero Veteris. — Ex iis autem, quæ dicta sunt, colligi potest, verum auxilium id esse, quod exterius appellavimus, cum interius utriusque generis nihil aliud sit, quam exterioris suggestio quædam et obsignatio, præsertim vero, cum nemini interius contingat, nisi prius exteriore recte usus sit. Credentibus enim et obedientibus Sp. s. datur.)

Cat. Rac. qu. 369 sq.: Omnibusne interior obsignatio contingit, quibus exterior, hoc est, quibus evangelium annunciatur? Nequaquam; verum iis tantum, qui evangelio sibi annunciato crediderint et exteriorem illam rationem, quam deus in confirmandâ promissione vitæ æternæ adhibet, amplexi eoque usi, quemadmodum oportet, fuerint. Etenim si illud donum Sp. s., quod ad tempus duravit, non dabatur nisi credentibus evangelio, multo magis id Sp. s. donum, quod perpetuum est, aliis non dari statuendum est, nisi qui et evangelio plane crediderint et illud ex animo amplexi fuerint. (Cf. Socin. *Opp.* i. p. 98 a.) — Nonne ad credendum evangelio Sp. s. interiore dono opus est? Nullo modo; nec enim in Scripturis sacris legimus, cuiquam id conferri donum nisi credenti evangelio.

Hence their doctrine is: 1. That man may, by means of the freewill indwelling in him, turn to faith and obedience towards God; 2. That God on His part furthers this return by threatenings and promises, especially the latter; 3. That God works in those who have become believing and obedient a certain hope (*obsignatio*), and thus completes the regeneration. The perfect fulfilment of the divine commandments depends on this obsignation, as Socinus says: Homo in hac vitâ . . . viribus sibi a deo per spem vitæ æternæ sibi ab eo factam subministratis, potest dei voluntatem *perficere*.

V. ARMINIAN.

Conf. Remonstr. xvii. 5: Homo non ex arbitrii sui liberi viribus regeneratur aut convertitur, quandoquidem in statu peccati nihil boni, quod quidem salutare bonum sit, ex se ipso vel a se ipso vel cogitare potest, nedum velle aut facere, sed necesse est, ut a deo in Christo per verbum evangelii eique adjunctam Spiritus sancti virtutem (cf. xvii. 2) regeneretur atque totus renovetur.—6: Gratiam itaque dei statuimus esse principium, progressum et complementum omnis boni, adeo ut ne ipse quidem regenitus absque praecedente istâ sive praeveniente, excitante, prosequente et co-operante gratiâ bonum ullum salutare cogitare, velle aut peragere possit. Cf. Curcell. *Rel. chr. instit.* vi. 12. 2 sq.—How far the natural ability of man may co-operate to conversion, the Conf. does not expressly say; but it requires of Christians *free* obedience, and consequently does not limit the power of the unregenerate to that of withstanding grace. In the natural man is, rather, a *facultas verbum div. amplectendi u. potestas illud rejiciendi.* S. Limborch, *Theol. chr.* iv. 13. 22.

Apol. Conf. Remonstr. p. 162 b: Gratia efficax vocatur ex eventu, quod tamen potest dupliciter accipi: primo sic, ut gratia statuatur ex se nullam habere vim ad producendum consensum in voluntate, sed tota efficacia ejus sit ex parte voluntatis humanae; secundo sic, ut statuatur gratia habere ex se sufficientem vim ad producendum consensum in voluntate, sed, quia vis illa partialis est, non posse exire in actum sine co-operatione liberae voluntatis humanae, ac proinde ut effectum habeat, pendere a liberâ voluntate. Alterum sensum suum esse volunt Remonstrantes. Here there is a co-operation of the human will with grace, as in Limborch, *Theol. chr.* iv. 12. 8: Sciendum vocationem triplici significatu solere dici efficacem (1) praecise secundum naturatam, quatenus actualis quaedam motio est voluntati a deo immissa, quae non tantum vim habet et efficacitatem formaliter excitandi in voluntate consensum, sed et effective concurrendi cum voluntate ad consensum. . . . (3) Ex parte effectus, quando voluntas illi co-operatur. Itaque sufficiens vocatio, quando per co-operationem liberi arbitrii sortitur suum effectum, vocatur efficax. iv. 13. 27: Si omnes actus et operationes, quibus verbum circa homines operatur, consideremus, liquet hominem in quovis instanti libertate tam rejiciendi verbum quam recipiendi praeditum. Et nisi ea semper adesset libertas, nulla esset virtus obedientiae, nullum vitium inobedientiae eet. iv. 14. 21: Recipit hic gratiam per rectum liberi arbitrii gratiâ divinâ excitati usum, ille eam rejicit per pravum liberi arbitrii abusum novamque contra gratiam divinam contumaciam. . . . Ergo liberum arbitrium co-operatur cum gratiâ? Fatemur, alias nulla obedientia aut inobedientia hominis locum habet. Dices: An co-operatio liberi arbitrii non est bonum salutare? Resp. omnino. Dices: Ergo gratia non est primaria causa salutis. Resp. non est solitaria, sed tamen primaria, ipsa enim liberi arbitrii co-operatio est a gratiâ tanquam primaria causa; nisi enim a præveniente gratiâ liberum arbitrium excitatum esset, gratiæ co-operari non posset.

Accordingly the Arminians hold a constant co-operation of the human will, awakened by grace, with the divine grace; but the influence of the latter appears to them by no means merely moral:[1] it is the power of the Holy Ghost connected with the divine word (*Con. Rem.* xvii. 2. 5) which influences the mind, and is in its nature supernatural, although the *kind* of operation is perfectly analogous with the natural power of all truth.

VI. The Mennonites.

The Mennonites ascribe to man a freedom whereby he can accept or refuse the good offered by God. This declares that man cannot *of himself* will or produce in himself good; so also what Schyn says of concupiscence. Hence he gives this view of their doctrine. Schyn, *Plen. deduct.* p. 240: Ista facultas NB. oblatam dei gratiam accipiendi vel rejiciendi ex gratiâ (dei) in omnibus remansit (Adami) posteris. — Mennonitæ non dicunt, per se et ex propriis sibi innatis

---

[1] *Canones Dordrac.* iii. 12: Regeneratio neutiquam fit per solam forinsecus insonantem doctrinam, moralem suasionem vel talem operandi rationem, ut post dei operationem in hominis potestate maneat, regenerari vel non regenerari; sed est plane supernaturalis, potentissima simul et suavissima mirabilis, arcana et ineffabilis operatio, . . . adeo ut omnes illi, in quorum cordibus admirando hoc modo deus operatur, certo, infallibiliter et efficaciter regenerentur et actu credant. What we find in *Conf. Rem.* vi. 2 treats of the general divine influence apart from Christianity, and the *hortationes, suasiones, signa, prodigia*, are the common experiences of life, tending to good, which do not exclude or render needless the *operatio Sp. sancti*.

viribus bonum posse præstari, sed non nisi primo a deo oblatum, qui hoc ex merâ suâ gratiâ largitur per verbum et suum spiritum . . ., ita ut sit gratia in principio, gratio in medio et mera gratia in fine ipsius salutis.

VII. QUAKER.

The Quakers hold the natural man to be altogether unable to release himself from evil by his own power, to free himself from the thraldom of the evil seed; and therefore ascribe regeneration entirely to the power of Christ, which first influences the mind as a call, then imparts the inner light to those who do not resist this power.

Barclay, *Apol.* Prop. vii. 3 : First, then, as by the explanation of the former thesis appears, we renounce all natural power and ability in ourselves, in order to bring us out of our lost and fallen condition and first nature; and confess that as of ourselves we are able to do nothing that is good, so neither can we procure remission of sins or justification by any act of our own, so as to merit it, or draw it as a debt from God due to us; but we acknowledge all to be *of* and *from* His *love*, which is the original and fundamental cause of our acceptance. . . . We consider, then, our redemption as a twofold respect or state, both which in their own nature are perfect, though in their application to us the one is not, nor cannot be, without respect to the other. . . . The first is the redemption performed and accomplished by *Christ for us* in His crucified body without us; the other is the redemption wrought by *Christ in us*, which no less properly is called and accounted a redemption than the former. The first, then, is that whereby a man, as he stands in the Fall, is put into a capacity of salvation, and hath conveyed unto him a measure of that power, virtue, spirit, life, and grace that was in Christ Jesus, which, as the free gift of God, is able to counterbalance, overcome, and root out the evil seed wherewith we are naturally, as in the Fall, leavened.

The second is that whereby we witness and know this pure and perfect redemption *in ourselves*, purifying, cleansing, and redeeming us from the power of corruption, and bringing us into unity, favour, and friendship with God. By the first of these two, we that were lost in Adam, plunged into the bitter and corrupt seed, unable of ourselves to do any good thing, but naturally joined and united to evil, forward and propense to all iniquity, servants and slaves to the power and spirit of darkness, are, notwithstanding all this, so far reconciled to God by the death of His Son, while enemies, that we are put into a capacity of salvation, having the glad tidings of the gospel of peace offered unto us, and God is reconciled unto us in Christ, calls and invites us unto Himself. . . . By the second we witness this capacity brought into act, whereby, receiving and not resisting the purchase of His death, to wit, the light, spirit, and grace of Christ revealed in us, we witness and possess a real, true, and inward redemption from the power and prevalency of sin. . . . 25: If all men have received a loss from Adam which leads to condemnation, then all men have received a gift from Christ which leads to justification. . . . That this saving light and seed, or a measure of it, is given to all, Christ tells us expressly in the parable of the sower. But this light or seed of God in man he cannot stir up when he pleaseth; but it moves, flows, and strives with man, as the Lord seeth meet. For, could there be a possibility of salvation to every man during the day of his visitation, yet cannot a man at any time when he pleaseth, or hath some sense of his misery, stir up that light and grace so as to procure to himself tenderness of heart, etc. . . . Prop. vii. 10 says of the works of righteousness which the justified perform, that they are the works of the Spirit of grace in the heart, wrought in conformity to the inward and spiritual law; *which works are not wrought on man's will, nor by his power and ability*, but in and by the power and Spirit of Christ in us.

Prop. v. and vi. 12: First, then, by this *day and time of visitation*, which we say God gives unto all, during which they may be saved, we do not understand the whole time of every man's life; though to some it may be extended even to the very hour of death, as we see in the example of the thief converted on the cross: but such a season at least as sufficiently exonerateth God of every man's condemnation, which to some may be sooner, and to others later, according as the Lord in

His wisdom sees meet. So that many men may outlive this day, after which there may be no possibility of salvation to them. . . . [The nature of the grace that works upon men is thus described:]—We understand not this seed, light, or grace to be an accident, as most men ignorantly do, but a real spiritual substance, which the soul of man is capable to feel and apprehend, from which that real, spiritual, inward birth in believers arises, called the *new creature*, the *new man in the heart*.

Prop. vii. thus defines the operations of this grace:—As many as resist not this light, but receive the same, it becomes in them an holy, pure, and spiritual birth, bringing forth holiness, righteousness, purity, and all those other fruits which are acceptable to God: by which holy birth, to wit, *Jesus Christ formed within us*, and working His works in us, as we are sanctified, so we are justified in the sight of God.

IX.

UNIVERSALITY OF GRACE: PREDESTINATION.

POINT OF DIVERGENCE.

THE influence of divine grace, which is, according to the common Protestant doctrine, indispensable to conversion, is in the Lutheran and Arminian confessions proffered to all men without distinction; may, however, be contemned by them (*gratia resistibilis*), which leaves them to bear the penalty of their eternal condemnation. According to the Reformed symbols, or most of them, based upon the Calvinistic principles and the decrees of the Synod of Dort, as also of the *Form. Cons. Helv.*, God imparts His renewing grace only to those whom He chose, in His eternal unconditional counsel and purpose (*decretum absolutum*), to save by grace; and in all these, grace works irresistibly conversion (*gratia irresistibilis*). All others, for whom that grace was not designed, are appointed by God to eternal damnation; but they suffer as the result of their own guilt, therefore righteously, because the unconverted man has deserved from God nothing but everlasting doom. In the Roman Church, the Jansenists hold the same doctrine of particular redemption. The other Roman Catholics, however, teach the universality of grace; as also do the Greeks, Mennonites, and Quakers.

Although Zwingli had not been a stranger to the predestinarian dogma, yet it was Calvin who introduced it into the Reformed Church, with all its consequences and all its sternness. Calv. *Institt.* iii. 21. After many vicissitudes, he was able to win acceptance for the doctrine agreed upon in the

Cons. past. eccl. Genevæ, among the other cantons of Switzerland, and the Reformed Churches of Germany and the Netherlands. The Church of Zurich held out longest. In the Netherlands, at the end of the sixteenth century, the Predestinarians were divided into two parties: the one, faithful to Calvin and Beza, so made the absolute decree of predestination precede the Fall, that this Fall itself, and with it, consequently, the everlasting ruin of the reprobate, was decreed by God at man's creation. These were the Supralapsarians. The others, of a milder type, regarded the decree of predestination as formed with reference to the Fall, as only permitted by Him. These were the Infralapsarians. The latter view carried the victory at the Synod of Dort. By the *Form. Cons. Helv.* the Calvin-Dort decrees were proclaimed as the faith of the Swiss Church, but only to be again renounced.

I. SYMBOLICAL TESTIMONIES.

Reformed Symbols.

a. Those which maintain a stricter Predestination.

Conf. Gall. art. 12: Credimus ex corruptione et damnatione universali, in quâ omnes homines naturâ sunt submersi, deum alios quidem eripere, quos videlicet æterno et immutabili suo consilio, solâ suâ bonitate et misericordiâ nulloque operum ipsorum respectu in Jesu Christo elegit; alios vero in eâ coruptione et damnatione relinquere, in quibus nimirum juste suo tempore damnandis justitiam suam demonstret, sicut in aliis divitias misericordiæ suæ declarat. Nec enim alii aliis sunt meliores, donec illos deus discernat ex immutabili illo consilio, quod ante seculorum creationem in Jesu Christo determinavit: neque posset quisquam suâ vi sibi ad bonum illud aditum patefacere, quum ex naturâ nostrâ ne unum quidem rectum motum vel affectum seu cogitationem habere possimus, donec nos deus gratis præveniat et ad rectitudinem formet.

Conf. Gall. ii. p. 8: God looketh upon us in grace, taketh compassion on us, and hath no other reason for showing His grace and mercy towards us, than only His kindness and pitifulness. Then we hold that the goodness which He hath shown towards us comes from this, that He before the world's creation chose us, . . . before we were born He elected us, and took us out of the common damnation in which all men were shut up. [Orig. in German.]

Conf. Belg. art. 16 : Credimus, deum, posteaquam tota Adami progenies sic in perditionem et exitium primi hominis culpâ præcipitata fuit, deum se talem demonstrasse, qualis est, nimirum misericordem et justum, misericordem quidem, eos ab hac perditione liberando et servando, quos æterno et immutabili suo consilio pro gratuitâ suâ bonitate in Jesu Christo elegit et selegit, absque ullo operum ipsorum respectu; justum vero, reliquos in lapsu et perditione, in quam sese ipsi præcipitaverant, relinquendo.[1]

Canon. Dordr. cap. i. art. 1 : Cum omnes homines in Adamo peccaverint et rei sint facti maledictionis et mortis æternæ, deus nemini fecisset injuriam, si universum genus humanum in peccato et maledictione relinquere ac propter peccatum damnare voluisset. Art. 3 : Ut autem homines ad fidem adducantur, deus clementer lætissimi hujus nuntii præcones mittit ad quos vult et quando vult, quorum ministerio homines ad resipiscentiam et fidem in Ch. vocantur.

Ib. art. 6 : Quod aliqui in tempore fide a deo donantur, aliqui non donantur, id ab æterno ipsius decreto provenit; . . . secundum quod decretum electorum corda, quantumvis dura, gratiose emollit et ad credendum inflectit, non-electos autem justo judicio suæ malitiæ et duritiæ relinquit. Atque hic potissimum sese nobis aperit profunda, misericors pariter

---

[1] F. Homm's edition has at the end this bracketed clause: Hac ratione declarat, se esse misericordem et clementem deum iis, quos salvos facit, quibus nihil debebat, uti quoque se declarat justum judicem ostensione justæ severitatis suæ erga reliquos. Atque interim illis nullam facit injuriam. Nam quod nonnullos salvos facit, non propterea fit, quod isti aliis sint meliores, cum omnes in exitium certum prolapsi sint, donec deus eos discernat et liberet secundum æternum atque immutabile propositum suum, quod in J. C. fundatum est, antequam mundus creatus fuit. Nemo itaque secundum hanc sententiam ad hanc gloriam pervenire per se ipsum potest, quoniam a nobis ipsis non sumus idonei ad cogitandum aliquid boni, nisi deus per gratiam ac meram bonitatem suam nos præveniat; adeo natura nostra corrupta est.

et justa hominum æqualiter perditorum discretio, sive decretum illud electionis et reprobationis in verbo dei revelatum.

Ib. art. 7: Est autem electio immutabile dei propositum, quo ante jacta mundi fundamenta ex universo genere humano, ex primæva integritate in peccatum et exitium suâ culpâ prolapso, secundum liberrimum voluntatis suæ beneplacitum, ex merâ gratiâ, certam quorundam hominum multitudinem aliis nec meliorum nec digniorum, sed in communi miseriâ cum aliis jacentium, ad salutem elegit in Christo, quem etiam ab æterno mediatorem et omnium electorum caput salutisque fundamentum constituit, atque ita eos ipsi salvandos dare et ad ejus communionem per verbum et spiritum suum efficaciter vocare ac trahere, seu verâ in ipsum fide donare, justificare, sanctificare et potenter in filii sui communione custoditos tandem glorificare decrevit, ad demonstrationem suæ misericordiæ et laudem divitiarum gloriosæ suæ gratiæ (Eph. i. 4, 5, 6; Rom. viii. 30).

Ib. art. 9: Electio facta est non ex prævisâ fide fideique obedientiâ, sanctitate, aut aliâ aliquâ bonâ qualitate et dispositione, tanquam causa seu conditione in homine eligendo prærequisita, sed ad fidem fideique obedientiam, sanctitatem cet. Ac proinde electio est fons omnis salutaris boni, unde fides, sanctitas et reliqua dona salvifica, ipsa denique vita æterna ut fructus et effectus ejus profluunt, secundum illud apostoli Ephes. i. 4.

Ib. art. 10: Causa hujus gratuitæ electionis est solum dei beneplacitum, non in eo consistens, quod certas qualitates seu actiones humanas ex omnibus possibilibus in salutis conditionem elegit; sed in eo, quod certas quasdam personas ex communi peccatorum multitudine sibi in peculium adscivit.

Ib. art. 15: Æternam et gratuitam electionis gratiam eo vel maxime illustrat scriptura sacra, quod porro testatur, non omnes homines esse electos, sed quosdam in æternâ dei electione præteritos, quos scilicet, deus ex liberrimo, justissimo et immutabili beneplacito decrevit in communi miseriâ, in quam se suâ culpâ præcipitarunt, relinquere nec salvificâ fide et conversionis gratiâ donare.

Ib. art. 16: Qui vivam in Christum fidem, studium filialis obedientiæ cet. in se nondum efficaciter sentiunt, mediis tamen, per quæ deus ista se in nobis operaturum promisit, utuntur, ii ad reprobationis mentionem non consternari, nec (se) reprobis accensere, sed in usu mediorum diligenter pergere ac horam uberioris gratiæ ardenter desiderare humiliterque exspectare debent cet.

Cap. ii. art. 8 : Fuit hoc dei patris liberrimum consilium et gratiosissima voluntas atque intentio, ut mortis pretiosissimæ filii sui vivifica et salvifica efficacia sese exsereret in omnibus electis, ad eos solos fide justificante donandos et per eam ad salutem infallibiliter perducendos, h. e. voluit deus, ut Ch. per sanguinem crucis ex omni populo, tribu, gente et linguâ eos omnes et solos, qui ab æterno ad salutem electi et a patre ipsi dati sunt, efficaciter redimeret, fide donaret, ab omnibus peccatis . . . sanguine suo mundaret, ad finem usque fideliter custodiret cet.

Cap. iii. et iv. art. 11 : Quando deus suum beneplacitum in electis exsequitur seu veram in iis conversionem operatur, non tantum evangelium illis externe prædicari curat, et mentem eorum per Spiritum sanctum potenter illuminat, ut recte intelligant et dijudicent, quæ sunt spiritus dei ; sed ejusdem etiam spiritus regenerantis efficacia ad intima hominis penetrat, cor clausum aperit, durum emollit, præputiatum circumcidit, voluntati novas qualitates infundit, facitque eam ex mortuâ vivam, ex malâ bonam, ex nolente volentem, ex refractaria morigeram, agitque et roborat eam, ut ceu arbor bona, fructus bonarum actionum proferre possit. — Art. 12 : Atque hæc est illa tantopere in scripturis prædicata regeneratio, nova creatio, suscitatio e mortuis et vivificatio, quam deus sine nobis in nobis operatur. Ea autem neutiquam fit per solam forinsecus insonantem doctrinam, moralem suasionem, vel talem operandi rationem, ut post dei (quod ipsum) operationem in hominis potestate maneat regenerare vel non regenerari, converti vel non converti, sed est plane supernaturalis, potentissima simul et suavissima, mirabilis, arcana et ineffabilis operatio virtute suâ, secundum scripturam (quæ ab auctore hujus operationis est inspirata) nec creatione, nec mortuorum resuscitatione minor aut inferior, adeo ut omnes illi, in quorum cordibus admirando hoc modo deus operatur, certo, infallibiliter et efficaciter regenerentur et actu credant. Atque tum voluntas jam renovata non tantum agitur et movetur a deo, sed a deo acta agit et ipsa. Quamobrem etiam homo ipse per gratiam istam acceptam credere et resipiscere recte dicitur.

Form. Cons. Helv. art. 4: Deus ante jacta mundi fundamenta in Chr. fecit propositum seculorum (Ephes. iii. 11), in quo ex mero voluntatis suæ beneplacito sine ullâ meriti, operum vel fidei prævisione ad laudem gloriosæ gratiæ suæ elegit certum ac definitum hominum, in eadem corruptionis massa . . . jacentium adeoque peccato corruptorum, numerum in tempore per Ch. ad salutem perducendum ejusque merito . . . efficaciter vocandum, regenerandum et fide ac resipiscentiâ donandum. Atque ita quidem deus gloriam suam illustrare constituit, ut decreverit, primo hominem integrum creare, tum ejusdem lapsum permittere ac demum ex lapsis quorundam misereri adeoque eosdem eligere, alios vero in corruptâ massâ relinquere æternoque tandem exitio devovere.—Art. 13: Ch. in tempore novi fœderis sponsor factus est pro iis solis, qui per æternam electionem dati ipsi sunt ut populus peculii cet. Pro solis quippe electis ex decretorio patris consilio propriâque intentione diram mortem oppetiit, solos illos in sinum paternæ gratiæ restituit, solos deo reconciliavit et a maledictione legis liberavit.—Art. 19: Deus nullum universale consilium inivit sine determinatione personarum, Christusque adeo non pro singulis sed pro solis electis sibi datis mortuus est. Quod soli electi credunt, reprobi vero indurantur, id a solâ gratiâ dei discriminante proficiscitur cet. Compare the sententia Helvetiorum de prædestinatione in the Actis Synodi Dordr. p. 537 sqq.

West. Conf. ch. iii. sec. 1: God from all eternity did, by the most wise and holy counsel of His own will, freely and unchangeably ordain whatsoever comes to pass; yet so as thereby neither is God the author of sin, nor is violence offered to the will of the creatures, nor is the liberty or contingency of second causes taken away, but rather established. Sec. 2: Although God knows whatsoever may or can come to pass upon all supposed conditions, yet hath He not decreed anything because He foresaw it as future, or as that which would come to pass upon such conditions. Sec. 3: By the decree of God for the manifestation of His glory, some men and angels are predestinated unto everlasting life, and others foreordained to everlasting death. Sec. 4: These angels and men, thus predestinated and foreordained, are particularly and unchangeably designed, and their number is so certain and definite, that it cannot be either increased or diminished. Sec. 5: Those of mankind that are predestinated unto life, God, before the foundation of the world was laid, according to His eternal and immutable purpose, and the secret counsel and good pleasure of His will, hath chosen in Christ unto everlasting glory, out of His mere free grace and love, without any foresight of faith or good works, or perseverance in either of them, or any other thing in the creature, as conditions or causes moving Him thereunto, and all to the praise of His glorious grace. Sec. 6: As God hath appointed the elect unto glory, so hath He, by the eternal and most free purpose of His will, foreordained all the means thereunto. Wherefore they who are elected, being fallen in Adam, are redeemed by Christ; are effectually called unto faith in Christ by His Spirit working in due season; are justified, adopted, sanctified, and kept by His power through faith unto salvation. Neither are any other redeemed by Christ, effectually called, justified, adopted, sanctified, and saved, but the elect only. Sec. 7: The rest of mankind, God was pleased, according to the unsearchable counsel of His own will, whereby He extendeth or withholdeth mercy as He pleaseth, for the glory of His sovereign power over His creatures, to pass by and to ordain them to dishonour and wrath for their sin, to the praise of His glorious justice. Sec. 8: The doctrine of this high mystery of predestination is to be handled with special prudence and care, that men attending the will of God revealed in His word, and yielding obedience thereunto, may, from the certainty of their effectual vocation, be assured of their eternal election. So shall this doctrine afford matter of praise, reverence, and admiration of God, and of humility, diligence, and abundant consolation to all that sincerely obey the gospel.

b. Confessions which have a milder Expression, or give Prominence to universal Redemption, or keep Silence on the Question.

Conf. Basil.: We confess that God, before He created the

world, chose those on whom He would bestow the inheritance of eternal salvation.

Helv. ii. cap. 10: Deus ab æterno prædestinavit vel elegit libere et merâ suâ gratiâ, nullo hominum respectu, sanctos quos vult salvos facere in Christo. Ergo non sine medio, licet non propter ullum meritum nostrum, sed in Ch. et propter Ch. nos elegit deus, ut, qui jam sunt in Christo insiti per fidem, illi ipsi etiam sint electi, reprobi vero, qui sunt extra Christum. . . . Et quamvis deus norit, qui sint sui et alicubi mentio fiat paucitatis electorum, bene sperandum est tamen de omnibus, neque temere reprobis quisquam est adnumerandus. — Further, the misunderstanding is obviated that any one need despair of his election. Not so much in this, however, as in the twofold fact, that God declares Himself repeatedly to desire the salvation of all men (x. 8, 9), and that faith is never spoken of as a specific gift to the elect alone,—there is a remarkable softening of the dogma. This Confession might be placed in the borderland of Predestinarianism.

Thirty-nine Artt. art. 17: Predestination to life is the everlasting purpose of God, whereby, before the foundations of the world were laid, He hath constantly decreed by His counsel, secret to us, to deliver from curse and damnation those whom He hath chosen in Christ out of mankind, and to bring them by Christ to everlasting salvation, as vessels made to honour. Wherefore, they which be endued with so excellent a benefit of God, be called according to God's purpose by His Spirit working in due season; they through grace obey the calling; they be justified freely; they be made sons of God by adoption; they be made like the image of His only-begotten Son Jesus Christ; they walk religiously in good works, and at length, by God's mercy, they attain to everlasting felicity.

Here it must be noted that reprobation, the severest side of the predestinarian dogma, is entirely passed over. Most distinguished theologians of the Episcopal Church have departed either stealthily or openly from the Calvin-Dort dogma. This was accepted, however, by the *Judicia theolog. Magn. Brit. de* V. *Artt. Remonst.* (in the *Actis Synodi Dordr.* p. 489), which coincide with the decrees of the Synod, and thus define reprobation: "It is the eternal decree of God, by which He determined, in the most free will, not so far to have mercy upon such a number of persons fallen in Adam, as efficaciously to snatch them, through Christ, from a state of misery, and lead them infallibly to salvation."

Conf. March. art. 14 (German): This is the most blessed of all the articles, as that on which not only do all the others rest, but our salvation is mostly based: that, namely, the Almighty God, out of pure grace and mercy, without any regard to human worthiness, before the world was, ordained and elected to eternal salvation all who perseveringly believe in Christ; that He knoweth all who are His, loved them from eternity, and therefore gives them in pure mercy saving faith and stedfast perseverance, so that none can pluck them out of the hand of Christ, or separate them from the Father's love; that all things good and evil must work their advantage, because they are the called according to His purpose. — Of no man's salvation is it to be doubted, so long as the means of grace are used, because none can know when God will mightily call His own. — We reject all who hold that God, *propter fidem prævisam*, on account of the faith which He foresaw, elected some, which is a Pelagian error. (That this Confession does not sustain the extreme particularism of Calvin is pretty generally acknowledged. The negative— God did not choose the elect *propter fidem prævisam*, which is expressly reckoned a Pelagian error—we must not misunderstand. The *propter* does not allow us to think of it as opposed to Lutheran dogma.)

II. ANTI-PREDESTINARIAN SYMBOLS.

I. ARMINIAN.

Art. Remonstr. 1: Deum æterno immutabili decreto in Jesu Christo filio suo ante jactum mundi fundamentum statuisse, ex lapso, peccatis obnoxio humano genere illos in Christo, propter Christum et per Christum servare, qui Spiritus sancti gratiâ in eundem ejus filium credunt et in ea fideique obedientia per eandem gratiam in finem perseverant: contra vero eos, qui non convertuntur, et infideles in peccato et irae subjectos relinquere et condemnare, tanquam a Christo alienos, secundum illud evangelii Joh. iii. 36, qui credit in filium, habet vitam aeternam, qui vero filio non assentitur, non videbit vitam aeternam, sed ira dei manet super eum. — Art. 2: Proinde Jesum Christum mundi servatorem pro omnibus et singulis mortuum esse atque ita quidem, ut omnibus per mortem Christi reconciliationem et peccatorum remissionem impetraverit, eâ tamen conditione, ut nemo illâ remissione peccatorum re ipsâ fruatur praeter hominem fidelem, et hoc quoque secundum evangelium.

Conf. Rem. xvii. 3: Est vocatio efficax ab eventu potius, quam a solâ intentione dei sic dicta, quae scil. effectum suum salutarem reipsâ sortitur, non quidem idcirco, quod ex praecisâ salvandi intentione per singularem et arcanam quandam dei sapientiam sic administretur, ut fructuose congruat voluntati ejus, qui vocatur, neque quod in eâ efficaciter per potentiam irresistibilem aut vim quantam omnipotentem voluntas ejus, qui vocatur, ad credendum ita determinetur, ut non possit non credere et obedire cet.

Ib. xvii. 7: Gratiam divinam aspernari et respuere ejusque operationi resistere homo potest, ita ut se ipsum, cum divinitus ad fidem et obedientiam vocatur, inidoneum reddere queat ad credendum et divinae voluntati obediendum; . . . irresistibilis enim gratia sive vis ejusmodi, quae actum ipsum fidei atque obedientiae eo modo efficiat, ut eâ positâ homo non possit non credere atque obedire, illic certe adhiberi non potest, nisi prorsus inepte atque insipienter, ubi obedientia libera serio mandatur.—8: Etsi vero maxima est gratiae disparitas, tamen Spiritus sanctus omnibus et singulis, quibus verbum fidei ordinarie praedicatur, tantum gratiae confert aut saltem conferre paratus est, quantum ad fidem ingenerandum et ad promovendum suis gradibus salutarem ipsorum conversionem sufficit. Itaque gratia sufficiens non tantum iis obtingit, qui actu credunt et convertuntur, sed etiam iis, qui actu ipso non credunt, nec re ipsâ convertuntur. Quoscunque enim deus vocat ad fidem et salutem, eos serio vocat, . . . ita ut nullum absolutae reprobationis aut impromeritae indurationis decretum dei istam præcedere unquam voluerit.—Cf. vii. 4 : Tenendum est, deum benignissimum isti generali malo (peccato orig.) gratuitum in filio suo dilecto J. C. remedium omnibus præparasse, ut vel hinc noxius illorum error satis appareat, qui decretum absolutæ reprobationis ab ipsis confictum in isto peccato fundare solent.

Apol. Conf. Remonstr. p. 102 : Decretum vocant Remonstrantes decretum prædestinationis ad salutem, quia eo decernitur, quâ ratione et conditione deus peccatores saluti destinet. Enuntiatur autem hoc decretum dei hac formulâ: deus decrevit salvare credentes, non quasi credentes quidam re ipsâ jam sint, qui objiciantur deo prædestinanti, sed ut, quid in iis, circa quos deus prædestinans versatur, requiratur, clare significetur. Tantundem enim valet atque si diceres, deus decrevit homines salvare sub conditione fidei. . . . Etiamsi hujusmodi prædestinatio non sit prædestinatio certarum personarum, est tamen omnium hominum prædestinatio, si modo credant, et in virtute prædestinatio certarum personarum, quæ et quando credunt. Ex vi enim prædestinationis ejusmodi generalis prædestinati ab æterno censeri possunt, quicunque in tempore credunt. . . . Etsi decretum istud de facto nullas certas personas prædestinet vel segreget (hoc enim fieri non potest, nisi intercedat divina scientia), tamen decreti ipsius natura talis est, ut ex vi ejus, quia generale est, prædestinati censeri debeant, quotquot in tempore conditionem præstant, adeo ut etiam, si nulla intercederet divina præscientia, recte dici posset ab æterno prædestinatos esse in vi generalis istius decreti divini, quo deus credentes salvare constituit, quotquot in tempore credunt.

Ib. p. 53 : Non mirum est, Remonstrantes doctrinam istam Calvin. (de absol. prædest.) rejecisse et quæ ex eâ consequuntur, impietates ac blasphemias damnasse ex professo. Istud ut facerent, gravissimas causas habebant, nam sententia ista hæretica Calvini jam nota erat vel pueris . . . patroni ejus non damnaverant tantum contrariam veritatem, sed etiam intolerabilem in ecclesiis suis judicaverant cet. Istam sententiam ut coloribus suis ad vivum depingerent Rem., necessarium erat, idque eo magis, quod eam, prout jacet, pestem credant et venenum religionis omnis, cum quâ forte hæresis nulla alia comparari mereatur et tamen nihilominus eam ut fundamentum religionis pæne totius christianæ statui ac propugnari videant.

Cf. Episcop. *Inst. Theol.* iv. 5; Curcell. *Inst.* vi.; Limborch, *Th. Ch.* iv. It has been common among the Arminians to distinguish vocation, as universal and sufficient, from election. The latter belongs to the converted believers, inasmuch as they are separated from the profane crowd of the condemned. *Vid. Conf. Remonst.* xvii. 2.

II. LUTHERAN.

As to the early judgments of Luther and Melanchthon on predestination, and the part taken by the latter against Calvin, and the history of this dogma in the Lutheran Church down to the *Form. Conc.*, see Planck, *Prot. Lehrb.* ii. 134.

F. C. p. 617: Primum omnium est, quod accurate observari oportet, discrimen esse inter præscientiam et prædestinationem sive æternam electionem dei.—Præscientia enim dei nihil aliud est, quam quod deus omnia noverit, antequam fiant.—Hæc dei præscientia simul ad bonos et malos pertinet, sed interim non est causa mali neque est causa peccati, quæ hominem ad scelus impellat. Peccatum enim ex diabolo et ex hominis pravâ et malâ voluntate oritur, neque hæc dei præscientia causa est, quod homines pereant, hoc enim sibi ipsis imputare debent. Sed præscientia dei disponit malum et metas illi constituit, quousque progredi et quam diu durare debeat, idque eo dirigit, ut, licet per se malum sit, nihilominus electis dei ad salutem cedat.

Ib. p. 618: Prædestinatio vero seu æterna dei electio tantum ad bonos et dilectos filios dei pertinet, et hæc est causa ipsorum salutis. Etenim eorum salutem procurat et ea, quæ ad ipsam pertinent, disponit.—Hæc dei prædestinatio non in arcano dei consilio est scrutanda, sed in verbo dei, in quo revelatur, quærenda est. Verbum autem dei deducit nos ad Christum, . . . Christus vero omnes peccatores ad se vocat et promittit illis levationem et serio vult, ut omnes homines ad se veniant et sibi consuli et subveniri sinant. His sese redemtorem in verbo offert et vult, ut verbum audiatur et ut aures non obdurentur nec verbum negligatur et contemnatur.

Et promittit, se largiturum virtutem et operationem Spiritus sancti et auxilium divinum, ut in fide constantes permaneamus, ut vitam æternam consequamur. P. 803: Deus illo suo consilio (electionis), proposito et ordinatione non tantum in genere salutem suorum procuravit, verum etiam omnes et singulas personas electorum, qui per Ch. salvandi sunt, clementer præscivit, ad salutem elegit et decrevit, quod eo modo, quem jam recitavimus, per suam gratiam, dona atque efficaciam salutis æt. participes facere, juvare, eorum salutem promovere, ipsos confirmare et conservare velit.

Ib. p. 619: Vera igitur sententia de prædestinatione ex evangelio Christi discenda est. In eo enim perspicue docetur, quod deus omnes sub incredulitatem concluserit, ut omnium misereatur, et quod nolit quemquam perire, sed potius ut omnes convertantur et in Christum credant.—Quod vero scriptum est (Matt. xxii. 14), multos quidem vocatos, paucos vero electos esse, non ita accipiendum est, quasi deus nolit, ut omnes salventur, sed damnationis impiorum causa est, quod verbum dei aut prorsus non audiant, sed contumaciter contemnant, aures obdurent et cor indurent, et hoc modo Spiritui sancto viam ordinariam præcludant, ut opus suum in eis efficere nequeat, aut certe quod verbum auditum flocci pendant atque abjiciant. Quod igitur pereunt, neque deus neque ipsius electio, sed malitia eorum in culpâ est.

[The link between prescience and predestination the other Lutherans find in 2 Thess. ii. 13 and 1 Pet. i. 2. Jo. Gerhard, *Loci*, ed. E. Preuss, ii. 86 B: Illos omnes et solos ab æterno a deo ad salutem electos esse dicimus, quos efficacia Spiritus sancti per ministerium evangelii in Christum redemtorem vere credituros et in fide usque ad vitæ finem permansuros prævidit; and J. A. Osiander, *Collegium theol. system*, Stutgardiæ 1686, 4, vi. 122 B: Electi sumus secundum præscientiam dei. E. Electio nostra nititur prænotione fidei nec absoluta, sed facta cum respectu ad applicationem correlativam mediorum gratiæ.]

III. SOCINIAN AND MENNONITE.

Cat. Rac. qu. 435: Ea de prædestinatione dei sententia

(quod deus ab æterno certos quosdam nominatim homines ad salutem, alios ad damnationem elegerit) prorsus fallax est, id vero duas ob causas potissimum, quarum una est, quod totam religionem corruere esset necesse; altera, quod deo multa inconvenientia attribui oporteret.

Ib. 440 : Prædestinatio dei in scripturis aliud nihil notat, quam dei ante conditum mundum de hominibus decretum ejusmodi, quod iis, qui in ipsum crederent eique obedirent, daturus esset vitam æternam, eos vero, qui in eum credere et ei parere recusarent, æternâ damnatione puniturus esset. Quod hinc apparet, quod Christus, divinæ voluntatis perfectus interpres, ita hoc dei consilium atque decretum nobis exposuerit: cum, qui in ipsum crederet, vitam æternam certo habiturum esse ; qui vero non crederet, eum certo condemnatum iri.

Cf. qu. 914, and Socin. *Prælect. theol.* c. 6 sqq.

Ris, *Conf.* art. 7 : Nullam creaturam prædestinavit (deus), ordinavit aut creavit, ut condemnaretur, nec voluit nec decrevit, ut peccarent aut in peccatis viverent, ut eas condemnationi subjiceret. Sed . . . omnes decrevit et creavit ad salutem, . . . inque Christo ordinavit et præparavit omnibus medicinam vitæ. . . . Qui oblatam gratiam dedignantur aut respuunt in impœnitentiâ et incredulitate, se ipsos per istam malitiam salutis reddunt indignos atque ideo . . . frustrantur isto fine, ad quem creati et in Christo erant destinati et vocati.

IV. Roman and Greek.

Conc. Trid. sess. vi. justificat. can. 17 : Si quis justificationis gratiam non nisi prædestinatis ad vitam contingere dixerit, reliquos vero omnes, qui vocantur, vocari quidem sed gratiam non accipere, utpote divinâ potestate prædestinatos ad malum : anathema sit. Cf. Bellarmin, *De gratia*, lib. 2.

Later, the Romish Church rejected predestination in Jansenism yet more decisively.

[Propositiones quinque Cornelii Jansenii ex ejus libro *Augustinus* excerptæ, damnatæ ab Innocentio x., ab Alexandro VII., Clemente XI. Propositio quinta: "Semipelagianum est dicere, Christum pro omnibus omnino hominibus mortuum esse aut sanguinem fudisse," damnata uti falsa, temeraria,

scandalosa et, intellecta eo sensu ut Christus pro salute dumtaxat prædestinatorum mortuus sit, impia, blasphema, contumeliosa, divinæ pietati derogans et hæretica. Denzinger, *Enchiridion,* S. 316, 317.]
Cf. Walch, *Religionsstreit. ausser der Luther. Kirche,* i. 233 ff., ii. 855 ff.; Schröckh, *KG. nach der Ref.* iv. 309 ff., vii. 375 ff. Of the Greek Conff., that of Metrop. Critop. alone contains the question, and only in one chapter, of which this is the sum:

Metr. Critop. p. 67: Πᾶσιν οὖν τοῖς τῷ φυσικῷ φωτὶ εὖ κατὰ λόγον χρωμένοις, τούτοις ὁ πανάγαθος θεὸς ἐπιλάμπει καὶ τὸ πνευματικὸν φῶς· τουτέστιν, ἐπανάγει αὐτοῖς τὴν τούτου ποριστικὴν καὶ καθεκτικὴν δύναμιν ἣν ἀπώλεσαν, καὶ τὸ περὶ ταύτην αὐτεξούσιον ἤδη νεκρωθὲν τῇ παραβάσει ἀνίστησι τῇ αὐτοῦ χάριτι. Οὓς καὶ πρὶν τοῦτο ποιῆσαι προγινώσκει τοῦτο ποιήσαντας, καὶ εἰς ἀγαθὸν τέλος τούτους προωρίζει, καὶ πρὸς ἑαυτὸν καλεῖ διὰ τοῦ ἁγίου πνεύματος, καὶ δικαιοῖ τῷ τοῦ μονογενοῦς αἵματι, καὶ δοξάζει τῇ αὐτοῦ χάριτι.—P. 68: Οὐ δυνάμεθα δὲ εἰπεῖν, τούτων τῶν ἀγαθῶν αἴτιον τὴν μετὰ λόγου χρῆσιν τοῦ φυσικοῦ φωτός· οὐ γὰρ παρὰ τοῦτο τοῖς σὺν λόγῳ τῷ ἐμφύτῳ νόμῳ χρωμένοις, ὀφείλει ὁ θεὸς τὰ προειρημένα ἀγαθὰ δοῦναι, ἀλλὰ φρόνιμος ὢν οὐ βούλετο τοῖς ἑκουσίως καταχρωμένοις τῷ φυσικῷ φωτὶ τὸ πνευματικὸν φῶς· ἐμπιστεῦσαι.—P. 70: Τοῦ μὲν γὰρ ἁπλῶς ἐθέλειν αὐτὸν μεταδιδόναι τισὶ τῆς ἑαυτοῦ χάριτος αἰτίαν μόνην λέγομεν τὴν αὐτοῦ ἀγαθότητα· τοῦ δὲ μὴ τούτοις, ἀλλὰ τούτοις, πρώτη μὲν καὶ μεγίστη ἐστὶν ἡ τοῦ θεοῦ φρόνησις καὶ σοφία, ἡ πάντα σοφῶς οἰκονομοῦσα, δευτέρα δὲ, τὸ τῶν λαμβανόντων δεκτικόν· καὶ περὶ οὐκ οἴκοθεν τοῦτο ἔχει τὸ ἰσχύον τοσοῦτον, ὥστε καὶ ἐπισωάσασθαι πρὸς ἑαυτὸ τὰ τηλικαῦτα μεγάλα καὶ αἰώνια τοῦ θεοῦ δῶρα· ἀλλὰ τῇ ἐκείνου σοφίᾳ καὶ ἀγαθότητι ἔδοξεν εἶναί τι.

Cf. Dosithei *Confess.* c. 3.

V. QUAKER.

The Quakers maintain the universality of the enlightenment proceeding from Christ so thoroughly, that they suppose even those who without their fault never heard of the historical Christ are under the influence of that grace.

Barclay, *Apol.* Prop. 6: Therefore Christ hath tasted death for every man—not only for all kinds of men, as some vainly talk, but for every man of all kinds—the benefit of whose offering is not only extended to such who have the distinct outward knowledge of His death and sufferings, as the same is declared in the Scriptures, but even unto those who are necessarily excluded from the benefit of this knowledge by some inevitable accident, which knowledge we willingly confess to be very profitable and comfortable, but not absolutely needful unto such from whom God Himself hath withheld it; yet they may be made partakers of the mystery of His death, though ignorant of the history, if they suffer His seed and light, enlightening their hearts, to take place, in which light communion with the Father and the Son is enjoyed, so as of wicked men to become holy, and lovers of that power, by whose inward and secret touches they feel themselves turned from the evil to the good, and learn to do to others as they would be done by, in which Christ Himself affirms all to be included. As they have then falsely and erroneously taught, who have denied Christ to have died for all men, so neither have they sufficiently taught the truth, who, affirming Him to have died for all, have added the absolute necessity of the outward knowledge thereof in order to obtain its saving effect. . . . As for that doctrine which these propositions chiefly strike at,—to wit, absolute reprobation, according to which some are not afraid to assert " that God, by an eternal and immutable decree, hath predestinated to eternal damnation the far greater part of mankind, not considered as made, much less as fallen, without any respect to their disobedience or sin, but only for the demonstrating of the glory of His justice; and that, for the bringing this about, He hath appointed these miserable souls necessarily to walk in their wicked ways, that so His justice may lay hold on them; and that God doth therefore not only suffer them to be liable to this misery in many parts of the world, by withholding from them the preaching of the gospel and the knowledge of Christ, but even in those places where the gospel is preached, and salvation by Christ is offered, whom, though He publicly invite them, yet He justly condemns for disobedience, albeit He hath withheld from them all grace, by which they could have laid hold of the gospel,—viz. because He hath by a secret will, unknown to all men, ordained and decreed (without any respect had to their obedience or sin) that they shall not obey, and that the offer of the gospel shall never prove effectual for their salvation, but only serve to aggravate and occasion their greater condemnation;"—I say, as to this horrible and blasphemous doctrine, our cause is common with many others, who have both wisely and learnedly, according to Scripture, reason, and antiquity, refuted it. [Accordingly, the resistibility of divine grace, as offered to man, is repeatedly asserted.] As the grace and light in all is sufficient to save all, and of its own nature would save all, so it strives and wrestles with all, in order to save them. He that resists its striving is the cause of his own condemnation; he that resists it not, it becomes his salvation. So that in him that is saved, the working is of the *grace*, and not of the *man*.

X.
JUSTIFICATION: FAITH, WORKS.

FIRST POINT OF DIVERGENCE.

The result of return to God under the influence of the Holy Ghost is justification. This is admitted by all Confessions; but they differ among themselves, partly in the definition of the very idea of justification, partly in the decision of the point in conversion at which justification follows as a consequence, and consequently of the strict condition under which it is imparted. As it respects the notion of justification, Protestants generally understand by it the absolution of a sinner in the sight of God, on the ground of the merit of Christ, and the imputation to faith of the righteousness of Christ. The Romanists, on the other hand, add to the forgiveness of sins sanctification also, that is, the internal change of the sinner into a righteous person, or a divine infusion of habitual righteousness, which makes the man capable of securing his salvation by good works. To the former, justification is an *actus forensis;* to the latter, an *actus physicus,* or *hyper-physicus.* With the Romanists on this point are ranged the Mennonites and the Quakers; whereas the Arminians and the Socinians, with Protestants generally, limit justification to the forgiveness of sins.[1]

[1] The Greek symbols never define justification. Kirpinski, *Comp. orth. theol.:* consistit forma justif. in remiss. pecc. et in mutatione hominis ex peccatore in justum

SYMBOLICAL TESTIMONIES.

I. Roman, Mennonite, and Quaker.

Conc. Trid. sess. vi. cap. 7 : Justificatio non est sola peccatorum remissio, sed et sanctificatio et renovatio interioris hominis per voluntariam susceptionem gratiae et donorum, unde homo ex injusto fit justus et ex inimico amicus, ut sit heres secundum spem vitae aeternae . . . justitia dei, quâ nos justos facit, quâ videlicet ab eo donati renovamur spiritu mentis nostrae et non modo reputamur, sed vere justi nominamur et sumus, justitiam in nobis recipientes. . . . Quanquam nemo possit esse justus, nisi cui merita passionis J. C. communicantur, id tamen in hac impii justificatione fit, dum ejusdem sanct. passionis merito per Spiritum s. caritas dei diffunditur in cordibus eorum, qui justificantur, atque ipsis inhaeret, unde in ipsâ justificatione cum remissione peccatorum haec omnia simul infusa accipit homo per J. Ch., cui inseritur, fidem, spem et caritatem. Cf. cap. 4.

Cf. can. 11; Bellarmin, *De justific.* ii. 2 sqq.; Bossuet, *Expos.* c. 6; Becan. *Man. Controv.* i. 16, 17.

On the relation of forgiveness to the Roman idea of justification, thus Bellarmin : Non potest haec translatio (in statum adoptionis filiorum dei) fieri, nisi homo per remissionem peccati desinat esse impius et per infusionem justitiae incipiat esse pius. Sed sicut aër cum illustratur a sole per idem lumen, quod recipit, desinit esse tenebrosus et incipit esse lucidus : sic etiam homo per eandem justitiam sibi a sole justitiae donatam atque infusam desinit esse injustus, delente videlicet lumine gratiae tenebras peccatorum cet.

Ris, *Conf.* art. 21 : Per vivam fidem acquirimus veram justitiam i. e. condonationem seu remissionem omnium tam praeteritorum quam praesentium peccatorum, ut et veram justitiam, quae per Jesum co-operante Spiritu sancto abundanter in nos effunditur vel infunditur, adeo ut ex malis . . . fiamus boni atque ita ex injustis revera justi.

Barclay, *Apol.* vii. 3 : We understand not by this justification by Christ, barely the good works even wrought by the Spirit of Christ, for they, as Protestants truly affirm, are rather an effect of justification than the cause of it; but we understand the formation of Christ in us, Christ born and brought forth in us, from which good works as naturally proceed as fruit from a fruitful tree. It is this inward birth in us, bringing forth righteousness and holiness in us, that doth justify us, which, having removed and done away the contrary nature and spirit that did bear rule and bring condemnation, now is in dominion over all *in* our hearts. Those, then, that come to know Christ thus formed in them, do enjoy Him wholly and undivided. [The whole section presses home the point that justification is a real internal renovation of mind; and the declarative sense of justification is absolutely rejected. The connection with forgiveness of sins is thus given.] The obedience, sufferings, and death of Christ, is that by which the soul obtains remission of sins, and is the procuring cause of that grace, by whose inward workings Christ comes to be formed inwardly, and the soul to be made conformable unto Him, and so just and justified. Comp. Prop. vii. 8.

II. Protestant.

Apol. A. C. p. 73: Quia *justificari* significat ex injustis justos effici seu regenerari, significat et justos pronuntiari seu reputari; utroque enim modo loquitur scriptura. Ideo primum volumus hoc ostendere, quod sola fides ex injusto justum efficiat, hoc est accipiat remissionem peccatorum cet. Again: consequi remissionem peccatorum est justificari; and p. 109: Justificari hic significat non, ex impio justum effici, sed usu forensi: justum pronuntiari.

Ibid. p. 125: Justificare h. l. (Rom. v. 1), forensi consuetudine significat reum absolvere et pronuntiare justum, sed propter alienam justitiam, videlicet Christi, quæ aliena justitia communicatur nobis per fidem. Cf. *Conf. Saxon.* p. 58 sqq.

F. C. p. 685: Vocabulum *justificationis* in hoc negotio significat justum pronuntiare, a peccatis et æternis peccatorum suppliciis absolvere propter justitiam Christi, quæ a deo fidei imputatur. Et sane hic vocabuli illius usus tam in V., quam in N. T. admodum frequens est (Prov. xvii. 15; Isa. v. 23; Rom. viii. 33).

Helv. ii. cap. 15 : *Justificare* significat apostolo (Paulo) in disputatione de justificatione peccata remittere, a culpâ et pœnâ absolvere, in gratiam recipere et justum pronuntiare.

Conf. Gall. art. 18 : In solâ Ch. obedientiâ prorsus acquiescimus, quæ quidem nobis imputatur, tum ut tegantur omnia nostra peccata, tum etiam ut gratiam coram deo nanciscamur.

Conf. Rem. xviii. 3 : *Justificatio* est : peccatoris vere resipiscentis ac credentis per et propter Christum verâ fide apprehensum misericors et quidem plenaria coram deo ab omni reatu absolutio sive gratuita peccatorum omnium per veram fidem in Jes. Ch. obtenta remissio.

Apol. Conf. Rem. p. 112 a : *Justificatio* est actio dei, quam deus pure pute in suâ ipsius mente efficit, quia nihil aliud est, quam volitio aut decretum, quo peccata remittere et justitiam imputare aliquando vult iis, qui credunt i. e. quo vult pœnas peccatis eorum promeritas iis non infligere eosque tanquam justos tractare et præmio afficere.

Cat. Racov. qu. 453 : Justificatio est, cum nos deus pro justis habet, quod eâ ratione facit, cum nobis et peccata remittit et nos vita æterna donat.

Cf. F. Socin. *Prælect. theol.* c. 15, and tract. de justific. (*Opp.* i. p. 602.) Ostorodt, *Unterricht.* c. 36, S. 296.

Observations.

1. [In evangelical doctrine justification is an act, an act of God; according to the Roman doctrine, it is a process. But the Evangelical Church does not teach that the act of justification occurs once only in the life of a man, as it were in baptism, or the so-called great conversion. It teaches that it is daily necessary. *Form. Conc.* p. 692. Further, justification, in the evangelical doctrine, is a judicial act; according to Rome, it is the communication or impartation of a substance.] The Romish Church teaches that there are degrees of justification (*alter justior altero*). Conc. Trid. sess. vi. 10.

2. The relation of justification, objectively, to the merits of Christ is defined by this, that justification is in some sense an imputation of the righteousness of Christ (*F. C.* p. 584). [Jo. Gerhard, *Loci*, ed. E. Preuss, iii. 501 A B : Quamvis enim meritum Christi nobis inhærere non possit, ut Bellarminus scribit, tamen nobis a Deo imputari potest, sicut Christo mediatori imputata sunt peccata nostra;

utrumque igitur justitiæ Christi tribuimus, quod sit causa justificationis meritoria et quod sit causa ejusdem formalis, nimirum ratione applicationis, quatenus per fidem nobis imputatur.] The Romanists consistently reject this definition,—Conc. Trid. sess. vi. can. 11; Bellarmin, *De justific.* ii. 7 sqq.—and thus teach, in accordance with their doctrine of justificatio, Trid. sess. vi. cap. 7: Chr. suâ sanctissimâ passione nobis justificationem meruit (cf. Becani *Manuale controv.* i. 16. 9); and the communicatio meriti Ch. is thus explained: Dum per Sp. s. caritas dei diffunditur in cordibus eorum, qui justificantur cet.; or as Bossuet, c. vi., says: Justitia Ch. non imputatur tantum fidelibus, sed actu ac reipsâ Sp. s. operatione communicatur, ut ejus gratiâ non justi tantum reputentur, sed fiant. Cf. Bellarmin, *Justific.* ii. 3, and Dosithei *Confess.* c. xiii. The antithesis to the Protestant imputation theory is thus briefly expressed: In justificatione peccata non teguntur tantum, sed tolluntur vere s. Becani *Manual.* i. p. 225. In another sense Arminians deny the imputatio justitiæ Christi. Curcell. *Rel. chr. instit.* vii. 9. 6: Nullibi docet scriptura, justitiam Chr. nobis imputari. Et id absurdum est. Nemo enim in se injustus alienâ justitiâ potest esse formaliter justus, non magis, quam alienâ albedine Æthiops esse albus cf. vii. 1. 7. *Apol. Conf. Remonstr.* p. 112 b: Remonstrantes phrasin illam: *Chr. justitiam nobis imputari* in declaratione suâ non usurparunt, non, quod eam benignâ interpretatione in commodum sensum flecti non posse credant, sed quod si rigide accipiatur, consistere non possit cum illâ, quæ propria est ecclesiarum reform. sententia, quâ justitia nobis imputari dicitur propter Chr. meritum et obedientiam. Nam si utramque in rigore velimus esse veram, necesse est ut dicamus, justitiam Ch. nobis imputari propter justitiam Ch., quæ locutio . . . manifestam in sese habet absurditatem. We should say, imputatur nobis justitia; but this consists (Limborch, *Theol. chr.* vi. 4. 17) in the fact that God credentem in filium suum, licet antea peccatorem et impium, nunc autem resipiscentem et per fidem opera pœnitentiâ digna producentem, eo loco reputat, ac si perfecte justus esset, . . . ac proinde eum ut talem tractare vult. It is at the same time clear from this, that the Arminian opposition to the imputation of Christ's righteousness springs from their divergent doctrine, not of justification, but of its ground.

The Socinians, though they teach no satisfaction, consistently reject the imputation of His righteousness. Justification springs from the sheer grace of God, who pardons those who believe in Christ, and obey. Barclay, *Apol.* vii. 2, shows how and why the Quakers reject this imputation.

3. The forgiveness of sins which is bestowed through the application of the merits of Christ, extends, in Protestant doctrine, to the guilt and all the punishment of sin. In Roman doctrine this comprehensive pardon is granted only in baptism: in the renewal of

justification in penance, only the guilt and eternal punishment of sin are remitted; the temporal punishments of sin must be expiated by Christians themselves. When, in either of these systems, forgiveness of sins is spoken of, we must understand original sin and actual transgressions. On the other hand, those systems which deny the reality of original sin refer forgiveness, of course, only to the personal sins of each individual.

SECOND POINT OF DIVERGENCE.

The standards agree that justification comes to man through Christ; but the manner of the appropriation is variously stated. Rome teaches that through man's faith, penitence, resolution of amendment, God is moved to infuse into one thus disposed justification, and with it the power to merit for himself by good works increase of grace and eternal life. [The evangelical church, on the contrary, teaches that the righteousness of Christ is laid hold on by the sinner, and calls this simple energy faith. Thus it is not our faith for the sake of which we are declared righteous, but Christ. Faith is only the means, the only one it is true, by which the righteousness of the God-man is applied. If a sinner is thus for the sake of the merit of Christ justified, then all the rest—love, and hope, and good works—necessarily follow.] Finally, the Greek and the Socinians, the Arminians and the Mennonites, occupying a middle place, would have faith and works unitedly (*fides obsequiosa*) the condition of righteousness. But the two latter parties reject absolutely all meritoriousness in the good works.

I. ROMAN.

Conc. Trid. sess. vi. cap. 6 : Disponuntur ad ipsam justitiam, dum excitati divinâ gratiâ et adjuti fidem ex auditu concipientes libere moventur in deum, credentes vera esse, quæ divinitus revelata et promissa sunt, atque illud inprimis, a deo justificari impium per gratiam ejus, . . . et dum, peccatores se esse intelligentes, a divinæ justitiæ timore, quo utiliter concutiuntur, ad considerandum dei misericordiam se convertendo in spem eriguntur, fidentes, deum sibi propter Christum propitium fore, illumque tanquam omnis justitiæ fontem diligere incipiunt ac propterea moventur adversus peccata per odium aliquod et detestationem.—C. 7: Hanc dispositionem s. præparationem justificatio ipsa consequitur cet.[1] See for what follows, above, I. —C. 10: Sic justificati et amici dei facti, euntes de virtute in virtutem renovantur de die in diem, h. e. mortificando membra carnis suæ et exhibendo ea arma justitiæ in sanctificationem per observationem mandatorum dei et ecclesiæ in ipsâ justitiâ per Ch. gratiam acceptâ, co-operante fide bonis operibus crescunt atque magis justificantur cet.—Can. 32: Si quis dixerit, justificatum bonis operibus, quæ ab eo per dei gratiam et J. Ch. meritum, cujus vivum membrum est, fiunt, non vere mereri augmentum gratiæ, vitam æt. et ipsius vitæ æt., si tamen in gratiâ decesserit, consecutionem atque etiam gloriæ augmentum, anath. sit.

Ibid. cap. 8: Per fidem ideo justificari dicimur, quia fides est humanæ salutis initium, fundamentum et radix omnis justificationis.

Ibid. cap. 9: Quamvis necessarium sit credere, neque remitti neque remissa unquam fuisse peccata, nisi gratis divinâ misericordiâ propter Christum, . . . tamen non illud asserendum est, . . . neminem a peccatis absolvi ac justificari, nisi eum, qui certo credat se absolutum et justificatum esse, *atque hac solâ fide absolutionem et justificationem perfici.*

Ibid. can. 9: Si quis dixerit, solâ fide impium justificari, ita ut intelligat nihil aliud requiri, quod ad justificationis gratiam consequendam co-operetur, . . . anathema sit.—Can. 12: Si quis dix., fidem justificantem nihil aliud esse, quam fiduciam divinæ misericordiæ peccata remittentis propter Christum, vel eam fiduciam solam esse, quâ justificamur, anathema sit.—Can. 14: Si quis dix., hominem a peccatis absolvi ac justificari ex eo, quod se absolvi ac justificari certo credat, aut

---

[1] Bellarmin, *Justif.* i. 12: Synod. Trid. septem actus enumerat, quibus impii ad justitiam disponuntur, videl. fidei, timoris, spei, dilectionis, pœnitentiæ, propositi suscipiendi sacramenti (baptismi) et propositi novæ vitæ atque observationis mandatorum dei. Cf. Becan. *Man. controv.* i. 17.

... hac solâ fide absolutionem et justificationem perfici, anathema sit.

Justification, the infusio justitiæ, is imparted gratuitously. Trid. sess. vi. cap. 8 : gratis justificari ideo dicimus, quia nihil eorum, quæ justificationis gratiam præcedunt, sive fides sive opera, ipsam justificationis gratiam promeretur. But it is usual, with the Romish divines, to term man's self-disposal towards justification a *meritum ex congruo* (*Eng. Art.* xiii.). Bellarmin, *Just.* i. 17, says : per fidem nos placere deo et impetrare atque *aliquo modo mereri* justificationem. (The meritum ex operibus is *e condigno.*) [And of the good works of the justified the Council of Trent says expressly that they must be regarded as properly meritorious.]

II. PROTESTANT.

A. C. art. 4 : Docent, quod homines non possint justificari coram deo propriis viribus, meritis aut operibus, sed gratis justificentur propter Christum per fidem, cum credunt, se in gratiam recipi et peccata remitti propter Christum ; ... hanc fidem imputat deus pro justitiâ coram ipso.

Apol. A. C. p. 67 : Cum justificatio contingat per gratuitam promissionem, sequitur, quod non possimus non ipsi justificare, alioqui quorsum opus erat promittere ? Cumque promissio non possit accipi nisi fide, evang. ... prædicat justitiam fidei in Chr.

Ib. p. 94 : Solâ fide nos justificamur coram deo, quia solâ fide accipimus remissionem peccatorum et reconciliationem, propter Christum, quia reconciliatio seu justificatio est res promissa propter Christum, non propter legem. S. *Apol.* pp. 73–82 ; cf. *A. Sm.* p. 304.

F. C. p. 584 : Confitemur, solam fidem esse illud medium et instrumentum, quo Christum salvatorem et ita in Christo justitiam illam, quæ coram judicio dei consistere potest, apprehendimus. — P. 689 : Neque contritio neque delectio neque ulla alia virtus, sed sola fides est illud unicum medium et instrumentum, quo gratiam dei, meritum Ch. et remissionem peccatorum apprehendere et accipere possumus. Recte etiam dicitur, quod credentes, qui per fidem in Ch. justificati sunt, in hac vita primum quidem imputatam sibi justitiam, deinde vero etiam inchoatam justitiam novæ obedientiæ s. bonorum operum habeant. Sed hæc duo non inter se permiscenda aut simul in articulum de justificatione fidei coram deo ingerenda sunt.

A. C. p. 18 : Nomen *fidei* non significat tantum historiæ notitiam, qualis est in impiis et diabolo, sed significat fidem, quæ credit non tantum historiam sed etiam effectum historiæ, videlicet hunc articulum, remissionem peccatorum cet.

Apol. A. C. p. 68 : Illa fides, quæ justificat, non est tantum notitia historiæ, sed est assentiri promissioni dei, in quâ gratis propter Christum offertur remissio peccatorum et justificatio. —P. 69 : Quoties de fide justificante loquimur, sciendum est, hæc tria objecta concurrere, promissionem et quidem gratuitam et merita Christi, tanquam pretium, et propitiationem. Promissio accipitur fide, gratuitum excludit nostra merita et significat, tantum per misericordiam offerri beneficium: Christi merita sunt pretium, quia oportet esse aliquam certam propitiationem pro peccatis nostris.—P. 72 : Id autem est credere, confidere meritis Christi, quod propter ipsum certo velit nobis deus placatus esse.

Ib. p. 172 : Adversarii, cum de fide loquuntur et dicunt, eam præcedere pœnitentiam, intelligunt fidem non hanc, quæ justificat, sed quæ in genere credit, deum esse, pœnas propositas esse impiis cet. Nos præter illam fidem requirimus, ut credat sibi quisque remitti peccata; de hac fide speciali litigamus, . . . hæc fides ita sequitur terrores, ut vincat eos et reddat pacatam conscientiam.

Cf. *Apol.* p. 131 ; *F. C.* pp. 585, 684.

Helv. ii. c. 15 : Docemus cum apostolo, hominem peccatorem justificari solâ fide in Christum ; . . . quia fides Christum justitiam nostram recipit et gratiæ dei in Christo omnia tribuit, ideo fidei tribuitur justificatio, maxime propter Christum et non ideo, quia nostrum opus est. Donum enim dei est.

Heidelb. Cat. Fr. 60 : How art thou justified before God? Only by a genuine faith in Jesus Christ, so that . . . God, without any merit of mine, out of pure grace, gives and reckons me the perfect satisfaction, righteousness, and holiness of Christ, as if I had never contracted any sin, and had myself accomplished the obedience which Christ rendered for me. Cf. 61.

Conf. Gall. art. 20 : Credimus, nos solâ fide fieri justitiæ participes ; . . . hoc autem ideo fit, quod promissiones vitæ nobis in ipso (Christo) oblatæ tunc usui nostro applicantur et nobis redduntur efficaces, cum eas amplectimur, nihil ambigentes nobis obventura, de quibus ore dei certiores fimus.

Thirty-nine Artt. art. xi.: We are accounted righteous before God, only for the merit of our Lord and Saviour Jesus Christ, by faith; and not for our own works or deservings. Wherefore, that we are justified by faith only is a most wholesome doctrine, and very full of comfort, as more largely is expressed in the Homily of Justification.

West. Conf. ch. xi. sec. 1: Those whom God effectually calleth He also freely justifieth, not by infusing righteousness into them, but by pardoning their sins, and by accounting and accepting their persons as righteous: not for anything wrought in them, or done by them, but for Christ's sake alone: not by imputing faith itself, the act of believing, or any other evangelical obedience, to them as their righteousness; but by imputing the obedience and satisfaction of Christ unto them, they receiving and resting on Him and His righteousness by faith : which faith they have not of themselves; it is the gift of God. Sec. 2: Faith, thus receiving and resting on Christ and His righteousness, is the alone instrument of justification ; yet is it not alone in the person justified, but is ever accompanied with all other saving graces, and is no dead faith, but worketh by love. Sec. 3 : Christ, by His obedience and death, did fully discharge the debt of all those that are thus justified, and did make a proper, real, and full satisfaction to His Father's justice in their behalf. Yet, inasmuch as He was given by the Father for them, and His obedience and satisfaction accepted in their stead, and both freely, not for anything in them, their justification is only of free grace; that both the exact justice and rich grace of God might be glorified in the justification of sinners.

Conf. Belg. art. 22 : Credimus, . . . Spiritum sanctum veram in cordibus nostris fidem accendere, quæ Jesum Christum cum omnibus suis meritis amplectitur eumque suum ac sibi proprium efficit nihilque amplius extra cum quærit. Merito igitur cum Paulo dicimus, nos solâ fide justificari seu fide absque operibus. Interim proprie loquendo nequaquam intelligimus ipsam fidem quæ nos justificat ut quæ sit duntaxat instrumentum, quo Christum, justitiam nostram, apprehendimus. Cf. *Conf. Anhalt.* 3.

Helv. ii. c. 16 : Fides christiana non est opinio ac humana persuasio, sed firmissima fiducia et evidens ac constans animi assensus, denique certissima comprehensio veritatis dei . . . atque adeo dei ipsius, summi boni et præcipue promissionis divinæ et Christi, qui omnium promissionum est colophon.

(Calvin, *Institutt.* iii. 2. 7 : Justa fidei definitio nobis constabit, si dicamus, esse divinæ erga nos benevolentiæ firmam certamque cognitionem, quæ gratuitæ in Christo promissionis veritate fundata per Spiritum sanctum et revelatur mentibus nostris et cordibus obsignatur.)

Cat. Heid. Fr. 21 (Germ.): What is true faith? It is not only a certain knowledge by which I hold all to be true that God hath revealed in His word, but also a hearty confidence which the Holy Ghost works in me through the gospel, that not only for others, but for me also, the forgiveness of sins, everlasting righteousness, and blessedness with God, are bestowed of His grace: of pure grace, for the merits alone of Jesus Christ.

Observations.

1. In order to express the manner or modes of justification by faith alone, the Protestant symbols use [in conjunction with the formula, *Justitia Christi nobis imputatur per fidem*] occasionally the Pauline words (Rom. iv. 5): *Fides a Deo imputatur (nobis)* pro justitiâ. *A. C.* art. 4; *Apol.* 121. [However, the sense in which they use these words is never this, that "on account of the acting of faith we are esteemed by God just," but always this, that "faith is reckoned for righteousness *quoad* its object, that is, the righteousness of Christ."] The Arminians do not approve of the statement that "the righteousness of Christ is imputed to us;" and the record, "Faith is reckoned to us by God for righteousness," they take in a sense different from that of the Lutheran formularies. Limborch, *Theol. Chr.* vi. 4. 39. So also, in some sense, the Socinians; *vid.* Ostorodt, *Unterr.* S. 304.

2. According to the Protestant doctrine, the true believer may be certified of his justification. *Apol. A. C.* 76; Calvin, *Instit.* iii. 2. 16; *Can. Dordr.* v. 9, 10; *Decl. Thorun.* 55. According to the Predestinarians, the believer is assured of his eternal salvation, since he cannot again lose his justification through unbelief. The Romanists deny both, in the interest of their doctrine both of faith and of justification. Trid. sess. vi. 9: Non asserendum est, . . . oportere eos, qui vere justificati sunt, absque ullâ omnino dubitatione apud semetipsos statuere, se esse justificatos cet. Nam sicut nemo pius de dei misericordiâ, de Christi merito . . . dubitare debet, sic quilibet, dum se ipsum suamque propriam infirmitatem et indispositionem respicit, de suâ gratiâ formidare et timere potest, cum nullus scire valeat certitudine fidei, cui non potest subesse falsum, se gratiam dei esse consecutum. Cf. Bellarm. *De Justif.* iii. 3; Möhler, *Symb.* 18; Klee, *Dogm.* iii. 71. The Arminians agree with other Protestants as to the assurance of justification (*vid.* Limb. *Th. Ch.* vi. 7. 1), but they reject the doctrine of an assured perseverance in faith as taught by the Calvinists.

3. What the Protestants understand by justifying faith may be seen from the foregoing symbolical evidences. The Romanists require, as a personal disposition on the part of him who shall attain justification, most assuredly faith; but that faith is not a trust in the merit of Christ, it is that general credence of the doctrines of the Christian revelation which is rooted in the understanding. But in the justified man, who seeks to attain increase of grace and eternal salvation, it is living faith, working by love, *fides formata*, or faith *with* good works, which attains to this completion of justification. (Conc. Trid. sess. vi. cap. 7.) The Socinians in this agree with the Arminians, that they refer justifying faith, the centre of which is personal trust, to the whole compass of the truth of redemption. It is in harmony with what has been said, that the Romish Church should be found maintaining that faith (as disposition towards justification) precedes repentance; while the Evangelical Church hold that penitence leads to faith, the latter indeed being in a broader sense part of repentance itself.

I. ROMAN CATHOLIC.

Concil. Trid. sess. vi. cap. 8: Fides est humanæ salutis initium, fundamentum et radix omnis justificationis, sine quâ impossibile est placere deo et ad filiorum ejus consortium pervenire. Cf. *Cat. Rom.* i. 3. 4.

Cat. Rom. i. 1. 1: Nos de eâ fide loquimur, cujus vi omnino assentimur iis, quæ tradita sunt divinitus. Hanc autem ad

salutem consequendam esse necessariam nemo jure dubitabit.
. . . Quum enim finis, qui ad beatitudinem homini propositus est, altior sit, quam ut humanæ mentis acie perspici possit, necesse ei erat ipsius a deo cognitionem accipere. Hæc vero cognitio nihil aliud est, nisi fides, cujus virtus efficit, ut id ratum habeamus, quod a deo traditum esse . . . ecclesiæ auctoritas comprobarit.

(Bellarmin, *Justif.* i. 4: (Catholici) fidem historicam et miraculorum et promissionum unam et eandem esse docent atque illam unam non esse proprie notitiam aut fiduciam, sed assensum certum atque firmissimum ob auctoritatem primæ veritatis. . . . Objectum fidei justificantis, quod hæretici restringunt ad solam promissionem misericordiæ specialis, Catholici tam late patere volunt, quam late patet verbum dei, quin potius certam promissionem specialis misericordiæ non tam ad fidem, quam ad præsumtionem pertinere contendunt. Deinde (dissentiunt) in facultate et potentiâ animi, quæ sedes est fidei. Siquidem illi fidem collocant in voluntate, cum fiduciam esse definiunt, ac per hoc eam cum spe confundunt. Fiducia enim nihil est aliud, nisi spes roborata, ut sanctus Thomas docet. Catholici fidem in intellectu sedem habere docent. Denique in ipso actu intellectus. Ipsi enim per notitiam fidem definiunt, nos per assensum. Assentimur enim deo, quamvis ea nobis credenda proponat, quæ non intelligimus. —Cap. 7: In eo, qui credit, duo sunt, apprehensio et judicium s. assensus. Sed apprehensio non est fides sed aliquid fidem præcedens. Præterea apprehensio non dicitur proprie notitia. . . . Nam accidere potest, ut rusticus catholicus non apprehendat nisi confuse tria illa nomina (trinitatis) et tamen vere credat. Judicium autem s. assensus duplex est, alter enim sequitur rationem et evidentiam rei, alter auctoritatem proponentis, prior dicitur notitia, posterior fides. Igitur mysteria fidei, quæ rationem superant, credimus, non intelligimus, ac per hoc fides distinguitur contra scientiam et melius per ignorantiam quam per notitiam definitur. Cf. Becani *Manual.* i. 233 sq. It is clear that Roman Catholic theology will not admit any elevation of faith in the promises of grace given by God in Christ out of and above the common round of faith in the Christian revelation. On that account, and also because they deny the possibility of a subjective and full assurance of forgiveness to the individual sinner, they will not regard the characteristic of faith as being confidence, or regard such confidence as the justifying element in faith. On all points the Protestant doctrine of faith contradicts that of the Romish system : see Möhler, *Symb.* 15.)

Conc. Trid. sess. vi. cap. 6 : Disponuntur ad justitiam, dum excitati divinâ gratiâ et adjuti fidem ex auditu concipientes libere moventur in deum, credentes vera esse, quæ divinitus revelata et promissa sunt, . . . et dum, peccatores se esse intelligentes a divinæ justitiæ timore ad considerandam dei misericordiam se convertendo, in spem eriguntur . . . ac propterea moventur adversus peccata per odium aliquod et detestationem h. e. per eam pœnitentiam, quam ante baptismum agi oportet cet.

Catech. Rom. ii. 5. 5 : Fides pœnitentiæ pars non est, verum in eo, quem pœnitet, fides pœnitentiam antecedat necesse est. Neque enim potest quisquam se ad deum convertere, qui fide careat.

Cf. Bellarmin, *Pœnit.* i. 19 ; *Confut. A. C.* p. 84 sq.

II. PROTESTANT.

Conf. A. p. 12 : Constat pœnitentia proprie his duabus partibus. Altera est contritio s. terrores incussi conscientiæ agnito peccato, altera est fides, quæ concipitur ex evangelio s. absolutione et credit propter Ch. remitti peccata et consolatur conscientiam et ex terroribus liberat. Cf. *A. Sm.* p. 319 sqq. ; *F. C.* pp. 816, 822.

The Reformed Symbols have not spoken on this point. Calvin, *Instit.* iii. 3. 3, brings some insignificant objections to Melanchthon's definitions.[1] When he himself asserts that faith ought to precede penitence, the difference rests upon a peculiar definition of penitence. Cf. Parci *Corp. doct. ch.* 482.

III. SOCINIAN.

Cat. Rac. qu. 418 : (Fides, quam necessario consequitur

---

[1] Melanch. had made the separation of penitence into *mortificatio* and *vivificatio*.

salus) est fiducia per Christum in deum. Unde apparet, eam in Christum fidem duo comprehendere, unum, ut non solum deo, verum et Christo confidamus. Deinde, ut deo obtemperemus, non in iis solum, quæ in lege per Mosen lata præcepit et per Christum abrogata non sunt; verum etiam in iis omnibus, quæ Christus legi addidit.

Ib. qu. 419 : Ergo tu obedientiam sub fide comprehendis? Sic est. Etenim res ipsa indicio est, neminem inveniri posse, qui spem certam vitæ æt. in animo concipiat, quam Ch. tantum sibi obtemperantibus promisit, qui non Christo dicto audiens sit cet.—*Ib.* qu. 420 : Cur vero ap. Paulus fidem operibus opponit? In iis locis, ubi ap. fidem opponit operibus, de operibus ejusmodi agit, quæ et perfectam et perpetuam obedientiam continent, qualem sub lege deus ab hom. requirebat, verum non de iis operibus, quæ obedientiam, quam deus a nobis, qui in Ch. credidimus, requirat, comprehendunt.

Ib. qu. 421 : (Obedientia est) ea, ut primum veterem hominem cum operibus ipsius exuentes ab omni peccato anteacto desistamus, quam quidem rem scriptura pœnitentiam vocat. Deinde, ut pro virili voluntatem dei exsequamur, adeo, ut non secundum carnem ambulemus, verum Spiritu opera carnis mortificemus, in summâ : nullius peccati habitum contrahamus, omnium vero virtutum christianarum habitum comparemus.

Socin. *De Chr. serv.* iv. 11 : Fides ergo in Christum, quâ justificamur, quamvis obedientiam, quam spe futuri boni, quod is nobis daturus sit, deo præstamus, et complectatur et significet atque idcirco opus omnino declaret, operibus tamen propterea merito opponitur, quia nec perpetuam et absolutissimam præceptorum dei conservationem ipsa per se continet, nec propriâ vi justificat, sed propter dei clementiam, qui ejusmodi opus facientibus, quod ob eam rem dei opus a Christo appellatum est, justitiam quantumvis antea injustis imputare dignatus est et ipsos pro justis coram se habere pro incomparabili suâ benignitate voluit.

IV. Arminian and Mennonite.

Apol. Conf. Remonstr. p. 113 : Mihi vide, an non mera logica pugna sit, si disputetur an fides, quæ est viva, an fides, quâ est viva, requiratur ad justificationem? Certe utrimque enim in describendâ fidei naturâ est consensio, utrimque bonorum operum praesentia necessaria esse statuitur, de respectu tantum, quem fides viva ad justificationem habet, quaestio manet, at de respectu statuere non est nostrum, sed judicis; deinde quid habet respectus ille merus, quod justam magnae liti causam dare possit, imo quid non habet, quod occasionem omnem liti debeat praecidere cet.? Sane si dicatur, fidem requiri ad justificationem, quatenus est viva fides, necessitas bonorum operum et pietatis christianae fortius adstruitur, quam si dicatur, fidem requiri, quae viva est. Natura rei id evincit.

Conf. Remonstr. xi. 1 sqq.: Fides in Christum est deliberatus et firmus animi assensus, verbo dei adhibitus et cum verâ in Christum fiduciâ conjunctus, quo non tantum doctrinae Christi tanquam verae ac divinae firmiter assentimus ac fidenter inhaeremus, sed in ipsum etiam Christum ad salutem a deo nobis ex purâ gratiâ datum toti recumbimus.—Itaque ad fidem veram et salvificam non sufficit sola notitia divinae voluntatis, . . . neque assensus etiam quilibet, puta, subitus, perfunctorius cet., sed requiritur omnino firmus et solidus voluntatisque deliberatae imperio roboratus, denique fiducialis et obsequiosus assensus, qui et fiducia dicitur. . . . Assensus ejusmodi fiducialis vel obsequiosa haec fiducia demum est vera ac viva fides, quae secum necessario trahit observationem mandatorum J. Ch. sive bona opera.

Limborch, *Theol. christ.* vi. 4. 22: Sciendum, quando dicimus, nos fide justificari, nos non excludere opera, quae fides exigit et tanquam foecunda mater producit; sed ea includere. . . . Sine operibus autem fides mortua et ad justificationem inefficax est. —4. 46: Acriter hic contendere, an fides quae viva, an vero quatenus viva est, nos justificet, sive, an opera ad justificationem requirantur necessitate solum praesentiae, an vero etiam efficientiae, inutile judicamus, dummodo utrimque in confesso est, deum ad justificationem exigere fidem vivam, fidemque non esse vivam, nisi per bona opera, neminemque justificationem consecuturum, nisi vivâ fide praeditum.—4. 31: Cum dicimus, fidem esse opus nostrum, tale non esse volumus opus, cui aut ex dignitate aut ex merito ullo suo aut denique ex intrinsecâ quadam efficaciâ remissio peccatorum et justitiæ imputatio debeatur, quique justitia nostra formalis sit, quæ in judicio dei per se subsistere possit. Male enim fides vocatur formalis justificationis causa, cum talis proprie non detur, quia justificatio est actus mentis divinæ purus putus, quâ deus nos habet pro justis. Sed fides est conditio in nobis et a nobis requisita, ut justificationem consequamur. Est itaque actus, qui licet in se spectatus perfectus nequaquam sit, sed in multis deficiens, tamen a deo gratiosâ et liberrimâ voluntate pro pleno et perfecto acceptatur et propter quem deus homini gratiose remissionem peccatorum et vivæ æternæ præmium conferre vult.

vi. 4. 29: Objectum fidei (justificantis) dicimus esse totum Jesum Christum tanquam prophetam, sacerdotem et regem, non tantum ipsius propitiationem, sed et præcepta, promissa et minas, quâ itaque totum Christum integramque ejus annuntiationem omniaque beneficia salutaria amplectimur; in illum tanquam prophetam, sacerdotem et regem credimus, ipsius doctrinam tanquam divinam recipimus, in ipsum spem ac fiduciam nostram collocamus et ab eo tanquam unico nostro redemtore vitam æternam eâ ratione ac conditione, quâ nobis eam promisit, sine ullâ dubitatione exspectamus. The *Confess. Remonstr.* xi. 2, thus negatively defines the idea of fiducia: Non quidem absoluta fiducia specialis misericordiæ, quasi re ipsâ jam perceptæ, qua scil. credo, mihi jam remissa esse peccata mea (hæc enim non est essentialis forma fidem justificantem constituens, sed quoddam tantum consequens adjunctum, imo ipsam salvificam fidem necessario tanquam præreqisitam sui conditionem præsupponit) sed quâ firmiter statuo, fieri non posse, ut aliter quam per J. Ch. et aliâ quam per ipsum præscriptâ ratione æternam mortem evadam et vitam sempiternam consequar cet.

Ris, *Conf.* art. 20: Fides est certissima cognitio sive scientia per gratiam dei ex S. s. acquisita, de deo nempe, de Christo atque aliis rebus cœlestibus, quorum cognitio et persuasio ad salutem necessaria est, debetque illa comitata esse amore dei et firmâ confidentiâ in unum deum cet. — 21: Per vivam ejusmodi fidem acquirimus veram justitiam cet.

V. Greek.

The older symbols of the Greek Church do not speak definitely on the ground of justification; indeed, no dogma is handled by them with less precision than that of justification and the methods of grace. The *Conf. orth.* declares generally that πίστις ὀρθή and ἔργα καλά are the essential and inseparable conditions of eternal salvation. On the other hand, Jeremias, in the *Act. Wirt.* p. 64, pressed by the Tübingen theologians, teaches that a living faith, active in good works, is necessary to *justification* · μόνῃ τῇ πίστει κυρίως τὴν ἄφεσιν τῶν ἁμαρτιῶν δίδοσθαι, διϊσχυρίζεσθε, ὡς δοκεῖ ὑμῖν· ἡ δὲ καθολικὴ ἐκκλ. τὴν πίστιν ζῶσαν ἀπαιτεῖ τὴν διὰ τῶν ἀγαθῶν ἔργων μαρτυρουμένην. And p. 288, he says: τελειοῦντες ὡς δυνατὸν τὸν κατὰ πνεῦμα νόμον, δικαιωθησόμεθα. More decided in relation to Calvinism is Dosithei *Conf.* c. 13 (s. also Parthenii *Decret. synod.* p. 122): πιστεύομεν οὐ διὰ πίστεως ἁπλῶς μόνης δικαιοῦσθαι τὸν ἄνθρωπον, ἀλλὰ διὰ πίστεως ἐνεργουμένης διὰ τῆς ἀγάπης, τ' αὐτὸν εἰπεῖν, διὰ τῆς πίστεως καὶ τῶν ἔργων· τὸ δὲ τὴν πίστιν χειρὸς ἔργον ἀποπληροῦσαν ἀντιλαμβάνεσθαι τῆς ἐν Χριστῷ δικαιοσύνης καὶ προσάπτειν ἡμῖν εἰς σωτηρίαν, πόρρω πάσης εὐσεβείας γινώσκομεν. That justification by faith was familiar to the Greeks, is shown by Heinecc. *Abbild.* ii. 165;—and Plato in *Catech.* S. 63 f. teaches in strict harmony with the Protestants.

VI. Quaker.

The Quaker system departs here in a striking manner from the ordinary theology of the churches. It teaches that justification is no other than the formation and growth of Christ in us. This finished stamp of Christ in us is wrought, however, by grace through the internal light; as God in the day of visitation causes the divine seed in man to germinate. To this, man of himself can contribute nothing; it is for him only not to reject the proffered grace, but to yield himself up believing to this enlightenment. This surrender is the faith that discerns and embraces Christ; faith is therefore by this internal enlightenment begotten: hence the man who may not have heard of the historical Christ or the external gospel, may yet be enlightened, accepted, and saved through Christ. To know Christ inwardly is the only and truly fruitful knowledge of Him. But he who is thus enlightened and regenerated through the light must needs live holily; in these his good works, therefore, which are the living signs of a Christ formed inwardly within, is he justified. See Barclay, *Apol.* Prop. v. 6 and 7.

THIRD POINT OF DIVERGENCE.

It is the common doctrine of Rome and Protestantism, that the will of God requires believers to walk in good works (*F. C.* p. 700). But Protestants will not admit that good works have in them any meritoriousness before God, assuming that they are the necessary consequences of a preceding justification. The Roman Church teaches that he who has become justified in Christ, merits for himself by his good deeds growth in the divine grace, everlasting life, and increase of his heavenly glory. In common with Protestants generally, the Arminians, Socinians, and Mennonites deny the meritoriousness of good works.

I. Roman Catholic.

Conc. Trid. sess. vi. cap. 16: Justificatis hominibus . . . proponenda sunt ap. verba; abundate in omni bono opere cet. Atque ideo bene operantibus usque in finem et in deo superantibus proponenda est vita æterna, et tanquam gratia filiis per Ch. misericorditer promissa, et tanquam merces ex ipsius dei promissione bonis ipsorum operibus et meritis fideliter reddenda. . . . Cum ille ipse Ch. tanquam caput in membra . . . in ipsos justificatos jugiter virtutem influat, quæ virtus bona eorum opera semper antecedit et comitatur et subsequitur, et sine quâ nullo pacto deo grata et meritoria esse possent, nihil ipsis justificatis amplius deesse credendum est, quominus plene illis quidem operibus, quæ in deo sunt facta, divinæ legi pro hujus vitæ statu satisfecisse et vitam æternam suo etiam tempore, si tamen in gratiâ decesserint, consequendam vere promeruisse censeantur.... Absit tamen, ut christianus homo in se ipso vel confidat vel glorietur ... et non in domino, cujus tanta est erga omnes homines bonitas, ut eorum velit esse merita, quæ sunt ipsius dona. Cf. sess. xiv. pœnit. cap. 8.

Ib. sess. vi. can. 24: Si quis dixerit, justitiam acceptam non conservari, neque etiam augeri coram deo per bona opera, sed opera ipsa fructus solummodo et signa esse justificationis adeptæ, non autem ipsius augendæ causam, anath. sit.—Can. 32: Si quis dixerit, hominis justificati bona opera ita esse dona dei, ut non sint etiam bona ipsius justificati merita, aut ipsum justificatum bonis operibus, quæ ab eo per dei gratiam et Christi meritum fiunt, non vere mereri augmentum gratiæ, vitam æternam et ipsius vitæ æternæ, si tamen in gratiâ decesserit, consecutionem atque etiam gloriæ augmentum, anath. sit.

Cat. Rom. ii. 5. 71: Tota pœnitentia a Christi passionis merito pendet. A quo etiam honestis actionibus duo illa maxima bona consequimur; alterum est, ut immortalis gloriæ præmia mereamur, ita ut calix etiam aquæ frigidæ, quam in ejus nomine dederimus, mercede non careat cet. Cf. qu. 72.

(Bellarmin, *Justific.* v. 1: Habet communis catholicorum omnium sententia, opera bona justorum vere ac proprie esse merita, et merita non cujuscunque præmii, sed ipsius vitæ æternæ.—iv. 7: Nos dicimus, opera bona homini justo esse necessaria ad salutem, non solum ratione præsentiæ sed etiam ratione efficientiæ, quoniam efficiunt salutem, et sine ipsis sola fides non efficit salutem. Intelligimus autem, hoc esse necessarium hominibus rationis usum habentibus.... Non enim negamus, quin infantes et etiam adulti recens baptizati salventur, si continuo ex hac vita decedant.) S. Klee, *Dogm.* iii. S. 58 ff.

Ib. v. 5: Merita justorum non opponuntur meritis Christi, sed ab illis nascuntur et quidquid ipsa justorum merita laudis habent, id totum redundat in laudem meritorum Christi.... Nemo nisi plane stultus dicere potest, detrahi de gloriâ Christi, si servi ejus per gratiam ejus, per spiritum ejus, per fidem et caritatem ab ipso inspiratam bona opera faciant, quæ ita vere sint justa, ut iis debeatur a justo judice corona justitiæ; ...

nec merita hominum requiruntur propter insufficientiam meritorum Christi, sed propter maximam eorum efficaciam. Meruerunt enim Christi opera apud deum non solum, ut salutem consequeremur, sed etiam ut eam per merita propria consequeremur. (In explanation of mereri . . . vitam æternam, Bellarmine adds, v. 20 : Nos existimamus, vitam æt. tum quoad primum gradum tum quoad ceteros reddi bonis meritis filiorum dei. Nam scriptura div. passim docet, non solum gloriæ incrementam sed ipsam gloriam simpliciter præmium esse operum bonorum. . . . Ex quo intelligimus, illum ipsum gradum gloriæ, qui debetur jure hæreditario, retribui etiam jure mercedis cet.)

II. Greek.

As to the confusion in the Greek dogma, see above. Salvation is by the Greek Church grounded on works. Jer. *in Act. Wirtemb.* p. 67 : παιδευόμεθα, ὅτι χρὴ πάντα ὁλοκλήρως καὶ νομίμως πληρώσαντα, οἷς ἡ ἐπαγγελεία τῆς βασιλείας τῶν οὐρανῶν ἐπαγγέλλεται καὶ ὧν ἄνευ ἀπηγόρευται, καὶ φυλαξάμενον, οὕτω προσδοκᾶν καταξιωθῆναι τῆς ἐπαγγελίας. Dositheus, *Conf.* 13, describes πίστις as justifying διὰ τῶν ἔργων; Cyrillus Lucaris (*Conf.* c. 9 and 13). Parthenius was condemned by misunderstanding of the Synod (Parthen. p. 123) : τὴν πίστιν γυμνὴν τῶν ἔργων σώζειν, εἶναι δὲ ταύτην οὐκ ἔργον ἡμέτερον ἀλλὰ τοῦ Χριστοῦ μόνου, ἔξωθεν δικαιοῦντος τὸν ἄνθρωπον διὰ τῆς ζωῆς καὶ θανάτου αὐτοῦ; and Cyr. L. : ἐκβάλλει τὰ καλὰ τῶν ἔργων τῆς τῶν ἀνθρώπων σωτηρίας, ἀναιροῦν διὰ τούτου τὸγ' ἐπ' αὐτῷ οὐ μόνον ἀρετὴν πᾶσαν καὶ βίον ἔνθεον ἀλλὰ πᾶσαν τὴν ἱερὰν γραφήν.

Observation.

The Romanists and Greeks agree in making prominent three good works : prayers, fasts, and alms. They are such religious acts as, resting upon free-will, may be reckoned among *satisfactions*, and assume, therefore, a very important place in the institute of penance. See below, XVII.

III. Protestant.

A. C. p. 11: Docent, quod fides debeat bonos fructus parere et quod oporteat bona opera mandata a deo facere propter voluntatem dei, non ut confidamus per ea opera justificationem coram deo mereri.—P. 12: Sequi debent (fidem) bona opera, quae sunt fructus poenitentiae.—P. 18: Quia per fidem accipitur Spiritus sanctus, jam corda renovantur et induunt novos affectus, ut parere bona opera possint.

Apol. A. C. p. 81: Nos quoque dicimus, quod dilectio fidem sequi debeat. Neque tamen ideo sentiendum est, quod fiducia hujus dilectionis aut propter hanc dilectionem accipiamus remissionem peccatorum et reconciliationem.—P. 83: Postquam fide justificati et renati sumus, incipimus deum timere, diligere, petere et exspectare ab eo auxilium, . . . et obedire ei in afflictionibus. Incipimus et diligere proximos, quia corda habent spirituales et sanctos motus.—P. 85: Falso calumniantur nos adversarii, quod nostri non doceant bona opera, cum ea non solum requirant, sed etiam ostendant, quomodo fieri possint.—P. 108: Nos loquimur de fide, quae resistit terroribus conscientiae, quae erigit et consolatur perterrefacta corda; talis fides neque facilis res est neque humana potentia, sed divina potentia, quâ vivificamur cet. Haec fides, cum sit nova vita, necessario parit novos motus et opera.— P. 133: Necesse est bene operari. Justificatis dicimus promissam esse vitam aet. Ideo justificamur, ut justi bene operari et obedire legi dei incipiamus; ideo regeneramur et Sp. sanctum accipimus, ut nova vita habeat nova opera, timorem, dilectionem dei cet.

F. C. p. 586: Confitemur, etsi antecedens contritio et subsequens nova obedientia ad articulum justificationis coram deo non pertinent, non tamen talem fidem justificantem esse fingendam, quae una cum malo proposito, peccandi videlicet, esse et stare possit. Sed postquam homo per fidem est justificatus, tum veram illam et vivam fidem esse per caritatem efficacem et bona opera semper fidem justificantem sequi. Fides enim vera nunquam sola est, quin caritatem et spem semper secum habeat.

Ib. p. 589: Nostra confessio est, quod bona opera veram

fidem certissime atque indubitato sequantur, tanquam fructus bonæ arboris; credimus etiam, quod bona opera penitus excludenda sint, non tantum cum de justificatione fidei agitur, sed etiam cum de salute nostrâ æternâ disputatur.—P. 688: Caritas fructus est, qui veram fidem certissime et necessario sequitur. Qui enim non diligit, de eo recte judicari potest, quod non sit justificatus, sed quod adhuc in morte detineatur, aut rursus justitiam fidei amiserit.

In the Evangelical Lutheran Church there arose a special discussion on the necessity of good works to salvation. This was the Majorist controversy. It was in reference to this that the above decision of the *Form. Conc.* was given.

F. C. p. 702: Propositiones hæ, bona opera esse necessaria et necesse esse bene agere, in commemoratâ piâ et genuinâ sententiâ immerito a quibusdam reprehenduntur et rejiciuntur. . . . Interim tamen de hoc etiam discrimine commonefactio observanda, quod per vocab. necessitatis intelligenda sit necessitas ordinis mandati et voluntatis Christi ac debiti nostri, non autem necessitas coactionis cet.

IV. Reformed.

Conf. Helv. ii. c. 15: Loquimur de fide vivâ vivificanteque, quæ propter Christum, qui vita est et vivificat quem comprehendit, viva est et dicitur ac se vivam esse vivis declarat operibus.—C. 16: Fides retinet nos in officio, quod deo debemus et proximo, et . . . ut uno verbo omnia dicam, omnis generis bonos fructus et bona opera progignit.—Quamvis doceamus cum apostolo, hominem gratis justificari per fidem in Chr. et non per ulla opera bona, non ideo tamen vilipendimus aut condemnamus opera bona.—Damnamus omnes, qui bona opera contemnunt. Interim non sentimus, per opera bona nos servari illaque ad salutem ita esse necessaria, ut absque illis nemo unquam sit servatus. Gratiâ enim soliusque Christi beneficio servamur. Opera necessario ex fide progignuntur.

Conf. Gall. art. 22: Tantum abest, ut bene et sancte vivendi studium fides exstinguat, ut etiam illud cieat et inflammet in nobis, unde bona opera necessario consequuntur.

Ceterum ... tamen profitemur, bona opera non respici a deo, ut per ea justificemur aut filii dei censeri mereamur.

Thirty-nine Artt. art. xii.: Albeit that good works, which are the fruits of faith, and follow after justification, cannot put away our sins, and endure the severity of God's judgment; yet are they pleasing and acceptable to God in Christ, and do spring out necessarily of a true and lively faith; insomuch that by them a lively faith may be as evidently known, as a tree discerned by the fruit.

Conf. Belg. art. 24: Tantum abest, ut fides justificans homines in rectâ sanctâque vitâ tepidiores efficiat, ut prorsus e contrario sine illâ ipsâ nemo unquam quidquam ex amore dei, sed amore tantum sui vel condemnationis metu effecturus sit. Fieri itaque non potest, ut sancta hæc fides in homine otiosa sit. . . . Atque hæc opera, quæ a bonâ fidei radice proficiscuntur, coram deo bona eique accepta sunt, quoniam omnia per illius gratiam sanctificantur; verumtamen ad nos justificandos in censum rationemque non veniunt.

Conf. Tetrapol. cap. 4.

Observations.

The grounds of the Protestant rejection of the merit of good works are the express words of Scripture. At the same time, the actual imperfectness of the good works of the saints is to be pointed to. On the Reformed side, especial reference is made to the fact that good works are not evidences of any good in man, but of the power of the Holy Ghost.

V. ARMINIAN.

Limborch, *Theol. chr.* v. 78. 12: Huic de obedientiæ seu bonorum operum necessitate quæstioni alia adhæret de bonorum opp. merito, utrum nimirum bona nostra opera mereantur vitam æternam. Quæstio hæc nobis intercedit cum pontificiis. Fatemur nos, si propriâ vocis meriti significatione neglectâ ampliorem et minus propriam illi tribuamus, posse bona fidelium opera catachrestice et in laxiori significatione merita vocari, quoniam deus ea vitâ æt. remunerari gratiose promisit cet. Sed quia hæc est significatio vocis meriti minus propria et pontificii in ea non acquiescunt, sed et opera nostra intrinseco suo valore vitam æt. mereri contendunt, præstat a voce meriti abstinere utpote quæ meritum proprie dictum involvere videatur, cum si meriti proprie dicti naturam inspiciamus, quæque ad meritum constituendum requirantur, consideremus, . . . manifestum futurum sit, ea omnia operibus nostris deesse ac proinde opera nostra vitæ æt. meritoria esse non posse. Cf. Simon. Episcop. *Op.* ii. 528 sqq.

VI. SOCINIAN.

F. Socin. *Opp.* i. p. 620 b: Diximus (opera) aliquo modo meritoria, ut ab ipsis operibus excludamus non modo absolutum et maxime proprium meritum, quod oritur ex ipsâ operum præstantiâ per se considerata, sed etiam illud, quod minus proprie et respective meritum est, quippe quod . . . ex solo dei promisso oritur, adeo ut nemo neque per illud neque per hoc meritum suorum operum justificationem adipiscatur. Ubi considerandum interea est, quod nihilominus merito dici potest, dari obedientiam, quæ possit dici causa justificationis nostræ propter dei promissum, nec tamen dicendum sit, operum merito tunc justificationem nobis concedi, quippe quod obedientia ista sub ipso N. T., si omnia præcepta in eâ nobis data considerentur, non possit dici perfecta, quamvis deus pro suâ bonitate velit, si eâ præditi fuerimus, nos justificatos pronuntiare.

Schyn, *Plen. deduct.* p. 232 : Fatemur, perfectam Christi obedientiam verâ et vivâ fide acceptam nostræ æternæ salutis unicam esse causam ; . . . non credimus, bona opera nos salvare, sed agnoscimus bona opera pro debitâ obedientiâ et fructibus fidei.

VII. QUAKER.

The Quakers assume to be midway between Protestants and Romanists in this matter. See Barclay, *Apol.* vii. 3. Although we place remission of sins in the righteousness and obedience of Christ, performed by Him in the flesh, as to what pertains to the remote procuring cause, and that we hold ourselves formally justified by Christ Jesus formed and brought forth in us, yet can we not, as some Protestants have unwarily done, exclude works from justification. For, though properly we be not justified *for* them, yet are we justified *in* them; and they are necessary, even as *causa sine quâ non*. . . . Since good works as naturally follow from this birth as heat from fire, therefore are they of absolute necessity to justification as *causa sine quâ non*, *i.e.* though not as the cause for which, yet as that *in which* we are, and without which we cannot be justified; and though they be not meritorious, and draw no debt upon God, yet He cannot but accept and reward them. For it is contrary to His nature to deny His own, since thay may be perfect in their kind, as proceeding from a pure, holy birth and root. . . . Against the merit of these works in the Romish sense, comp. vii. 12. We are far from thinking or believing that man merits anything by His works from God, all being of free grace; and therefore do we and always have denied that Popish notion of merit *de condigno*. Nevertheless we cannot deny but that God, out of His infinite goodness wherewith He hath loved mankind, after He communicates to him His holy grace and spirit, doth, according to His own will, recompense and reward the good works of His children; and therefore this merit of congruity or reward, in so far as the Scripture is plain and positive for it, we may not deny.

Observation.

The acceptableness of the good works of the justified, and even their rewardablenesss, is not denied by Protestants.[1] Under what restrictions, however, they assert both, will be seen in the Confessions.

Apol. A. C. p. 96: Docemus, operibus fidelium proposita et promissa esse præmia; docemus bona opera meritoria esse, non remissionis peccatorum gratiæ aut justificationis, hæc enim tantum fide consequimur, sed aliorum præmiorum corporalium et spiritualium in hac vitâ et post hanc vitam.— P. 135: Nos non rixamur de vocabulo mercedis, de hac re

---

[1] The *Conf. Wirtem.* p. 106, does not hesitate to use this expression: Bona opera *mereri* gratuitâ dei clementiâ sua quædam sive corporalia sive spiritualia præmia.

litigamus, utrum bona opera per se sint digna gratiâ et vitâ æternâ, an vero placeant tantum propter fidem, quæ apprehendit mediatorem Christum. Adversarii nostri non solum hoc tribuunt operibus, quod sint digna gratiâ et vitâ æternâ cet.—P. 136: Nos fatemur, vitam æt. mercedem esse, quia est res debita propter promissionem, non propter merita nostra. Est enim promissa justificatio, et huic dono dei conjuncta est promissio vitæ æt. Hanc promissionem scire sanctos oportet, non ut propter suum commodum laborent, . . . sed ne desperent in afflictionibus cet. Cf. p. 138; *F. C.* p. 700; *Conf. Saxon* (art. 9 and 10), p. 65 sqq.

Conf. Helv. ii. c. 16: Placent approbanturque a deo opera, quæ a nobis fiunt per fidem, quia illi placent deo propter fidem in Christum, qui faciunt opera bona, quæ insuper per Spiritum sanctum ex gratia dei sunt facta.—Docemus, deum bona operantibus amplam dare mercedem.—Referimus tamen mercedem hanc, quam dominus dat (bonis operibus), non ad meritum hominis accipientis, sed ad bonitatem vel liberalitatem et veritatem dei promittentis atque dantis, qui, cum nihil debeat cuiquam, promisit tamen, se suis cultoribus fidelibus mercedem daturum.

Conf. Belg. art. 24: Non negamus, deum bona opera remunerari, verum gratiæ esse dicimus, quod coronet sua dona. Cf. *Catech. Heidelb.* 63.

West. Conf. ch. xvi. sec. 2: These good works, done in obedience to God's commandments, are the fruits and evidences of a true and lively faith; and by them believers manifest their thankfulness, strengthen their assurance, edify their brethren, adorn the profession of the gospel, stop the mouths of the adversaries, and glorify God, whose workmanship they are, created in Christ Jesus thereunto, that, having their fruit unto holiness, they may have the end eternal life.

XI.
THE HOLINESS OF THE REGENERATE, AND WORKS OF SUPEREROGATION.

POINT OF DIVERGENCE.

ACCORDING to the Roman and Greek doctrine, the regenerate may not only keep perfectly the commandments of God, but also perform certain good works, which are not commanded, counselled only by Christ (*consilia evangelica*), and these as done are *opera supererogationis*, or works of supererogation.[1] The Protestants deny any distinction between the commandments of God and evangelical counsels; and the rather, because no regenerate man even perfectly fulfils the law of God. (This, however, the Quakers and some others deny.) Consequently the Protestants consistently reject the system of monkery, so far as this is regarded as a higher perfection, and something meritorious in itself in the sight of God.

SYMBOLICAL TESTIMONIES.

a. As to whether the Justified may perfectly fulfil the Law of God.

I. ROMAN AND QUAKER.

Conc. Trid. sess. vi. cap. 11 : Nemo temerariâ illâ . . . voce uti debet, dei præcepta homini justificato ad observandum esse impossibilia. . . . Licet enim in hac mortali vitâ quan-

---

[1] The expression *opera supererogationis* is sometimes used of the *satisfactiones superabundantes sanctorum*, which, however, Bellarmine, *De indulg.* ii. 9, does not approve.

tumvis sancti et justi in levia saltem et quotidiana, quæ etiam venialia dicuntur, peccata quandoque cedant, non propterea desinunt esse justi.

Cf. can. 18; *Catech. Rom.* iii. 1. 7.

(Bellarmin, *De justific.* iv. 10 sqq., gives these as the rational grounds of the Romish doctrine: 1. Si præcepta essent impossibilia, neminem obligarent, ac per hoc præcepta non essent præcepta. Neque enim fingi potest, quomodo aliquis peccet in eo, quod vitare non potest. 2. Si lex domini esset impossibilis, sequeretur, deum omni tyranno esse crudeliorem et stultiorem, quippe qui ab ipsis etiam amicis tributum exigeret, quod nemo solvere posset, et leges ferret, quas sciret a nemine observandas.—Hence it may be seen how much of what Möhler urges against the Protestant doctrine is new and peculiar to him.)

Barclay, *Apol.* Prop. vii. 3: For though we judge so of the best works performed by man, endeavouring a conformity with the outward law by his own strength and in his own will, yet we believe that such works as naturally proceed from this spiritual birth and formation of Christ in us are pure and holy, even as the root from which they come; and therefore God accepts them, justifies us in them, and rewards us for them of His own free grace. . . . Wherefore their judgment is false and against the truth, that say that the holiest works of the saints are defiled and sinful in the sight of God. For these good works are not the works of the law excluded by the apostle from justification.

II. PROTESTANT.

Apol. A. C. p. 91: Tota scriptura, tota ecclesia clamat, legi non satisfieri. Non igitur placet illa inchoata legis impletio propter se ipsam, sed propter fidem in Christum. Alioqui lex semper accusat nos. . . . Semper in hac infirmitate nostra adest peccatum, quod imputari poterat.—P. 92: Sentire nos oportet, quod procul a perfectione legis absimus.—P. 121: Vix imbecillis et exigua legis impletio contingit etiam sanctis. —P. 191: Nemo tantum facit, quantum lex requirit. Cf. p. 89, *Conf. Saxon.* p. 65 sq.

F. C. p. 678: (Rejicitur) pontificum et monachorum doctrina, quod homo, postquam regeneratus est, legem dei in hac vitâ perfecte implere possit. S. against Schwenkfeld's followers, p. 829.

Conf. Helv. ii. c. 16: Sunt multa indigna deo et imperfecta plurima inveniuntur in operibus etiam sanctorum.

Conf. Belg. art. 24: Nullum opus facere possumus, quod non sit carnis vitio pollutum ac proinde pœnis dignum.

Conf. Scot. 15: Affirmamus, neminem in terrâ (Christo solo excepto) opere et revera ita præstitisse, præstare aut præstiturum eam in opere obedientiam legi, quam lex requirit.

West. Conf. ch. xvi. sec. 6: Yet notwithstanding, the persons of believers being accepted through Christ, their good works also are accepted in Him, not as though they were in this life wholly unblameable and unreprovable in God's sight, but that He, looking upon them in His Son, is pleased to accept and reward that which is sincere, although accompanied with many weaknesses and imperfections.

Catech. Heid. 62: Our best works in the present life are all imperfect and stained with sin. Cf. *Declar. Thorun.* ii. 4. 10; *Conf. Remons.* xi. 6.

[The grounds on which the Evangelical Church thus teaches are simply these: The law of God commands, *Thou shalt not covet.* Who keeps this? The sum of the law is to love God with all the soul and with all the strength, and the neighbour as self (Luke x. 26). Who keeps this? Therefore all are sinners, and come short of the glory of God (Rom. iii. 23).]

b. *Whether the Justified can do more than keep the Commandments:*

I. ROMAN AND GREEK.

In the symbols of the Roman Church there is no doctrine of the *consilia evangelica*, and the consequent *opera supererogationis*. The *Cat. Rom.* iii. 3 only hints at it in passing. Hence we turn to Bellarmine.

Bellarm. *De monachis*, cap. 7: Consilium perfectionis vocamus opus bonum, a Christo nobis non imperatum sed demonstratum, non mandatum sed commendatum. Differt autem a praecepto ex parte materiae, ex parte subjecti, ex parte formae, ex parte finis. Ex parte materiae dupliciter. Primo quia materia praecepti est facilior, consilii difficilior : illa enim sumta est ex principiis naturae, haec superat quodammodo naturam, nam ad servandam conjugii fidem natura inclinat, at non ita ad abstinendum a conjugio. . . . Secundo quia materia praecepti bona est, consilii melior et perfectior, loquendo de praeceptis, quae circa eandem materiam versantur, circa quam versantur consilia : consilium enim includit praeceptum et aliquid supra praeceptum addit. . . . Ex parte subjecti differunt consilia et praecepta, quod praeceptum commune sit omnium, consilium non item. . . . Ex parte formae, quod praeceptum vi suâ obliget, consilium in arbitrio hominis positum sit. . . . Ex parte finis sive effectus, quod praeceptum observatum habet praemium, non observatum habet poenam ; consilium autem si non servetur, nullam habet poenam, et si servetur, majus habet praemium.—Cap. 8 : Sententia est catholicor. omnium, multa esse vere et proprie consilia evang. (cf. *Apol. A. C.* p. 191), sed praecipue tria, continentiam, obedientiam et paupertatem, quae nec sint praecepta nec indifferentia, sed deo grata et ab illo commendata (cf. Matt. xix. 11 sq., 21 ; 1 Cor. vii. 1, 7).— Cap. 12 : Videmus in omnibus bene institutis rebuspublicis praeter praemia et poenas . . . esse etiam praemia quaedam decreta heroicis operibus ; . . . ita ergo non abhorret a ratione, imo potius conforme est rationi, ut praeter vitam aeternam, promissam observatoribus legis divinae, sint etiam certa praemia et singulares honores pro iis, qui non solum dei legem servant, sed etiam virtutes heroicas ostendunt.

Cf. Möhler, *neue Untersuch.* S. 295 ff.

Metroph. Critop. *Conf.* c. 19, p. 142 : τῶν τῆς Χριστ. διδασκαλίας τὰ μέν ἐστιν ἐπιταγματικὰ ὡς ἀναγκαῖα, οἷον τὸ μὴ φονεύειν, . . . τὰ δὲ ἐπιταγμ. μὲν ὡς ἀναγκαῖα οὐκ ἂν εἴη, ἐπαινετὰ δὲ ἄλλως καὶ πολλῶν ἐγκωμίων ἄξια, οἷον τὰ τῆς ἀληθοῦς παρθενίας κατόρθωμα, ἡ ἐσχάτη ἀκτημοσύνη, ἡ ἄκρα ὑπομονὴ ὡς καὶ τὴν ἑτέραν παρειὰν προτείνειν τῷ ἤδη θατέραν παίσαντι καὶ τελευταῖον αὐτὸ ἡ παντελὴς ἀπαλλαγὴ τῶν τοῦ κόσμου θορύβων. Ἐχρῆν δὲ εἶναι τινὰς ἐν τῇ ἐκκλησίᾳ, οἳ καὶ ταῦτα μετέλθοιεν, ἵνα μὴ παντελῶς ἀργὰ ᾖ τὰ κυριακὰ ῥήματα. . . . ὅπερ πάρεστιν ἰδεῖν παρ' ἡμῖν, οἱ πάντες μὲν μοναχοὶ τελοῦσι. τοὺς ὄντας δὲ οἱ λοιποὶ ἀποδέχονται καὶ ἄγανται.

II. Protestant.

A. C. p. 33: Addebant (Pontificii), vitam monasticam non tantum justitiam mereri coram deo, sed amplius etiam, quia servaret non modo præcepta, sed etiam consilia evangelica.
Apol. A. C. p. 190 sq.: De lege sic dicunt: Deus condescendens nostræ infirmitati constituit homini mensuram eorum, ad quæ de necessitate tenetur, quæ est observatio præceptorum, ut de reliquo i. e. de operibus supererogationis possit satisfacere de commissis. Hic fingunt, homines legem dei ita facere posse, ut plus etiam, quam lex exigit, facere possimus. . . . Nemo tantum facit, quantum lex requirit.—P. 282: Falsum et hoc est, quod observationes monasticæ sint opera consiliorum evangelii. Nam evangelium non consulit discrimina vestitus, ciborum, abdicationem rerum propriarum; hæ sunt traditiones humanæ. Cf. p. 282.
Conf. Wirtemb. p. 105: Quod nonnulli sentiunt, hominem posse in hac vitâ eo pervenire, ut non tantum impleat suis operibus decalogum, verum etiam possit plura et majora opera facere, quam in decalogo præcepta sunt, quæ vocant opera supererogationis, alienum est a propheticâ et apostolicâ doctrinâ.
Thirty-nine Artt. art. 14: Voluntary works, besides over and above God's commandments, which they call works of supererogation, cannot be taught without arrogancy and impiety; for by them men do declare that they do not only render unto God as much as they are bound to do, but that they do more for His sake than of bounden duty is required; whereas Christ saith plainly, When ye have done all that are commanded to you, say, We are unprofitable servants. Cf. *Conf. Scot.* negat. p. 127; *Declar. Thorun.* ii. 4. 15.
West. Conf. ch. xvi. sec. 4: They who in their obedience attain to the greatest height which is possible in this life, are so far from being able to supererogate, and to do more than God requires, as that they fall short of much which in duty they are bound to do. Sec. 5: We cannot by our best works merit pardon of sin or eternal life at the hand of God, by

reason of the great disproportion that is between them and the glory to come, and the infinite distance that is between us and God, whom by them we can neither profit nor satisfy for the debt of our former sins; but when we have done all we can, we have done but our duty, and are unprofitable servants; and because, as they are good, they proceed from His Spirit; and as they are wrought by us, they are defiled and mixed with so much weakness and imperfection, that they cannot endure the severity of God's judgment.

Limborch, *Theol. christ.* v. 76. 17 : Colligimus, vota monastica non esse a deo, utpote nuncupantiores, quas deus nullo præcepto fatentibus ipsis Pontificiis sibi gratas declaravit. Dices: Consulit tamen eas ut perfectius quid ? Resp. nulla ejusmodi consiliorum in scripturis mentio est. Fatemur quidem, in scripturis aliquando consilia quædam proponi, quæ a præceptis necessario observandis distinguenda sunt, eorum tamen observationem, prout in se nude spectantur, indifferentem esse ; posse autem ejusmodi incidere speciales circumstantias, quæ consilium mutant in præceptum et rem alioquin naturâ suâ liberam necessariam faciunt. Nihil autem hoc cum consiliis, quorum observatio majorem gloriæ gradum mereri dicitur, commune habet.

c. *Monasticism and Vows.*

On the dogma of evangelical counsels is founded the institute of monasticism, which still exists in the Roman and Greek Churches. Bellarmine, *De monach.* c. 8, says that it is the opinion of all Catholics, that there are many evangelical precepts, but especially three,—those of continence, obedience, and poverty, the three well-known monastic vows. And he defines the estate of the religious as that state of men which tends to Christian perfection through these three vows. The Council of Trent did not treat of monasticism in a dogmatically connected way ; it takes for granted the existence of the institute, and issues only some reformatory decrees (*e.g.* sess. 25) *de regularibus et monialibus.* Against the Protestants the *Confut. A. C.* p. 108 protested. Cf. also Eck, *Loci*, c. 17. As to the doctrinal views of the Greek Church, see Metroph. Critop. *Conf.* p. 142. Jeremias, *in Act. Wirtem.*, says : εἰ τὰ ἀγαθὰ ἔργα στέργετε πάντα, ὡς λέγετε, καὶ ταῦτα (τὴν μοναχικὴν πολιτείαν), ἀγαθὰ ὄντα, στέργειν ὀφείλετε; cf. also pp. 132, 136. The Protestant refutation rested mainly on the character of meritoriousness, which the monastic estate was supposed to possess. But this led to a consideration of the lawfulness of such vows generally. We shall only give a few condensed references from the symbols.

Protestant Symbols.

Apol. C. A. p. 279 sq.: Primum hoc certissimum est, non esse licitum votum, quo sentit is, qui vovet, se mereri remissionem peccatorum coram deo aut satisfacere pro peccatis coram deo. Nam hæc opinio est manifesta contumelia evangelii, quod docet, nobis gratis donari remissionem peccatorum propter Christum. . . . Secundo obedientia, paupertas et cœlibatus, si tamen non sit impurus, exercitia sunt adiaphora et sancti viri usi sunt (iis) propter utilitatem corporalem, ut expeditiores essent ad docendum et ad alia pia officia, non quod opera ipsa per se sint cultus, qui justificent aut mereantur vitam æternam. . . . Tertio in votis monasticis promittitur castitas. Supra autem diximus de conjugio sacerdotum, non posse votis aut legibus tolli jus naturæ in hominibus, . . . quare hoc votum non est licitum in his, qui non habent donum continentiæ, sed propter imbecillitatem contaminantur.

Art. Sm. p. 336: Quia vota monastica e diametro pugnant cum primo principali articulo, ideo plane abroganda sunt; . . . qui enim votum facit in monasterio vivendi, is credit, se vitæ rationem sanctiorem initurum esse, quam alii Christiani ducunt et suis operibus non tantum sibi, sed etiam aliis cœlum mereri vult. Hoc vero quid aliud est, quam Christum negare?

Conf. Wirtemb. p. 126 sq.: Non est dubium, quin vota pia, justa et legitima sint servanda ac solvenda et vota impia sint rescindenda. Sed haud immerito disputatur, in quo votorum genere collocanda sint vota monachorum. Nam manifestum est, quod cœlibatus non sit verbo dei præceptus; manifestum etiam est, . . . quod non est sentiendum, quod hoc genus vitæ per se sit coram tribunali dei excellentius et sanctius, quam conjugium. . . . Qui vovet virginitatem vel cœlibatum aut vovet eum, ut singularem cultum dei: tunc quia status coelibum non est verbo dei mandatus, pertinet hoc votum ad mandata hominum cet.; aut vovet cum, ut meritum remissionis peccatorum et vitæ æternæ, et tunc est manifeste impium votum. . . . Aut possides facultates et voves te iis relictis acturum vitam pauperem, ut victum quæras mendicitate et consequaris hujus voti merito vitam æternam : tunc hoc votum primum quidem pugnat cum caritate proximi, quæ exigit, ne cui sis præter necessitatem mendicimonio molestus; deinde pugnat cum fide in Christum, quod is solus sit meritum æternæ vitæ. . . . Facultates autem tuas sic deserere, ut eas in commune conferas, non est paupertatem sectari, sed de certiori et copiosiori victu tibi prospicere. . . . Obedientia aut refertur ad deum, tunc non est arbitrarii voti, sed debitæ necessitatis; . . . aut refertur ad hominem, tunc sua sunt obedientiæ officia, quæ subditus magistratui, liberi parentibus cet. debent. Hæc sive voveantur sive non voveantur, certe divinitus exiguntur. Vovere autem homini obedientiam sine certâ vocatione dei, ut operibus talis obedientiæ non solum præstes deo singularem cultum, sed etiam expies coram deo peccata tuo, supervacaneum est et impium, quia solius Ch. obedientia expiavit peccata nostra cet.

Conf. Helv. ii. c. 18: Cum sciamus certo, monachos et monachorum ordines vel sectas neque a Christo, neque ab apostolis esse institutas, docemus, nihil eas ecclesiæ dei utiles esse, imo perniciosas. *Conf. Tetrapol.* c. 12; *Conf. Helv.* i. art. 27; *Conf. Gall.* art. 24.

Cf. Zwingli, *Op.* iii. p. 276 sqq.; Calvin, *Instit.* iv. 13. 8 sqq.; Limborch, *Theol. chr.* v. 76. 15 sqq.

Observations.

The doctrine of vows generally is not to be sought so much in the Protestant symbols as in the private writings of Luther and Calvin. There are *licita vota* (cf. *Declar. Thorun.* p. 57): these must, according to *A. C.* p. 34, be *in re possibili, voluntarium, sponte et consulto conceptum,* and of things especially not forbidden by the divine law. The use of such vows is only moral, and consequently subjective; they must never be held for part of the divine service, or be undertaken to prepare for or merit grace. As *cultus divinus* must that vow only be reckoned which belongs to baptism. It is to this restriction that the negation of the Conc. Trid. sess. vi. *de Baptism.* refers: Si quis dixerit, ita revocandosesse homines ad baptismi suscepti memoriam, ut vota omnia, quæ post baptismum fiunt, vi promissionis in baptismo ipso jam factæ irrita esse intelligant, quasi per ea et fidei, quam professi sunt, detrahatur et ipsi baptismo, anathema sit. Bellarmine lays down the general principle of his Church thus: Omne, quod fit ex voto, etiamsi alioqui non sit a deo præceptum, vere et proprie est cultus dei.

XII.

LOSS OF GRACE: MORTAL AND VENIAL SINS.

POINT OF DIVERGENCE.

ALL Christian Confessions which reject the dogma of predestination agree in this, that the converted man, in whom the evil concupiscence is not perfectly extinguished, may sink again into the condition of the unconverted, and lose even for ever the grace obtained in justification. It has been usual, in theological language, to term those sins which are fatal to a state of grace mortal sins, *peccata mortalia*, or *mortifera*. But here there is a divergence: 1. As to whether mortal sins may co-exist with faith, or *ipso facto* exclude faith: the former is asserted by the Romanists; the latter by the Protestants, in harmony with their respective differences as to the nature of faith. 2. Whether venial sins, *peccata venialia*, are venial in themselves (*ex naturâ suâ, ex fundamento materiali*), which the Roman theologians maintain, or in themselves deserve eternal death, but are to Christians on account of their faith forgiven by God, which is the Protestant doctrine.

SYMBOLICAL TESTIMONIES.

a. The Defectibility of Justification.

I. ROMAN, LUTHERAN, AND ARMINIAN.

Conc. Trid. sess. vi. cap. 15: Asserendum est, . . . quocunque mortali peccato . . . acceptam justificationis gratiam amitti. Cf. can. 23; Bellarmin, *Justific.* iii. 14 sq.

Conf. orth. p. 280: Ἡ τοιαύτη ἐπιθυμία (θανάσιμον ἁμάρτημα) ξεχωρίζει τὸν ἄνθρωπον ἀπὸ τὴν χάριν τοῦ θεοῦ καὶ φονεύει τον, ἀφ' οὗ πληρωθῇ μὲ τὸ ἔργον. Cf. p. 283.

A. C. p. 13: Damnant Anabaptistas, qui negant, semel justificatos posse amittere Spiritum sanctum.

F. Conc. p. 705: Falsa illa opinio graviter redarguenda atque rejicienda est, quod quidam fingunt, fidem et acceptam justitiam atque salutem non posse ullis peccatis aut sceleribus . . . amitti.

Ib. p. 591: Damnamus dogma illud, quod fides in Christum non amittatur et Spiritus sanctus nihilominus in homine habitet, etiamsi sciens volensque peccet et quod sancti atque electi Spiritum sanctum retineant, tametsi in adulterium aut in alia scelera prolabantur et in iis perseverent.

Conf. Remonstr. xi. 7: Fieri omnino posse, imo non raro factum esse credimus, ut (renati) paulatim relabantur ad pristinam vitæ profanitatem et tandem etiam a priori fide et caritate suâ plane deficiant desertâque viâ justitiæ ad pristina, quæ vere reliquerant, mundi inquinamenta . . . revertantur, . . . et sic totaliter tandemque etiam finaliter . . . divina gratia excidant. Cf. xviii. 6; *Apol. Confess.* p. 133 sqq.; Limborch, *Theol. chr.* lib. v. cap. 81.[1] Here belongs the Arminian contradiction of the sentence that the regenerate commit no mortal sins. Curcell. *Instit.* iv. 4. 19. Limborch, *Theol. christ.* v. 4. 21.

Socin. *biblioth. fratr. Pol.* i. p. 604 a: Si eveniat, ut ab hac obedientiâ deficiamus et in unum plurave peccata relabamur, in eisque permaneamus, justificati esse desinimus.

II. Reformed.

Calvin, *Instit.* iii. 2. 12: Hoc tenendum est, quantumvis exigua sit ac debilis in electis fides, quia tamen spiritus dei certa illis arrha est ac sigillum suæ adoptionis, nunquam ex eorum cordibus deleri posse ejus sculpturam. 21: Asserimus, fidei radicem nunquam e pio pectore avelli, quin imâ in parte

---

[1] In the 5 Artic. the matter is left doubtful: utrum regeniti et rursus deficere possint, prius ex scripturâ diligentius et accuratius inquirendum esse, quam id sine dubitatione alii doceantur.

defixa hæreat, utcunque decussa huc aut illuc inclinare videatur, ejus lumen ita nunquam exstingui aut præfocari, quin saltem velut sub favilla delitescat. Cf. Parei, *Corp. doctr.* p. 49.

Can. Dordrac. v. 3 : Propter peccati inhabitantis reliquias . . . non possent conversi in gratiâ perstare, si suis viribus permitterentur. Sed fidelis est deus, qui ipsos in gratiâ semel collatâ misericorditer confirmat et in eadem usque ad finem potenter conservat. . . . 4 : Etsi autem illa potentia dei major est, quam quæ a carne superari possit, non semper tamen conversi ita a deo aguntur et moventur, ut non possint in quibusdam actionibus particularibus a ductu gratiæ suo vitio recedere et a carnis concupiscentiis seduci iisque obsequi. In peccata etiam gravia et atrocia abripi possunt. . . . 5 : Talibus autem enormibus peccatis deum valde offendunt, reatum mortis incurrunt, Spiritum s. contristant, fidei exercitium interrumpunt, conscientiam gravissime vulnerant, sensum gratiæ nonnunquam ad tempus amittunt, donec per seriam resipiscentiam in viam revertentibus paternus dei vultus rursum affulgeat.

Ib. v. 6 : Deus ex immutabili electionis proposito Spiritum sanctum etiam in tristibus lapsibus a suis non prorsus aufert nec eo usque prolabi sinit, ut gratiâ adoptionis ac justificationis statu excidant aut peccatum ad mortem sive in Spiritum sanctum committant et ab eo penitus deserti in exitium æternum sese præcipitent. v. 8 : Ex gratuitâ dei misericordiâ id obtinent (electi), ut nec totaliter fide et gratiâ excidant, nec finaliter in lapsibus maneant. Cf. *Rejectio errorum* 3, 4, 8, *Declar. Thorun.* ii. 4. 11.

Heidegger, *Corp.* xxiv. 57 : Regenitorum status prorsus immutabilis est, quia regeneratio unica est et semen ejus in regenitis sic manet, ut peccare seu peccata semen regenerationis excutientia et condemnantia committere, adeoque finaliter vel etiam totaliter deficere non possint. . . . Hoc enim criterio regeniti ab irregenitis discernuntur . . . ; in regenito semper aliquid latet, quod manum injicit, ut a peccando retrahat. Semen igitur hoc indelebilis character et hereditatis arrhabo est, quo renati ad redemtionem obsignantur.

West. Conf. ch. xxvii. sec. 1 : Sacraments are holy signs and seals of the covenant of grace, immediately instituted by God, to represent Christ and His benefits, and to confirm our interest in Him; as also to put a visible difference between those that belong unto the Church and the rest of the world; and solemnly to engage them to the service of God in Christ, according to His word. Sec. 2: There is in every sacrament a spiritual relation, or sacramental union, between the sign and the thing signified; whence it comes to pass, that the names and effects of the one are attributed to the other. Sec. 3: The grace which is exhibited in or by the sacraments, rightly used, is not conferred by any power in them; neither doth the efficacy of a sacrament depend upon the piety or intention of him that doth administer it, but upon the work of the Spirit, and the word of institution; which contains, together with a precept authorizing the use thereof, a promise of benefit to worthy receivers.

Observations.

The point of contention between the advocates of universal and particular redemption is in the above references of the *F. C.* and the *Can. Dordr.* correctly and definitely exhibited. That, namely, the truly elect cannot possibly fall for ever from grace, is acknowledged also by the *Form. Conc.;* for they were elected in the divine prevision of their unchangeable faith. But whether all who once truly believed and were justified are simply assured of their faith, and consequently of their justification, even though they fall into deadly sin, is here the vital question. The Particularists answer that question in the affirmative, and regard faith and the Holy Ghost as somewhat that cannot be entirely lost even in sin, that is, as a *character indelebilis* of the elect. This system has no place for sins that destroy and root out faith. Here we may refer what is said in *Conf. Gall.* 21: fidem electis dari, non ut semel tantum in rectam viam introducantur, quin potius ut in eâ ad extremum usque pergant cet. In the scientific theology of the Reformed Church this is now always treated under the rubric *Perseverantia sanctorum.* Cf. Baumgarten, *Polem.* ii. 633; Schubert, *Theol. Polem.* iii. 302; Limborch, *Th. chr.* v. 80.

III. Quaker.

The Quakers admit that the " possibility of sinning " abides in the regenerate "in some part where the mind doth not most diligently and watchfully attend unto the Lord." But they regard it as possible to attain a state in which sin is excluded.

Barclay, *Apol.* Prop. viii.: In whom this pure and holy birth is fully brought forth, the body of death and sin comes to be crucified and removed, and their hearts united and subjected to the truth; so as not to obey any suggestions or temptations of the evil one, and to be free from actual sinning and transgressing of the law of God, and in that respect perfect. Yet doth this perfection still admit of a growth; and there remaineth always in some part a possibility of sinning, where the mind doth not most diligently and watchfully attend unto the Lord. . . . Prop. ix.: Although this gift and inward grace of God be sufficient to work out salvation, yet in those in whom it is resisted it both may and doth become their condemnation. Moreover, they in whose hearts it hath wrought in part to purify and sanctify them in order to their further perfection, may by disobedience fall from it, turn to wantonness, Jude 4; make shipwreck of faith, 1 Tim. i. 19; and, after having tasted the heavenly gift, and been made partakers of the Holy Ghost, again fall away, Heb. vi. 4, 5, 6. Yet such an increase and stability in the truth may in this life be attained, from which there can be no total apostasy.

b. Relation of Mortal Sins to Faith.

I. ROMAN CATHOLIC.

Conc. Trid. sess. vi. cap. 15: Asserendum est, non modo infidelitate, per quam et ipsa fides amittitur, sed etiam quocunque alio mortali peccato, quamvis non amittatur fides, acceptam justificationis gratiam amitti cet.

Ib. can. 27: Si quis dixerit, nullum esse mortale peccatum, nisi infidelitatis aut nullo alio, quantumvis gravi et enormi præterquam infidelitatis peccato semel acceptam gratiam amitti, anath. sit.

Ib. can. 28: Si quis dix., amissâ per peccatum gratiâ, simul et fidem semper amitti, . . . a. s.

II. PROTESTANT.

Apol. A. C. p. 71: Fides non stat cum peccato mortali.

Ib. p. 86: Fides illa, quæ accipit remissionem peccatorum,

. . . non manet in his, qui obtemperant cupiditatibus, nec exsistit cum mortali peccato. Comp. p. 291, and *Conf. Saxon.* p. 67.

(Luther, *Captiv. babyl.*: Christianus volens non potest perdere salutem suam quantiscunque peccatis, nisi nolit credere. Nulla enim peccata eum possunt damnare nisi sola incredulitas.)

Observations.

The Roman definition of mortal sin runs thus: quæ sunt contraria caritati dei et proximi (cf. also *Conf. orthod.*). The Protestant thus: quæ fidem excutiunt. The Roman casuists reckoned a series of mortal sins; so also the *Conf. orthod.* p. 284.

c. *Venial Sins, and their Proper Nature.*

I. ROMAN AND GREEK.

The Concil. Trid. sess. vi. cap. 12 defines *peccata venialia* as *levia et quotidiana*, on account of which we do not cease to be just, and leaves it optional whether they are to be confessed or not. Nothing is said as to the nature of such sins. But Bellarmine, *De amiss. gr.*, following the schoolmen, gives a more definite theory; as thus:—Sess. xiv. cap. 5, cf. *Cat. Rom.* ii. 5. 46 : 1. Peccatum ven. *ex naturâ suâ* distingui a mortali, ac sine ullâ relatione vel ad prædestinationem vel ad misericordiam dei vel ad statum renatorum esse ejusmodi, ut pœnam quidem mereatur sed non æternam. 2. These peccata ven., which proprie and absolute are opposed to peccatis mortal., are either venialia ex genere suo (quæ habent pro objecto rem malam et inordinatam, sed quæ caritati dei vel proximi non repugnet, v. c. verbum otiosum) or ven. ex imperfectione operis, *i.e.* (*a*) quæ non sunt perfecte voluntaria v. c. subiti motus cupiditatis, iræ cet. (*b*) quæ in re parvâ ac levi committuntur v. c. furtum unius oboli. Cf. Bellarmin, *Eccles. milit.* c. 2; Möhler, *neue Untersuch.* S. 209 ff.

Conf. orth. p. 305, merely says: ἁμαρτία συγγνωστὴ εἶναι ἐκείνη, τὴν ὁποίαν οὐδένας ἄνθρωπος ἠμπορεῖ νὰ φύγῃ, ἔξω ἀπὸ τὸν Χριστὸν καὶ τὴν παρθένον Μαρίαν· μὰ δὲν μᾶς στερεύει ἀπὸ τὴν χάριν τοῦ θεοῦ, μήτε μὰς καθυποβάλλει εἰς τὸν αἰώνιον θάνατον.

II. Protestant.

The Protestant counter-statements, which are to be found rather in the writings of the Reformers than in the symbols,[1] are as follows: In the unregenerate there are no venial sins; and in the regenerate these sins are not in themselves or *ex naturâ suâ* venial. Every sin deserves from God eternal death, but for Christ's sake a portion of our sins are forgiven graciously; that is, those which are consistent with the existence of faith, inasmuch as by faith we are justified. But with faith can coexist only unpremeditated sins: these, therefore, are the *peccata venialia;* and the difference between them and *peccata mortalia*[2] is not in the matter of the sin itself, but in the spirit and thought of the sinner—in the *formalis qualitas subjectiva peccantium*. Cf. Melanc. *Loci*, i. 271; Chemnic. *Ex.* i. 10; Calvin, *Instit.* ii. 8, *Decl. Thorun.* 2, 3. As to the objection urged against Protestants, that they made all sins equal, *vid.* Helv. ii. 8; Calvin, *Instit.* ii. 8. 58.

III. Arminian.

The *Conf. Rem.* vii. 6 gives no exact point of connection here. But the Arminian theologians, although opposed in a certain sense to the Calvinists on the question, by no means agree with the Romanists that venial sins are in themselves, and therefore in the unregenerate, venial. Curcell. *Instit.* iv. 4. 18: Animadvertendum est, nullum fingi posse peccatum tam exiguum, quod deus, si vellet cum hominibus summo jure agere, non posset exclusione e regno cœlorum punire. 20: Dico, peccata venialia esse leviora illa, ad quæ deus *in gratuito suo fœdere* connivere decrevit, etiamsi in illa subinde per in-

---

[1] *Helv.* ii. cap. 8: The distribution into *peccata mortalia* and *venialia* occurs only in passing.

[2] Luther, *Gal.* c. v.: Peccatum distinguitur in mortale et veniale, non ob substantiam facti sed personam, non juxta differentiam peccatorum admissorum sed peccatorum ea committentium.

firmitatem aut incogitantiam labamur et eorum habitum non plane exuerimus; . . . talibus enim peccatis fideles plerumque in hac vita obnoxios esse testatur scriptura. Cf. a. Limborch, *Theol. christ.* v. 4. 20 sqq. In entire harmony with this is the positive teaching of *Apol. Conf. Rem.* on this subject.

XIII.

THE MEANS OF GRACE: THE WORD OF GOD.

ROMANISTS and Protestants agree in regarding as the ordinary means, appointed in the church, through which the grace of God in Christ flows to man, the word of God, as it is proclaimed in the church or read in the Scriptures, and the sacraments. The Socinians and Mennonites include only the word. The Quakers, even the older Anabaptists, are of opinion that the Holy Ghost enlightens man without the word immediately by an internal light; every man in this matter having his day of visitation, when this internal light, if rightly used, enables him to apprehend the word of God, which otherwise is only a dead letter.

The mutual relations of word and sacrament are not definitely treated in the symbols of the Protestant Church. But we must not omit what is found in *Conf. Helv.* ii. c. 19 : Verbum dei habetur instar tabularum vel literarum, sacramenta vero instar sigillorum, quæ literis deus appendit solus. How far the Roman Catholic Church exalts the sacraments above the word may be seen in Nitzsch, *Stud.* 1834, iv.

SYMBOLICAL TESTIMONIES.

I. ROMAN.

The Roman Catholic symbols speak only by the way of the *verbum Dei*. The *Cat. Rom.* calls it *cibus animi* (iv. 13. 18), and places it by the side of the sacraments (ii. 1. 32). However, this is understood primarily of the preaching of the word, which in the Conc. Trid. sess. vi. cap. 6 is mentioned only among the preparatory means of conversion; and in sess. xxiv. cap. 4 is imposed on bishops as a duty *ad fidelium salutem.* The reading of the written word of God is, as observed above, to say the least, not favoured by the Roman Catholic Church.

II. PROTESTANT.

A. C. p. 11: Per verbum et sacramenta, tanquam per instrumenta donatur Spir. s., qui fidem efficit, ubi et quando visum est deo, in iis, qui audiunt evangelium cet. Damnant Anabaptistas et alios, qui sentiunt, Spiritum s. contingere sine verbo externo hominibus per ipsorum præparationes et opera. Cf. *Apol. A. C.* p. 268.

Cat. maj. p. 426: Dei verbum thesaurus ille et gaza est pretiosissima, quæ omnia sanctificat, cujus adminiculo etiam ipsi sancti omnes sanctimoniam consecuti sunt. Jam quacunque horâ verbum dei docetur, auditur, legitur, consideratur aut repetitur memoriâ, eâ hujus tractatione audientis persona, dies et opus sanctificatur, non externi quidem operis gratiâ, sed propter verbum, quo omnes nos sancti reddimur et efficimur.—*Ib.* p. 502: Qui (Spiritus s.) quotidie nos divini verbi prædicatione attrahit et adsciscit fidemque impertit, auget atque corroborat, per verbum illud et remissionem peccatorum, ut nos . . . prorsus per omnia sanctos faciat, id quod jam per verbum in fide exspectamus.

A. Sm. p. 331: Constanter tenendum est, deum nemini spiritum vel gratiam suam largiri nisi per verbum et cum verbo externo et præcedente, ut ita præmuniamus nos adversum enthusiastas i. e. spiritus, qui jactitant se ante verbum et sine verbo spiritum habere. [P. 333: Quare in hoc nobis est constanter perseverandum, quod Deus non velit nobiscum aliter agere, nisi per vocale verbum et sacramenta, et quod, quidquid sine verbo et sacramentis jactatur, ut spiritus, sit ipse diabolus. Nam Deus etiam Mosi voluit apparere per rubum ardendum et vocale verbum. Et nullus propheta, sive Elias sive Elisæus, Spiritum sine Decalogo sive verbo vocali accepit.]

F. C. p. 670: Prædicatio verbi dei et ejusdem auscultatio

sunt Sp. s. instrumenta, cum quibus et per quæ efficaciter agere et homines ad deum convertere atque in ipsis et velle et perficere operari vult. — Cf. p. 671 : Per prædicationem et auditionem verbi deus operatur, emollit corda nostra trahitque hominem eet. Etsi autem utrumque, tum concionatoris plantare et rigare, tum auditoris currere et velle frustra omnino essent neque conversio sequeretur, nisi S. s. virtus et operatio accederet, qui per verbum prædicatum et auditum corda illuminat et convertit, ut homines verbo credere et assentiri possint: tamen neque concionator neque auditor de hac Sp. s. gratiâ et operatione dubitare debent. — P. 818 : Ad conciones itaque sacras miseri peccatores conveniant, verbum dei accuratâ diligentiâ audiant neque dubitent, quin pater eos ad filium suum sit pertracturus. Spiritus enim sanctus virtute suâ ministerio adesse et per illud ad hom. salutem vult operari. Et hic est tractus ille patris, de quo sacræ lit. loquuntur.

Ib. p. 581 : Rejicimus enthusiastarum errorem, qui fingunt, deum immediate absque verbi dei auditu et sine sacramentorum usu homines ad se trahere, illuminare, justificare et salvare.

Conf. Helv. ii. cap. 1 : Cum hodie dei verbum per prædicatores legitime vocatos annuntiatur in ecclesiâ, credimus, ipsum dei verbum annuntiari et a fidelibus recipi, neque aliud dei verbum vel fingendum vel cœlitus esse exspectandum. Neque arbitramur, prædicationem illam externam tanquam inutilem ideo videri, quoniam pendeat institutio veræ religionis ab interna spiritus illuminatione. Quanquam enim nemo veniat ad Christum, nisi trahatur a patre cœlesti ac intus illuminetur per spiritum, scimus tamen, deum omnino velle prædicari verbum dei, etiam foris. Equidem potuisset per spiritum suum sanctum aut per ministerium angeli absque ministerio sancti Petri instituisse Cornelium in Actis deus, ceterum rejicit hunc nihilominus ad Petrum. Agnoscimus interim, deum illuminare posse homines etiam sine externo ministerio, quos et quando velit, id quod ejus potentiæ est. Nos autem loquimur de usitatâ ratione instituendi homines, et præcepto et exemplo tradita nobis a deo.—Cap. 18 : Credamus, deum verbo suo nos docere foris per ministros suos, intus autem et commovere electorum suorum corda ad fidem per Spir. s.

Conf. Belg. art. 24: Credimus, veram fidem per auditum verbi dei et Sp. sancti operationem homini insitam eum regenerare.

Cat. Heid. Fr. 65 (Germ.): Whence comes saving faith? It is wrought by the Holy Ghost in our hearts through the preaching of the holy gospel, and He confirms it by the use of the sacraments. — Against the enthusiasts or mystics see Calv. *Instill.* i. 9, on the Word as the means of the Divine Call.

Conf. Remonstr. xvii. 2: Efficitur et perficitur vocatio per prædicationem evangelii eique adjunctam virtutem Spiritus sancti. 8: Spiritus s. omnibus et singulis, quibus verbum fidei ordinarie prædicatur, tantum gratiæ confert, aut saltem conferre paratus est, quantum ad fidem ingenerandum et ad promovendum suis gradibus salutarem ipsorum conversionem sufficit. . . .

Apol. Conf. p. 159 b: Verba: *quibus verb.* . . . *prædicatur* addita sunt a Remonstrantibus, . . . ut significarent, se extraordinarias dei vocationes in computum hunc recensere nolle, in quibus fieri potest, ut deus excellentiore et nobiliore aliquâ virtute quosdam vocatos dignetur, inpr. eos, quorum opera ad aliorum hominum conversionem uti vult. Cf. Limborch, *Theol. christ.* iv. 13. 20.

III. SOCINIAN.

As to the Socinian theory, the *Cat. Racov.* distinguishes in the conversion of men a duplex auxilium dei: an *exterius*, consisting in the promises and threatenings of the New Testament; and an *interius*, when God by His Spirit more and more writes and seals what He promised in the hearts of the faithful. This influence of the Holy Spirit has not only the substance of the divine word for its object and material, but is strictly connected with it. Then comes into view also what the *Cat. Racov.*, p. 251, says of the perpetual gift of the Spirit: "It is an afflatus of God, by which our minds are filled either with a richer knowledge of divine things, or with a more certain hope of eternal life, and consequently with a joy and relish in the prospect of future blessedness. This hope of eternal life, indeed, we conceive through the preaching of the gospel; but it seems to be necessary, in order to implant in the mind a firmer and more certain hope, that the promise externally set forth in the Gospels should be internally sealed by the Holy Spirit in our hearts." Ostorodt, *Unterricht.* c. 34, expressly declares that this ordinary and regular influence of the Divine Spirit does not exclude one that is extraordinary on individual men.

In the Confessions of the Mennonites there are no express clauses touching the word of God as the means of grace. But this *Conf.* 20, says of faith that it is "a most certain apprehension and knowledge derived by the grace of God from the Holy Scriptures."

IV. Arminian.

The symbolical books do not enter into particulars as to the connection between the word of God and the divine energy. Against the Predestinarians, who distinguish between the power of the Holy Ghost as only operative in the elect, and the word of God, in fact separating off that power as a specific element (see Calvin, *Institt.* iv. 14. 10), Arminianism maintains an inseparable union between the influence of the Spirit and the divine word. Limborch, *Theol. christ.* iv. 12 : Externa vocatio dei fit per externum dei verbum vel ore prolatum vel scripto traditum. . . . Interna vocatio est, quæ fit per spir. dei, qui in corda hominum influens ea movet, excitat et exstimulat, ut vocationi externæ per verbum factæ obtemperent. Hæc autem int. vocatio non est virtus sp. seorsim operans a verbo, sed per verbum et verbo semper inest, adeo ut revera una eademque sit vocatio, sed quæ secundum diversos respectus vocatur externa et interna. Quia enim spir. nunquam operatur absque verbo neque verbum unquam destitutum est spiritu, hinc qui verbo vocantur, etiam spiritu, quantum ad conversionem et fidem sufficit, donantur. . . . Non dicimus duas esse (verbi et spiritus) actiones specie distinctas, sed unam eandemque actionem, quoniam verbum est spiritus, h. e. spiritus verbo inest verbumque propterea spiritualem nos convertendi vim habet. Et quæcunque hic sit spiritus actio, ea alia non esse videtur, quam sensus ex verbo percepti validior in mente hominis impressio, quo et de officio suo et magnitudine ac certitudine divinorum promissorum plenius persuasus excitatur ad fidem et perpetuum sanctimoniæ studium. — Similarly, the older Lutheran theologians, and with the same true instinct, maintained *Spiritum sanctum cum verbo dei indivulse conjunctum esse.*

Law and Gospel.

The Protestant symbols, noting the manner and process of individual renewal as effected through the instrumentality of the word of God, not only distinguish between the two constituents of the divine word, commandments and promises, terming the former as a whole the Law,[1] and the latter the Gospel,[2] but they also define the influence which each exerts on conversion, and the value which the law as such has for the regenerate,—a point to which the Lutheran divines were directed by the antinomistic controversies.

I. PROTESTANT.

Apol. A. C. p. 60: Universa scriptura in hos duos locos præcipuos distribui debet, in legem et promissiones. Alias enim legem tradit, alias tradit promissionem de Christo, videlicet, cum aut promittit Christum venturum esse et pollicetur propter eum remissionem peccatorum, justificationem et vitam æternam, aut in evangelio Christus, postquam apparuit, promittit remissionem peccatorum, justificationem et vitam æternam. Vocamus autem legem in hac disputatione decalogi

---

[1] The foundation of the law, the substance and compend of the divine commandments, is the Decalogue: *Apol. A. C.* 60; *Helv.* ii. c. 12. As to the division of this into ten precepts, there was between the Lutherans and the Reformed (Calvin, *Instit.* ii. 8) the same difference as that between the Roman and the Greek Churches. This has been expressed in the symbolical catechisms. Against the Roman and Lutheran distribution there is a circumstantial protest in *Cat. Rac.* p. 176.

[2] This is the distinction which has been predominant, and has entered into the symbols. It is scarcely of any moment that Luther in the Greater Catechism says *præcepta et fides* instead of *lex et evangelium;* and the designation *lex* for the whole of the Old Testament is peculiar to the *Artt. Smalc.* p. 313.

præcepta, ubicunque illa in scripturis leguntur; de ceremoniis et judicialibus legibus Moisi in præsentiâ nihil loquimur.

Ib. p. 170 : Hæc sunt duo præcipua opera del in hominibus, perterrefacere et justificare ac vivificare perterrefactos. In hæc duo opera distributa est universa scriptura. Altera pars lex est, quæ ostendit, arguit et condemnat peccata. Altera pars evangelium, hoc est promissio gratiæ in Christo donatæ, et hæc promissio subinde repetitur in totâ scripturâ, primum tradita Adæ postea patriarchis, deinde a prophetis illustrata, postremo prædicata et exhibita a Christo inter Judæos, et ab apostolis sparsa in totum mundum. Cf. pp. 68, 166.[1]

A. Sm. p. 319 sq : Præcipuum officium et ἐνέργεια legis est, ut peccatum originale et omnes fructus ejus revelet et homini ostendat, quam horrendum in modum natura ejus lapsa sit et funditus ac totaliter depravata, ita ut lex ei dicat, hominem nec habere nec curare deum et adorare alienos deos, id quod antea et sine lege homo non credidisset. Hac ratione perterrefit, humiliatur, prosternitur, desperat de se ipso, et anxie desiderat auxilium nec scit, quod fugiat, incipit irasci deo et obmurmurare præ impatientiâ. — Hoc officium legis retinetur in N. T., et in eo exercetur. — Huic officio Novum Test. statim adjungit consolationem et promissionem gratiæ evangelii, cui credendum est.

F. C. p. 592 : Credimus, legem esse proprie doctrinam divinitus revelatam, quæ doceat, quid justum deoque gratum sit; quæ etiam quicquid peccatum est et voluntati divinæ adversatur, redarguat. . . . Quare, quicquid exstat in sacris literis, quod peccata arguit, id revera ad legis concionem pertinet. Evangelion vero proprie doctrinam esse censemus, quæ doceat, quid homo credere debeat, qui legi dei non satisfecit et idcirco per eandem damnatur, videlicet, quod illum credere oporteat, Jesum Christum omnia peccata expiasse atque pro iis satisfecisse et remissionem peccatorum, justitiam coram deo consistentem et vitam æternam, nullo interveniente peccatoris illius merito, impetrasse. . . . Cum autem vocabulum (evangelii) non semper in unâ eademque significatione in sacrâ

---

[1] It is no contradiction, only another phraseology, when, *Apol.* p. 71, the *Evangelium* is said *arguere peccata.* But this confession, which in the *Conf. Aug.* is repeated, gave occasion for suspicion as to the changed text of the *Conf.*

scripturâ usurpetur, docemus et confitemur, si vocabulum (evangelii) de totâ Christi doctrinâ accipiatur, quam ipse in ministerio suo (quemadmodum et ejus apostoli) professus est (in quâ significatione Mrc. i. [15] et Act. xx. 24 vox illa usurpatur) recte dici et doceri, evangelium esse concionem de pœnitentiâ et remissione peccatorum.

Ib. p. 593: Etsi concio illa de passione et morte Christi, filii dei, severitatis et terroris plena est, quæ iram dei adversus peccata ostendit, unde demum homines ad legem dei propius adducuntur, postquam velum illud Moisis ablatum est, ut tandem exacte agnoscant, quanta videlicet dominus in lege sua a nobis exigat, quorum nihil nos præstare possumus, ita ut universam nostram justitiam in solo Christo quærere oporteat: tamen, quam diu nobis Christi passio et mors iram dei ob oculos ponunt et hominem perterrefaciunt, tam diu non sunt proprie concio evangelii, sed legis et Moisis doctrina, et sunt alienum opus Christi, per quod accedit ad proprium suum officium, quod est, prædicare de gratiâ dei, consolari et vivificare. Hæc propria sunt prædicationis evangelicæ.

Ib. p. 595: Credimus, etsi vere in Christum credentes et sincere ad deum conversi a maledictione et coactione legis per Christum liberati sunt, quod ii tamen propterea non sint absque lege, quippe quos filius dei eam ob causam redemit, ut legem dei diu noctuque meditentur atque in ejus observatione sese assidue exerceant. . . . Credimus, concionem legis non modo apud eos, qui fidem in Christum non habent et pœnitentiam nondum agunt, sed etiam apud eos, qui vere in Christum credunt, vere ad deum conversi et renati et per fidem justificati sunt, sedulo urgendam esse. . . . Etsi enim renati et spiritu mentis suæ renovati sunt, tamen regeneratio illa et renovatio in hac vitâ non est omnibus numeris absoluta, sed duntaxat inchoata. Et credentes illi spiritu mentis suæ perpetuo luctantur cum carne, hoc est cum corruptâ naturâ, quæ in nobis ad mortem usque hæret. Et propter veterem Adamum, qui adhuc in hominis intellectu, voluntate et in omnibus viribus ejus infixus residet, opus est, ut homini lex dei semper præluceat, ne quid privatæ devotionis affectu in negotio religionis confingat et cultus divinos verbo dei non institutos eligat; item, ne vetus Adam pro suo ingenio agat, sed potius contra suam voluntatem, non modo admonitionibus et minis legis, verum etiam pœnis et plagis coerceatur, ut spiritui obsequatur seque ipsi captivum tradat.

Ib. p. 596 : Ad hunc modum una eademque lex est manetque, immota videlicet dei voluntas, sive pœnitentibus sive impœnitentibus, renatis aut non renatis proponatur. Discrimen autem, quoad obedientiam, duntaxat in hominibus est: quorum alii non renati legi obedientiam qualemcunque a lege requisitam præstant, sed coacti et inviti id faciunt (sicut etiam renati faciunt, quatenus adhuc carnales sunt); credentes vero in Christum, quatenus renati sunt, absque coactione, libero et spontaneo spiritu talem obedientiam præstant, qualem alias nullæ quantumvis severissimæ legis comminationes extorquere possent.

Conf. Helv. ii. c. 13 : Evangelium opponitur legi. Nam lex iram operatur et maledictionem annuntiat, evangelium vero gratiam et benedictionem prædicat. — Quamvis patres nostri in scripturis prophetarum habuerint evangelium, per quod et salutem in Christo per fidem consecuti sunt, evangelium tamen proprie illud dicitur lætum et felix nuntium, quo nobis primum per Joannem baptistam, deinde per ipsum Christum dominum, postea per apostolos ejus apostolorumque successores prædicatum est, mundo deum jam præstitisse, quod ab exordio mundi promisit, ac misisse, imo donavisse nobis filium unicum, et in hoc reconciliationem cum patre, remissionem peccatorum, omnem plenitudinem et vitam æternam. Historia ergo descripta a quatuor evangelistis, explicans quomodo hæc sint facto vel adimpleta a Christo, quæ docuerit et fecerit Christus, et quod in ipso credentes omnem habent plenitudinem, recte nuncupatur evangelium. Prædicatio item et scriptura apostolica, qua nobis exponunt apostoli, quomodo nobis a patre datus sit filius et in hoc vitæ salutisque omnia, recte dicitur doctrina evangelica, sic ut ne hodie quidem, si sincera sit, appellationem tam præclaram amittat. — *Ib.* 12 : Docemus, legem non datam esse hominibus, ut ejus justificentur observatione, sed ut ejus judicio infirmitatem potius, peccatum atque condemnationem agnoscamus, et de viribus nostris desperantes, convertamur ad Christum in fide. — Hactenus itaque abrogata est lex dei, quatenus nos amplius non damnat, nec iram in nobis operatur. Sumus enim sub gratiâ, et non sub lege. — Attamen legem non ideo fastidientes rejicimus. Meminimus enim verborum domini discentis: non veni legem et prophetas solvere, sed implere (Mt. v. 17). Scimus, lege nobis tradi formulas virtutum atque vitiorum; scimus, scripturam legis, si exponatur per evangelium, ecclesiæ esse utilem, et idcirco ejus lectionem non exterminandam esse ex ecclesiâ.

Conf. Gall. art. 23: Credimus, omnes legis figuras adventu Jesu Christi sublatas esse, quamvis earum veritas et substantia nobis in eo constet, in quo sunt omnes impletæ. Legis tamen doctrinâ et prophetis nobis utendum est, tum ad vitam nostram formandam, tum ut eo magis in promissionibus evangelicis confirmemur. — Similarly *Conf. Belg.* art. 25. *Conf. Hungar.* (Czenger.) p. 157: Lex ad peccata arguenda et evangelium propter annunciandam remissionem peccatorum prædicandum est. Neque enim pœnitentia prædicari potest neque peccata argui possunt sine lege. Compare, as to the use and obligation of the Mosaic law for Christians, Calvin, *Institt.* ii. 7. 14; *Thirty-nine Artt.* vii. Why the Predestinarians do not willingly term the gospel a law, is shown in the *Apol. Conf. Rem.* p. 143.

II. Socinians.

The Socinians, who regard Judaism, like Christianity, as a legislation based on divine promises, might, like the Protestants generally, have distinguished their whole Bible into law and gospel; but they would not have placed the promises on the same line with the commandments, and therefore used the terms law and gospel for the Old and New Testaments respectively. So also the Arminians: Curcell. *Rel. ch. inst.* v. 16; Limborch, *Th. ch.* iii. 17. Among the Romanists, Bellarmine, *Justif.* iv. 2, in order to maintain the necessity of good works to salvation, declares himself against the Protestant distinction between law and gospel, and seeks (cap. 3 and 4) to give another definition of these ideas. On the other hand, Plato, *Catech.* S. 49, joins the Protestants here.

XIV.
SACRAMENTS GENERALLY.

FIRST POINT OF DIVERGENCE.

WITH the sole exception of the Quakers, who are opposed to externality in religion, referring all to the life of the spirit, and its only source the internal light, Christian communities celebrate certain holy ordinances appointed by Christ Himself. But they differ as to the design of these institutions: while the Romanists, Greeks, and the greater portion of Protestants, regard them as means of grace,[1] the Arminians, Mennonites, and some other Protestant communities, join the Socinians in giving up the notion that they are directly such. The older Socinians discerned in the sacraments, which they preferred to call *cerimoniæ*, only external acts (*præcepta cerimonialia Christi*), which primarily betoken a profession of the Christian faith: the Christian man not receiving aught in them, but rather doing something himself. The Arminians and others, on the contrary, regard the sacraments as sacred signs of Christian profession, and of grace promised by God; which signs as such exert a moral influence on the mind. The Zwinglians teach in harmony with the Socinians.

SYMBOLICAL TESTIMONIES.

I. QUAKER.

The Quakers reject both the idea and the name of sacraments. Barclay, *Apol.* Prop. xii., declares that the Scripture

[1] As signs of profession, they are by these still regarded; but this end is subordinate to their use as means of grace.

names nothing the signature and pledge of our gospel inheritance save the Spirit of God. Compare their Catechism, where the baptism of Christ is distinguished from the water-baptism of John as a baptism of the Holy Ghost; and the Lord's Supper is said, with allusion to Rom. xiv. 17, Col. ii. 16–22, not to have been designed for perpetual observance.

Barclay, *Apol. Prop.* xii.: As there is one Lord, and one Faith, so there is one Baptism; which is not the putting away of the filth of the flesh, but the answer of a good conscience before God, by the resurrection of Jesus Christ. And this baptism is a pure and spiritual thing, to wit, the baptism of the Spirit and fire, by which we are buried with Him, that, being washed and purged from our sins, we may walk in newness of life.—*Comm.* sec. 6: But to make water-baptism a necessary institution of the Christian religion, which is pure and spiritual, and not carnal and ceremonial, is to derogate from the new covenant dispensation, and set up the legal rites and ceremonies, of which this of baptism, or washing with water, was one.

Prop. xiii. on the Eucharist: The communion of the body and blood of Christ is inward and spiritual, which is the participation of His flesh and blood, by which the inward man is daily nourished in the hearts of those in whom Christ dwells. Of which things the breaking of bread by Christ with His disciples was a figure, which even they who had received the substance used in the church for a time, for the sake of the weak; even as abstaining from things strangled and from blood, the washing one another's feet, and the anointing of the sick with oil: all which are commanded with no less authority and solemnity than the former [Baptism and the Lord's Supper]; yet, seeing they are but shadows of better things, they cease in such as have obtained the inheritance. —*Comm.* sec. 3: So that the Supper of the Lord, and the supping with the Lord, and partaking of His flesh and blood, is no ways limited to the ceremony of breaking bread and drinking wine at particular times, but is truly and really enjoyed as often as the soul retires into the light of the Lord, and feels and partakes of that heavenly life by which the inward man is nourished; which may be and is often witnessed by the faithful at all times.

II. Roman, Greek, and Lutheran.

Conc. Trident. sess. 7: Sacramenta per quæ omnis vera justitia vel incipit vel cœpta augetur vel amissa reparatur.

Cat. Rom. ii. 1. 11: Ut explicatius quid sacramentum sit declaretur, docendum erit, rem esse sensibus subjectam, quæ ex dei institutione sanctitatis et justitiæ tum significandæ tum efficiendæ vim habet: ex quo sequitur, ut facile quivis possit intelligere, imagines sanctorum, cruces et alia id genus, quamvis sacrarum rerum signa sint, non ideo tamen sacramenta dicenda esse.

Conf. orthod. p. 155: Τὸ μυστήριον (Sacrament) εἶναι μία τελετὴ ἡ ὁποία ἀποκάτω εἰς κάποιον εἶδος ὁρατὸν εἶναι αἰτία καὶ φέρει εἰς τὴν ψυχὴν τοῦ πιστοῦ τὴν ἀόρατον χάριν τοῦ θεοῦ· διαταχθὲν ὑπὸ τοῦ κυρίου ὑμῶν, δι' οὗ ἕκαστος τῶν πιστῶν τὴν θείαν χάριν λαμβάνει.

A. C. [P. 11: Per verbum et sacramenta, *tanquam per instrumenta*, donatur Spiritus sanctus, qui fidem efficit, ubi et quando visum est Deo, in iis, qui audiunt evangelium.] P. 13: Sacramenta instituta sunt, non modo ut sint notæ professionis inter homines, sed magis ut sint signa et testimonia voluntatis dei erga nos ad excitandum et confirmandam fidem in his, qui utuntur, proposita.

Apol. A. C. p. 200: Sacramenta vocamus ritus, qui habent mandatum dei et quibus addita est promissio gratiæ. *Ib.* p. 253: Sacramentum est cerimonia vel opus, in quo deus nobis exhibet hoc, quod offert annexa cerimoniæ promissio. Cf. p. 267.

III. Reformed.

Conf. Helv. i. art. 20: Asserimus, sacramenta non solum tesseras quasdam societatis chr., sed et gratiæ div. symbola esse, quibus ministri domino ad eum finem, quem ipse promittit, offert et efficit, co-operentur.

Conf. Helv. ii. c. 19: Sunt sacramenta symbola mystica vel

ritus sancti aut sacræ actiones a deo ipso institutæ, constantes verbo suo, signis et rebus significatis, quibus in ecclesiâ summa sua beneficia homini exhibita retinet in memoriâ et subinde renovat, quibus item promissiones suas obsignat et quæ ipse nobis interius præstat, exterius repræsentat ac veluti oculis contemplanda subjicit, adeoque fidem nostram, spiritu dei in cordibus nostris operante, roborat et auget: quibus denique nos ab omnibus aliis populis et religionibus separat sibique soli consecrat et obligat, et quid a nobis requirat, significat.
—Sacr. sunt rerum sacrarum symbola mystica, et signa et res significatæ inter se sacramentaliter conjunguntur, conjunguntur, inquam, vel uniuntur per significationem mysticam et voluntatem vel consilium ejus, qui sacramenta instituit.

Thirty-nine Artt. art. xxv.: Sacraments ordained of Christ be not only badges or tokens of Christian men's profession, but rather they be certain sure witnesses and effectual signs of grace, and God's goodwill towards us, by the which He doth work invisibly in us, and doth not only quicken, but also strengthen and confirm our faith in Him.

Conf. Scot. art. 21 : (Confitemur) sacramenta . . . non tantum visibiliter inter populum dei et eos qui extra fœdus sunt, distinguere, sed etiam fidem suorum filiorum exercere; et participationem eorundem sacramentorum in illorum cordibus certitudinem promissionis ejus et felicissimæ illius conjunctionis, unionis et societatis, quam electi cum Ch. habent, obsignare.

West. Conf. ch. xxvii. sec. 1 : Sacraments are holy signs and seals of the covenant of grace, immediately instituted by God, to represent Christ and His benefits, and to confirm our interest in Him; as also to put a visible difference between those that belong unto the church and the rest of the world; and solemnly to engage them to the service of God in Christ, according to His word. Sec. 2 : There is in every sacrament a spiritual relation, or sacramental union, between the sign and the thing signified; whence it comes to pass, that the names and effects of the one are attributed to the other.

Conf. Gall. art. 34: Credimus, adjuncta esse verbo sacramenta amplioris confirmationis causâ, gratiæ dei nimirum pignora et tesseras, quibus infirmæ et rudi fidei nostræ subveniatur. Fatemur enim, talia esse signa hæc exteriora, ut deus per illa sancti sui spiritus virtute operetur, ne quidquam ibi frustra nobis significetur.

[*Conf. Belgica*, art. xxxiii.: Sunt sacramenta signa ac symbola visibilia rerum internarum et invisibilium, per quæ ceu per media, Deus ipse virtute Spiritus sancti in nobis operatur.]

Heidelb. Cat. Fr. 66: Sacraments are visible, sacred signs and seals appointed of God, that in their use we may have the promise of the gospel made clearer and sealed: to wit, that God for the sake of the one oblation of Christ bestows on us forgiveness of sins and eternal life.

Catech. Genev. p. 519: Sacramentum est externa divinæ erga nos benevolentiæ testificatio, quæ visibili signo spirituales gratias figurat ad obsignandas cordibus nostris dei promissiones, quo earum virtus melius confirmetur. Vim et efficaciam sacramenti non in externo elemento inclusam esse existimas, sed totam a spiritu dei manare? Sic sentio, nempe, ut virtutem suam exercere domino placuerit per sua organa, quem in finem ea destinavit.

Observations.

[The older Reformed Confessions, which were drawn up by Zwingli, teach in another strain. Zwingli, *Fid. Ratio ad Car. Rom. imper.* No. vii.: Credo, imo scio, omnia sacramenta tam abesse, ut gratiam conferant, ut ne adferant quidem aut dispensent. See Niemeyer, *Coll.* S. 24. The doctrine afterwards taught, under the influence of Calvin, may be summed under the following heads:] 1. They are Symbola *mystica*. 2. They are signs of His grace, instituted *of God:* consequently more than mere moral remembrances of the heavenly, bringing it near, for these the church itself could have ordained. 3. They are signs of that which *the Holy Ghost* inwardly effects: sign and operation coincide, although in an incomprehensible manner (*Conf. Belg.* art. 35); indeed, according to *Helv.* ii., the symbola et res significatæ are *sacramentaliter* united by God. The *Decl. Thorun.* ii. 6 speaks of their gratiam exhibere mediantibus illis signis, and of a vera et infallibilis rerum promissarum modo ipsis convenienti et proprio exhibitio. The *Conf. Gall.* art. 37, however, says: deum nobis reipsa i. e. vere et efficaciter donare, quidquid sacramentaliter figurat ac proinde cum signis conjungimus veram possessionem ac fruitionem ejus rei, quæ ibi nobis offertur. Add to this what the *Conf. Helv.* ii.

says: sacramenta verbo, signis et rebus significatis constantia manent vera et integra sacramenta, non tantum significantia res sacras sed deo offerente etiam res significatas, tametsi increduli res oblatas non percipiant.

1. Although the sacraments are to the Roman as to the Evangelical means of grace, there is much difference in their respective views of the special grace which they are the means of imparting. The Evangelical Church teaches that the grace of the forgiveness of sins is presented through the sacraments; also that their effect is that of quickening and strengthening faith (*Apol. C. A.* p. 200; *Helv.* ii. c. 19). The Roman Catholic Church, on the other hand, regards sacraments generally as channels through which sanctifying and saving grace in its rich and manifold diversity flows: we have only to think of the altar, penance, marriage, orders! The Council of Trent says, sess. vii. can. 5, *de sacr.*: Si quis dixerit, sacramenta propter solam fidem nutriendam instituta fuisse, anathema sit. For the positive side, see *Cat. Rom.* ii. 1. 11 and 14; Bellarmine, *de sacr.* ii. 2; Becani *Manuale controv.* i. 173. Thus it appears how much the Roman Church has misinterpreted the Protestant faith, in making it teach only that the sacraments were intended for the strengthening of faith.

2. The symbols do not dwell at length on the relation between the operation of grace in the sacraments and the sacramental elements themselves. But in the Reformed Confessions, the Holy Ghost, who makes that real in the heart which the elements figure, is not indistinctly described as an independent power, which however is strictly connected through the sacramental institution with the external rite; and that which is laid down in Calv. *Instit.* iv. 14 is stated in them without controversy. Luther gives a closer internal connection between water in baptism and the word of God in *Cat. maj.* 538, 539: By the word the baptismal water first becomes a sacrament and means of grace. And this doctrine, as the opposite of a *virtus Sp. s. extrinsecus accedens*, as the Reformed view is characterized, is accepted heartily by Chemnitz, Gerhard, and others.

IV. SOCINIAN.

For the Socinian doctrines, see on Baptism and the Supper. We remark here only: 1. According to the fundamental principles of Socinus on baptism, as laid down in his treatise *de baptismo aquæ*, the *Cat. Racov.* introduced in the first edition only one præceptum Christi cærimoniale, that is, the Supper, and baptism was treated only as an appendage, and in a negative way. But when the Socinians afterwards sought to conform more to the leading Confessions in respect to baptism, it was discussed as a second ceremonial commandment; hence in the second edition (1644) we read: Actus externi religiosi sui ritus sacri in eccl. Ch. semper usurpati sunt baptismus et fractio panis. And baptism takes the precedence. So also, in the *Confess.* p. 24, Baptism and the Supper are reckoned together among the res sanctæ, quarum communionem habere quisque debet. 2. Socinus declares against the expression sacrament as unbiblical. 3. The *Summa theol. Unit.* iii. 8 enlarges the sacramental idea in the Arminian way, defining sacraments thus: Mutuæ inter deum ac homines sacræ confœderationis tesseræ; non enim sunt tantum testimonia obedientiæ christ., sed etiam gratiæ div. in nos collatæ et conferendæ signa.

V. Arminian.

Conf. Remonstr. xxiii. 1: Sacramenta cum dicimus, externas ecclesiæ cæremonias seu ritus illos sacros ac solennes intelligimus, quibus veluti fœderalibus signis ac sigillis visibilius deus gratiosa beneficia sua in fœdere præsertim evangelico promissa non modo nobis repræsentat et adumbrat, sed et certo modo exhibet atque obsignat, nosque vicissim palam publiceque declaramus ac testamur, nos promissiones omnes divinas verâ, firmâ atque obsequiosâ fide amplecti et beneficia ipsius jugi, et gratâ semper memoriâ celebrare velle. Cf. *Apol. Confess.* p. 245, b.

Limborch, *Theol. chr.* v. 66. 31: Restat, ut dicamus, deum gratiam suam per sacramenta nobis exhibere, non eam actu per illa conferendo sed per illa tanquam signa clara et evidentia eam repræsentando et ob oculos ponendo ... tanquam præsentem, ut ita in signis istis tanquam in speculo quodam exhibitionem illam gratiæ, quam deus nobis concessit, quasi conspiciamus. Estque hæc efficacia nulla alia, quam objectiva, quæ requirit facultatem cognitivam rite dispositam, ut apprehendere possit illud, quod signum objective menti offert. — Operantur in nobis tanquam signa repræsentantia menti nostræ rem, cujus signa sunt. Neque alia in illis quæri debet efficacia. Sic sacramentum confirmat fidem, quia magis persuadet, veram esse promissionem, cui confirmandæ comparatum est, quia sigilli instar est, quo deus promissum suum verbo testatum visibili quodam signo confirmat nosque certos reddit, se nos fœdere suo comprehendisse, seque a suâ parte promissis staturum, si nos officio nostro non desimus. Nam licet in sacramento res, quæ promittitur, futura spectetur, promissum tamen est præsens, et res futura ita spectatur, ut sacramentum ferme eam repræsentet. (In § 29 L. had refuted the dogma of a spiritualis perceptio rerum ipsarum.)

Ris, *Conf.* art. 30 : Sacramenta sunt externæ visibilesque actiones et signa immensæ benignitatis dei erga nos, nobis ex parte dei ob oculos ponentia internam spiritualemque actionem, quam deus per Christum exsequitur regenerando, justificando, spiritualiter nutriendo. — Nos vero quod attinet, iisdem confitemur religionem, pœnitentiam, fidem et obedientiam nostram.

The Feet-washing.

The Mennonites placed by the side of the sacraments, as a holy usage prescribed by Christ, the washing of the feet. *Vide Conf. der Friesen u. Deutsch.* art. 13 ; and Cornelis, *Bekenntn.* art. 11. In the former passage the feet-washing is only in a distant manner indicated, as in reference to the communion of believers. But it is well known that the Frisian or rigid Mennonites practised this mutual feet-washing.

SECOND POINT OF DIVERGENCE.

The Roman Church, like the Greek, reckons seven sacraments: that is, baptism, confirmation, eucharist, penance, extreme unction, orders, marriage. The Protestant Church, including all parties, admit only two : baptism and the holy supper. But the Roman Church does not attribute an equal dignity to all the seven.

SYMBOLICAL REFERENCES.

I. Roman and Greek.

Conc. Trid. sess. 7. sacram. can. 1: Si quis dixerit, sacramenta novæ legis ... esse plura vel pauciora quam septem (videlicet baptismum, confirmationem, eucharistiam, pœnitentiam, extremam unctionem, ordinem et matrimonium), aut etiam aliquod horum septem non esse vere et proprie sacramentum: anathema sit.

Cat. Rom. ii. 1. 20: Cur neque plura neque pauciora (sacramenta) numerentur, ex iis etiam rebus, quæ per similitudinem a naturali vitâ ad spiritualem transferuntur, probabili quadam ratione ostendi poterit. Homini enim ad vivendum vitamque conservandam et ex suâ reique publicæ utilitate traducendam hæc septem necessaria videntur, ut scilicet in lucem edatur, augeatur, alatur, si in morbum incidat, sanetur, imbecillitas virium reficiatur; deinde, quod ad rempublicam attinet, ut magistratus nunquam desint, quorum auctoritate et imperio regatur, ac postremo legitima sobolis propagatione seipsum et humanum genus conservet. Quæ omnia quoniam vitæ illi, qua animo deo vivit, respondere satis apparet, ex iis facile sacramentorum numerus colligetur.

Conf. orthod. p. 154: Ἑπτὰ μυστήρια τῆς ἐκκλησίας· τὰ ὁποῖα εἶναι ταῦτα· τὸ βάπτισμα, τὸ μύρον τοῦ χρίσματος, ἡ εὐχαριστία, ἡ μετάνοια, ἡ ἱερωσύνη, ὁ τίμιος γάμος καὶ τὸ εὐχέλαιον· ταῦτα τὰ ἑπτὰ μυστήρια ἀναβιβάζονται εἰς τὰ ἑπτὰ χαρίσματα τοῦ ἁγίου πνεύματος.

Cf. Jerem. *in Actis Wirtemb.* p 77; Dosithei *Confess.* c. xv.; Plato, *Catech.* p. 122.

Conc. Trid. sess. 7, can. 3: Si quis dixerit, hæc septem sacramenta ita esse inter se paria, ut nullâ ratione aliud sit alio dignius, anath. sit. (Bellarmin, *De sacram. in genere*, ii. 28: Concilium præcipue intendit damnare errorem Lutheranorum de paritate baptismi et eucharistiæ.)

Cat. Rom. ii. 1. 22: Sacramenta non parem omnia et æqualem necessitatem aut dignitatem habent, atque ex iis tria sunt, quæ, tametsi non eadem ratione, tamen præ ceteris necessaria dicuntur, baptismus, pœnitentia, ordo; verum si dignitas in sacramentis spectetur, eucharistia sanctitate et mysteriorum numero ac magnitudine longe ceteris antecellit (s. Conc. Trid. sess. xiii. cap. 3).

Baptism and the Eucharist are esteemed by the Greeks the chief sacraments: Plato, *Catech.* p. 122; Jerem. *in Actis Wirtemb.* p. 240. Metroph. Critopulus, c. 5, p. 72 sq., adds penance, and calls the three τὰ πρὸς σωτηρίαν ἀναγκαῖα μυστήρια. Cf. Heinecc. ii. 239 f., against Cyrill. Lucar., who, in *Conf.* c. 15, says that only two sacraments were ordained by Christ. Cyrill. Berrhœens. *Censura synod.* p. 77, and Parthen., p. 127, utter an anathema. In both decrees there is no difference in the dignity of the seven sacraments.

II. Protestant.

The Catechisms of Luther and the *Conf. Aug.* treated only of two sacraments, baptism and the Supper, without excluding the others expressly from the number of the sacraments.[1] On penance, the *Catech. major.* 594: Vides, baptismum æque et virtute et significatione suâ tertium quoque sacramentum comprehendere, quod pœnitentiam appellare consueverunt, quæ proprie nihil aliud est, quam baptismus aut ejus exercitium. (Melanchthon's (*Apol.* p. 167) explanation: Absolutio proprie dici potest sacramentum pœnitentiæ, cf. p. 159, is by this modified. Against the seven we have the following testimonies:—

Apol. C. A. p. 200: (Adversarii) jubent nos etiam septem sacramenta numerare. Nos sentimus præstandum esse, ne negligantur res et cerimoniæ in scripturis institutæ, quotcunque sunt. Nec multum referre putamus, etiamsi docendi causâ alii numerant aliter, si tamen recte conservent res in scripturâ traditas. Nec veteres eodem modo numeraverunt.

Conf. Helv. ii. c. 19: Novi populi sacramenta sunt baptismus et cœna dominica. Sunt qui sacramenta novi populi septem numerent. Ex quibus nos pœnitentiam, ordinationem ministrorum, non papisticam quidem illam sed apostolicam, et matrimonium agnoscimus instituta esse dei utilia, sed non

---

[1] Only the *Conf. Wirtemb.* expressly argues against the five Roman sacraments. On the Reformed side, this is done in the *Declar. Thorun.* ii. 6.

sacramenta. Confirmatio et extrema unctio inventa sunt hominum, quibus nullo cum damno carere potest ecclesia.

Conf. Gall. art. 35: Agnoscimus duo tantum sacramenta, toti ecclesiæ communia cet.

Conf. Belg. art. 33: Sufficit nobis is sacramentorum numerus, quem Christus magister noster instituit: quæ duo duntaxat sunt, nimirum sacramentum baptismi et sacræ cœnæ Jesu Christi.

Thirty-nine Artt. art. 25: Sacraments ordained of Christ be not only badges or tokens of Christian men's profession, but rather they be certain sure witnesses and effectual signs of grace, and God's goodwill towards us, by the which He doth work invisibly in us, and doth not only quicken, but also strengthen and confirm our faith in Him. There are two sacraments ordained of Christ our Lord in the gospel: that is to say, baptism and the Supper of the Lord. Those five, commonly called sacraments, that is to say, confirmation, penance, orders, matrimony, and extreme unction, are not to be counted for sacraments of the gospel, being such as have grown partly of the corrupt following of the apostles, partly are states of life allowed in the Scriptures; but yet have not like nature of sacraments with baptism and the Lord's Supper, for that they have not any visible sign or ceremony ordained of God. The sacraments were not ordained of Christ to be gazed upon, or to be carried about; but that we should duly use them. And in such only as worthily receive the same they have a wholesome effect or operation: but they that receive them unworthily, purchase to themselves damnation, as Saint Paul saith.

West. Conf. ch. xxvii. sec. 4: There be only two sacraments ordained by Christ our Lord in the gospel, that is to say, baptism and the Supper of the Lord; neither of which may be dispensed by any but by a minister of the word, lawfully ordained.

III. ARMINIAN.

The Arminians (*Conf.* xxiii. 2) acknowledge only two sacraments, although they approve of other holy observances, *e.g.* imposition of hands in ordination and confirmation, the blessing in marriage, etc., *modo absit vana superstitio seu opinio divini cultus, item præcisæ necessitatis cet.* Limborch, *Th. chr.* v. 77, opposes at large the five additional Roman sacraments.

As it regards the Mennonites, Ris admits only two sacraments (*Conf.* art. 30); but the *Conf.* of the united Frisians and Germans (art. 13) adds to the sacraments the feet-washing (John xiii.) as a *ritus præceptus.* Cf. Schyn, *Plen. deduc.* p. 183.

Observations.

Of the seven sacraments of the Roman Church, three—baptism, confirmation, and orders—have an indelible character (*character indelebilis*), and may on no account be repeated: Conc. Trid. sess. vii. sacr. can. 9; *Cat. Rom.* ii. 1. 30; Bellarmini *Sacr.* ii. 19–22. The Protestants also reject the repetition of baptism, — without, however, attributing to the sacrament an indelible character. Chemn. *Exam. C. T.* ii. 1.

THIRD POINT OF DIVERGENCE.

The question as to what the operation of the sacraments, as distinguished from their power, depends upon, the two leading communions answer differently. 1. The Romanists teach that all sacraments exert their influence *ex opere operato*, through the objective sacred performance of them, yet only when the priests perform them with intention: and in this last the Greeks agree with them. 2. The Protestants, on the other hand, assert that the effect of the sacraments, the power indwelling in them, has its operation in the receivers by means of their faith, nothing being dependent on the intention of the administering pastor. But both churches agree (in opposition to the Donatists, *A. C.* art. 10; and Anabaptists, *F. C.* 829)[1] that the spiritual character of the administrant is without any influence in this matter, and an unconverted priest may as effectually minister the sacrament as a converted one.

[1] Cf. Luther's *deutsche Werke,* xix. 685. In general, the Quakers also are of the opinion that man cannot without the true grace of God be a minister of the gospel and profit souls. Barcl. *Apol.* Prop. iv.

SYMBOLICAL TESTIMONIES.

I. Roman.

Conc. Trid. sess. vii. sacram. can. 8 : Si quis dixerit, per ipsa novæ legis sacramenta ex opere operato non conferri gratiam, sed solam fidem divinæ promissionis ad gratiam consequendam sufficere, anathema sit.

(Bellarmin, *De sacram.* ii. 1 : Id quod active et proxime atque instrumentaliter efficit gratiam justificationis est sola actio illa externa, quæ sacramentum dicitur, et hæc vocatur *opus operatum*, accipiendo passive (operatum), ita ut idem sit sacramentum conferre gratiam ex opere operato, quod conferre gratiam ex vi ipsius actionis sacramentalis a deo ad hoc institutæ, non ex merito agentis vel suscipientis. . . . Voluntas dei, quæ sacramento utitur, concurrit quidem active, sed est causa principalis. Passio Christi concurrit, sed est causa meritoria, non autem effectiva, cum non sit actu, sed præterierit, licet maneat objective in mente dei. Potestas et voluntas ministri concurrunt necessario, sed sunt causæ remotæ, requiruntur enim ad efficiendam ipsam actionem sacramentalem, quæ postea immediate operatur. Probitas ministri requiritur, ut ipse minister non peccet sacramenta ministrando, non tamen ipsa est causa gratiæ in suscipiente nec juvat suscipientem per modum sacramenti, sed solum per modum impetrationis et exempli. Voluntas, fides et pœnitentia in suscipiente adulto necessario requiruntur ut dispositiones ex parte subjecti, non ut causæ activæ, non enim fides et pœnitentia efficiunt gratiam sacramentalem neque dant efficaciam sacramenti, sed solum tollunt obstacula, quæ impedirent, ne sacramenta suam efficaciam exercere possent, unde in pueris, ubi non requiritur dispositio, sine his rebus fit justificatio. Exemplum esse potest in re naturali. Si ad ligna comburenda primum exsiccarentur ligna, deinde excuteretur ignis ex silice, tum applicaretur ignis ligno et sic tandem fieret combustio : nemo diceret, causam immediatam combustionis esse siccitatem aut excussionem ignis ex silice aut applicationem ignis ad ligna, sed solum ignem ut causam primariam et solum calorem s. calefactionem ut causam instrumentalem. Cf.

Bossii *Institt. theol.* ii. 279, and what is said, Conc. Trid. sess. vi. cap. 6, as to the disposition in the adult towards baptism. According to this, the controversy in its main point would disappear; for, that their power indwells in the sacraments in virtue of the Lord's institution, Protestantism has never even distantly denied.[1] Meanwhile, 1. It has been shown that the Melanchthonian explanation of the *ex opere operato* had not been unusual before the Reformation in the schools of theology. 2. It appears that what is demanded of the recipient is rather something negative than positive, the *non ponere obicem*: cf. Conc. Trid. sess. vii. *sacr.* can. 6 (in peccato mortali non esse constitutum?). 3. Even admitted that this *non ponere obicem* must be interpreted of positive qualities, the faith demanded by the Roman teachers is not identical with the *faith* of Protestants. *Vide* Baur, *Gegensatz*, S. 299.)

The Greek Confessions contain nothing of an influence of the sacraments *ex opere operato*. Compare, on the contrary, the requirement of a firm faith in the communicant, Plato, *Catech.* p. 129.

Cat. Rom. ii. 1. 25: Ministri, quoniam in sacrâ illâ functione non suam, sed Christi personam gerunt, eâ re fit, ut, sive boni sive mali sint, modo eâ formâ et materiâ utantur, quam ex Christi instituto semper ecclesia catholica servavit, idque facere proponant, quod ecclesia in eâ administratione facit, vere sacramentum conficiant et conferant: ita, ut gratiæ fructum nulla res impedire possit, nisi, qui ea suscipiunt, se ipsos tanto bono fraudare et Spiritui sancto velint obsistere. Cf. ii. 4. 68.

Conf. Trid. sess. vii. sacram. can. 11: Si quis dixerit, in ministris, dum sacramenta conficiunt et conferunt, non requiri intentionem saltem faciendi, quod facit ecclesia, anath. sit.

(Bellarmin. *de sacram.* i. 27: Sententia Catholicorum est, requiri intentionem faciendi, quod facit ecclesia. Ita enim expresse habent concilium Tridentinum et concilium Florentinum in instructione Armenorum. Sunt autem hoc loco quædam notanda. Primo non ita requiri, ut minister habeat

---

[1] *Vide* esp. *Conf. Helv.* ii. cap. 19 : Sicut a dignitate vel indignitate ministrorum non æstimamus integritatem sacramentorum, ita neque a conditione sumentium. Agnoscimus enim, sacramentorum integritatem ex fide vel veritate meraque bonitate dei dependere.

intentionem generalem faciendi, quod facit ecclesia, ut non possit habere particularem: immo melius est habere particularem, id est, conferendi sacramentum baptismi, absolutionis cet. Sed qui non nosset nostra mysteria, satis esset, si in generali intenderet facere, quod facit ecclesia: et hoc docent evangelia. Secundo non est opus, intendere, quod facit ecclesia Romana, sed quod facit vera ecclesia, quaecunque illa sit, vel quod Christus instituit, vel quod faciunt Christiani: ista enim in idem recidunt. . . . Qui intendit facere, quod facit ecclesia Genevensis, intendit facere, quod fait ecclesia universalis, . . . quia putat illam esse membrum ecclesiae verae universalis. . . . Non tollit efficaciam sacramenti error ministri circa ecclesiam, sed defectus intentionis. Atque hinc est, quod in ecclesiâ catholicâ non rebaptizantur baptizati a Genevensibus. . . . Tertio non requiritur necessario actualis intentio, nec sufficit habitualis, (qualis etiam in dormiente inesse potest; . . . alioqui baptizatus diceretur, si quis a dormiente vel ebrio baptizatus esset) sed virtualis requiritur et sufficit, quamvis danda sit opera, ut actualis habeatur. . . . Virtualis dicitur, cum actualis intentio in praesenti non adest ob aliquam evagationem mentis, tamen paulo ante adfuit et in virtute illius fit operatio. Cf. Bossii *Institutt. theol.* ii. p. 334 sqq.)

Conf. orthod. p. 156: ὁ ἱερεὺς ἁγιάζει τὸ μυστήριον τῇ δυνάμει τοῦ ἁγίου πν., μὲ γνώμην ἀποφασισμένην τοῦ νὰ τὸ ἁγιάσῃ.

Conc. Trid. sess. vii. sacram. can. 12: Si quis dixerit, ministrum in peccato mortali exsistentem, modo omnia essentialia, quae ad sacramentum conficiendum aut conferendum pertinent, servaverit, non conficere aut conferre sacramentum: anathema sit. Cf. Klee, *kathol. Dogmat.* ii. 87 ff.

II. Protestant.

C. A. p. 13: Damnant igitur illos, qui docent, quod sacramenta *ex opere operato* justificent, nec docent, fidem requiri in usu sacramentorum, quae credat remitti peccata.

Apol. C. A. p. 203: Damnamus totum populum Scholasticorum doctorum, qui docent, quod sacramenta non ponenti obicem conferant gratiam *ex opere operato*, sine bono motu utentis. Hæc simpliciter judaica opinio est, sentire, quod per cerimoniam justificemur, sine bono motu cordis, hoc est sine fide. . . . At sacramenta sunt signa promissionum. Igitur in usu debet accedere fides.—Loquimur hic de fide speciali, quæ præsenti promissioni credit, non tantum, quæ in genere credit deum esse, sed quæ credit offerri remissionem peccatorum.

(*Conf. Bohem.* art. 11 : Docent, quod sacramenta per se vel ex opere operato his, qui prius bono motu non sunt præditi et intus per Spiritum sanctum vivificati, non conferunt gratiam nec fidem illam justificantem largiuntur. Præcedere enim fidem oportuit (de adultis loquimur), quæ hominem per Sp. s. vivificet et cordi bonos motus injiciat; sine fide enim . . . nec ulli sacramenta prosunt.)

Helv. ii. cap. 19 : Non approbamus istorum doctrinam, qui docent, gratiam et res significatas signis (sacram.) ita alligari et includi, ut quicunque signis exterius participent, etiam interius gratiæ rerumque significatarum participes sint, quales sint.—The positive side is laid down in many places: Habent Symbola (in sacram.) promissiones adjunctas, quæ requirunt fidem. . . . Sacramenta . . . manent vera et integra, . . . tametsi increduli res oblatas non percipiant. Fit hoc non dantis aut offerentis dei vitio, sed hominum sine fide illegitimeque accipientium culpâ.

Conf. Gall. art. 37 : Affirmamus, eos, qui ad sacram mensam domini puram fidem tanquam vas quoddam afferunt, vere recipere, quod sibi signa testificantur.

Conf. Scot. art. 21 : Totum hoc ex verâ fide Jesum Ch. apprehendente, qui solus facit sacramenta nobis efficacia, provenire dicimus.

Declar. Thorun. ii. 6. 4 : Non operantur sacr. aut conferunt gratiam ex opere operato sine bono motu utentis, sed virtute promissionis, quæ verâ fide acceptanda est.

West. Conf. ch. xxvii. sec. 3 : The grace which is exhibited in or by the sacraments, rightly used, is not conferred by any power in them ; neither doth the efficacy of a sacrament depend upon the piety or intention of him that doth administer it, but upon the work of the Spirit, and the word of institution ;

which contains, together with a precept authorizing the use thereof, a promise of benefit to worthy receivers.

Helv. ii. cap. 19 : Minime probamus eos, qui sanctificationem sacramentorum attribuunt nescio quibus characteribus et recitationi vel virtuti verborum pronuntiatorum a consecratore et qui habeat *intentionem consecrandi.*

Declar. Thorun. ii. 6. 5 : Efficacia sacramenti non pendet ab intentione ministri, modo in ipsâ actione s. administratione servetur formæ divinæ institutionis.

A. C. p. 12 : Sacramenta propter ordinationem et mandatum Ch. sunt efficacia, etiamsi per malos exhibeantur.

Apol. A. C. p. 144 : Non sacramenta ideo non sunt efficacia, quia per malos tractantur, imo recte uti possumus sacramentis, quae per malos administrantur.

Cf. *F. C.* p. 732.

Conf. Helv. ii. c. 19 : (Ut) fideles agnoscant, operari deum in suo instituto, ideoque sacramenta perinde ac ex ipsius dei manu percipere et ipsis ministri vitium, si quod insigne ipsi insit, non obesse, quando agnoscant, sacramentorum integritatem dependere ab institutione domini.

Thirty-nine Artt. art. xxvi.: Nevertheless, it appertaineth to the discipline of the church that inquiry be made of evil ministers, and that they be accused by those that have knowledge of their offences ; and finally, being found guilty, by just judgment be deposed.

The Lutheran Confessions contain no counter-statement as to Intention. But Protestantism, laying all the stress on the subjectivity of the recipient, does not apologize for or regard with indifference the evil character of the administrant who thoughtlessly dispenses the sacrament. As, according to our fundamental principles, the sacraments have not their effect *ex opere operantis* (administrantis), we may say in *this* sense that they effect their purpose *ex opere operato,* as even Bellarmine, *de bon. oper.* ii. 12, uses the phrase. But, on account of its ambiguity, Protestants have always avoided the term.

XV.

BAPTISM.

FIRST POINT OF DIVERGENCE.

ALL Christian communities, the Quakers excepted, hold baptism with water as applied by Christ to be a religious ordinance of perpetual obligation in the church. But they differ in many points, and with regard to this one. The Socinians believe that it was not ordained by Christ to be continual, and that, according to the usage of the apostles, it is to be administered only to those who pass over from outside Christianity to the Christian faith. The Romanists and Greeks and Protestants regard this sacrament as instituted by the Lord for perpetual observance, and to be administered to those born in Christendom as well as to those who enter it.

SOCINIAN SYMBOLS.

Cat. Rac. qu. 345 : Quid sentis de aquæ baptismo ? Id, quod sit ritus initiationis, quo homines, agnitâ Christi doctrinâ et susceptâ in eum fide, Christo auctorantur et discipulis ejus seu ecclesiæ inseruntur, renuntiantes mundo et moribus erroribusque ejus, profitentes vero, se patrem et filium et Spiritum sanctum, qui per apostolos locutus est, pro unico duce et magistro religionis totiusque vitæ et conversationis suæ habituros esse, ipsaque sui ablutione et immersione ac remersione declarantes ac veluti repræsentantes, se peccatorum sordes deponere, Christo consepeliri, proinde commori et ad vitæ novitatem resurgere velle, utque id reipsâ præstent sese obstringentes, simul etiam hoc professione et obligatione factâ symbolum et signum remissionis peccatorum ipsamque adeo remissionem accipientes (literally the same in the last revision).

Socin. *De bapt. aq.* c. 16, p. 734, b : Abunde probatum, non fuisse omnibus, qui Christi discipuli esse velint peræque et in perpetuum aquæ baptismum suscipiendi præceptum datum, et ob eam rem posse quempiam et nominari et revera esse Christianum, licet aquæ baptismum vel nunquam vel non rite, cum tamen posset, acceperit.—C. 17, p. 736, a : Quoniam passim receptum est, ut qui ecclesiæ annumerari debeant, aquæ baptismo sint tincti : tingantur porro aquæ baptismo omnes, qui pro jam tinctis non habentur ; nihil enim prohibet, quo minus id fieri possit, quamvis ut fiat, præceptum non fuerit. — P. 736, b : Dico censere me, ut quicunque ex Judæis vel Turcis vel aliis, qui J. Ch. religionem minime profitentur, ad ipsum Chr. convertuntur, in ipsius J. Ch. nomen omnino aquâ baptizentur ipsique eâ ratione initientur. Etsi enim eâ de re nullum expressum et perpetuum mandatum exstat, apostolos tamen qui id facere consueverunt, imitari decet.—P. 737, a : Porro qui infantes ex fratribus nati baptizati non fuerint, ii, quoniam ut dicimus, adhuc baptismum aquæ a nemine negligi debere, plerique omnes censent, omnino postquam ita adoleverint, ut suæ fidei rationem reddere possint, in J. C. nomen aquâ tingantur. *Opp.* i. p. 351, a.

Socinus, *De aq. bapt.*, seeks to show that Christ did not Himself (not even in Matt. xxviii. 19) institute baptism as a rite of initiation ; and that the apostles, without any command of Christ, applied it only to adult Jews and Gentiles, and not always to them.

SECOND POINT OF DIVERGENCE.

The Socinians regard baptism only as a ceremony by means of which the baptized publicly testifies his entrance into the

Christian church, and his assumption of all its obligations.[1] The Arminians and Mennonites discern in it further a figurative assurance of the divine grace. The Romanists, Greeks, and other Protestants, on the other hand, without denying to the sacrament the significance of a rite of reception and profession, attribute to it a divine energy for regeneration, and therefore hold it to be a means of grace. But with this difference: the Romanists and Greeks maintain that in baptism original sin is destroyed; while the Protestants, in accordance with their stricter view of original sin, teach that original sin still remains even in the baptized, though not as condemnable in the sight of God, or not regarded by Him as such, and not imputed.

SYMBOLICAL TESTIMONIES.

The Signification and Virtue of Baptism generally.

I. Socinian Symbols.

Cat. Rac. qu. 348 (last revision): Falluntur vehementer, (qui putant, homines ritu baptismi regenerari). Etenim regeneratio est rationis et voluntatis nostræ transmutatio et ad Christi doctrinam compositio, ut ipsa vox regeneratio indicat. Verum ejusmodi transformatio in infantibus locum habere nequit. Qui ignorant, quæ dextra et sinistra sit, tantum abest, ut res tanti momenti in eos cadat. Adultos vero, in quibus mentis et voluntatis transformatio locum habet, aquâ vel ritu regenerari posse, tantum a veritate abest, ut etiam videatur quidpiam hoc idololatriæ simile, cum aquæ vel ritui hoc vel adscribitur vel sine expressâ dei voluntate adstringitur, quod ipsi deo et sacro ejus verbo, eorum qui regenerandi sunt mentibus percepto, adscribi debet.

Compare, however, the following words of Socinus, *Disput.*

---

[1] Zwingli's somewhat similar view is expressed in the *Conf. ad Carolum V.* briefly thus: The matter in baptism is the union with the church and people of God. Baptism is a sacrament signifying, to wit, that the recipient belongs to the church: not that it makes him belong to it, but that it testifies to the people that he already belongs to it.

de bapt. aquæ, c. 7 (in *Opp.* i. 724): Considerandum est, me non negare, quin in bapt. aquæ post. Ch. resurrectionem instituto aliquid sit, quod ad peccatorum remissionem s. ad peccata delenda aliquo modo pertineat. Est enim in ipso, cum in J. Ch. nomine ministretur, publica et aperta J. C. nominis professio, quæ nullo pacto omitti debet, alioquin a peccatorum reatu liberatio non continget. Verum professio ista externæ illi ablutioni alligata non est, adeo ut etiam alio modo fieri non queat cet.—P. 744, b: Quod attinet ad peccatorum remissionem, eam per aquæ bapt. adumbratam quidem fuisse et dari quodam modo consuevisse, hoc ipso loco (Heb. vi. 1, 2) fatetur scriptura. Verum hoc posterius non aliâ ratione intelligendum est, quam id, quod de donatione Sp. s. per manuum impostionem commemorat, ut scil. res, quæ dabatur, nullo modo ipsi ritui externo alligata esset, nec ab ipsius vi aliquâ proficisceretur, quamvis, eâ cerimoniâ rite peractâ, ex div. benignitate omnino dari consuevisset.

II. ARMINIAN AND MENNONITE.

Conf. Remonstr. xxiii. 3: Baptismus est primus Novi Test. publicus et sacer ritus, in quo fœderati omnes (nullo aut ætatis, aut sexus discrimine) per solennem aquæ ablutionem ecclesiæ inseruntur et cultui divino initiantur, sive idcirco in nomen patris et filii et Spiritus sancti aquæ immerguntur vel aquâ abluntur, ut hoc veluti symbolico signo ac sacrâ tesserâ confirmentur de gratiosâ dei erga ipsos voluntate, quod sicut aqua sordes corporis abluuntur, ita ipsi per sanguinem et spiritum Christi (modo sua ipsorum culpa gratiosum hoc fœdus irritum non fecerint) intus purgandi, sive a reatu omnium peccatorum plenissime liberandi, et tandem gloriosâ filiorum dei immortalitate atque æternâ felicitate donandi sint; ac simul etiam ex alterâ parte ipsi obligentur, eoque palam declarent, se omnem salutem suam a solo deo et domino Jesu Christo, unico mediatore, sacerdote ac rege suo constanter exspectare, ipsi ex animo confidere, eique, abjectis peccatorum omnium sordibus atque inquinamentis, virtute Spiritus sancti per omnem vitam obedire velle. Cf. Limborch, *Theol. christ.* v. 67. 5.

Ris, Confess. art. 31, 32: Sacer baptismus est externa,

visibilis et evangelica actio, in quâ sec. Christi præceptum et praxin apostolorum ad finem sanctum aqua baptizantur, . . . qui doctrinam evangelii audiunt, credunt et libenter pœnitenti corde accipiunt. — Tota externi baptismi actio nobis ante oculos ponit, testatur et significat, J. Chr. pœnitentem et credentem hominem interne baptizare in lavacro regenerationis et renovatione Sp. sancti, abluens per virtutem et merita sanguinis sui effusi omnes animæ maculas atque peccata et per virtutem et operationem Sp. s., qui vera . . . aqua est, internam animæ malitiam redditque eam cœlestem, spiritualem cet. Cf. a. Cornelis, *Bekenntn.* art. vii.

III. Roman, Greek, Protestant.

Concil. Trid. sess. xiv. pœn. cap. 2 : Per baptismum Christum induentes nova prorsus in illo efficimur creatura, plenam et integram peccatorum omnium remissionem consequentes. Cf. sess. vi. cap. 7.

Cat. Rom. ii. 2. 5 : Recte et apposite definitur, baptismum esse sacramentum regenerationis per aquam in verbo. Naturâ enim ex Adam filii iræ nascimur, per baptismum vero in Christo filii misericordiæ renascimur. Cf. ii. 2. 42, 45. (More definitely Bellarmin, *Bapt.* c. 12 : Confert ex opere op. gratiam et dona divina, quibus vere et formaliter justificatur homo. Cf. Klee, *Dogmat.* iii. S. 106.)—*Ib.* ii. 2. 44 : Baptismi proprius effectus est peccatorum omnium, sive originis vitio sive nostrâ culpâ contracta sint, remissio.—45 : In baptismo non solum peccata remittuntur, sed peccatorum etiam et scelerum pœnæ omnes a deo benigne condonantur.—50. Exponendum est, hujus sacramenti virtute nos non solum a malis, quæ vere mala dicenda sunt, liberari, verum etiam eximiis bonis et muneribus augeri. Animus enim noster divinâ gratiâ repletur, qua justi et filii dei effecti æternæ quoque salutis heredes instituimur. Est autem gratia non solum, per quam peccatorum fit remissio, sed divina qualitas in anima inhærens . . ., quæ animarum nostrarum maculas omnes delet ipsasque animas pulchriores et splendidiores reddit.

Conf. orthod. p. 159 sq. : Τὸ βάπτισμα τόσην δύναμιν ἔχει, ὅπου ἔστωντας καὶ νὰ μὴ δίδεται δεύτερον, εἶναι ἀναμφίβολος σφραγὶς τῆς σωτηρίας τῆς αἰωνίου, καὶ ποῖος νὰ εἶναι ὁ καρπὸς καὶ τὸ κέρδος τοῦ μυστηρίου τούτου, εὔκολα καθ' ἕνας τὸ γνωρίζει. Διατὶ πρῶτον σικώνει ὅλα τὰ ἁμαρτήματα, εἰς μὲν τὰ βρέφη τὸ προπατορικόν, εἰς δὲ τοὺς μεγάλους καὶ τὸ προπατ. καὶ τὸ προαιρετικόν· δεύτερον ὁ ἄνθρωπος ἀνακαινίζεται καὶ ἀποκαθίσταται εἰς τὴν δικαίωσιν ἐκείνην, ὅπου εἶχεν ὅταν ἦτον ἀθῶος καὶ ἀναμάρτητος. . . . ἔπειτα οἱ βαπτισθέντες γίνουνται μέλη τοῦ σώματος τοῦ Χριστοῦ καὶ τὸν κύριον ἡμῶν ἐνδυόμεθα.

Cf. Jerem. *in Act. Wirtcmb.* p. 248.

Luth. *Cat. min.* p. 376: Baptismus operatur remissionem peccatorum, liberat a morte et a diabolo et donat æternam beatitudinem omnibus et singulis, qui credunt hoc, quod verba et promissiones divinæ pollicentur.—*Cat. maj.* p. 543: . . . quæcunque baptismo promittuntur et offeruntur, victoria nempe mortis ac diaboli, remissio peccatorum, gratia dei, Christus cum omnibus suis operibus et Sp. sanctus c. omnibus suis dotibus.

Conf. Helv. ii. cap. 20: Nascimur omnes in peccatorum sordibus et sumus filii iræ; deus autem purgat nos a peccatis gratuito per sanguinem filii sui et in hoc adoptat nos in filios . . . et variis donis ditat, ut possimus novam vivere vitam. Obsignantur hæc omnia baptismo; nam intus regeneramur, purificamur et renovamur a deo per Spiritum sanctum, foris autem accipimus obsignationem maximorum donorum in aquâ, qua etiam maxima illa beneficia repræsentantur et veluti oculis nostris conspicienda proponuntur.

Thirty-nine Artt. art. xxvii.: Baptism is not only a sign of profession, and mark of difference, whereby Christian men are decerned from others that be not christened; but it is also a sign of regeneration or new birth, whereby, as by an instrument, they that receive baptism rightly are grafted into the church; the promises of forgiveness of sin, and of our adoption to be the sons of God by the Holy Ghost, are visibly signed and sealed; faith is confirmed, and grace increased by virtue of prayer unto God. The baptism of young children is in any wise to be retained in the church, as most agreeable with the institution of Christ.

West. Conf. ch. xxviii. sec. 1: Baptism is a sacrament of

the New Testament, ordained by Jesus Christ, not only for the solemn admission of the party baptized into the visible church, but also to be unto him a sign and seal of the covenant of grace, of his ingrafting into Christ, of regeneration, of remission of sins, and of his giving up unto God through Jesus Christ, to walk in newness of life; which sacrament is, by Christ's own appointment, to be continued in His church until the end of the world. Sec. 2: The outward element to be used in this sacrament is water, wherewith the party is to be baptized in the name of the Father, and of the Son, and of the Holy Ghost, by a minister of the gospel, lawfully called thereunto. Sec. 3: Dipping of the person into the water is not necessary; but baptism is rightly administered by pouring or sprinkling water upon the person.

Conf. Gall. art. 35: Baptismus nobis testificandæ nostræ adoptioni datus, quoniam in eo inserimur Christi corpori, ut ejus sanguine abluti simul etiam ipsius spiritu ad vitæ sanctimoniam renovemur.

Catech. Genev. p. 522: Baptismi significatio duas partes habet. Nam ibi remissio peccatorum, deinde spiritualis regeneratio figuratur. . . . Annon aliud aquæ tribuis, nisi ut ablutionis tantum sit figura? Sic figuram esse sentio, ut simul annexa sit veritas. Neque enim sua nobis dona pollicendo nos deus frustratur. Proinde et peccatorum veniam et vitæ novitatem offerri nobis in baptismo et recipi a nobis, certum est.

Cf. *Catech. Heidelb. Fr.* 69 ff.; *Declar. Thorun.* p. 61.

THIRD POINT OF DIVERGENCE.

From the foregoing it will be assumed that the Romanists, Greeks, and most Protestants hold baptism necessary, that is, generally necessary to salvation. On that account they teach that even the children of Christians must be baptized. The Anabaptists and Mennonites entirely deny this, however; while the Arminians and Socinians hold it to be matter of indifference,—not necessary, but permissible and decent.

SYMBOLICAL TESTIMONIES.

I. Romish.

Conc. Trid. sess. v. 4 : Si quis parvulos recentes ab uteris matrum baptizandos negat, etiamsi fuerint a baptizatis parentibus orti, aut dicit, in remissionem quidem peccatorum eos baptizari, sed nihil ex Adam trahere originalis peccati, quod regenerationis lavacro necesse sit expiari ad vitam aeternam consequendam, unde fit consequens, ut in iis forma baptismatis in remissionem peccatorum non vera sed falsa intelligatur, anathema sit.

Ib. sess. vii. can. 5 : Si quis dixerit, baptismum liberum esse, hoc est non necessarium ad salutem, anathema sit.— Can. 12 : Si quis dixerit, neminem esse baptizandum, nisi eâ aetate quâ Christus baptizatus est, vel in ipso mortis articulo, anath. sit.—Can. 13 : Si quis dixerit, parvulos eo quod actum credendi non habent, suscepto baptismo inter fideles computandos non esse, ac propterea, cum ad annos discretionis pervenerint, esse rebaptizandos, aut praestare omitti eorum baptisma, quam eos non actu proprio credentes baptizari in sola fide ecclesiae, anath. sit.

Cat. Rom. ii. 2. 31 : Doceantur (fideles), omnibus hominibus baptismi legem a domino praescriptam esse, ita ut, nisi per baptismi gratiam deo renascantur, in sempiternam miseriam et interitum a parentibus, sive illi fideles sive infideles sint, procreentur.

Ib. ii. 2. 33 : Non dubitare licet, quin infantes fidei sacramenta, cum abluuntur, accipiant : non quia mentis suae assensione credant, sed quia parentum fide, si parentes fideles fuerint, sin minus, fide, (ut d. Augustini verbis loquamur), universae societatis sanctorum muniuntur. Etenim ab iis omnibus recte dicimus eos baptismo offerri, quibus placet, ut offerantur, et quorum caritate ad communionem sancti Spiritus adjunguntur.

II. Protestant.

A. C. p. 12 : De baptismo docent, quod sit necessarius ad

salutem, . . . et quod pueri sint baptizandi, qui per baptismum oblati deo recipiantur in gratiam dei.

Apol. A. C. p. 156: Certissimum est, quod promissio salutis pertinet etiam ad parvulos. . . . Igitur necesse est baptizare parvulos, ut applicetur iis promissio salutis, . . . quia salus cum baptismo offertur.

A. Sm. p. 329: De pædobaptismo docemus, infantes esse baptizandos. Pertinent enim ad promissam redemtionem per Christum factam, et ecclesia debet illis baptismum et promissionis illius annunciationem.

Conf. Helv. ii. c. 20: Damnamus Anabaptistas, qui negant baptizandos esse infantulos recens natos a fidelibus. Nam juxta doctrinam evang. horum est regnum dei et sunt in fœdere dei, cur itaque non daretur iis signum fœderis dei?

Conf. Gall. art. 35: Quamvis bapt. sit fidei et resipiscentiæ sacramentum, tamen cum una cum parentibus posteritatem etiam illorum in ecclesiâ deus recenseat, affirmamus, infantes sanctis parentibus natos esse ex Chr. auctoritate baptizandos.

Thirty-nine Artt. art. 27: Baptism is not only a sign of profession and mark of difference, whereby Christian men are discerned from others that be not christened, but it is also a sign of regeneration, or new birth, whereby, as by an instrument, they that receive baptism rightly are grafted into the church; the promises of forgiveness of sin, and of our adoption to be the sons of God by the Holy Ghost, are visibly signed and sealed; faith is confirmed, and grace increased by virtue of prayer unto God. The baptism of young children is in anywise to be retained in the church, as most agreeable with the institution of Christ.

West. Conf. ch. xxviii. sec. 4: Not only those that do actually profess faith in and obedience unto Christ, but also the infants of one or both believing parents, are to be baptized. Sec. 5: Although it be a great sin to contemn or neglect this ordinance, yet grace and salvation are not so inseparably annexed unto it, as that no person can be regenerated or saved without it, or that all that are baptized are undoubtedly regenerated. Sec. 6: The efficacy of baptism is not tied to that moment of time wherein it is administered; yet, notwithstanding, by the right use of this ordinance, the grace promised is not only offered, but really exhibited and conferred by the Holy Ghost, to such (whether of age or infants) as that grace belongeth unto, according to the counsel of God's own will, in His appointed time. Sec. 7: The sacrament of baptism is but once to be administered to any person.

Conf. Belg. art. 34: Credimus, omnem hominem, qui id satagit, ut vitam æternam consequatur, semel unico baptismo illo, qui in posterum non iteretur, baptizari debere.—(Infantes fidelibus parentibus natos) baptizandos et fœderis signo obsignandos esse credimus, sicuti olim infantes circumcidebantur in Israele propter easdem promissiones infantibus nostris factas cet.

Cf. *Cat. Heidelb. Fr.* 74; *Cat. Genev.* p. 524 sq.

The Salvation of Infants.

The necessity of baptism to salvation is carried so far by the Roman Catholic Church, that they regard Christian children unbaptized as forfeiting heavenly blessedness. Against this the *Conf. Scot.* expressly protests, nor does the *Declar. Thorun.* admit the absolute necessity of baptism. [The *Form. Conc.* does not pronounce definitively. However, the framers of that formula, in common with other dogmatic theologians, taught that not the deprivation, but the contempt, of the sacrament condemns.]

I. ROMAN.

Cat. Rom. ii. 2. 34: Hortandi sunt magnopere fideles, ut liberos suos, cum primum id sine periculo facere liceat, ad ecclesiam deferendos et solennibus cerimoniis baptizandos curent. Nam cum pueris infantibus nulla alia salutis comparandæ ratio, nisis eis baptismus præbeatur, relicta sit, facile intelligitur, quam gravi culpâ illi sese obstringant, qui eos sacramenti gratiâ diutius, quam necessitas postulet, carere patiantur cet.

Bellarmine, *Bapt.* i. 4, represents the question in controversy between Catholics and Protestants, whether baptism is necessary as a means of salvation, so that he who is not baptized perishes, notwithstanding the excuse of his neglect of the precept having sprung from ignorance. He asserts that the church has always believed that infants perish if they depart this life without baptism, and seeks further to demonstrate this faith of the church by copious argument, ending by this: Etiamsi parvuli sine suâ culpâ non baptizantur, non tamen sine suâ culpâ pereunt, cum habeant peccatum originale.— Though they are not guilty of neglecting baptism, they do not perish without guilt, for they have original sin. Cf. also Klee, *kath. Dogm.* iii. 114. As to the Limbus Infantum, see No. xvii.

II. PROTESTANT.

Conf. Scot. neg. p. 127: Detestamur crudele (rom. Antichristi) judicium contra infantes sine baptismo morientes.

Declar. Thorun. ii. 6, bapt. 2: Necessitatem baptismi adeo absolutam non statuimus, ut quicunque sine bapt. externo ex hac vitâ excesserit sive infans sive adultus, quocunque in casu etiam citra omnem contemtum accidat, propterea necessario damnandus sit. Hic potius regulam illam maxime valere credimus, quod non privatio sed contemtus sacramenti damnet.

Calvin, *Institt. christ.* iv. 16. 26: Explodendum esse eorum commentum palam est, qui omnes non baptizatos æternæ morti adjudicant. Solis ergo adultis administrari baptismum ex eorum postulato fingamus: quid puero fieri dicent, qui pietatis rudimentis rite probeque imbuitur, dum tinctionis dies appetit, si subitâ morte præter spem omnium abripi contingat? Clara est domini promissio, quicunque in filium credidit, non visurum mortem, nec in judicium venturum, sed transiisse a morte in vitam; nondum baptizatum nullibi damnasse comperitur. Quod in eam a me partem accipi nolo, perinde ac si baptismum contemni impune posse innuerem (quo contemtu violatum iri domini fœdus affirmo, tantum abest ut excusare sustineam), tantum evincere sufficit, non esse adeo necessarium, ut periisse protinus existimetur, cui ejus obtinendi ademta fuerit facultas. Atqui si eorum commento assentimur, eos omnes citra exceptionem damnabimus, quos a baptismo casus aliquis prohibuerit, quantacunque alioqui fide præditos, per quam Christus ipse possidetur. Insuper infantes omnes æternæ mortis reos peragunt, quibus baptismum negant suâ ipsorum confessione ad salutem necessarium. Viderint nunc, quam belle sibi cum Christi verbis conveniat, quibus regnum cœlorum illi ætati adjudicatur. Atque ut nihil illis non concedamus, quantum ad hujus loci intelligentiam attinet, nihil tamen inde elicietur, nisi prius, quod jam constitutum est a nobis, dogma de infantium regeneratione everterint. S. Heidegger, *Corp. theol.* xxv. 60 sq.

Cf. Limborch, *Theol. chr.* v. 68. 7.

Observations.

As it is the prevalent Protestant doctrine, that only believers experience the sacramental virtue of baptism (above, xiv. 3), the question naturally arose, whether baptized infants could have faith. In the symbols this point has never been discussed or set forth at length. But the older dogmatists taught, in harmony with Luther's well-known utterance, *Cat. Maj.* p. 546, that baptism itself wrought faith in infants. They appeal to Matt. xix. 13–15, xviii. 6; Mark xv. 16.

III. SOCINIAN.

Catech. Racov. p. 222 (final revision): Numquid ad baptismum infantes pertinent? Si quidem veteris apost. eccl. morem spectes et finem, in quem hic ritus fuit ab apostolis institutus, ad infantes non pertinet, cum in scripturis nec mandatum nec exemplum ullum hac de re habeamus, nec ipsi fidei in Chr. . . . adhuc capaces sint. . . . Tamen errorem (pædobaptismi) adeo inveteratum et pervulgatum christiana caritas tolerare suadet.

Socin. *Bapt. aquæ*, c. 17, p. 737, a: De eorum baptismo, qui ex parentibus pro fratribus agnitis et receptis nascuntur, ita statuo, ut, quando . . . non, vel si infantes baptizentur, id per se ipsum quidquam mali parere posse videtur, potestas unicuique fiat suos infantes vel baptizandi vel secus. . . . Hanc infantium suorum baptizandi vel non baptiz. libertatem ad eos etiam extendimus, qui tum primum ad Ch. ecclesiam sunt aggregandi.

IV. ARMINIAN.

Apolog. Remonstr. c. xxiii. p. 247: Remonstrantes ritum baptizandi infantes ut perantiquum . . . haud illubenter etiam in cœtibus suis admittunt adeoque vix sine offensione et scandalo magno intermitti posse statuunt; tantum abest, ut eum seu illicitum aut nefastum improbent ac damnent. Sed nec arbitrantur tamen propterea, eum ut præcise observatu necessarium vel ex præcepto Ch. vel ex traditione apost. vel aliâ aliquâ certâ atque indubitatâ auctoritate tenendum, urgendum aut imperandum esse.

Cf. Curcellæus, *De pecc. orig.* lvi. p. 913. Limborch, *Theol. christ.* v. 68. 19 sqq., although he zealously defends infant baptism against the Anabaptists, reaches the same issue. But he contends earnestly against the error that unbaptized Christian children are condemned (iii. 5. 2), and says: Omnes infantes, sicut per Adamum moriendi necessitati subjiciuntur, ita nostro judicio ex morte liberantur per Chr., sive baptizati sint sive non; non enim gratia div. ita huic signo alligata est, ut deus extra illud eam non communicet. John vii. 5 is referred to adults only.

V. ANABAPTIST.

As to the older Anabaptists, *vid. F. C.* 826. From the Mennonite symbols we extract a few notes:—

Ris, *Conf.* art. 31: Aquâ baptizantur in nomine patris et Sp. s., qui doctrinam sancti evangelii audiunt, credunt et libenter pœnitenti corde accipiunt. Tales enim jussit Christus baptizari, *sed neutiquam infantes.*

In the *Conf. of the Frisians and Germans* the baptism of adults is alone mentioned. And in the *Frank. Verh.* infant baptism is rejected, as not ordained by Christ: Infantes salvari absque baptismo per merita Christi, et nemini signum baptismi convenire quam credenti. Schyn, *P. D.* 236.

Horn. *Bek.* art. 21 (Germ.): The baptism of young and unintelligent infants is by good reasons rejected. We hold it for a plant of man from the kingdom of Antichrist, which ought to be clean rooted out, since nowhere in the New

Testament is it commanded, or any trace of it in the apostles' words or writings. It is, in truth, no other than a contempt and violation of Christ's true baptism, and in many respects its very antagonist.

Re-baptism, which was usual among the Anabaptists and Mennonites, is condemned, *A. C.* p. 12; *Apol.* 156; *F. C.* 623; *Conf. Helv.* ii. c. 20. It concerned partly those who, as the children of Christians, had already been baptized, but as adults entered their church, partly those who had been excommunicated or cast out of the Mennonite congregations. The re-baptism of these latter was soon abandoned by the Mennonites themselves as an unscriptural abuse. The rebaptism of the former, however, continued long a usage, but is now relinquished very generally by these churches. The *Confession of the Frisians* says only: Hominem sub conditione veræ pœnitentiæ et scripturæ conformis fidei semel baptizatum nunquam rebaptizamus.

VI. QUAKER.

The Quakers hold the baptism of infants to be a mere human tradition, of which there is neither example nor precept in the whole Scripture. Barclay, *Apol.* Prop. 12.

Observations.

I. HERETICAL BAPTISM.

The baptism of heretics, if performed in the name of the Holy Trinity, and with intention, is accepted as valid by the Roman and Greek Churches: *Conc. Trid.* sess. vii. can. 4; *Conf. orth.* 157. But in the Russian Church there prevailed for a long time the rebaptization of the converts: Heinecc. ii. 256. Even in the Roman Church, here and there zealous priests have thought fit to rebaptize their converts from Protestantism. The Protestant Church has never practised this. Sim. Episcop., *Resp. ad Dilemm.*, holds it for indifferent, whether those baptized in heresy be rebaptized or not. The validity of baptism performed in the Roman Church is expressly admitted in *Conf. Gall.* art. 28.

II. FORM OF BAPTISM.

The Greek Church has always adopted a triple immersion (κατάδυσις, καταδύεσθαι τρὶς ἐν τῷ ὕδατι). *Conf. orth.* p. 157; Metr. Critop.

Conf. 86; Jeremias, *in Actis*, 238. In the Western Church, Roman and Protestant, with the exception of the Baptists, sprinkling is alone adopted, although in *Cat. Maj.* p. 548 in aquam *mergi* is spoken of. The Greeks lay great stress on the immersion; but to the Westerns, the manner in which the water is applied to the baptized is matter of indifference. Cf. *Cat. Rom.* ii. 2. 17; Limborch, *Th. ch.* v. 68. Jeremias condemns in the Romanists their single sprinkling; but cf. Bossii *Inst. th.* ii. 380. The Socinians are opposed to sprinkling generally. *Cat. Rac.* p. 222.[1] Exorcism has been practised always by the Roman Church among the ceremonies of baptism; and the older Protestants retained it.

III. LAY BAPTISM.

The Roman, Greek, and Protestant Churches permit, under pressing circumstances, baptism by unordained hands, including those of the midwife, or even of persons not Christians. *Conf. orth.* p. 159 : εἰς καιρόν τινος ἀνάγκης ἠμπορεῖ νὰ τὸ κάμῃ τὸ μυστήριον τοῦτο καὶ κοσμικὸν πρόσωπον ἀνδρὸς ἢ γυναικός. *Cat. Rom.* ii. 2. 24 : Cogente necessitate baptizare possunt omnes etiam de populo sive mares sive fœminæ, quamcunque illi sectam profiteantur. Nam Judæis quoque, infidelibus et hæreticis cum necessitas cogit, hoc munus permissum est. But in these cases the baptismal ceremonies must be pretermitted. Bellarm. *De bapt.* i. 7; Gerhard, *Loc. theol.* ix. 95. The Reformed Church has declared against this baptism in distress. *Conf. Helv.* ii. 20; *Conf. Scot.* 22; Calvin, *Institt.* iv. 15.

IV. BAPTISM OF BELLS.

This, which is a kind of benediction, *vid. A. Smalc.* p. 337; *Conf. Scot. neg.* 127.

---

[1] Non recte dicis, eos infantes baptizare; non enim baptizant, quod sine totius corporis in aquam immersione et ablutione fieri nequit, sed verticetenus tantum leviter adspergunt . . . quem tamen errorem . . . christiana caritas tolerare suadet.

XVI.
THE LORD'S SUPPER.

FIRST POINT OF DIVERGENCE.

THE Christian communities which celebrate the Lord's Supper as a religious ordinance instituted by Christ, regard it either as a mere ceremony of thanksgiving and profession, or as a means of grace in which is imparted to the recipients some heavenly blessing. The former is the view of the Socinians, the Arminians, and the Mennonites. The latter is that of the Romanists, Greeks, and Protestants generally; although with many differences as to the definition of the nature of what is imparted.

SYMBOLICAL TESTIMONIES.

I. SOCINIAN.

Cat. Rac. qu. 334: (Cœna domini) est Christi institutum, ut fideles ipsius panem frangant et comedant et ex calice bibant, mortis ipsius annuntiandæ causâ. Quod permanere in adventum ipsius oportet.

Ib. qu. 335: (Annuntiare mortem domini) est publice ac sacrosancte Christo gratias agere, quod is pro ineffabili suâ erga nos caritate corpus suum torqueri et quodammodo frangi et sanguinem suum fundi passus sit, et hoc ipsius beneficium laudibus tollere et celebrare.

Ib. qu. 337: Nonne alia causa, ob quam cœnam instituit dominus, superest? Nulla prorsus. Etsi homines multas excogitarint, cum alii dicant esse sacrificium pro vivis et mortuis. Alii usu ipsius se consequi peccatorum remissionem et firmare fidem sperant, et quod eis mortem domini in mentem revocet, affirmant.

Ib. qu. 344: Verum sensum (verborum *hoc est corpus meum*) facile intelliges, si animadverteris, et in sacris literis et vulgo admodum esse usitatum, ut figuræ et imagines et signa memorialia appellentur earum rerum nominibus, quarum sunt imagines cet. Quare cum Ch. vellet hoc ritu a nobis annuntiari mortem suam cruentam cum quadam illius adumbratione et repræsentatione, ideo dixit, panem hunc, qui frangitur, esse corpus suum, . . . h. e. signum memoriale et figuram quandam esse corporis sui cet.

Socin. *De cœnâ dom.* p. 753 b: Quod omnes fere opinantur, hoc ritu . . . confirmari saltem fidem nostram, ne id quidem verum censeri debet, cum nec ullo sacro testimonio comprobetur nec ratio ulla sit, cur id fieri possit. Quomodo enim confirmare potest nos in fide id, quod nos ipsi facimus cet.— P. 754 b: Animadvertendum est, posse quidem in ipsâ cœnâ dom. celebrandâ confirmari et augeri fidem, sed non ex ipsâ panis et vini sumtione, nec ex virtute aliquâ divinâ . . ., sed ex mutuis cohortationibus mutuoque Ch. præceptis obedientiæ exemplo, ex solenni illâ commemoratione et concelebratione beneficiorum dei et Christi, et denique ab ipso divino verbo toti cerimoniæ adjuncto.

II. ARMINIAN.

Conf. Remonstr. xxiii. 4: S. cœna est alter Novi Test. sacer ritus, a Jesu Christo eâ quâ proditus fuit nocte institutus, ad celebrandum eucharisticam et solennem mortis suæ commemorationem, in quo fideles, postquam se ipsos explorarunt inque verâ fide approbarunt, sacrum panem in cœtu publice fractum edunt et simul vinum publice fusum bibunt, idque ad cruentam domini mortem pro nobis obitam (qua sicut corpora nostra cibo et potu seu pane et vino sustentantur, ita corda nostra in spem vitæ æternæ aluntur et nutriuntur) cum solenni gratiarum actione annuntiandum, suamque vicissim cum crucifixo Christi corpore et effuso sanguine (sive cum ipso Jesu Ch. pro nobis crucifixo et mortuo), eoque beneficiis omnibus per mortem Jesu Christi partis atque acquisitis, vivificam et spiritualem communionem et mutuam simul inter se caritatem coram deo et ecclesiâ publice testificandam. Against the orthodox Reformed doctrine, *vide* Limborch, *Theol. christ.* v. 71. 9 sqq.

Ris, *Conf.* art. 34: Tota externæ cœnæ actio nobis ante oculos ponit, testatur et significat, Christi sanctum corpus in cruce fractum . . . esse ad remissionem peccatorum nostrorum, illum jam in cœlis glorificatum animarum nostrarum esse panem vivificantem.—Per eam docemur inter externam illam actionem corda nostra sursum elevare sanctis supplicationibus, atque verum et summum bonum hac cœnâ adumbratum a Christo petere; tandemque nos adhortatur, ut deo agamus gratias atque unitatem et caritatem inter nos exerceamus.

III. Greek and Roman.

Conf. orthod. p. 169 sq.: Οἱ καρποὶ τοῦ μυστηρίου τούτου εἶναι τούτοι· πρῶτον ἡ ἀνάμνησις τοῦ ἀναμαρτήτου πάθους καὶ τοῦ θανάτου τοῦ Χριστοῦ . . . τὸ δεύτερον κέρδος εἶναι, διατὶ τὸ μυστ. τοῦτο γίνεται ἱλασμὸς καὶ καλοσύνημα πρὸς τὸν θεὸν διὰ τὰς ἁμαρτίας ἡμῶν εἴτε ζώντων εἴτε καὶ ἀποθαμένων . . . τὸ τρίτον διάφορον εἶναι ὅπου ὅποιος χριστιανὸς εὑρίσκεται παρὼν συχνὰ εἰς τὴν θυσίαν ταύτην καὶ νὰ κοινωνᾶ τοῦ μυστηρ. τούτου, ἐλευθερώνεται δι' αὐτοῦ ἀπὸ κάθα πειρασμὸν καὶ κίνδυνον διαβόλου cet.

Concil. Trid. sess. xiii. euchar. cap. 2: Sumi voluit Ch. sacramentum altaris tanquam spiritualem animarum cibum, quo alantur et confortentur viventis vitâ illius, qui dixit: qui manducat me cet (Joh. vi.) et tanquam antidotum, quo liberemur a culpis quotidianis et a peccatis mortalibus præservemur. Pignus præterea id esse voluit futuræ nostræ gloriæ et perpetuæ felicitatis adeoque symbolum unius illius corporis, cujus ipse caput exsistit cet.—Can. 5: Si quis dixerit vel præcipuum fructum eucharistiæ esse remissionem peccatorum vel ex eâ non alios fructus provenire, anath. sit.

Catech. Rom. ii. 4. 47 sqq.—Bellarmine, against the Protestants: Eucharistiam non remittere peccata mortalia, quorum homo conscientiam habet, et ideo requiri, ut antea purgentur (sacramento pœnitentiæ). We give a more precise statement than is generally found, from Bossii *Institutt. theol.* iii. p. 155 sq.: Primus effectus est augmentum gratiæ sanctificantis s. vitæ spiritualis, quod scholastici gratiam secundam vocant homini justo per modum nutritionis collatam; secundus est remissio peccatorum venialium (cf. *Cat. Rom.* ii. 4. 52), non autem mortalium; tertius est diminutio fomitis et concupiscentiæ; quartus perseverantia in justitiâ; quintus est remissio pœnæ tempor. peccato debitæ: accedentes enim ad ejusmodi sacram. commemoramus deo sacrificium illud, quo mirum in modum divina justitia delinita fuit per superabundantem satisfactionem; sextus est immortalitas carnis nostræ; septimus est suavitas, dulcedo ac delectatio mirifica, qua justorum animæ perfunduntur cet.

IV. PROTESTANT.

Apol. A. C. p. 99 : Instituta est cœna domini, ut recordatione promissionum Christi, quarum in hoc signo admonemur, confirmetur in nobis fides et foris confiteamur fidem nostram et prædicemus beneficia Christi.

Cat. maj. p. 555 : Ideo ad sacramentum (altaris) accedimus, ut ejusmodi thesaurum ibi accipiamus, per quem et in quo peccatorum remissionem consequamur. Siquidem propterea a Christo jubeor edere et bibere, ut meum sit mihique utilitatem adferat veluti certum pignus et arrabo, imo potius res ipsa, pro peccatis meis, morte et omnibus malis ille opposuit et oppignoravit.

Conf. Helv. ii. c. 21 : Retinere vult dominus ritu hoc sacro in recenti memoriâ maximum generi mortalium præstitum beneficium, nempe quod tradito corpore et effuso suo sanguine omnia nobis peccata nostra condonavit ac a morte æternâ et potestate diaboli nos redemit, jam pascit nos suâ carne et potat suo sanguine, quæ verâ fide spiritualiter percepta alunt nos ad vitam æternam. Et hoc tantum beneficium renovatur toties, quoties cœna domini celebratur. . . . Obsignatur item hac cœnâ s., quod revera corpus domini pro nobis traditum et sanguis ejus in remissionem peccatorum nostrorum effusus est, ne quid fides nostra vacillet. Et quidem visibiliter hoc foris sacramento per ministrum repræsentatur et veluti oculis contemplandum exponitur, quod intus in animâ invisibiliter per ipsum Spiritum s. præstatur.

Conf. Belg. art. 35: Convivium hoc mensa est spiritualis, in quâ Christus seipsum nobis cum omnibus bonis suis communicat efficitque, ut in illâ tam ipsomet, quam passionis mortisque ipsius merito fruamur, miseram nostram animam omnique solatio destitutam carnis suæ esu nutriens corroborans et consolans sanguinisque sui potu reficiens ac recreans.

Cat. Heidelb. Fr. 76: What is it to eat the crucified body, and to drink His shed blood? It is not only with believing hearts to appropriate the suffering and death of Christ, and thereby receive forgiveness and eternal life, but also to become more and more incorporated with His blessed body, through the Holy Ghost, who liveth at once in Him and in us.

Thus the main difference between the Romanists and Protestants in respect to the virtue of the Supper is this, that the Protestants refer it, though not alone, to the forgiveness of sins; while the Romanists, excluding the forgiveness, refer it to the grace of sanctification.

SECOND POINT OF DIVERGENCE.

The Confessions of the Protestant Churches differ from one another in this, that the Lutherans, like the Romanists and Greeks, teach a substantial presence of the body and blood of Christ in the Supper, and a corporeal participation of the same by the mouth under the bread and wine, or their forms. The Reformed Churches deny both.

[As it regards the positive doctrine of the Reformed, Zwingli contends against the presence of the body of Christ in the Supper, and any partaking of it. Calvin endeavoured to mediate between the Zwinglian view and that of the Augsburg Confession. He maintains, it is true, that the body of Christ is in heaven, and thus cannot be present in, with, and under the bread; but still he thinks that the believing soul rises to heaven in the participation of the bread and wine, and there unites itself with Christ. Calvin interprets the words of institution as Zwingli does, that the *is* means *signifies*, and, like him, contends against the notion that unbelievers partake in the Supper of the body and blood of Christ.] Before giving the testimonies of the symbols, we shall insert the teachings of Zwingli and Calvin from their private writings.

I. THE EUCHARISTIC DOCTRINE OF ZWINGLI AND CALVIN, AS TAKEN FROM THEIR WRITINGS.

Zwingli's views were pronounced in 1523, in the following words of the address sent by the Council of Zurich to pastors and preachers: "The Supper of the Lord is no other than a feast of the soul; and Christ instituted it as a remembrance of Himself. When a man entrusts himself to the passion and redemption of Christ, he is saved. A sure visible sign of this He has left in the emblems of His body and blood; and bids them both eat and drink in remembrance of Himself." Further, we may quote:

Zwingli, *De verâ et falsâ rel.* (*Opp.* iii. 263): Est ergo sive eucharistia sive synaxis sive coena dominica nihil aliud, quam commemoratio, quâ ii, qui se Christi morte et sanguine firmiter credunt patri reconciliatos esse, hanc vitalem mortem annunciant, hoc est laudant, gratulantur et prædicant. Jam ergo sequitur, quod qui ad hunc usum aut festivitatem conveniunt mortem domini commemoraturi, hoc est annunciaturi, sese unius corporis esse membra, sese unum panem esse ipso facto testentur. . . . Qui ergo cum Christianis commeat, quum mortem domini annunciant, qui simul symbolicum panem aut carnem edit, is nimirum postea secundum Christi præscriptum vivere debet, nam experimentum dedit aliis, quod Christo fidat; qui ergo eo fidunt, debent ambulare, sicut et ipse ambulavit.

Epist. ad princip. German. (*Opp.* ii. p. 545 b): In eucharistiâ res est, ex fide gratias agere domino pro beneficiis, quæ nos per filium suum redimendo præstitit; panis et vini sacrorum symbolorum divinis verbis sanctificatorum sumtio ejus rei sacramentum est; gratiarum ergo actio non est vel peccatorum remissio vel panis et vinum Christi corpus naturale, sed ea tantummodo significat atque in rem præsentem velut adducit repræsentando et contemplationi fidei offerendo.—P. 546 a: Cum panis et vinum, quæ ipsis domini verbis consecrata sunt, simul fratribus distribuuntur, an non jam totus Chr. velut sensibiliter (ut etiam si verba requirantur, plus dicam, quam vulgo solet) sensibus etiam offertur? Sed quomodo? anne corpus ipsum naturale, manibus et palato tractandum? Minime, sed animo offertur istud contemplandum, sensui vero sensibile ejus rei sacramentum.—P. 546 b: Nos nunquam negavimus, corpus Ch. sacramentaliter ac in mysterio esse in cœnâ, tum propter fidei contemplationem tum propter symboli, ut diximus, totam actionem.

Calvin, *Instit.* iv. 17. 10: Summa sit non aliter animas nostras carne et sanguine Christi pasci, quam panis et vinum corporalem vitam tuentur et sustinent. Neque enim aliter quadraret analogia signi, nisi alimentum suum animæ in Christo reperirent, quod fieri non potest, nisi nobiscum Christus vere in unum coalescat nosque reficiat carnis suæ esu et sanguinis potu. Etsi autem incredibile videtur in tantâ locorum distantiâ penetrare ad nos Christi carnem, ut nobis sit in cibum, meminerimus, quantum supra sensus omnes nostros emineat arcana Spiritus sancti virtus et quam stultum sit, ejus immensitatem modo nostro velle metiri. Quod ergo mens nostra non comprehendit, concipiat fides, spiritum vere unire, quæ locis disjuncta sunt. Jam sacram illam carnis et sanguinis sui communicationem qua vitam suam in nos transfundit Christus, non secus, ac si in ossa et medullas penetraret, in cœnâ etiam testatur et obsignat, et quidem non objecto inani aut vacuo signo, sed efficaciam spiritus sui illic proferens, qua impleat quod promittit. Et sane rem illic signatam offert et exhibet omnibus, qui ad spirituale illud epulum accumbunt, quanquam a fidelibus solis cum fructu percipitur, qui tantam benignitatem verâ fide animique gratitudine suscipiunt.—11: Dico igitur, in cœnæ mysterio per symbola panis et vini Christum vere nobis exhiberi adeoque corpus et sanguinem ejus, in quibus omnem obedientiam pro comparandâ nobis justitiâ adimplevit, quod scilicet primum in unum corpus cum ipso coalescamus, deinde participes substantiæ ejus facti, in bonorum omnium communicatione virtutem quoque sentiamus. —16: Alii fatentur, panem cœnæ vero substantiam esse terreni et corruptibilis elementi nec quidquam in se pati mutationis, sed sub se habere inclusum Chr. corpus. Si ita sensum suum explicarent, dum panis in mysterio porrigitur, annexam esse exhibitionem corporis, quia inseparabilis est a signo suo veritas, non valde pugnarem.—18 : *Si oculis animisque in cœlum evehimur, ut Christum illic in regni sui gloriâ quæramus, quemadmodum symbola nos ad cum integrum invitant, ita sub panis symbolo pascemur ejus corpore, sub vini symbolo distincte ejus sanguine potabimur,* ut demum toto ipso perfruamur. Nam tametsi carnem suam a nobis sustulit et corpore in cœlum ascendit, ad dextram tamen patris sedet, hoc est in potentiâ et majestate et gloriâ patris regnat. Hoc regnum nec ullis locorum spatiis limitatum nec ullis dimensionibus circumscriptum, quin Christus virtutem suam, ubicunque placuerit, in cœlo et in terra exserat, quin se præsentem potentiâ et virtute exhibeat.—19 : Nos vero talem Christi præsentiam in cœnâ statuere oportet, quæ nec panis elemento ipsum affigat nec in panem includat nec ullo modo circumscribat (quæ omnia derogare cœlesti ejus gloriæ, palam est), deinde quæ nec mensuram illi suam auferat vel pluribus simul locis distrahat vel immensam illi magnitudinem affingat, quæ per cœlum et terram diffundatur; hæc enim naturæ humanæ veritati non obscure repugnant. Istas, inquam, duas exceptiones nunquam patiamur nobis eripi: ne quid cœlesti Christi gloriæ derogetur quod fit, dum sub corruptibilia hujus mundi elementa reducitur, vel alligatur ullis terrenis creaturis; ne quid ejus corpori affingatur humanæ naturæ minus consentaneum, quod fit dum vel infinitum esse dicitur, vel in pluribus simul locis ponitur. Cæterum his absurditatibus sublatis, quicquid ad exprimendam veram *substantialemque* corporis ac sanguinis domini communicationem, quæ sub sacris cœnæ symbolis fidelibus exhibetur, facere potest, libenter recipio; atque ita ut non imaginatione duntaxat aut mentis intelligentia percipere, sed ut te ipsa frui in alimentum vitæ æternæ intelligantur.

II. SYMBOLICAL TESTIMONIES.

Conf. Basil. 7 (Germ.): As in baptism, wherein the washing away of sins is declared, water remains, so in the Lord's

Supper, wherein . . . the true body and blood of Christ is figured and offered, bread and wine remain. But we stedfastly hold that Christ Himself is the food of believing souls unto eternal life; and that our souls, through a true faith in the crucified Christ, are fed and refreshed by the flesh and blood of Christ; and thus that we, members of His body who is our Crown, Head, live in Him, and He in us. And therefore we confess that Christ in His holy Supper is present to all those who truly believe; [and conclude that the natural and true body of Christ, which was born of the pure Virgin, suffered for us, and ascended to heaven, is not in the bread and wine given by the Lord.]

Wahrh. Bek. der D. d. K. in Zurich, 1545: "We teach that the remembrance of the body offered and blood shed for the forgiveness of sins, is the great substance and end of the Supper, and that the great hope of the sacrament reaches simply to that. But this remembrance cannot be without a true faith. And although the things of which we preserve the remembrance cannot be again corporeally seen or become present, not the less is renewed therein. The believing apprehension and the assurance of faith make in some sense present to the believing mind the past transactions of our soul's redemption. He hath verily eaten the flesh of Christ . . . who truly believeth in Christ, God and man, for us crucified, whose faith is eating, and whose eating is faith. . . . Believers have in the Supper no other lifegiving food than they have without it. . . . The believer there and not there receives in *one* manner and in one *way* of faith *one* food, which is Christ: save that in the Supper the act is performed and the sign observed according to the command of Christ, with testimony and thanksgiving and consecration to duty. . . . Christ's flesh accomplished our salvation on earth; it is no more conversant on earth; it is not here below."

Conf. Helv. i. art. 22: . . . cœnam mysticam (esse), in quâ dominus corpus et sanguinem suum, i. e. se ipsum suis vere ad hoc offerat, ut magis magisque in illis vivat et illi in ipso; non quod pani et vino corpus domini et sanguis vel naturaliter uniantur vel hic localiter includantur vel ullâ huc carnali præsentiâ statuantur, sed quod panis et vinum ex institutione

domini symbola sint, quibus ab ipso domino per ecclesiæ
ministerium vera corporis et sanguinis ejus communicatio
non in periturum ventris cibum sed in æternæ vitæ alimoniam
exhibeatur.

Conscns. Trigur. No. 21 : Tollenda est quælibet localis
præsentiæ imaginatio. Nam quum signa hic in mundo sint,
oculis cernantur, palpentur manibus : Christus quatenus homo
est, non alibi quam in cœlo, nec aliter quam mente et fidei
intelligentiâ quærendus est. Quare perversa et impia superstitio est, ipsum sub elementis hujus mundi includere.

Ib. No. 22 : Proinde, qui in solennibus cœnæ verbis : hoc
est corpus meum, hic est sanguis meus, præcise literalem, ut
loquuntur, sensum urgent, eos tanquam præposteros interpretes
repudiamus. Nam extra controversiam ponimus, figurate accipienda esse, ut esse panis et vinum dicantur id quod significant. Neque vero novum hoc aut insolens videri debet, ut
per metonymiam ad signum transferatur rei figuratæ nomen,
quum passim in scripturis ejusmodi locutiones occurrant, et
nos sic loquendo nihil asserimus ; quod non apud vetustissi-
mos quosque et probatissimos ecclesiæ scriptores exstet.—No.
23 : Quod autem carnis suæ esu et sanguinis potione, quæ hic
figurantur, Christus animas nostras per fidem Spiritus sancti
virtute pascit, id non perinde accipiendum, quasi fiat aliqua
substantiæ vel commixtio vel transfusio, sed quoniam ex
carne semel in sacrificium oblatâ et sanguine in expiationem
effuso vitam hauriamus.—[No. 25 : *Quia—corpus Christi, ut
fert humani corporis natura et modus, finitum est et cœlo, ut
loco continetur, necesse est a nobis tanto locorum intervallo
distare, quanto cœlum abest a terrâ.* And in the same Conf.,
in Niemeyer, S. 15 : *Abest igitur Christus a nobis secundum
corpus;* spiritu autem suo in nobis habitans, in cœlum ad se
ita nos attollit, ut vivificum carnis suæ vigorem in nos trans-
fundat. . . . Sensus pietatis clare dictat, non aliter vitam ex
carne suâ in nos stillare, quam dum, *totus secundum corpus in
cœlo manens, ad nos suâ virtute descendit.*]

Conf. Gall. art. 36 : Quamvis (Christus) nunc sit in cœlis,
ibidem etiam mansurus donec veniat mundum judicaturus,
credimus tamen, eum arcanâ et incomprehensibili spiritus sui
virtute nos nutrire et vivificare sui corporis et sanguinis (sub-

stantiâ) per fidem apprehensâ. Dicimus autem hoc spiritualiter fieri, non ut efficaciæ et veritatis loco imaginationem aut cogitationem supponamus, sed potius, quoniam hoc mysterium nostræ cum Christo coalitionis tam sublime est, ut omnes nostros sensus totumque adeo ordinem naturæ superet, denique quoniam cum sit divinum ac cœleste, non nisi fide percipi et apprehendi potest.—Art. 37 : Affirmamus, eos, qui ad sacram mensam domini puram fidem afferunt, vere recipere, quod sibi signa testificantur, nempe corpus et sanguinem J. Ch. cet.

Conf. Helv. ii. c. 21 : Ut rectius et perspicacius intelligatur, quomodo caro et sanguis Christi sint cibus et potus fidelium percipianturque a fidelibus ad vitam æternam, paucula hæc adjiciemus. Manducatio non est unius generis. Est enim manducatio corporalis, qua cibus in os percipitur ab homine, dentibus atteritur et in ventrem deglutitur. Hoc manducationis genere intellexerunt olim Capernaitæ sibi manducandam carnem domini, sed refutantur ab ipso Joan. 6. Nam, ut caro Christi corporaliter manducari non potest citra flagitium aut truculentiam, ita non est cibus ventris. Est et spiritualis manducatio corporis Christi, non eâ quidem, existimemus cibum ipsum mutari in spiritum, sed quâ manente in suâ essentiâ et proprietate corpore et sanguine domini ea nobis communicantur spiritualiter, utique non corporali modo, sed spirituali per Spiritum sanctum, qui videlicet ea, quæ per carnem et sanguinem domini pro nobis in mortem tradita, parata sunt, ipsam inquam remissionem peccatorum, liberationem et vitam æternam, applicat et confert nobis, ita ut Christus in nobis vivat et nos in ipso vivamus, efficitque ut ipsum, quo talis sit cibus et potus spiritualis noster, id est vita nostra, verâ fide percipiamus. Sicut enim cibus et potus corporalis corpora nostra non tantum reficiunt ac roborant, sed et in vitâ conservant, ita et caro Christi tradita pro nobis et sanguis ejus effusus pro nobis non tantum reficiunt et roborant animas nostras, sed etiam in vitâ conservant, non quatenus quidem corporaliter nobis a spiritu dei communicantur, dicente domino : Et panis, quem ego dabo, caro mea est, quam dabo pro mundi vita. Caro (nimirum corporaliter manducata) non prodest quidquam, spiritus est, qui vivificat.—Et hic esus carnis et potus sanguinis domini ita est necessarius ad salutem, ut sine ipso nullus servari possit. Fit autem hic esus et potus spiritualis etiam extra domini cœnam et quoties aut ubicunque homo in Christum crediderit.

Ib. c. 21 : Præter superiorem manducationem spiritualem est et sacramentalis manducatio corporis domini, quâ fidelis non tantum spiritualiter et interne participat vero corpore et sanguine domini, sed foris etiam accedendo ad mensam domini accipit visibile corporis et sanguinis domini sacramentum. Prius quidem, dum credidit fidelis, vivificum alimentum percepit et ipso fruitur adhuc, sed ideo, dum sacramentum quoque accipit, nonnihil accipit. Nam in continuatione communicationis corporis et sanguinis domini pergit, adeoque magis magisque incenditur et crescit fides ac spirituali alimoniâ reficitur. Dum enim vivimus, fides continuas habet accessiones. Et qui foris verâ fide sacramentum percipit, idem ille non signum duntaxat percipit, sed re ipsâ quoque, ut diximus, fruitur.

Conf. Belg. art. 35 : Christus testificatur, nos, quam vere hoc sacramentum manibus nostris accipimus et tenemus illudque ore comedimus et bibimus, unde postmodum vita nostra sustentatur, tam vere etiam nos fide (quæ animæ nostræ et manus et os est) in animis nostris recipere verum corpus et verum sanguinem Christi, unici servatoris nostri, ad vitam nostram spiritualem. Nequaquam erraverimus dicentes, id quod comeditur esse proprium et naturale corpus Christi, idque quod bibitur proprium esse sanguinem. At manducandi modus talis est, ut non fiat ore corporis, sed spiritu per fidem.

Conf. Angl. p. 94 : Panem et vinum dicimus esse sacra et cœlestia mysteria corporis et sanguinis Christi, et illis Christum ipsum, verum panem æternæ vitæ, sic nobis præsentem exhiberi, ut ejus corpus sanguinemque per fidem vere sumamus. Non tamen id ita dicimus, quasi putemus, naturam panis et vini prorsus immutari atque abire in nihilum, quemadmodum multi proximis istis seculis somniarunt neque adhuc potuerunt unquam satis inter se de suo somnio convenire.— P. 95 : Nec tamen, quum ista dicimus, extenuamus cœnam domini, aut eam frigidam tantum cerimoniam esse docemus et in eâ nihil fieri, quod multi nos docere calumniantur. Christum enim asserimus vere sese præsentem exhibere ... in cœnâ, ut eum fide et spiritu comedamus et de ejus cruce ac sanguine habeamus vitam æternam. Idque dicimus non perfunctorie et frigide, sed re ipsâ et vere fieri. Etsi enim Christi corpus dentibus et faucibus non attingimus, eum tamen fide, mente, spiritu tenemus et premimus. Neque vero vana ea fides est, quæ Christum complectitur, nec frigide percipitur, quod mente, fide, et spiritu percipitur. Ita enim nobis in illis mysteriis Christus ipse totus, quantus quantus est, offertur et traditur, ut vere sciamus, esse jam nos carnem de ejus carne et os de ossibus ejus, et Christum in nobis manere et nos in illo.— *Thirty-nine Artt.* art. xxviii.: The body of Christ is given, taken, and eaten in the Supper, only after a heavenly and spiritual manner; and the mean whereby the body of Christ is received and eaten in the Supper is faith.

West. Conf. ch. xxix. sec. 7: Worthy receivers, outwardly partaking of the visible elements in this sacrament, do then also inwardly by faith, really and indeed, yet not carnally and corporally, but spiritually, receive and feed upon Christ crucified, and all benefits of His death: the body and blood of Christ being then not corporally or carnally in, with, or under the bread and wine; yet as really, but spiritually, present to the faith of believers in that ordinance, as the elements themselves are to their outward senses.—8: Although ignorant and wicked men receive the outward elements in this sacrament, yet they receive not the thing signified thereby; but by their unworthy coming thereunto are guilty of the body and blood of the Lord, to their own damnation. Wherefore all ignorant and ungodly persons, as they are unfit to enjoy communion with Him, so are they unworthy of the Lord's table, and cannot, without great sin against Christ, while they remain such, partake of these holy mysteries, or be admitted thereunto.

Conf. Scot. art. 21: Credimus . . ., quod in cœnâ domini rite usurpatâ Chr. ita nobis conjungitur, quod sit ipsissimum animarum nostrarum nutrimentum et pabulum, non quod panis in naturale Ch. corpus . . . transsubstantiationem ullam imaginemur . . ., sed unio hæc et conjunctio, quam habemus cum corpore et sanguine J. C. . . ., operatione Sp. s. efficitur, qui nos verâ fide supra omnia quæ videntur quæque carnalia et terrestria sunt, vehit et ut vescamur corpore et sanguine J.

Ch. semel pro nobis effusi et fracti efficit, quodque nunc est in cœlo, et in præsentiâ patris pro nobis apparet. Et quamvis magna sit loci distantia inter corpus ipsius nunc in cœlis glorificatum et nos nunc in his terris mortales, nihilominus tamen firmiter credimus, panem quem frangimus, esse communionem corporis cet. Sic, quod fideles in recto usu cœnæ dom. ita edere corpus et bibere sanguinem J. Ch. confitemur, et certo credimus, quod ipse in illis et illi in ipso manent, imo ita fiunt caro de carne et os de ossibus ejus, quod sicut æterna deitas carni J. Ch. vitam et immortalitatem tribuit, ita etiam caro et sanguis ejus, dum a nobis editur et bibitur, easdem nobis prærogativas confert.

Cat. Gen. p. 525 sqq.: Cœna s. ideo a Chr. instituta est, ut corporis et sanguinis sui communicatione educari in spem vitæ æt. animas nostras nos doceret idque nobis certum redderet. — Nam cum in eo sita sit tota salutis nostræ fiducia, ut accepta nobis feratur obedientia ipsius, quam patri præstitit, perinde ac si nostra foret: ipsum a nobis possideri necesse est. Neque enim bona nobis sua aliter communicat, nisi dum se nostrum facit. — Illa communicatio (in c. s.) nobis confirmatur et augetur. Tametsi enim tum in baptismo tum evangelio nobis exhibetur Christus, eum tamen non recipimus totum sed ex parte tantum. Quid ergo in symbolo panis habemus? Corpus Ch., ut semel pro nobis ad nos deo reconciliandos immolatum fuit, ita nunc quoque nobis dari, ut certo sciamus, reconciliationem ad nos pertinere. . . . Cum dominus Chr. ipsa sit veritas, minime dubium est, quin promissiones, quas dat illic nobis, simul etiam impleat et figuris suam addat veritatem. Quam ob rem non dubito, quin, sicuti verbis et signis testatur, ita etiam suæ nos substantiæ participes faciat, quo in unam cum eo vitam coalescamus. — Hoc mirifica arcanaque spiritus sui virtute efficit, cui difficile non est sociare, quæ locorum intervallo alioqui sunt disjuncta.

Catech. Heidelb. Fr. 76: What is it to eat the crucified body of Christ, and to drink His shed blood? It means, not only with thankful hearts to appropriate the passion of Christ, and thereby receive forgiveness of sins and eternal life, but also and therein, through the Holy Ghost, who dwelleth in Christ and in us, to be more and more united to His blessed body;

so that, although He is in heaven, and we are upon earth, we nevertheless are flesh of His flesh and bone of His bones, and live for ever one spirit with Him.

Confess. Palat. p. 152 sq.: Credo, in sacrâ cœnâ credentibus non minus quam discipulis in primâ cœnâ verum traditumque et crucifixum Ch. corpus una cum omnibus ejus cœlestibus thesauris et donis, quæ suâ morte suis acquisivit, ut sit famelicæ ipsorum animæ cibus, . . . a Ch. ipso porrigi et distribui. . . . Credentes nihil impedit distantia loci, quo minus corpus illud Ch. edamus et sanguinem ejus bibamus, etiamsi Ch. illo ipso naturali suo corpore nunc non sit amplius in terris cet. Sufficit scire nos ex ejus verbo, ipsum suo illo corpore neque visibili neque invisibili, neque comprehensibili neque incomprehensibili modo in terris esse velle, et tamen nihilo minus tanquam omnipotens dei filius et semper et ubique suâ gratiâ et Sp. sancto præsto est suis, imprimis autem in sacrâ suâ cœnâ, ubi ipse et cibi præbitor et cibus ipse est.

Declar. Thor. p. 61: Nequaquam statuimus nuda, vacua, inania signa, sed potius id quod significant et obsignant simul exhibentia, tanquam certissima media et efficacia instrumenta, per quæ corpus et sanguis Christi adeoque Christus ipse, cum omnibus suis beneficiis, singulis vescentibus exhibetur seu offertur, credentibus vero confertur, donatur et ab ipsis in cibum animæ salutarem et vivificum acceptatur.—Nequaquam etiam negamus veram corporis et sanguinis Christi in cœnâ præsentiam, sed tantum localem et corporalem præsentiæ modum et unionem cum elementis substantialem, ipsam vero nobiscum præsentiam sancte credimus, et quidem non imaginariam, sed verissimam, realissimam et efficacissimam, nempe ipsam illam Christi nobiscum unionem mysticam, quam ipsemet, ut per verbum promittit et per symbola offert, ita per spiritum efficit, quamque nos per fidem acceptamus, per caritatem sentimus, secundum vetus illud dictum: motum sentimus, modum nescimus, præsentiam credimus. — Unde et patet, non solam virtutem, efficaciam, operationem aut beneficia Christi nobis præsentari et communicari, sed inprimis ipsam substantiam corporis et sanguinis Christi seu ipsam illam victimam, quæ pro mundi vitâ data est et in cruce mactata, ut per fidelem hujus victimæ communionem et cum Christo ipso unionem consequenter etiam meritorum et beneficiorum sacrificio ejus partorum participes simus et sicut ipse in nobis, ita nos in ipso maneamus.—Et quidem non tantum quoad animam, sed etiam quoad corpus nostrum, etsi enim, ut ore corporis rem terrenam, ita fide cordis ceu organo proprio rem cœlestem acceptamus, tamen fide illâ mediante non solum animæ, sed et ipsa corpora nostra Christi corpori per ejusdem spiritum ad spem resurrectionis et vitæ æternæ inseruntur et uniuntur, ut simus caro de carne ejus et os de ossibus ejus adeoque unum cum ipso corpus mysticum.

Confess. Brand. 8: Two things are found there: the external signs, and the true body of Christ which was given to death for us, with the sacred blood, which was also poured out for us. These are partaken of in a double manner also,—the bread and wine with the mouth, the true body and blood properly only by faith. The words of institution make no difference to the bread and wine which still remain: these are His holy body and blood sacramentally, in the same way as God instituted and appointed the holy sacraments of both the Old and the New Testaments, that they might be His visible and true signs of invisible grace. And the Lord Christ Himself shows that the Holy Supper is a sign, yet not a bare and empty sign, of the new covenant, instituted in remembrance of Christ; or, as the Apostle Paul, 1 Cor. xi. 26, declares, for an abiding memorial and setting forth of His death, that it might be a remembrance of consolation, of thanksgiving, and of love.—9: And inasmuch as faith is the mouth, as it were, by which the crucified body and His poured-out blood are taken and received, Sr. Churf. Gn. strongly insist that to the unbelievers and impenitent such a sacrament signifies nothing; they are not partakers of the true body and blood of Christ.

The Reformed doctrine of the Supper cannot be any further illustrated from the documents; and, in fact, the manifold particular Confessions which the literature of the Reformed Church contains on this dogma, present nothing different from what these universal Confessions exhibit. We mention only two of these particular Confessions. The one is a fundamental account of the Supper of the Lord drawn from the clear writings of Scripture, of the early church, and compared with the

Augsburg Confession, by theologians of the University of Heidelberg, 1574. The other is the *Apologia modesta* of the Swiss churches, 1575, which is a defence against the Articles on the Supper, issued at Torgau, and printed 1574.

THIRD POINT OF DIVERGENCE.

Those Confessions which maintain a real presence of the body of Christ in the Supper are again once more divided. 1. The Roman and Greek Churches assert a change of the substance of the bread and wine, consequent upon the consecration of the priest, into the substance of the body and blood of Christ, the result of which only the *accidens* of the elements remain. 2. The Lutheran Church, however, teaches only a presence of the body and blood of Christ—further not capable of explanation, being sacramental, and wrought by the omnipotence of God—in, with, and under the bread and wine, which, as received, retain their substance.

SYMBOLICAL TESTIMONIES.

I. Roman Catholic.

Conc. Trid. sess. xiii. eucharist. cap. 4: Quoniam Christus redemtor noster corpus suum id, quod sub specie panis offerebat, vere esse dixit, ideo persuasum semper in ecclesiâ dei fuit, idque nunc denuo sancta hæc synodus declarat, per consecrationem panis et vini conversionem fieri totius substantiæ panis in substantiam corporis Christi, et totius substantiæ vini in substantiam sanguinis ejus: quæ conversio convenienter et proprie a sanctâ catholicâ ecclesiâ *transsubstantiatio* est appellata.

Ib. cap. 1: Principio docet synodus in almo sanctæ eucharistiæ sacramento post panis et vini consecrationem Jesum Christum, verum deum atque hominem, vere, realiter ac substantialiter sub specie illarum rerum sensibilium contineri; nec enim hæc inter se pugnant, ut ipse salvator noster semper ad dexteram patris in cœlis assideat juxta modum exsistendi naturalem, et ut multis nihilominus aliis in locis sacramentaliter præsens suâ substantiâ nobis adsit, eâ exsistendi ratione, quam etsi verbis exprimere vix possumus, possibilem tamen esse deo, cogitatione per fidem illustratâ assequi possumus et constantissime credere debemus.

Ib. can. 2 : Si quis dixerit, in sacrosancto eucharistiæ sacramento remanere substantiam panis et vini, una cum corpore et sanguine Jesu Christi, negaveritque mirabilem illam et singularem conversionem totius substantiæ panis in corpus et totius substantiæ vini in sanguinem, manentibus duntaxat speciebus panis et vini, quam quidem conversionem catholica ecclesia aptissime *transsubstantiationem* appellat, anathema sit.

Cat. Rom. ii. 4. 37 : Docebunt (pastores), panis et vini substantiam in sacramento (euchar.) post consecrationem non remanere. Hoc vero quamvis maximam admirationem merito habere possit, tamen cum eo, quod prius demonstratum est, necessario conjungitur. Etenim si est verum Chr. corpus sub panis et vini specie post consecrationem, omnino necesse est, cum ibi antea non esset, hoc vel loci mutatione vel creatione vel alterius rei in ipsum conversione factum esse. At vero fieri non posse constat, ut corpus Ch. in sacramento sit, quod ex uno in alium locum venerit. Ita enim fieret, ut a cœli sedibus abesset, quoniam nihil movetur, nisi locum deserat, a quo movetur. Creari autem corpus Ch. minus credibile est ac ne in cogitationem quidem cadere hoc potest ; relinquitur ergo, ut in sacramento sit corpus domini, quod panis in ipsum convertatur. Quare nulla panis substantia remaneat necesse est. Cf. 41, 26. . . . A marvellous deduction from this change is thus stated in qu. 45, perpetua et constans cathol. eccl. doctrina : Cum demonstratum sit, corpus dom. et sanguinem vere in sacramento esse, ita ut amplius nulla subsit panis et vini substantia, quoniam ea accidentia, Ch. corpori et sanguini inhærere non possunt, relinquitur, ut supra omnem naturæ ordinem ipsa se nullâ aliâ re nisa sustentent.

II. GREEK.

Down to the unsettlement of faith occasioned by Cyril Lucar, there was in the Greek Orthodox Church only the doctrine of the early Greek Fathers on the Eucharist, with the ancient and customary formulas; and the explanatory comments of Jeremias will not mislead any who are familiar with that doctrine and its phraseology, into the notion that this divine had in his thoughts any proper transubstantiation, or any change of the sacramental elements whereby the substance of the latter should cease to exist. Cf. Heinecc. ii. 278.

Jerem. *in Act. Wirtemb.* p. 86 : Δοξάζει ἡ καθολικὴ ἐκκλησία, ὅτι μετὰ τὸν ἁγιασμὸν ὁ μὲν ἄρτος μεταβάλλεται εἰς αὐτὸ τὸ σῶμα τοῦ Χριστοῦ, ὁ δὲ οἶνος εἰς αὐτὸ τὸ αἷμα, διὰ πνεύματος ἁγίου. Ὁ γὰρ κύριος τῇ νυκτὶ ᾗ παρεδίδοτο, λαβὼν ἄρτον . . . ἔκλασε καὶ εἶπε . . . οὔτε μὴν τότε δοθείσης τῆς σαρκὸς τοῦ κυρίου, ἣν ἐφόρει, εἰς βρῶσιν τοῖς ἀποστόλοις, . . . ἢ νῦν ἐν τῇ θείᾳ μυσταγωγίᾳ καταβαίνοντος τοῦ κυριακοῦ σώματος ἐξ οὐρανοῦ . . ., ἀλλὰ καὶ τότε καὶ νῦν μεταποιούμενον καὶ μεταβαλλόμενον τῇ ἐπικλήσει καὶ χάριτι τοῦ πνεύματος διὰ τῶν θείων καὶ ἱερῶν εὐχῶν καὶ λογίων, τοῦ μὲν ἄρτου εἰς αὐτὸ τὸ κυρίου σῶμα, τοῦ δὲ οἴνου εἰς αὐτὸ τὸ κυρίου αἷμα. Cf. p. 102.

Still more simply does Metr. Critop. express himself, but not hinting at any change. *Confess.* p. 100 : Ἔστι ὡς ἀληθῶς σῶμα Χριστοῦ ὁ ἱερουργούμενος ἄρτος, καὶ τὸ ἐν τῷ ποτηρίῳ αἷμα Χριστοῦ ἀναμφιβόλως· ὁ δὲ τρόπος τῆς τοιαύτης μεταβολῆς ἄγνωστος ἡμῖν καὶ ἀνερμήνευτος· τεταμίευται γὰρ τοῖς ἐκλεκτοῖς ἡ περὶ τῶν τοιούτων σαφήνεια ἐν τῇ βασιλείᾳ τῶν οὐρανῶν, ἵνα διὰ τῆς ἁπλῆς καὶ ἀπεριέργου πίστεως μείζονος χάριτος τύχοιεν παρὰ τοῦ θεοῦ.

In polemical opposition, as against Cyril Lucar,[1] was the Romish notion of a *mutatio substantiæ*, or μετουσίωσις (already current among the Greeks), sanctioned as a dogma.

Conf. orthod. p. 166 : Πρέπει νὰ ἔχῃ ὁ ἱερεὺς τοιαύτην γνώμην εἰς τὸν καιρόν, ὁποῦ ἁγιάζει τὰ δῶρα, πῶς αὐτὴ ἡ οὐσία

---

[1] Cyrilli Lucaris *Conf.* p. 38 : Ἐν τῇ ἐγχειρίσει τοῦ μυστηρίου τούτου (of the Supper) καὶ διακονίᾳ τὴν ἀληθῆ καὶ βεβαίαν παρουσίαν τοῦ κυρίου ἡμῶν Ἰησοῦ Χριστοῦ ὁμολογοῦμεν καὶ πιστεύομεν· πλὴν ἣν ἡ πίστις ἡμῖν παρίστησι καὶ προσφέρει, οὐχ ἣν ἡ ἐφευρεθεῖσα εἰκῆ διδάσκει μετουσίωσις· πιστεύομεν γὰρ τοὺς πιστοὺς μεταλαμβάνοντας ἐν τῷ δείπνῳ τὸ σῶμα τοῦ κυρίου ἡμῶν Ἰησοῦ Χριστοῦ ἐσθίειν· οὐκ αἰσθητῶς τοῖς ὀδοῦσι τρύχοντας καὶ ἀναλύοντας τὴν μετάληψιν, ἀλλὰ τῇ τῆς ψυχῆς αἰσθήσει κοινωνοῦντας· τὸ γὰρ σῶμα τοῦ κυρίου οὐκ ἔστιν ὅπερ ἐν τῷ μυστηρίῳ τοῖς ὀφθαλμοῖς ὁρᾶταί τε καὶ λαμβάνεται, ἀλλ᾿ ὅπερ πνευματικῶς ἡ πίστις λαβοῦσα ἡμῖν παριστάνει τι καὶ χαρίζεται·

τοῦ ἄρτου καὶ ἡ οὐσία τοῦ οἴνου μεταβάλλεται εἰς τὴν οὐσίαν τοῦ ἀληθινοῦ σώματος καὶ αἵματος τοῦ Χριστοῦ, διὰ τῆς ἐνεργείας τοῦ ἁγίου πνεύματος, οὗ τὴν ἐπίκλησιν κάμει τὴν ὥραν ἐκείνην. *Ib.* p. 167: Μετὰ τὰ ῥήματα ταῦτα ἡ μετουσίωσις παρευθὺς γίνεται, καὶ ἀλλήσει ὁ ἄρτος εἰς τὸ ἀληθινὸν σῶμα τοῦ Χριστοῦ, καὶ ὁ οἶνος εἰς τὸ ἀληθινὸν αἷμα· ἀπομένονται μόνον τὰ εἴδη ὁποῦ φαίνουνται, καὶ τοῦτο κατὰ τὴν θείαν οἰκονομίαν.

On the subsequent fates of the doctrine of transubstantiation in the Greek Church, cf. Schröckh. It is clearly laid down in Dosithei *Conf.* c. 17, and the Lutheran doctrine is to him λίαν ἀμαθὴς καὶ ἄθλιος!

The doctrine of transubstantiation is rejected, *A. Sm.* p. 330; *F. C.* pp. 602, 756; *Conf. Wirtemb.* p. 115; *Declar. Conf. Helv.* i. art. 22; *Conf. Angl.* p. 94 sq.; *Eng. Artt.* 28; *Conf. Scot.* art. 21; *Heidelb. Fr.* 78; *Declar. Thorun.* p. 62 (Calvin, *Institut.* iv. 17. 12 sqq.); *Conf. Remonst.* xxiii. 5; *Cat. Racov.* qu. 341.

III. Lutheran Symbols.

C. A. p. 12: De cœnâ domini docent, quod corpus et sanguis Christi vere adsint et distribuantur vescentibus in cœnâ domini, et improbant secus docentes.

A. Sm. p. 330: De sacramento altaris sentimus, panem et vinum in cœnâ esse verum corpus et sanguinem Christi, et non tantum dari et sumi a piis sed etiam ab impiis christianis. — De transsubstantiatione subtilitatem sophisticam nihil curamus, quâ fingunt, panem et vinum relinquere et amittere naturalem suam substantiam et tantum speciem et colorem panis et non verum panem remanere. Optime enim cum s. s. congruit, quod panis adsit et maneat, sicut Paulus ipse nominat: panis quem frangimus, et: ita edat de pane.

Apol. A. C. p. 157: Confitemur, nos sentire, quod in cœnâ domini vere et substantialiter adsint corpus et sanguis Christi

ὅτιν ἀληθές ἐστιν ἐσθίειν ἡμᾶς καὶ μετέχειν καὶ κοινωνοὺς εἶναι, ἐὰν πιστεύσωμεν· ἐὰν οὐ πιστεύωμεν, πάντως ἡμᾶς τοῦ μυστηρίου κέρδους ἀφίστασθαι cet. The following antithesis retains the early traditional view:—Cyrilli Berrhœens. *Cens. synod.* p. 76: Ἀνάθεμα Κυρίλλῳ δογματίζοντι καὶ πιστεύοντι μὴ μεταβάλλεσθαι τὸν ἐπὶ τῆς προθέσεως ἄρτον, καὶ ἔτι τὸν οἶνον διὰ τῆς τοῦ ἱερέως εὐλογίας καὶ πνεύματος ἁγίου ἐπιφοιτήσεως εἰς ἀληθὲς σῶμα καὶ αἷμα Χριστοῦ. And Parthen., p. 129, vindicates, against Lucaris, only the præsentia vera corporis Christi.

et vere exhibeantur cum illis rebus, quæ videntur, pane et vino, his, qui sacramentum accipiunt.

Cat. maj. p. 553 : Quid est itaque sacramentum altaris? Resp. est verum corpus et sanguis domini nostri Jesu Christi in et sub pane et vino per verbum Christi nobis christianis ad manducandum et bibendum institutum et mandatum.

F. C. p. 599 : Credimus, quod in cœnâ domini corpus et sanguis Christi vere et substantialiter sint præsentia, et quod una cum pane et vino vere distribuantur atque sumantur. Credimus, verba testamenti Christi non aliter accipienda esse, quam sicut verba ipsa ad literam sonant, ita, ne panis absens Christi corpus et vinum absentem Christi sanguinem significent, sed ut propter sacramentalem unionem panis et vinum vere sint corpus et sanguis Christi. Cf. p. 736. Docent, quemadmodum in Christo duæ distinctæ et non mutatæ naturæ inseparabiliter sunt unitæ, ita in sacrâ cœnâ duas diversas substantias, panem videlicet naturalem et verum naturale corpus Christi in institutâ sacramenti administratione hic in terris simul esse præsentia.

Ib. p. 604: Prorsus rejicimus atque damnamus capernaiticam manducationem corporis Christi, quam nobis sacramentarii contra suæ conscientiæ testimonium post tot nostras protestationes malitiose affingunt, ut doctrinam nostram apud auditores suos in odium adducant, quasi videlicet doceamus, corpus Christi dentibus laniari et instar alterius cujusdam cibi in corpore humano digeri. Credimus autem et asserimus secundum clara verba testamenti Christi veram, sed supernaturalem manducationem corporis Christi quemadmodum etiam vere, supernaturaliter tamen, sanguinem Christi bibi docemus. Hæc autem humanis sensibus aut ratione nemo comprehendere potest, quare in hoc negotio, sicut et in aliis fidei articulis, intellectum nostrum in obedientiam Christi captivare oportet. Hoc enim mysterium in solo dei verbo revelatur et solâ fide comprehenditur.

Cf. *Conf. Wirtemb.* p. 115.

Reservation and Adoration of the Host.

Since, in Roman doctrine, through consecration the true body of Christ has for ever and substantially taken the place of the bread and wine, that Church appoints the consecrated Host: 1. To be exhibited in the mass to the faithful for their adoration, as also the cup; 2. To be reserved as *venerabile* (in the monstrance or sanctuary), to be exhibited to veneration, to be carried round in processions for the same purpose. [According to evangelical doctrine, any reservation of the body and blood of Christ is out of the question; for it is present only *in ipso usu*. As it regards the adoration, the Book of Concord shows that this belongs, not to the bread and the wine, but to Christ the God-man, who is present in His Supper truly and substantially.]

I. Romish Symbols.

Conc. Trid. sess. xiii. cap. 3 : Illud in eucharistiâ excellens et singulare reperitur, quod reliqua sacramenta tunc primum sanctificandi vim habent, cum quis illis utitur, at in eucharistiâ ipse sanctitatis auctor ante usum est.

Ib. can. 4 : Si quis dixerit, peractâ consecratione in eucharistiæ sacramento non esse corpus et sanguinem Jesu Christi, sed tantum in usu, dum sumitur, non autem ante vel post et in hostiis seu particulis consecratis, quæ post communionem reservantur vel supersunt, non remanere verum corpus domini, anathema sit.—Can. 6 : Si quis dixerit, in eucharistiæ sacramento Christum non esse cultu latriæ etiam externo adorandum atque ideo nec festivâ peculiari celebritate venerandum neque in processionibus solenniter circumgestandum vel non publice, ut adoretur, populo proponendum et ejus adoratores esse idololatras, anathema sit. Cf. cap. 5, where among other things we read : Declarat præterea sancta synodus, pie et religiose admodum in dei ecclesiam inductum fuisse hunc morem, ut singulis annis peculiari quodam et festo die præcelsum hoc et venerabile sacramentum singulari veneratione ac solemnitate celebraretur, utque in processionibus reverenter et honorifice illud per vias et loca publica circumferretur.

Ib. can. 7 : Si quis dixerit, non licere sacram eucharistiam in sacrario reservari, sed statim post consecrationem adstantibus necessario distribuendam, aut non licere, ut illa ad infirmos honorifice deferatur, anathema sit.

The Greeks also reserve the remainder of the consecrated elements as λείψανα σώματος καὶ αἵματος Χριστοῦ, but they do not bear them about in processions for adoration: Metr. Critop. *Conf.* c. 9, p. 103. It is taught in Dosithei *Conf.* c. 15, that already before the use, that is, in the consecration, Christ is bodily present in the Supper.

II. PROTESTANT.

F. C. p. 729: Extra usum, dum reponitur aut asservatur in pixide aut ostenditur in processionibus, ut fit apud Papistas, sentiunt non adesse corpus Christi, [. . . tamen porrecto pane sentiunt simul adesse et vere exhiberi corpus Christi.]—P. 760: Negamus, elementa illa seu visibiles species benedicti panis et vini adorari oportere. [Quod autem Christus ipse, verus deus et homo, qui in cœnâ suâ, in legitimo nimirum ejus usu, vere et substantialiter præsens est, in spiritu et in veritate . . . adorari debeat, id nemo, nisi Arianus hæreticus negaverit.] Cf. p. 749.

Thirty-nine Artt. art. xxviii.: The sacrament of the Lord's Supper was not by Christ's ordinance reserved, carried about, lifted up, or worshipped. Cf. *Conf. Scot.* art. 22; *Dec. Thor.* 63.

West. Conf. ch. xxix. sec. 2: In this sacrament Christ is not offered up to His Father, nor any real sacrifice made at all for remission of sins of the quick or dead; but only a commemoration of that one offering up of Himself, by Himself, upon the cross, once for all, and a spiritual oblation of all possible praise unto God for the same; so that the Popish sacrifice of the mass, as they call it, is most abominably injurious to Christ's one only sacrifice, the alone propitiation for all the sins of the elect.—Sec. 3: The Lord Jesus hath, in this ordinance, appointed His ministers to declare His word of institution to the people, to pray, and bless the elements of bread and wine, and thereby to set them apart from a common to a holy use; and to take and break the bread, to take the cup, and (they communicating also themselves) to give both to the communicants, but to none who are not then present in the congregation.—Sec. 4: Private masses, or receiving this sacrament by a priest, or any other alone; as likewise the denial of the cup to the people; worshipping the elements, the lifting them up, or carrying them about for adoration, and the reserving them for any pretended religious use; are all contrary to the nature of this sacrament, and to the institution of Christ.—Sec. 5: The outward elements in this sacrament, duly set apart to the uses ordained by Christ, have such relation to Him crucified, as that truly, yet sacramentally only, they are sometimes called by the name of the things they represent, to wit, the body and blood of Christ; albeit in substance and nature they still remain truly and only bread and wine, as they were before.—Sec. 6: That doctrine which maintains a change of the substance of bread and wine into the substance of Christ's body and blood (commonly called transubstantiation) by consecration of a priest, or by any other way, is repugnant not to Scripture alone, but even to common sense and reason; overthroweth the nature of the sacrament; and hath been and is the cause of manifold superstitions, yea, of gross idolatries.

Conf. Remonstr. xxiii. 5: . . . tantum abest, ut symbola quasi corporis et sanguinis Christi latibula religiose nobis adoranda sint hocque ipso fine aut publice in templis proponenda aut ciboriis includenda, aut in processionibus circumgestanda cet.

FOURTH POINT OF DIVERGENCE.

While the Greeks, Protestants, Arminians, Mennonites, and Socinians believe that the Lord's Supper is perfectly received only in its twofold form, the Romish Church limits its dispensation to the bread in the case of the laity and of the *sacerdotes non conficientes* or priests not officiating,[1] maintaining that Christ is altogether present under each of the two forms.

[1] Sacerdos conficiens is the minister who consecrates and dispenses. Why he, and he alone, communicates *sub utráque* is explained thus by Eck, *Loci*, c. 9: Consecrans utramque speciem consecrat, quia agitur repræsentatio dominicæ passionis, ideo corpus et sanguis simul sub utráque sp. consecrantur, et sacerdos in personâ populi offert et sumit sub utráque sp., in cujus personâ totus populus quadam spiritali sumtione se sanguinem Ch. bibere, gaudenter debet credere.

I. Romish Symbols.

Concil. Constant. sess. xiii.: Concil. declarat, quod, licet . . . in primitivâ eccl. hujusmodi sacramentum reciperetur a fidelibus sub utrâque sp., tamen hæc consuetudo ad evitandum aliqua pericula et scandala est rationabiliter introducta, quod a conficientibus sub utrâque sp., et a laicis tantummodo sub sp. panis suscipiatur. . . . Præcipimus sub pœnâ excommunicationis, quod nullus presbyter communicet populum sub utrâque specie panis et vini.

Conc. Trid. sess. xiii. euchar. can. 3: Si quis negaverit, in venerabili sacramento eucharistiæ sub unaquaque specie et sub singulis cujusque speciei partibus separatione factâ totum Christum contineri, anath. sit. Cf. sess. xxi. cap. 3, can. 3.

Ib. sess. xxi. cap. 1: Sancta synodus, a Spiritu sancto . . . edocta atque ipsius ecclesiæ judicium et consuetudinem secuta, declarat ac docet, nullo divino præcepto laicos et clericos non conficientes obligari ad eucharistiæ sacramentum sub utrâque specie sumendum, neque ullo pacto salvâ fide dubitari posse, quin illis alterius speciei communio ad salutem sufficiat. — Cap. 2: Agnoscens ecclesia suam in administratione sacramentorum auctoritatem, . . . gravibus et justis de caussis adducta hanc consuetudinem sub alterâ specie communicandi approbavit et *pro lege habendam decrevit*, quam reprobare aut sine ipsius ecclesiæ auctoritate pro libito mutare non licet. Cf. can. 2.

Cat. Rom. ii. 4. 6: Multis et iis quidem gravissimis rationibus adductam esse ecclesiam patet, ut hanc potissimum sub alterâ specie communicandi consuetudinem non solum approbaret, sed etiam decreti auctoritate firmaret. Primum enim maxime cavendum erat, ne sanguis domini in terram funderetur: quod quidem facile vitari posse non videbatur, si in magnâ populi multitudine eum ministrare oportuisset. Præterea, cum sacrâ eucharistiâ ægrotis præsto esse debeat, magnopere timendum erat, ne si diutius vini species asservaretur, coacesceret. Permulti præterea sunt, qui vini saporem ac ne odorem quidem perferre ullo modo possint. Quare ne quod spiritualis salutis causâ dandum est, corporis valetudini noceret, prudentissime sancitum est ab ecclesiâ, ut panis tantummodo speciem fideles acciperent. Accedit ad alias rationes, quod in pluribus provinciis summâ vini penuriâ laboratur: neque id aliunde sine maximis inpensis, ac non nisi longissimis ac difficillimis itineribus convehi potest. Deinde, quod maxime omnium ad rem pertinet, convellenda erat eorum hæresis, qui negabant, sub utrâque specie totum Christum esse, sed corpus tantum exsangue sub panis, sanguinem autem sub vini specie contineri asserebant. Ut igitur fidei catholicæ veritas magis ante omnium oculos poneretur, sapientissimo consilio alterius speciei hoc est panis communio inducta est.

Cf. *Confut. A. C.* p. 93 sq.; Bellarmin. *Sacr. euchar.* iv. 20–28; Klee, *Dogmat.* iii. S. 185 ff. Many voices have recently pleaded in the Romish Church for the restoration of the cup. Schmid, *Liturg.* i. 274, says: It must not be suppressed that the majority of sincere Catholics, who are capable of a judgment on this point, heartily wish that the supreme apostolical ruler of the Church would give back the use of the cup to those who wish it.

II. GREEK AND PROTESTANT.

Conf. orthod. p. 168: Ἡ δὲ κοινωνία τοῦ μυστηρίου τούτου (τῆς εὐχαριστίας) πρέπει νὰ γίνεται καὶ κατὰ τὰ δύο εἴδη τοῦ ἄρτου καὶ τοῦ οἴνου· τόσον ἀπὸ τοὺς πνευματικούς, ὅσον καὶ ἀπὸ τοὺς κοσμικούς.

Metroph. Critopul. *Conf.* p. 98: Μετέχουσι πάντες ἑκατέρου εἴδους τῶν ἐν τῇ δεσποτικῇ τραπέζῃ, τοῦ τε ἄρτου φημὶ καὶ τοῦ ποτηρίου, ἐκκλησιαστικοί τε καὶ λαϊκοί, ἄνδρες καὶ γυναῖκες.

Cf. also Jerem. *in Actis Wirtemb.* p. 129.

C. A. p. 21: Laicis datur utraque species sacramenti in cœnâ domini, quia hic mos habet mandatum domini Matth. xxvi. 27. Bibite ex hoc omnes.

Apol. C. A. p. 233: Non potest dubitari, quin pium sit et consentaneum institutioni Christi et verbis Pauli, uti utrâque parte in cœnâ domini. Christus enim instituit utramque partem, et instituit, non pro parte ecclesiæ, sed pro totâ ecclesiâ.

Art. Sm. p. 330: Non tantum unam speciem esse dandam sentimus. . . . Etsi enim verum esse possit, quod sub unâ tantum sit, quantum sub utrâque, tamen una species non est tota ordinatio et institutio per Ch. facta.

F. C. p. 602 : Rejicimus sacrilegium, quo laicis una tantum pars sacramenti datur, cum nimirum contra expressa verba testamenti Christi calice illis interdicitur atque ita sanguine Christi spoliantur.

Conf. Helv. ii. cap. 21: Improbamus illos, qui alteram speciem, poculum inquam domini, fidelibus subtraxerunt. Graviter enim peccant contra institutionem domini.

Conf. Angl. p. 94: (Agnoscimus), populo ad sacram communionem accedenti utramque partem eucharistiæ tradendam esse. Id enim et Christum jussisse et apostolos ubique terrarum instituisse, et omnes veteres patres et catholicos episcopos secutos esse : et si quis contra faciat, eum, ut Gelasius ait, committere sacrilegium.

Thirty-nine Artt. art. xxx.: The cup of the Lord is not to be denied to the lay-people : for both the parts of the Lord's sacrament, by Christ's ordinance and commandment, ought to be ministered to all Christian men alike.

Conf. Scot. art. 22: Pontificii ... suffurando a populo poculum illud benedictionis horrendum sacrilegium commiserunt.

S. also *Declar. Thorun.* p. 64.

Observation.

Infant Communion ; Unleavened Bread ; Water mingled with the Wine.

Differences of less importance concern the following points: 1. The communion of children, which only the Greek Church permits, all others rejecting it. 2. The use of leavened or unleavened bread,—the former being customary in the Greek, and the latter in the Romish and the Lutheran. 3. The use of wine mixed with water or unmixed: the former is preferred by the Roman and Greek, the latter by the Protestant Churches.

SYMBOLICAL REFERENCES.

I. GREEK.

(*a*) Metroph. Critopul. *Conf.* p. 98: Καὶ αὐτὰ τὰ βρέφη ἀρξάμενα εὐθὺς ἀπὸ τοῦ ἁγίου βαπτίσματος μετέχει τοῦ λοιποῦ ὁσάκις οἱ γονεῖς βούλονται.

Cf. Jerem. *in Act. Wirtemb.* p. 89.

(*b* and *c*) *Conf. orthod.* p. 166 : Ἡ πρεπουμένη ὕλη, ἤγουν ἄρτος σίτινος ἔνζυμος . . . καὶ οἶνος ἄμικτος . . ., καὶ εἰς τὴν προσκομιδὴν ἐγχεῖται καὶ ὕδωρ.

Metroph. Critopul. *Conf.* p. 90 : Ἡ ὕλη . . . ἐστὶ ἄρτος ἔνζυμος καὶ κρᾶμα, τουτέστιν οἶνος ὕδατι κεκραμμένος. Cf. p. 98.

Jerem. *in Actis Wirtemb.* p. 129 : Οὐκ ἐν ἀζύμῳ ἀλλ' ἐν ἄρτῳ ἐνζύμῳ τῷ τοῦ ἄρτου εἴδει χρώμεθα. Cf. p. 86.

II. ROMISH.

(*a*) *Cat. Rom.* ii. 4. 62 : Quamvis hæc lex dei et ecclesiæ auctoritate sancita ad omnes fideles pertineat, docendum est, eos tamen excipi, qui nondum rationis usum propter ætatis imbecillitatem habent. Hi enim neque sacram eucharistiam a communi et profano pane sciunt discernere, neque ad eam accipiendam pietatem animi et religionem afferre possunt. Atque id etiam a Christi institutione alienissimum videtur.

(*b* and *c*) *Ib.* ii. 4. 13 : Quemadmodum nullus panis nisi triticeus apta sacramenti materia putandus est, (hoc enim apostolica traditio nos docuit et ecclesiæ catholicæ auctoritas firmavit), ita etiam ex iis, quæ Christus gessit, azymum esse debere, facile intelligitur.—14 : Neque tamen ea qualitas adeo necessaria existimanda est, ut, si illa pani desit, sacramentum confici non possit.

Ib. ii. 4. 15 : (Altera sacramenti materia) est vinum ex vitis fructu expressum, cui modicum aquæ permixtum sit. Nam dominum salvatorem vino in hujus sacramenti institutione usum esse cet. Cf. Trid. sess. xxii. cap. 7. S. Klee, *Dogmat.* iii. S. 190 ff.

III. PROTESTANT.

The Protestant symbols contain no express declarations on these points, which is easily to be explained. The practice of the Church, however, is plain enough.

FIFTH POINT OF DIVERGENCE.

It is peculiar to the Greek and Roman Churches to regard the Eucharist not merely as a sacrament, but at the same time as a true sacrifice (especially a *sacrificium propitiatorium*). They believe, namely, that the same Christ who once offered Himself to God for mankind in a bloody oblation on the cross, is continually offered in an unbloody oblation by the hand of the priest, for the living and the dead, the present and the absent, for the expiation of sin. The solemn rite, adorned with a multitude of ceremonies, by which the priest accomplishes the unbloody sacrifice on the altar, is called the mass, or *missa*. No part of the Roman Catholic faith has been so vehemently assaulted as this; and in the symbols of both Protestant Churches the mass is rejected in the most decided manner, and sometimes with expressions of abhorrence.

Observation.

How the two aspects under which the Eucharist may be viewed on this theory are to be united, the Council of Trent does not say; but it is the idea of the personal presence of Christ, and the transubstantiation which lies at the basis of it, which unites sacrament and sacrifice. That is to say, the Christ made present through the consecration is not merely partaken of by the communicants, with which participation, according to the Protestants, the sacrament ends, but at the same time is as a sacrifice ever anew offered to God,—a sacrifice, that is, which He in His collective work ever is. It is of no importance that the two are separated in the sessions of Trent; the Catechism and all Roman theologians treat the Eucharist in one section, first as sacrament, then as sacrifice. The mutual relation between the two is thus defined by the *Cat. Rom.* ii. 4. 71: Sacr. consecratione perficitur, omnis vero sacrificii vis in eo est, ut offeratur. Quare sacra euchar., dum in pyxide continetur vel ad ægrotum defertur, sacramenti, non sacrificii rationem habet. Deinde etiam ut sacramentum est, iis, qui div. hostiam sumunt, meriti causam affert et omnes illas utilitates, quæ commemoratæ sunt; ut autem sacrific. est, non merendi solum sed satisfaciendi quoque efficientiam continet. The celebration at the altar is always sacrament and sacrifice at once; but the communion may be separated from the sacrifice, as for the sick.

I. SYMBOLICAL TESTIMONIES.

I. Romish and Greek Symbols.

Conc. Trid. sess. xxii. cap. 1 : Dominus noster, etsi semel se ipsum in arâ crucis deo patri oblaturus erat, ut æternam illis redemtionem operaretur, quia tamen per mortem sacerdotium ejus exstinguendum non erat, in cœnâ novissimâ, ut suæ ecclesiæ visibile, sicut hominum naturæ exigit, relinqueret sacrificium, quo cruentum illud semel in cruce peragendum repræsentaretur ejusque memoria in finem usque sæculi permaneret atque illius salutaris virtus in remissionem eorum, quæ a nobis quotidie committuntur, peccatorum[1] applicaretur, . . . corpus et sanguinem suum sub speciebus panis et vini deo patri obtulit ac sub earundem rerum symbolis apostolis, quos tunc N. T. sacerdotes constituebat, ut sumerent, tradidit et iisdem eorumque in sacerdotio successoribus, ut offerrent, præcepit.

Ib. cap. 2 : Quoniam in divino hoc sacrificio, quod in missâ peragitur, idem ille Christus continetur et incruente immolatur, qui in arâ crucis semel se ipsum cruente obtulit, docet synodus, sacrificium istud vere propitiatorium esse per ipsumque fieri, ut, si cum vero corde et rectâ fide, cum metu et reverentiâ, contriti ac pœnitentes ad deum accedamus, misericordiam consequamur et gratiam inveniamus in auxilio opportuno. Hujus quippe oblatione placatus dominus gratiam et donum pœnitentiæ concedens, crimina et peccata, etiam ingentia, dimittit; una enim eademque est hostia, idem nunc offerens sacerdotum ministerio, qui seipsum tunc in cruce obtulit, sola offerendi ratione diversa. Cujus quidem oblationis cruentæ, inquam, fructus per hanc incruentam uberrime percipiuntur: tantum abest, ut illi per hanc quovis modo derogetur. Quare non solum pro fidelium vivorum peccatis, pœnis, satisfactionibus et aliis necessitatibus, sed et pro defunctis in Christo nondum ad plenum purgatis, rite juxta apostolorum traditionem offertur.

Ib. can. 1 : Si quis dixerit, in missâ non offerri deo verum et proprium sacrificium, aut quod offerri non sit aliud, quam nobis Christum ad manducandum dari, anathema sit.—Can. 3 :

---
[1] Cf. *A. C.* p. 25.

Si quis dixerit, missæ sacrificium tantum esse laudis et gratiarum actionis, aut nudam commemorationem sacrificii in cruce peracti, non autem propitiatorium, vel soli prodesse sumenti, neque pro vivis et defunctis, pro peccatis, pœnis, satisfactionibus et aliis necessitatibus offerri debere, anathema sit.

For clearer view of the virtue and operation of the mass, we select from Bellarmine (*Controv. de euchar.* v. 6): Sacrif. missæ non habet vim ex opere operato ad modum sacramentorum. Non operatur sacrificium efficienter et immediate, neque est proprie instrumentum dei ad justificandum. — Non immediate justificat, ut baptismus et absolutio faciunt, sed donum pœnitentiæ impetrat, per quod homo peccator ad sacramentum accedere velit et per illud justificetur. . . . Non majorem vim habere potest sacrif. missæ quam sacrificium crucis; . . sacrif. autem crucis non efficienter et immediate justificavit, sed tantum impetratorie et meritorie, alioqui omnes homines continuo justi effecti essent; cum dom. pro omnibus hominibus se deo in sacrificium obtulerit. . . . Sacrif. missæ vim habet per modum impetrationis et ejus propria efficientia est impetrare. — Sacrif. crucis fuit meritorium, satisfactorium et impetratorium vere et proprie, quia Ch. tunc mortalis erat et mereri ac satisfacere poterat; sacrif. missæ proprie solum est impetratorium, quia Ch. nunc immortalis nec mereri nec satisfacere potest. Cum autem dicitur propitiatorium vel satisfactorium, id est intelligendum ratione rei, quæ impetratur. Dicitur enim propitiatorium, quia impetrat remissionem culpæ, satisfactorium, quia impetrat remissionem pœnæ, meritorium, quia impetrat gratiam benefaciendi ac merita acquirendi. Quanquam non negaverim, dici etiam satisfactorium, quod ex Christi institutione per sacrificium hoc applicetur ejusdem Christi passio ad pœnas tollendas seu viventium seu mortuorum, quæ post culpam remissam aliquando remanent, vel in hac vitâ vel in purgatorio luendæ.— Valor sacrificii missæ finitus est. Hæc est communis sententia theologorum et probatur apertissime ex usu ecclesiæ. Nam si missæ valor infinitus esset, frustra multæ missæ præsertim ad rem eandem impetrandam offerrentur. Si enim una infiniti valoris est, certe ad omnia impetranda sufficiet, quorsum igitur aliæ? Et confirmatur ex sacrificio crucis, quod non aliâ de causâ unum tantum fuit neque unquam repetitur, nisi quia illud unum infiniti valoris fuit et pretium acquisivit pro omnibus peccatis præteritis et futuris remittendis. — Etiamsi posset Ch. per unam oblationem sacrificii incruenti sive per se sive per ministrum oblati quælibet a deo et pro quibuscunque impetrare, tamen noluit petere nec impetrare, nisi ut pro singulis oblationibus applicaretur certa mensura fructus passionis suæ sive ad peccatorum remissionem sive ad alia beneficia, quibus in hac vitâ indigemus. Cur autem id voluerit, non est nostrum curiosius inquirere. — Sacrificium missæ non solum impetratorium est spiritualium beneficiorum, sed etiam temporalium, ed idcirco offerri potest pro peccatis, pro poenis et pro quibuscunque aliis necessitatibus.

Conf. orthod. p. 165: The Eucharist is called ἀναίμακτος θυσία, p. 170, and among its καρποῖς are reckoned: Τὸ μυστήριον τοῦτο προσφέρεται θυσία ὑπὲρ πάντων τῶν ὀρθοδόξων χριστιανῶν ζώντων τε καὶ κεκοιμημένων ἐπ' ἐλπίδι ἀναστάσεως ζωῆς αἰωνίου· ἡ ὁποία θυσία δὲν θέλει τελείως ἕως τῆς τελευταίας κρίσεως. — Τὸ δεύτερον κέρδος ὅπου μὲν δίδῃ εἶναι, διατὶ τὸ μυστήριον τοῦτο γίνεται ἱλασμὸς καὶ καλοσύνημα πρὸς τὸν Θεὸν διὰ τὰς ἁμαρτίας ἡμῶν εἴτε ζώντων εἴτε καὶ ἀποθαμένων.

Jerem. *in Act. Wirtemb.* p. 104: Διττῶς ἁγιάζουσα φαίνεται ἡ θεία τελετή (εὐχαριστία)· ἕνα μὲν τρόπον τῇ μεσιτείᾳ· προσφερόμενα γὰρ τὰ δῶρα αὐτῷ τῷ προσφέρεσθαι ἁγιάζει τοὺς προσφέροντας καὶ ὑπὲρ ὧν προσφέρουσι καὶ ἵλεον αὐτοῖς ἐργάζονται τὸν Θεόν· ἕτερον δὲ τῇ μεταλήψει cet. Τούτων τῶν τρόπων ὁ μὲν πρῶτος κοινὸς γίνεται ζῶσι καὶ τεθνηκόσι, καὶ γὰρ ὑπὲρ ἀμφοτέρων τῶν μερῶν ἡ θυσία προσφέρεται. Cf. also p. 97 sq.

Dositheï *Conf.* c. 17: Πιστεύομεν, εἶναι θυσίαν ἀληθῆ καὶ ἱλαστικὴν προσφερομένην ὑπὲρ πάντων τῶν εὐσεβῶν ζώντων καὶ τεθνεώτων καὶ ὑπὲρ ὠφελείας πάντων cet.

See also Heinecc. *Abbild.* ii. 296: The practice of the Greek orthodox Church is distinguished from that of the Romish by this, that the former duly celebrates the office only once in the same church, and accordingly tolerates in every church only one altar; Metrop. Critop. *Conf.* c. ix. p. 102. On Romish principles, masses may be said on the several altars of *one* church from dawn to mid-day. *Vid.* Schmid, *Liturgik,* i. 263.

From the idea of the mass as a sacrifice, it is easily explained how in the Roman Catholic Church private masses (*missæ privatæ*, but *vid. Cat. Rom.* ii. 4. 79), at which no communicant is present, may be held. Trid. sess. xxii. can. 8: Si quis dixerit, missas, in quibus solus sacerdos sacramentaliter communicat, illicitas esse adeoque abrogandas, a. s. The masses for the dead, missæ pro defunctis, are yet to be mentioned; they are connected with the doctrine of Purgatory, and will be treated hereafter.

The Council of Trent did not approve of masses in the vernacular. Sess. xxii. cap. 8: Etsi missa magnam contineat populi fidelis eruditionem, non tamen expedire visum est patribus, ut vulgari passim linguâ celebraretur. Against this use of a foreign tongue in divine service protests were uttered by *Apol. A. C.* p. 250; *Helv.* ii. cap. 22; *Thirty-nine Artt.* art. xxiv.

II. Protestant.

The references in the Protestant and Socinian symbols to the mass, and remonstrances against it, are very diffuse, and cannot therefore be cited in full. Cf. *A. C.* p. 23; *Art. Smalc.* 305; *F. C.* p. 602; *Conf. Helv.* ii. 21; *Eng. Artt.* art. xxxi.

XVII.
PENANCE.

DIVERGENCE.

The Sacrament of Penance corresponds with that of Baptism, inasmuch as the baptized, having lost by sin his justification, can regain it only by means of penance. Romanists and Protestants are at one on this, that the sinner must experience deep repentance on account of his sins, and exhibit it before God, if he would be a partaker of forgiveness through Christ, and therefore of a renewed justification. But they part asunder at this point. 1. Protestants hold penitence to be a matter purely internal, and any verbal confession to a human minister as non-essential. The Romanists and Greeks, on the contrary, regard this confession of sin, *confessio oris*, as an essential element, the second part in repentance. 2. Protestants teach that the forgiveness of such a penitent sinner is perfect at once for Christ's sake; they require no contribution of the sinner's own. The Romanists and Greeks, on the contrary, require for the removal of the temporal punishments of sin personal *satisfactiones* of the absolved, holding that these constitute the third element in repentance. 3. The Romanists and Greeks regard repentance, thus viewed, and connected with priestly absolution, as a sacrament. The Protestants deny this altogether.

Although the evangelical Church holds confession not to be a law of Christ, and therefore not as essentially necessary, it has nevertheless retained it as a permanent institute, mainly on account of its connection with absolution. As such, it is always the preparation of the Lord's Supper.[1] (The Reformed Church, it is true, avows that common confession of sins in the congregation is sufficient; but it permits, and for some cases of special need enjoins, a private confession to the minister as the means of consolation and instruction.) The evangelical Church is distinguished from the Roman and Greek by this, that it regards a confession of sin in the general by the penitent as sufficient;[2] on the contrary, the latter require a specific detail of all mortal sins, so far as the penitent can remember them, with their essential circumstances (*confessio auricularis*). With their principle, that the priest is in the place of a judge appointed by God for the penitent, Protestantism cannot be reconciled, especially as it knows nothing of satisfaction that might be imposed. The confessor is the servant or organ of God, the announcer of divine mercy: his absolution flows from the power of the keys entrusted to him. (No. XX.)

a. Repentance, and the Sacrament of Penance generally; and Satisfactions in particular.

SYMBOLICAL TESTIMONIES.

I. ROMAN AND GREEK.

Conc. Trid. sess. xiv. pœnit. cap. 3 : Sunt quasi materia hujus sacramenti (pœnitentiæ) ipsius pœnitentis actus, nempe contritio, confessio et satisfactio. Qui, quatenus in pœnitente ad integritatem sacramenti ad plenamque et perfectam peccatorum remissionem ex dei institutione requiruntur, hac ratione pœnitentiæ partes dicuntur.

Ib. can. 4: Si quis negaverit, ad integram et perfectam

---

[1] *A. C.* p. 27 ; *Conf. Sax.* p. 73. Confession was, down to the middle of the past century, merely a private confession,—the individual went alone to his minister. Latterly, however, the public and general confession has been introduced, and almost entirely superseded the former. That private confession was an efficacious means of furthering piety in individuals, especially in the hands of intelligent ministers, is generally acknowledged. Many even of the Reformed theologians have expressed a wish that it could be introduced into their churches.

[2] In case any man desired to confess his individual sins, the Church, in its earlier regulations at least, by no means prohibited this.

peccatorum remissionem requiri tres actus in pœnitente, quasi materiam sacramenti pœnitentiæ, videlicet contritionem, confessionem et satisfactionem, quæ tres pœnitentiæ partes dicuntur; aut dixerit, duas tantum esse pœnitentiæ partes, terrores scilicet incussos conscientiæ agnito peccato, et fidem conceptam ex evangelio vel absolutione, qua credit quis sibi per Christum remissa peccata: anathema sit.

Cat. Rom. ii. 5. 21: Est hujus sacramenti (pœnitentiæ) proprium, ut præter formam et materiam, quæ omnibus sacramentis communia sunt, partes etiam illas habeat, quæ tanquam totam integramque pœnitentiam constituant, contritionem scilicet, confessionem et satisfactionem. . . . Hæ autem partes ex earum partium genere esse dicuntur, quæ ad aliquod totum constituendum necessariæ sunt, quoniam, quemadmodum hominis corpus ex pluribus membris constat, manibus, pedibus, oculis et aliis hujusmodi partibus, quarum aliqua si desit, merito imperfectum videatur, perfectum vero, si nulla desideretur; eodem etiam modo pœnitentia ex hisce tribus partibus ita constituitur, ut, quamvis, quod ad ejus naturam attinet, contritio et confessio, quibus homo justus fit, satis sit, tamen nisi tertia etiam pars, id est, satisfactio accedat, aliquid ei omnino ad perfectionem desit necesse sit. Quare adeo hæ partes inter se connexæ sunt, ut contritio confitendi et satisfaciendi consilium et propositum inclusum habeat, confessionem contritio et satisfaciendi voluntas, satisfactionem vero duæ reliquæ antecedant.

Conc. Trid. sessio xiv. pœnit. can. 1: Si quis dixerit, in catholicâ ecclesiâ pœnitentiam non esse vere et proprie sacramentum pro fidelibus, quoties post baptismum in peccata labuntur, ipsi deo reconciliandis a Christo institutum, anathema sit.

Conf. orthod. p. 178: Τὸ πέμπτον μυστήριον εἶναι ἡ μετάνοια, ἡ ὁποῖα εἶναι ἕνας πόνος τῆς καρδίας διὰ τὰ ἁμαρτήματα ὁποῦ ἔσφαλεν ὁ ἄνθρωπος, τὰ ὁποῖα κατηγορᾷ ἔμπροσθεν τοῦ ἱερέως μὲ γνώμην βεβαίαν νὰ διορθώσῃ τὴν ζωήν του εἰς τὸ μέλλον, καί, μὲ ἐπιθυμίαν νὰ τελειώσῃ ὅ, τι τὸν ἐπιτιμήσει ὁ ἱερεὺς ὁ πνευματικός του· τοῦτο τὸ μυστήριον ἰσχύει καὶ πέρνει τὴν δύναμίν του, ὁπόταν ἡ λύσις τῶν ἁμαρτιῶν γίνεται διὰ τοῦ ἱερέως, κατὰ τὴν τάξιν καὶ ξυνήθειαν τῆς ἐκκλησίας· ὁποῦ παρευ-

θὺς ὡς αν πάρῃ τὴν συγχώρησίν του, ἀφέωνται τὰ ἁμαρτήματα τὴν ὥραν ἐκείνην ὅλα ἀπὸ τὸν Θεὸν διὰ τοῦ ἱερέως.
Ib. p. 179 sq.: Εἶναι ἀναγκαῖαν νὰ ἔχῃ συντριβὴν καρδίας ὁ μετανοῶν καὶ λύπην διὰ τὰ ἁμαρτήματά του. — Εἰς τὴν συντριβὴν τούτην τῆς καρδίας πρέπει νὰ ἀκολουθᾷ καὶ ἡ διὰ στόματος ἐξομολόγησις πάντων τῶν ἁμαρτημάτων καθ' ἕκαστον. . . . Τὸ τρίτον μέρος τῆς μετανοίας πρέπει νὰ εἶναι ὁ κανόνας καὶ τὸ ἐπιτίμιον cet.

Concil. Trid. sess. xiv. pœnit. cap. 8 : Quoad satisfactionem (quæ ex omnibus pœnitentiæ partibus, quemadmodum a patribus nostris christiano populo fuit perpetuo tempore commendata, ita una, maxime nostrâ ætate, summo pietatis prætextu impugnatur ab iis, qui speciem pietatis habent, virtutem autem ejus abnegarunt) synodus declarat, falsum omnino esse et a verbo dei alienum, culpam a domino nunquam remitti quin universa etiam pœna condonetur. . . . Sane et divinæ justitiæ ratio exigere videtur, ut aliter ab eo in gratiam recipiantur, qui ante baptismum per ignorantiam deliquerint, aliter vero, qui semel a peccati et dæmonis servitute liberati et accepto Spiritus sancti dono, scientes templum dei violare et Spiritum sanctum contristare non formidaverint. Et divinam clementiam decet, ne ita nobis absque ullâ satisfactione peccata dimittantur, ut occasione acceptâ, peccata leviora putantes, velut injurii et contumeliosi Spiritui sancto in graviora labamur, thesaurizantes nobis iram in die iræ. Procul dubio enim magnopere a peccato revocant et quasi freno quodam coërcent hæ satisfactoriæ pœnæ cautioresque et vigilantiores in futurum pœnitentes efficiunt: medentur quoque peccatorum reliquiis, et vitiosos habitus male vivendo comparatos contrariis virtutum actionibus tollunt. . . . Neque vero ita nostra est satisfactio hæc, quam pro peccatis nostris exsolvimus, ut non sit per Christum Jesum: nam qui ex nobis tanquam ex nobis nihil possumus, eo co-operante, qui nos confortat, omnia possumus. Ita non habet homo unde glorietur, sed omnis gloriatio nostra in Christo est: in quo vivimus, in quo meremur, in quo satisfacimus, facientes fructus dignos pœnitentiæ; qui ex illo vim habent, ab illo offeruntur patri et per illum acceptantur a patre. Debent ergo sacerdotes domini, quantum spiritus et prudentia suggesserit, pro qualitate criminum et poenitentium facultate salutares et convenientes satisfactiones injungere, ne, si forte peccatis conniveant et indulgentius cum poenitentibus agant, levissima quædam opera pro gravissimis delictis injungendo, alienorum peccatorum participes efficiantur.

Ibid. can. 13 : Si quis dixerit, pro peccatis quoad poenam temporalem minime deo per Chr. merita satisfieri poenis ab eo inflictis et patienter toleratis vel a sacerdote injunctis sed neque sponte susceptis, ut jejuniis, orationibus, eleemosynis vel aliis etiam pietatis operibus, . . . anath. sit.—Can. 14 : Si quis dix., satisfactiones, quibus poenitentes per Ch. Jes. peccata redimunt, non esse cultus dei sed traditiones hominum, doctrinam de gratiâ et verum dei cultum atque ipsum beneficium mortis Ch. obscurantes, anathema sit.

Cf. *Confut. A. C.* p. 85 ; *Cat. Rom.* ii. 5. 62 sqq.

Conf. orthod. p. 181 : Τὸ τρίτον μέρος τῆς μετανοίας πρέπει νὰ εἶναι ὁ κανόνας καὶ τὸ ἐπιτίμιον, ὁποῦ δίδη καὶ διορίζῃ ὁ πνευματικός, ὡς ἂν εἶναι προσευχαὶ, ἐλεημοσύναι, νηστεῖαι, ἐπίσκεψις ἁγίων τόπων, αἱ γονυκλισίαι καὶ τὰ ὅμοια, ὁποῦ θέλουσι φανεῖ ἁρμόδια εἰς τὴν κρίσιν τοῦ πνευματικοῦ.

Metroph. Critop. *Conf.* cap. x. p. 105 : Εἶτα καὶ ποινή τις ἐπάγεται τοῖς μετανοοῦσι παρὰ τῶν ἀκροασαμένων τὰ τούτων· εἴς τε σωφρονισμόν τ' οὐ μηκέτ' ἀτάκτως βιοῦν, καὶ ἵνα διὰ τῆς ἑκουσίου καὶ προαιρετικῆς θλίψεως μετριωτέρας πειραθῶσι τῆς τοῦ Θεοῦ προσκαίρου ῥάβδου.

II. PROTESTANT.

C. A. p. 12 : Constat. poenitentia proprie his duabus partibus : altera est contritio seu terrores incussi conscientiæ agnito peccato ; altera est fides, quæ concipitur ex evangelio seu absolutione, et credit propter Christum remitti peccata, et consolatur conscientiam, et ex terroribus liberat.

A. Sm. p. 321 : Poenitentiæ adjungunt tres partes, contritionem, confessionem et satisfactionem, addita grandi consolatione et pollicitatione remissionis peccatorum, meriti, expiationis peccatorum ac plenariæ redemtionis coram deo, si homo vere doleat, confiteatur et satisfaciat. Sic in poenitentiâ homo ad fiduciam propriorum operum ducitur. Hinc orta est vox, quæ in suggestis, cum prælegeretur vulgo publica absolutio, usurpata fuit: Prolonga deus vitam meam, donec pro meis peccatis satisfecero et vitam meam emendavero.

Conf. Helv. ii. cap. 14: Per pœnitentiam intelligimus mentis in homine peccatore resipiscentiam, verbo evangelii et Spiritu sancto excitatam fideque verâ acceptam, qua protinus homo peccator agnatam sibi corruptionem peccataque omnia sua, per verbum dei accusata, agnoscit ac de his ex corde dolet, eademque coram deo non tantum deplorat et fatetur ingenue cum pudore, sed etiam cum indignatione exsecratur, cogitans jam sedulo de emendatione et perpetuo innocentiæ virtutumque studio, in quo sese omnibus diebus vitæ reliquis sancte exerceat. Et hæc quidem est vera pœnitentia, sincera nimirum ad deum et omne bonum conversio, sedula vero a diabolo et ab omni malo aversio.

Apol. A. C. p. 163: Tertius actus (pœnitentiæ) de satisfactionibus. Hic vero habet confusissimas disputationes. Fingunt æternas pœnas mutari in pœnas purgatorii et harum partem remitti potestate clavium, partem docent redimendam esse satisfactionibus. Addunt amplius, quod oporteat satisfactiones esse opera supererogationis et hæc constituunt in stultissimis observationibus, velut in peregrinationibus, rosariis aut sim. observationibus, quæ non habent mandata dei. . . . Inter hæc scandala et doctrinas dæmoniorum jacet obruta doctrina de justitiâ fidei in Chr. et de beneficio Christi cet.

Ib. p. 184: Nunc more (ecclesiæ vet.) antiquato manet nomen satisfactionis et vestigium moris, quod in confessione præscribuntur certæ satisfactiones, quas definiunt esse opera non debita, nos vocamus satisfactiones canonicas. De his sic sentimus sicut de enumeratione, quod satisfactiones can. non sint necessariæ jure divino ad remissionem peccatorum. . . . Retinenda est enim sententia de fide, quod fide consequamur remissionem peccatorum propter Chr., non propter nostra opera præcedentia aut sequentia.

Ib. p. 189: Cum scripturæ non dicant, quod operibus non debitis pœnæ æternæ compensandæ sint, temere affirmant adversarii, quod per satisfactiones canonicas pœnæ illæ compensentur, nec habent claves mandatum pœnas aliquas commutandi, item partem pœnarum remittendi.

Cf. *Conf. Saxon.* p. 77 sqq.; *Conf. Wirtemb.* p. 111 sqq.
Conf. Helv. ii. cap. 14: Improbamus illos, qui suis satisfactionibus existimant se pro commissis satisfacere peccatis. Nam docemus, Christum unum morte vel passione suâ esse omnium peccatorum satisfactionem, propitiationem vel expiationem: interim tamen, quod et ante diximus, mortificationem carnis urgere non desinimus; addimus tamen, hanc non obtrudendam esse deo superbe pro peccatorum satisfactione, sed præstandam humiliter, pro ingenio filiorum dei.
Cf. *Declar. Thorun.* p. 65 sq.

b. *Confession and Absolution.*

I. Roman and Greek.

Conc. Trid. sess. xiv. pœnit. cap. 5: Colligitur, opertere a pœnitentibus omnia peccata mortalia, quorum post diligentem sui discussionem conscientiam habent, in confessione recenseri, etiamsi occultissima illa sint; . . . nam venialia, quanquam recte et utiliter citraque omnem præsumtionem in confessione dicantur, taceri tamen citra culpam multisque aliis remediis expiari possunt. . . . Itaque dum omnia, quæ memoriæ occurrunt peccata, Christi fideles confiteri student, procul dubio omnia divinæ misericordiæ agnoscenda exponunt. Qui vero secus faciunt et scienter aliqua retinent, nihil divinæ bonitati per sacerdotem remittendum proponunt. . . . Colligitur præterea, etiam eas circumstantias in confessione explicandas esse, quæ speciem peccati mutant, quod sine illis peccata ipsa neque a pœnitentibus integre exponantur nec judicibus innotescant, et fieri nequeat, ut de gravitate criminum recte censere possint et pœnam, quam oportet, pro illis pœnitentibus imponere.

Ib. can. 6: Si quis negaverit, confessionem sacramentalem vel institutam vel ad salutem necessariam esse jure divino, aut dixerit, modum secrete confitendi soli sacerdoti . . . alienum esse ab institutione et mandato Ch. et inventum esse humanum, anathema sit. — Can. 7: Si quis dixerit, in sacramento pœnitentiæ ad remissionem peccatorum necessarium non esse jure divino, confiteri omnia et singula peccata mortalia, quorum memoriâ cum debitâ et diligenti præmeditatione habeatur, etiam occulta . . . et circumstantias, quæ peccati speciem mutant, . . . aut demum non licere confiteri peccata venialia, anathema sit. — Can. 8 : Si quis dixerit, confessionem omnium peccatorum, qualem ecclesia servat, esse impossibilem et traditionem humanam a piis abolendam, aut ad eam non teneri omnes et singulos utriusque sexus Ch. fideles semel in anno cet., anathema sit.

Conf. orthod. p. 180 : Εἰς τὴν συντριβὴν τῆς καρδίας πρέπει νὰ ἀκολουθᾷ καὶ ἡ διὰ στόματος ἐξομολόγησις πάντων τῶν ἁμαρτημάτων καθ' ἕκαστον· διατὶ δὲν ἠμπορεῖ ὁ πνευματικὸς νὰ λύσῃ τίποτες, ἂν δὲν ἠξεύρῃ ποῖα πρέπει νὰ λυθοῦσι.

Metroph. Critop. *Conf.* p. 107 : Ἐρωτῶσι μὲν οἱ ἀκροαταὶ τῆς τῶν ἁμαρτημάτων ἐξομολογήσεως κατ' εἶδος τὰ ἁμαρτήματα καὶ τὴν τούτων ποιότητα, ἵνα τὸ πρόσφορον φάρμακον ἐπάξωσι τῷ νοσοῦντι· ἐπεὶ καὶ ἰατρὸς οὐκ ἂν θεραπεύσειεν οἰονδήποτε νόσημα, μὴ κατανοήσας πρότερον τὸ ποιὸν τοῦ νοσήματος· οὐ μὴν τε καὶ τὰ πρόσωπα, μεθ' ὧν ἡ ἁμαρτία ἐπράχθη, τόν τε τρόπον καὶ τόπον· περιττὸν γὰρ τοῦτο, καὶ λίαν πονηρὰν ὑπόληψιν τῷ πολυπραγμονοῦντι καὶ περιεργαζομένῳ προσάπτον.

Cf. Jerem. *in Act. Wirtemb.* p. 87 ; Plato, *Catech.* p. 132. Auricular confession is μυστηριακὴ ἐξομολόγησις (Dosithei *Conf.* c. 15).

Conc. Trid. sess. xiv. pœnit. cap. 6 : Quamvis absolutio sacerdotis alieni beneficii sit dispensatio, tamen non est solum nudum ministerium vel annuntiandi evangelium, vel declarandi remissa esse peccata, sed ad instar actus judicialis, quo ab ipso velut a judice sententia pronuntiatur. Cf. can. 9.

II. Protestant.

A. C. p. 12 : De confessione docent, quod absolutio privata in ecclesiis retinenda sit, quanquam in confessione non sit necessaria omnium delictorum enumeratio, est enim impossibilis (Ps. xix. 13). — P. 27 : Docentur homines, ut absolutionem plurimi faciant, quia sit vox dei et mandato dei pronuntietur.

Apol. A. C. p. 163 : Quantum negotii est in illâ infinitâ

enumeratione peccatorum, quæ tamen magnâ ex parte consumitur in traditionibus humanis! Et quo magis crucientur bonæ mentes, fingunt hanc enumerationem esse juris divini.— P. 181 : De enumeratione delictorum in confessione diximus, quod sentiamus, eam non esse jure divino necessariam. Nam quod objiciunt quidam, judicem prius debere cognoscere causam, priusquam pronuntiat, hoc nihil ad hanc rem pertinet, quia ministerium absolutionis beneficium est seu gratia, non est judicium seu lex. — P. 159 : Etiamsi prodest rudes assuefacere, ut quædam (peccata) enumerent, ut doceri facilius possint : verum disputamus nunc, quid sit necessarium jure divino.

Ib. p. 167 : Potestas clavium administrat et exhibet evangelium per absolutionem, quæ est vera vox evangelii ; . . . et quia deus vere per verbum vivificat, claves vere coram deo remittunt peccata. Quare voci absolventis non secus ac voci de cœlo sonanti credendum est. — P. 181 : Impium esset, ex ecclesiâ privatam absolutionem tollere. Neque quid sit remissio peccatorum aut potestas clavium intelligunt, si qui privatam absolutionem aspernantur.

Art. Sm. p. 323 : Confessio sic instituebatur, ut homines juberentur omnia sua peccata enumerare (quod factu impossibile est). Hæc ingens carnificina fuit. Et si quis quorundam peccatorum oblitus esset, is eatenus absolvebatur, ut si in memoriam illa recurrerent, ea postea confiteretur. Nemo igitur scire poterat, num unquam sufficienter, pure et recte confessus esset et quando confessionis finis futurus esset.

Ib. p. 331 : Cum absolutio et virtus clavium etiam sit consolatio et auxilium contra peccatum et malam conscientiam in evangelio ab ipso Christo instituta, nequaquam in ecclesiâ confessio et absolutio abolenda est, præsertim propter teneras et pavidas conscientias ; . . . enumeratio autem peccatorum debet esse unicuique libera, quid. enumerare aut non enumerare velit.

Cf. also *Cat. min.* p. 378 ; *Conf. Wirtemb.* p. 111 sq.

Conf. Helv. ii. cap. 14 : Credimus, confessionem ingenuam, quæ soli deo fit vel privatim inter deum et peccatorem vel palam in templo, ubi generalis illa peccatorum confessio recitatur, sufficere nec necessarium esse ad remissionem peccatorum consequendam, ut quis peccata sua confiteatur sacerdoti susurrando in aures ipsius, ut vicissim cum impositione manuum ejus audiat ab ipso absolutionem.—Si quis vero peccatorum mole et tentationibus perplexis oppressus velit consilium, institutionem et consolationem privatim vel a ministro ecclesiæ aut aliquo fratre in lege dei docto petere, non improbamus, quemadmodum et generalem et publicam illam in templo ac cœtibus sacris recitari solitam peccatorum confessionem utpote scripturis congruam maxime approbamus. Cf. *Conf. Tetrap.* art. 20; *Declar. Thorun.* p. 65.

Calvin, *Institutt. christ.* iii. 4. 12: Duas privatæ confessionis formas scriptura probat. Unam, quæ nostrâ causâ fiat, quo pertinet illud Jacobi, ut alter alteri peccata confiteamur: sentit enim, ut nostras infirmitates alter alteri detegentes, consilio et consolatione muta nos juvemus; alteram, quæ in promixi gratiam facienda est, ad ipsum placandum et nobis reconciliandum, si quâ in re nostro vitio læsus fuerit. Ac in priore quidem specie, tametsi Jacobus neminem nominatim assignando, in cujus sinum nos exoneremus, liberum permittit delectum, ut ei confiteamur, qui ex ecclesiæ grege maxime idoneus fuerit visus. Quia tamen pastores præ aliis ut plurimum judicandi sunt idonei, potissimum etiam nobis eligendi erunt. Dico autem ideo præ aliis appositos, quod ipsâ mysterii vocatione nobis a domino designantur, quorum ex ore erudiamur ad subigenda et corrigenda peccata, tum consolationem ex veniæ fiduciâ percipiamus. . . . Ergo id officii sui unusquisque fidelium esse meminerit, si ita privatim angitur et afflictatur peccatorum sensu, ut se explicare nisi alieno adjutorio nequeat, non negligere, quod illi a domino offertur remedium, nempe ut ad se sublevandum privatâ confessione apud suum pastorem utatur, ac ad solatia sibi adhibenda privatam ejus operam imploret, cujus officium est et publice et privatim populum dei evangelicâ doctrinâ consolari. Verum eâ moderatione semper utendum est, ne, ubi deus nihil certum præscribit, conscientiæ certo jugo alligentur. Hinc sequitur, ejusmodi confessionem liberam esse oportere, ut non ab omnibus exigatur, sed iis tantum commendetur, qui eâ se opus habere intelligent. Deinde ne hi ipsi, qui illa utuntur pro suâ necessitate, ad enumeranda omnia peccata vel præcepto aliquo cogantur vel arte inducantur, sed quoad interesse sua putabunt, ut solidum consolationis fructum referant.[1]

Ibid. 14: Non minoris (quam publica) efficaciæ aut fructus est privata absolutio, ubi ab iis petitur, qui singulari remedio ad infirmitatem suam sublevandam opus habent. Accidit enim non raro, ut qui generales promissiones audit, quæ ad totam fidelium congregationem destinantur, maneat nihilominus in aliquâ dubitatione, ac velut remissione nondum impetrata inquietum adhuc animum habeat. Idem si pastori suo secretum animi vulnus aperuerit atque illam evangelii vocem peculiariter ad se directam audierit: remittuntur tibi peccata tua, confide, . . . animum confirmabit ad securitatem illâque quâ prius æstuabat trepidatione liberabitur. S. Heidegger, *Corp. theol.* xxiii. 23.

Against Romish auricular confession, s. *Conf. Angl.* p. 97; *Conf. Scot. neg.* p. 127; and Limborch, *Theol. christ.* v. 77. 9 sqq.

Penances.

The penances which are usually imposed on penitents in the Roman Catholic Church are chiefly prayers, fastings, and alms. Protestants are, of course, not indisposed to assign their due importance to these performances,—to prayer and charity as Christian duties, and to fasting as a bodily discipline helpful to piety. But they attach no merit to these things. They deny to them the character of making satisfaction, because they hold personal satisfaction and personal expiation as having no place in Christianity.

[1] Zwingli *Exposit. articulor.* (*Opp.* i. p. 405): Confessio libera esse debet, nec quisquam ad eam cogendus erit. Qui infirmi sunt et imbecilles, hi adeant episcopum suum et pastorem, consilium petant aut consolationem aut aliud, quo egent. Qui firmi sunt in fide et satis docti, sacerdote hac in parte nihil opus est iis. Hac libertate permissâ non raro et firmi accedent consulturi sacerdotem, nam nemo tam firmus est, qui non admonitione egeat. Venient autem sponte, ut quum quis fratrem in rebus dubiis adit et aliquando etiam delictum fatetur proximo cui fidit, quærens, qua peccatum effugiat (nam quisque suis in rebus cæcus est), ut et rogans pro ipso deum precetur, ut peccatum remittat et fidem augeat.

SYMBOLICAL TESTIMONIES.

I. Romish and Greek.

Concil. Trid. sess. xiv. de pœnit. 13, s. above.

Cat. Rom. ii. 5. 74 : Omne satisfactionis genus pastores docebunt ad hæc tria præcipue conferendum esse, orationem, jejunium et eleemosynam, quæ quidem tribus bonis animæ, corporis et iis, quæ externa commoda dicuntur, quæ omnia a deo accepimus, respondent. Nihil vero aptius et convenientius ad exstirpandas omnium peccatorum radices esse potest. Nam cum omne, quod est in mundo, concupiscentia carnis sit aut concupiscentia oculorum aut superbia vitæ, nemo non videt, his tribus morbi causis totidem medicinas, priori scilicet jejunium, alteri eleemosynam, tertiæ orationem rectissime opponi.

(Bellarmin, *Pœnit.* iv. 6 : Opera satisfactoria ex communi theologorum sententia sunt oratio, jejunium et eleemosyna ac præterea illa omnia, quæ ad hæc tria tanquam ad quædam præcipua capita revocantur. Cur autem hæc tria præcipue a theologis statuantur, duæ sunt causæ. Una est, quod debeamus satisfacere per ea bona, quæ nostra sunt, quoad ejus fieri potest. Habemus autem tria genera bonorum, animi, quæ deo damus per orationem, corporis, quæ deo damus per jejunium, externa, quæ deo damus per eleemosynam. Altera ratio est, quod omnia vitia revocantur ad illa tria, concupiscentiam carnis, conc. oculorum et superbiam vitæ. Jejunium comprimit concupiscentiam carnis, eleemosyna concup. oculor. i. e. avaritiam, oratio superbiam vitæ.

Id. Bon. oper. i. 3 : Tres sunt primarii fructus orationis, satisfactio, meritum, impetratio. Ex quibus duos priores adversarii funditus tollunt.—Oratio sive impetret quod postulat sive non impetret, semper est meritoria majoris gratiæ et gloriæ, quando ab homine justo et sicut oportet funditur.— ii. 6 : Jejunium generatim sumtum habet divinum præceptum, quamvis in particulari ab ecclesia determinetur tempus modusque jejunii. — C. 12 : Jejunium utile est ad deum colendum.—Loquimur de abstinentia, quæ ex electione assumitur ad bonum aliquem finem, sic enim jejunium non est res media sed actus virtutis. — Jejunium est utile ad satis-

faciendum deo vel ad eum placandum. — *Ibid.* iii. 5 : Error est hæreticorum, qui tametsi eleemosynas utiles esse non negant, tamen negant eas ad merendam vitam æternam aut ad satisfaciendum pro peccatis aliquam vim habere.)
Conf. orthod. p. 181, s. above.
Ib. p. 268 : Ἀπὸ τὰς γενικὰς καὶ ἐξαιρέτους τρεῖς ἀρετὰς ποῖαι ἄλλαι γεννοῦνται; αἱ τρεῖς αὗται, ἡ προσευχὴ, ἡ νηστεία καὶ ἡ ἐλεημοσύνη.
On Fasting in particular, *Conf. orthod.* p. 268 sq.: ἡ νηστεία, λογιζομένη κατὰ τὰς χριστιανὰς ἀρετάς, εἶναι μία ἐγκράτεια ἀπὸ ὅλα τὰ φαγητὰ ἢ ἀπὸ κάποια . . ., ὁμοίως καὶ ἀπὸ τὰ ποτὰ καὶ ἀπὸ ὅλα τὰ πράγματα τοῦ κόσμου καὶ ἀπὸ ὅλαις ταῖς ἐπιθυμίαις ταῖς κακαῖς, διὰ νὰ ἠμπορῇ ὁ χριστιανὸς νὰ κάνῃ τὴν προσευχὴν του μὲ τρόπον εὐκολώτερον καὶ νὰ ἱλάσκεται τὸν Θεὸν ἀκόμι διὰ νὰ νεκρώνῃ τὰς τῆς σαρκὸς ἐπιθυμίας καὶ νὰ ἀποδέχεται τὴν χάριν τοῦ Θεοῦ. . . . Ἡ νηστεία αὕτη ὅταν γίνεται κατὰ τοὺς προσήκοντας τρόπους, κάνει μεγάλον ἱλασμὸν εἰς τὸν Θεὸν διὰ τὰς ἁμαρτίας μας. Cf. Metroph. Critop. *Conf.* c. 18 ; Jerem. *in Actis Wirtemb.* p. 126 sq.

II. PROTESTANT.

As to fasting, the Protestant principles, so far as the symbols refer to it, may be thus stated :—

C. A. p. 31 : Docent, quod quilibet christianus debeat se corporali disciplinâ aut corporalibus exercitiis et laboribus sic exercere et coercere, ne saturitas aut desidia exstimulet ad peccandum, non ut per illa exercitia mereamur gratiam aut satisfaciamus peccatis. . . . Itaque non damnantur ipsa jejunia, sed traditiones, quæ certos dies, certos cibos præscribunt cum periculo conscientiæ, tanquam istiusmodi opera sint necessarius cultus. Cf. *Apol. C. A.* pp. 191, 209 sq.

Conf. Wirtemb. p. 113 : De oratione, jejunio, eleemosynâ et aliis id genus operibus sentimus, ea diligentissime sectanda esse, sed longe alium habere usum, quam quod vel meritis suis satisfaciant deo pro peccatis nostris, vel applicent nobis meritum Christi.

Ib. p. 114 : Jejunium sentimus utile esse non in hoc, ut

vel operis sui merito expiet peccata coram deo, vel applicet jejunanti meritum Christi, sed ut sobrietate injiciat carni frenum cet.

Ib. p. 128 : Veteres jejunarunt aliquoties totis diebus, ut vacarent publicæ precationi et hac disciplinâ admonerent ecclesiam suam ac præsertim juventutem de præteritis vel de præsentibus vel de imminentibus periculis ac excitarent eam ad agendam pœnitentiam, quâ ira dei mitigaretur. Hic est pius et utilis horum jejuniorum finis.

Conf. Helv. ii. c. 14 : See above, S. 148, 149, cap. 24 : Omnia jejunia proficisci debent ex libero spontaneoque spiritu et vere humiliato, nec composita esse ad plausum vel gratiam hominum consequendam, multo minus eo, ut per ipsa velit homo justitiam demereri. Jejunet autem in hunc finem quilibet, ut fomenta carni detrahat et ferventius deo inserviat.

Cf. *Conf. Tetrapol.* cap. 7–10 ; *Declar. Thorun.* ii. 5. 12 ; Calvin, *Institutt.* iv. 12. 14 sqq.; Limborch, *Theol. chr.* v. 75.

Purgatory.

The pious Christian, who dies without having made full satisfaction for his sins,[1] is, according to the Roman Catholics, placed in purgatory (*ignis purgatorius*), that there he may suffer the temporal punishment of sin, and thus, purged from all impurity, be fit to enter heaven. The Greek Church and the Protestant entirely reject this doctrine of a purifying fire.[2]

[1] Bellarmin, *Purgator.* ii. 9 : Restat reatus pœnæ et peccata venialia, quæ proprie dici possunt reliquiæ peccatorum, ob quas est purgatorium. Has autem reliquias aliquando certum est in morte purgari (in the case of martyrs), aliquando certum est non purgari, aliquando dubium est quid fiat, et probabilissimum est, partim purgari, partim non purgari. S. Becan. *Manual. controv.* i. p. 197 sqq. These satisfactions not made refer partly to mortal sins, the pardon of which has been obtained through the sacrament of penance only so far as concerns eternal punishment, partly to venial sins, which are only temporally to be expiated, which, however, cling to the most pious. Cf. Becani *Man. controv.* i. p. 199 sq.

[2] The Latinizing Greeks at Florence, 1439, went so far as this (Harduin. *Collect. Concil.* ix. p. 421) : ἐὰν οἱ ἀληθῶς μετανοήσαντες ἀπεθάνωσιν ἐν τῇ τοῦ Θεοῦ ἀγάπῃ, πρὶν τοῖς ἀξίοις τῆς μετανοίας καρποῖς ἱκανοποιῆσαι περὶ τῶν ἡμαρτημένων ὁμοῦ καὶ ἡμιλημένων, τὰς τούτων ψυχὰς θαρτικαῖς τιμωρίαις καθαίρεσθαι μετὰ θάνατον cet. But it is well known what a slight value this Florentine compromise had for the Greek Church.

SYMBOLICAL TESTIMONIES.

I. ROMISH.

Conc. Trid. sess. vi. justificat. can. 30 : Si quis post acceptam justificationis gratiam cuilibet peccatori pœnitenti ita culpam remitti et reatum æternæ pœnæ deleri dixerit, ut nullus remaneat reatus pœnæ temporalis exsolvendæ vel in hoc sæculo vel *in futuro, in purgatorio,* antequam ad regna cœlorum aditus patere possit : anathema sit.

Ib. sess. xxv. purgator.: Cum catholica ecclesia, a Sp. s. edocta, ex. s. litteris et antiqua patrum traditione, in s. conciliis et novissime in hac œcumenica synodo docuerit, purgatorium esse animasque ibi detentas fidelium suffragiis potissimum vero acceptabili altaris sacrificio juvari, præcipit s. synodus episcopis, ut sanam de purgatorio doctrinam, a. s. patribus et s. conciliis traditam, a Christi fidelibus credi, teneri, et ubique prædicari diligenter studeant : apud rudem vero plebem difficiliores ac subtiliores quæstiones, quæque ad ædificationem non faciunt, et ex quibus plerumque nulla fit pietatis accessio, a popularibus concionibus secludantur; incerta item, vel quæ specie falsi laborant, evulgari ac tractari non permittant ; ea vero, quæ ad curiositatem quandam aut superstitionem spectant vel turpe lucrum sapiunt, tanquam scandala et fidelium offendicula prohibeant.

Cat. Rom. i. 6. 3 : Est *purgatorius ignis,* quo piorum animæ ad definitum tempus cruciatæ expiantur, ut eis in æternam patriam ingressus patere possit, in quam nihil coinquinatum ingreditur. Ac de hujus quidem doctrinæ veritate, quam et scripturarum testimoniis et apostolicâ traditione confirmatam esse sancta concilia declarant, eo diligentius et sæpius parocho disserendum erit, quod in ea tempora incidimus, quibus homines sanam doctrinam non sustinent.

Observation.

Fire, the purgatorial agent, or means of purification, the Romish Church has not defined. According to Klee, *kath. Dogm.* iii. 425, the fire has been assumed as a mere matter of opinion. But Bellarmine, *Purgat.* ii. 10, says: Certum est in purgatorio sicut etiam in inferno esse pœnam ignis, sive iste ignis accipiatur proprie sive metaphorice. He himself decides for the corporeal fire, c. 11.

The *Limbus infantum*. Children dying immediately after baptism do not enter purgatory (Bellarm. *Purgat.* ii. 1), but, as the schoolmen taught, into the limbus infantum, which is placed in loco inferni altiore, ita ut ad eum ignis non perveniat: in a higher part of the Infernus, which the fires cannot reach, they undergo a pœnam damni, a penalty of loss; *vid.* Bellarmine, *Purgat.* ii. 6. The symbols say nothing of this. The *Limbus patrum*, where the præ-Christian pious until the descent of Christ were supposed to wait (Bellarmine, *de Christo*, iv. 10), is mentioned only in *Cat. Rom.* i. 6. 3.

II. Greek.

Conf. orthod. p. 112 : Πῶς πρέπει νὰ γροικοῦμεν διὰ τὸ πῦρ τὸ καθαρτήριον; οὐδεμία γραφὴ διαλαμβάνει περὶ αὐτοῦ· νὰ εὑρίσκεται δηλαδὴ κἂν μία πρόσκαιρος κόλασις καθαρτικὴ τῶν ψυχῶν, ὕστερα ἀπὸ τὸν θάνατον. — P. 113 : Τοὺς μύθους τινῶν ἀνθρώπων, ὅπου λέγουσι περὶ ψυχῶν, πῶς ὅταν μισεύσουσιν ἀμετανόητας ἀπὸ τὸν κόσμον, κολάζονται εἰς σουβλία, εἰς νερὰ καὶ λίμναις, ποτέ δὲν τοὺς ἐδέχθηκεν ἡ ἐκκλησία.

Metroph. Critop. *Conf.* c. xx. p. 149 : οὔκ ἐστι πῦρ καθαρτήριον παρ' ἡμῶν, ἀλλὰ θλίψις τις ἀπὸ συνειδήσεως (καὶ αὕτη μέντοι μετὰ πάνυ χρηστῆς ἐλπίδος) διήκουσ' ἕως ἂν ὁ Θεὸς θέλῃ. S. Heinecc. ii. 410 f.

The notion of an intermediate state is found in Metroph. Critop. *Conf.* c. xx. p. 147 sq.: εἶναί τινας μὴ μετὰ θάνατον εὐθέως τῆς ἐνεργείᾳ σωτηρίας τυγχάνειν ἀλλὰ δυνάμει καὶ ἐν ἐλπίδι ταύτην ἐκδέχεσθαι, ἐλπίδι λέγω βεβαίᾳ ἀναντιρρήτῳ· οἱ πειραθέντες πρότερον τῆς τοῦ Θεοῦ πατρικῆς ῥάβδου ἀξιοῦνται ἐν καιρῷ καὶ τῆς ἐνεργείᾳ σωτηρίας. . . . Λέγει ἡ ἐκκλησία τὴν ἐκείνων ποινὴν μὴ ὑλικὴν εἶναι, εἴτ' οὖν ὀργανικὴν μὴ διὰ πυρός, μήτε δι' ἄλλης ὁποιασοῦν ὕλης, ἀλλὰ διὰ θλίψεως καὶ ἀνίας τῆς ἀπὸ συνειδήσεως, συμβαίνουσαν τούτοις ἐκ τοῦ μιμνήσκεσθαι τῶν ὅσα ἐν τῷ κόσμῳ μὴ κατὰ λόγον μηδὲ ὁσίως ἔπραξαν. Prayers of survivors may soften or shorten this condition. *Confess.* Dositheis, c. 18 : ταύτων (those who have not expiated their sins upon earth) τὰς ψυχὰς ἀπέρχεσθαι εἰς ᾅδου (πιστεύομεν) καὶ ὑπομένειν τὴν ἕνεκα ὧν εἰργάσαντο ἁμαρτημάτων ποινήν· εἶναι δ' ἐν συναισθήσει τῆς ἐκεῖθεν ἀπαλλαγής· ἐλευθεροῦσθαι δὲ ὑπὸ τῆς ἄκρας ἀγαθότητος διὰ τῆς δεήσεως τῶν ἱερέων καὶ εὐποιῶν, ἃ τῶν ἀποιχομένων ἕνεκα οἱ ἑκάστου συγγενεῖς ἀποτελοῦσι· μεγάλα δυναμένης μάλιστα τῆς ἀναιμάκτου θυσίας, ἣν ἰδίως ὑπὲρ τῶν κεκοιμημένων συγγενῶν ἕκαστος καὶ κοινῶς ὑπὲρ πάντων ἡ καθολ. ὁσημέραι ποιεῖ ἐκκλησία.

Confess. orthod. p. 108, says, on the contrary: ἀποθνήσκουσι τάχα καὶ ἄνθρωποι ὅπου νὰ εἶναι ἀνάμεσα τῶν σωζομένων καὶ ἀπολλυμένων; τοιαύτης τάξεως ἄνθρωποι δὲν εὑρίσκονται, μὰ βέβαια πολλοὶ ἀπὸ τοὺς ἁμαρτωλοὺς ἐλευθερώνουνται ἀπὸ τῶν δεσμῶν τοῦ ᾅδου, ὄχι μὲ μετάνοιαν ἢ ἐξομολόγησιν ἐδικήν τους . . ., ἀλλὰ μὲ τὰς εὐποιΐας τῶν ζώντων καὶ προσευχὰς ὑπὲρ αὐτῶν τῆς ἐκκλησίας καὶ μὲ τὴν ἀναίμακτον μάλιστα θυσίαν, ὅπου καθ' ἡμέραν προσφέρει ἡ ἐκκλησία διὰ τοὺς ζῶντας καὶ τεθνηκότας κοινῶς ὅλους. . . .—P. 110 : μόνον αἱ θεῖαι λειτουργίαι, αἱ προσευχαὶ καὶ ἐλεημοσύναι, ὅπου γίνουνται διὰ τὴν ψυχὴν ἀπὸ τοὺς ζῶντας, ἐκεῖνα τὴν ὠφελοῦσι πολλότατα καὶ ἀπὸ τὰ δεσμὰ τοῦ ᾅδου τὴν ἐλευθεροῦσιν.

Philaret, n. 18, rejects both purgatory and every other purification of the soul after death.

III. PROTESTANT.

A. Sm. p. 307 : Purgatorium et quidquid ei solennitatis, cultus et quæstus adhæret, mera diaboli larva est. Pugnat enim cum primo articulo, qui docet, Christum solum et non hominum opera animas liberare. S. *Conf. Wirtemb.* p. 123 sq.

Conf. Helv. ii. cap. 26 : Quod quidam tradunt de igne purgatorio, fidei christianæ : credo remissionem peccatorum et vitam æternam, purgationique plenæ per Christum et Christi sententiis adversatur.

Conf. Gall. art. 24 : Purgatorium arbitramur figmentum esse, ex eâdem officinâ profectum, unde etiam manarunt vota monastica, peregrinationes, interdicta matrimonii et usus ciborum, ceremonialis certorum dierum observatio, confessio auricularis, indulgentiæ, ceteræque res omnes ejusmodi, quibus opinantur quidam, se gratiam et salutem mereri. Ea vero omnia non tantum rejicimus propter falsam meriti opinionem ipsis adjunctam, sed etiam quoniam sunt humana commenta et jugum ex hominum auctoritate conscientiis impositum.

Thirty-nine Artt. art. xxii.: The Romish doctrine concerning purgatory, pardons, worshipping, and adoration as well of images as of relics, and also invocation of saints, is a fond thing, vainly invented, and grounded upon no warranty of Scripture, but rather repugnant to the word of God.

S. *Declar. Thorun.* p. 66, and, as it concerns the Arminians, Curcellæi *Op.* p. 655 sqq.; Limborch, *Theol. christ.* vi. 10. 10 and 16.

Indulgence.

Release, perfect or partial, from the temporal penances which are exacted even after the remission of eternal punishments, as also from the pains of purgatory *per modum suffragii* or by prayer, may, according to Romish doctrine, be obtained by believers out of the treasure of superabundant merit which the Church has at her disposal. Such a dispensation is called Indulgence. The pains of purgatory, however, may also, by way of supplication, be abridged through masses for the dead, prayers, satisfactions (fasts, alms, pilgrimages, etc.) of the living. The Greeks reject all indulgences, as well as all vicarious satisfaction for the dead. The evangelical church, rejecting temporal satisfactions, rejects as a consequence the need of indulgence; denying the treasury of superabundant merit, it denies the source of indulgence.

ROMISH SYMBOLS.

The doctrine of indulgences is not dogmatically exhibited in the Romish symbols. The Council of Trent only obviates perversions.

Conc. Trid. sess. xxv. *De indulgent.:* Cum potestas conferendi indulgentias a Christo ecclesiæ concessa sit, atque hujusmodi potestate, divinitus sibi tradita, antiquissimis etiam temporibus illa usa fuerit: synodus indulgentiarum usum, christiano populo maxime salutarem et sacrorum conciliorum auctoritate probatum, in ecclesiâ retinendum esse docet et præcipit; eosque anathemate damnat, qui aut inutiles esse asserunt vel eas concedendi in ecclesiâ potestatem esse negant. In his tamen concedendis moderationem juxta veterem et probatam in ecclesiâ consuetudinem adhiberi cupit, ne nimiâ facilitate ecclesiastica disciplina enervetur. Abusus vero, qui in his irrepserunt, quorum occasione insigne hoc indulgentiarum nomen ab hæreticis blasphematur, emendatos et correctos cupiens, præsenti decreto generaliter statuit, pravos quæstus omnes pro his consequendis, unde plurima in christiano populo abusuum causa fluxit, omnino abolendos esse. Ceteros vero, qui ex superstitione, ignorantiâ, irreverentiâ aut aliunde quomodocunque provenerunt, cum ob multiplices locorum et provinciarum, apud quas hi committuntur, corruptelas commode nequeant specialiter prohiberi, mandat omnibus episcopis, ut diligenter quisque hujusmodi abusus ecclesiæ suæ colligat cet.

We may give the dogmatic grounds on which indulgences rest in Bellarmine's words, *De indulg.* i. 1 : Ecclesia et scholæ theologorum indulgentias vocant remissiones pœnarum, quæ sæpe remanent eluendæ post remissionem culparum et reconciliationem in sacramento pœnitentiæ adeptam, quas remissiones summi pontifices ex paternâ lenitate . . . certis temporibus et non sine justâ aliquâ et rationabili causâ concedere solent. — Cap. 2 : Opus bonum, quâ parte meritorium est, non potest alii applicari, potest tamen, quâ satisfactorium est ; . . . exstat in ecclesiâ thesaurus satisfactionum ex Christi passionibus infinitus, qui nunquam exhauriri poterit. . . . Ad hunc thesaurum superfluentium satisfactionum pertinent etiam passiones b. Mariæ virginis et omnium aliorum sanctorum, qui plus passi sunt, quam eorum peccata requirerent. — Cap. 3 : Satisfactiones Christos et sanctis supervacaneæ applicari possunt aliis, qui rei sunt pœnæ temporalis. Docemur enim in Symbolo apostolico, fideles omnes esse invicem membra et quasi vivum quoddam corpus et, sicut membra viva se invicem juvant, ita fideles inter se bona sua communicare, præsertim cum ea, quæ uni superflua sunt, alteri necessaria vel valde utilia esse possunt. — As to the manner and efficacy of indulgences, c. 5 : Indulgentia proprie est absolutio judiciaria annexam habens solutionem ex thesauro. — Dat (pontifex) vere indulgentiam subditis suis . . . ; contra autem defunctis non dicitur dare simpliciter indulgentiam sed per modum suffragii, quia non ipse sed deus acceptat compensationem pro defunctis et eosdem defunctos absolvit, pontifex autem solum offert ex thesauro justam compensationem. . . .—C. 7: Per indulg. non absolvimur nec solvimur a reatu culpæ ullius i. e. nec letalis nec venialis . . . ; per indulg. non tollitur nisi reatus pœnæ temporalis, qui remanet culpa dimissa. — Indulgentiæ liberant homines a reatu pœnæ non solum coram ecclesiâ sed etiam coram deo. — Cap. 14: Res certissima est et ap. Catholicos indubitata, indulgentiis juvari posse animas, quæ in purgatorio pœnas luunt. — Vera sententia est, indulgentias prodesse (defunctis) per modum suffragii, quia non prosunt per modum absolutionis juridicæ, sed per modum solutionis, quo modo prosunt suffragia, quæ pro defunctis fieri solent. Sed cum suffragia tribus modis defunctos juvent, per modum meriti de congruo, per mod. impetrationis et per mod. satisfactionis, indulgentiæ autem non sint nisi satisfactoriæ, intelligendum est, indulgentias dari defunctis per modum suffragii tantum satisfactorii. Comp. Bellarmin. *Purgat.* c. 16.

Bellarmine admits that unanimity is not to be found among Romish theologians as to the virtue of indulgences. Many denied that remission of the temporal punishments of sin was obtained, that is, of sin as such and as punished by God, and also that the power of indulgences extended to purgatory. We have given the more general view, which Bellarmine maintains, and which modern theologians do not scruple at. Eck, *Loci,* c. 23; Bossii *Institutt. theol.* iii. p. 226 sqq.; Bossuet, *Exposit.* p. 20 sq.; Möhler, *neue Untersuch.* § 65 f.; Klee, *Dogmat.* iii. S. 280 f.

Prayers for the Dead.

The *suffragia fidelium pro defunctis* are briefly mentioned in the Conc. Trid. sess. xxv. *Purg.;* and among them prominence is given to the *acceptabile altaris sacrificium.* As to the latter, the masses for the dead, vid. *Cat. Rom.* ii. 4. 78; and on the whole subject, Bellarm. *Purgat.* c. 15. He says among other things: Tria sunt genera suffragiorum, sacrificium missæ, oratio et opera quælibet pœnalia et satisfactoria, ut eleemosyna, jejunia, peregrinationes et similia.

Evangelical Protests.

A. Sm. p. 310 : (Draconis cauda ista, missam intelligo, peperit multiplices abominationes et idololatrias.) Huc pertinent indulgentiæ vivis et defunctis pro pecunia attributæ, quibus sacrilegus et damnatus ille Judas seu papa meritum Christi et merita superflua omnium sanctorum et totius ecclesiæ vendidit, quæ omnia et singula nequaquam ferenda sunt, quia carent verbo dei, non sunt mandata, non sunt necessaria, sed pugnant cum articulo primo. Meritum enim Christi non nostris operibus aut nummis, sed per fidem ex gratiâ apprehenditur et obtinetur, sine pecuniâ et merito, non per papæ potestatem sed per prædicationem verbi dei oblatum et propositum.

The Reformed Confessions reject indulgences only in a few simple terms, as the matter had been thoroughly sifted already. *Helv.* ii. c. 14; *Gall.* art. 24; *Eng. Art.* xxii.: *Conf. Scot.* 128. Barclay, for the Quakers, is very strong, *Apol.* vii.

XVIII.

CONFIRMATION; MARRIAGE; SUPREME UNCTION; ORDERS.

THE Protestant Church rejects these four sacraments as such, because the scriptural arguments adduced in their favour appear untenable. Supreme unction is indeed absolutely renounced; ordination and confirmation are retained as useful rites, which exert a moral influence; lastly, on the marriage obligations, whose connection with the religious life is recognised, the Protestant Church pronounces an ecclesiastical consecration. What the Greek and Latin Churches have taught concerning the matter and form of these four sacraments will appear in the following extracts from their symbols.

a. Confirmation.

I. GREEK AND LATIN.

The difference between the Romish and the Greek Confirmation does not affect the internal sacramental elements, but the external. 1. In the Greek Church, confirmation may be validly administered by every priest. 2. The Greeks attach confirmation immediately to baptism; while the Roman Catholic Church requires that confirmation should be administered not before the seventh year at least.

Conc. Trid. sess. vii. confirmat. can. 1: Si quis dixerit, confirmationem baptizatorum otiosam esse ceremoniam et non

potius verum et proprium sacramentum, aut olim nihil aliud fuisse, quam catechesin quandam, quâ adolescentiœ proximi fidei suœ rationem coram ecclesiâ exponebant: anathema sit.
— Can. 3 : Si quis dixerit, sanctœ confirmationis ordinarium ministrum non esse solum episcopum, sed quemvis simplicem sacerdotem, anathema sit. Cf. sess. xxiii. can. 7.

Cat. Rom. ii. 3. 2 : *Confirmationem* ab ecclesiâ hoc sacramentum idcirco vocari docendum est, quoniam, qui baptizatus est, cum ab episcopo sacro chrismate unguitur, additis solemnibus illis verbis : *Signo te signo crucis et confirmo te chrismate salutis, in nomine patris et filii et Spiritus sancti,* nisi aliud efficientiam impediat, novœ virtutis robore firmior atque adeo perfectus Christi miles esse incipit.

Ib. ii. 3. 5 : Cum baptismi gratiâ homines in novam vitam gignantur, confirmationis autem sacramento, qui jam geniti sunt, viri evadant, evacuatis quœ erant parvuli : satis intelligitur, quantum in naturali vita generatio ab incremento distat, tantundem inter se differre baptismum, qui regenerandi vim habet, et confirmationem, cujus virtute fideles augescunt et perfectum animi robur assumunt.

Ib. ii. 3. 18 : Observandum est, omnibus quidem post baptismum confirmationis sacramentum posse administrari, sed minus tamen expedire, hoc fieri, antequam pueri rationis usum habuerint. Quare si duodecimus annus exspectandus non videatur, usque ad septimum certe hoc sacramentum differre maxime convenit. Neque enim confirmatio ad salutis necessitatem instituta est, sed ut ejus virtute optime instructi et parati inveniremur, cum nobis pro Christi fide pugnandum esset : ad quod sane pugnœ genus pueros, qui adhuc usu rationis carent, nemo aptos judicarit.

Ib. ii. 3. 20 : Hœc sacra et mystica signa ejusmodi esse demonstratum est, quœ gratiam declarant atque efficiunt. Ex quo sequitur, ut peccata etiam condonet ac remittat, quoniam gratiam simul cum peccato ne fingere quidem nobis licet. Sed præter hæc, quæ cum aliis communia censenda sunt, primum quidem illud proprie confirmationi tribuitur, quod baptismi gratiam perficit. Qui enim per baptismum christiani effecti sunt, quasi infantes modo geniti, teneritatem adhuc et mollitiem quandam habent ac deinde chrismatis sacramento adversus omnes carnis, mundi et diaboli impetus robustiores fiunt: et eorum animus in fide omnino confirmatur ad confitendum et glorificandum nomen Jesu Christi: ex quo etiam nomen ipsum inventum esse nemo dubitat.

Ib. ii. 3. 23: Habet confirmatio eam vim, ut characterem imprimat; quo fit, ut nullâ unquam ratione iterari possit.

The theology of confirmation is very fully handled by Bellarmine, as also by Klee, *K. D.* iii.

Conf. orthod. p. 161: Τὸ δεύτερον μυστήριον εἶναι τὸ μύρον τοῦ χρίσματος, τὸ ὁποῖον ἤρχισεν ἀπὸ τὸν καιρὸν ἐκεῖνον, ὅπου τὸ πνεῦμα τὸ ἅγιον ἐκατάβηκεν εἰς τοὺς ἀποστόλους, σφραγίζοντὰς τοὺς μὲ τὴν θείαν τοῦ χάριν, διὰ νὰ κηρύττουσι σταθερῶς καὶ ἀδιαλείπτως τὴν πίστιν τοῦ Χριστοῦ.

Ib. p. 163: Πρῶτον ζητεῖται (εἰς τὸ μυστήριον τοῦ μύρου τοῦ χρίσματος) νὰ γίνεται ἀπὸ τὸν ἀνωτάτῳ ἐπίσκοπον τὸ μύρον τοῦτο. Δεύτερον νὰ ἔχῃ τὴν πρεπουμένην τοῦ ὕλην, ἤγουν τὸ ἔλαιον, τὸ βάλσαμον καὶ τὰ λοιπὰ μυρίσματα. Τρίτον ζητεῖται ὅτι παρευθὺς μετὰ τὸ βάπτισμα νὰ χρίῃ ὁ ἱερεὺς τὸν βαπτιζόμενον εἰς τὰ διωρισμένα μέλη, ἐπιλέγων τὰ λόγια ἐκεῖνα· σφραγὶς δωρεᾶς πνεύματος ἁγίου, ἀμήν. Ἀπὸ τὸ μυστήριον τοῦτο γενοῦνται οἱ καρποὶ τοῦτοι· Πρῶτον διατὶ καθὼς μετὰ βάπτισμα ἀναγενόμεθα τέτοιας λογῆς, μὲ τὸ ἅγιον μύρον γενόμεθα μέτοχοι τοῦ ἁγίου πνεύματος, βεβαιωθέντες εἰς τὴν πίστιν τοῦ κυρίου, καὶ αὐξάνομεν εἰς τὴν θείαν χάριν κατὰ τὸν ἀπόστολον. Δεύτερον διατὶ μὲ τὴν δύναμιν τοῦ ἁγίου πν. οὕτως εὔμεσθεν βέβαιοι καὶ στερεοὶ ὅπου δὲν ἠμπορεῖ νὰ βλάψῃ καθόλου ὁ νοητὸς ἐχθρὸς τὴν ψυχήν μας.

Cf. Metroph. Critop. *Conf.* c. 8, p. 87 sqq.; Jerem. *in Act. Wirtemb.* p. 79. The latter confesses that this sacrament rests upon no scriptural authority, but upon apostolical tradition.

II. PROTESTANT.

The Protestant Confessions mention Confirmation (the Romish) only to reject it. *Apol. A. C.* p. 201: Confirmatio et extrema unctio sunt ritus accepti a patribus, quos ne ecclesia quidem tanquam necessarios ad salutem requirit, quia non habent mandatum Dei. *Conf. Saxon.* p. 82: Ritus confirmationis, quem nunc episcopi retinent, quid est nisi inanis umbra? *Conf. Helv.* ii. c. 19: Confirmatio et extrema unctio inventa sunt hominum, quibus nullo cum damno carere potest ecclesia. But the earliest theologians recommended Confirmation as freed from papistical superstition (Chemnicius, *Exam. Conc. Trid.* ii. 3. 25; Calvin, *Instit.* iv. 19. 4; cf. a. *Declar. Thorun.* ii. 14. 1); and since the middle of the seventeenth century, this ceremony, which our Church has never held to be essential, has been everywhere either introduced or brought into publicity. S. Limborch, *Theol. chr.* v. 77. 2 sq.

b. *Marriage: Divorce.*

I. ROMISH.

Conc. Trid. sess. xxiv. matrim.: Gratiam, quæ naturalem amorem perficeret et indissolubilem unitatem confirmaret conjugesque sanctificaret, ipse Christus, sacramentorum institutor atque perfector, suâ nobis passione promeruit. . . . Cum igitur matrimonium in lege evangelicâ veteribus connubiis per Christum gratia præstet, merito inter novæ legis sacramenta annumerandum patres, concilia et universalis ecclesiæ traditio semper docuerunt.

Ib. can. 1: Si quis dixerit, matrimonium non esse vere et proprie unum ex septem legis evangelicæ sacramentis a Christo institutum, sed ab hominibus in ecclesiâ inventum neque gratiam conferre: anathema sit.

Cat. Rom. ii. 8. 3: Ita ex communi theologorum sententiâ definitur: matrimonium est viri et mulieris maritalis conjunctio, inter legitimas personas individuam vitæ consuetudinem retinens.—*Ib.* ii. 8. 15: Quemadmodum matrimonium, ut naturalis conjunctio ad propagandum humanum genus ab initio institutum est, ita deinde, ut populus ad veri dei et salvatoris nostri Christi cultum et religionem procrearetur atque educaretur, sacramenti dignitas illi tributa est. Cum enim Christus vellet arctissimæ illius necessitudinis, quæ ei cum ecclesiâ intercedit, suæque erga nos immensæ caritatis certum aliquod signum dare, tanti mysterii dignitatem hac potissimum maris et feminæ sanctâ conjunctione declaravit. Quod quidem aptissime factum esse, ex eo intelligi potest, quod ex omnibus humanis necessitudinibus nulla inter se homines magis quam matrimonii vinculum constringit, maximâque inter se vir et uxor caritate et benevolentiâ devincti sunt. Atque idcirco fit, ut frequenter sacræ literæ nuptiarum similitudine divinam hanc Christi et ecclesiæ copulationem nobis ante oculos proponant.

Ib. ii. 8. 23: Primum matrimonii bonum est proles, hoc est liberi, qui ex justâ et legitimâ suscipiuntur uxore. Id enim tanti fecit apostolus, ut dicerit: Salvabitur mulier per filiorum generationem. Nec vero hoc de procreatione solum, sed de educatione etiam et disciplinâ, quâ filii ad pietatem erudiuntur, intelligendum est.—24: Sequitur fides, quod est alterum matrimonii bonum, non ille virtutis habitus, quo imbuimur, cum baptismum percipimus, sed fidelitas quædam, quâ mutuo vir uxori et uxor viro se ita obstringit, ut alter alteri sui corporis potestatem tradat, sanctumque illud conjugii fœdus nunquam se violaturum pollicetur.—25: Tertium bonum sacramentum appellatur, vinculum scilicet matrimonii, quod nunquam dissolvi potest. Nam, ut est apud apostolum, dominus præcipit uxorem a viro non discedere: quod si discesserit, manere innuptam aut viro suo reconciliari: et vir uxorem non dimittat. Si enim matrimonium, ut sacramentum est, Christi conjunctionem cum ecclesia signat, necesse est, ut Christus se nunquam ab ecclesiâ disjungit, ita uxorem a viro, quod ad matrimonii vinculum attinet, separari non posse.

As to the matter and form of this sacrament, it has been the most common opinion of theologians that the matter is the *corpora* or *personæ contrahentium*, and the form the *verba* or *signa mutuum consensum exprimentia*. Consequently the bridal pair are the *ministri sacramenti*. Against this opinion the dignity of the priestly benediction has been urged by Berg and others. See, on this controversy, Bossius and Schmid.

II. GREEK.

Conf. orthod. p. 183: Ὁ τίμιος γάμος, ὁ ὁποῖος γίνεται πρῶτον μὲν μὲ τὴν εἰς ἀλλήλους συμφωνίαν τοῦ ἀνδρὸς καὶ τῆς γυναικὸς χωρίς τινος ἐμποδίσματος· ἡ ὁποία συμφωνία δὲν φάνισεν διὰ ἀληθινοῦ γάμου σύββασις, παρὰ ἐκεῖνοι οἱ ἴδιοι νὰ μαρτυρήσωσιν ἀλλήλους τῶν ἔμπροσθεν τοῦ ἱερέως τὴν ὑπόσχεσίν τως· . . . ὕστερον δὲ βεβαιώνεται καὶ εὐλογῆται ἀπὸ τὸν ἱερέα τούτῃ ἡ συμφωνία καὶ ὑπόσχεσίς των. Cf. Metroph. Critop. *Conf.* c. 12, p. 114 sqq.; Jerem. *in Actis Wirtemb.* pp. 78, 80, 241.

The Greek Church permits no fourth marriage, and makes the second and third difficult (Met. Critop. *Conf.* 12).

Divorce.

The Roman Catholic Church declares every dissolution of marriage, or *divortium* (which allows another marriage), even after adultery resulting, to be unlawful, and permits only a separation of the pair. The Greeks, on the contrary, like the Mennonites, admit adultery to be a reason, and the only sufficient reason, for divorce. Metrop. Critop. *Conf.* c. 13 : "The married pair must not be separated for any reason save that of adultery, according to the gospel." As to the law principles which regulate the practice of the Greek Church, *vide* Heincee. ii. 393. The Protestant doctrine will appear below.

I. Roman Symbols.

Concil. Trid. sess. xxiv. can. 7 : Si quis dixerit, ecclesiam errare, cum docuit et docet juxta evangelicam et apostolicam doctrinam, propter adulterium alterius conjugum matrimonii vinculum non posse dissolvi, et utrumque, vel etiam innocentem, qui causam adulterio non dedit, non posse, altero conjuge vivente, aliud matrimonium contrahere : mœcharique eum, qui dimissâ adulterâ aliam duxerit, et eam, quæ dimisso adultero alii nupserit : anathema sit.

Cat. Rom. ii. 8. 20 sq.: Christi testimonio (Matt. xix. 9) facile comprobatur, nullo divortio vinculum matrimonii dissolvi posse. Si enim post libellum repudii mulier a viri lege soluta esset, liceret ei sine ullo adulterii crimine alteri viro nubere. Atqui dominus aperte denunciat: omnis, qui dimittit uxorem suam et alteram ducit, mœchatur. Quare conjugii vinculum nullâ re nisi morte disrumpi, perspicuum est. . . . Ac ne forte alicui videatur durior matrimonii lex, quod nullâ

unquam ratione dissolvi possit, docendum est, quæ sint cum
eâ utilitates conjunctæ. Primum enim homines in conjungendis matrimoniis virtutem potius et morum similitudinem,
quam divitias et pulchritudinem spectandam esse hinc intelligent, quâ quidem re communi societati maxime consuli nemo
dubitare potest. Præterea, si divortio matrimonium dissolveretur, vix unquam dissidendi causæ hominibus, quæ iis ab
antiquo pacis et pudicitiæ hoste quotidie objicerentur, deessent. Nunc vero, cum fideles secum cogitant, quamvis etiam
conjugii convictu et consuetudine careant, se tamen matrimonii
vinculo constrictos teneri omnemque alterius uxoris ducendæ
spem sibi præcisam esse, eâ re fit, ut ad iracundiam et dissidia
tradiores esse consueverint. Quod si interdum etiam divortium faciant et diutius conjugis desiderium ferre non possint,
facile per amicos reconciliati ad ejus convictum redeunt.

Cf. Bellarmin, *De sacram. matrim.* c. 14–17; Klee, *kath.
Dogmat.* iii. 317 ff.; Walter, *Kirchenrecht.* S. 620 ff.

II. PROTESTANT.

The Protestant symbols recognise in marriage a divine institution (*Conf. Aug.* p. 33; *Apol. A. C.* p. 238; *Cat. maj.*
455; *Conf. Helv.* i. art. 27; *Helv.* ii. 29), but without admitting that it is a sacrament. *Apol.* p. 202: Matrimonium non
est primum institutum in novo Testamento, sed statim initio,
creato genere humano. "It has the commandment of God,
it has also the promises, not indeed peculiar to the New Testament, but pertaining to life universal in the body. Wherefore, if any one wishes to call it a sacrament, he ought to
distinguish it from those more proper sacraments which are
signs in the New Testament, testimonies of grace and of the
remission of sins." Cf. Calvin, *Instit.* iv. 19. 34; *Conf. Helv.*
ii. cap. 19; *Dec. Thor.* p. 67. The ecclesiastical benediction
was, however, always usual in the Protestant Church, with the
exception of Holland (Luther's *Traubüchlein* became an appendix of the Catechism), but not as necessary, rather as an
edifying usage.[1]

[1] In the Harmon. Conf., the *Conf. Helv.* ii. c. 29 has: confirmentur (conjugia) publice in templo cum precatione et benedictione.

As to divorce, the Protestant symbols contain nothing complete. Generally, we read in *A. Sm.* p. 355 : injusta est traditio, quæ prohibet conjugium personæ innocenti post factum divortium. The *Conf. Sax.*, p. 80, is more copious : De divortiis firmissime tenetur regula : peccare eos, qui vel adulterio vel desertione initium faciunt distractionis et adulteri et adulteræ, et desertores et desertrices condemnamus voce docentium in ecclesiis et judicum in consistoriis, et a magistratibus severe puniuntur. Sed personæ innocenti, cum re cognitâ pronuntiatur esse libera, non prohibetur conjugium, ut deum invocare et pie vivere possit. . . . Hæc nostra consuetudo et cum veteri ecclesiâ congruit. *Vide Conf. Wirtemb.* p. 120 ; Chemnicius, *Exam. Conc. Trid.* ii. 14, p. 600 sqq. ; Limborch, *Theol. chr.* v. 60. 33 sqq.

c. Extreme Unction: Extrema Unctio.

ROMISH AND GREEK.

Conc. Trid. sess. xiv. *Proœm. de. sacr. extr. unct.* : Visum est synodo, præcedenti doctrinæ de pœnitentiâ adjungere ea, quæ sequuntur de sacramento extremæ unctionis : quod non modo pœnitentiæ, sed et totius christianæ vitæ, quæ perpetua pœnitentia esse debet, consummativum existimatum est a patribus. Primum itaque circa illius institutionem declarat et docet, quod clementissimus redemtor noster, quemadmodum auxilia maxima in sacramentis aliis præparavit, quibus christiani conservare se integros, dum viverent, ab omni graviori spiritus incommodo possint, ita extremæ unctionis sacramento finem vitæ tanquam firmissimo quodam præsidio munivit.

Ib. cap. 1 : Instituta est sacra unctio infirmorum tanquam vere et proprie sacramentum N. T., a. Christo Marc. vi. 13, quidem insinuatum, per Jacobum autem (v. 14 sq.) fidelibus commendatum ac promulgatum. . . . Intellexit ecclesia, materiam esse oleum ab episcopo benedictum. Nam unctio aptissime Spiritus sancti gratiam repræsentat ; formam deinde esse illa verba : per istam unctionem cet.

Ib. cap. 2 : Oratio fidei salvabit infirmum et alleviabit eum dominus et, si in peccatis sit, dimittentur ei. Res etenim hæc gratia est Spiritus sancti, cujus unctio delicta, si quæ sint adhuc expianda, ac peccati reliquias abstergit et ægroti animam alleviat et confirmat, magnam in eo divinæ misericordiæ fiduciam excitando, quâ infirmus sublevatus . . . et sanitatem corporis interdum, ubi saluti animæ expedierit, consequitur.

Ib. cap. 3 : Declaratur, esse hanc unctionem infirmis adhibendam, illis vero præsertim, qui tam periculose decumbunt, ut in exitu vitæ constituti videantur. Quod si infirmi post susceptam hanc unctionem convaluerint, iterum hujus sacramenti subsidio juvari poterunt, cum in aliud simile vitæ discrimen inciderint.

Cat. Rom. ii. 6. 9 : Docendi sunt fideles, quamvis hoc sacramentum ad omnes pertineat, quædam tamen hominum genera excipi, quibus administrandum non est. Ac primum excipiuntur, qui sano et firmo corpore sunt. Iis enim extremam unctionem tribuendam non esse, et apostolus docet, cum inquit : Infirmatur quis in vobis, . . . et ratio ostendit, siquidem ob eam rem instituta est, non modo ut animæ, sed etiam ut corpori medicinam afferat. Cum igitur illi tantum, qui morbo laborant, curatione indigeant, idcirco iis etiam, qui adeo periculose ægrotare videntur, ut, ne supremus illis vitæ dies instet, metuendum sit, hoc sacramentum præberi debet. Nemini igitur, qui graviori morbo affectus non sit, sacramentum unctionis dare licet, tametsi vitæ periculum adeat, vel quia periculosam navigationem paret, vel quia prœlium initurus sit, a quo illi certa mors impendeat, vel etiam si capitis damnatus ad supplicium raperetur. Omnes præterea, qui rationis usu carent, ad hoc sacramentum suscipiendum apti non sunt ; et pueri, qui nulla peccata admittunt, quorum reliquias sanare hujus sacramenti remedio opus sit ; amentes item et furiosi, nisi interdum rationis usum haberent, et eo potissimum tempore pii animi significationem darent peterentque, ut sacro oleo unguerentur.

Ib. ii. 6. 11 : In quibus illud observare oportet, unâ eademque ægrotatione, cum æger in eodem vitæ periculo positus est, semel tantum unguendum esse. Quod si post susceptam hanc unctionem æger convaluerit, quoties postea in id vitæ discrimen inciderit, toties ejusdem sacramenti subsidium ei poterit adhiberi.

Conf. orthod. p. 185 sq.: Τὸ εὐχέλαιον τὸ ὁποῖον εἶναι διατεταγμένον ἀπὸ τὸν Χριστόν (Mr. vi. 13).... Πρῶτον πρέπει νὰ προσέχωμεν, νὰ γίνεται τὸ μυστήριον τοῦτο (εὐχέλαιον) ἀπὸ ἱερεῖς μὲ τὰ ἀκόλουθα τοῦ μυστηρίου καὶ ὄχι ἀπό τινα ἄλλον· δεύτερον νὰ εἶναι τὸ ἔλαιον καθαρὸν χωρίς τινος ἀρτύματός, καὶ νὰ εἶναι ὁ ἀσθενὴς ὀρθόδοξος καὶ καθολικῆς πίστεως, νὰ εἶναι ἐξομολογούμενος τὰ ἁμαρτήματά του ἔμπροσθεν εἰς τὸν ἱερέα τὸν πνευματικόν του· καὶ τρίτον εἰς τὸν καιρὸν τοῦ χρίσματος νὰ διαβάζεται ἡ εὐχὴ ἐκείνη, εἰς τὴν ὁποῖαν ἑρμηνεύεται τοῦ μυστηρίου τούτου ἡ δύναμις. — Τὰ διάφορα καὶ καρποὺς ὁποῦ γεννοῦνται ἀπὸ τὸ μυστήριον τοῦτο, ὁ ἀπόστολος Ἰάκωβος (v. 14) τοὺς ἑρμηνεύει, λέγωντας ἄφεσιν ἁμαρτιῶν ἢ σωτηρίαν ψυχῆς, ἔπειτα ὑγείαν τοῦ σώματος καλὰ καὶ πάντοτε ἡ θεραπεία τοῦ σώματος νὰ μὴν γίνεται, ἀλλ' ἡ ἄφεσις τῶν ἁμαρτιῶν τῆς ψυχῆς πάντοτε εἰς τὸν μετανοοῦντα ἀκολουθῇ.

Cf. Metroph. Critop. *Conf.* c. 13, p. 117 sqq.; Jerem. *in Act. Wirtemb.* pp. 81, 242. The Greek Church deviates from the Roman, in that it does not defer the anointing till deadly peril. *Vid.* Metroph. Critop. *Conf.* p. 121, οὐ μένομεν τὰ λοίσθια τοῦ κάμνοντος καὶ τότ' εἰς ταύτην (χρίσιν) ἐρχόμεθα, ἀλλ' ἔτι ἐλπίδας ἀγαθὰς ἔχοντες ὑπὲρ τῆς ὑγιείας ἐκείνου χρώμεθα τούτῳ τῷ μυστηρίῳ.... ὥστε οὐχ ἅπαξ τοῦ βίου ἀλλὰ καὶ πολλάκις ἔξεστι χρῆσθαι τούτῳ, καθὰ καὶ τοῖς ἰαματικοῖς φαρμάκοις τοσαυτάκις χρώμεθα, ὁσάκις νοσήσομεν.

Against extreme unction as a sacrament, see *Apol. A. C.* p. 201; *Conf. Helv.* ii. c. 19; *Conf. Wirtemb.* p. 121 sq.; *Conf. Saxon.* p. 82; *Declar. Thorun.* p. 66.

d. *Orders: Ordinatio.*

I. Roman and Greek.

Con. Trid. sess. xxiii. *Sacram. ordin.* cap. 3: Cum scripturæ testimonio, apostolicâ traditione et patrum unanimi consensu perspicuum sit, per sacram ordinationem, quæ verbis et signis exterioribus perficitur gratiam conferri: dubitare nemo debet, ordinem esse vere et proprie unum ex septem sanctæ ecclesiæ sacramentis. Cf. can. 3.

Ib. can. 4: Si quis dix., per sacram. ordinationem non dari

Spiritum sanctum, . . . aut per eam non imprimi characterem, vel eum qui sacerdos semel fuit, laicum rursus fieri posse, an. sit.

Ib. can. 7: Si quis dix., episcopos non esse presbyteris superiores, vel non habere potestatem confirmandi et ordinandi, vel eam quam habent, illis esse cum presbyteris communem, . . . an. sit.

Cat. Rom. ii. 7. 34: Constat, quamvis ordinis sacramentum maxime ad ecclesiæ utilitatem et pulchritudinem spectet, tamen in ejus quoque animo, qui sacris initiatur, sanctificationis gratiam efficere, qua idoneus habilisque ad recte munere suo fungendum sacramentaque administranda reddatur; quemadmodum etiam baptismi gratia quilibet ad alia sacramenta percipienda aptus efficitur.

The question to what grade of clerical order consecration is a sacrament, is answered by Bellarmin, *Sacram. ord.* c. 5 sqq.: Convenit inter omnes catholicos, ordinem presbyterorum esse vere ac proprie sacramentum, de aliis non omnino convenit. De diaconis valde probabile et omnino tenendum est, eorum ordinationem sacramentum esse, licet id non sit certum ex fide (i. e. non potest evidenter deduci ex verbo dei scripto vel tradito). De subdiaconatu non est tanta certitudo, quanta de diaconatu. Nam nec in scripturis de eo fit mentio, nec ejus ordinatio habet manus impositionem, nec subdiaconi ministrant eucharistiam aut alia facere possunt quæ diaconi, et denique non pertinent proprie ad hierarchiam, nisi ut ministri heirarcharum. Est tamen valde probabile, etiam hunc ordinem esse sacramentum tum, quia videtur imprimere characterem, cum sit initerabilis, tum quia habet annexum solenne votum continentiæ, tum denique quia hæc est communis theologorum sententia cet. De minoribus ordin. minus probabile est, quod sacramenta sint, quam de subdiaconatu, nam neque est ita communis sententia cet. Absolute tamen probabilior sententia est, quæ ordines omnes sacramenta esse docet, quam ea, quæ id negat cet.

Conf. orthod. p. 173: Ἡ ἱερωσύνη, ὁποῦ εἶναι μυστήριον, διετάχθη τοῖς ἀποστόλοις ἀπὸ τὸν Χριστόν, καὶ διὰ τῆς ἐπιθέσεως τῶν χειρῶν αὐτῶν μέχρι τῆς σήμερον γίνεται ἡ χειροτονία, διαδεξαμένων τῶν ἐπισκόπων αὐτοὺς πρὸς διάδοσιν τῶν θείων μυστηρίων καὶ διακονίαν τῆς σωτηρίας τῶν ἀνθρώπων.

Cf. Jerem. *in Actis Wirtemb.* pp. 78, 241.
Ordination is called by the Greeks χειροτονία.

II. PROTESTANT.

Apol. A. C., p. 201 sq., admits that orders may be a sacrament in the wider sense; that is, if *ordo* means the ministry of the word.

A. Sm. p. 352: Cum jure divino non sint diversi gradus episcopi et pastoris, manifestum est, ordinationem a pastore in suâ ecclesiâ factum jure divino ratam esse.

The evangelical doctrine of ordination is best given by Chemnicius, *Examen Concilii Tridentini*, ed. E. Preuss, S. 479, 480.

Conf. Helv. ii. cap. 18: Qui electi sunt (ab ecclesiâ vel ad hoc deputatis ab ecclesiâ), ordinentur a senioribus cum orationibus publicis et impositione manuum.

Ib. cap. 19: Sunt, qui sacramenta septem numerent. Ex quibus nos . . . ordinationem ministrorum non papisticam quidem illam sed apostolicam . . . agnoscimus institutum esse dei utile, sed non sacramentum.

Declar. Thorun. p. 67.

XIX.
THE CHURCH: ITS IDEA AND AUTHORITY.

FIRST POINT OF DIVERGENCE.

THE Romanists term the Church the fellowship of those baptized into Christ, as founded upon earth by Christ under His representative, the Pope, as its visible head. The Protestants, on the contrary, term it the fellowship of the saints, in which the gospel is purely preached and the sacraments are duly, that is, in harmony with their institution, administered.

Observations.

The preaching of the word of God and administration of the sacraments, as open to observation and scriptural test, have been regarded by Protestants as the *externæ notæ* of the Church. *Apol. A. C.* 144; *Helv.* ii. c. 17. That which lies at the basis of the fellowship of saints, true faith, is something internal. With reference to this in particular, and to the doctrine of election, some Reformed Confessions term the Church *invisibilis*: *Helv.* ii. c. 17; *Conf. Scot.* art. 16. Cf. Calvin, *Institt.* iv. 1. 7. The German Reformers rather avoided this term *invisible*, on account of Anabaptist and Romanist perversions: cf. *e.g.* Melanch. *Loc.* i. p. 283. [That the Church is at once a fellowship and an institution, is not doubted by either the Romanist or the Evangelical Church. The question is only as to which of the two is the foremost and most essential element. The Roman Church teaches that the Church is *principaliter* institution; the Protestants, that it is *principaliter* fellowship.]

SYMBOLICAL TESTIMONIES.

I. Roman Catholic.

Confut. A. C. 7 : Septimus Conf. A. artic., quo affirmatur ecclesiam congregationem esse sanctorum, non potest citra fidei præjudicium admitti, si per hoc segregentur ab ecclesiâ mali et peccatores. Nam articulus ille in Constantiensi damnatus est concilio inter errores damnatæ memoriæ J. Huss et plane contradicit evangelio (Matt. xiii. 47 sq., xxv. 1 sqq.).

Cat. Rom. i. 10. 7 : In ecclesiâ militanti duo sunt hominum genera, bonorum et improborum, et improbi quidem eorundem sacramentorum participes, eandem quoque, quam boni, fidem profitentur, vitâ ac moribus dissimiles ; boni vero in ecclesiâ dicuntur ii, qui non solum fidei professione et communione sacramentorum sed etiam spiritu gratiæ et caritatis vinculo inter se conjuncti et colligati sunt. . . . Bonos igitur et improbos ecclesia complectitur, quemadmodum et divinæ litteræ et sanctorum virorum scripta testantur.—8 : Quamvis autem bonos et malos ad ecclesiam pertinere catholica fides vere et constanter affirmet, ex iisdem tamen fidei regulis fidelibus explicandum est, utriusque partis diversam admodum rationem esse ; ut enim paleæ cum frumento in areâ confusæ sunt vel interdum membra varie intermortua corpori conjuncta, ita etiam mali in ecclesiâ continentur. — 11 : Unus est ecclesiæ rector ac gubernator, invisibilis quidem Christus . . ., visibilis autem is, qui Romanam cathedram Petri, apostolorum principis, legitimus successor tenet.

(Bellarmini *Eccles. milit.* c. 2 : Nostra sententia est, ecclesiam unam tantum esse, non duas, et illam unam et veram esse cœtum hominum, ejusdem christianæ fidei professione et eorundem sacramentorum communione colligatum, sub regimine legitimorum pastorum ac præcipue unius Christi in terris vicarii, Romani pontificis. Ex quâ definitione facile colligi potest, qui homines ad ecclesiam pertineant, qui vero ad eam non pertineant. Tres enim sunt partes hujus definitionis. Professio veræ fidei, sacramentorum communio et subjectio ad legitimum pastorem, Romanum pontificem. Ratione primæ partis excluduntur omnes infideles, tam qui nunquam fuerunt in ecclesiâ, ut Judæi, Turcæ, Pagani, tam qui fuerunt et recesserunt, ut hæretici et apostatæ. Ratione secundæ excluduntur catechumeni et excommunicati, quoniam illi non sunt admissi ad sacramentorum communionem, isti sunt dimissi. Ratione tertiæ excluduntur schismatici, qui habent fidem et sacramenta, sed non subduntur legitimo pastori, et ideo foris profitentur fidem et sacramenta percipiunt. Includuntur autem omnes alii, etiamsi reprobi, scelesti et impii sunt. Atque hoc interest inter sententiam nostram et alias omnes, quod omnes aliæ requirunt internas virtutes ad constituendum aliquem in ecclesiâ, et propterea ecclesiam veram invisibilem faciunt; nos autem et credimus, in ecclesiâ inveniri omnes virtutes, fidem, spem, caritatem et ceteras, tamen ut aliquis aliquo modo dici possit pars veræ ecclesiæ, de quâ scripturæ loquuntur, non putamus requiri ullam internam virtutem, sed tantum externam professionem fidei et sacramentorum communionem, quæ sensu ipso percipitur. Ecclesia enim est cœtus hominum ita visibilis et palpabilis, ut est cœtus populi Romani, vel regnum Galliæ aut respublica Venetorum.)

II. Greek.

In the Confessions of the Greeks there is no permanent definition of Church: even Metr. Critop., c. 7, leaves it undecided whether ἐκκλησία signifies σύστημα πάντων τῶν τῷ εὐαγγελικῷ κηρύγματι ὁπωσοῦν πεισθέντων, ὀρθοδόξων καὶ αἱρετικῶν, or, according to others, σύστημα μόνων τῶν ὀρθοδόξων καὶ περὶ τὸν χριστιανισμὸν κατὰ πάντα ὑγιαινόντων. On the other hand, a synod pronounced against Cyril Lucar's assertion that the ἐκλεκτοί alone constituted the Church of Christ (ecclesia invisibilis); vide Parthenii Dec. syn. p. 123; and cf. Dosithei Conf. c. 11.[1]

III. Protestant.

C. A. p. 11: Est ecclesia congregatio sanctorum, in quâ evangelium recte docetur et recte administrantur sacramenta.

[1] Πιστεύομεν τὰ μέλη τῆς καθολ. ἐκκλησίας εἶναι τοὺς ἁγίους τοὺς εἰς τὴν αἰώνιον ζωὴν ἐκλελεγμένους, ὧν τοῦ κλήρου καὶ τῆς μετοχῆς ἀποκλείεσθαι τοὺς ὑποκριτάς, εἰ καὶ καταλαμβάνομεν καὶ ὁρῶμεν ἐν ταῖς μερικαῖς ἐκκλησίαις τὸν σῖτον τοῖς ἀχύροις συναναμιγνύμενον.

Apol. C. A. p. 144 : Ecclesia non est tantum societas externarum rerum ac rituum, sicut aliae politiae, sed principaliter est societas fidei et Sp. s. in cordibus, quae tamen habet externas notas, ut agnosci possit, videlicet puram evangelii doctrinam et administrationem sacramentorum consentaneam evangelio Christi. — Quare illi, in quibus nihil agit Christus, non sunt membra Christi.

Ib. p. 148 : Non somniamus nos Platonicam civitatem, ut quidam impie cavillantur, sed dicimus exsistere hanc ecclesiam, videlicet vere credentes ac justos, sparsos per totum orbem. Et addimus notas puram doctrinam evangelii et sacramenta. Et haec ecclesia proprie est columna veritatis. Retinet enim purum evangelium et, ut Paulus inquit, fundamentum, hoc est, veram Christi cognitionem et fidem, etsi sunt in his etiam multi imbecilles, qui supra fundamentum aedificant stipulas perituras, hoc est, quasdam inutiles opiniones, quae tamen, quia non evertunt fundamentum, tum condonantur illis tum etiam emendantur. Cf. *Conf. Saxon.* p. 68.

Ib. p. 144 : Addiderunt adversarii longam declamationem, quod mali non sint ab ecclesiâ segregandi. . . . Nos ob hanc ipsam causam adjecimus octavum articulum, ne quis existimaret, nos segregare malos et hypocritas ab externâ societate ecclesiae.—P. 146 : In decretis inquit glossa ecclesiam large dictam complecti bonos et malos, it. malos nomine tantum in ecclesiâ esse, non re, bonos vero re et nomine. (Accordingly the *F. C.*, p. 827, makes it Anabaptist error to say : non esse eam veram et christ. ecclesiam, in quâ peccatores reperiantur.)

Ib. p. 149 : Fortassis adversarii sic postulant definiri ecclesiam, quod sit monarchia externa suprema totius orbis terrarum, in quâ oporteat Romanum pontificem habere potestatem ἀνυπεύθυνον, de quâ nemini liceat disputare aut judicare, condendi articulos fidei, abolendi scripturas, quas velit, instituendi cultus et sacrificia, item condendi leges, quas velit, dispensandi et solvendi quibuscunque legibus velit divinis, canonicis et civilibus ; a quo imperator et reges omnes accipiant potestatem et jus tenendi regna, de mandato Christi. — Atque haec definitio, non ecclesiae Christi sed regni Pontificii, habet auctores non solum canonistas, sed etiam Danielem cap. xi.

Conf. Helv. ii. cap. 17 : Oportet semper fuisse, esse et futuram esse ecclesiam, id est e mundo evocatum vel collectum coetum fidelium, sanctorum inquam omnium communionem, eorum videlicet, qui deum verum in Christo servatore per verbum et Spiritum sanctum vere cognoscunt et rite colunt, denique omnibus bonis per Christum gratuito oblatis fide participant. . . . Illam docemus veram esse ecclesiam, in quâ signa vel notæ inveniuntur ecclesiæ veræ, inpr. vero verbi divini legitima vel sincera prædicatio.

Conf. Basil. art. 5: (Germ.) We believe in one holy, Christian Church: that is, the fellowship of the saints, the congregation of spiritual believers, which is holy and the bride of Christ, in which all are citizens who confess truly [1] that Jesus is Christ the Lamb of God . . . and approve that faith by works.

Conf. Gall. art. 27: Affirmamus ex dei verbo, ecclesiam esse fidelium coetum, qui in verbo dei sequendo et purâ religione colendâ consentiunt, in quâ etiam quotidie proficiunt cet. Minime tamen infitiamur, quin fidelibus hypocritæ et reprobi multi sint permixti, sed quorum malitia ecclesiæ nomen delere non possit.

Conf. Belg. art. 27: Credimus unicam ecclesiam catholicam seu universalem, quæ est congregatio sancta seu coetus omnium vere fidelium christianorum, qui totam suam salutem in uno Jesu Christo exspectant, sanguine ipsius abluti et per spiritum ejus sanctificati atque obsignati. . . . Sancta hæc ecclesia certo in loco non est sita vel limitata aut ad certas singularesque personas alligata, sed per totum mundum sparsa atque diffusa. — Art. 29: Nequaquam hic de hypocritarum coetu loquimur, qui quanquam bonis in ecclesia permixti sint, de ecclesia tamen non sunt, etiamsi corpore in ea sint. — Notæ quibus vera ecclesia cognoscitur, hæ sunt: si ecclesia pura evangelii prædicatione, si sincera sacramentorum ex Chr. præscripto administratione utatur, si disciplina ecclesiastica, ut vitia corrigantur, obtineat.

Ris, *Conf.* art. 24: Fideles et regenerati homines per totum terrarum orbem dispersi sunt verus dei populus sive ecclesia Jesu Ch. in terra cet. Quamvis hanc inter ecclesiam ingens simulatorum et hypocritarum lateat et versetur multitudo, illi

[1] In the Latin text of the Syntagma, it is only qui confitentur.

tamen soli sunt vera corporis Ch. membra atque capropter beatorum promissorum hæredes cet.

Cf. *Thirty-nine Artt.* xix.; *Conf. Scot.* art. xvi.; [*West. Conf.* ch. xx. 2, 3, 4]; *Declar. Thor.* p. 68. The definition of the Church in the style of Predestinarianism runs thus: Ecclesia est societas fidelium, quos deus ad vitam æternam prædestinavit. *Cat. Gen.* p. 480.

IV. ARMINIAN.

The Arminians agree with the Lutherans in the definition of the true Church: Limborch, *Th. ch.* 7; Curcellæi *Tr. de eccl.* p. 659. What is found in the *Apol. Conf. Rem.* p. 241 has nothing to do with the definition of the Church, and may be passed over.

V. QUAKER.

The Quakers call the Church:—1. In the wider sense, the community of all, of whatever nation, or race, or tongue, including those who are far off and strangers to the knowledge and profession of the Christian faith, who follow the divine light within them, and the testimony of God in their hearts, that they may be sanctified by it and delivered from evil. Such men have always been upon earth, even before the coming of Christ; and they are still to be found among Turks, and heathens, and Jews. 2. In the stricter sense, the Church is to be considered a certain number of persons gathered by God's Spirit, and by the testimony of some of His servants raised up for that end, unto the belief of the true principles and doctrines of the Christian faith, who, through their hearts being united by the same love, and their understandings informed in the same truths, gather, meet, and assemble together to wait upon God, to worship Him, etc. Barclay, *Apol.* Prop. x. sec. 3.

The Quakers unite with the Anabaptists and Mennonites in so interpreting the life of God in the soul, and so applying the words of Christ, as to refuse certain observances and duties which others practise, such as some political offices, taking the oath in courts of justice, serving in war. Barclay, *Apol.* xv.; Ris, *Conf.* art. 37; *F. C.* 827.

VI. SOCINIANS.

The Socinians, placing all religion in the knowledge and obedience of the divine will, and thinking that both these may be attained without the Church, hold the idea of the Church to be unimportant. They understand by it the fellowship of those who adhere to the true doctrine of Christian salvation. This they call the *invisible* Church, as embracing those who trust in Christ and obey Him, and the *visible* as embracing those who hold and profess this doctrine together (*Cat. Rac.* qu. 488). The trusting and obeying are to them altogether internal; while the profession is external, and constitutes the visible Church. But they hold the Church proper to be the visible; the word is used of the invisible only by metonymy. But then the visible Church is of course something very different from that of Rome. *Cat. Rac.* 352.

SECOND POINT OF DIVERGENCE.

Outside the Church of Christ, which is led by the Spirit of God into all the truth, there is for men no eternal salvation. Romanists and Protestants agree in this. But their several view of the Church affects the meaning of this expression. Hence the proposition has a very different meaning and application in the two systems.

SYMBOLICAL TESTIMONIES.

a. Extra ecclesiam nulla salus.

I. ROMAN CATHOLIC.

Conc. Trid. sess. v. Decr. de pecc. orig.: Ut fides nostra catholica, sine quâ impossibile est placere deo, . . . permaneat.

Cat. Rom. i. 10. 16 : Universalis etiam ob eam causam dicitur (ecclesia), quod omnes, *qui salutem æternam consequi cupiunt*, eam tenere et amplecti debeant, non secus ac qui arcam, ne diluvio perirent, ingressi sunt.

Ib. i. 10. 19 : . . . In solâ dei ecclesiâ, neque extra eam usquam, verus cultus verumque sacrificium reperitur, quod deo placere ullo modo possit.

Profess. fid. Trid.: Catholica fides, extra quam nemo salvus esse potest cet.

S. Klee, *kathol. Dogmat.* i. S. 123 f.

II. PROTESTANT.

C. A. p. 10 : Neque vero pertinet (promissio salutis) ad illos, qui sunt extra ecclesiam Christi, ubi nec verbum nec sacramenta sunt, quia regnum Christi tantum cum verbo et sacramentis exsistit.

Cat. maj. p. 500 sq. : Extra christianitatem, ubi evangelio locus non est, neque ulla est peccatorum remissio, quemadmodum nec ulla sanctificatio adesse potest. Cf. p. 503.

Conf. Helv. ii. c. 17 : Communionem cum ecclesiâ Ch. verâ tanti facimus, ut negemus, eos coram deo vivere posse, qui cum verâ dei ecclesiâ non communicant, sed ab eâ se separant. Nam ut extra arcam Noë non erat ulla salus, pereunte mundo in diluvio, ita credimus extra Christum, qui se electis in ecclesia fruendum præbet, nullam esse salutem certam, et proinde docemus, vivere volentes non oportere separari a verâ Christi ecclesiâ.

Conf. Belg. art. 28 : Credimus, quod cum . . . extra ecclesiam nulla sit salus, neminem, cujuscunque ordinis aut dignitatis fuerit, sese ab eâ subducere debere, ut se ipso contentus separatim degat; sed omnes pariter teneri huic se adjungere eique uniri, ecclesiæ unitatem conservare cet.

Conf. Gall. art. 28 : Papisticos conventus damnamus, quod pura dei veritas ab illis exsulet, in quibus etiam sacramenta fidei corrupta sunt cet. Ac proinde arbitramur, omnes eos, qui sese ejusmodi actionibus adjungunt et iis communicant, a Chr. corpore se ipsos separare.

S. *Conf. Scot.* art. 16.

Y

b. *Infallibility of the Church.*

I. Roman Catholic.

Catech. Rom. i. 10. 18: Quemadmodum hæc una ecclesia (cathol.) errare non potest in fidei ac morum disciplinâ tradendâ, cum a Spir. s. gubernetur: ita ceteras omnes, quæ sibi ecclesiæ nomen arrogant, ut quæ diaboli spiritu ducantur, in doctrinæ et morum perniciosissimis erroribus versari necesse est.

(Bellarmini *Eccl. milit.* c. 14: Nostra sententia est, ecclesiam absolute non posse errare nec in rebus absolute necessariis nec in aliis, quæ credenda vel facienda nobis proponit, sive habeantur expresse in scripturis sive non; et cum dicimus, ecclesiam non posse errare, id intelligimus tam de universitate fidelium quam de universitate episcoporum, ita ut sensus sit ejus propositionis: ecclesia non potest errare i. e. id quod tenent omnes fideles tanquam de fide, necessario est verum et de fide, et similiter id quod docent omnes episcopi tanquam ad fidem pertinens, necessario est verum et de fide. Cf. Klee, *kathol. Dogm.* i. S. 111 ff.)

[The Encyclical of 8th Dec. 1864: Romani pontifices et concilia œcumenica a limitibus suæ potestatis recesserunt, jura principum usurparunt, atque etiam in rebus fidei et morum definiendis errarunt. The present Vatican Council makes Papal Infallibility an article of faith.]

II. Protestant.

Apol. C. A. p. 148: Hæc ecclesia proprie est columna veritatis, p. 150. Non est ad pontifices transferendum, quod ad veram ecclesiam pertinet, quod videlicet sint columnæ veritatis.

[Hutterus, *Compendium locorum theologicorum loc.* xvii. No. 18: Ergone errare potest ecclesia? Potest. No. 19. Sic statuendum est, errare non posse ecclesiam si totam ac universam ecclesiam sive catholicam ecclesiam respicias. . . . Cæterum quoad hanc vel illam particularem ecclesiam, imo quoad maximam etiam ejus partem errare potest ecclesia, imo enormiter erravit sæpissime, id quod patet exemplo ecclesiæ tempore diluvii, tempore Eliæ prophetæ, tempore nati Christi, tempore Arianismi per totum orientem ecclesias occupantis.]

Conf. Helv. ii. c. 17 : Ecclesia dei . . . non errat, quamdiu innititur petræ Christo et fundamento prophetarum et apostolorum.

Against the infallibility of the Romish Church, see *Thirty-nine Artt.* art. xix.

THIRD POINT OF DIVERGENCE.

The Christian Church upon earth (*ecclesia militans*) has, according to the Protestants and the Greeks, only one invisible Head, Christ. In the Romish system there is a visible head, the Roman Bishop or Pope, as the successor of Peter appointed by Christ as chief Bishop and Vicar of Himself. The power of the Pope in the Church has, however, not been defined, as to its extent, in the symbols.

SYMBOLICAL TESTIMONIES.

I. ROMISH.

Concil. Florent. diffinit. (in Harduin, ix. p. 986) : Diffinimus, sanctam apostol. sedem et Romanum pontificem in universum orbem tenere primatum et ipsum pontificem Rom. successorem esse Petri, principis apostolorum, et verum Christi vicarium totiusque ecclesiæ caput et omnium Christianor. patrem ac doctorem exsistere cet.

In the Conc. Trid. is ascribed to the Pope (Christi in terris vicario, sess. vi. ref. cap. 1) suprema in ecclesiâ universali potestas (sess. xiv. cap. 7) ; the confirmation of bishops (sess. xxiii. can. 8) ; the decision as to indulgences and Communio sub utrâque (sess. xxv. de indulg., sess. xxii. super petitione concess. calic.).

In the Profess. fid. Trid. the Pope is called Petri apostolorum principis successor ac I. Ch. vicarius.

Cat. Rom. i. 10. 11: Unus est ecclesiæ rector ac gubernator, invisibilis quidem Christus, ... visibilis autem is, qui Romanam cathedram, Petri apostolorum principis legitimus successor, tenet.— *Ib.* i. 10. 12: (De Romano pontifice) fuit illa omnium patrum ratio et sententia, hoc visibile caput ad unitatem ecclesiæ constituendam et conservandam necessarium fuisse.

Ib. ii. 7. 28: Catholica ecclesia Romanum pontificem maximum, quem in Ephesinâ synodo Cyrillus Alexandrinus archiepiscopum totius orbis, terrarum patrem et patriarcham appellat, semper venerata est. Cum enim in Petri apostolorum principis cathedrâ sedeat, in quâ usque ad fidem sedisse constat, summum in eo dignitatis gradum et jurisdictionis amplitudinem, non quidem ullis synodicis aut uliis humanis constitutionibus sed divinitus datam agnoscit. Quamobrem omnium fidelium et episcoporum ceterorumque antistitum, quocunque illi munere et potestate præditi sint, pater ac moderator universali ecclesiæ ut Petri successor Christique verus et legitimus vicarius in terris præsidet.

II. Greek and Protestant.

Conf. orthod. p. 138 sq.: Διδασκόμεθα, πῶς μόνος ὁ Χριστὸς εἶναι κεφαλὴ τῆς ἐκκλησίας κατὰ τὴν διδασκαλίαν τοῦ ἀποστόλου (Eph. v. 32).

Metroph. Critop. *Conf.* c. xxiii. p. 159: Ἔστι δὲ τοιαύτη κεφαλὴ τῆς καθολικῆς ἐκκλησίας ὁ κύριος Ἰησοῦς Χριστός, ὅς ἐστιν ἡ κεφαλὴ πάντων, ἐξ οὗ πᾶν τὸ σῶμα συναρμολογεῖται. ἧς κεφαλῆς ζώσης διὰ παντὸς συζῇ ταύτῃ καὶ ἡ ἐκκλησία, κυβερνωμένη καὶ διευθυνομένη ὑπὸ τοιαύτης ἀθανάτου καὶ τεθεωμένης κεφαλῆς, καὶ οὐδένα τῶν πολεμίων φοβουμένη. κἂν μυρία κακὰ ταύτῃ ἐπανασταίη, πάντων αὕτη περιγίνεται δυνάμει τῆς ἑαυτῆς θείας κεφαλῆς. Previously: οὐδέποτε ἠκούσθη, παρὰ τῇ καθολ. ἐκκλησίᾳ ἄνθρωπον θνητὸν καὶ μυρίαις ἁμαρτίαις ἔνοχον κεφαλὴν λέγεσθαι τῆς ἐκκλησίας. As to the opinion of the Greeks concerning the primacy of the Roman bishop, cf. Heinecc. ii. 371 ff.; s. Philaret, n. 16.

In the Greek symbols the Pope is not mentioned. The four patriarchs have equal rank.

A. Sm. p. 312: Quod papa non sit jure divino seu secundum verbum dei caput totius christianitatis (hoc enim nomen uni et soli Jesu Christo debetur), sed tantum episcopus et pastor ecclesiæ, quæ est Romæ, et eorum qui voluntarie et sponte vel per humanam creaturam, id est politicum magistratum, se ad eum conferunt, . . . vetera concilia et ætas Cypriani ostendunt.

Ib. p. 313: Hinc sequitur, omnia, quæ papa ex tam arrogante, temeraria, mendace, blasphema et furto accepta potestate suscepit et fecit et adhuc facit, fuisse et esse mere diabolica acta et instituta (excepta politici regni administratione, ubi deus etiam sæpe per tyrannos et perfidos nebulones populo alicubi benefacit) ad perditionem totius sanctæ ecclesiæ catholicæ seu christianæ (quantum in ipso est) et ad destructionem primi et præcipui articuli de redemtione facta per Jesum Christum.

Ib. p. 314: Ecclesia nunquam melius gubernari et conservari potest, quam si omnes sub uno capite, quod est Christus, vivamus.

Ib. p. 340 (tr. de potestate et primatu papæ): Rom. pontifex arrogat sibi, quod jure div. sit supra omnes episcopos et pastores; deinde addit etiam, quod jure div. habeat utrumque gladium, h. e. auctoritatem etiam regna conferendi et transferendi; et tertio dicit, quod hæc credere sit de necessitate salutis. Et propter has causas Rom. episcopus vocat se vicarium Christi in terris. Hos tres articulos sentimus falsos, impios, tyrannicos et perniciosos ecclesiæ esse.

Cf. also *Conf. Wirtemb.* p. 131 sq.

Conf. Helv. ii. cap. 27: Caput est, quod in corpore eminentiam habet et unde vitam haurit, cujus spiritu regitur in omnibus, unde et incrementa et ut crescat habet. Unicum item est corporis caput et cum corpore habet congruentiam. Ergo ecclesia non potest ullum aliud habere caput quam Christum. Nam ut ecclesia corpus est spirituale, ita caput habeat sibi congruens spirituale utique oportet. Nec alio potest regi spiritu, quam Christi. Non probamus ergo doctrinam cleri Romani, facientis suum illum Rom. pontificem catholicæ in terris ecclesiæ militantis pastorem universalem et caput summum, adeoque verum Christi vicarium, qui habeat in ecclesiâ plenitudinem, ut vocant, potestatis et dominium supremum. Docemus enim, Christum dominum esse et manere unicum pastorem universalem, summum item pontificem coram deo patre, ac in ecclesiâ ipsum omnia pontificis vel pastoris obire munia ad finem usque seculi, ideoque nullo indigere vicario, qui absentis est. Christus vero præsens est ecclesiæ et caput vivificum.

Confess. Angl. p. 91: Credimus, ecclesiam esse regnum, esse corpus Christi, ejus regni Christum solum esse principem, ejus corporis Christum solum esse caput cet. . . . Caput ecclesiæ totius aut universalem episcopum non magis aut illum (Roman. episcopum), aut alium quemvis mortalem esse posse, quam sponsum, quam lucem, quam salutem, quam vitam ecclesiæ: hæc enim esse Christi unius privilegia et nomina et illi uni proprie atque unice convenire.

See *Conf. Gall.* art. 30; *Belg.* art. 29; *Declar. Thorun.* p. 70; and Limborch, *Theol. chr.* vii. 10.

Apologia Conf. Aug. S. 149 and 208.

Art. Smalc. S. 347: Constat, Romanos pontifices cum suis membris defendere impiam doctrinam et impios cultus. Ac plane notæ Antichristi competunt in regnum papæ et sua membra. Paulus enim ad Thessalonicenses describens Antichristum, vocat eum adversarium Christi, extollentem se super omne, quod dicitur aut colitur Deus, sedentem in templo Dei, tanquam Deum. Loquitur igitur de aliquo regnante in ecclesiâ, non de regibus ethnicis: et hunc vocat adversarium Christi, quia doctrinam pugnantem cum evangelio excogitaturus sit, et is arrogabit sibi auctoritatem divinam. Primum autem constat, papam regnare in ecclesiâ, et prætextu ecclesiasticæ auctoritatis et ministerii sibi hoc regnum constituisse. . . . Deinde doctrina papæ multipliciter pugnat cum evangelio, et arrogat sibi papa auctoritatem divinam tripliciter: primum quia . . ., secundo quia . . ., tertio quia . . . Hoc autem est se Deum facere, nolle ab ecclesiâ aut ab ullo judicari. . . . Hæc quum ita sint, cavere omnes Christiani debent, ne fiant participes impiæ doctrinæ, blasphemiarum et injustæ crudelitatis papæ. Ideo papam cum suis membris, tanquam regnum Antichristi, deserere et exsecrari debent.

Cf. *Confessio et expositio brevis et simplex sinceræ rel. christ.* cap. xi. in Augusti, S. 28; *Confessio Bohæmica*, art. 8; Niemeyer, S. 798; *Confessio Sigismundi*, c. xiii.; Niemeyer, S. 649

XX.

THE MINISTRY.

FIRST POINT OF DIVERGENCE.

THAT the Church might exert its energies for the advantage of its members, certain special organs, chosen from the body of Christians, are necessary: the *ministri ecclesiæ*, or an appointed ministerial function. With the exception of the Quakers and Anabaptists, all Christian communities have been agreed in this. But a divergence of sentiment has obtained as to the relation of the ministerial order to the general body of Christians. The Protestants ascribe to that order a distinction from other believers, grounded only on the function of their office; but the Romish Church vindicates for its priesthood an indelible character, imparted in ordination, which for ever separates them from the laity. It sharply opposes the clergy as the governing, to the laity as the governed body.

SYMBOLICAL TESTIMONIES.

I. QUAKER.

As by the light or gift of God all true knowledge in things spiritual is received and revealed, so by the same, as it is manifested and received in the heart, by the strength and power thereof, every true minister of the gospel is ordained, prepared, and supplied in the work of the ministry; and by the leading, moving, and drawing hereof ought every evangelist and Christian pastor to be led and ordered in his labour and work of the gospel, both as to the place where, as to the persons to whom, and as to the time wherein, he is to be minister. Moreover, they who have this authority may and ought to preach the gospel, though without human commission or literature; as, on the other hand, they who want the authority of the divine gift, however learned, or authorized by the commission of men or churches, are to be esteemed but as deceivers, and not true ministers of the gospel. Also, they who have received this holy and unspotted gift, as they have freely received it, so are they freely to give it without hire or bargaining, far less to use it as a trade to get money by; yet if God hath called any one from their employment or trades by which they acquire their livelihood, it may be lawful for such, according to the liberty which they feel given them in the Lord, to receive such temporals (to wit, what may be needful for them for meat or clothing) as are given them freely and cordially by those to whom they have communicated spirituals.

As to the first part of the objection, viz., that I seem to make no distinction between the minister and the people, I answer, if it is understood of a liberty to speak or prophesy by the Spirit, I say all may do that, when moved thereunto, as above is shown. But we do believe and affirm that some are more particularly called to the work of the ministry, and therefore are fitted of the Lord for that purpose; whose work is more constantly and particularly to instruct, exhort, admonish, oversee, and watch over their brethren; and that as there is something more incumbent upon them in that respect than upon every common believer, so also, as in that relation, there is due to them from the flock such obedience and subjection as is mentioned in these testimonies of the Scripture: Heb. xiii. 17; 1 Thess. v. 12, 13; 1 Tim. v. 17; 1 Pet. v. 5. Also, besides those who are particularly called to the ministry, and constant labour in the word and doctrine, there are also the elders, who, though they be not moved to a frequent testimony by way of declaration in words, yet, as such are grown up in the experience of the blessed work of truth in their hearts, they watch over and privately admonish the young, take care for the widows, the poor and fatherless, and look that nothing be wanting, but that peace, love, unity, concord, and soundness be preserved in the Church of Christ; and this answers to the deacons mentioned, Acts vi.

That which we oppose is the distinction of laity and clergy, which in the Scripture is not to be found, whereby none are admitted into the work of the ministry but such as are educated at schools on purpose, and instructed in logic, philosophy, etc., and so are at their apprenticeship to learn the art and trade of preaching, even as a man learns any other art, whereby all other honest mechanic men who have not got this heathenish art are excluded from having this privilege.

Seeing male and female are one in Christ Jesus, and that He gives His Spirit no less to one than to the other, when God moveth by His Spirit in a woman, we judge it no ways unlawful for her to preach in the assemblies of God's people.

Accordingly, the fundamental principle of the Quakers is, that speaking in their assemblies, the end of which is edification, is not and cannot be limited to any special order or office. Hence the preacher in their meetings is only a provision or surrogate for the case in which no one in the congregation is moved by the Spirit.

II. Romish and Protestant.

The relation of the clergy to the laity has been laid down in no one precise statement of the Romish symbols (it is hinted only in *Cat. Rom.* ii. 7. 24); but it may without difficulty be gathered from what will be adduced below as to the priesthood and hierarchy, and from what has been adduced on the sacrament of orders. The works of the theologians and of the writers on ecclesiastical law plainly distinguish between the clerical order and the people. Nor do the Protestant symbols enter fully into the matter. The avoidance of the terms *clerici* and *laici*, however, teaches that the Reformers were averse to it (Calvin, *Inst.* iv. 4. 9; *vid.* Bellarmine, *De clcr.* i. 1[1]); and the proposition that all the power of

[1] Prima inter nos et hæreticos quæstio nascitur, rectene, an secus quidam inter Christianos clerici, quidam laici nominentur. Lutherani enim et Calvin-

the ministry flows from the Church primarily, that is, from the fellowship of believers, is not reconcilable with the division of the Church into two essentially different classes. Finally, where the *communio sub unâ* is in question, the Romish doctrine is contradicted. *Apol. A. C.* p. 235.

SECOND POINT OF DIVERGENCE.

In the Roman and Greek Churches the ministerial office is regarded as, in its essential character, a true priesthood. But as various classes of ecclesiastical officers are subordinated to the priests, so also among the priests themselves there is, *jure divino*, a spiritual distinction of rank and office; that is, there exists in the Romish Church a hierarchy, instituted by Christ Himself, and continued in unbroken succession, which consists of bishops, priests, and deacons. The evangelical Church not only rejects the priestly character of the ministers of the Church—having no sacrifice, needing therefore no priests—but attributes to all ministers, *jure divino*, equal official status.

Observations.

For the sake of better order than has been introduced into the evangelical Church, a distinction of rank and function and ordination has almost everywhere been reserved for the higher ministry, the bishops, general superintendents, etc. But this ordinance exists only *jure humano*. It affects not so much the spiritual office itself, as the supervision of the clergy. The general superintendent has, as minister ecclesiæ, no more comprehensive authority than the parochial pastor; hence, in the elevation of a deacon to a pastorate, or of a pastor to the superintendency, there is no new consecration. The English Episcopal Church approximates in this to the Romish constitution; it has not only three separate orders, but also for each a special conse-

istæ, tametsi minime negant, quod ad rem attinet, ministerium verbi et sacramentorum non ex æquo ad omnes pertinere, et habent ipsi quoque suos quosdam ministros et pastores, . . . tamen quod eorum contentiones et schismata ab odio clericorum et laicorum favore initium duxerint, et vocabulum cleri non obscure excellentiam quandam ac dignitatem præ se ferre videatur, nullo modo ferunt, ut ministri ecclesiastici clerici, ceteri laici appellentur.

cration, and a special and exclusive circle of official functions. The English Articles, however, have nothing on this point.

SYMBOLICAL TESTIMONIES.

I. Romish and Greek.

Concil. Trid. sess. xxiii. cap. 1 : Sacrificium et sacerdotium dei ordinatione conjuncta sunt, ut utrumque in omni lege exstiterit. Cum igitur in N. T. sanctum eucharistiæ sacrificium visibile ex domini institutione catholica ecclesia acceperit, fateri etiam oportet, in eâ novum esse visibile et externum sacerdotium. Hoc autem ab eodem domino institutum esse atque apostolis eorumque successoribus in sacerdotio potestatem traditam consecrandi, offerendi et ministrandi corpus et sanguinem ejus nec non et peccata dimittendi et retinendi, sacræ literæ ostendunt et catholicæ eccl. traditio semper docuit. Cf. can. 1.

Ib. cap. 2 : Cum autem divina res sit tam sancti sacerdotii ministerium, consentaneum fuit, quo dignius et majori cum veneratione exerceri potest, ut in ecclesiæ ordinatissimâ dispositione plures et diversi essent ministrorum ordines, qui sacerdotio ex officio deservirent, et ita distributi, ut, qui jam clericali tonsurâ insigniti essent, per minores ad majores adscenderent. Nam non solum de sacerdotibus, sed et de diaconis sacræ litteræ apertam mentionem faciunt, et quæ maxime in illorum ordinatione attendenda sunt, gravissimis verbis docent. Et ab ipso ecclesiæ initio sequentium ordinum nomina atque uniuscujusque eorum propria ministeria, subdiaconi scilicet, acoluthi, exorcistæ, lectoris et ostiarii, in usu fuisse cognoscuntur, quamvis non pari gradu. Nam subdiaconatus ad majores ordines a patribus et sacris conciliis refertur, in quibus et de aliis inferioribus frequentissime legimus.—Can. 6 : Si quis dixerit, in ecclesiâ catholicâ non esse hierarchiam divinâ ordinatione institutam, quæ constat ex episcopis, presbyteris et ministris: anathema sit.

Cat. Rom. ii. 7. 26 : Tametsi unus est ordo sacerdotalis, varios tamen dignitatis et potestatis gradus habet. Primus est eorum, qui sacerdotes simpliciter vocantur. Secundus est episcoporum, qui singulis episcopatibus præpositi sunt, ut non solum ceteros ecclesiæ ministros, sed fidelem populum regant et eorum saluti summâ cum vigilantiâ et curâ prospiciant. . . . Tertius gradus est archiepiscoporum, qui pluribus episcopis præsunt, qui metropolitani etiam vocantur, quod illarum urbium antistites sint, quæ tanquam matres habeantur illius provinciæ. Quare superiorem, quam episcopi, locum et ampliorem potestatem habent, tametsi ab episcopis ordinatione nil differunt. In quarto gradu patriarchæ collocantur, id est primi supremique patres.

Conc. Trid. sess. xxiii. cap. 4 : S. synodus declarat, præter ceteros ecclesiasticos gradus episcopos, qui in apostolorum locum successerunt, ad hunc hierarchicum ordinem præcipue pertinere et positos a Spiritu s. regere ecclesiam dei, eosque presbyteris superiores esse ac sacramentum confirmationis conferre, ministros ecclesiæ ordinare atque alia pleraque peragere ipsos posse, quarum functionum potestatem reliqui inferioris ordinis nullam habent.

Conf. orthod. p. 173 : Ἡ ἱερωσύνη ὁποῦ εἶναι μυστήριον, διετάχθη τοῖς ἀποστόλοις ἀπὸ τὸν Χριστόν, καὶ διὰ τῆς ἐπιθέσεως τῶν χειρῶν αὐτῶν μέχρι τῆς σήμερον γίνεται ἡ χειροτονία, διαδεξαμένων τῶν (ἀποστόλων) ἐπισκόπων αὐτοὺς πρὸς διάδοσιν τῶν θείων μυστηρίων καὶ διακονίαν τῆς σωτηρίας τῶν ἀνθρώπων.

Ib. p. 176 : Ἡ ἱερωσύνη περικρατεῖ εἰς τὴν ἑαυτὴν τῆς ὅλους τοὺς βαθμούς· μὲ ὅλον τοῦτο πρέπει κατὰ τὴν τάξιν νὰ δίδονται· οἷον ἀναγνώστης, ψάλτης, λαμπαδάριος, ὑποδιάκονος, διάκονος. Cf. Metroph. Critop. *Conf.* c. xi. p. 108 sq.

Metroph. Critop. *Conf.* c. xi. p. 110 : Ὁ ἐπίσκοπος δύναται τὰ τῶν πρεσβυτέρων, ἔξοχον δι' αὐτοῖς ἔργον ἡ χειροτονία τῶν ὑφ' αὐτοὺς τάξεων. Οὗτοι μὲν γὰρ χειροτονοῦνται ὑπὸ τριῶν ἐπισκόπων τοὐλάχιστον· ἕκαστος δὲ τούτων τὰς ὑποδεεστέρας τάξεις, συμπαρόντων αὐτῷ πρεσβυτέρων τε καὶ διακόνων ἀδιορίστων. Against the Protestant doctrine as to the equality of ministers, s. Dosithei *Confess.* c. 10.

II. PROTESTANT.

Apol. A. C. p. 201 : Sacerdotium intelligunt adversarii non de ministerio verbi et sacramentorum aliis porrigendorum, sed intell. de sacrificio, quasi oporteat esse in N. T. sacerdotium simile levitico, quod pro populo sacrificet et mereatur aliis remissionem peccatorum. Nos docemus, sacrificium Ch. morientis in cruce satis fuisse cet. Ideo sacerdotes vocantur non ad ulla sacrificia velut in lege pro populo facienda, . . . sed ad docendum evang. et sacramenta porrigenda populo. Nec habemus nos aliud sacerdotium, simile levitico. Cf. p. 265, and *Conf. Wirtemb.* p. 119.

Conf. Helv. ii. cap. 18 : Diversissima inter se sunt sacerdotium et ministerium. Illud enim commune est christianis omnibus, hoc non item. Nec e medio sustulimus ecclesiæ ministerium, quando repudiavimus ex ecclesiâ Christi sacerdotium papisticum. . . . In Novo Testam. Christi non est amplius tale sacerdotium, quale fuit in populo veteri, quod unctionem habuit externam, vestes sacras et cærimonias plurimas, quæ typi fuerunt Christi, qui illa omnia veniens et adimplens abrogavit. Manet autem ipse solus sacerdos in æternum, cui ne quid derogemus, nemini inter ministros sacerdotis vocabulum communicamus. Ipse enim dominus noster non ordinavit ullos in ecclesiâ Novi Testam. sacerdotes, qui acceptâ potestate a suffraganeo offerant quotidie hostiam, ipsam inquam carnem et ipsum sanguinem domini pro vivis et mortuis, sed qui doceant et sacramenta administrent.

Art. Sm. p. 314: Ecclesia nunquam melius gubernari et conservari potest, quam si omnes sub uno capite, quod est Christus, vivamus et episcopi omnes pares officio, licet dispares sint quoad dona, summâ cum diligentiâ cet. Cf. p. 352.

Conf. Helv. ii. cap. 18 : Data est omnibus in ecclesiâ ministris una et æqualis potestas sive functio. . . . Interea propter ordinem servandum unus aut certus aliquis ministrorum cœtum convocavit et in cœtu res consultandas proposuit, sententias item aliorum collegit, denique ne qua oriretur confusio, pro virili cavit.

Conf. Gall. art. 30 : Credimus omnes veros pastores, ubicunque locorum collocati fuerint, eadem et æquali inter se potestate esse præditos sub unico illo capite summoque et solo universali episcopo Jesu Christo.

Conf. Belg. art. 31 : Quantum attinet divini verbi ministros, ubicunque locorum sint, eandem illi potestatem et auctoritatem habent, ut qui omnes sint Christi unici illius episcopi universalis unicique capitis ecclesiæ ministri.

Conf. Remonstr. xxi. 7 : Cum episcoporum et presbyterorum omnium munus atque officium sit juxta propositam ab apostolis formam ecclesias docere ac regere, manifestum satis esse videtur, aliis in alios imperium ac potestatem proprie dictam nullo jure div. competere. Neque idcirco tamen omnino improbamus . . . gradus illos docentium ac regentium, qui . . . ordinis et decori caussâ jam olim instituti sunt et passim hactenus obtinent, si modo ii tandem non degenerent in tyrannidem cet.

Observations.

The bishops, on Romish principles, constitute, when they are assembled under their Primus the Pope in an Œcumenical Council, the *ecclesia repræsentans*, to which belongs an infallible decision as to the faith and morals of the Church out of the word of God. In the Protestant symbols the synodal constitution is only touched (*A. Sm.* p. 351 ; *Conf. Helv.* ii. c. 18 ; *Eng. Art.* xxi.) ; yet the idea of a general council is not foreign to Protestantism, though for infallible as such it could not be held, *Conf. Wirt.* p. 134. On the foregoing premises, however, all ministers without exception would be eligible for election.

THIRD POINT OF DIVERGENCE.

All Christian communities, which hold a separated order of ministry as necessary, require also (the Socinians excepted) a special call on the part of each individual. The prerogative of this call Protestants generally assign to the Church ; while the Romanists and Greeks vindicate it *lege divinâ* for the episcopate, that is, in the final resort, for the head of the Church, from whom all ecclesiastical jurisdiction flows. (The possible committal of this right to an ecclesiastical selection, or to the civil power, cannot be entered upon here, as the symbols have not decided it.)

SYMBOLICAL TESTIMONIES.

I. Romish.

Concil. Trid. sess. xxiii. cap. 4 : Docet s. synodus, in ordinatione episcoporum, sacerdotum et ceterorum ordinum nec populi nec cujusvis secularis potestatis et magistratus consensum sive vocationem sive auctoritatem ita requiri, ut sine eâ irrita sit ordinatio; quin potius decernit, eos, qui tantummodo a populo aut seculari potestate ac magistratu vocati et instituti ad hæc ministeria exercenda ascendunt, . . . non ecclesiæ ministros, sed fures et latrones per ostium non ingressos habendos esse.

(Bellarmin, *De cleric.* c. 2: Exsistit inter nos et adversarios controversia, cui potissimum jus sit in ecclesiâ episcopos creandi, id est eligendi, vocandi, atque initiandi. . . . Sunt autem tres de hac totâ quæstione sententiæ. . . . Altera sententia est M. Lutheri, J. Calvini, Matthiæ Illyrici, Jo. Brentii, Mart. Chemnicii aliorumque hujus temporis sectariorum, qui electionem et vocationem jure divino ad ecclesiam universam, hoc est ad clerum et populum spectare volunt, ita prorsus ut sine populi consensu ac suffragio nemo legitime electus aut vocatus ad episcopatum habeatur. — Contra autem doctores catholici summâ consensione docent, jus episcopos ordinandi ac vocandi ad plebem nullo modo pertinere posse, jus autem eligendi fuisse aliquando et aliquo modo penes populum, sed pontificum concessione vel conniventiâ, non lege divinâ. Ex quo nos longe verius colligemus, nullam esse apud hæreticos veram ordinationem, nullam vocationem, nullam electionem, proinde nullos episcopos, nullam ecclesiam.

The Greek Confessions say nothing on this point; but Jeremias shows from the decrees of councils that the people have no part in the choice and vocation of the clergy.

II. PROTESTANT.

A. Sm. p. 353 (de potestate et primatu papæ): Ubicunque est ecclesia, ibi est jus administrandi evangelii. Quare necesse est, ecclesiam retinere jus vocandi, eligendi et ordinandi ministros. Et hoc jus est donum proprie datum ecclesiæ, quod nulla humana auctoritas ecclesiæ eripere potest. . . . Idque etiam communissima ecclesiæ consuetudo testatur. Nam olim populus eligebat pastores et episcopos cet.

Conf. Helv. ii. cap. 18: Vocentur et eligantur electione ecclesiasticâ et legitimâ ministri ecclesiæ, i. e. eligantur religiose ab ecclesiâ vel ad hoc deputatis ab ecclesiâ, ordine justo cet.

Conf. Belg. art. 31: Credimus, ministros divini verbi, seniores et diaconos ad functiones suas legitimâ ecclesiæ electione . . . eligi debere.

Cf. *Eng. Art.* xxiii.

III. SOCINIAN.

Catech. Racov. qu. 505: Nonne ii, qui docent in ecclesiâ et ordini tuendo et conservando invigilant, ut singulari aliquâ ratione mittantur, opus habent? Nullo modo. Etenim illi nunc nullam novam nec antea inauditam doctrinam afferunt. Sed apostolicam antiquitus ab omnibus exceptam tantum proponunt, inculcant, utque secundum eam vitam instituant homines hortantur. Unde etiam apostolus describens diserte omnia, quæ ad constituendas personas ejusmodi pertinent, nullam missionis facit mentionem. Nihilominus tamen, cum personæ ejusmodi ex præscripto apostolicæ doctrinæ constituuntur et his duabus rebus præstant, vitæ innocentiâ et ad docendum aptitudine, propter ejusmodi constitutionem merito apud omnes auctoritatem justam invenire debent.

FOURTH POINT OF DIVERGENCE.

According to the fundamental principle of all Christian bodies, the ministry thus called are ordained to their office by imposition of hands and prayer. Differences of view obtain only: 1. As to the dignity of this usage; the Romish Church holding ordination as a sacrament, which impresses an indelible character, while Protestants regard it only as an observance continued from the apostles. 2. As to the person whose office it is to ordain; the Romanists and Greeks assigning that prerogative to the bishops alone, while Protestants hold every minister competent and justified in imparting consecration to others, most individual Protestant churches attaching the office of ordination to special superior functionaries only for the sake of order. *Vide* No. XVIII.

FIFTH POINT OF DIVERGENCE.

The Roman Catholic Church has imposed on consecrated priests the law of perpetual celibacy; the Protestant Church leaves marriage free to its ministers. The Greek Church tolerates no married bishops, but allows other clergy to marry under certain restrictions.

SYMBOLICAL TESTIMONIES.

I. ROMISH.

Conc. Trid. sess. xxiv. *Sacram. matrimon.* can. 9 : Si quis dixerit, clericos in sacris ordinibus constitutos vel regulares castitatem solemniter professos posse matrimonium contrahere contractumque validum esse, non obstante lege ecclesiasticâ vel voto, et oppositum nil aliud esse, quam damnare matrimonium; posseque omnes contrahere matrimonium, qui non sentiunt se castitatis, etiamsi eam voverint, habere donum: anathema sit, cum deus id recte petentibus non deneget nec patiatur nos supra id, quod possumus, tentari.

Confut. A. C. p. 94 : Quod memorant inter abusus cælibatum cleri, et quo pacto sacerdotes eorum uxores ducant et alios ducere suadeant, res profecto est admiratione digna, quod cælibatum sacerdotalem abusum vocent, cum potius e diverso violatio cælibatus et illicitus ad conjugium transitus in sacerdotibus pessimus abusus dici mereatur. Etenim sacerdotes nunquam debere uxores ducere, testatur Aurelius in concilio 2 Carthaginiensi, ubi inquit: quia sic docuerunt apostoli exemplo et ipsa servavit antiquitas, nos quoque custodiamus. Et paulo ante talis legitur canon: placet, ut episcopi, presbyteri et diaconi vel qui sacramenta contrectant pudicitiæ custodes ab uxoribus se abstineant. Ex quibus verbis liquet, ab apostolis receptam esse hanc traditionem, non ab ecclesiâ noviter inventam. . . . Ad hæc sacerdotes veteris legis tempore officii et ministerii sui in templo separabantur ab uxoribus. Cum autem sacerdos novæ legis semper debeat esse in ministerio, sequitur, semper eum debere continere. Amplius, conjuges non debent se fraudare officio conjugali, nisi ad tempus (1 Cor. vii.), ut vacent orationi. Cum ergo sacerdos semper debeat orare, semper debet continere. . . . Continentia sacerdotalis cum sit a conciliis, a pontificibus praecepta et a deo revelata, proprio voto a sacerdote deo promissa, non est rejicienda. Nam hanc exigit sacrificii, quod tractant, excellentia, orationis frequentia, libertas et puritas spiritus, ut curent, quomodo deo placeant, juxta S. Pauli doctrinam. . . . Habet sacerdos medium, ut neque uratur neque nubat, sed per gratiam dei contineat, quam oratione devotâ et castigatione carnis, jejuniis et vigiliis a deo impetret. Amplius, dum aiunt, Christum docuisse, non omnes homines ad caelibatum idoneos esse, hoc quidem verum, ideoque nec omnes idonei sunt ad sacerdotium, sed sacerdos oret, et poterit capere verbum Christi de continentia.

Comp. Eck, *Loci*, c. 18; Bellarmin, *De cleric.* c. 18-22; Eichhorn, *Kirchenrecht*, i. S. 516 ff.

II. Protestant.

A. C. p. 23: Cum exstet mandatum dei, cum mos ecclesiae notus sit, cum impurus caelibatus plurima pariat scandala, adulteria et alia scelera, digna animadversione boni magistratus, tamen mirum est, nullâ in re majorem exerceri saevitiam, quam adversus conjugium sacerdotum. Deus praecepit honore afficere conjugium. Leges in omnibus rebus publicis bene constitutis etiam apud ethnicos maximis honoribus ornaverunt. At nunc capitalibus poenis excrucientur, et quidem sacerdotes, contra canonum voluntatem, nullam aliam ob causam, nisi propter conjugium. Paulus vocat doctrinam daemoniorum, quae prohibet conjugium 1 Tim. iv. 3. Id facile nunc intelligi potest, cum talibus suppliciis prohibitio conjugii defenditur.

Apol. A. C. p. 237: Non legem de caelibatu, quam defendunt adversarii, ideo non possumus approbare, quia cum jure divino et naturali pugnat et ab ipsis canonibus conciliorum dissentit, et constat, superstitiosam et periculosam esse. Parit enim infinita scandala, peccata et corruptelam publicorum morum.

A. Sm. p. 334: Quod conjugium prohibuerunt et divinum

ordinem sacerdotum perpetuo coelibatu onerarunt, malitiose sine omni honestâ causâ fecerunt, et in eo antichristi, tyrannorum et pessimorum nebulonum opus exercuerunt ac causam praebuerunt multis horrendis, abominandis, innumeris peccatis tetrarum libidinum, in quibus adhuc volutantur. . . . Quare ipsorum spurco coelibatui assentire nolumus, nec etiam illum feremus, sed conjugium liberum habere volumus, sicut deus illud ipse ordinavit et constituit, cujus opus nec rescindere nec destruere nec impedire volumus.

Comp. *Conf. Wirtemb.* p. 120 sq.

Conf. Helv. ii. cap. 29: Qui coelitus donum habent coelibatus, ita ut ex corde vel toto animo puri sint ac continentes nec urantur graviter, serviant in eâ vocatione domino, donec senserint se divino munere praeditos, et ne efferant se ceteris: sed serviant domino assidue, in simplicitate et humilitate. Aptiores autem hi sunt curandis rebus divinis, quam qui privatis familiae negotiis distrahuntur. Quod si ademto rursus dono ustionem senserint durabilem, meminerint verbi apostolici: melius esse nubere, quam uri.

Art. Angl. 32: Episcopis, presbyteris et diaconis nullo mandato divino praeceptum est, ut aut coelibatum voveant aut a matrimonio abstineant. Licet igitur etiam illis ut ceteris omnibus christianis, ubi hoc ad pietatem magis facere judicaverint, pro suo arbitratu matrimonium contrahere. Cf. *Conf. Angl.* p. 92.

S. Calvin, *Institut.* iv. 12. 23 sq.

III. GREEK.

Metroph. Critop. *Conf.* c. 11, p. 111: Πάσαις ταῖς τάξεσι (of the ministry) πλὴν τῶν ἐπισκόπων συγκεχώρηται ὁ γάμος, οὐχ ὡς ἔτυχε δέ, ἀλλὰ μετὰ λόγου πάνυ ἐπαινετοῦ. Πρῶτον μὲν οἱ βουλόμενοι γαμεῖν, πρὸ τῆς χειροτονίας τοῦτο ποιοῦσιν. Δεύτερον, εἴ τινος γυνὴ ἔφθη τὸ ζῆν ἐκμετρήσασα, εἰ μὲν πρεσβύτερος ἢ διάκονός ἐστιν ὁ χηρεύσας καὶ βούλεται δευτέρᾳ γυναικὶ προσομιλῆσαι, παύει τῆς τῶν μυστηρίων ἱερουργίας. ἔχουσι δὲ μόνον εἰς παραμυθίαν . . . ὁ μὲν τὴν μετὰ τῶν πρεσβυτέρων, ὁ δὲ τὴν μετὰ τῶν διακόνων καθέδραν. Οἱ δὲ μετὰ τούτους, οἷον ὑποδιάκονοι, ἀναγνῶσται cet. Τῆς μὲν τάξεως αὐτῶν οὐ καθαιροῦνται δὶς γαμήσαντες, προαχθῆναι δὲ εἰς μείζονα οὐ δύνανται, μένει οὖν ἕκαστος ἐν ᾗ εὑρέθη. Τοὺς δὲ ἐπισκόπους ἐκλέγει ἡ ἐκκλησία πάντοτε ἐκ τῆς τάξεως τῶν μοναχῶν ἤτοι ἐκ παρθένων ἢ ἐκ σωφρόνων· παρθένους μὲν καλοῦμεν τοὺς μηδέποτε γυναῖκα ὁπωσοῦν ἐγνωκότας, σώφρονες δὲ λέγονται οἱ μιᾷ καὶ μόνῃ νομίμῳ γυναικὶ συναφθέντες cet.

Cf. Jerem. *in Actis Wirtemb.* p. 129.

SIXTH POINT OF DIVERGENCE.

The ministerial authority committed to the pastorate consists, on Romish and Protestant principles, in the preaching of the word of God, the administration of the sacraments, and the power to forgive or retain sins. But as the Romish Church has reserved the administration of two sacraments, ordination and confirmation, and the Greek Church that of ordination, to the bishops, so both limit still further, and more than they limit preaching, the offering of the sacrifice on the altar. Excommunication, that is, exclusion from the communion of the Church, is regarded as issuing from the power of the keys, and has consequently never been considered *in praxi* to be the function of any particular minister. The excommunication practised in the Roman Church, the major and the minor, has always been held to belong to the episcopate. But the power of jurisdiction given by that Church to the bishops, as by divine right, is rejected by Protestants.

SYMBOLICAL TESTIMONIES.

I. ROMISH AND GREEK.

Catech. Rom. ii. 7. 6 : Potestas ecclesiastica est duplex, ordinis et jurisdictionis. Ordinis potestas ad verum Christi domini corpus in sacrosanctâ eucharistiâ refertur, jurisdictionis vero potestas tota in Christi corpore mystico versatur. Ad eam enim spectat christianum populum gubernare et moderari et ad æternam cœlestemque beatitudinem dirigere.

Ib. ii. 7. 2 : Sacerdotibus potestas tum corpus et sanguinem domini nostri conficiendi et offerendi, tum peccata remittendi collata est.—32 : In sacerdote non solum ea cognitio requirenda est, quæ ad sacramentorum usum et tractationem pertinet, sed etiam sacrarum literar. scientiâ ita instructum esse oportet, ut populo christianæ fidei mysteria et divinæ legis præcepta tradere, ad virtutem et pietatem excitare, e vitiis revocare fideles possit. Cf. præfat. 5.

Ib. i. 11. 4 : Cum necesse fuerit, in ecclesiâ potestatem esse peccata remittendi, aliâ etiam ratione, quam baptismi sacramento, claves regni cœlorum illi concreditæ sunt, quibus possint unicuique pœnitenti, etiamsi usque ad extremum vitæ diem peccasset, delicta condonari.—5 : Neque vero existimandum est, hanc potestatem certis quibusdam peccatorum generibus definitam esse, nullum enim tam nefarium facinus vel admitti vel cogitari potest, cujus remittendi potestatem sancta ecclesia non habeat.

Conc. Trid. sess. xxv. *d. reformat.* cap. 3 : Quamvis excommunicationis gladius nervus sit ecclesiasticæ disciplinæ et ad continendos in officio populos valde salutaris : sobrie tamen magnaque circumspectione exercendus est, cum experientia doceat, si temere aut levibus ex rebus incutiatur, magis contemni, quam formidari, et perniciem potius parere, quam salutem. Quapropter excommunicationes illæ, quæ monitionibus præmissis ad finem revelationis ut aiunt pro deperditis seu subtractis rebus ferri solent, a nemine prorsus præterquam ab episcopo decernantur, et tunc non alias quam ex re non vulgari causâque diligenter ac magnâ maturitate per episcopum examinatâ, quæ ejus animum moveat ; nec ad eas concedendas cujusvis sæcularis etiam magistratus auctoritate adducatur cet.

As to the distinction between excommunicatio major and minor, s. Walter, *Kirchenrecht*, S. 365 ff.

Conf. orthod. p. 174 : Εἰς τὴν οἰκονομίαν ταύτην (μυστηρίων Θεοῦ, 1 Cor. iv. 1) δύο πράγματα περιέχονται, πρῶτον ἡ δύναμις καὶ ἡ ἐξουσία τοῦ λύειν τὰς τῶν ἀνθρώπων ἁμαρτίας, . . . δεύτερον ἡ ἐξουσία καὶ ἡ δύναμις τοῦ διδάσκειν.—Metroph. Critop. *Conf.* c. 11, p. 108, διακονία τοῦ λόγου καὶ τῶν μυστηρίων ἱερουργία, cf. p. 110, and Jer. *in Actis Wirtemb.* p. 105.

Excommunication is not in the Greek Confessions. But it

is customary in that Church, though attended by much superstition and abuse.

II. PROTESTANT.

Apol. A. C. p. 294 : Habet episcopus potestatem ordinis, hoc est ministerium verbi et sacramentorum, habet et potestatem jurisdictionis, hoc est auctoritatem excommunicandi obnoxios publicis criminibus et rursus absolvendi eos, si conversi petant absolutionem.

A. Sm. p. 351: Evangelium tribuit his, qui præsunt ecclesiis, mandatum docendi evangelii, remittendi peccata, administrandi sacramenta, præterea jurisdictionem, videlicet mandatum excommunicandi eos, quorum nota sunt crimina, et resipiscentes rursum absolvendi. Ac omnium confessione etiam adversariorum liquet, hanc potestatem jure divino communem esse omnibus, qui præsunt ecclesiis, sive vocentur pastores, sive presbyteri, sive episcopi.

A. C. p. 39 : Secundum evangelium s. de jure divino nulla jurisdictio competit episcopis ut episcopis h. e. his, quibus est commissum ministerium verbi et sacramentorum, nisi remittere peccata, item cognoscere doctrinam et doctrinam ab evangelio dissentientem rejicere et impios, quorum nota est impietas, excludere a communione ecclesiæ sine vi humanâ sed verbo. . . . Si quam habent aliam vel potestatem vel jurisdictionem in cognoscendis certis causis videl. matrimonii aut decimarum cet., hanc habent humano jure.

Conf. Helv. ii. cap. 18 : In hoc sunt vocati ministri ecclesiæ, ut evangelium Christi adnunciant fidelibus et sacramenta administrent.—Potestas ecclesiastica ministrorum ecclesiæ est functio illa, qua ministri ecclesiam dei gubernant quidem, verum omnia in ecclesiâ sic faciunt, quemadmodum verbo suo præscripsit dominus, quæ cum facta sunt, fideles tanquam ab ipso domino facta reputant.—Officia ministrorum sunt varia, quæ tamen plerique ad duo restringunt, in quibus omnia alia comprehenduntur, ad doctrinam Christi evangelicam et ad legitimam sacramentorum administrationem.

A. Sm. p. 333 : Majorem illam excommunicationem, quam papa ita nominat, non nisi civilem pœnam esse ducimus, non pertinentem ad nos ministros ecclesiæ : minor autem, quam nominat, vera et christiana est excommunicatio, quæ manifestos et obstinatos peccatores non admittit ad sacramentum et communionem ecclesiæ, donec emendentur et scelera vitent. Et ministri non debent confundere hanc ecclesiasticam pœnam seu excommunicationem cum pœnis civilibus.—*Ib.* (de potest. et prim. papæ) p. 354 : Constat, jurisdictionem illam communem excommunicandi reos manifestorum criminum pertinere ad omnes pastores.

Conf. Gall. 33 : Excommunicationem approbamus, et una cum suis appendicibus necessariam esse arbitramur.

Eng. Artt. art. xxxiii. : That person which by open denunciation of the Church is rightly cut off from the unity of the Church, and excommunicated, ought to be taken of the whole multitude of the faithful as an heathen and publican, until he be openly reconciled by penance, and received into the Church by a judge that hath authority thereunto.

Conf. Angl. p. 91 : Ministris a Christo datum esse dicimus ligandi, solvendi, aperiendi, claudendi potestatem. Ac solvendi quidem munus in eo situm esse, ut minister vel dejectis animis et vere resipiscentibus per evangelii prædicationem merita Christi absolutionemque offerat et certam peccatorum condonationem ac spem salutis æternæ denunciet, aut ut eos, qui gravi scandalo et notabili publicoque aliquo delicto fratrum animos offenderint et sese a communi societate ecclesiæ et a Christi corpore quodammodo abalienarint, resipiscentes reconciliet et in fidelium cœtum atque unitatem recolligat ac restituat. Ligandi vero illum claudendique potestatem exercere dicimus, quoties vel incredulis et contumacibus regni cœlorum januam occludit illisque vindictam dei et sempiternum supplicium edicit, vel publice excommunicatos ecclesiæ gremio excludit. Sententiam autem, quamcunque ministri dei ad hunc modum tulerint, deus ipse ita comprobat, ut quidquid illorum opera solvitur et ligatur in terris, idem ipse solvere et ligare velit et ratum habere in cœlis.

From the passages of the Reformed symbols it is clear that excommunication is understood of an exclusion from church fellowship, but without civil consequences. *Vid. A. C.* 39. The distinction in practice between the major and minor excommunication is post-symbolical.

THE POWER OF THE KEYS.

Observations.

The power of forgiving or retaining sins is termed, both in Romish and in Protestant formularies, after Matt. xvi. 19, *potestas clavium.* Yet this expression is by no means limited to that meaning. The Reformed Confessions, almost without exception, and the Lutheran here and there, refer it to the ministry of the gospel generally, by which the entrance of the kingdom of heaven is opened or shut. The power of the keys, then, includes in it that binding or loosing, since the preaching of the word is either an announcement of forgiveness or threatening of condemnation. The disciplinary power of the keys is proved from Matt. xviii. 17 by Calvin, *Inst.* iv. 11. Bellarmine, *De Rom. Pont.* c. 13, refers Matt. xvi. to Peter's primacy, and understands by the *claves* (cœli) the summa potestas in omnem ecclesiam.

SYMBOLICAL TESTIMONIES.

I. Protestant.

A. C. p. 37 : Sic sentiunt, potestatem clavium seu potestatem episcoporum juxta evangelium potestatem esse seu mandatum dei prædicandi evangelii, remittendi et retinendi peccata et administrandi sacramenta. Nam cum hoc mandato Christus mittit apostolos.

Conf. Helv. ii. cap. 14 : De clavibus regni dei traditis a domino apostolis multi admiranda garriunt et ex his cudunt enses, lanceas, sceptra et coronas, plenamque in maxima regna, denique in animas et corpora potestatem. Nos simpliciter judicantes secundum verbum dei dicimus, omnes ministros legitime vocatos habere et exercere claves vel usum clavium, cum evangelium adnunciant, id est populum suæ fidei creditum docent, hortantur, consolantur et increpant inque disciplinâ retinent. Ita enim regnum cœlorum aperiunt obsequentibus et inobsequentibus claudunt. . . . Rite itaque et efficaciter ministri absolvunt, dum evangelium Christi et in hoc remissionem peccatorum, quæ singulis promittitur fidelibus, sicuti et singuli sunt baptizati, prædicant et ad singulos peculiariter pertinere testantur.

Cat. Heidelb. Fr. 83 : What is the office of the keys? The preaching of the holy gospel and Christian discipline, by which the kingdom of heaven is opened to believers and shut against unbelievers.

Cf. *Conf. Helv.* i. art. 16 ; *Conf. Angl.* p. 91 sq.; *Conf. Tetrap.* c. 13 ; Calvin, *Instit.* iv. 6. 3 and xi. 1.

II. Romish.

Bellarmin, *l.c.*: Nos et catholici omnes per claves datas Petro intelligimus summam potestatem in omnem ecclesiam. Id tribus rationibus confirmamus. Primum ipsa metaphora clavium, ut in scripturis accipi solet, cf. Isa. xxii. 15–22. Hic aperte per claves non intelligitur remissio peccatorum aut ministerium verbi, sed principatus ecclesiasticus. . . . Secundo probatur verbis illis *quodcunque ligaveris* cet., nam in scripturis ligare dicitur, qui præcipit et qui punit, Matt. xxiii. 4, xviii. 18. Tertio probatur ex patribus cet.

XXI.

DIVINE WORSHIP: LITURGY.

With the exception of the Quakers, all Christian communions have an appointed order of divine service. The necessary constituents of this are the preaching of the word of God, and the administration of the sacraments, with the sacrifice of the mass in the Romish and Greek Churches. These essential elements may be clothed with edifying ceremonies, and, as in a liturgy, made compact and harmonious. Such religious ceremonies appear to Protestants as in their nature *adiaphora*, indifferent, that is, as not necessary to the attainment of salvation; and every particular Church has the right to appoint them, according to its necessities, and in accordance with the word of God. The Papists and Greeks regard the ritual and ceremonial of the Church as commandments necessary to be observed; and derive them, or those of them which are connected with the sacrifice of the mass, from apostolical or ecclesiastical tradition. Their worship is at the same time complicated with much more abundant ceremonies than that of the Protestants. The Reformed Church among the latter is almost entirely free from ceremonial; and its symbols appoint but few ecclesiastical usages of any kind.

Observations.

Parallel with ecclesiastical ceremonies are the pious exercises which are appointed in the Romish Church *ad promerendam gratiam*, such as fastings, pilgrimages, etc. For the protests of the evangelical Church against these human traditions, see No. I. The priestly consecrations of various things are contended against in *Conf. Wirt.* p. 129. Many matters of this kind are usually by Papists summed up under the term *sacramentalia* or *ritus sacramentales*.

SYMBOLICAL TESTIMONIES.

1. Quaker.

Barclay, *Apol.* Prop. xi. : All true and acceptable worship to God is offered in the inward and immediate moving and drawing of His own Spirit, which is neither limited to places, times, nor persons. For though we are to worship Him always, and continually to fear before Him; yet as to the outward signification thereof, in prayers, praises, or preachings, we ought not to do it in our own will, where and when we will, but where and when we are moved thereunto by the stirring and secret inspiration of the Spirit of God in our hearts; which God heareth and accepteth of, and is never wanting to move us thereunto when need is, of which He Himself is the alone proper judge. All other worship, then, both praises, prayers, or preachings, which man sets about in his own will and at his own appointment, which he can both begin and end at his pleasure, do or leave undone as himself seeth meet, whether they be a prescribed form, as a liturgy, etc., or prayers conceived extempore by the natural strength or faculty of the mind,—they are all but superstition, will-worship, and abominable idolatry in the sight of God, which are now to be denied and rejected, and separated from, in this day of His spiritual arising. However, it might have pleased Him (who winked at the times of ignorance, with a respect to the simplicity and integrity of some, and of His own innocent seed, which lay as it were buried in the hearts of men under that mass of superstition) to blow upon the dead and dry bones, and to raise some breathing of His own, and answer them; and that until the day should more clearly dawn and break forth.

In that these particular men come not thither to meet with the Lord, and to wait for the inward motions and operations of His Spirit; and so to pray as they feel the Spirit breathe through them, and in them; and to preach as they find themselves actuated and moved by God's Spirit, and as He gives utterance, so as to speak a word in season to refresh weary souls, and as the present condition and state of the people's hearts require, suffering God by His Spirit both to prepare people's hearts, and also give the preacher to speak what may be fit and seasonable for them.

To come, then, to the state of the controversy as to the public worship, we judge it the duty of all to be diligent in the assembling of themselves together, and when assembled, the great work of one and all ought to be to wait upon God; and returning out of their own thoughts and imaginations, to feel the Lord's presence, and know a gathering into His name indeed, where He is in the midst, according to His promise. And as every one is thus gathered, and so met together inwardly in their spirits, as well as outwardly in their persons, there the secret power and virtue of life is known to refresh the soul, and the pure motions and breathings of God's Spirit are left to arise; from which, as words of declaration, prayers and praises arise, the acceptable worship is known, which edifies the Church, and is well-pleasing to God. And no man here limits the Spirit of God, nor bringeth forth his own conned and gathered stuff; but every one puts that forth which the Lord puts into their hearts; and it is uttered forth not in man's will or wisdom, but in the evidence and demonstration of the Spirit and of power. Yea, though there be not a word spoken, yet is the true spiritual worship performed, and the body of Christ edified; yea, it may, and hath often fallen out among us, that divers meetings have passed without one word, and yet our souls have been greatly edified and refreshed, and our hearts wonderfully overcome with the secret sense of God's power and Spirit, which without words hath been ministered from one vessel to another.

II. Roman and Greek.

Conc. Trid. sess. xxii. Sacrific. missæ, cap. 5 : Cum natura hominum ea sit, ut non facile queat sine adminiculis exterioribus ad rerum divinarum meditationem sustolli, propterea pia mater ecclesia ritus quosdam, ut scilicet quædam summissâ voce, alia vero elatiore in missâ pronunciarentur, instituit; ceremonias item adhibuit, ut mysticas benedictiones, lumina, thymiamata, vestes aliaque id genus multa ex apostolicâ disciplinâ et traditione, quo et majestas tanti sacrificii commendaretur et mentes fidelium per hæc visibilia religionis et pietatis signa ad rerum altissimarum, quæ in hoc sacrificio latent, contemplationem excitarentur.

Ib. can. 7 : Si quis dixerit, ceremonias, vestes et externa signa, quibus in missarum celebratione ecclesia catholica utitur, irritabula impietatis esse magis, quam officia pietatis, anathema sit.

Ib. sess. vii. sacram. can. 13 : Si quis dixerit, receptos et approbatos ecclesiæ catholicæ ritus, in solemni sacramentorum administratione adhiberi consuetos aut contemni aut sine peccato a ministris pro libito omitti, aut in novos alios per quemcunque ecclesiarum pastorem mutari posse : anathema sit.

Cat. Rom. ii. 2. 59 : These ceremonies in the sacraments are not obscurely referred to the apostles' origination.

(Bellarmin, *De sacram.* ii. 30 : Fatemur omnes catholici, ceremonias ecclesiasticas non esse præcipuum cultum, nec ab iis pendere essentiam et efficaciam sacramentorum, nec habere vim justificandi, ut habent sacramenta, proinde inferiora esse sacramentis nec esse approbandos ritus, qui pugnant cum verbo dei, nec esse nimis multiplicandas, ita ut suâ multitudine obruant quodammodo religionem, cui servire debent. Nota, totam controversiam consistere in sex capitibus. Primum est, an sint aliquæ ceremoniæ a Christo vel apostolis institutæ, quæ non habeantur in scripturâ, sed ex traditione solâ cognoscantur ; secundum est, an ceremoniæ, quæ non sunt sacramenta, habeant vim aliquam spiritualem, ut coërcendi dæmones ; tertium est, an ecclesia possit instituere novas ceremonias: quartum an possit eas ita instituere, ut teneantur fideles in conscientiâ eas servare etiam circa scandalum ; quintum, an ejusmodi ceremoniæ sint res bonæ et meritoriæ et pars aliqua divini cultus ; sextum, an linguâ latinâ sacramenta celebranda et ministranda sint. Ad hæc omnia catholici respondent affirmative, ad eadem capita solo excepto tertio omnes fere Lutherani et Calvinistæ respondent negative. *Id. De missa*, ii. 13 : Chemnicius dicit, apud catholicos ita necessariam existimari ceremoniarum observantiam, ut pronuncient mortaliter peccare, qui aliquid in illis neglexerint. At hoc mendacium est, non enim ap. nos quælibet negligentia peccatum est mortale, sed contemtus aut notabilis negligentia in rebus gravibus.)

The Greeks not only regard their liturgy as perfect, but attach to ceremonies as much importance as the Romans do. Comp. Simeon Thessalon. περὶ τοῦ ναοῦ καὶ ἐξήγησις εἰς τὴν λειτουργίαν in Goari *Euchol.* p. 212 sqq.; s. also Heineccii *Abbild.* i. 28; Augusti *Progr.* i. p. 6 sqq.—The ritual of the mass is carried back to the apostles, Jerem. *in Act. Wirtemb.* p. 103; but Metroph. Critop., *Conf.* ch. vii. p. 85, refers the sacramental ceremonies to a tradition of the Church, under the influence of the Holy Ghost.

III. PROTESTANT.

C. A. p. 13 : De ritibus ecclesiasticis docent, quod ritus illi servandi sint, qui sine peccato servari possunt et prosunt ad tranquillitatem et bonum ordinem in ecclesiâ, sicut certæ feriæ, festa et similia. De talibus rebus tamen admonentur homines, ne conscientiæ onerentur, tanquam talis cultus ad salutem necessarius sit.

Apol. A. C. p. 151 : Damnant adversarii . . ., quod diximus ad veram unitatem ecclesiæ satis esse consentire de doctrinâ evangelii et administratione sacramentorum, nec necesse esse, ubique similes traditiones humanas esse seu ritus et ceremonias ab hominibus institutas. Cf. *A. C.* p. 19 sq.

F. C. p. 615: Credimus, . . . quod ceremoniæ s. ritus ecclesiastici, qui verbo dei neque præcepti sunt neque prohibiti, sed tantum decori et ordinis causâ instituti, non sint per se cultus divinus aut aliqua saltem pars cultus divini. — Credimus, ecclesiæ dei ubivis terrarum et quocunque tempore licere pro re natâ ceremonias tales mutare juxta eam rationem, quæ ecclesiæ dei utilissima et ad ædificationem ejusdem maxime accommodata judicatur.—P. 616 : Credimus, . . . quod ecclesia alia aliam damnare non debeat propterea, quod hæc vel illa plus minusve externarum ceremoniarum, quas dominus non instituti, observet, si modo in doctrinâ ejusque articulis omnibus et in vero sacramentorum usu sit inter eas consensus. Hoc enim vetus et verum dictum est: Dissonantia jejunii non dissolvit consonantiam fidei.

Conf. Angl. p. 96 : De multitudine otiosarum ceremoniarum scimus Augustinum graviter suo tempore conquestum esse. Itaque nos magnum earum numerum resecavimus, quod illis sciremus affligi conscientias hominum et gravari ecclesiam dei. Retinemus tamen et colimus non tantum ea, quæ scimus tradita fuisse ab apostolis, sed etiam alia quædam, quæ nobis videbantur sine ecclesiæ incommodo ferri posse.

Eng. Artt. art. xxxiv.: It is not necessary that traditions and ceremonies be in all places one, and utterly like; for at all times they have been diverse, and may be changed according to the diversities of countries, times, and men's manners, so that nothing be ordained against God's word. Whosoever through his private judgment willingly and purposely doth openly break the traditions and ceremonies of the Church, which be not repugnant to the word of God, and be ordained and approved by common authority, ought to be rebuked openly (that others may fear to do the like), as he that offendeth against the common order of the Church, and hurteth the authority of the magistrate, and woundeth the consciences of the weak brethren. Every particular or national Church hath authority to ordain, change, and abolish ceremonies or rites of the Church, ordained only by man's authority, so that all things be done to edifying.

Conf. Belg. art. 32: Rejicimus omnia humana inventa omnesque leges, quæ pro cultu dei a quocunque introduci possunt, ut iisdem conscientiæ ullo omnino modo devinciantur atque constringantur. Illud itaque solum suscipimus, quod ad conservandam et alendam concordiam atque unitatem omnesque in dei obedientiâ retinendos idoneum est. Ad id vero inprimis requiritur excommunicatio juxta verbum dei usurpata cet.

Conf. Helv. i. art. 23 : Ceteras vero (preaching, eucharist, etc., had been referred to) ceremoniarum ambages inutiles ac innumerabiles, vasa, vestes, vela, faces, aras, aurum, argentum, quatenus pervertendæ religioni serviunt, idola præsertim, quæ ad cultum prostant et offensionem præbent, ac id genus omnia prophana a sacro nostro cœtu procul arcemus.

Conf. Helv. ii. cap. 27: Quanto magis accedit cumulo rituum in ecclesiâ, tanto magis detrahitur non tantum libertati christianæ, sed et Christo et ejus fidei, dum vulgus ea quærit in ritibus, quæ quæreret in solo Jesu Christo per fidem. Sufficiunt itaque piis pauci moderati, simplices nec alieni a verbo dei ritus. Quod si in ecclesiis dispares inveniuntur ritus, nemo ecclesias existimet ex eo esse dissidentes. . . . Et nos hodie ritus diversos in celebratione cœnæ domini et in aliis nonnullis rebus habentes in nostris ecclesiis, in doctrinâ tamen et fide non dissidemus, neque unitas societasque ecclesiarum nostrarum eâ re discinditur. Semper vero ecclesiæ in hujusmodi ritibus, sicut mediis, usæ sunt libertate. Id quod nos hodie quoque facimus.

See *Conf. Bohem.* art. 15 ; *Declar. Thorun.* p. 59 ; and the *Conf. Remonstr.* xxiii. 6–8.

THE VERNACULAR.

Observations.

As in Protestant worship all is ordered for edification through the divine word, the Confessions ordained the use of the language of the country in public service. The Romish Church has permitted the Latin language in the performance of holy rites. The Council of Trent expressly prescribed this tongue for the Mass.

SYMBOLICAL TESTIMONIES.

I. ROMISH.

Conc. Trid. sess. 22, sacrific. missæ, cap. 8 : Etsi missa magnam contineat populi fidelis eruditionem, non tamen expedire visum est patribus, ut vulgari passim linguâ celebraretur. Quamobrem retento ubique cujusque ecclesiæ antiquo et a sanctâ Rom. ecclesiâ, omnium ecclesiarum matre et magistrâ, probato ritu, ne oves Christi esuriant neve parvuli panem petant et non sit, qui frangat eis, mandat s. synodus pastoribus et singulis curam animarum gerentibus, ut frequenter inter missarum celebrationem, vel per se vel per alios, ex iis, quæ in missâ leguntur, aliquid exponant atque inter cetera sanctissimi hujus sacrificii mysterium aliquod declarent, diebus præsertim dominicis et festis. Comp. Bellarmin, *Controv. de missâ*, ii. 11 sq.

Confut. A. C. p. 99 sq.: Cum persona communis sit sacerdos totius ecclesiæ, non solum circumstantium, ideo non mirum, quod sacerdos latine in latinâ celebrat ecclesiâ. Proficit autem auditori, si in fide ecclesiæ audit missam. . . . Neque necessarium est, ut omnia verba missæ audiat vel intelligat et etiam intelligens semper attendat: præstat enim intelligere et attendere finem, quia missa celebratur, ut offeratur eucharistia in memoriam passionis Christi.

II. PROTESTANT.

A. C. p. 23 sq.: Servantur usitatæ cerimoniæ fere omnes (in missâ) præterquam quod latinis concionibus admiscentur alicubi germanicæ, quæ additæ sunt ad docendum populum cet.

A. C. p. 250: Adversarii longam declamationem habent de usu latinæ linguæ in missâ, in quâ suaviter ineptiunt, quomodo prosit auditori indocto in fide ecclesiæ missam non intellectam audire; videlicet fingunt, ipsum opus audiendi cultum esse et prodesse sine intellectu.—Latinam linguam retinemus propter hos, qui latine discunt et intelligunt. Et admiscemus germanicas cantiones, ut habeat et populus, quod discat et quo excitet fidem et timorem. *Conf. Wirtcmb.* p. 118.

Conf. Helv. ii. c. 22: Taceant omnes peregrinæ linguæ in cœtibus sacris. Omnia proponantur linguâ vulgari et quæ eo in loco ab hominibus in cœtu intelligatur.

Conf. Angl. p. 122: Precamur eâ linguâ, quam nostri, ut par est, omnes intelligant, ut populus, quemadmodum Paulus monet, a communibus votis utilitatem communem capiat, quemadmodum omnes pii patres et catholici episcopi, non tantum in veteri, verum etiam in novo testamento, et precati sunt ipsi et populum precari docuerunt: ne, ut Augustinus ait, tanquam psittaci et merulæ videamur sonare, quod nescimus. Comp. *Eng. Art.* xxiv.

See *Declar. Thorun.* p. 57.

Images and Pictures.

Observations.

The most important difference between the Lutheran and the Reformed Churches in the matter of divine worship concerns the adornment of churches by pictures (and altars). The former holds these permissible, though indifferent. The latter rejects them.

I. Reformed.

Conf. Helv. ii. cap. 4 : Rejicimus . . . Christianorum simulacra. Tametsi enim Ch. humanam assumserit naturam, non ideo tamen assumsit, ut typum præferret statuariis atque pictoribus. . . . Ut instituantur homines in religione prædicare jussit evangelium dominus, non pingere et picturâ laicos erudire ; sacramenta quoque instituit, nullibi statuas constituit.

Cat. Heidelb. Fr. 98 : May not pictures be endured in the church as the books of the people ? No ; for we should not be wiser than God, who will teach His Christendom not by dumb figures, but by the living preaching ot His word.

Comp. *Conf. Czenger.* p. 158 ; Calvin, *Institut.* i. 11. 13. The altars are particularly mentioned, *Conf. Helv.* i. art. 23.

II. Lutheran.

The Lutheran symbols give no utterance concerning pictures in churches. But Luther's own opinion is plain from the following :—

Werke v. Walch, vi. 2747 : When the worship of them is out of the question, we may use figures, like letters, which remind us of good things, and put them as it were before our eyes. Who is so stone blind as not to see that, as Christian stories may be told without sin and to the profit of the hearers, so for the good of the simple such histories may without sin be painted and carved, not only at home in our houses, but publicly in the churches ? I assuredly know that God will have His word to be heard and read, especially concerning the passion of Christ. But if I hear and think of this, it is impossible but that I form images of those things in my mind. For, will I or will I not, if I hear of Christ, the figure of a man is drawn in my heart, hanging on the cross; just as my countenance is pictured in the water when I look into it. If then it is not sin, but a good thing, to have Christ's image in my heart, why should it be sin to have it before my eyes? For, the heart is more than the eyes, and ought more than the eyes to be preserved from sin: since there is the true dwelling-place and seat of God Himself.

Cf. Chemnicius, *Exam.* iv. 2. 9.

TABLES OF COMPARATIVE THEOLOGY.

COMPARATIVE

ROMISH.	GREEK.	LUTHERAN.	REFORMED.
\multicolumn{4}{c}{Christianity is a Divine Revelation communicated}
\multicolumn{4}{c}{the saving truths of which}
\multicolumn{2}{c}{from the Bible and tradition;}		from the
which, under the special influence of the Holy Ghost, have been, the former written, the latter continued uncorrupt.			
The interpretation of the Bible rests with the Church, led by the Holy Ghost, and finally with the Pope.		There exists in the Church contents unfold	
\multicolumn{2}{c}{According}	\multicolumn{2}{c}{to the}
\multicolumn{2}{c}{God is}	\multicolumn{2}{c}{a}
that is, the divine essence exists in in dignity		Three Persons, both in nature and perfectly equal.	
(The Holy Ghost proceeds from Father and Son.)	(The Holy Ghost proceeds from the Father alone.)		(The Holy Ghost proceeds
\multicolumn{2}{c}{Besides this Triune God}	\multicolumn{2}{c}{there is no}
Yet it is wholesome to invoke Mary, who was conceived without sin, and	the saints as intercessors with God, and to reverence their pictures and relics.	All service of saints,	
\multicolumn{4}{c}{Man is born with a corrupt bias, which was not his}
\multicolumn{2}{c}{the first man,}	\multicolumn{2}{c}{that is, as he came}
(besides natural faculties of his soul) habitual holiness and immortality (gifts of divine grace).	immortality, perfect wisdom, and a will regulated by reason.	a *justitia originalis* inwrought, and belonging to his nature (and immortality).	
\multicolumn{2}{c}{Through}	\multicolumn{2}{c}{the}

THEOLOGY.—TABLE I.

ARMINIAN.	SOCINIAN.
to mankind	through Christ,
must be	derived
Bible alone,	from the New Testament.
no infallible tribunal of interpretation of themselves to	Holy Scripture; its divine every Christian.
Christian	Revelation
Trinity;	God, the eternal and absolute Being, is one
that is, the divine essence exists in Three Persons, equal in nature, but in dignity admitting subordination.	Jesus, the Man, was in time exalted by God to divine majesty; and to Him, who now in eternity is God, belongs divine honour; the Holy Ghost is nothing personal in God, but the divine power working unto sanctification.
from Father and Son.)	
object of divine worship.	Besides Him there is no object of divine worship.
pictures, and relics is	contrary to Scripture.
property from the	beginning of the race;
from the hands of his	Creator, possessed
innocence, and hope of	continuance in being.
first	sin

TABLE I.—*continued.*

ROMISH.	GREEK.	LUTHERAN.	REFORMED.
Adam and his posterity lost those divine gifts of grace, and his will (towards good) was weakened.	Adam and his posterity lost immortality, and his will received a bias towards evil.	Adam and his posterity lost the *justitia originalis*, and there entered a total corruption of his nature (in spiritual things).	
	In this state the natural man, even	before he commits actual sin, is a	
	sinner before God	(in original or inherited sin).	
Original sin consists in the *carentia justitiæ originalis*; evil concupiscence, however, is not itself sin, but only leads to sin.		Evil concupiscence is positively original sin.	
	and commits,	following his evil desire,	
although not absolutely without power of will towards good, well pleasing to God, and not in his natural state doing only evil.		being altogether unable to do what is pleasing to God, and able to do nothing but sin.	

TABLE I.—*continued*.

ARMINIAN.	SOCINIAN.
Adam and his posterity lost their destined freedom from death; and now, in consequence of repeated sinning, man's nature is firmly held by a bias to evil.	
The natural man is affected with an inherited evil, which, however, does not involve guilt.	
The bias to evil is not in itself sin.	
manifold sins,	
although not absolutely unable to do anything good.	

COMPARATIVE

Romish.	Greek.	Lutheran.	Reformed.
			Chr
	the Son of God (became man)	(who appeared in the flesh	as the
			con-
	of two natures (the Divine and the	Human), which, most internally and insepar-
		so that the properties of the one nature belong also to the other (*communicatio idiomatum*),	yet so that no mutual communication of the properties of the two natures takes place,
	has, according to the	eternal purpose of God, obtained for
		im- me-	diate-
	inasmuch as He	by His vicarious death has made satisfaction
His satisfaction was perfectly commensurate The satisfaction of Christ was indeed more than sufficient; and the superabundant merit of the Redeemer is committed to the Church as a precious treasure.		with the sins of the world, and had before God a sufficient value.	
	The condition	under which man is made partaker of which
	attains to, being moved upon and sustained by the Holy Ghost.	lacking all power of his own to good, can begin and complete only through the influence of the Holy Ghost.
	But	this Divine
	offered to all men	without distinction ;	offered only to those whom God has by His eternal absolute decree elected to salvation.
	but may by them	be rejected.	It cannot be resisted by the elect.
	In	order to attain to

THEOLOGY.—TABLE II.

ARMINIAN.	SOCINIAN.
1st Son of God)	a man, conceived by the Holy Ghost and born as the Son of God,
sisting ably united, make **one** only Person,	of **one** nature, the Human, exalted to divine majesty.
mankind reconciliation with God and ly;	eternal life, mediately;
to God for the world's sins;	in that by His teaching and work He has opened the way for an amendment acceptable to God, which He rewards of His grace with forgiveness and eternal salvation.
although His death had not in itself this satisfying power, but received it through the mercy of God, who reckoned the satisfaction, imperfect of itself, as perfect for man.	His death was not expiatory: it gave to men a great motive to amendment; and also led Christ Himself to divine dignity and heavenly authority on behalf of His own.
reconciliation with God and eternal salvaman	tion is spiritual regeneration,
by the help of the Holy Ghost begins and finishes.	begins by his own strength, but can finish only by the aid of the Holy Ghost.
help	is
imparted to all men	without distinction,
but may by them	be rejected.
salvation, man is	justified;

TABLE II.—*continued*.

ROMISH.	GREEK.	LUTHERAN.	REFORMED.
that is, habitual righteousness is infused into him; and by the good works which he thereby performs, he merits increase of grace and eternal salvation.		of grace for Christ's sake. But the merit of Christ is appropriated by faith.	that is, he receives
	The justified		can, however, do no
may do more than the commandments of God demand, and, by observing the evangelical counsels, may obtain a higher degree of moral perfection and of heavenly salvation.			
But the venial sins, which do not in their nature work condemnation, may be expiated by personal satisfactions.	may, however, fall from a state of grace;	through mortal sins, The lighter sins (of inadvertence), which might indeed bring condemnation, are forgiven by God's grace for Christ's merits' sake.	but never, even through great sins, can altogether lose the grace of God.
Mortal sins do not necessarily destroy faith.		Mortal sins consist not with faith.	

TABLE II.—*continued.*

ARMINIAN.	SOCINIAN.
from God forgiveness of sins (and hope of	eternal salvation).
more than the commands of	God require.
may, however, sink the unre-	again into the state of generate.

COMPARATIVE

ROMISH.	GREEK.	LUTHERAN.	REFORMED.
The by means and by means		Regeneration of man of the word of the Sacraments,	
which under visible signs communicate to Christians the invisible grace of God.		which under and in visible signs communicate to Christians the invisible grace of God.	which in the communication of visible signs seal to the Christian divine grace.
The Sacraments exhibit this power,		administered by godly or ungodly ministers,	
in every partaker *ex opere operato*,		only in believers,	the elect,
if the administrator does it *cum intentione*.		without the intention of the minister being necessary.	
Of		such Sacraments	
seven: Baptism; Confirmation; Eucharist; Penance; Marriage; Orders; Extreme Unction.			only two,
Baptism must be		administered to children of Christians,	
and it entirely destroys original sin.		and it abolishes the guilt of original sin, without destroying the sin itself.	
In the Eucharist the veritable body and the Christ are substantially		veritable blood of present,	In the Supper, bread
that is, under the elements, which on consecration lose their substance, and are changed into the substance of Christ.		that is, in and under the elements; which do not lose their substance, nor are changed into the body of Christ.	
The body and blood of Christ are by corporeally partaken		communicants of;	The body and blood of Christ are partaken of by recipients spiritually in faith;
and this participation increases sanctifying grace, confirms the forgiveness of remissible sins, preserves from mortal sins, etc.		and this participation assures of forgiveness of sins, life, and salvation.	
The laity need to receive only the body of Christ.	All Christians	must receive the	

THEOLOGY.—TABLE III.

ARMINIAN.	SOCINIAN.
is	effected
of	God;
The Sacraments are ceremonies which sensibly exhibit the spiritual covenant between God and man.	The Sacraments are ceremonies by means of which the Christian publicly avows his faith in Christianity.
there	are
that is, Baptism and the Lord's	Supper. Baptism was not ordained as a permanent rite.
Baptism may be administered	to the children of Christians.
and wine are signs of the substantial, not	present, body and blood of Christ.
the communicants	receiving both,
and thus make thankful confession of the union with	death of Christ suffered for men, and their Christ.
bread and the	wine.

TABLE III.—*continued.*

ROMISH.	GREEK.	LUTHERAN.	REFORMED.
The Eucharist is also an expiatory sacrifice, in which the priest presents unbloody to God the body of Christ, which was offered in blood on the cross; and this oblation of Christ in the mass procures benefit for the living and the dead.			
	Justification		**lost may be restored**
Penance consists not merely (*a*) in sincere repentance, but also (*b*) in confession of sin to the priest, in which the individual mortal sins of which a man is conscious must be recounted, and (*c*) in the discharge of penances imposed by the priest for the removal of the temporal punishments which may have been imposed by God.		but useful, and therefore as an ecclesiastical institute to be retained.	Repentance consists essentially Confession of sin to the but in certain cases useful, and therefore to be permitted to such as desire. Yet no enumeration of Ecclesiastical penances
With the absolution of the priest, who here acts as judge, penance makes a proper sacrament.		Absolution is bestowed by the minister, not as judge, but as announcer of the divine will.	
He who dies without having made full satisfaction is placed in purgatory, where, before he can enter heaven, he must undergo discipline of purification. Indulgence dispensed by the Church secures dispensation from penance to those who know true repentance. Indulgence also, like masses for the dead and other pious works, abridge (*per modum suffragii*) the pains of purgatory.	There is no purgatory.		Penance is by no means Purgatory, and all

TABLE III.—*continued.*

ARMINIAN.	SOCINIAN.
through repentance.	
of sincere sorrow for sin.	
priest is not necessary,	
particular sins is to be required.	
disparage the merit of Christ.	
a Christian sacrament.	
that is connected with it, is of human	invention.

COMPARATIVE

ROMISH.	GREEK.	LUTHERAN.	REFORMED.
		The Church	
is the fellowship of all confessors of Christ, good and evil, united under Christ and His visible representative the Pope.	is the fellowship of all those who accept and profess all the articles of faith transmitted by the apostles, and approved by general synods.	is the fellowship of saints united under the pure gospel is preached and the	
Without this visible church is no salvation.		Without this church	
The same is under the abiding influence of the Holy Ghost, and therefore cannot err as to matters of faith.		The same is by the Holy	
		In the service of the Church specially	
which form an order essentially distinguished from other Christians. This order has many gradations of spiritual offices and dignities, which *jure divino* are distinguished in their prerogatives: that is, bishops, priests, and ministers.		which form There and all	
Among the bishops, the first (*Primas*) is the Bishop of Rome, as successor of the Apostle Peter, and therefore the visible head of the Church.	Among the bishops the four patriarchs have the highest rank, but are of equal dignity among themselves.	There is no [rather is the	
The bishops under the Pope,	The bishops,		
united in a general council, represent the Church, and infallibly decide, under the guidance of the Holy Ghost, concerning all matters of faith and ecclesiastical life.		and, if united in a Synod,	
		All ministers of Christ must be regularly called	
		To their office, however, they are	
by the sacrament of orders, which		by the apostolic ordinance of imposition of	
impresses upon them an indelible character, but			
can be administered only by the bishop,			

THEOLOGY.—TABLE IV.

ARMINIAN.	SOCINIAN.
of	Christ
Christ as their invisible Head, in which sacraments are duly administered.	is the fellowship of those who hold fast in faith and obedience, and outwardly confess, the doctrines of salvation announced by Christ.
is no salvation.	
Ghost led into all truth.	
appointed persons are	necessary,
an order only officially distinguished from	other Christians.
are no	priests,
(*jure divino*) have the same vocation and	official rights.
first among these (*jure divino*), and no visible	head of the Church
Pope Antichrist].	
they must decide only according to the	written word of God.
and appointed.	Christian ministers need no specific call
consecrated	
hands, which may be exercised by all ministers,	

TABLE IV.—*continued.*

Romish.	Greek.	Lutheran.	Reformed.
and entails the obligation of celibacy.	Bishops must be unmarried, but priests and deacons must not contract a second marriage: otherwise they lose their right to exercise spiritual functions.		and
To all priests in common belongs, besides the preaching of the gospel, the administration			The office of the ministry administration
of five sacraments: baptism, penance, Eucharist, marriage, and extreme unction;	of six sacraments: baptism, confirmation, penance, Eucharist, marriage, unction of sick;		
and the presentation of the sacrifice of the mass.			as also the exercise of
To the bishops alone belongs the administration			
of the sacraments of confirmation and orders.	of the sacrament of orders.		
Ecclesiastical ceremonies are part of the divine service, most of them having apostolical origin; and those connected with the sacraments must not be omitted by the priests, on pain of mortal sin.		Ecclesiastical ceremonies, which are not Pictures and altars may be set up in churches.	the need of but they need be few; and pictures and altars are not to be suffered in churches.

TABLE IV.—*continued.*

ARMINIAN.	SOCINIAN.
does not involve the obligation of	celibacy.
consists in the preaching of the gospel, of the	and in sacraments;
the power of the keys.	
part of the divine worship, may be ordered the community, in harmony with the word	by every particular church according to of God;

INDEX.

ABILITY, human, 148.
Absolution, 303, 357.
Acceptatio, acceptilatio, 138.
Adoration of the host, 284.
Anabaptists, 29.
Antichrist, 353.
Arminianism, 28.
Altars in churches, 363.
Apocrypha, O.T., 60.
Atonement of Christ, 138.
Augsburg Confession, 15.

BAPTISM, meaning, 249; necessity, 255; infant, 258; of heretics, 262.
Barclay's Apology, 35.
Bible, 41, 56.
Bishops in general council, 351; jurisdiction, 352; celibacy of, in Greek Church, 354.
Bread in the Eucharist, 290.
Bullarium Romanum, 10.

CALVIN'S doctrine of the Eucharist, 269.
Canon, 45.
Canonization of saints, 72.
Catechismus Romanus, 9.
Celibacy, 354.
Ceremonies of the Church, 361.
Chemnitz, *Examen*, 1.
Christ, divinity, 116 seq.; person, 116; body, 124; impeccability and sinlessness, 130; mediator in one or both natures, 132; exaltation, 133; merit, 138.
Church, 330.
Clerici et laici, 346.
Communio sub unâ, 347.
Communicatio idiomatum, 116 seq.
Conception, immaculate, 98.
Concilia evangelica, 205.
Concupiscentia, 99.
Confessio Augustana, 15.
Confession, 303.
Confirmation, 318.
Consubstantiation, 280.
Councils, œcumenical, 56.

Cup, withdrawal of, 287.
Cultus of the Virgin, 68.

DECALOGUE, 227.
Decrees, divine, 161.
Divine image in man, 82.
Divine worship, 366.

ECCLESIA repraesentans, 351.
Election, 161.
Elevation and adoration of the host, 284.
Eucharistic sacrament and sacrifice, 292.
Excommunication, major et minor, 357.
Exorcism, 263.
Extreme unction, 325.

FAITH, in justification, 179; in children, and mortal sin, 219.
Fall, effects of, 86 seq.
Fasting, 309.
Fathers and tradition, 49.
Feet-washing, 239, 243.
Fides formata, 189.
Filioque, 67.
Flacius' doctrine of original sin, 91.
Forensic justification, 178.
Formula Concordiæ, 17.
Free will, 48; its co-operation in regeneration, 50.

GHOST, Holy, divine personality, 16; procession, 57; in regeneration, 146.
Grace, 145; and ability, 148.
Grace, means of, 223.
Grace, resistible and irresistible, 146.

HEATHEN, perdition of, 333.
Hierarchy, 347.
Host, reservation and adoration of, 284.

IMAGE of God in man, 78 seq.
Immaculate conception, 198.
Imposition of hands, 353.

INDEX.

Imputation of Adam's sin, 106; to faith, 188.
Inability, moral, 111.
Indelibility in sacrament, 243.
Indulgences, 143, 314.
Infralapsarians, 161.
Inspiration, 57.
Intention of priest, 243.
Invocation of saints, 68.

JUSTIFICATION, 178.
Justitia originalis, 82.

KEYS, power of the, 357.

LAW and gospel, 227.
Light, internal, 46.
Limbus infantum and patrum, 312.
Liturgy, 345.
Lutheran confessions, 15.

MARRIAGE and divorce, 321.
Mary, immaculate conception, 198.
Mass, 292.
Masses, private, 296.
Means of grace, 222.
Merit, 201.
Meritum, de condigno and de congruo, 185.
Ministry, the, 340; degrees, 347; equality, 347; Quaker, 344.
Monasticism, 210; and evangelical counsels, 210.

NOTES of the Church, 330.

OATH, 346.
Obedience, active and passive, 130.
Ordination, 329, 353.
Original sin, 86; guilt, 106; and baptism, 108.

PAPAL infallibility, 354.
Penance, 297.
Penances, 307.
Perseverance, 217.
Person of Christ, 116.
Pictures and relics, 75.
Pope, the, 353.
Prayers for the dead, 316.
Predestination, 161.
Presence, the real, 286.

Private masses, 296.
Purgatory, 310.

QUAKER confessions, 34.

READING of Scripture by laity, 57.
Redemption, 127 seq.
Reformed Church, 20.
Relics, 75.
Renewal and conversion, 150.
Repentance, 298.
Restoration of the cup, 289.
Righteousness of Christ, 181.

SACRAMENTS, 232.
Sacrifice of the Mass, 280.
Saints, invocation of, 68; pictures and relics, 75.
Satisfaction of Christ, 138.
Satisfactions, 198.
Scripture, sufficiency of, 41; interpretation, 56.
Sinlessness of Christ, 130.
Sin, mortal and venial, 219.
Sin, original, 106; and baptism, 108.
State, original, of man, 80 seq.
Subordination in Trinity, 63 seq.
Supererogation, 205.
Supralapsarianism, 161.
Symbola Œcumenica, 45.
Synergism, 145.
Synods, 45.

TESTAMENT, Old, its validity, 45.
Tradition, 41.
Transubstantiation, 280.
Trinity, 63 seq.
Treasure of merits, 127.

UNLEAVENED bread in Eucharist, 290.

Vows, 210, 212.
Vulgate, 58.

WORD and sacrament, 223.
Word of God, 222.
Works, good, 196, 198, 203.
Wine in Eucharist, 290.

ZWINGLIAN doctrine of the Eucharist, 269.

www.ingramcontent.com/pod-product-compliance
Lightning Source LLC
Chambersburg PA
CBHW022102300426
44117CB00007B/549